The Elements of
Cognitive Aging

The Elements of Cognitive Aging

*Meta-Analyses of Age-Related Differences
in Processing Speed and Their Consequences*

PAUL VERHAEGHEN

OXFORD
UNIVERSITY PRESS

OXFORD
UNIVERSITY PRESS

Oxford University Press is a department of the University of
Oxford. It furthers the University's objective of excellence in research,
scholarship, and education by publishing worldwide.

Oxford   New York
Auckland   Cape Town   Dar es Salaam   Hong Kong   Karachi
Kuala Lumpur   Madrid   Melbourne   Mexico City   Nairobi
New Delhi   Shanghai   Taipei   Toronto

With offices in
Argentina   Austria   Brazil   Chile   Czech Republic   France   Greece
Guatemala   Hungary   Italy   Japan   Poland   Portugal   Singapore
South Korea   Switzerland   Thailand   Turkey   Ukraine   Vietnam

Oxford is a registered trademark of Oxford University Press
in the UK and certain other countries.

Published in the United States of America by
Oxford University Press
198 Madison Avenue, New York, NY 10016

Library of Congress Cataloging-in-Publication Data
Verhaeghen, Paul.
The elements of cognitive aging : meta-analyses of age-related differences in processing
speed and their consequences / Paul Verhaeghen.
pages cm
Includes bibliographical references and index.
ISBN 978–0–19–536869–7 (alk. paper)
1. Cognition—Age factors.   2. Ability, Influence of age on.
3. Aging.   4. Human beings.   I. Title.
BF724.55.C63V47 2013
155.67′13—dc23
2013016058

1 3 5 7 9 8 6 4 2
Printed in the United States of America
on acid-free paper

This book is dedicated to
John Cerella, mentor and collaborator extraordinaire

TABLE OF CONTENTS

PREFACE

Every human life, I hope, is marked by one great love. Those among us lucky enough to be scientists can get away with being smitten twice—once in real life, once in the life of the mind. I vividly remember falling in scientific love on a gorgeously sunny afternoon in late Spring of 1989. (Sunny afternoons are rare in Leuven, Belgium, where I did my graduate work, so it stands out.) I was leaning against the shelves in the "J" section ("Developmental Psychology") in the Psychology Library, and the tome balanced in my hand was *Aging in the 1980s*, edited by Lenny Poon.

I was staring at a graph, and I was completely blown away.

I was sent to the stacks by one of the members of my PhD committee. He had heard rumors about a paper in that book at a conference; he thought it could be helpful. (The original rumormonger turned out to be Pat Rabbitt, so it made sense to follow that up.) The paper, unpromisingly titled "Aging and the complexity hypothesis," turned out to be completely unhelpful for my dissertation, but it set me off on a new, wilder, much more exciting path, following the Zen-like promise of its second graph, the one I was staring at with the disbelief that often characterizes the beginnings of any deep romance.

At the time, I was steeped in a tradition of aging research that was derived from traditional developmental psychology, with its qualitative jumps, its classification schemes, and its penchant for iconoclasm vis-à-vis intuitive ideas about development, including aging. This was the era of the competent neonate, and the infirmities of old age were just an oppressive fiction perpetrated by a cruel society, including psychologists, researchers first and foremost among them. Older adults suffered from mere "production deficits"—many if not most of the age-related differences in the literature were ascribed to easily remediable differences in strategy use, and so simple instruction and encouragement could bring older adults up to the level of performance of younger adults. (I exaggerate, of course.)

Cerella, Poon, and Williams's (but really Cerella's) Figure 24-2, reproduced here as Figure 1.4, told a very different story. It plotted response times of groups of older adults performing bare-bones cognitive tasks as a function of response times of groups of younger adults performing the same tasks. What emerged was a slender cloud of 99 points, almost a line, a whiff of smoke signifying (perhaps) the demise of any qualitative theory about age differences in these elementary tasks as well as any hope that these basic tasks might be age-invariant.

As often happens when one falls in love, I was initially seduced by sheer beauty, but I kept coming back for the smarts, the attitude and, yes, the complications. These complications are what this book is all about. It is nothing but a long meditation on and an even longer expansion of this initial graph—more studies, more tasks, more pitfalls, more theory, more models, more fractionations, and maybe here and there even some explanations.

One of the luckier coincidences of my scientific life was that I was able to walk the most significant part of this journey alongside John Cerella himself. (Actually, it was more like I was perpetually limping a few steps behind.) When I applied for a faculty position at Syracuse University, I had no idea John was working there; when I found out he was, I almost didn't dare take the airplane to interview; after I got the job, I was delighted to be housed in the same suite as John. John was, and is, a precise, relentlessly questioning, deeply serious mentor and collaborator; someone who gladly discovers the problem in any solution, and then builds a new and unexpected solution from scratch, which then in turn leads to more exquisite problems. The end product was/is always fascinating (exhibit one: Figure 1.4). It was even more breathtaking to be witness to the process, for instance, to be the increasingly bewildered recipient of a stream of slender, equation-riddled memos slid daily under my office door, each numbered consecutively, each supplanting and outdating the previous one, and then (after a month or so) to be gently but firmly quizzed on their content.

One of the things John and I have in common is a love for the music of Johann Sebastian Bach. I consider John Cerella the Johann Sebastian Bach of cognitive aging—underneath all that mathematical meticulousness, that clockwork precision, that unyielding yearning for beauty (which just *has* to be truth), lays a tremendous sensitivity and the greatest of hearts.

So, I dedicate this book to John—I couldn't have wished for a better mentor. I know he will find fault with it, and rightfully so, but those faults are entirely my own. Whatever in these pages that is good exudes John's spirit, if it is not his actual handiwork—the rest is me.

There have been other companions on this road as well—this work has benefitted greatly from discussions and collaborations with friends and colleagues at Leuven (Paul De Boeck, Lieve de Meersman, Luc Goossens, Fons Marcoen), Syracuse University (Chandramallika Basak, Kara Bopp, Bill Hoyer, Elke Lange, Marty Sliwinski, Rob Stawski, Dave Steitz, Christina Wasylyshyn), Georgia Tech (Tianyong Chen, Greg Colflesh, Audrey Duarte, Randy Engle, Amanda Gilchrist, Chris Hertzog, Dan Spieler) and beyond (Sandy Hale, Reinhold Kliegl, Ralf Krampe, Shu-Chen Li, Ulrich Mayr, Joel Myerson, Tania Singer, Jacqui Smith), as well as from the help and support of my current lab mates (Shivangi Jain, Jessie Martin, Didem Pehlivanoglu, John Price, Shriradha Sengupta). The National Institute on Aging graced our lab with a grant on *Aging and Varieties of Cognitive Control* (AG 16201), which was/is extremely helpful; the grant is especially relevant for Chapters 6 and 9.

A special thank you goes to the Interlibrary Loan Librarian at Georgia Tech, Katharine Calhoun. I sent far too many crazy last-minute requests for papers (invariably late on Friday); Katharine was always graceful, and she always delivered much faster than promised. Without her and her staff this book would not be. We never met, but the day this book comes out, I'll go visit her with a box of chocolates.

A very special thank you goes to Tim Salthouse. Without his invitation to spend the month of April 1996 at Georgia Tech, I simply would not have a career. Tim quasi-ordered me to write a book like this 10 years ago. It's finally here.

An extra-special thank you goes to Shelley Aikman and Bodhi Aikman Verhaeghen. Family is always said to proverbially suffer when the spouse/parent is Working on The Book. If Shelley and Bodhi did, they did not complain. On the contrary, I felt incredibly supported and loved throughout this whole long, drawn-out process. If I didn't suffer more than I did, it is because of them. (And that is true for my real life as well.)

Finally, I will heed the words of one of my illustrious colleagues at Syracuse who told me during breakfast at the time of my interview, while repeatedly sneezing into my hash browns, that "All meta-analysts are leeches!" I don't know about others, but I am—I could not have done this book without the hard work of the roughly 2,000 scientists cited in these pages. I will not likely ever meet most of you, but if I do, remind me to buy you a drink, or bake you a cookie.

Aging and Processing Speed: History, Methodology, and Outlook

Human aging is a phenomenon as old as humankind itself, and its study is likely just as old. Plato (who died at age 80) wrote about it in his *Republic*; Cicero (who died at age 62) devoted a whole book to it (*De Senectute*; Cicero, 1923); and the Buddha (who died at age 80) has a teaching on it (the *Jara Sutta*). None of these sages seemed to have been particularly enamored with the bodily and mental changes that accompanied their advancing age ("I spit on you, old age," the *Jara Sutta* says), except for being freed of what Cicero called "the bondage of passion."

These men were, of course, unlucky enough to be born in an age when aging was rarer than it is today and was not the happiest of occurrences either: Life expectancy was low and morbidity rampant. Medical advances since then, especially throughout the 20th century, have changed the demographics of society considerably. Old age is no longer an exception. I am, as I write this sentence, in my late 40s. If I had been born in 1900, my probability of being dead at my current age would have exceeded 50%. Over the last century, life expectancy for White males born in the United States has risen from 48 for those born in 1920, over 66 for those born in 1950, 71 for those born in 1980, to 75 for those born in 2000 (Department of Health and Human Services, 2006). Part of the tremendous increase in life expectancy is, of course, due to lower mortality in the early part of the life span. But it is not all situated there. If one reached the grand old age of 50 in 1900 (and one was a U.S.-born White male), one had, on average, 21 more years to look forward to. In 1950, those became 23 years; by 1980, 25 more years, and in 2000, 28 more years. One can even, to some extent, manipulate the length of one's lifespan. Using a handy online app[1] that allows users to plug in different details of their and their family's health history and habits, I just calculated my current life expectancy to be another 38 years. (Interestingly, the app also suggests that by giving up sex and repenting from my vegetarian diet, I could add one year and one month to that number. I conferred with my spouse; she doesn't think it's worth it.)

But is this rise in life expectancy past 50 really something to look forward to?

People's perception of old age—what they expect to happen to themselves or others when they grow older—often involves negative changes in not just the physical, but also the behavioral and mental realm. A recent study by the Pew Research Center (Taylor, Morin, Parker, Cohn, & Wang, 2009) shows that adults between the ages of 18 and 64 expect that aging implies memory loss (57% of respondents), the inability to drive (45%), sexual inactivity (34%), depression or sadness (29%), and loneliness (29%). Clearly, aging is seen as a bracing challenge. (It also happens relatively late: only 32% of respondents were willing to call someone 65 years old "old," although that changed with age—young adults in their 20s consider a sexagenarian "old"; sexagenarians disagree with that sentiment.) The good news is that the actual older adults in the same survey (65 years of age or older) indicated experiencing these negative aspects much less often than the younger adults expect them to—the gap between actual reality and dreaded reality is, on average, 19%.

Expectations are especially harsh with regard to the aging of cognitive functioning. Another survey, published in 2006 by the MetLife Foundation, found that while Americans fear getting cancer more than they fear getting any other disease, for those 55 years or older Alzheimer's (the ultimate insult to cognitive functioning) is the most dreaded disease. Older adults routinely complain about memory loss (e.g., Blazer, Hays, Fillenbaum, & Gold, 1997; Cutler & Grams, 1988). The association between aging and cognitive decline is even encoded in our language. The term *senior moment*, for instance, does not refer to a revelatory flash of increased maturity but to brief memory lapses, experiences of cognitive impairment, and even to functional incompetence (Bonnesen & Burgess, 2004).

For these and other reasons, psychologists have become quite interested in what happens to cognition as people age—what changes occur in how we gather, store, and use information? This topic of study is now known as "cognitive aging." We do know a lot about cognitive aging and the amount of our knowledge is, as it should in science, ever increasing. Late May 2012, I queried *Web of Science* for papers that have "cognitive aging" as their topic. *Web of Science* returned 54,375 citations. This is arguably a large number. Even more revealing is Figure 1.1, which plots the number of citations as a function of year of publication (up until 2011). Panel A shows all the data. It is immediately noticeable that few papers on the topic appear before 1990. This does not indicate an absolute lack of interest; it mostly reflects that the field, small as it was, had not yet converged on a term to name itself—the first major conference in the field, the 1988 *Cognitive Aging Conference*, organized by the Experimental Psychology faculty at the Georgia Institute of Technology, served that purpose. Since 1992 or so, the publication trend matches an exponential growth model (Panel B). It is also instantly clear that it has now effectively become impossible to keep up with the field—more than 10% of the papers on the topic (5,778 to be exact) have been published in the last year. If she would be doing even a mere cursory 10-minute scan of each paper, a researcher working in 2011 would have been spending 2 hours per day reading, just to keep up with the literature as it was being published. This also implies, I would argue, that reviews of the field and of selected subsections thereof will become increasingly important, not just for outsiders looking in, but for insiders as well.

1.1. Reviewing the Field: Meta-analyses of Aging and Speed of Processing

There is no lack of overview papers in the field. The last three years alone have yielded three excellent book-length reviews: Salthouse's (2010) *Major Issues in Cognitive*

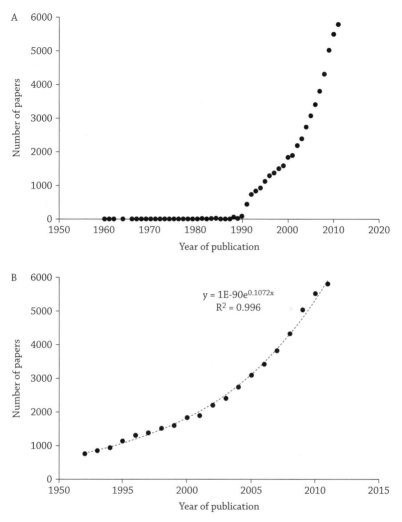

Figure 1.1 Number of papers on the topic "cognitive aging," plotted as a function of year of publication as retrieved from *Web of Science*, May 2012; Panel A shows all the data; Panel B zooms in on post-1992 segment and overlays an exponential curve.

Aging and Hertzog, Kramer, Wilson, and Lindenberger's (2009) *Enrichment Effects on Adult Cognitive Development*; a more popular-science type of overview is given in Carstensen's (2011) *A Long Bright Future*. At least two older monographs—Kausler's (1991) *Experimental Psychology, Cognition, and Human Aging* and Salthouse's (1991c) *Theoretical Perspectives on Cognitive Aging*—present near-encyclopedic overviews of the data to date.

Why add one more?

One unique feature of the present book is its emphasis on meta-analysis, that is, on the statistical combination and analysis of existing results to review a field or topic. Most large-scale reviews in cognitive aging have taken a narrative approach; that is, they compress the data into conclusions that essentially are, or fit, a story (typically: who and what ages and why, and what can potentially be done about this). Such reviews are by necessity subjective in the conclusions offered and in their suggestions for particular future directions. This subjectivity is, of course, a large part of what makes these books valuable—they inform others, whether inside the field or outside, of the point of view of someone deeply and successfully immersed in the subject. I would assume that this also is the reason why these books get written: These authors have a unique, or at least strong, point of view to impart.

My goal here is slightly different: to provide not a narrative review of the field, but a *quantitative review*, in particular by collecting a rather extensive set of meta-analyses, most of them conducted for the express purpose of being included in this book (and thus reported here for the first time). Meta-analysis simply implies bringing together the results of multiple studies, each aggregated at the group level (typically, the unit of analysis is the mean of a group of individuals), and conducting some form of statistical analysis on these results. In this kind of review, the reviewer ideally disappears behind the data and lets conclusions emerge from the analyses themselves. The end result of this endeavor is not so much a story as a set of tables and figures—a catalog of effects. There is obviously still a subjective component to this endeavor, of course, if only in the selection of the question or type of questions to examine, and in what to highlight from the results.

In my view, there are some clear advantages to quantification. I would argue that only when we quantify effects can we reliably and precisely answer crucial questions such as: What is the size of the age-related effect in task/process/test X, and how does it compare to the age-related difference in task/process/test Y? (Questions of this sort are taken up in Chapters 2, 4, and 6 of this book.) When does cognitive aging start? And what course does the decline in a specific task/process/test—if any—take over the adult life span? (Such questions are tackled in Chapters 7 and 8.) How are the age-related effects in different tasks/processes/tests interrelated? (Chapter 9 examines this question.) And how are these effects related to physiological/biological parameters like neurotransmitter efficacy or regional brain volume? (This question is addressed mainly in Chapter 5 and Chapter 9.)

The latter type of questions shows that quantitative integration does not only serve a descriptive purpose, but that it can also meaningfully be applied to theoretical questions, although I would still surmise that meta-analysis is typically better suited to constrain theory than to provide definitive tests of very specific hypotheses. (This issue will be tackled in Chapter 10.) The level of explanation I am aiming for is clearly higher than the micro-level typically attempted in experimental psychology (where process is often the purported unit of analysis), but lower than the macro-level often considered in individual-differences work (where latent ability is the desirable object of scrutiny)—a meso-level of explanation. The meso-level revolves around the concepts of task, task domain, and task families, of dissociations between them (i.e., what sets of tasks belong together when age-related differences are considered, and what sets of tasks reliably split off from others), and of the relationships between them. What I mean by this will hopefully become clear over the course of this book.

Second, once the decision was made to present a quantitative overview, it seemed wise to concentrate on a single but broad aspect of behavior that is easy to quantify, namely the *speed* of its execution. Many aspects of cognition are or can be measured under the aspect of speed, thus yielding the potential of a broad overview of tasks and task domains. Additionally, all speeded data are scaled on the same metric—chronological time—making speed of processing a ready candidate for cross-study quantification. The upshot is that this approach allows us to directly compare age-related effects across different tasks, with crisp, straight conclusions attached. (It is harder to derive such conclusions from accuracy data, especially keeping in mind that for simple tasks like the ones considered here, performance is often relatively error-free.)

There are also more substantive reasons to focus on speed.

First, speed of processing is often considered one of the more basic aspects of cognitive behavior. Some have even argued it is the single most basic parameter of cognitive functioning (e.g., Jensen, 2006). Speed of processing is also a variable that appears eminently age-sensitive—aging is often associated with considerable slowing, even in very basic tasks (e.g., Birren, 1960; Salthouse, 1996b). For instance, in a large meta-analysis of studies using continuous age samples (updated here in Chapter 9), Verhaeghen and Salthouse (1997) reported an age-speed correlation of –.52, stronger than any other age-ability correlation (speed here was measured as perceptual speed, the ability to quickly and accurately compare letters, numbers, objects, pictures, or patterns). Welford (1977) observed that each additional year of adult age increases choice reaction time by 1.5 ms. Cerella and Hale (1994) estimated that the average 70-year-old functions at the speed of the average 8-year-old. The sheer size of the effect and its near-omnipresence (for both examples and counterexamples of this, see Chapters 4 and 6) makes speed of processing an obvious target variable for researchers interested in cognitive aging.

1.2. Meta-analysis: Boons and Biases

Meta-analysis is a methodological approach, and like any such approach, it has its advantages and blind spots. I would also argue that, like any approach, it engrains a modus operandi in the regular user that translates into certain habitual ways of examining data and certain biases in interpretations.

The standard meta-analytic method (e.g., Hedges & Olkin, 1985) is to pool the data, compute the average of the study averages, and construct a confidence interval around that mean. In aging research, the effect of interest is typically the difference between a group of younger and a group of older adults on some measure of interest. Once the average effect, in this case the age-related effect, is computed and its confidence interval established, the second step in meta-analysis is to assess the homogeneity of the variance around that average (typically by a *chi*-square test on the weighted sum of squared differences between individual study effects and the pooled effect across studies). A homogeneous average effect size implies that the average can be considered a good estimate of the true effect; a heterogeneous average effect suggests that there is so much variance that the data cannot be represented by a single point estimate. The latter result should encourage the meta-analyst to dig deeper and examine potential moderators or mediators of the effect. Meta-analysts accordingly have a double reflex at the outset of each research project: to assess the common effect and to immediately distrust it.

This attitude implies that the data are effectively tested against two successive null hypotheses. The first null hypothesis is that the data show no effect; in our case, that implies: Younger and older adults perform at the same speed. The second null hypothesis is that the aggregate effect size (regardless of whether it differs from zero or not) is an adequate description of the data. In the context of aging and speed of processing this second null hypothesis translates into the claim that the data can be explained through a single age-related effect. This hypothesis has been succinctly labeled as the *general slowing hypothesis*—the idea that aging slows all processes and tasks to the same degree (e.g., Cerella, 1994). It is important to stress here that the general slowing hypothesis is a hypothesis, not a theory (i.e., there are no serious claims that general slowing is, indeed, a viable way to describe the aging mind), and that it is the *null* hypothesis; that is, it is the default setting that the analysis is ultimately trying to reject. This still means that the onus (so to speak) is on the alternative hypothesis, and that the bias of our testing is toward accepting the general slowing hypothesis. (I will return to this point later in this chapter.)

Note that within a cognitive aging context, this lump-then-split approach is not restricted to meta-analysis per se. Many primary researchers have used similar approaches—examining large data sets for communalities among age effects on different tasks assumed to represent a certain class of processes, and for dissimilarities between age effects operating across classes (e.g., Hale & Myerson, 1996; Kliegl, Mayr, & Krampe, 1994; Verhaeghen et al., 2002).

A second reflex of the meta-analyst—rare among experimental psychologists but more common among individual-differences psychologists—is to emphasize the size of an effect rather than its sheer significance. Statistical significance is a function of both sample size and effect size (larger samples and larger effect sizes yield statistical significance more easily), but also, to some extent, luck (good or bad). Luck's role in statistical testing is an inbuilt risk: Tests are typically set up so that the researcher accepts that the result may be due to chance in 5% of the cases. This implies that in 1 out of 20 studies a significant effect will emerge purely on the basis of chance. Publication bias may have an additional hand in swinging fate's pendulum. Meta-analysis, by gathering data from multiple experiments, minimizes the role of chance and offers a more balanced view. A classic example of this balancing principle outside the field of aging is the Mozart effect—people allegedly perform better on tests of spatial ability after listening to classical music (an effect first discovered by Rauscher, Shaw, & Ky, 1993). An early meta-analysis (Steele et al., 1999) showed that the average effect was small (2.1 IQ points), not reliable, and that the initial study was the one with the largest effect. It is then likely that the original Mozart-effect paper was published exactly because the effect was so large, probably due to chance; subsequent replications helped to put this result in perspective.

This leads to a third reflex of the meta-analyst, which is to mistrust (by which I mean to refuse to accept at face value) any single result obtained in any single study. The reasoning is simple. If the average effect of a set of studies is zero, then by definition half of the studies will show a positive effect and the other half a negative effect; some of these effects will be significant at the level of the individual study. In my experience, experimentalists confronted with diverging results tend to blame methodological differences between studies. Meta-analysis teaches us to first assess whether the point estimate is tight enough to warrant a single conclusion. If it is, the variation in results might simply be due to chance.

Meta-analysis has one additional, and often hidden, advantage over narrative reviews: It can bring very disparate sets of results together in a single analysis, allowing for comparisons and contrasts never intended by the original designers of the primary studies. This, in turn, might reduce some of the biases inherent in publications of direct tests of an interaction hypothesis (such as publication bias—an effect will often only be submitted and/or accepted for publication if it is significant in the expected direction). It can also increase statistical power, confidence in one's inferences, or both. My favorite example here is Henry, MacLeod, Phillips, and Crawford's (2004) meta-analysis on aging and prospective memory. Prospective memory, briefly, is memory for intentions to be carried out in the future (such as picking up a quart of milk from the store on the way home). It is often contrasted with retrospective memory (also called episodic memory), memory for events that have occurred in the past. In real life, older adults outperform younger adults on such tasks, presumably because of excellent strategy use. In the laboratory, clear age-related differences in the opposite direction are the typical outcome: Older adults struggle more with such tasks than younger adults. The field, therefore, originally rallied around the question of why this deficit occurs. Henry et al.'s meta-analysis, however, uncovered a very interesting new fact: The effect size for laboratory-based prospective memory tasks was actually smaller than that typically obtained for retrospective memory tasks. The analyses indicated that although the field of prospective memory had been focused on identifying the causes of the age-related deficits in prospective memory, the real puzzle might be why older adults show smaller age-related effects in these types of tasks than would be expected on the basis of their retrospective memory performance—exactly the opposite question. Only the use of meta-analysis allowed the researchers to bring these two types of studies together and to draw comparisons between the age-related effects.

Meta-analysis has obvious drawbacks as well. For example, one can analyze only what has been published. For some of the tasks investigated here, there might be a file-drawer problem: Maybe some tasks are sparsely covered because they tend to not yield age-related differences and therefore stand a lower change of getting published in peer-reviewed journals (Rosenthal, 1979). One consequence would be that average age-related effects for seemingly rarely investigated tasks would then generally be an overestimation of the real age-related effect.

Another drawback of meta-analysis is that the inherent bias toward lumping by necessity skims over a lot of very real detail, often detail that primary researchers build expressly and expertly into their research to answer a question of import. Thus, a meta-analysis's level of aggregation often feels uncomfortably vague to many practitioners of primary research. For instance, in a meta-analysis on aging and the Stroop effect (people are slower to name the ink color of color words if that color is incongruent; e.g., the word "green" printed in red vs. green), we (Verhaeghen & De Meersman, 1998b) concluded that the age difference in the incongruent condition ("green" printed in red) is not larger than that in the congruent condition ("green" printed in green). Reaching this conclusion necessitated averaging over many different kinds of manipulations (vocal vs. manual response time (RT), different proportions of congruent vs.

incongruent trials, different number of potential responses, and so on). Researchers in the field are very much interested in the effect of these manipulations because they change the amount of explicit executive control the subject needs to exert over the task (e.g., Kane & Engle, 2003). Likewise, some researchers (e.g., Spieler, Balota, & Faust, 1996) have argued that merely inspecting means is misleading, and that specific age-related differences can be observed in the slow tail of the distribution (i.e., older adults have many more exceptionally slow trials in the interference condition than younger adults). Meta-analysis averages group averages derived from individual averages, and thus loses all this important detail. There is, however, often no alternative to such aggregation. Readers who feel uncomfortable with this lack of detail are encouraged to read the original papers.

1.3. The Allometrics of Aging: General Slowing and Its Discontents

The goal I set myself for this book, then, is to examine age-related differences and similarities in processing speed in a quantitative fashion. Specifically, I am interested in average age effects for particular tasks and/or processes (the list of these tasks/processes is long; it includes sensorimotor tasks, spatial tasks, lexical tasks, and executive control tasks; skimming the section headings for Chapters 4 and 6 will give a clearer idea), in variations around these average effects and how these might be explained, and in how different types of families of tasks differ from or resemble each other in their age-related effects. To do so, I will adopt an allometric framework. In describing this framework, I will take a historical perspective, because it seems to add good insight as to why and how these methods have been applied. The data will be described graphically and in equations. Nothing here is too complicated, I hope: The mathematical reasoning never progresses beyond simple linear algebra. Readers not interested in the actual mathematical arguments preferred in this section should feel free to skip or skim the equations; they will not lose too much information. It does seem to me that explicating the reasons why the different parameters and models are interpreted the way they are might be helpful.

Allometry is a term originally referring to the study of biological scaling (Shingleton, 2010, offers a brief overview); that is, how body parts or biological processes scale as a function of the body as a whole or of other body parts. The term has also been used in a more narrow sense to describe developmental (within-species) or evolutionary (across-species) changes in organs or organisms (Needham & Lerner, 1940; Von Bertalanffy & Pirozynski, 1952). Allometry involves the mathematical description of such changes; the inspiration for the mathematical functions often comes from graphing the data—organ size against organism size (e.g., brain weight vs. body weight in different species of mammals), or organ size against organ size (e.g., wing area by thorax length as a function of age in *Drosophila melanogaster*).

In the present case, the allometry concerns the comparison of younger and older adults on their speed of processing as measured in a set of cognitive tasks. Cognitive aging researchers interested in allometry typically rely on one (or both) of two types of graphs for its assessment: Brinley plots and state traces. A *Brinley plot* is a scatter plot with mean performance of younger adults on the X-axis and mean performance of older adults on the Y-axis; typically, performance on different tasks is plotted separately. A *state trace* plot is, in a sense, the inverse of the Brinley plot: It plots performance on one task as a function in performance on another, and performance of younger and older adults is plotted separately.

One clear assumption here is that allometry is a valid approach; that is, it is assumed that performance of older adults can indeed be linked by a mathematical function to that of younger adults, or, in other words, that aging results in a mere rescaling of response times. This assumption is testable, and Chapters 2, 4, 5, and 6 are heavily concerned with such tests. The testability is not absolute, because it relies on having a formal or informal criterion as to what is considered a good enough fit to assume that the assumption holds (I return to this issue in Section 1.3.2.4.2.3). In practice, as we shall see, this isn't much of a problem: Fits of allometric functions of processing speed data in aging studies are habitually excellent by any standards.

In the remainder of this section, I will discuss the two types of allometric graphs, giving a brief sense of their history and of the interpretations that have been derived from them. These are the tools that form the basis for most of this book (Chapters 2 through 6).

1.3.1. Brinley Plots: Brinley (1965)

In a Brinley plot, performance of older adults is plotted as a function of performance of younger adults performing the same task. (In the present context, performance is measured as response time, but accuracy can be used as well.) The Brinley plot is named after the author who originated it, Joseph Brinley (1965). It is not clear who first starting calling these plots Brinley plots (perhaps Perfect, 1994). Although the technique originated in cognitive aging research, the term is now also used more widely for any plot that charts performance of one group against another (e.g., children against adults, Kail, 1991; children with attention-deficit hyperactivity disorder (ADHD) against non-ADHD children, Pocklington & Maybery, 2006; video gamers against non-video gamers, Dye, Green, & Bavelier, 2009; schizophrenics against non-schizophrenics, Meiran, Levine, Meiran, & Henik, 2000; HIV patients against non-HIV patients, Hardin & Hinkin, 2002).

The original Brinley plot (reproduced in Figure 1.2) almost seems to have happened by accident. It is one graph of a few in a chapter apparently derived from Brinley's dissertation, which went otherwise unpublished. The chart is presented rather drily, with no indication that the author was aware he was presenting a novel and/or important analysis technique. The figure shows experimental data derived from a single study: performance of a group of older adults on 12 different task-switching tasks and 9 non-switch tasks plotted against performance of a group of younger adults performing the same tasks. The striking finding, as the figure illustrates, is that all 21 dots fall neatly along the same straight line, as testified by a very high correlation, $r = .99$. This line, or "Brinley function," has a slope of 1.68 and an intercept of −270 ms. Brinley's interpretation of his result is sparse: "The slope of the regression line for shift [i.e., task-switching] tasks appears identical with the one for nonshift tasks. Consequently

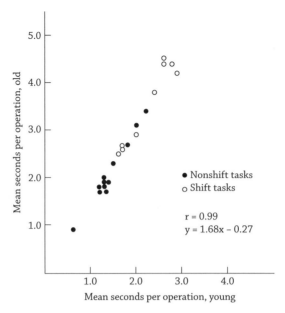

Figure 1.2 The original Brinley plot (reproduced from Brinley, 1965): Performance of a group of older adults on 12 different task-switching tasks and 9 non-switch tasks plotted against performance of a group younger adults performing the same tasks. Note the striking regularity of the plot. Copyright © 1965 by Charles C. Thomas Publisher LTD. Reprinted by permission of Charles C. Thomas Publisher, Ltd.

response times for both groups and for each type of task variation may be conceived as varying along a single dimension which might be termed 'task difficulty'." (p. 131)

Brinley notes an important consequence of this finding, one I will return to in this book often: "[D]espite the fact that older individuals, on the average, had more difficulty in shifting . . . it might be possible to conclude from these data alone that more 'rigid' behavior of older individuals reflected nothing more than the fact that shift tasks were more difficult" (p. 138).[2]

This statement deserves some unpacking. Brinley notes two effects in his data. The first is that older adults take longer to switch between tasks than younger adults do. This can be concluded from the cost associated with task switching: When latencies in the version of the task where no switching is required are subtracted from latencies in the version of the task where switching is required, an age difference emerges. The traditional interpretation of this result—one step removed from the data—is that older adults show a deficit in task switching compared with younger adults. Brinley's second result, however, casts doubt on this at first glance uncontroversial conclusion. This second result is that both types of tasks, switch and non-switch, fall along the same line in the RT_{older} by $RT_{younger}$ graph. This finding demonstrates that the relationship between older and younger adults' response times is exactly the same for tasks involving a task-switching component and tasks not involving this component. This implies that all we need to know to predict the average response time of older adults in any given condition in this study is the average response time of younger adults for the same condition. Crucially, no task information whatsoever is needed for this prediction. Hence, the interpretation is that older adults have no specific deficit in task switching over and beyond the deficit found in the non-switching conditions.

If there is no difference in the young-old relationships between the two tasks, how do we end up with larger task switching costs for older adults? The seeming discrepancy can be explained by examining the figure more closely. Note that the conditions involving switching are located more to the right of the graph and more toward the upper portion. This is because they take more time (presumably because they include the additional switching component, which is likely to be time-consuming); tasks that take longer are situated more to the right for younger adults, and more upward for older adults. (One would expect to see similar effects in both age groups; there is no reason to assume that the added requirement to switch would not be time-consuming for everyone, regardless of age). It is this geographical detail combined with the nature of the Brinley equation that leads to the greater observed cost in older adults. Consider the equation that describes these data:

$$\text{RT}_{older} = 1.68 \, \text{RT}_{younger} - 270.$$

Judging from Brinley's graph, the eyeballed median for the non-switching tasks for younger adults is around 1,500 ms; the eyeballed median for the switching tasks is around 2,300 ms. From the equation, the predicted median for the non-switching tasks for older adults is around 2,066 ms; the predicted median for the switching tasks is around 3,410 ms. The task-switching cost of younger adults is then about 800 ms (the difference between the two eyeballed medians), the predicted task-switching cost for older adults is about 1,344 ms (the difference between the two predicted medians)—much larger. Thus, the larger observed cost in older adults is simply due to a difference in task difficulty between switch tasks and non-switch tasks, coupled with the nature of the equation governing the younger-older RT relationship in this study. In other words: It is an artifact, and not informative about an underlying specific age-related deficit in the task-switching operation. Put yet differently: The group difference in the task-switching cost, in this case, is simply the wrong metric to assess group differences, because it will—with this Brinley function—lead to false positives. (For the reader who is still not convinced: Note that in the region of the graph where the two tasks overlap "horizontally," that is, where switch tasks and non-switch tasks yield similar response times in younger adults—between 1800 ms and 2100 ms—the data points for switch and non-switch tasks overlap.)

What is true for "costs" within an age group is also true, conversely, for age differences compared across conditions. The average absolute age difference across the task-switch conditions is larger than that obtained in the non-task switch conditions, but this is again an artifact of the former taking, on average, longer than the former in either age group. We can calculate the expected age difference using the Brinley equation, as above. Recall that if younger adults need 1,500 ms for non-switch tasks and 2300 ms for the switching tasks, the Brinley equation predicts that older adults will need 2,066 ms and 3,410 ms, respectively. Thus, even under this one-dimensional (i.e., single-line) model with no actual difference between the two conditions in their age-relatedness, the age difference is projected to differ across condition: 566 ms in the non-switch condition and 1,110 ms in the switch condition.

What this exercise demonstrates is that relying on the standard (i.e., additive) model to test for age differences across conditions, or condition differences across age groups, or, more generally, age group by condition interactions might yield spurious results—a bias toward false positives when the Brinley slope is larger than 1 and a bias toward false negatives when the slope is smaller than 1. (We will see one such case in the next chapter.)

Thus, at a higher level of abstraction, Brinley's radical departure from received wisdom was that he shifted the understanding of what defines a dissociation or a "true" (as opposed to "observed") age-by-condition/task/process interaction. The standard view, with its assessment of absolute differences between conditions as a function of age (or of age-related differences as a function of condition), typically in the form of an age-by-condition interaction, has been replaced by an examination of the underlying relationship between the response times of older and younger adults in each of the conditions. If all conditions are governed by the same equation, the conclusion must necessarily be that there is only a single age-related effect present in the data—regardless of differential age differences across conditions, differential condition effects across ages, or the presence of an age-by-condition interaction (a situation now known as "general slowing" or "generalized slowing"; e.g., Cerella, 1985, 1990; Hale, Myerson, & Wagstaff, 1987; Myerson, Hale, Wagstaff, Poon, & Smith, 1990).

Finding that a single Brinley function suffices to explain the data strongly suggests that processing differences between young and older adults in the given study are quantitative, rather than qualitative. Conversely, if the Brinley functions diverge, we would conclude that the two conditions/tasks/processes diverge in their age-related effects. The point can also be proven analytically. For instance, Cerella (1994) has shown that if a single information-processing mechanism drives the performance of both age groups, then the resulting plot of points in Brinley space is by necessity monotonic (i.e., it forms a single line). Dunn and Kirsner (1988) have shown that the inverse is also true: Monotonicity in two variables (in this case, older adults' mean latency and younger adults' mean latency) implies that a third variable (e.g., general cognitive efficiency) can be constructed to which both are monotonically related. (Put more understandably, if a single line describes the data in a Brinley plot, then response times of both younger and older adults are guided by the exact same principles.) Conversely, a non-monotonic Brinley plot—the emergence of two or more lines—implies, by mathematical necessity, the existence of distinct underlying age-sensitive mechanisms, one for each distinct line on the Brinley plot.

Brinley's paper thus reveals a clear tension between *phenomenology* and *theory* that is still very much alive within the field: The presence of clear and significant age-by-condition interactions does not preclude that the data may be governed by a single underlying function and thus, possibly, a single underlying causal mechanism. Part of my hope for this book is that it might instill the reflex in aging researchers to use general slowing (rather than numerical equivalence of age-related effects) as the null hypothesis and to use the appropriate measures to verily test for deviations from the general slowing pattern.

This being said, the years I spent doing the analyses described in this book also made me realize that some of us—and I certainly include myself in the roster of the guilty—have a tendency to focus solely on these theoretical aspects of the Brinley functions, to the detriment of the effects actually observed in the data. In this book, I will report both, because ultimately both are necessary for a complete understanding of age-related effects. The observed effects, after all, are what we perceive in the real world, and they have valid real-world consequences. For instance, in Chapter 6, I will argue that there are few, if any, age-related differences in tasks of selective attention such as the Stroop task. This conclusion is based on the finding that for all tasks purporting to measure selective attention, a single Brinley function suffices to capture both the slowing in the baseline and the selective attention conditions. This finding has obvious theoretical implications. The observed age effects, however, still differ across conditions, with larger observed slowing in the more difficult selective attention versions of the tasks. In real life, it is the larger absolute cost, not the Brinley function, that older adults have to deal with—the reality that they are at a particular disadvantage, for instance, when picking out speech in background noise, or when driving through neon-lit Las Vegas at night than when driving down a quiet village street on a sunny day. Cocktail party strangers or cars suddenly barging out of side streets don't care about general slowing; their cut-offs are absolute. One area in which observed age differences are more useful than modeled age differences is in consumer-oriented design or human factors. In human factors modeling, for instance (see Chapter 4), total time needed for a task is calculated from the steps that are necessary and the time needed for each step. In that case, absolute times, calculated from observed data, are just as useful, and probably more so, than generalizations drawn from theory (Jastrzembski & Charness, 2007).

Before moving on to descriptions of post-Brinley developments on Brinley plots, I would like to offer two more additional comments about Brinley's results.

A first note is that there is nothing a priori empirically or theoretically compelling about the type of young-old relationship that Brinley uncovered—a linear function with a slope larger than one and a negative intercept. There is no a priori reason, for instance, why the relationship should be linear. In fact, subsequent work has shown that reasonable theories can be constructed that predict a nonlinear relationship. One such theory is the Myerson et al. (1990) information-loss model. This model proposes that information is transferred through the cognitive system in a series of discrete steps; if a fixed proportion of information gets lost on each step, and this proportion differs by age, the expected Brinley function will be a power function rather than a straight line. Second, there is no a priori reason why the function should have a negative intercept and a slope larger than 1. For instance, one might well envision a scenario (and I will show some in Chapter 4) under which older adults are simply slowed by a fixed amount compared with younger adults. In that case (and only that case), one is allowed to apply standard ANOVA to examine deviations from this "additive" Brinley function.

The second comment is that Brinley was only able to recover the underlying relationship between younger and older adults' RTs because his study included a large number of conditions. This was, and is, an unusual situation. The field typically embraces much more minimal designs, often subjecting participants to no more than two or three task conditions. Such designs leave the nature of the young-old relationship uncovered. This, in turn, risks limiting the strength of the theoretical conclusions that can be drawn from any single study.

Figure 1.3 illustrates the conundrum. It shows fictitious data from a fictional study using three conditions, A, B, and C, in ascending order of difficulty as measured by RT of younger adults. (This is only one fictitious example among many such possible.) The pattern of fictitious results is one that is entirely plausible: A and B yield identical absolute age-related effects (in the Brinley plot, this means they have the same distance to the diagonal, which is the line of zero age effects), C yields a larger age-related effect. The standard interpretation (if one is ANOVA-minded) is that whatever process or component constitutes the difference between task C and the other tasks is differentially age-sensitive, that is, it slows down more with aging

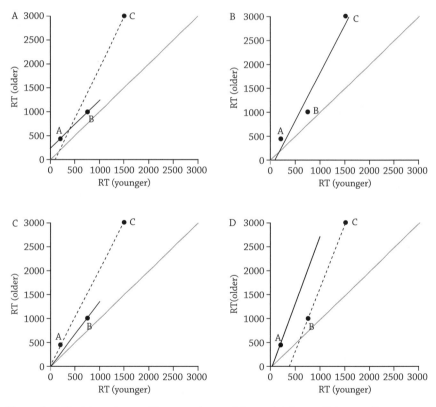

Figure 1.3 Fictitious data to illustrate the need for multiple-condition studies to assess Brinley configurations. Data from three fictitious experimental conditions (A, B, and C) represented in four Brinley plots, each with a distinct potential theoretical configuration of the data. Dots represent the data, solid and dashed lines the assumed Brinley functions; the dotted line is the equality diagonal. A sparse configuration of data, such as represented here (and in many experiments in the literature) puts almost no constraints on the theory to explain it.

than the processes involved in A and B. Depending on the underlying Brinley functions, however, this interpretation may or may not be correct. Panel A shows the circumstances under which this interpretation is correct: A and B both fall on the same Brinley function, parallel to the diagonal; C lies outside this function. Panel B shows a pattern where all three points are simply noisy approximations of the same Brinley function. Panel C shows the case where B is the outlier, and A and C are located on the same Brinley function. Finally, Panel D effectively shows the opposite pattern of what would be the traditional conclusion: Here, B and C fall along the same function, and A, the easiest task, shows an age effect that is larger than that in B and C.

I don't mean to suggest that any set of results can be interpreted any which way and to raise doubts about any set of findings in the literature. Rather, my point is that in order to make reasonable interpretations for a set of data, we need more information than is routinely afforded by our typically sparse designs. Where can we get that information? In Brinley's case, the additional information comes from the design itself. Although only two types of tasks are contrasted, each type of task is implemented at different levels of task difficulty, thus allowing for a nice window into the Brinley function for each. Some tasks have these difficulty manipulations quasi built-in. For instance, in iterative tasks, that is, tasks in which a set of operations is simply repeated, a natural difficulty manipulation is to vary the number of repetitions (e.g., the size of the memory set to be searched, or the number of distractor items to be ignored). This allows the researcher to quickly sweep out a detailed Brinley function. (I will go into more detail on iterative tasks in Chapter 4.) A second source of information is the existing literature, with the assumption that similar tasks yield similar types of Brinley functions. If the Brinley function, or at least its shape, is known, this additional information can assist the researcher with picking the right analytical technique to take the "general slowing" effect into account when testing whether the age differences vary by condition. (See below, e.g., Section 2.2.3, or Faust, Balota, Spieler, & Ferraro, 1999, for more detail.) This—I hope—is where meta-analysis in general and this book in particular can be helpful: I will recover Brinley functions for quite a number of tasks over the course of this book (especially in Chapters 4 and 6), and these might give researchers a good idea of what type of young-old relationship to expect.

1.3.2. Brinley Plots after Brinley: Interpretations of the Parameters and the Quest for Dissociations

Brinley's claims in his original paper were modest and rather informal. Brinley did not attach meaning to the shape of the function he uncovered—a straight line—nor was he interested in interpreting its parameters. These questions were tackled by the next generation of researchers (Salthouse, Cerella, and Myerson/Hale), after a period of delay during which Brinley's work lay forgotten.

1.3.2.1. Salthouse (1978): Aging in Critical Stages versus Aging as a Universal Decrement

The first attempt at more formal analysis appears in an unpublished 1978 paper by Salthouse. Salthouse's concern was theoretical rather than descriptive—what is the nature of age-related differences observed in speeded processes and how do these differences inform theories about cognitive processes?

Salthouse's paper starts from the then relatively uncontroversial postulate that the information-processing chain in any task can be parsed into three assumedly serial components—an input (or sensory) stage, a decision (or central, or computational, or cognitive) stage, and an output (or motor) stage. Turning to the literature, Salthouse observed that studies that have attempted to isolate specific age-related decrements in any of those three components have failed: Impairments have been reported in all three stages. This led Salthouse to posit that "the nature of the group difference is general or universal rather than localized or specific" (p. 13). He verifies this assumption with a simple linear model that estimates older adults' performance from younger adults' performance—a Brinley function.

Salthouse reasoned that if age differences were localized in a single stage (he calls this the *critical stage* model, p. 13), one would expect additivity; that is, aging would simply add a constant to one's response time. If so, the equation, or Brinley function, would be:

$$RT_{older} = RT_{younger} + k$$

The reasoning behind this assertion is not made explicit in the paper, but the finding would follow from (subscripted numbers indicate the three hypothetical processes—input, decision, output):

$$RT_{younger} = RT_{1,younger} + RT_{2,younger} + RT_{3,younger}$$

If only one of the three processes (let's say, process 2) would be impaired by an age-related factor a, one would expect:

$$RT_{older} = RT_{1,younger} + a\, RT_{2,younger} + RT_{3,younger}$$

or, rearranged:

$$RT_{older} = RT_{1,younger} + RT_{2,younger} + RT_{3,younger} + (a-1)\, RT_{2,younger}$$

and thus:

$$RT_{older} = RT_{younger} + (a-1)\, RT_{2,younger}$$

or (simplifying):

$$RT_{older} = RT_{younger} + k$$

This Brinley function describes a line parallel to the diagonal.

The second possibility is what Salthouse labels a *universal decrement* (p. 13), in which all processes are affected equally by age. This would lead to a Brinley function that passes through the origin, and has a slope larger than 1. This is a multiplicative model—aging adds a proportional or relative cost to response time:

$$RT_{older} = k\, RT_{younger}$$

Again, the reasoning is not made explicit, but it follows from the same principles. If

$$RT_{younger} = RT_{1,younger} + RT_{2,younger} + RT_{3,younger}$$

and all three processes would be impaired by age to the same degree, one would expect:

$$RT_{older} = a\ RT_{1,younger} + a\ RT_{2,younger} + a\ RT_{3,younger}$$

which simplifies to:

$$RT_{older} = a\ (RT_{1,younger} + RT_{2,younger} + RT_{3,younger})$$

or:

$$RT_{older} = a\ RT_{younger}$$

Armed with this small set of simple equations, Salthouse examined eight different data sets from the literature, each of which included three or more conditions. (By keeping the comparisons within-study, Salthouse hoped to eliminate part of the measurement error, namely the noise due to task and method variance.) Linear correlations within each data set were high: The lowest correlation was .84 (and this is an outlier, the second lowest was .96); the median was .99. This finding suggests that linear models fit the within-study data extremely well: The linear component explains, on average, 98% of the variance.

The parameter values for the Brinley functions resembled the universal decrement model best: Slopes were larger than 1 (varying between 1.58 and 2.26), and only one intercept was technically larger than zero (4 ms), the others varied between –35 ms and –430 ms. Salthouse took the slopes as clear evidence for the multiplicative model; he rejected the negative intercepts as measurement error.

1.3.2.2. *Cerella: Age-related Slowing Factors*

One obvious extension of Salthouse's paper (and one he suggested himself) would be to test the limits of this universal decrement—exactly how universal is universal? This was the question taken up by the next generation of researchers in this area—Cerella and colleagues (e.g., Cerella, Poon, & Williams, 1980; Cerella, 1985, 1990; Verhaeghen, Steitz, Sliwinski, & Cerella, 2003), Hale and Myerson and colleagues (e.g., Myerson & Hale, 1993) and Sliwinski and colleagues (e.g., Sliwinski & Hall, 1998).

1.3.2.2.1. Cerella, Poon, and Williams (1980): The First Brinley Meta-Analysis
    Cerella (Cerella, Poon, & Williams, 1980) was the first to combine findings obtained from different studies into a single analysis—the first meta-analytic Brinley plot, reproduced here in Figure 1.4. The plot contains data from 18 different studies, 99 conditions in total. Again, the main conclusion was that a single line fitted the data well (ordinary least-squares, or OLS, regression was used for fitting). The slope of this line

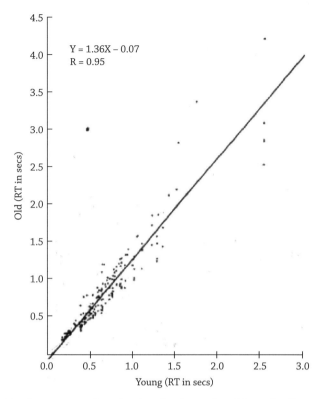

Figure 1.4 The first meta-analytic Brinley plot (reproduced from Cerella, Poon, & Williams, 1980). Average latencies of groups of older adults are plotted as a function of average latencies of groups of younger adults performing the same tasks (data were sourced from 18 studies, 99 points in total). Again, note the striking regularity of the plot.

was 1.36; its intercept –70 ms. The correlation between average response times of older adults and those of younger adults was .95; the Brinley function thus explained 90% of the variance. Like Salthouse before them, Cerella and colleagues simply ignored the intercept and stressed the multiplicative nature, or proportionality, of the young-old relationship: Rather than needing task-specific explanations for age-related slowing, the data seem governed by "a single mechanism operating equally in difficult and easy conditions, the mechanism of performance slowing" (p. 337). Brinley derived his conclusion from a single data set; Cerella and colleagues' result adds weight to Brinley's original conclusion by showing that the single-line result can also be obtained from an analysis that combines multiple samples of subjects and tasks.

Despite the presence of this strong "single mechanism," Cerella et al. set out to refine their explanation by explicitly examining the data for furcations—that is, different equations for different subject groups or for different families of tasks. They found a clear age-related furcation: The slope of the Brinley function was larger for participants over age 60 ($RT_{older} = 1.62\ RT_{younger} - 130$) than for adults younger than 60 years ($RT_{older} = 1.16\ RT_{younger} - 40$). Adding age to the equation increased the amount of variance explained from 90% to 96%. Thus (and quite unsurprisingly), the older the groups of older adults were on average, the larger the age-related effect in the data.

In a second sweep over the data, Cerella et al. added task-specific parameters to the equation. The authors identified five tasks—card sorting, memory scanning, S-R mapping, choice reaction time, and proactive interference—plus a miscellaneous class. The different tasks did yield a variety of slopes, ranging from 1.1 to 1.7, but the authors discarded this variation, on the grounds that adding the new parameters (six slopes, six intercepts) to the model did not increase the proportion of variance explained substantially—it went from 90% to 91%. (The paper itself is mum on whether this increase is statistically significant.)

The third sweep separated out all sensorimotor conditions ($RT_{older} = 1.14\ RT_{younger} - 10$) from all "mental processing" conditions ($RT_{older} = 1.62\ RT_{younger} + 0$). This increased the proportion of variance explained to 92%.

The conclusion from these analyses, as Cerella et al. saw it, is that age-related slowing in the peripheral, sensorimotor apparatus is less outspoken than age-related slowing in central, truly cognitive tasks, and that further refinement within those central tasks does not add significantly to this picture—"slowing appears to affect all mental processes equally" (p. 339).

1.3.2.2.2. Cerella (1985, 1990): Central and Peripheral Slowing Factors

The next theoretical advance was again provided by Cerella (1985). This paper contains the first attempt at incorporating an interpretation of the Brinley intercept. It is also the first paper to explicitly acknowledge the nested nature of multiple-studies Brinley plots. That is, studies often contribute multiple data points to the Brinley plot, making the resulting regression line an unknown mixture of within-study and between-study effects (a theme later taken up more formally by Sliwinski and colleagues, e.g., Sliwinski & Hall, 1998; Verhaeghen et al., 2003; Wasylyshyn, Sliwinski, & Verhaeghen, 2011; see Section 1.3.2.3.2 below). Consequently, Cerella fitted separate regression lines for each experiment in his data base.

This within-study fitting led to two striking conclusions: (a) All of the intercepts for the fitted functions were negative; and (b) a strong negative correlation between intercepts and slope emerged. The regression plot is reproduced in Figure 1.5 (the 35 lines in the graph represent regression analyses on a total of 189 data points from 35 experiments). The geometry is clear: The data take the shape of a fan emanating from the point where RT of younger adults equals 464 ms and that of older adults 568 ms:

$$RT_{older} - 568 = k\ (RT_{younger} - 464).$$

To explain this fan, Cerella returned to his earlier distinction between peripheral (sensorimotor) and central (computational, or cognitive) task processes. More specifically, if it is assumed (a) that different tasks are comprised of different mixtures of these two components (i.e., some tasks rely more heavily on peripheral processing, others more on central processing); and (b) that there is a single central and a single peripheral age-related slowing factor, the end result would, naturally, be a fan, with the slopes driven by the relative proportion of the two types. (For more details, including the mathematical argument, see the original publication.)

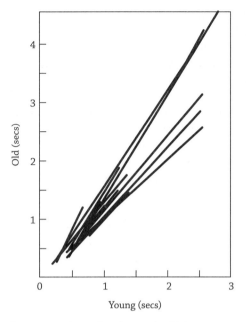

Figure 1.5 Individual regression lines fitted to each of 35 experiments (189 data points total) illustrating the fan effect often obtained in Brinley plots (reproduced from Cerella, 1985).

In his next paper, Cerella (1990) introduced a special case of the fan model—the *multilayered slowing model*. (This is a bit of a misnomer: In reality, the model contains merely two layers.) The simplifying assumption to arrive at this model is to assume that the sensorimotor stage is constant across tasks. This assumption derives from the observation that the tasks included in the database all were quite alike in their perceptual and motor requirements—they all involve the perception of a visual stimulus and the pressing of a button. Thus, Cerella argued, the sensorimotor processes can all be considered to be identical enough to make the assumption that they are constant across tasks. What varies is the time needed for central processing. More formally:

$$\mathrm{RT}_{\mathrm{younger}} = \textbf{central} + \textbf{peripheral,}$$

and:

$$\textbf{central} = \mathrm{RT}_{\mathrm{younger}} - \textbf{peripheral.}$$

Using the term c to describe the age-related slowing factor in central processing, and p to denote age-related slowing in peripheral processing:

$$\mathrm{RT}_{\mathrm{older}} = c\ \textbf{central} + p\ \textbf{peripheral.}$$

Substituting for central in this equation yields:

$$\mathrm{RT}_{\mathrm{older}} = p\ \textbf{peripheral} + c\ (\mathrm{RT}_{\mathrm{younger}} - \textbf{peripheral}).$$

This can be rearranged as:

$$\text{RT}_{\text{older}} - p \text{ peripheral} = c \, (\text{RT}_{\text{younger}} - \text{peripheral}),$$

which is, in effect, the fan as described above. The equation immediately explains the origin of the fan: It is the time needed for peripheral processing in younger and older adults. The ratio of the older/younger fan-origin points gives us the peripheral slowing factor p. The parameter c that governs the fan is the age-related slowing present in the central task component.

Note that the next-to-last equation can also be rearranged as:

$$\text{RT}_{\text{older}} = c \, \text{RT}_{\text{younger}} + (p \text{ peripheral} - c \text{ peripheral}),$$

or, simplified:

$$\text{RT}_{\text{older}} = c \, \text{RT}_{\text{younger}} + (p - c) \text{ peripheral}$$

This final equation is a Brinley function: It expresses RT_{older} as a function of $\text{RT}_{\text{younger}}$. What this mathematical excursion then demonstrates is that the slope of the Brinley function (under the assumptions detailed above, viz. that peripheral and central processes are additive, and that all tasks in the data set share the same sensorimotor processes) can be interpreted directly as c, that is, the average slowing factor in central processing in the task or tasks at hand. The intercept, that is $(p - c)$ peripheral, is messier—it is a mixture of two slowing factors (p and c) and the time younger adults need for the peripheral components. Its form, however, makes clear why it so often turns out to be negative: Whenever the age-related slowing factor in central processing c is larger than the age-related slowing factor in peripheral processing p, $(p - c)$ will be negative, and hence $(p - c)$ peripheral, the intercept, will be smaller than zero as well. The equation also explains the negative correlation between intercept and slopes in empirical Brinley functions: The larger the age-related slowing factor in central processing c, the more negative the intercept will become. (Geometrically, this will translate into a steeper line in the fan.)

In sum, Cerella (1990) provides us with a succinct interpretation of both the slope and the intercept of the Brinley function—the former is the age-related slowing factor in central processing; the latter is not noise, as Salthouse (1978) assumed, but it carries meaning, and it will often by necessity be smaller than zero.

1.3.2.3. Brinley Plots in the 1990s and the 2000s: Further Developments

In terms of theory, in the sense of understanding of what the Brinley parameters mean, the Cerella multilayered slowing model is essentially where the field stands. Significant advances, however, have been made in the application of Brinley plots to research questions, with a clear thrust toward the examination of age-related dissociations, as well as in methodology, where standard regression procedures have been abandoned in favor of multilevel modeling. Throughout the 1990s and 2000s, doubts about the suitability and accuracy of Brinley plotting have been raised as well; I will address these in the next section.

1.3.2.3.1. Dissociations and the Question of Dimensionality; Efficiency Modes

Enthusiasm for Cerella's claim of a single general age-related slowing factor in central computational processes waned considerably in the 1990s and 2000s. As more Brinley plots became available, the scatter in these plots became conspicuous, raising the possibility that the degree of slowing might be less than uniform from task to task. At the same time, researchers started noticing clear similarities in the age-related slowing factors of tasks thought to represent similar kinds or families or domains of processes, spurring the study of dissociations in age-related slowing.

At least three such dissociations have now been posited.

The first of these has been mentioned above. It concerns the bifurcation of age-related effects in peripheral (i.e., perceptual and motor processes; a slope around 1.2), and central (i.e., computational and decision; a slope around 1.5) processes (Cerella, 1985).

Second, Hale and Myerson and colleagues (e.g., Hale & Myerson, 1996; Jenkins, Myerson, Joerding, & Hale, 2000; Lima, Hale, & Myerson, 1991; Myerson & Hale, 1993; see also Sliwinski & Hall, 1998) uncovered another dissociation: They consistently found shallower Brinley slopes for tasks measuring lexical/verbal processes (a slope of about 1.5) than for tasks tapping spatial processing (a slope of about 2.0).

Finally, some have proposed that aging brings about deficits in the basic executive control processes that govern working memory (for a review, see McDowd & Shaw, 2000). This claim has taken many forms. For instance, Kliegl, Mayr, and colleagues have consistently found smaller slowing factors for tasks that do not require coordination within working memory ("sequential" tasks) than for tasks that do ("coordinative" tasks) (e.g., Kliegl, Mayr, & Krampe, 1994; Mayr, Kliegl, & Krampe, 1996; Verhaeghen, Kliegl, & Mayr, 1997). Sequential tasks involve processing that proceeds in a chain-like fashion, with intermediate results immediately feeding into the next step. Coordinative processing occurs when intermediate results have to be stored in working memory while additional processing is carried out concurrently. For instance, Verhaeghen et al. (1997) found no age difference in mental arithmetic for chain-like sums (e.g., $5 + 2 + 1 - 3 - 4 + 2$) but a rather large age difference for sums in which parentheses introduced a concurrent storage-and-processing requirement (e.g., $[6 - (2 + 1)] + [8 - (4 + 2)]$). Other researchers have made more explicit claims about age-related deficits in specific aspects of executive control—inhibitory control, dual-task performance, and/or task switching. Not all of these dissociations, however, have been confirmed in either primary research or meta-analytic Brinley plots. In meta-analyses from my lab, we obtained null results—equal effects in baseline conditions and critical conditions—for Stroop and negative priming (Verhaeghen & De Meersman, 1998a and 1998b) as well as for task switching (Wasylyshyn et al., 2011); a positive result was observed for task mixing (Wasylyshyn et al., 2011).

(The present book is, among other things, a replication and extension of this search for dissociations. The former two [central/peripheral and verbal/spatial] are revisited in Chapters 2 and 4; the latter [low vs. high executive control] in Chapter 6.)

One remarkable result from the dissociation studies cited above (as well as Verhaeghen et al., 2002, and Verhaeghen, Cerella, & Basak, 2006) is that these dissociations appear as qualitative, all-or-none jumps in processing ability, to the exclusion of intermediary values. To underscore the quantal character of the deficits,

Verhaeghen et al. (2002) and Verhaeghen, Cerella, and Basak (2006) labeled these strata *efficiency modes*.

All of this work conducted throughout the 1990s and 2000s has made it clear that the assumption of general slowing is untenable; it has now yielded to the reality of major dissociations. At this juncture in time, the interesting question is no longer to what extent a single factor can predict the data, but rather what the minimum number of factors is that is needed to account for slowing on a particular set of tasks. In other words: What is the *dimensionality* of age-related slowing?

For the study of dissociations to be interesting from the point of view of cognitive aging theory, more is needed than the mere demonstration that they exist. It should also be possible to capture these dissociations in a coherent model or framework that, after the fact, should be able to reliably classify new tasks into each of the posited dimensions. In this book, I will attempt to build such a framework, most noticeably in Chapters 5 and 6.

1.3.2.3.2. Multilevel Modeling of Brinley Functions

The 1990s also saw a push for more methodological sophistication in the estimation of Brinley functions. The first of these, by Myerson and colleagues (e.g., Myerson, Ferraro, Hale, & Lima, 1992), was a fine-tuning: Ordinary least-squares (OLS) regression was replaced with weighted least-square regression (WLS), weighting for sample size within study. This gives studies with larger samples more weight, potentially reducing measurement noise that arises more prominently in smaller samples.

The second and more incisive change was introduced by Sliwinski and Hall (1998). Sliwinski and Hall (like Cerella, 1985, and, more implicitly, Salthouse, 1978, before them) noted that studies often contribute more than a single point to any Brinley data set. One problem is that this creates a double imbalance in the data set. First, different studies contribute different numbers of data points to the equation, introducing differential weighting, and, second, the levels of the independent variable (i.e., latencies of younger adults) potentially vary widely across studies.

A bigger problem still is that standard regression procedures like OLS and WLS fail to take the nested nature of the data into account. When the nesting of the data points within studies is ignored, the regression coefficients are hard to interpret because they represent a mixture of within-study and between-study effects. Moreover, Sliwinski and Hall argue that analyses are only meaningful at the within-study level, because the within-study regression coefficient is the coefficient directly associated with the actual manipulation of the independent variable of interest. The between-study coefficient is contaminated with other sources of variation—sample differences as well as differences in task and procedure. OLS and WLS will also lead to less precise parameter estimates, and tend to introduce a negative bias in the standard errors, potentially leading to overly lenient significance testing.

The solution is simple: to adopt multilevel modeling (also know as hierarchical linear modeling), distinguishing a within-study level from a between-study level. "Study" here means an independent sample of subjects; a single paper might contain multiple samples (e.g., multiple experiments on independent subjects, or the same task performed by males and females, or the like). The approach (see Sliwinski & Hall, 1998, or Verhaeghen, Steitz, Sliwinski, & Cerella, 2003 for some more detail) requires the specification of a within-study model, representing response times of older adults as a function of the corresponding response times of younger adults, and can be implemented in any analysis package that supports multilevel modeling (HLM, MLWin, etc.):

$$\text{RT}_{\text{older},it} = \beta_{0t} + \beta_{1t}\,\text{RT}_{\text{younger},it} + R_{it},$$

where $\text{RT}_{\text{older},it}$ is the average response time of older adults from condition i in study t, $\text{RT}_{\text{younger},it}$ is the average response time of younger adults from condition i in study t, β_{0t} is the intercept for study t, β_{1t} is the slope relating older to younger RTs for study t, and R_{it} is the residual for condition i in study t.

The between-study level model represents each regression parameter as a function of the overall mean and each study's unique effect as follows:

$$\beta_{0t} = \bar{\beta}_0\,U_{0t},$$

$$\beta_{1t} = \bar{\beta}_1\,U_{1t}$$

where $\bar{\beta}_0$ is the average intercept across all studies, $\bar{\beta}_1$ is the average slopes across all studies, U_{0t} and U_{1t} are the increments to intercept and slope associated with study t. The fixed effects, $\bar{\beta}_0$ and $\bar{\beta}_1$, provide precision-weighted estimates of the average within-study intercept and slope; the random effects, U_{0t} and U_{1t}, provide estimates of the within-study regression parameter variance.

These equations implement the general slowing model. Task effects are examined in the within-study-level model by introducing a dummy variable that codes for task (task = 0 if task A, task = 1 if task B):

$$\text{RT}_{\text{older},it} = \beta_{ot} + \beta_{1t}\text{RT}_{\text{younger},it} + \alpha_{0t}\,(\text{task}) + \alpha_{1t}\,(\text{task} * \text{RT}_{\text{younger},it}) + R_{it},$$

The parameter α_{0t} conveys the effect of task on the intercept of the Brinley function, and the parameter α_{1t} conveys the effect of task on the slope. If the average $\bar{a}_0$ is statistically different from zero, coupled with an absence of age difference in $\bar{a}_1$, then the difference between the Brinley functions for the two tasks is situated in the intercept only. If $\bar{a}_1$ is significantly larger than 1, then the slopes of the Brinley functions for the two tasks are significantly different. If more than two tasks are tested against each other, the number of dummy variables is increased accordingly; with k tasks, $(k - 1)$ dummy variables are necessary. (This is standard practice in testing main effects and interactions involving categorical variables in regression analysis; Jaccard & Turrisi, 2003, offer a nice tutorial.) For instance, if there are three tasks A, B, and C, two dummy variables, task_1 and task_2, will be constructed, task A represented by $\text{task}_1 = 0$ and $\text{task}_2 = 0$; task B by $\text{task}_1 = 1$ and $\text{task}_2 = 0$; and task C by $\text{task}_1 = 0$ and $\text{task}_2 = 1$. Pairwise comparisons of the fitted parameters can then determine which Brinley functions are statistically different from each other.

Model fit in multilevel modeling is based on a deviance statistic, that is, it is an index of lack of fit (specifically, it is -2 times the value of the log likelihood at its maximum). This statistic is not very useful in and of itself, but it can be used to test the relative fit of nested models; that is, models where some of the parameters are fixed (e.g., set to zero) versus models where more, sometimes all, of the parameters are estimated freely. The difference between the two deviance values has a *chi*-square distribution with the difference in the number of parameters estimated as its degrees of freedom. In the text, I will refer to this difference statistic as ΔLR χ^2 (*k*), with *k* denoting the degrees of freedom.

A second useful statistic is R^2, the amount of variance accounted for by the model. This value is calculated as a pseudo-R^2; that is, the ratio of the difference in within-study variance when the model of interest is fitted versus when the empty model (i.e., $RT_{older} = \beta_{0t}$) is fitted over the within-study variance when the empty model is fitted. (The empty model just claims that response times of older adults equal a constant.) The R^2 value expresses how much of the within-study variance is accounted for by the introduction of younger adults' latency and the task parameters, if any. Note that, unlike the OLS and WLS estimates of R^2, which are a mixture of variance accounted for at the between-study and within-study level, this quantity is evaluated solely at the within-study level.

Throughout this book, I will use multilevel modeling for all Brinley analyses (as well as state-trace analyses, explained below). To unclutter the text, I will report only the within-study level equations. These are the equations of interest, and they can be read like the standard regression equations with which most of us are familiar. This is also the approach Sliwinski and I and our colleagues have taken in our collaborative meta-analyses using this approach (Verhaeghen et al., 2003; Wasylyshyn et al., 2011).

Sliwinski and Hall introduced one novelty that has gone unfollowed: They centered the data points around the mean of each study to facilitate parameter estimation. Centering creates a less biased estimate of the Brinley slopes, but it also leads to a considerable loss of information—lost are both the actual geometry of the data points, that is, their location in the Brinley plot, as well as the function's intercept, which, as we have seen above, is a meaningful quantity. In subsequent work, Sliwinski and I and our collaborators have reverted back to the customary practice of using actual response times rather than centered values (Verhaeghen et al., 2003; Wasylshyn et al., 2011). I will follow that practice here.

1.3.2.4. *Brinley Plots: Potential Issues and Problems*

Brinley plots, like any other methodology, should not be applied blindly. In this section, I gather a few known potential issues and problems (as well as one non-issue), and discuss how I will address them (or not) in this book. The issues concern potential contamination of the data by age-related strategy differences, the difference between Brinley plots and quantile-quantile plots (Q-Q plots), as well as a few technical/methodological issues that could lead to an underestimation of the number of dimensions present in the data (task restriction, lack of data overlap, reliance on proportion of variance explained, and affirming the null hypothesis).

1.3.2.4.1. Age-related Strategy Shifts and Brinley Plots:
The Correspondence Assumption

The interpretation of the age differences observed in Brinley plots is quantitative in nature: Older adults are slower than younger adults in this or that task or process by a certain amount. Hidden underneath this reading is the assumption that younger and older adults are approaching the tasks in the same way; that is, that they perform the same operations in the same fashion (e.g., in parallel or serially). Cerella (1990) has labeled this the correspondence axiom—the idea that age-related differences observed in Brinley plots should reflect defects in the "component hardware" rather than a shift in "software strategies" (p. 215), or defects in the "integrity" of the cognitive system, not its "logic." This assumption isn't exclusive to the Brinley plot. It also lies at the heart, for instance, of many modeling efforts in cognitive psychology, such as the diffusion model and its many variations, one of which will be explored in Chapter 3. In such endeavors, individual or group differences are modeled as changes in the values of specific parameters that govern the duration or precision of specific aspects of processing, and the assumption is that the task itself—its constituent processes and their chaining—is performed identically across individuals or groups.

The issue of correspondence becomes especially important when investigating age-related dissociations. If we find, for instance (as we will; Chapters 2, 4, and 5) that there are larger age-related differences in processing spatial information than in processing linguistic information, do those differences reflect a larger age-related deficit in the cognitive processes underlying spatial tasks than in the processes underlying linguistic tasks, or could it be the case that older adults simply use less efficient strategies for spatial processing than younger adults?

There is no easy way out of this conundrum. Cerella (1990) advises to examine within-study Brinley plots for non-monotonicity. (He calls this a less rigorous test, p. 215, compared with what would be the ideal, but rather unpractical, test, that is, to exhaustively build a cognitive model for each task in the plot.) The reasoning behind the monotonicity idea is that if younger and older adults do perform the same computations, they should exhibit the same rank ordering of task difficulty. The problem of false dissociations, however, still remains: If monotonicity is obtained, one can be reasonably sure that correspondence holds; if it is not (as in the spatial/linguistic example), the interpretation is ambiguous: It may signal a true dissociation or a non-correspondence.

In the present book, I take two approaches I hope will minimize the risk of non-correspondence. The first is to include only tasks that could be reasonably assumed not to be subject to individual differences in strategy use. Take, for instance, a lexical decision task. In lexical decision task, subjects decide whether a string of letters ("BUY," "BIY") form a word or not. It seems reasonable to assume that there are few individual differences in the way this task is performed. (In fact, I cannot think of any top-down strategy to use here, other than to read and see if the mental lexicon retrieves an entry.) Take, as another example, a mental rotation task. Subjects are shown a rotated object (typically an abstract shape or a letter or the mirror image of a letter) and have to decide whether the stimulus, when rotated back, matches a comparison stimulus or not (mismatches are typically mirror images). Again, it is difficult to conceive of what subjects could be doing other than mentally rotate. (There is some debate in the mental rotation literature. It mostly concerns what type of representation—holistic or feature-based—is used for the rotation; e.g., Raabe, Höger, & Delius, 2006.) Chapter 4 will model age differences in such fast, elementary tasks. Related is the assumption that shorter tasks are less likely to be amenable to strategic variation. For that reason, I will limit myself in this book (with a few exceptions) to tasks that take on average 2,000 ms or less to perform in younger adults.

A second approach to avoid potential non-correspondence is to examine convergence of results across tasks. Consider the example above of an observed age-related dissociation between linguistic and spatial processing. If this observation is based on a comparison between a single linguistic task and a single spatial task, it should probably not carry too much weight. If we continue to probe more and more tasks, however, and consistently keep finding this dissociation (ideally with more or less identical slowing factors for tasks fitting within the same category), it becomes harder and harder to maintain that the results would be produced by age-related differences in strategy use: The more tasks are included within a task family, the less likely that there will be overlap in the actual strategies applied to them. For instance, one could argue that visual search, mental rotation, subitizing (i.e., the rapid counting of a small number of elements, typically four or less), and mouse movement to one of multiple targets are all tasks that fit into a spatial task family. It is, however, hard to imagine what strategic behaviors they would have in common. Yet, I will conclude in Chapter 4 that this set of tasks shares a common age-related slowing factor. The lack of strategic overlap in the tasks makes it more likely that the similarity in the age-related slowing factors across tasks is due to the spatial processes per se.

1.3.2.4.2. Brinley Plots are not Q-Q Plots

A second issue that needs to be addressed is a simple misunderstanding that should not have been. It concerns a confusion between Brinley plots and Q-Q plots, originating in a paper by Ratcliff and colleagues (Ratcliff, Spieler, & McKoon, 2000), which has led to grave doubts about the interpretation of the former. The source of the confusion is that Ratcliff and colleagues claim that Brinley plots *are* Q-Q plots—and this is simply not the case. (Readers interested in a more detailed treatment of this topic might wish to consult Myerson, Adams, Hale, & Jenkins, 2003; and Myerson, Robertson, & Hale, 2007.)

What is the difference?

A Brinley plot, as I hope is clear by now, represents an ordered sequence of pairs of data points. Each pair represents the average response time of a group of younger adults coupled with the average response time of a group of older adults *performing the exact same task*. A Q-Q plot, in contrast, is a quantile-quantile plot. In the context of a meta-analysis, a Q-Q plot would be constructed from the same data as the Brinley plot—groups of younger and older adults performing a set of identical tasks—but the direct coupling between points within each pair would be destroyed. Instead, in the Q-Q plot, the data would be reorganized such that the response times within each age group—younger and older adults—are rank-ordered from fastest to slowest, and then paired up again, so that the fastest mean for younger adults is plotted against the fastest mean for older adults, the second-fastest mean of younger adults against the second-fastest mean for older adults and so on. Thus, the new pairings are artificial and make no reference to the actual tasks being performed.

As an illustration, consider we have four tasks, requiring 250 ms, 300 ms, 700 ms, and 900 ms for younger adults to perform. Assume these same tasks take 750 ms, 500 ms, 1400 ms, and 1200 ms in a group of older adults. The Brinley plot pairs would be: (250, 750), (300, 500), (700, 1400), and (900, 1200), respectively, simply lining up the tasks. The Q-Q plot would look very different. First rank-ordering the data within each age group would result in the following pairings: (250, 500), (300, 750), (700, 1200), and (900, 1400). It is easy to see from this example that a Q-Q plot will be monotonic by definition (in other words, whatever the plot actually shows, it cannot show dissociations), whereas a Brinley plot need not be.

It is not clear where Ratcliff's confusion comes from—prior to Ratcliff et al., the term "Brinley plot" had been used for reordered data exactly once, by Maylor and Rabbitt (1994), and they took care to use the term "Brinley plots of distributions" to distinguish their plot (a plot of rank-ordered individual means) from the standard Brinley plots based on non-reordered condition means.

This distinction is not academic—the toy example above shows that the same set of data, Brinley-plotted, can look very different from the same set of data, Q-Q-plotted. The difference is between a plot that is informative of the structure of age-related differences in tasks or processes (the Brinley plot), and a plot that isn't (the Q-Q plot). A Q-Q plot is highly regular, by definition monotonic; Ratcliff et al. demonstrated quite nicely that the slope of the Q-Q plot is simply the ratio of the standard deviation of the older over younger adult condition means, and that its intercept is a measure of the relative speed of the two groups. Neither of those pieces of information tells us anything new. The Q-Q plot is informative, however, about the difference in shape between the distribution of mean response times of older adults and younger adults (Myerson et al., 2007; Wilk & Gnanadesikan, 1968). How nonacademic the difference between Brinley plots and Q-Q plots is, is illustrated in Figure 1.6. The figure shows the exact same data plotted as a Brinley plot (Panel A) and a Q-Q plot (Panel B). The data are 575 data pairs, foreshadowed from Chapter 4, representing a meta-analysis of two sets of tasks. The first set is comprised of perceptual tasks—fixation duration, flicker fusion, gap detection, and P300. The second set contains spatial tasks—subitizing, movement time, feature and conjunction visual search, and mental rotation. In the Brinley plot, a bifurcation is clearly visible—we have two lines, one with a slope of 1.1, the other with a slope of 1.8. This plot allows us to make the interpretation that perceptual tasks are characterized by age-related effects that are much less outspoken than the age-related effects visible in spatial tasks. Additionally, the Brinley plot tells us something about the dispersion of the points: The second factor especially appears to show large variability around its mean, inviting us, perhaps, to examine more closely what the source of that variability might be. Now consider the Q-Q plot: All of this information is simply and irretrievably lost. The plot inspires exactly nothing; it leads to no follow-up questions. In that very narrow sense, Ratcliff and colleagues were right: *If* Brinley plots were Q-Q plots, they would not tell us much. But they are not, and they do.

1.3.2.4.2. Technical/Methodological Issues

Finally, there are a few potential technical/methodological issues concerning Brinley plots that are very much worth mentioning. These technical issues can interfere with a correct assessment of the dimensionality in the plots, misleading one (typically) into concluding that fewer dimensions are present in the data, the world, or both, than actually are.

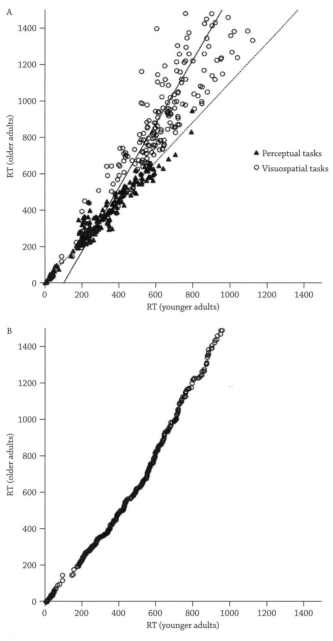

Figure 1.6 Brinley plots are not Q-Q plots. The exact same meta-analytical data (sets of perceptual and visuospatial tasks culled from Chapter 4) represented in two formats: a Brinley plot (Panel A), which preserves the original grouping of (young, old) pairs, and a Q-Q plot (Panel B), which destroys the original grouping in favor of rank-ordering the data within each set (i.e., within the young and within the old) before forming pairs. Each data point represents a condition within an experiment. The Brinley plot is informative about the perceptual/visuospatial dissociation in the data (the dotted line is the regression line for the perceptual data the solid line for the visuospatial data); the Q-Q plot is not.

1.3.2.4.2.1. TASK RESTRICTION   A first potential methodological issue is possible task restriction. Whether or not a dissociation will emerge in the data is obviously a function of what tasks are included in the data set, and whether or not the
researcher is able to set up a meaningful contrast between those tasks. For instance,
the data sets used by Cerella et al. (1980) and Cerella (1985) included tasks that were
mostly of the choice reaction time variety, as well as tasks of memory scanning, a
rather sparse subset of all possible latency tasks. The R^2 of the equation might then
have been unnaturally inflated compared with the R^2 of an equation for a data set that
would have tapped a wider variety of tasks.

In this book, I will take two measures to weaken the deleterious effects of task
restriction. First, in Chapter 2, which provides a first, mostly exploratory pass over a
representative sample of aging studies, I will apply no censorship to the tasks whatsoever, except for the latency range restriction introduced above (i.e., younger adults
should, on average, be able to perform the tasks in 2 seconds or less). Presumably,
the only reason for not including a particular task would then be that the field has
not been interested in it. This analysis should afford a rather good estimate of how
much variance different models, including the single-line model, truly account for.
Second, whenever feasible and appropriate, I will use targeted contrasts to test for dissociations. This technique is used most extensively in Chapters 4 and 6, where I investigate an amalgam of elementary tasks and the role of executive control demands,
respectively.

1.3.2.4.2.2. LACK OF RANGE OVERLAP   A related problem is potential lack
of overlap in the range of data points for different tasks, a problem first noted by
Perfect (1994), and recently re-examined by Prince, Brown, and Heathcote (2012).
Figure 1.7 illustrates the point. The graph depicts meta-analytic data, again foreshad-
owing Chapter 4. Consider Panel A. It shows results from the four perceptual tasks
earlier illustrated in Figure 1.6—fixation duration, flicker fusion, gap detection, and
P300, now split up by task. These four tasks have little or no horizontal overlap, but
they seem to fall along a single Brinley line (and they do—see Chapter 4). The conclusion, just by eye, is that general slowing is all there is to the graph—all data are part
of one elongated cloud. Contrast this with Panel B, where the peak time of the P300
component of event-related potentials in (mostly) oddball tasks[3] is compared with the
time needed to move the arm or a computer mouse to one of several potential target
locations. Now there is almost absolute overlap between the horizontal locus of the
two data clouds, but their vertical position is markedly different—it would be hard to
argue, by eye, that the two clouds fall along a single line. Finally, Panel C shows yet a
different situation, the one to which Perfect was alerting the field. Here we have two
sets of tasks with no horizontal overlap—a set of fast tasks (fixation duration, flicker
fusion, and gap detection) on the one hand, and a slow one (mental rotation) on the
other. In Chapter 4, we will see that these tasks reliably split into two factors (the
fast tasks loading on one, the slow on another factor), and this can be gleaned from
the figure as well: The three former tasks have a shallow Brinley slope, the latter task
a steep slope. Yet, a single equation (with a slope of 1.67 and an intercept of –49 ms)
fits these data very well, with 98% of the variance explained in an OLS model. (We
can explain an extra percent of variance by fitting a nonlinear model, such as Myerson

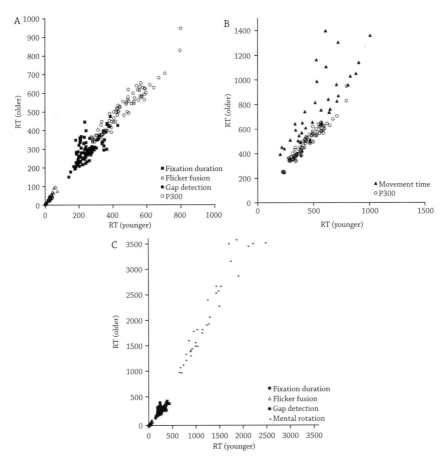

Figure 1.7 Illustration of the lack of range overlap problem. Data are culled from Chapter 4; each data point represents a condition in an experiment. Panel A shows lack of overlap in tasks that reliably fall along the same Brinley function; Panel B shows range overlap for two tasks that clearly do not fall along the same Brinley function; Panel C shows the interesting case: One might be tempted to conclude that all four tasks fall along the same line, but statistically they do not.

et al.'s information-loss model.) Noting this large R^2, we might be tempted to conclude that only a single dimension is present in the data. Were we to run an explicit interaction analysis (including an interaction term for slow and fast tasks, and testing for its significance), this analysis would indeed show the presence of a dissociation. But there is a circularity here: We can only detect this dissociation if we know it is likely to be there, that is, if we suspect what tasks group into one factor, and what into the other. What if there are more than two groupings? Worse, what if we don't have any a priori idea of how to group the data? (The latter situation will happen in Chapter 2, where I will attempt to cluster a large set of tasks into meaningful categories; a large category of tasks will remain unclassified.) We can run more descriptive diagnostics, such as plotting residuals as a function of task or as a function of younger adults' mean

RT, but this is only helpful if we can then devise a scheme to categorize the data. The most fruitful way around this problem (implemented in Chapter 5) is to explicitly build a set of models that incorporates the lowest level of categorization possible, that is, the level of tasks.

1.3.2.4.2.3. BLIND RELIANCE ON R^2 VALUES   This problem brings us to a related issue, and that is blind reliance on high R^2 values to assess the fit of Brinley models (Fisk & Fisher, 1994; Perfect, 1994). High values of R^2 are obviously needed before we can conclude that a given model fits the data, but high values of R^2 are not sufficient—correlations in Brinley plots tend to be high, partially for trivial reasons.

One contributor to high correlations in Brinley plots is the nature of the data: Young-old data pairs have a correlation built in simply because latency of older adults is typically slower than that of younger adults. In a Brinley plot, that means that the data are confined to the region above the diagonal. This by necessity creates an elongated data cloud and thus, again by necessity, a positive correlation. The size of that spurious correlation will vary with the number of data points (fewer data points, higher correlation) and their horizontal dispersion (more dispersion, higher correlation). As an illustration, I calculated, by repeated simulation, the expected value for the correlation for the data set included in the next chapter. The empirical data set contains 1,354 data pairs, with latencies ranging from approximately 300 ms to 2000 ms for younger adults. In my simulation, I created 50 data sets, randomly drawing 1,354 data pairs, one from the [350–2,000] uniform distribution, one from the [350–4,000] uniform distribution. The former would simulate the data for younger adults, the latter the data for older adults. In case the data point that was supposed to be the younger-adult point was larger than the older-adult point, they were swapped, so that within each young-old pair the young-adult latency was always shorter than the older-adult latency. One of the 50 data sets is shown in Figure 1.8, Panel A. The range of correlations was surprisingly restricted—between .26 and .38 (and thus nowhere near zero), with a median of .33, yielding a median R^2 of .11. This simulation is obviously naïve, and some of its assumptions (the use of uniform distributions, the abrupt cut-offs) can be rightfully challenged. What this quick armchair exercise does show is that the null hypothesis in a Brinley plot is not that the correlation is zero; that is simply an unrealistic scenario. It also suggests that the R^2 values typically observed (R^2s above .90 in the studies mentioned above; .79 in the studies in Chapter 5) are quite a bit higher than would be expected if the generating process is anything like the process used here. Thus, the simple fact that older adults are slower than younger adults forces a positive correlation upon the Brinley plot, but not of the magnitude that is typically observed, strongly suggesting that Brinley plots are more than random arrangements.

To provide a fairer evaluation of the size of the Brinley correlation, a less naïve model, however, would be preferable. Figure 1.8, Panel B, illustrates a more realistic null model, again with a sample data set. This model takes into account that the 1,354 data pairs from the next chapter are not completely independent, but are nested within studies. More specifically, the data points were nested within 175 studies, each then contributing, on average, 8 data points to the Brinley plot. If we assume that these points are derived from different difficulty levels of the same task, and if we assume that the correspondence assumption holds, then a more realistic expectation would be that

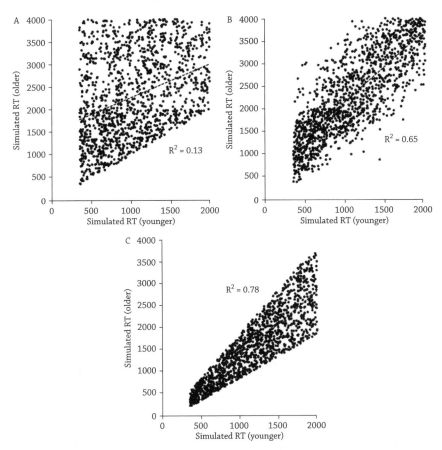

Figure 1.8 Three simulations, 1,354 data points each, to illustrate expected values of R^2 under different generating models for the data. Panel A: Younger-adult and older-adult data are generated randomly and independently, then randomly paired; Panel B: Younger-adult and older-adult data are generated such that random groupings of 8 pairs are created to simulate 8-condition studies; within groupings, pairings were rearranged so that the within-study data are monotonic; Panel C: Random data were generated for younger adults, these were randomly grouped in clusters of 8, and then a random slowing factor between 1 and 2 was applied to these data points to yield the older adult data. The actual data conform better to the latter model.

there is monotonicity within the mini-Brinley plots formed by each of these clusters of 8 points. I simulated 1,354 young-old data pairs as described above, and then created random groupings of 8. Within each of these groupings, the data points were re-paired, such that the fastest young-adult point was paired with the fastest old-adult point, the second-fastest young-adult point was paired with the second-fastest old-adult point, and so on. (In effect, this creates mini Q-Q plots, of 8 data pairs each.) Figure 1.8, Panel B, clearly shows that this restriction imposes more structure on the data—the band is now much narrower, and the correlation goes up correspondingly, to .81, implying an R^2 of.65. Thus, if we assume that older adults perform cognitive tasks in the same way as younger adults do—with monotonicity within task within study as a conse-quence—the expected correlation is quite high, and ultimately not that much smaller than the observed correlation. This new null hypothesis certainly makes an R^2 of .79 or even .90 look a lot less impressive. It is interesting to note, however, that the shape of the simulated data cloud is not that of the data cloud typically observed, which is much more fan-shaped. This, then, suggests that mere monotonicity—or correspondence—is unlikely to produce the kind of data we typically see.

What is needed to reproduce the usual fan shape more tightly is a specific kind of monotonic relationship—one in which younger and older adults' latencies are tied by a multiplicative function ($RT_{older} = a\ RT_{younger}$). Figure 1.8, Panel C, shows results from a simulation where this relationship is implemented. For this simulation, I created 1,354 young-adult data points as described above, and then created random group-ings of 8. Within those groupings, I simulated older-adult data points by multiply-ing the young-adult data with a slowing factor drawn from the uniform distribution [1.00–2.00]. Within each grouping, the same slowing factor was applied; between groupings, the slowing factors differed. This simulation produced data that look very much like the typical Brinley plot. The correlations between the simulated younger and older adult data is very high, varying from .87 to .90 in 50 simulated data sets, with a median of .89, and thus a median R^2 of .79—exactly the fit obtained for the empirical data. This does not logically imply that the empirical data are generated by a multiplicative model, but it certainly makes this a hypothesis worth exploring—just what I will attempt in Chapters 2, 4, and 6.

It also bears repeating that a high R^2 value in and of itself (unless it is actually 1) can never prove that there is only a single dimension to the data (Fisk, Fisher, & Rogers, 1992). The previous exercise shows that even one rather modest assumption about the data—correspondence within studies—leads to a high R^2 value (.65). Clearly the mere size of the (squared) correlation alone shouldn't be taken as an indicator that (a) the data are linear, and/or (b) a single Brinley function suffices to explain the data. Both of these assertions need to be explicitly tested; I will do this later in this book. For instance, in Chapter 4, I will gather data from 15 different tasks, combining them in a single plot. R^2 for the single-line model will be .96, impressive by any measure. It is still, however, reliably smaller than the R^2 obtained for a four-dimensional model, although the gain in R^2 is nominally small (.016). Thus, although a single-line model clearly fits those data, it is at the same time also roundly refuted by the data, and this is what counts, at least from a theoretical perspective.

Finally, it is worthwhile to consider exactly what it is we are predicting here—behavior at the level of the group, not at the level of the individual. The ultimate knowledge we gain from this enterprise is information on how the mean of a group of older adults is related to the mean of a group of younger adults. This does not imply that we can predict the behavior of an individual older adult from the behavior of a group of younger adults, let alone that we can predict behavior of an individual older adult from that of a single younger adult. Likewise, finding dissociations at the group level does not imply that similar dissociations exist at the level of the individual. For instance, although lexical decision tasks, on average, show smaller age-related slowing than mental rotation tasks, individual older adults may well show the inverse effect, or similar effects on both measures.

1.3.2.4.2.4. AFFIRMING THE NULL HYPOTHESIS   A final problem is that tests involving Brinley plots may be too conservative, because they ultimately revolve around affirming the null hypothesis. To determine the dimensionality of a data set, one examines dissociations. One concludes that dissociations exist if an appropriate test flags a significant age by task interaction; the *alpha* level of this test is typically set at .05. Thus, the burden is on the dissociations to reveal themselves; the general slowing model is the default. The analyses are then de facto biased toward simpler, lower-dimensionality explanations of age-related cognitive slowing. At the same time, there is also the challenge that one can never prove the null hypothesis, only fail to disprove it (Prince et al., 2012).

What to do? In this book, I attempt to maximize the chance of finding dissociations. First, I will use multilevel modeling rather than standard linear regression; the former tends to be more sensitive to dissociations (Sliwinski & Hall, 1998). Second, I will explicitly examine targeted dissociations. This is true for Chapter 2, where I will categorize tasks into three broad domains, and even more so for Chapters 4 and 6, where very specific tasks will be pitted against each other. Third, whenever possible, I will supplement the Brinley analyses with state-trace analysis (see the next section), not only to provide converging evidence, but also because state-trace analysis tends to be more sensitive to dissociations.

Let's turn to these state traces next.

1.3.3. State Traces

Brinley plots are one way to represent young-old data. When data on two (or more) related tasks are available, a second type of plot can also be constructed—a state trace or state-space plot (Bamber, 1979; Dunn & Kirsner, 1988; such plots were introduced in the aging literature by Mayr, Kliegl, & Krampe, 1996; for a recent excellent overview on the technique, see Prince et al., 2012).

In a state-trace plot, performance on one task (task A) is plotted against performance on another (task B). Such plots, of course, make sense only if the relationship between the two tasks provides meaningful information. Typically, that implies that the task on the Y-axis (task B) contains a process of interest that is examined (or perhaps even isolated) by comparing it to a baseline task that does not involve this process, plotted on the X-axis (task A). For instance, one might wonder whether there is an age-related decline in the ability to perform multiple tasks. One could then compare the relationship between single-task performance as a baseline, plotted on the X-axis, and multiple-task performance, plotted on the Y-axis, and see if this relationship is different in older adults compared with younger adults. The core logic of the analyses is the same as for the Brinley plot: If a single line suffices to explain the data, the conclusion is that the relationship between task A and task B is identical across age groups. This in turn implies that there are no age-related differences in the process purported to drive the difference between the two tasks. Conversely, if two distinct lines were to emerge (one for younger adults, one for older adults), the conclusion would be that there are specific age-related differences in the processes that make up the difference between the two tasks.

There are two advantages to complementing a Brinley analysis with a state-trace analysis. The first is that state traces often provide a more sensitive test for group differences than Brinley analysis does (an observation first made by Perfect, 1994). This is because state traces involve within-study comparisons, and Brinley functions involve both within-study and between-study comparisons. Compared with Brinley functions, state traces then reduce the amount of variance due to sampling or individual differences. This can be particularly useful when sampling variance is large compared with the size of the experimental effect (Verhaeghen & De Meersman, 1998a).

The second advantage concerns cognitive theory. Unlike Brinley analysis, state-trace analysis is directly informative about the type of effect imposed by the added process. I will label this added effect the "complexity" effect, a term coined by Cerella (1990). Cerella and collaborators have distinguished two types of complexity effects, *additive* and *multiplicative complexity* (e.g., Verhaeghen & Cerella, 2002; Appendix B and C in Verhaeghen et al., 2003, authored by Cerella, provides a complete formal mathematical treatment). In the next subsections, I examine both, in isolation and in combination.

1.3.3.1. State Traces: The Case of Additive Costs

One effect of a complexity manipulation might be to add an extra processing stage to the baseline task, or prolong one of its existing stages. In this case, we expect an additive effect—a constant cost will be added to the baseline RT. Algebraically, starting from the earlier decomposition (Section 1.3.2.2.1):

$$RT_{younger,baseline} = \text{central} + \text{peripheral},$$

and therefore:

$$RT_{younger,complex} = \text{central} + \text{peripheral} + \text{cost}.$$

The state-trace equation, which predicts younger adults' latency in the complex condition from that in the baseline condition, is then:

$$RT_{younger,complex} = RT_{younger,baseline} + \text{cost}.$$

Here is what we expect for older adults, with slowing factors c and p in central and peripheral processing, respectively:

$$RT_{older,baseline} = c \text{ central} + p \text{ peripheral},$$

and, with a slowing factor k for the cost:

$$RT_{older,complex} = c \text{ central} + p \text{ peripheral} + k \text{ cost},$$

which leads to the following state-trace equation:

$$RT_{older,complex} = RT_{older,baseline} + k \text{ cost}.$$

Thus, an additive complexity effect leads to a state trace that is parallel to the diagonal (i.e., its slope is 1). The state trace's intercept is a direct reflection of the complexity cost. I built in the expectation of a larger cost in older adults than in younger adults, with an inflation factor k. This expectation seems reasonable to me, and it allows for the testing of null hypotheses that are more interesting than the hypothesis that the costs are equal across age groups (i.e., the hypothesis that $k = 0$). For instance, one can compare the age-related slowing factor associated with the complexity cost with the slowing observed in the central component of the baseline task (i.e., H_0: $k = c$). One way to do this is to calculate c and k from the data and establish an appropriate confidence interval around the obtained values to assess significance. An alternative and perhaps simpler way is to resort to the Brinley plot of the same data. For the baseline condition (again from Section 1.3.2.2.1):

$$\text{RT}_{\text{older,baseline}} = c\ \text{RT}_{\text{younger,baseline}} + (p - c)\ \textbf{peripheral.}$$

We know that:

$$\text{RT}_{\text{younger,complex}} = \textbf{central} + \textbf{peripheral} + \textbf{cost,}$$

which we can rearrange to obtain:

$$\textbf{central} = \text{RT}_{\text{younger,complex}} - \textbf{peripheral} - \textbf{cost.}$$

Substitute this in:

$$\text{RT}_{\text{older,complex}} = c\ \textbf{central} + p\ \textbf{peripheral} + k\ \textbf{cost,}$$

and we obtain:

$$\text{RT}_{\text{older,complex}} = c\ (\text{RT}_{\text{younger,complex}} - \textbf{peripheral} - \textbf{cost)} + p\ \textbf{peripheral} + k\ \textbf{cost,}$$

which rearranges to:

$$\text{RT}_{\text{older,complex}} = c\ \text{RT}_{\text{younger,complex}} - c\ \textbf{peripheral} - c\ \textbf{cost} + p\ \textbf{peripheral} + k\ \textbf{cost,}$$

and finally to:

$$\text{RT}_{\text{older,complex}} = c\ \text{RT}_{\text{younger,complex}} + (p - c)\ \textbf{peripheral} + (k - c)\ \textbf{cost.}$$

Thus, if we assume that the complexity manipulation inserts a new process, or prolongs an existing one, the associated Brinley function for the complex condition will be equal to that of the baseline condition with the addition of a constant (viz. $(k - c)$ cost). This constant will be zero if and only if $k = c$, that is, if the age-related slowing factor for the complexity cost equals the age-related slowing factor in the central component of the baseline task. Thus, if the Brinley plot shows two coinciding lines, the conclusion must be that the two slowing factors k and c are identical. If slowing in the complexity cost is larger than slowing observed in the baseline task, the two lines will be parallel, with the function for the complex task elevated above that for the baseline condition. Conversely, if the age-related slowing in the complexity cost is smaller than the age-related slowing observed in the baseline task, the function for the complex task will be parallel to and below the function for the baseline condition.

Figure 1.9 (top row) illustrates an additive complexity effect (the data are from Verhaeghen, Cerella, and Basak, 2006). In the baseline condition, 6, 7, 8, or 9 Xs were scattered over the screen; the subject's task was simply to count the number of Xs. In the more complex condition, several Os appeared as distractors among the Xs. The upper left panel shows latency as a function of the number of elements to be counted. Three basic findings stand out: The functions are quite linear, indicating that counting likely proceeds in discrete steps; older adults are slower than younger adults, with the added peculiarity that the duration of each counting step is longer (as indicated by a steeper slope); and the task takes longer when distractors are added. What is of interest here is that the presence of the distractors simply elevates the baseline function. This strongly suggests that the need to ignore or bypass the distractors adds a step to the processing stream without affecting the actual counting rate (i.e., the slope of response time over set size remains unchanged). This is true for both younger and older adults. The upper right panel confirms that the resulting state trace is a line elevated above and parallel to the diagonal. As expected, the line for older adults is elevated above that of younger adults, indicating that older adults need more time to remove distractors from attention than younger adults do. The Brinley plot is provided in the upper center panel. It shows two (parallel) lines rather than one. Thus, the complexity manipulation indeed provoked an age-related dissociation, and the age-related slowing factor associated with distractor interference is larger than that associated with counting.

1.3.3.2. State Traces: The Case of Multiplicative Costs

A second possible effect of adding complexity to a task is to prolong or inflate each step in the original central processing stream. In that case, central-processing latencies in the complex conditions will be a fixed ratio (larger than unity) of central-processing latencies in the baseline conditions, as follows:

$$RT_{younger,baseline} = \textbf{central} + \textbf{peripheral},$$

and

$$RT_{younger,complex} = \textbf{central} * \textbf{cost} + \textbf{peripheral}.$$

After rearrangement, we obtain:

$$\textbf{central} = RT_{younger,baseline} - \textbf{peripheral}.$$

Substitution results in:

$$RT_{younger,complex} = \textbf{cost} \; (RT_{younger,baseline} - \textbf{peripheral}) + \textbf{peripheral},$$

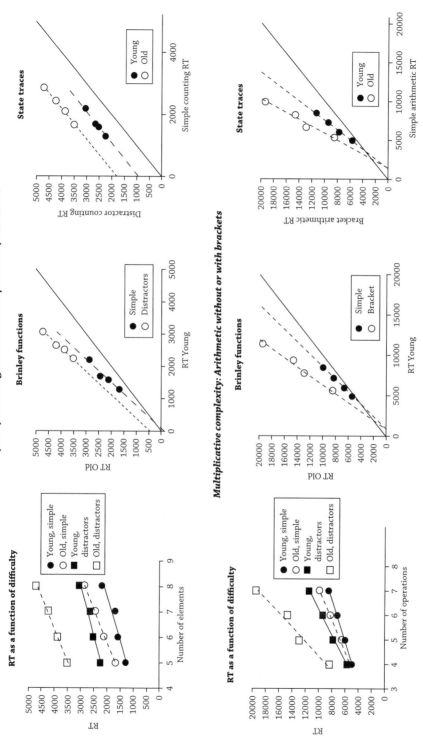

Figure 1.9 Illustration of additive and multiplicative complexity effects in two experimental tasks: Experimental data, Brinley plots, and state traces along with regression lines (in the latter two plots, the equality diagonal is indicated as a solid line). Figure reproduced from Verhaeghen and Cerella (2002).

which simplifies to:

$$RT_{younger,complex} = cost\ RT_{younger,baseline} + (1 - cost)\ peripheral.$$

Thus, the state trace is again a linear function, and its slope provides a direct estimate of the multiplicative cost involved in the complexity manipulation. The intercept should be smaller than zero, at least if the cost is larger than 1 (as one expects it to be).

Setting up the equations for older adults yields:

$$RT_{older,baseline} = c\ central + p\ peripheral,$$

and

$$RT_{older,complex} = c\ central * k\ cost + p\ peripheral.$$

The variable k here relates directly to the specific age-related effect of complexity. If $k = 1$, there is no effect, and age-related slowing in the complex condition is identical to age-related slowing in the baseline condition.

Rearrangement gives us:

$$c\ central = RT_{older,baseline} - p\ peripheral,$$

and substitution results in:

$$RT_{older,complex} = (RT_{older,baseline} - p\ peripheral) * k\ cost + p\ peripheral,$$

which simplifies to:

$$RT_{older,complex} = k\ cost\ RT_{older,baseline} + (1 - k\ cost)\ p\ peripheral.$$

As for younger adults, the state trace for older adults provides a direct estimate of the complexity cost in its slope. The state trace also allows for an easy appraisal of the size of the age-related effect inherent in the complexity manipulation (viz., k): It is the ratio of the state-trace slope for older adults over the state-trace slope of younger adults (i.e., $k\ cost/cost = k$). Thus, in the case of multiplicative complexity, the state trace results are informative about an age-related dissociation: If the two state traces diverge, there must be a specific age-related complexity effect (i.e., $k \neq 1$), and vice versa.

The associated Brinley plot uncovers the same effect. For the baseline condition:

$$RT_{older,baseline} = c\ RT_{younger,baseline} + (p - c)\ peripheral.$$

We know that:

$$RT_{younger,complex} = central * cost + peripheral,$$

which we can rearrange to obtain:

$$\text{central} = (\text{RT}_{\text{younger,complex}} - \text{peripheral})/\text{cost}.$$

Substitute this in:

$$\text{RT}_{\text{older,complex}} = c \text{ central} * k \text{ cost} + p \text{ peripheral},$$

and we obtain:

$$\text{RT}_{\text{older,complex}} = c \left[(\text{RT}_{\text{younger,complex}} - \text{peripheral})/\text{cost}\right] * k \text{ cost} + p \text{ peripheral},$$

which rearranges to:

$$\text{RT}_{\text{older,complex}} = c\, k \,(\text{RT}_{\text{younger,complex}} - \text{peripheral}) + p \text{ peripheral},$$

and finally to:

$$\text{RT}_{\text{older,complex}} = c\, k \,(\text{RT}_{\text{younger,complex}}) + (p - c\, k) \text{ peripheral}.$$

Thus, the Brinley functions for the baseline condition and for the complex condition will be identical if and only if $k = 1$, that is, when there is no specific age-related deficit in the multiplicative cost.

Figure 1.9 (bottom row) provides an illustration of a multiplicative complexity effect (data, like those for the illustration of additive effects, are from Verhaeghen et al., 2006). The round symbols in the left panel show data from a simple mental arithmetic task. Addition/subtraction problems consisting of 4, 5, 6, or 7 signed digits were displayed on a screen, and participants had to determine whether the indicated sum was correct or off by one unit (e.g., $5 + 2 - 3 - 2 + 6 - 3 = 5$). The figure shows the mean RTs for both age groups as a function of the number of digits in the problem. The square symbols show data from a version of the task in which parentheses were introduced (e.g., $[5 - (1 + 2)] + [(2 + 6) - 3] = 7$). This manipulation should force participants to store intermediate results and to reorder operations, something that likely would interfere with central processing. As can be seen in the lower left panel, the latency by number-of-operations functions were indeed steeper for the arithmetic condition with parentheses than for the simple conditions. Thus, negotiating the parentheses likely slowed the rate of the addition process itself. The state trace of older adults (lower right panel) diverged from that of the young, showing that the multiplicative cost in the older adults is greater than the multiplicative cost in the young. The Brinley functions (lower center panel) reinforce the finding of an age-related deficit in the multiplicative cost associated with the introduction of parentheses: Two lines are necessary to fully capture the data.

1.3.3.3. State Traces: The Full Model

A third possibility exists—a full, or mixed, complexity model, in which both additive and multiplicative effects are present. The full complexity model and the multiplicative model share a similar signature: a change in slope, and, possibly, a change in intercept of the information-processing function. Thus the two models are potentially indistinguishable. If the intercept of the state trace increases from baseline to complex conditions, this implicates the full complexity model and rules out a simple multiplicative model. If, on the other hand, the intercept is constant or reduced, either model—multiplicative or mixed—could be responsible, and the data are inconclusive.

1.3.4. Allometric Meta-Analyses of Age-related Slowing: A Brief Summary

As stated above, allometry is the tool I will use for most of this book. In the previous sections, I tried to offer some general idea of the usefulness as well as the limitations of the technique.

The analyses in the preceding three sections clearly show that when the interest is in examining age-related dissociations, Brinley plots suffice. I will re-emphasize here that although a simple, but incisive interpretative apparatus for Brinley plots is available, all that is needed for theory, at least when one is interested in the mere presence of dissociations or in investigating the dimensionality of the age-related effects in a particular data set, is a monotonicity assessment. Often, of course, we are also interested in a description of the age-related effects, and then the specific values of the slopes and intercepts are of interest as well.

State trace plots, when available, provide additional insight into what type of complexity effect is introduced with the experimental manipulation. For that reason alone, one could argue that they should be included in allometric analyses whenever possible—and in this book, I will. This supplementary piece of information would certainly also be useful for cognitive psychologists, neuropsychologists, or psychometricians in general. Often, the default assumption is that complexity costs are additive, as testified by the rampant use of difference scores to establish such effects (e.g., Stroop interference scores, or scores on the Trail Making Test). This assumption often goes simply unexamined, and we will see that it is often wrong. State trace plots may also be useful, as stated above, because they typically yield a higher signal-to-noise ratio than Brinley plots, and thus might be more sensitive to age-related effects.

1.4. Age-related Slowing: Four Main Questions

This chapter has been mostly concerned with the tools that will be deployed in the remainder (or at least a large part of the remainder) of this book.

The more important question is: What can these tools do for us? What questions can they help us answer?

This book will tackle three major questions, all of which, it seems to me, arise naturally out of age-related data. (Some will even receive answers, although some answers will be more tentative than others.)

The first question is: *What tasks and/or processes decline with age, why, and by how much?* This question will be taken up in Chapters 2, 4, and 6. After the discussion of allometrics, it will come as no surprise that a pervasive issue throughout these chapters is the question of data reduction and data dimensionality.

Chapter 2 is devoted to a first, broad-stroke treatment. I report a meta-analysis on seven year's worth of data culled from the three top journals in the psychology of aging. The only criterion for inclusion into the data set is that latency is reported, and that mean latency for younger adults does not exceed two seconds. This data set allows for a close look at an unbiased sample of tasks.

Chapter 3 takes up alternative explanations for these data, that is, explanations that would cast doubt on the reality of age-related slowing, or on the interpretation of domain-differential age-related slowing as domain-differential age-related slowing. These alternatives include age-related differences in speed-accuracy trade-offs, increased interindividual variability with advancing age (which may be indicative of divergence of individual trajectories in speed over the adult lifespan, or simply be reflective of a practice of less selective sampling in older cohorts), the presence of nonlinear effects, or test unreliability.

Chapter 4 provides a more systematic look at age-related difference in a number of elementary tasks and processes in the perceptual, cognitive, and motor domains—17 in total. Practice effects also will be investigated.

In Chapter 5, I will fit different data-reduction models that place these tasks into different types of groupings based on the geometry of the Brinley plot, on a statistical cluster analysis, on a priori models from the literature, and on the suspected underlying brain anatomy.

Chapter 6 adds a systematic look at processes of executive or cognitive control, comparing age-related differences in latency on tasks or conditions requiring cognitive control with baseline versions of the same task that minimize the control requirement. More specifically, I will examine age-related differences in resistance to interference, also often called inhibition (unintentional inhibitory control, control over access into working memory, and restraint inhibition, also known as inhibition of habitual responses), task shifting, and task coordination.

The second question concerns *the trajectory of these age-related differences over the adult lifespan*. This question will be tackled in Chapter 7, under three guises. First, what is the shape of the relationship between adult age and response time? (Is it, for instance, linear, accelerated, decelerated, or inverse-U shaped?) Second, when does decline, if any, start? Third, do trajectories differ by task or by task domain?

Chapter 8 deals with an additional and equally important question, namely, whether these curves describe age differences, generational differences, or both.

The final question concerns *the role of age-related decline in processing speed in more complex aspects of cognition*. As I observed at the outset of this chapter, speed is often considered a very basic aspect of cognition. If so, one might expect that age-related cognitive slowing would have consequences for other aspects of cognition as well. (This idea was popularized by Salthouse in the 1990s; e.g., Salthouse, 1996b.) Chapter 9 investigates the correlations and tests a few mediational models. It also includes analyses of longitudinal data, which allow for a direct assessment of the direction of influence.

A final note. One overarching principle I will use in this book is that of triangulation, that is, of empirical convergence between data sets, methods, or both. The reader will quickly note, for instance, that all and each of the techniques, designs, and/or methods of analysis used in this book have been criticized at one point or other on methodological grounds. (This includes, among others, allometrics [I discussed a few of the criticisms earlier in this chapter], the use of simplified versions of the diffusion model to decompose response time and accuracy into true speed and bias parameters, the use of partial correlations to partition variance, and the use of longitudinal methods to assess true age differences.) If the field were to give up these methods because of these criticisms, no work at all could be done. One line of attack of this book will be to circumvent these criticisms by using multiple approaches to investigate the same phenomenon. For instance, the next chapter will present three methods to look at speed-accuracy trade-offs; the final chapter will use both cross-sectional and longitudinal data to examine the influence of speed on more complex aspects of cognition. The expectation is that although all our methods are to some degree flawed, getting convergent results when applying different methods should increase our confidence in the findings. That is, if independent analyses (where possible on independent data sets) all point to the same conclusion, it seems more natural to bow before Ockham's razor and accept these conclusions to be highly likely than to assume that the flaws in the methods all by accident lead to the same bias. I hope the reader will forgive this penchant for convergence and see it as an abundance of caution rather than excess.

Notes

1. http://gosset.wharton.upenn.edu/mortality/perl/CalcForm.html
2. As we will see in Chapter 4, there is a small irony involved here: Meta-analysis (Wasylyshyn, Sliwinski, & Verhaeghen, 2011) has shown that this type of task switching typically leads to age-related dissociations after all.
3. See Chapter 3 for more details on this task.

Age-related Slowing in a Quasi-Random Sample of Studies

Meta-analyses of aging and processing time can be approached in many ways. One line of attack would be the top-down route, that is, to conduct a principled analysis based on a precise question concerning a specific type or set of data. For instance, a researcher might be interested in the effect of adult age on the Stroop interference effect. Answering that question entails collecting and analyzing all studies that have investigated adult age-related differences in the Stroop effect. Chapters 4 and 6 present analyses of this kind. A second possibility—the one I will use in this chapter—is to go broad and inductive: to cast as wide a net as possible and collect a large sample of studies, and explore this data set from the bottom up.

2.1. The Sample of Studies

Ideally, an enterprise of this sort would require the universe of studies on aging and response times. Collecting these is a humanly impossible task. As of June 2012, a search on *Web of Science* for papers that contain both the keywords "cognitive aging" and "speed" yielded 3,241 publications. To make matters worse, a lot of the literature is hidden from keyword searches. A cursory exploration of journals quickly taught me that many articles do contain one or the other measure of processing speed without being flagged in academic search engines, simply because the measure is not the main focus of the paper or because the response time or speed aspect of the measure is understood implicitly (e.g., in the case of Stroop interference).

Instead of using the keyword method, I opted for a systematic search through the three arguably most important journals in the field of cognitive aging, namely *Psychology and Aging, Journals of Gerontology: Psychological Sciences,* and *Aging, Neuropsychology, and Cognition.* I assumed that seven years worth of data would yield a nice sample, and restricted myself to issues published between 1997 and 2004. (This ensured that the data collected were independent of those from most previous untargeted meta-analyses, which were collected in the 1980s and early 1990s, with Sliwinski & Hall, 1998, an exception. I am also embarrassed to admit that 2005 was the year when I collected these studies and thus started this book. Part of the analyses was reported in Verhaeghen & Cerella, 2008.)

Each article was hand-searched for response time (RT) data, with the following restrictions: (a) the average age of the group of younger adults in the study was 30 or under; (b) the average age of the group of older adults in the study was 60 or over; and (c) only ($RT_{younger}$, RT_{older}) pairs for which the younger adult's mean RT was faster than 2,000 ms were recorded for analysis. The latter restriction (identical to Kail's, 1991, and Cerella and Hale's, 1994) was implemented for three reasons, in keeping with the principles outlined in Chapter 1. First, keeping the range of response times relatively narrow almost guarantees overlap of data points along the abscissa of the Brinley plot, a necessary precondition for an accurate analysis of dissociations (Perfect, 1994). Second, although 2,000 ms is admittedly an arbitrary criterion, it ensures that most of the tasks examined will be relatively simple in their information-processing content. This, in turn, facilitates the classification into domains that I will attempt below. Finally, fast tasks tend to be less amenable to differential strategy use. One further restriction was that when studies examined practice effects only the data from the first trial or block were entered in the data analysis. (The practice effects, and age-related differences therein, will be examined in Chapter 4.) When available, accuracy and/or *SD* were also recorded. My definition of response time is the most generic definition possible: A stimulus had to be presented, and the subject had to emit a response of some kind; the elapsed time between stimulus onset and behavioral response is the response time.

The final sample is rather large. It consists of 1,354 distinct ($RT_{younger}$, RT_{older}) pairs, contained in 175 distinct (i.e., between-subject) studies culled from 118 articles. (These studies are indicated in the reference list by an asterisk. An overview of the task included in the sample is presented in Section 2.2.2.) This is by far the largest meta-analysis of its kind: The Cerella et al. (1980) analysis contained 99 data points; Cerella (1985) had 94; Myerson et al. (1990) 115. Average age of younger adults in the sample of studies was 21.6 (*SD* of the mean age was 2.6), average age for older adults was 70.7 (*SD* = 3.0); the average age difference was thus 49.3 years (*SD* = 4.7). Number of years of education completed was reported in 129 studies for younger adults, and in 136 studies for older adults; it was 14.4 (*SD* = 1.2) and 15.3 years (*SD* = 1.3), respectively. A paired-samples *t*-test revealed no significant difference between age groups on this variable, $t(128) = 1.32$. Average sample size was 26.3 for younger adults (*SD* = 15.7), and 26.6 for older adults (*SD* = 16.4). Average RT was 770 ms for younger adults (*SD* = 324), and 1,046 ms for older adults (*SD* = 529); the difference was, as expected, significant in a one-tailed test, $t(1,353) = 1.81$.

2.2. Brinley Plots

As described in Chapter 1, I analyzed the data using multilevel linear modeling, nesting data-points within studies. Data were not centered prior to analysis, so that the equations describe RT in millisecond units. My analyses progressed from the single-line general slowing model, which assumes that all tasks or processes yield identical age-related slowing factors to a model that tried to capture the major dissociations that have been proposed in the field—models that assume differential slowing for sensorimotor tasks versus cognitive tasks, and for linguistic/verbal tasks versus spatial tasks. More detailed models that would capture the slowing factor in individual tasks are hard to assess with the present data set—they will be attempted in Chapters 4 and 6 with more targeted data sets.

2.2.1. Brinley Plots: Fitting the General Slowing Model

Figure 2.1 (top left) shows the Brinley plot of all available data points. In a first analysis, merely to allow for comparison with previous Brinley fittings, I applied OLS regression to all data points ($k = 1,354$). The resulting linear equation (*SE* of the parameters indicated within parentheses) was:

$$RT_{older} = -74 \ (17) \ ms + 1.46 \ (0.02) \ RT_{younger}.$$

This model fit the data well, $R^2 = .79$.

The OLS technique assumes that all data points are independent, that is, that each data point derives from a different sample of subjects. This is not the case—most studies yield more than a single data point, sometimes because more than one task is assessed, and sometimes because a study includes multiple conditions within a task (e.g., different numbers of distractors in visual search, or baseline and interference conditions of a Stroop task).

Figure 2.1 (top right and bottom left) clearly demonstrates the nested nature of the data. In the top right panel, all data points within a single study are joined by dotted lines; the bottom left panel shows within-study regression lines for those studies that included more than a single data point. The resulting best fitting multilevel regression line ($k = 1,354$; *SE* of the parameters indicated within parentheses) was:

$$RT_{older} = -52 \ (26) \ ms + 1.44 \ (0.04) \ RT_{younger}.$$

This line had an intercept that was reliably smaller than 0, and a slope that was reliably larger than 1. The model, at least nominally, explains a little more of the variance: Compared with the empty model (i.e., the model that simply states that older adults' response time is a constant) the general slowing equation explained 83% of the variance.

The value of the multilevel slope—the age-related slowing factor—is quite close to values previously reported in the literature for such broad data sets, that is, 1.36 (Cerella et al., 1980), and 1.46 (Cerella, 1985, for central processing in groups over 60 years of age). It is also close to the OLS estimate obtained from the same data set. The standard error around the slope is about twice as large in this model as in OLS (0.04 vs. 0.02). This is likely because OLS fails to account for the dependency between means derived from the same study, thereby underplaying within-study variance. The convergence between OLS and multilevel estimates is reassuring—it suggests that whatever drives the age-related differences within a study (the level we are primarily interested in; see Section 1.3.2.3.2 and Sliwinski & Hall, 1998) might be the same mechanism that drives age-related differences between studies. This, in turn, suggests that results from previous OLS or WLS Brinley analyses (which model a mixture of both within and between-study effects) can, after all, be trusted.

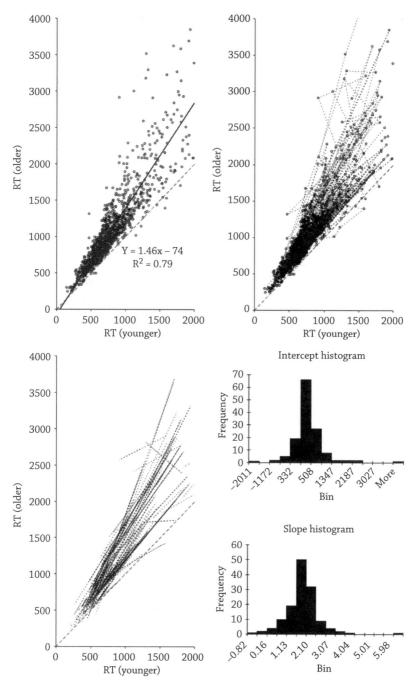

Figure 2.1 Brinley plots of the main corpus of data (k = 1,354). The top left-hand panel shows all data, along with the best-fitting ordinary least-squares (OLS) regression line. The top right-hand panel shows all data points within a study connected with dotted lines. The bottom left-hand panel shows all within-study regression lines. In all three panels, the dashed line indicates the equality diagonal. The bottom right-hand panels show the distribution of within-study regression intercepts and slopes.

Another noteworthy result is that the correlation between slope estimates and intercept estimates is large and negative, namely –.86. The regression lines in Figure 2.1 show why this is the case: There is a clear fanning effect in the data, such that the actual data radiate from a point well into the first quadrant, rather than from the Cartesian origin (i.e., the (0, 0) point), as was the case in Cerella (1985).

As explained in Section 1.3.2.2.2, the existence of an alternative origin makes eminent sense: The Cartesian origin is arbitrary, and, in fact, senseless for response time data—any cognitive task requires time. A much more natural origin of the fan would be the pair of points that describes the fastest possible RT for younger and older adults, that is, the time needed for the simplest task relevant to the current data set. Such a task would share sensorimotor requirements and simple response decisions with most of the tasks in the sample, but would include little or none of their cognitive requirements. Given that most of the tasks require binary manual responses, two-choice manual reaction time seemed a good candidate for the origin of the fan. The present data set contains 12 two-choice reaction time data points. The average two-choice RT (2CRT) for younger adults was 398 ms (ranging from 318 ms to 725 ms); for older adults, the mean was 520 ms (ranging from 318 ms to 858 ms). Refitting the Brinley equation for all data points, correcting for simple sensorimotor and decision processes by simply subtracting 398 ms from each RT value of the young and 520 ms from each RT value of the old, resulted in the following best-fitting model:

$$\text{RT(adjusted for 2CRT)}_{older} = 2\ (13)\ ms + 1.44\ (0.04)$$
$$\text{RT(adjusted for 2CRT)}_{younger.}$$

The intercept of this model is just about as close to zero as possible and not significantly different from it. Importantly, the covariance between slopes and intercepts now dropped to nonsignificance, LR χ^2 (1) = 1.91. This suggests two things. First, the correlation between slopes and intercepts is indeed an artifact of using the (0, 0) point as the origin for the data fan, and, second, the time needed for two-choice decisions is indeed a viable alternative point of origin for the fan. The implication is that age-related slowing can be described as a true ratio, or a simple age-related slowing factor, once the time needed for sensorimotor processes and simple response decisions is subtracted from the total RT. One consequence of this finding is that using sensorimotor control conditions can help clarify age effects in the central or cognitive processes involved in our tasks (see Lange & Verhaeghen, 2009, for an application).

Visual inspection of the bottom left panel of Figure 2.1 also suggests that there is considerable variability in slopes and intercepts. The multilevel results indeed indicate significant variability in the random component of both the intercepts (level 2 variance component = 36,583, LR χ^2 (1) = 596.4) and the slopes (level 2 variance component = 0.13; LR χ^2 (2) = 399.2). This indicates that both the intercepts and slopes vary significantly (and considerably) between experiments. The range is rather large, with intercepts ranging all the way from –2,011 ms (admittedly an outlier) to 3,867 ms (likewise an outlier); slopes range from –0.82 to 6.46.

Interestingly, although the variance components are significant, inspection of the slope and intercept histograms in Figure 2.1 shows single-peaked distributions, with peaks that are sharper than expected from a normal distribution. Deviation from the normal distribution was confirmed by a Kolmogorov-Smirnov test for the intercepts (Kolmogorov-Smirnov $Z = 2.02$, $p = .001$); the same test proved marginally significant for the distribution of slopes (Kolmogorov-Smirnov $Z = 1.35$, $p = .053$). For both intercepts and slopes, a significant positive skew and kurtosis was also obtained (intercept: skew = 2.04, $SE = 0.21$; kurtosis = 11.58, $SE = 0.41$; slope: skew = 1.53, $SE = 0.21$; kurtosis = 9.85, $SE = 0.41$). The conclusion is that both the intercept and slope distribution have an elongated right tail and are sharply peaked. Distributional analysis, however, is notoriously sensitive to outliers. Removing outliers, defined as studies with intercepts or slopes outside three interquartile ranges from the mean, resulted in a sample of 129 studies; the distribution of this sample did not deviate significantly from the normal distribution (intercepts: Kolmogorov-Smirnov $Z = 1.07$, ns; slopes: Kolmogorov-Smirnov $Z = 0.91$, ns).

We are faced, then, with two seemingly conflicting results: (a) There is a significant random variance component in within-study slopes (as testified by the multilevel analysis), accompanied by (b) a peaked or normal distribution of said slopes (as indicated by the Kolmogorov-Smirnov test). Proponents of the idea of generalized slowing can point to the latter result to justify their position: A normal or peaked distribution suggests that a single slope value may suffice to characterize the young-old relationship (after all, the distribution is unimodal and not an obvious mixture of two or three distributions with distinct peaks). The observed variation around the mean may then be due, as is usual in cognitive measures, to random processes such as measurement unreliability, sampling differences, and the like, and not at all to the cognitive content of the tasks. Proponents of the idea of task-specific, process-specific, or domain-specific slowing can point to the significant between-study variability in slopes, which indicates that a single-point estimate of the slope is unwarranted. From this point of view, then, the variability in slopes might very much be due (at least in part) to different slowing factors for distinct tasks or processes.

There is only one way to settle this debate and that is to examine the data set further. In the next section, I examine slowing factors for discrete a priori domains. Finding reliable dissociations between domains would invalidate the idea of generalized slowing.

2.2.2. Brinley Plots: Fitting Major Dissociations

As noted in the previous chapter, multiple meta-analytic data sets (e.g., Cerella, 1985; Lima, Hale, & Myerson, 1991; Sliwinski & Hall, 1998) as well as primary data sets (e.g., Hale & Myerson, 1996; Jenkins, Myerson, Joerding, & Hale, 2000; Verhaeghen et al., 2002; Verhaeghen et al., 2006) have demonstrated that a single Brinley function does not suffice to capture all of the variability in the available data. More specifically, the authors cited have argued for the existence of reliable age-related dissociations between different families of tasks and/or processes. Some have noted dissociations between sensorimotor (sometimes called peripheral) and cognitive (sometimes called central or computational) processing (e.g., Cerella et al., 1980); others have noted dissociations between linguistic and spatial processing (e.g., Hale & Myerson, 1996; Jenkins, Myerson, Joerding, & Hale, 2000; Lima, Hale, & Myerson, 1991; Verhaeghen et al., 2002). Cerella (1985) and Cerella et al. (1980) estimate the Brinley slopes for sensorimotor slowing to be between 1.1 and 1.2 and those of cognitive slowing to be between 1.6 and 2.0. Slowing factors for linguistic processing are estimated to be between 1.2 and 1.5, and those for spatial processing to be between 2.6 and 3.0 (Hale & Myerson, 1996; Jenkins et al., 2000; Lima et al., 1991; Myerson & Hale, 1993). Putting these two results together suggests that we might expect shallow slowing factors for sensorimotor tasks (1.15 or so), more pronounced slowing factors for linguistic tasks (1.35 or so), and very large slowing factors (in excess of 2.5) for spatial tasks. (The latter two are both cognitive, or central, tasks in Cerella's scheme.)

To explore the slowing factors for these three domains, I separated all data points (k = 1,354) into four categories. The first category contains tasks that primarily tap sensorimotor processes and the simple decisions associated with response selection. This category is close to Cerella's sensorimotor/peripheral category. The second category contains linguistic tasks, that is, tasks that require processing of language stimuli (typically words) at a language level (i.e., making judgments about lexicality or semantics). The third category consists of spatial tasks performed on spatial stimuli. The fourth category contains tasks that did not seem to fit easily into any of the other three categories. To ensure that the former three categories are as pure as possible, I applied this fourth category quite liberally. Note again that categories 2–4 (linguistic, spatial, unclassified) would be considered cognitive or central in Cerella's scheme.

More specifically, the four categories contained the following tasks:

1. *Sensorimotor/simple response decisions* (104 observations): single reaction times, choice reaction times, saccadic reaction times, digit-digit reaction times, vocal reaction times, initiation time for single reaction times, preparation times for target detection, attentional capture, and mouse movement times;

2. *Linguistic* (252 observations): letter reading, lexical decision, word naming, picture naming, semantic category judgment, semantic matching, semanticity judgment, synonym matching, synonym-antonym production, reading rate, speech discrimination, spoken word identification, grammatical judgment, and generating an appropriate verb for a noun;

3. *Spatial* (646 observations): visual search, visual marking, location discrimination or detection, line length discrimination, orientation detection, shape classification, pattern detection, shape identity judgment, distance judgment, matrix scanning, pro-saccade tasks and the Simon task;

4. *Unclassified* (352 observations): enumeration, arithmetic, alphabet arithmetic, memory retrieval, letter cancellation, digit-symbol substitution, auditory classification of consonants, color naming, odd/even judgments on digits, Stroop or other kinds of response-inhibition, and the like.

For the analysis, I used the dummy-coding system as described in Section 1.3.2.3.2. The fitted model (*SE* of the parameters within parentheses) yielded the following parameters:

$$RT_{older} = 300\ (55) + 0.78\ (0.07)\ RT_{younger} - 345\ (83)\ \text{(Sensorimotor/}$$
$$\textbf{Simple response decisions dummy)} - 574\ (62)\ \textbf{(Spatial dummy)}$$
$$- 367\ (48)\ \textbf{(Unclassified dummy)} + 0.78\ (0.16)\ \textbf{(Sensorimotor/}$$
$$\textbf{Simple response decisions dummy} * RT_{younger}) + 1.21\ (0.07)$$
$$\textbf{(Spatial dummy} * RT_{younger}) + 0.70\ (0.06)\ \textbf{(Unclassified dummy}$$
$$* RT_{younger}).$$

This model could be simplified at no significant cost to fit, LR χ^2 (2) = 2.95, by allowing a single intercept and a single slope to represent both sensorimotor and unclassified tasks. An attempt at further simplification of this model by allowing a single intercept and slope for all nonlinguistic tasks led to a significant decrease in fit, LR χ^2 (2) = 101.11, and was therefore abandoned.

The final model fits as follows:

$$RT_{older} = 301\ (55) + 0.78\ (.07)\ RT_{younger} - 350\ (45)\ \text{(Sensorimotor/}$$
$$\textbf{Simple response decision or Unclassified dummy)}$$
$$- 571\ (61)\ \textbf{(Spatial dummy)} + 0.68\ (0.06)\ \textbf{(Sensorimotor/}$$
$$\textbf{Simple response decision or Unclassified dummy} * RT_{younger})$$
$$+ 1.20\ (0.07)\ \textbf{(Spatial dummy} * RT_{younger}).$$

This final model can more readably be represented as a set of three equations:

1. $RT(\textbf{Linguistic})_{older} = 301 + 0.78\ RT(\textbf{Linguistic})_{younger};$

2. $RT(\textbf{Sensorimotor/Simple response decision or Unclassified})_{older} =$ $-49 + 1.46\ RT(\textbf{Sensorimotor/Simple response decision and}$ $\textbf{Unclassified})_{younger};$

3. $RT(\textbf{Spatial})_{older} = -270 + 1.98\ RT(\textbf{Spatial})_{younger}.$

The data and the multilevel regression line for each of the three categories are represented in Figure 2.2. I show the full data range in the left-hand panel, and zoom in on the [0–1000, 0–1600] region for enhanced visibility. The three lines form a fan that seems to emanate from a common point not too far from the point that describes the average single reaction time for younger and older adults. Setting this point, the point (398, 520), as the origin for all three lines did, however, reduce fit significantly, LR χ^2 (3) = 13.04. By eye, I found another likely origin for the fan at the point (470, 640); forcing all three lines through this point did not reliably reduce fit compared with the final model, LR χ^2 (3) = 2.01, and reduced the percentage of explained variance only slightly, to 91%. In this model, the slope for linguistic tasks was 0.82; the slope for sensorimotor/simple response decisions and unclassified tasks was 1.46, and the slope for spatial tasks was 2.02. This demonstrates that the data can indeed be described as a fan.

Note that the slope for linguistic tasks is reliably smaller than 1, LR χ^2 (1) = 9.62 in the final model; the upper limit of the 95% confidence interval is 0.92. This is a

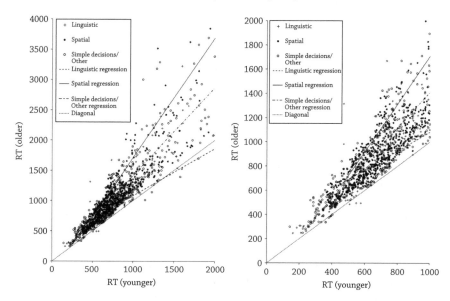

Figure 2.2 Final results from the multilevel Brinley analysis on the latency data
(*k* = 1,354); full data range (left panel); restricted range, for visibility (right panel).
Three different regression lines were obtained: one for linguistic tasks, one shared
between sensorimotor/simple response decision tasks and the unclassified tasks, and
one for spatial tasks. The equality diagonal is indicated as a dotted line.

decidedly odd result. Two additional observations put this finding in perspective. The
first one is that although the slope may be smaller than unity, indicating a significant
speed-up in the age-related "slowing" factor, only 11 out of 252 data points for linguistic data points (a mere 4% of the data) are situated below the diagonal. Thus, the
large majority of the data does indicate that age-related slowing is present, at least at
the level of raw RT. Part of the explanation for this seeming discrepancy between raw
RT and the Brinley function lies in the large intercept of the function (355 ms), which
"allows" the slope to become smaller than unity without losing contact with data that
clearly show age-related slowing. The second observation is that when I tried to verify
this unexpected slowing factor by fitting the linguistic data only, the model failed to
converge. (This was not the case for the two other groupings, which did yield converging models.) Fitting the data using OLS rather than multilevel regression yielded a
slope of 1.36 (and a negative intercept, –0.52 ms), with an R^2 of .85. My interpretation is then that the trifurcating model demonstrates that there is reliable trifurcation, but that the model's estimate of the linguistic slowing factor is most probably
off the mark, likely underestimating the slope and overestimating the intercept. In
Chapter 4, I will estimate this slowing factor more precisely, using a partially independent data set, and concentrating on lexical decision tasks only; this slowing factor will
turn out to be significantly larger than 1 (Section 4.4.5).

The final trifurcating model fits the data very well: It explains 92% of the variance
compared with the empty mode, or 8% more than the general slowing model. There is,
however, still considerable and significant variance in the random slope component

(level 2 variance component = 0.28, LR χ^2 (2) = 765.47), signifying that the trifurcation does not capture all of the variance present in the data.

To examine whether the model captures the amount of variance adequately within each of the groupings, I estimated a multilevel model for each. If the groupings were truly homogeneous, we would expect no random component to the slopes within each grouping. Only for the sensorimotor grouping (k = 104) did the random component to the slope fail to reach significance, LR χ^2 (2) = 0.00; the two other groupings for which the models converged both showed significant random variance in slopes: for spatial, k = 646, LR χ^2 (2) = 815.76, and for unclassified, k = 352, LR χ^2 (2) = 121.31. The variability in the "unclassified" category is to be expected—this category contains an amalgam of different tasks. The variability in spatial processing is markedly larger than that for the unclassified tasks. Inspection of the studies and their individual slowing factors suggested that tasks of spatial identification (shape discrimination, line length discrimination, location discrimination) might show less age-related slowing than tasks of spatial manipulation (mental rotation, visual search). This further bifurcation, however, did not stand up to formal analysis: A model that included a separate slope for the 77 tasks of spatial identification clearly did not fit the spatial data significantly better than a model without this separate slope, LR χ^2 (1) = 0.00. I will take up the theme of within-domain variability again in Chapters 4 through 6, where I will descend my analyses to the level of the task.

2.2.3. Major Dissociations in Brinley Plots: Repercussions for Study Design and Data Analysis

One unexpected finding from the present meta-analysis was the relatively large age-related slowing factor for tasks involving sensorimotor processes and simple response decisions. Ever since Cerella's analyses, received wisdom seems to be that these tasks show much less slowing than cognitive tasks. Here, I found that some cognitive tasks—namely linguistic tasks—yield smaller age-related effects than traditional sensorimotor tasks; age-related sensorimotor slowing was also not reliably smaller than slowing in the set of "unclassified" cognitive tasks.

This finding suggests that slowing in sensorimotor tasks (a field of study that has been relatively neglected since the 1970s) is more severe than researchers in the field have typically assumed, and perhaps tied to the same brain mechanism that governs slowing in a number of cognitive tasks. I will investigate this possibility in some more depth in Section 5.2.4. I would also suggest that this finding should encourage those of us conducting experimental research to include sensorimotor control conditions in our aging studies. I would argue that aging effects in cognitive tasks are only truly interesting if they exceed the deficit obtained in sensorimotor and simple response decision processes.

There is a second reason to include sensorimotor control conditions in experimental designs, and this has to do with the fan found in the Brinley plot. The origin of the fan is not the (0, 0) point, but the (sensorimotor $RT_{younger}$, sensorimotor RT_{older}) point. Including a sensorimotor control condition allows us to estimate that point, and this, in turn, allows us to easily test for age by condition interactions. In a first step, one subtracts this sensorimotor control RT from all experimental RTs; in a second step, these corrected RTs are subjected to a logarithmic transformation. The logic is to "reset" the ($RT_{younger}$, RT_{older}) coordinate system to its true origin, from where age deficits are truly multiplicative. In a third step, ANOVA is applied.

Here is a more formal justification of this analysis. Assume we have two tasks or conditions, A and B, each with their associated slowing factor c_A and c_B.

If we reduce the young-old relationship to multiplicative relationship by correcting all RTs (by simply subtracting this sensorimotor control RT from all experimental RTs), then:

$$RT(corrected)_{A,older} = c_A\ RT(corrected)_{A,younger},$$

and:

$$RT(corrected)_{B,older} = c_B\ RT(corrected)_{B,younger}.$$

Remember that: $\log(a * b) = \log(a) + \log(b)$. Log-transforming both sides of the equations, we get:

$$Log(RT[corrected]_{A,older}) = \log(c_A\ RT[corrected]_{A,younger}),$$

and

$$Log(RT[corrected]_{B,older}) = \log(c_B\ RT[corrected]_{B,younger}),$$

which simplifies to:

$$Log(RT[corrected]_{A,older}) = \log(c_A) + \log(RT[corrected]_{A,younger}),$$

and

$$Log(RT[corrected]_{B,older}) = \log(c_B) + \log(RT[corrected]_{B,younger}).$$

We have now isolated the age-related slowing factors as an additive factor, and testing for the age by condition interaction on the log-transformed corrected RTs will tell us if $\log(c_A) = \log(c_B)$, and, thus, if $c_A = c_B$.

The usefulness of the transformation can also be illustrated with an example. The equation relating RT of younger and older adults in spatial tasks is: $RT_{older} = 2\ RT_{younger} - 270$ ms. Assume we have a group of younger and older adults perform a simple spatial task, for instance visual search with five distractors. If we assume that younger adults need 1,000 ms to perform this task, then we expect older adults to need (1,000 * 2 − 270) ms, or 1,730 ms. The absolute age difference is therefore 730 ms. Assume we make the task more difficult, perhaps by simply lowering the contrast on the display, so that the task now takes younger adults 2,000 ms to complete. The expected RT for older adults is then (2,000 * 2 − 270) ms, or 3,730 ms. The absolute age difference is now 1,730 ms, much larger than in the first condition, and it is likely that an ANOVA will flag the age by condition interaction as significant, leading the researcher to conclude that older adults have a particular difficulty with degraded displays. In reality, however, the age-related slowing equation is exactly the same across the two conditions, implying that no additional mechanism needs to be invoked to explain the difference in the absolute age difference across conditions. Simple log transformation on the original RTs does not completely correct the problem (in log units, the age difference is 0.55 in the baseline condition, and 0.62 in the low-contrast condition, a difference that might still become significant in an ANOVA); correction for sensorimotor slowing does, however, remove the spurious interaction (after subtracting 470 ms from the younger adults' RTs, and 640 from the older adults' RTs, the age difference expressed in logarithmic units is 0.69 in the baseline condition, and 0.70 in the low-contrast condition).

2.3. Age-related Slowing in a Quasi-random Sample of Studies: Conclusions

The goal of the present chapter was to provide a first, bottom-up look at age-related slowing. Following in the footsteps of the pioneers of these types of analyses (e.g., Cerella et al., 1980; Salthouse, 1978), I purposely cast a wide net and collected a large sample of studies on adult age differences in response time, regardless of the tasks tested. The Brinley analysis suggested that age-related cognitive slowing proceeds along three dissociable dimensions: (a) linguistic tasks show positive age-related effects, or age-related "speed-up," in the Brinley slope (0.80 in the main analysis, with an upper limit of 0.92; this is a curious finding, and I will re-examine it in Chapter 4); (b) sensorimotor tasks are modestly sensitive to aging (slowing factor of about 1.5); and (c) spatial tasks show relatively large age-related deficits (slowing factor of about 2.0 over both analyses). This does not imply that these three dimensions explain all of age-related slowing (although the further furcations I attempted all failed), but it does imply that the hypothesis of general slowing is clearly falsified. Thus, general slowing, although a good first approximation of the data, is not cognitive aging's ultimate underlying truth.

3

Is Age-related Slowing Real?

Investigating Threats to the Validity of Brinley Slopes

Although the data reported in the previous chapter clearly show an age-related increase in processing speed as measured by Brinley slopes, doubts could be raised whether such increases truly reflect age-related effects, whether or not the dissociations obtained are true dissociations, and/or whether the decline (if any) is measured correctly. For instance, doubts have been raised as to the validity of the estimates of age-related differences as obtained from Brinley plots. Is there evidence for a differential speed-accuracy trade-off in old age, potentially leading to an overestimation or underestimation of age-related declines in processing speed? Are older adults more variable in their response times (RTs) than younger adults, potentially due to sampling heterogeneity? Is there evidence for nonlinearity in the Brinley slopes? Are Brinley slope estimates reliable? Can part of the variability in estimates be explained through sampling differences?

Note that some of these doubts cannot be examined within the present data set. For instance, it can be (and has been, e.g., Flynn, 1998) argued that age-related slowing is not due to aging per se, but that it mainly reflects *speed differences between successive generations*. (In the aging literature, this artifact is labeled a "cohort" effect.) The present data set spans only 7 years, so it does not allow for a good comparison between generations. I will, however, examine this hypothesis in Chapter 8, where I investigate studies using continuous age ranges, some of which have been conducted in a longitudinal context. This allows us to disentangle the effects of aging from the effects of generational shifts (Sections 8.1 and 8.2).

Likewise, one might argue that younger and older adults bring *differential life experiences* to the testing booth. Younger adults (in practice often undergraduate students) live in an environment that encourages regular practice of the type of skills required to do well on standard laboratory tests of cognition; older adults tend to live in an environment that might be less geared toward the deployment of such skills (e.g., Baron & Cerella, 1993; the oldest account of this "disuse" hypothesis is probably Thorndike, Bregman, Tilton, & Woodyard, 1928). According to this account, older adults might need more practice with the task than younger adults before they reach their full potential. In cognitive experiments, age differences are typically measured without extensive practice, and this might then inflate the observed slowing factors. At its most extreme, this theory would predict that age differences in RT would disappear after sufficient practice; a more moderate version would predict shrinkage of the age-related slowing factor over the course of practice. The present data set contains only a few practice studies, so this question will have to wait. I will take it up with a more extensive data set in Section 4.5.

The present data set does, however, allow for the investigation (sometimes directly, sometimes in an indirect fashion) of quite a few potential threats to the validity of the Brinley slopes obtained in the previous section.

A first family of alternative explanations concerns the validity of the very conclusion that there is an age-related decline in processing speed at all. The argument is that the decrease in processing speed observed with advancing age may be an artifact, or—less extreme—that the estimates of age-related slowing obtained from Brinley plots (or any other measure) are greatly exaggerated. One concern is that the observed age-related slowing may be an artifact of *differential speed-accuracy trade-offs* in younger and older adults. Perhaps younger adults focus more on speed than on accuracy, and perhaps older adults do the opposite and sacrifice speed for accuracy. This differential trade-off would then lead to slower processing in older adults, not because they are intrinsically slower than younger adults, but because they wait longer to emit a response, for unknown strategic reasons or out of an overabundance of caution (e.g., Ratcliff et al., 2004).

A second potential issue is *differential sample heterogeneity*. The samples of younger adults included in our studies are typically quite homogeneous (more often than not undergraduate students registered at major research universities in the United States); our samples of older adults might not be. For instance, older adult samples might very well be contaminated with participants who suffer from undetected preclinical dementia (e.g., Sliwinski, Lipton, Buschke, & Stewart, 1996), or with individuals who suffer from the ill effects of declining cardiovascular health (e.g., Verhaeghen, Borchelt, & Smith, 2003); neither of these pathologies are part of the actual aging process, and neither is likely present in individuals in our younger-adult samples. This heterogeneity would likely lead to an inflation of the slowing factors, simply because some proportion of the older adults tested will be slower for reasons other than the aging process per se. Although the present meta-analysis cannot address the question of sampling heterogeneity directly, it can tackle one symptom of such heterogeneity: increased interindividual variability in RT.

A second family of alternative explanations centers around the question whether or not the observed variability in Brinley slopes (and hence any potential dissociations in Brinley slopes between tasks or task domains) could be due to task-unrelated factors. Even if one would conclude (as I will) that age-related slowing is a real phenomenon and not an artifact of speed-accuracy trade-offs, increased interindividual heterogeneity in the older adult samples, generational differences and the like, it remains to be demonstrated that the variability observed in age-related slowing factors is, in fact, interesting, that is, related to the cognitive content or components of the task. There are quite a few possible uninteresting ways to explain the variability in Brinley slopes.

One is the potential presence of *nonlinear effects*, and how these might influence the conclusion of dissociations in Brinley space. At least one model (the information-loss model formulated by Myerson et al., 1990) has posited such nonlinear effects.

A potential source of nonlinearity in age-related slowing factors could be the complexity of the task, regardless of its component processes. Given that task complexity is likely to be monotonically related to RT (more complex tasks tend to yield longer RTs), one might then expect nonlinear effects in the data, with longer mean RTs of younger adults associated with steeper within-study slopes. Simpler tasks (such as sensorimotor tasks) might then show shallower slopes than more complex tasks (such as central, or cognitive, tasks), simply because of this proposed nonlinear complexity effect.

A second threat under this heading concerns *measurement reliability*. Little (in fact, nothing) is known about the reliability of Brinley slopes.

Finally, I will investigate the influence of *sampling characteristics* on the slopes. I will focus on two sampling characteristics that are typically reported in experimental studies: age and level of educational attainment. Younger-adult groups tend to be sampled from a constricted age range; this is less the case for older adults. This likely creates some heterogeneity in slope estimates. Also, and perhaps more importantly, generational shifts in educational opportunities and educational attainments may influence slopes as well, if one assumes that education and speed of processing are positively related to each other.

3.1. Age-related Slowing Cannot be Fully Explained by differential Speed-accuracy Trade-offs.

The ideal test for age differences in speed-accuracy trade-offs would entail mapping out the entire speed-accuracy function for both age groups. Studies that have done so are scarce (for a few exceptions, see Kliegl, Mayr, & Krampe, 1994; Kumar, Rakitin, Nambisan, Habeck, & Stern, 2008; Mayr, Kliegl, & Krampe, 1996; Verhaeghen, Kliegl, & Mayr, 1997). The current meta-analytic data set is essentially mute on this account. There are, however, at least three ways in which speed-accuracy trade-offs can be inferred from meta-analytic conglomerates. The first is *quadrant analysis* (Cerella, 1990), which is simply a redescription of the data based on a simultaneous analysis of age differences in speed and those in accuracy. The second is to fit a mathematical model that aims to simultaneously recover age differences in "true" speed and in decision criterion (i.e., whether subjects are more liberal or more conservative—more reckless or more cautious—in the amount of information they require before they are willing to make a decision). The model I will fit is the *EZ diffusion model* (Wagenmakers, Van der Maas, & Grasman, 2007), which is a simplified version of Ratcliff's (e.g., Ratcliff, 1978) diffusion model. A third tool is at our disposal as well: *Domain-specific dissociations in accuracy* can be used to infer whether or not the dissociations found in response times could logically be due to speed-accuracy trade-offs. If they were, we would expect an inverse relation: Tasks that yield smaller age-related slowing factors should yield large effects in accuracy.

I will investigate quadrant analysis first, then turn to dissociations as found in accuracy data, and finally fit the EZ diffusion model to the data.

3.1.1. Examining Speed-Accuracy Trade-offs
using Quadrant Analysis

Quadrant analysis (Cerella, 1990) is an ad hoc technique to assess the likelihood of differential speed-accuracy trade-offs by examining age differences in speed and accuracy simultaneously. Age differences in RT are plotted against age differences in accuracy in the same task (thus defining a $RT_{age\ difference} \times Accuracy_{age\ difference}$ space), and the average RT and accuracy difference is computed from these data.

Three hypothetical cases may illustrate the usefulness and limitations of this technique. (Given that older adults are generally slower than younger adults, I concentrate here on the two possibilities that matter in practice: Older adults are either slower and more accurate than younger adults, or slower and less accurate.) Consider the three sets of hypothetical speed-accuracy curves depicted in the top row of Figure 3.1. A speed-accuracy trade-off curve represents accuracy as it relates to speed of processing within a task within a person (or group of people, as is the case here). The relationship between the two is typically monotonic—slower performance makes one more accurate, and faster response might lead to more mistakes. The left-most panel shows the case where both younger and older adults are situated on the same speed-accuracy curve—the case typically subsumed under the notion of age-differential speed-accuracy trade-offs. In this case, there is only one possibility for younger adults to be faster than older adults, and that is by being less accurate. When we plot the two data points in $RT_{age\ difference} \times Accuracy_{age\ difference}$ space (the middle row of Figure 3.1), the resulting data point is situated in the first (i.e., top-right) quadrant. The two other cases assume that younger and older adults operate on different speed-accuracy trade-off functions, and that the speed-accuracy function of older adults is less efficient than that of younger adults. This is not an assumption—it is the consistent finding in age-comparative speed-accuracy research (Kliegl et al., 1994; Kumar et al., 2008; Verhaeghen, 2002; Verhaeghen et al., 1997). The center panel of the top row of Figure 3.1 shows the case in which older adults are slower and less accurate than younger adults; this translates into a data point in the fourth (i.e., bottom-right) quadrant in $RT_{age\ difference} \times Accuracy_{age\ difference}$ space. The right-most panel shows that even if the speed-accuracy curve of older adults is less efficient than that of younger adults, older adults can still be more accurate, resulting in a data point in the first quadrant in $RT_{age\ difference} \times Accuracy_{age\ difference}$ space.

This brief exercise teaches us that, given that older adults are slower than younger adults and assuming that the speed-accuracy curves for older adults are not more efficient than those of younger adults, plotting the data in $RT_{age\ difference} \times Accuracy_{age\ difference}$ space can be informative, but only up to a point. Data points in the fourth quadrant can be interpreted unequivocally: The speed-accuracy curve of older adults is less efficient than that of older adults. There simply is no other way for data to fall within the fourth quadrant. Data points that fall in the first quadrant, however, can be interpreted in two ways: Either (1) younger and older adults perform along the same speed-accuracy curve and older adults are trading off speed for accuracy; or (2) older adults operate on a less efficient speed-accuracy curve and set a higher accuracy criterion. Both of those outcomes would signify that older adults do sacrifice speed in return for higher accuracy.

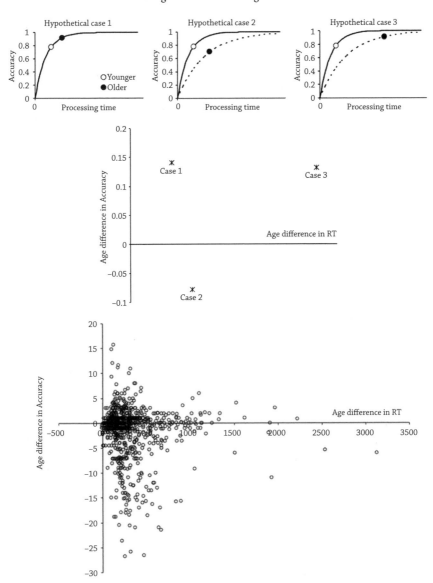

Figure 3.1 Quadrant analysis to determine possible age-differential speed-accuracy trade-off effects. The top row presents three hypothetical speed-accuracy cases, as explicated in the text (Case 1: Younger and older adults are situated on the same speed-accuracy function and older adults sacrifice speed for accuracy; Case 2: Older adults are situated on a less efficient speed-accuracy function, and older adults are both less accurate and slower; Case 3: Older adults are situated on a less efficient speed-accuracy function, and older adults are slower but more accurate); the center row plots these hypothetical cases in the space described by the age difference in RT and the age difference in accuracy. The bottom row plots the available data (*k* = 1,036) in the same space, indicating that the majority of the data are compatible with Case 2, where older adults are slower and less accurate than younger adults and do not trade off speed for accuracy.

Figure 3.1, bottom panel, provides a plot of all 1,036 studies in the current data set for which both accuracy and RT data were available. The average age difference in accuracy, expressed as a percentage point, was –1.30 (SD = 4.78) for all data points (k = 1,036); it was –1.76 (SD = 3.97) when data were first averaged within experiments (k = 120). Both values are significantly different from zero, t (1,035) = –8.77 and t (119) = –4.87, respectively, indicating that older adults are, on average, less accurate than younger adults. This finding shows that the average data point falls within the fourth quadrant, not the first quadrant. This is not just the mean, but also the modal finding: When all data points are considered, 59.7% of the 1,036 points fall on or below the abscissa; when data are first averaged within experiments, 72.5% of the 120 points fall on or below the abscissa.

The data thus strongly suggest that the age-related slowing observed in the full data set cannot be due to a simple speed-accuracy trade-off taking place on an identical speed-accuracy trade-off curve. Most of the data, as well as the average data point, fall in the fourth quadrant, indicating that older adults generally perform on a speed-accuracy curve that is less efficient than that of younger adults. This does not imply that they use the same speed-accuracy trade-off criterion as younger adults, but it does show that they typically do not prioritize accuracy to the point where they perform equally well as younger adults, let alone better. Speed-accuracy trade-offs therefore cannot be the sole reason for the observed age-related slowing, although such trade-off mechanisms may have been operating in some studies (at best in 27% of the present sample).

3.1.2. Examining Differential Speed-Accuracy Trade-offs by Examining Dissociations in Accuracy

The quadrant analysis shows that speed-accuracy trade-offs cannot explain all of the age-related differences in speed. It is still possible, however, that the dissociations obtained in Chapter 2 are due to differential settings of trade-off criteria across domains. For instance, slowing factors might be smaller for lexical-decision tasks than for visual-search tasks because older adults are more willing to tolerate errors in the linguistic domain than in the spatial domain.

This conjecture can be easily tested. I fitted the same model I used for the response time data (using the four categories: sensorimotor/simple response decisions, linguistic tasks, spatial tasks, and the unclassified tasks) to the available accuracy data. Accuracy was operationalized as error rate; as was the case for the quadrant analysis, the number of data points was 1,036. The fitted equation was:

$$\text{Error}_{\text{older}} = 0.014\ (0.005) + 0.891\ (0.098)\ \text{Error}_{\text{younger}} - 0.003\ (0.015)$$

(Sensorimotor/Simple response decisions dummy)
+ 0.000 (0.006) (Spatial dummy) – 0.001 (0.005)
(Unclassified dummy) – 0.367 (0.311) (Sensorimotor/Simple response decisions dummy * $\text{Error}_{\text{younger}}$)
+ 0.394 (0.120) (Spatial dummy * $\text{Error}_{\text{younger}}$)
+ 0.239 (0.123) (Unclassified dummy * $\text{Error}_{\text{younger}}$).

Of the dummy and interaction predictors, only the interaction terms associated with spatial and unclassified tasks reached significance. Deleting the other predictors

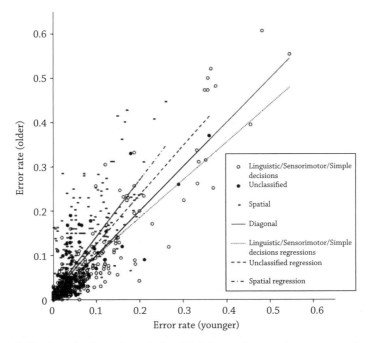

Figure 3.2 Final results from the multilevel Brinley analysis on the error rate data (*k* = 1,036). Each of the four groupings of data points is shown, as well as the equality diagonal (solid line). Three different regression lines were obtained, one for linguistic and sensorimotor/simple response decision tasks, one for unclassified tasks, and one for spatial tasks.

did not significantly decrease fit, LR χ^2 (4) = 2.56. The final fitted model (represented in Figure 3.2) is then:

$$\text{Error}_{\text{older}} = 0.014\ (0.003) + 0.854\ (0.086)\ \text{Error}_{\text{younger}}$$
$$+\ 0.421\ (0.086)\ (\text{Spatial dummy} * \text{Error}_{\text{younger}})$$
$$+\ 0.254\ (0.096)\ (\text{Unclassified dummy} * \text{Error}_{\text{younger}}).$$

The model explains 75% of the variance compared with the empty model. The fit is at least nominally worse than the fit for response time, but still quite handsome. Note that the confidence interval for the joint linguistic and sensorimotor/simple response decisions slope contains 1, indicating that there is no significant age difference in error rates for these two types of tasks. The two interaction terms differed reliably from each other, LR χ^2 (1) = 6.90. This final model can be represented as set of three equations:

1. **Error (Linguistic or Sensorimotor/Simple response decision)**$_{\text{older}}$
   **= 0.854 Error (Linguistic or Sensorimotor/Simple response
   decision)**$_{\text{younger}}$ **+ 0.014;**

2. **Error (Unclassified)**$_{\text{older}}$ **= 1.11 Error (Unclassified)**$_{\text{younger}}$ **+ 0.014;**

3. **Error (Spatial)**$_{\text{older}}$ **= 1.28 Error (Spatial)**$_{\text{younger}}$ **+ 0.014.**

Like the RT data, the accuracy data show a trifurcation. The nature of the trifurcation is not identical to that found in the response time data, however: The error function for sensorimotor/simple response decision tasks now groups with the linguistic tasks; the unclassified data form their own grouping. Linguistic and spatial tasks dissociate in accuracy as they do in response time, with larger error rates for spatial tasks. These data suggest that the trifurcation in age-related slowing is not a consequence of differential speed-accuracy trade-offs: Tasks that show larger age-related slowing factors also tend to show larger age differences in error rates favoring the young. This finding is the exact opposite of what would be expected were an age-differential speed-accuracy trade-off responsible for the response time dissociations. A possible exception is the dissociation between linguistic processing and sensorimotor slowing, which show identical age differences in accuracy, but different slowing factors.

3.1.3. Examining Differential Speed-Accuracy Trade-offs by Fitting the Data to an EZ Diffusion Model

A more principled way to investigate age-differential speed-accuracy trade-offs is to explicitly model the data. The dominant framework to model speed and accuracy in simple decision tasks in the past 50 years (starting with Stone, 1960) is the sequential-sampling model. Many flavors of this model exist; perhaps the best-known sequential-sampling model is Ratcliff's diffusion model (Ratcliff, 1978; Ratcliff & Tuerlinckx, 2002). The underlying assumption of this model (as of all sequential-sampling models) is that when a participant is confronted with a decision, she will repeatedly sample information from the environment to guide this decision. Information accumulates from a *starting point* toward one of two response *boundaries*; when a boundary is reached, a decision is triggered and a response is emitted. The mean rate at which information accumulates in the cognitive system is called the *drift rate*; higher values of the drift rate parameter indicate that more information is absorbed per time unit. There is variability associated with this drift rate—processes wander over a wide range, which will mean that occasionally the wrong boundary will be reached and an error will be made. The variability in drift rates coupled with the simple geometry of the model creates an RT distribution with a longer right-hand tail.

Under the diffusion model, there are at least three ways in which processes or individuals can be fast or slow. First, smaller drift rates lead to slower responses, and also to a larger probability of hitting the wrong boundary, and thus to higher error rates. This would be the way in which proponents of the age-related slowing hypothesis tend to see slowing: as a limitation on an intrinsic processing rate. A second way to slow down processing is by boundary placement. The placement of the boundaries indicates how much evidence needs to be accumulated before a decision is triggered. When the boundaries are spaced far apart, the individual is cautious: Decisions will be reached slowly, but the wide boundary placement also reduces the probability of reaching the wrong boundary. Conversely, closely spaced boundaries indicate rash behavior: Responses will be fast and errors many. The placement of the boundaries thus indicates the speed-accuracy trade-off the individual is willing to make. The third way of slowing down is related to the speed of processing prior to and after the decision has been reached. The diffusion model combines the times required for these other processes—stimulus encoding, response selection and response output, and, depending on the task, memory access, retrieval cue assembly, and so on—into one parameter, namely, nondecision time. This time is considered independent of the decision processes; it is simply additive to them; that is, decision time plus nondecision time equals total response time. Subjects can be faster or slower on these nondecision times, and this will obviously influence total response time. (There is a fourth way to be fast or slow as well: The starting point, which is essentially the bias toward saying "yes" or "no" when no evidence is present, can work for or against the individual depending on what the correct response is, and what the proportion of a specific response is over the course of a experiment.)

Thus, with the aid of this model, we can distinguish whether older adults are slower than younger adults because of increased caution (i.e., they set wider boundaries), or because of inherent differences in mental tempo (i.e., they have lower drift rates, slower nondecision times, or both). The original diffusion model is very complex (the Ratcliff & Tuerlinckx version has 16 free parameters) and needs the full RT distributions of both correct and incorrect responses for its estimation. Needless to say, this information is rarely available in published articles. Fortunately, a simplified version of the diffusion model is available, the EZ diffusion model (Wagenmakers et al., 2007), and this version can be applied to meta-analytic data sets. It takes as its input the mean and variance of correct response times, as well as the proportion of correct answers—information routinely reported in scientific articles. The drawback is that the EZ model only estimates the three core parameters (drift rate, boundary, and nondecision time); it achieves its simplification, among other things, by assuming that the starting point is midway between the boundaries for all subjects.

The diffusion model only fits binary response data, so only studies that required subjects to choose between two response alternatives were included. The binary-decision criterion excluded multiple-choice RT measures, tasks in which stimuli have to be read or named (including Stroop tasks and negative priming tasks), and arithmetic production tasks. It left lexical decision tasks, category judgment tasks (including color judgments), synonym and antonym judgment tasks, visual search tasks, arithmetic verification tasks, and the like. The final sample for fitting the EZ diffusion model consisted of 42 studies (contained in 32 papers), with a total of 333 younger-older adult response time pairs, and the associated variances and error rates.

The average drift rate in these studies (averaged first within studies, then weighted for sample size) was 0.288 for younger adults, and 0.224 for older adults. (The drift rate units are arbitrary; that is, they carry no meaning that can be directly translated into response time.) Thus, at least nominally, older adults show smaller drift rates, that is, slower accumulation of evidence leading to slower decision speed. The average boundary separation was 0.127 for younger adults and 0.149 for older adults. At least nominally, older adults set more conservative criteria than younger adults. (Boundary separation, too, is measured in arbitrary units.) Finally, average nondecision times were 511 ms for younger adults and 731 ms for older adults. Here, too, older adults are nominally slower. The conclusion is that there are suspected age differences in all three parameters of the EZ diffusion model.

To test for age-related differences, I conducted Brinley analyses on each of the EZ diffusion parameters (333 data pairs for each; see Figure 3.3). Note that the average RT in this data set (first averaged within studies, then weighted for sample size) is

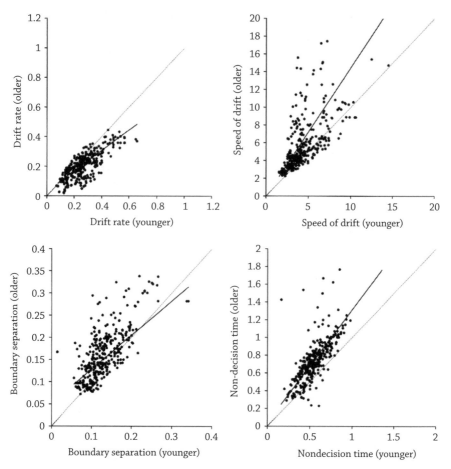

Figure 3.3 Brinley plot of the four parameters of the EZ diffusion model as obtained from the meta-analytic data set: drift rate, speed of drift (i.e., 1/drift rate), boundary separation, and nondecision time ($k = 333$). Within each panel, the equality diagonal is depicted as a dotted line; the solid line is the multilevel regression line.

785 ms for younger adults, and 1,108 ms for older adults. The "decision times" that are being modeled by drift rate and boundary separation are the difference between this response and the nondecision times, that is, 274 ms in younger adults and 377 ms in older adults. The Brinley equation for observed RT in this data set was:

$$RT_{older} = -67\ (69) + 1.45\ (0.10)\ RT_{younger}.$$

The *SE* for this intercept is about the same size as the parameter itself. The model could be simplified to a purely multiplicative model at no significant cost to fit, $\Delta LR\ \chi^2\ (1) = 2.48$:

$$RT_{older} = 1.36\ (0.03)\ RT_{younger}.$$

Thus, we have an age-related slowing factor of about 1.4 in observed response time in this subset of the data. Compared with the empty model, the final equation explained 73% of the variance in RT_{older}.

The Brinley function for drift rate was:

$$\text{Drift rate}_{older} = 0.031 \ (0.012) + 0.69 \ (0.03) \ \text{Drift rate}_{younger}.$$

Because smaller drift rates indicate faster speed, this equation should be mirrored around the 45° diagonal to make it comparable to the other analyses in this book. (That is, if older adults absorb information at a rate that is 0.69 times that of younger adults, they are $1/0.69 = 1.45$ times slower to absorb each unit of information.) I computed speed of drift as 1/drift rate. Doing so yielded the following equation:

$$\text{Speed of drift}_{older} = -0.031 \ (0.012) + 1.45 \ (0.03) \ \text{Speed of drift}_{younger}.$$

This equation implies that older adults' speed of drift is significantly slower than that of younger adults (i.e., the slope is larger than 1). The age-related slowing factor in the speed of drift is 1.45—quite similar to the age-related slowing factor observed in total response time. Compared with the empty model, this model explained 64% of the variance in older adults' drift rate.

It makes theoretical sense to assume a multiplicative model for drift rates rather than a full linear model—unlike response times, drift rates can go down to zero and remain interpretable (Wagenmakers et al., 2008). Such a model fitted the data significantly less well, however, $\Delta LR \ \chi^2 \ (1) = 22.30$:

$$\text{Speed of drift}_{older} = 1.26 \ (0.03) \ \text{Speed of drift}_{younger}.$$

Turning to boundary separation, a first thing to note from the figure is that most points lie above the diagonal, indicating that in the large majority of the studies, older adults were more cautious than younger adults. The actual equation shows a complex reality:

$$\text{Boundary separation}_{older} = 0.051 \ (0.012) + 0.77 \ (0.10) \ \text{Boundary separation}_{younger}.$$

The intercept of this function is significantly positive. This implies that when boundary separation is zero in younger adults (signifying a completely reckless instant decision) older adults do show significant separation or caution. The slope, however, is reliably smaller than 1. This implies that the younger-older gap that is visible at zero boundary separation for younger adults gets smaller as the boundary widens in younger adults; when younger adults become more cautious, so do older adults, but to a lesser degree. The slope of 0.77 implies that for every "step" younger adults take in the direction of increased caution, older adults take 77% of a step. Note that boundary separation for younger adults in the present data set is effectively constrained between 0.05 and 0.35, with only a handful of data points situated above 0.25. The equation above implies that the younger-older gap will close at a younger-adult boundary value of

0.22. Thus, older adults are just as cautious as younger adults when younger adults are about as cautious as they (empirically) will get; but, in all other cases, older adults are the more cautious group. Compared with the empty model, the equation explained 34% of the variance in boundary separation in older adults.

The Brinley equation for nondecision times was:

$$\text{Nondecision time}_{\text{older}} = 44\ (900) + 1.27\ (0.15)\ \text{Nondecision time}_{\text{younger}}.$$

The SE of the intercept is quite large compared with its estimate. Fixing the intercept to zero did not significantly affect fit, $\Delta\text{LR } \chi^2 (1) = 3.66$. The resulting equation was:

$$\text{Nondecision time}_{\text{older}} = 1.33\ (0.06)\ \text{Nondecision time}_{\text{younger}}.$$

Thus, compared with those of younger adults, older adults' nondecision times are slowed by a factor of about 1.3. Compared with the empty model, this model explained 65% of the variance in nondecision times of older adults.

How does the age-related slowing in nondecision times compare to the age-related slowing in decision times? Given that decision time equals total response time minus nondecision time, mean decision time for each measurement in each study can be calculated and subjected to Brinley analysis as well. The resulting equation was:

$$\text{Decision time}_{\text{older}} = -13\ (24) + 1.51\ (0.11)\ \text{Decision time}_{\text{younger}}.$$

The intercept is not significantly different from zero, $\Delta\text{LR } \chi^2 (1) = 0.30$. The purely multiplicative model was:

$$\text{Decision time}_{\text{older}} = 1.47\ (0.08)\ \text{Decision time}_{\text{younger}}.$$

This model explained 36% of the variance in decision times of older adults.

The age-related slowing factor for decision times seems to be larger than that for nondecision times. To test for this conjecture, I fitted a Brinley model to the 666 estimated latency data points (333 nondecision times, 333 decision times), using a purely multiplicative model and including the interaction between a decision dummy (0 = nondecision time; 1 = decision time) and estimated latency for younger adults. The interaction term tests whether the Brinley slope for decision times is larger than that for nondecision times. The ratio of the interaction parameter estimate over its SE was 1.84. If we accept a one-tailed test (which is not unreasonable, given that some researchers have argued that age-related sensorimotor slowing—which likely makes up the bulk of the nondecision times—is less pronounced than "central" slowing), then we would conclude the age-related slowing factor in decision times (viz., 1.47) is indeed larger than that in nondecision times (viz., 1.33).

The end conclusion here is that age-related differences in response times cannot be simply traced to an age-related difference in a single parameter of the EZ diffusion model—all three parameters are affected. Previous work with the full diffusion model (e.g., Ratcliff, 2008; Ratcliff et al., 2004; Ratcliff, Thapar, & McKoon, 2001, 2006a,

2006b, 2007; Starns & Ratcliff, 2010; Thapar et al., 2003) has claimed that there are no or only small age differences in drift rate, but large age differences in boundary setting (as well as an increase in nondecision times). These studies then suggest that there is, in fact, no age-related slowing in the central/computational aspect of cognitive processing; the observed differences in RT can be explained completely through age differences in speed-accuracy trade-offs. (Allow me to observe here that if these results were true, one should be able to make young-old differences in response speed disappear by simple speed-accuracy instructions. To my knowledge, Ratcliff and colleagues have never explicitly tested this corollary of their finding. Existing results do not seem to conform to this prediction. For instance, Brébion [2001] found that age differences remained identical after subjects were instructed to emphasize speed; Forstmann et al. [2011] obtained the opposite result—larger effects of speed-emphasis instructions on response thresholds in younger adults than in older adults.) The discrepancy between Ratcliff's studies and the meta-analytic results is puzzling. It may be that the EZ diffusion model (the only version of the diffusion model that can be applied to the present data set) is too simple (e.g., Ratcliff, 2008, obtained age differences in the variability of the drift rate, a parameter not modeled in the EZ diffusion model). It might also be possible that choices made in the fitting of the full 16-parameter model lead to trade-offs within parameter space that may mask age-related differences in drift rate. In this context, it may be meaningful to point out that drift rates of younger and older adults are quite nicely correlated, and so are their nondecision times (the younger-adult parameter explains about 65% of the variance of older-adult parameter at the group level); this is much less the case for the boundary setting parameter (34% of the variance explained). This might imply that boundary separation is simply measured or modeled with less precision, or it might mean that it is less important to explain age-related differences. The first of these conclusions could be taken as support for the necessity to fit the full diffusion model; the latter could be seen as support for the position that aging leads primarily to an intrinsic change in information accumulation rather than a strategic retreat into cognitive conservativism.

Is it possible to explain the Brinley slope dissociations between task domains through only one (or two) of the diffusion parameters? Of the 333 pairs, less than half (127) concerned lexical decision tasks; the rest concerned spatial tasks. Figure 3.4 represents the data. The task domain dummy was set as 0 = linguistic and 1 = spatial. For drift rate:

$$\text{Drift rate}_{older} = 0.025 \ (0.009) + 0.77 \ (0.03) \ \text{Drift rate}_{younger}$$
$$- 0.14 \ (0.02) \ \text{Drift rate}_{younger} \ \text{by task domain.}$$

This model then shows that there is a reliable dissociation (i.e., the interaction term is significant), and that spatial processing further depresses the drift rate slope; that is, it leads to larger age-related slowing in the drift rate compared with the slowing observed in the linguistic task. Rotated around the 45° diagonal:

$$\text{Speed of drift}_{older} = -0.025 \ (0.009) + 1.30 \ (0.03) \ \text{Speed of drift}$$
$$+ 0.14 \ (0.02) \ \text{Speed of drift}_{younger} \ \text{by task domain.}$$

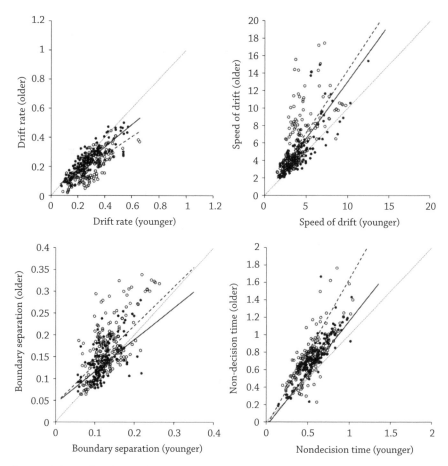

Figure 3.4 Brinley plot of the four parameters of the EZ diffusion model as obtained from the meta-analytic data set: drift rate, speed of drift (i.e., 1/drift rate), boundary separation, and nondecision time (*k* = 333), separated out for linguistic (black dots) versus spatial (open circles) tasks. The equality diagonal is depicted as a dotted line, the solid line is the multilevel regression line for linguistic tasks, and the dashed line is the multilevel regression line for spatial tasks.

The dissociation was also obtained for the boundary separation parameter:

$$\text{Boundary separation}_{older} = 0.043\ (0.012) + 0.73\ (0.11)\ \text{Boundary separation}_{younger} + 0.16\ (0.04)\ \text{Boundary separation}_{younger}\ \text{by task domain.}$$

The interaction term is significant, showing that the age difference in boundary separation is larger for the spatial tasks than the lexical decision tasks, again echoing the dissociation found in response times (and drift rate). Note that this equation predicts that for more cautious settings, older adults will, in fact, become more liberal than younger adults in linguistic tasks from boundary values of 0.16 onwards (i.e., for more than half the range of boundary values); older adults remain more cautious than younger adults for the spatial tasks.

Finally, the nondecision times show the same dissociation effect, with larger age effects for spatial tasks:

$$\text{Nondecision time}_{\text{older}} = -0.05\ (0.04) + 1.21\ (0.09)\ \text{Nondecision time}_{\text{younger}}$$
$$+ 0.48\ (0.04)\ \text{Nondecision time}_{\text{younger}}\ \text{by task domain.}$$

This set of analyses then suggests that there is no single locus of the age-related dissociation between linguistic and spatial tasks within the EZ diffusion model parameters. Rather, all three parameters—drift rate, boundary separation, and nondecision time—showed more pronounced age-related effects for spatial tasks than for linguistic tasks. Additionally, the converging evidence for the separability of the two domains in the EZ diffusion analysis can be taken as evidence for the validity of that analysis.

One additional result of interest is that the nondecision times (in the present sample of studies and tasks) makes up the larger part of total RT—about 65% in both age groups. This result does not mean that studying decision processes is not important, but it does imply that age-related slowing in peripheral factors is worthy of study, too, especially given that nondecision times show considerable age-related slowing as well, echoing the age-related effects in decision times—a slowing factor of about 1.2 for linguistic tasks and 1.7 for spatial tasks. It also underscores the need to include sensorimotor control conditions in experimental studies; otherwise, what is being explained is a mixture of central and peripheral processing times that is typically more skewed toward the latter.

3.1.4. Age Differences in Speed-Accuracy Trade-offs: Summary and Conclusion

The results from the three analyses performed here all converge rather strongly on the conclusion that there is little evidence that age-related slowing can be ascribed to speed-accuracy trade-offs alone.

The quadrant analysis showed that older adults are both slower and less accurate, on average, than younger adults. This result alone refutes claims that younger and older adults are situated on the same speed-accuracy function. Rather, these results are compatible only with a model where older adults are situated on a less efficient speed-accuracy trade-off function than younger adults.

The Brinley analyses of accuracy data largely echoed the Brinley analyses of response times: Tasks that have large age-related slowing factors also tend to have larger age effects in error rates—the exact opposite of what would be expected if a speed-accuracy trade-off was at play.

Finally, the EZ diffusion analysis obtained age differences in all three parameters of the model—nondecision times, boundary separation, and drift rate. The boundary separation result does indicate that older adults tend to be more cautious than younger adults, but this is only true for spatial tasks. For both linguistic and spatial tasks, the rate at which information accumulates in the system (the drift rate), as well as the time needed to encode incoming information and emit a response (the nondecision time), is slower in older adults than in younger adults. Moreover, age-related slowing in both those parameters is larger in spatial tasks than in linguistic tasks, again echoing the bifurcation observed in latency data. Thus, if we accept the EZ diffusion fits as truthful, increased caution is clearly not the only reason for age-related slowing, and differential cautiousness is not the only reason for the age-related dissociation between linguistic and spatial tasks. One issue that is still very much open is whether these effects—increased slowing and increased cautiousness—are independent. It seems possible, for instance, that with advancing age individuals might notice their drift rate deteriorating and react by deliberately withholding a response until they are certain that enough information has accumulated. Resetting the decision boundaries could then be an adaptive strategy, secondary to the slowing down of information accumulation. The finding that the conservative resetting does not seem to be a general phenomenon, but only occurs for the task domain that is slowing down most might lend some credence to this conclusion.

3.2. Age-related Slowing Cannot be Explained by Increased Interindividual Variability

A second threat to the validity of our conclusions is potential incomparability of the typical younger and older adult samples in the literature. Under the scientific adage of "all else equal," older adults recruited for experimental studies should be as close to the average undergraduate college student as possible in every personal characteristic but age. This is unlikely. For one, the typical sample of younger adults tends to be rather homogenous (typically undergraduate students at research universities in the United States); the same cannot be said for our typical samples of older adults. If there is increased heterogeneity in our older samples, and if that heterogeneity were due to sampling differences that disadvantage older adults, and/or if our samples of older adults included large proportions of individuals who represent negative deviations from the normal aging process (individuals with clinical or preclinical dementia or other forms of central nervous system pathology, for instance), the end result would be an overestimation of the age-related slowing factor. It can also be argued, inversely, that the older-adult samples in the literature (at least in the journals from which I culled the present data set) are more highly selected than the younger adult samples. For instance, in one meta-analysis on aging and vocabulary scores, I found an age-related increase in vocabulary scores, with an effect size (mean standardized difference) of 0.80; the older adults had also, on average, completed 15 years of education (vs. 14 years for younger adults; Verhaeghen, 2003). Similarly, the data set collected here shows high levels of education for the older adults (15.3 years vs. 14.4 years for the younger adults in this sample). This result suggests that the older-adult samples typically involved in cognitive aging research are a subset of the very highly educated and, if we take vocabulary scores as measures of crystallized (i.e., stable) intelligence, inherently smarter than the younger adults recruited for the same studies.

Although it is nearly impossible to ascertain the equality of samples after the fact, it is quite possible to examine whether there is significantly larger variability in response times in the older adult samples collected here—a very direct measure of heterogeneity in the measure of interest.

A first thing to note is that, when examined at the level of within-group standard deviations, older adults are indeed clearly more variable than younger adults. The present sample of studies allowed me to collect 710 younger-older pairs of standard deviations (*SD*) from a total of 111 experiments. At the study level (k = 111), the average *SD* for the younger adults was 172 ms (*SD* = 152), compared with an average *SD* for older adults of 264 ms (*SD* = 262). At the level of individual conditions (k = 710), average *SD* for younger adults was 168 ms (*SD* = 151), compared with an average *SD* for older adults of 259 ms (*SD* = 247). In both cases, a paired-samples t-test indicated larger variability for older adults, $t(110)$ = 6.42 and $t(709)$ = 14.99, respectively.

Directly comparing *SD* may not be the best way to assess heterogeneity, however. It is well-known that variability of response time measures increases with mean RT of the group. An alternative measure of variability is the coefficient of variability (*CV*). *CV* is obtained by scaling *SD* on the mean, $CV = SD/M \times 100$. It is thus an indicator of relative rather than absolute variability. There is a precedent to using *CV* in meta-analysis. Morse (1993) collected *CV* measures from 93 different conditions contained within 15 experiments. She found no significant age difference in *CV* when *CV*s were first averaged within each study ($CV_{younger}$ = 29.5; CV_{older} = 33.4, or a nonsignificant age-related increase in variability of 13%), but the age difference was significant when all individual data points were considered ($CV_{younger}$ = 21.3; CV_{older} = 26.0, or an age-related increase in variability of 22%). The present corpus of data is much larger than Morse's. I was able to extract a total of 739 pairs of younger-older *CV*s, contained in a total of 118 experiments. When first averaged within each study, average $CV_{younger}$ was 20.1 (*SD* = 10.3) and CV_{older} 22.1 (*SD* = 10.9), indicating a (significant) 10% increase in variability, $t(117)$ = 3.01. When all data points were considered individually, $CV_{younger}$ = 20.1 (*SD* = 10.8); CV_{older} = 22.5 (*SD* = 11.3), indicating a (significant) 12% increase in variability, $t(738)$ = 7.58.

It can be argued, however, that even *CV* may not be precise enough. A third type of technique to analyze variability has been proposed by Hale, Myerson, Smith, and Poon (1988). They reasoned that because *SD* and mean RT are related, the best test for an age-related increase in diversity would be to examine the linear relation between *SD* and RT in both age groups and then to test for age differences in the parameter estimates of the *SD* by RT regression line. In a later paper, Myerson, Hale, Zheng, Jenkins, and Widaman (2003) presented a mathematical model (the "difference engine") to account for this mathematical relationship, predicting, among other things, a negative intercept for the function relating *SD* to RT. The result of the Hale et al. meta-analyses (23 data points for manual RT, 30 for vocal RT), was that the relationship between *SD* and RT did not differ as a function of age. Chen, Hale, and Myerson (2007) provided further evidence for this claim within a single experiment with 18 different tasks.

I replicated the Myerson et al. (2003) analysis (using multilevel regression) on all available data from the main corpus (k = 1,420, i.e., 710 SD-RT pairs for younger adults and 710 SD-RT pairs for older adults). The upper panel of Figure 3.5 presents the data. The resulting equation was:

$$SD = -73 \ (18) \ \text{ms} + 0.31 \ (0.02) \ \text{RT} + 4 \ (10) \ \text{ms} * \text{Age group}$$
$$- 0.01 \ (0.01) \ (\text{Age group by RT}).$$

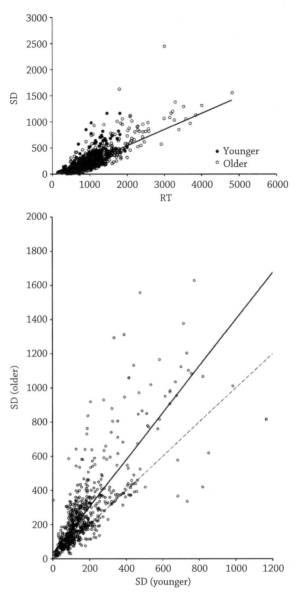

Figure 3.5 Analyses of differential variability in the two age groups. The top panel shows mean *SD* of RT of older and younger adults (*k* = 1,420) as a function of mean RT, indicating that a single function (shown as a solid bold line) fits the data well. The bottom panel presents the Brinley plot (*k* = 710), with the equality diagonal indicated by a dashed line and the regression line in solid.

The age group and the age group by RT interaction were not significant, indicating that a single line fits the data best, LR χ^2 (2) = 4.52. The equation describing this single line was:

$$SD = -60 \ (17) \ \text{ms} + 0.30 \ (0.02) \ \text{RT.}$$

This equation explains 80.03% of the variance compared with the empty model. The negative intercept explains why the *CV* analysis yielded larger *CV*s for older adults: Slower tasks or individuals or groups will yield larger *CV*s than faster tasks, individuals, or groups if the relationship between *SD* and RT is over-proportional. In the present sample of studies, mean RT of the younger adults was 770 ms, yielding a predicted *SD* of 165 ms, and a predicted CV of 21.42; for older adults, a mean RT of 1,046 ms leads to a predicted *SD* of 250 ms, and a predicted CV of 23.88. Therefore, under the (now verified) assumption that the same linear function applies to the relation between *SD* and mean RT in younger and older adults, we expect an increase in CV for older adults of about 11%. This value corresponds nicely to the observed age difference reported above.

One additional result is that the *SD*s of younger and older adults are highly correlated (see the bottom panel of Figure 3.5). The equation is:

$$\text{SD}_{older} = 31 \ (16) \ \text{ms} + 1.37 \ (0.11) \ \text{SD}_{younger}.$$

This equation explains 61% of the variance compared with the empty model, corresponding to a correlation at the within-study level of .78. Thus, it seems that the aging of variability shares some characteristics with the aging of response times: (a) Mean *SD* of the old can be predicted quite well from mean *SD* of the young; and (b) the relationship is quite linear, with a slope of about 1.4, quasi-identical to the slope found in mean RT data. This result is not surprising, given the relationship between mean RT and *SD*.

The main conclusion from this analysis, then, is that, once age differences in mean response time are taken into account, older-adult samples are not more variable than younger-adult samples, within the confines of the present meta-analysis. The observed increase in between-subject variability can simply be ascribed to age-related slowing.

3.3. Variability in Age-related Slowing Factors Cannot be Explained through Nonlinear effects

One potential source of variability in age-related slowing factors is the complexity of the task, regardless of the nature of its component processes. Task complexity is likely to be monotonically related to RT. If more complex tasks also yield larger age differences, we would expect larger slowing factors—steeper within-study Brinley slopes—for tasks that are associated with longer RTs in younger adults. One mathematical model that explicitly predicts this possibility is Myerson et al.'s (1990) information-loss model. This model begins with the assumption that processing occurs in discrete steps; with some probability, with each step a small quantity of information is lost. The claim is that older adults lose more information per step than younger adults. Myerson and colleagues showed that this leads to a positively accelerated Brinley function, closely approximated by a power function.

I conducted two analyses to test for nonlinear effects.

The first test examines nonlinear effects by examining within-study slopes. If longer mean $RT_{younger}$ values were associated with a larger age-related slowing factor, one would expect a positive correlation between the within-study Brinley slope and its horizontal location in the overall Brinley plot. I operationalized horizontal location as either the minimum younger adults' RT within the study, the maximum younger adults' RT within the study, or the mean of younger adults' RT within the study (the latter option is visualized in Figure 3.6). There was no positive correlation between within-study slopes and either operationalization of location: $r = -.24, .02$, and $-.19$, respectively ($k = 135$). (In fact, the first correlation is significantly negative.)

The second test for nonlinear effects is more direct. If the age effect increases with younger adults' RT, one would expect a significant quadratic effect of younger adults' RT. Adding a quadratic term to the multilevel regression line ($k = 1,354$) yielded:

$$RT_{older} = -88 \ (37) \ ms + 1.54 \ (0.08) \ RT_{younger} + 0.00 \ (0.00) \ RT_{younger}^{\ 2}.$$

The quadratic component was equal to zero, and not significant, LR $\chi^2 \ (1) = 1.8$. This result implies that any model that posits nonlinear effects—including the information-loss model—appears to be misgiven.

One potential problem with this finding is the obvious range restriction in the present sample—2,000 ms of processing time or less. It is possible that nonlinear effects might appear if a larger range of RTs were considered. I examined this possibility by conducting an analysis for nonlinear effects in the iterative tasks considered in Chapter 4. Iterative tasks are tasks that have their central processing (likely) occurring in discrete, looping steps; the number of steps can be varied parametrically. Examples of such variations include set size in memory search, the number of elements to be

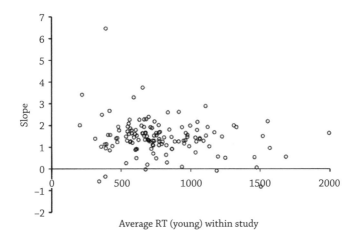

Figure 3.6 Results from one analysis to test for nonlinear effects: within-study Brinley slope as a function of average young-adult within-study RT ($k = 135$). If more complex tasks led to larger slopes, we would expect a positive correlation between the two variables; none is evident.

enumerated in a counting task, the number of distractors in visual search, and the degree of rotation in mental rotation tasks. Even though the RT range is larger in these iterative tasks, nonlinear effects were still negligible. The fitted model (k = 210) was:

$$RT_{older} = -169\ (49)\ ms + 1.74\ (0.09)\ RT_{younger} + 0.00\ (0.00)\ RT_{younger}^{2}.$$

Although the quadratic component was significant, LR χ^2 (1) = 4.40, the coefficient associated with the nonlinear effect was equal to zero to (at least) the third decimal.

The conclusion is very simple: There is very little evidence for nonlinear effects in Brinley plots.

3.4. Variability in Age-related Slowing Factors is Partially Due to Unreliability

Unreliability, or measurement error, is by definition a source of variability in psychological measurement, and, moreover, one that should give rise to a normal distribution of slopes, just like the one observed in the present sample (but only after outliers were removed). Measurement reliability is rarely reported in experimental studies, and the present sample of articles is no exception. Therefore, there is no direct way to assess the effect of measurement unreliability on the variability of slopes.

There are, however, some techniques to assess the effects of unreliability indirectly: We can examine the influence of study characteristics that are likely to affect measurement reliability. Figure 3.7 presents scatterplots of within-study OLS slopes with three such characteristics: (a) the range of RT in younger adults; (b) the number of conditions within each study, that is, the number of data points used for the slope estimate, and (c) the number of participants in each study. One might expect more reliable, and hence less variable, estimates, with larger RT ranges, with an increasing number of data points within a study, and with a larger number of participants. As an explicit test, I performed a median split on each of these three variables (viz., at an RT range of 223 ms, at 4 data points, and at 48 participants, respectively), and conducted a Levene's test for equality of variance of the OLS slopes. This test was significant for the range of RTs, $F(1, 132) = 5.90$, indicating that shorter ranges lead to more variable estimates, as well as for the number of data points, $F(1, 132) = 10.69$, indicating that studies with fewer data points yield more variable slope estimates. The Levene's test was not significant for the median split on the number of participants, $F(1, 132) = 0.26$.

These results suggest that part of the variability in slopes is indeed, and unsurprisingly, associated with study characteristics that might influence reliability. The pressing question is whether the reliability problem is sufficiently large to explain all of the observed variability in slopes. To test for this assumption, I returned to multilevel modeling. There is a small subset of the data (19 studies, k = 211) that lies above the median on all three dimensions. The conclusion that unreliability is an important component of the variability in slopes would be strengthened if it could be demonstrated that there is no random variability in slopes in this selected subsample of presumably quite reliable studies.

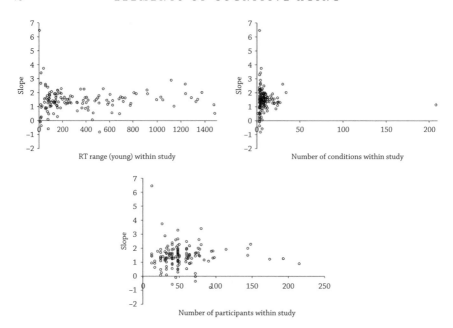

Figure 3.7 Examination of select threats to internal validity. Within-study slopes (*k* = 135) as a function of the range of RT in younger adults, the number of conditions within each study, and the number of participants in each study. One might expect more reliable, and hence less variable, estimates, with larger RT ranges, with an increasing number of data points within a study, and with a larger number of participants.

The best fitting regression line for this subsample studies is:

$$\text{RT}_{older} = -129\ (84)\ \text{ms} + 1.59\ (0.11)\ \text{RT}_{younger}.$$

This model still exhibits significant variance in the random slope component (level 2 variance component = 0.012, LR χ^2 (2) = 26.63), indicating that even in this subset of presumably highly reliable studies some variance remains to be accounted for.

It should be noted that although a smaller range of younger adults' response time and a smaller number of conditions within the experiments were significantly associated with larger variability in slope estimates, these two variables (or the number of participants) did not bias the slope estimates. Slope estimates correlated .16 with RT range, –.02 with the number of conditions, and –.02 with the number of participants; none of these correlations are significant (*k* = 135). Likewise, the confidence interval around the slope of the multilevel model on the 19 most reliable studies, 1.59, comprises the slope of the full data set, 1.44.

The conclusion is that part of the variability in slope estimates is indeed likely due to unreliability, but that the estimate of the mean of the slope appears to be unbiased.

3.5. Variability in Age-related Slowing Factors Cannot be Explained through Average Age or Level of Education of the Older Adult Samples

Previous meta-analyses (Cerella, 1985; Cerella et al., 1980) have concluded that the age of the older-adult subgroup influences the slope estimate—groups of older adults that are on average younger than 60 produced shallower Brinley slopes than groups that were on average older than 60. In the present data asset, the relevant equation, testing for the effects of age within the older adult subgroups on intercept and slope, is:

$$RT_{older} = 300\ (652)\ ms + 0.20\ (1.04)\ RT_{younger} - 4.97\ (9.26)\ (\text{Age of older group}) + 0.02\ (0.02)\ (\text{Age of older group by } RT_{younger}).$$

Neither the age parameter (indicating the influence of age on the intercept of the Brinley function) nor the age by RT interaction term (indicating the influence of age on the slope of the Brinley function) were significant. The model did not fit better than the general slowing model, LR χ^2 (2) = 3.5, k = 1,354. Thus, age of the older samples did not reliably influence either the slope or the intercept estimates. This may be due to range restriction, to selection effects in the older subgroups (older adults who sign up for and complete a typical cognitive psychology experiment are likely to be a more selected subpopulation of their age peers than younger older adults who do the same), or both.

It can be argued that the absolute age of the groups of older adults might matter less than the age difference between the younger adults and the older adults in a study. I set up a model that included this age difference rather than absolute age as a predictor of Brinley slopes and intercepts. Again, neither the age difference term (–2.1, SE = 5.7) nor its interaction with $RT_{younger}$ (0.010, SE = 0.009) were significant, and the model did not fit the data better than the general slowing model, LR χ^2 (2) = 3.5, k = 1,348. (Six data points were missing because the corresponding article did not contain information about younger adults' age.) Thus, the average age difference between the younger and older adults in the study did not reliably influence either the slope or intercept of the Brinley function.

Another group characteristic that could potentially moderate age effects is education. I set up two models, analogous to the age models, to test for the influence of education on the Brinley slope and intercept. In a model using absolute level of education (i.e., years of schooling completed), neither the education term itself (–39, SE = 39) nor its interaction with $RT_{younger}$ (0.04, SE = 0.04) were significant, and the model did not fit better than the corresponding general slowing model, LR χ^2 (2) = 1.0, k = 1,109, indicating that the number of years of education of the older group did not reliably influence either the slope or the intercept estimate. Likewise, a model that used the difference in years of education rather than the absolute number of years of education produced nonsignificant education difference (2, SE = 29) and education difference by $RT_{younger}$ (–0.01, SE = 0.03) parameters, and did not fit better than the general slowing model, LR χ^2 (2) = 0.1, k = 1,082, further indicating that education, within the confines of the present data set, did not influence either the slope or the intercept of the Brinley function. Note that one previous meta-analysis examining one measure of processing speed, namely the WAIS Digit Symbol Substitution Test (Hoyer, Stawski, Wasylyshyn, & Verhaeghen, 2004) likewise found no moderating effect of education on the observed age differences.

Thus, there is no evidence that the variability in Brinley slope estimates is tied to either the average age or the average level of education in the samples included in the meta-analysis.

3.6. Summary and Outlook

In this chapter, I investigated potential threats to the validity of the conclusions derived in Chapter 2. The news is quite good. There is little evidence that speed-accuracy trade-offs play the major role in explaining age-related slowing. Fitting the data using the EZ diffusion model suggested that age is associated with differences in all three parameters—older adults are slower at reaching decisions, set more conservative boundaries (but only for spatial tasks, not for linguistic tasks), and have longer non-decision times than younger adults. The dissociation between linguistic and spatial tasks was replicated in the EZ diffusion analysis. Variability in response times was identical for younger and older adults once the effect of mean RT was removed. There was no evidence of nonlinearity in the data. Some of the variability in slope estimates is indeed due to unreliability, but unreliability does not appear to bias the estimate of the average slope. Age and level of education within the older-adult groups in the meta-analysis had no influence on the slope estimates.

All in all, these analyses suggest that age-related slowing in general, and the dissociations obtained here, are real, and not an artifact of low validity.

4

The Aging Model Human Processor

Age-related Differences in the Speed of Elementary Operations

In Chapter 2, I presented a rather global look at age-related differences in processing speed by collecting a large anthology of tasks and examining possible dissociations between broad task domains. In this chapter and in Chapter 6, I will zoom in on age-related differences in specific tasks. I will build multiple models for age-related dissociations at more aggregate levels as determined bottom-up by the data as well as top-down by theory. The goal is to reach some sensible form of dimensionality reduction—to determine, if possible, the minimal number of distinct dimensions present in these data. In the current chapter and the next, I will focus on tasks that tap the speed of elementary sensory, motor, and cognitive processes. Chapter 6 adds tasks purportedly measuring cognitive or executive control—mostly tasks dealing with the ability to resist interference and to switch efficiently between tasks.

4.1. Elementary Processes of the Human Mind

One basic assumption in cognitive psychology is that it is possible to identify a set of discrete elementary processes and measure their speed of execution as well as their accuracy or fidelity. Much of the work on elementary processes has its roots in the information-processing framework. The information-processing framework views the mind as software—a set of procedures (lines of code, if one wishes) to transform input from the senses into actionable knowledge and memory representations. These procedures are the elementary operations; the basic characteristics of the hardware (e.g., how many chunks of information it can handle at any given time) are likewise essential for a full understanding of the mind's workings.

One complication for the researcher interested in identifying these elementary processes is that they, like any cognitive process, can never be observed directly; they only exist within the context of specific tasks, which combine multiple processes in either serial or parallel fashion, or both. Each task and each task situation also comes with its own specific set of demands and affordances, which are channeled through specific participants—participants in cognitive experiments are apt to bring specific skill sets and strategies to the table, and these might influence performance. All of this complicates the "pure" measurement of any "pure" elementary process.

A further, and potentially more problematic, complication is that the literature offers little in terms of a definitive list of these elementary processes. One recent crowd-sourced taxonomy, Russel Poldrack's Cognitive Atlas (http://www.cognitiveatlas. org/) is promising, but for the present purposes a tad overwhelming (more than 600 concepts and more than 400 tasks). Broader mathematical models, such as Alan Newell's Soar architecture (Soar originally stood for State, Operator And Result; 1990), John Anderson's ACT-R model (Adaptive Control of Thought—Rational; Anderson, 1983), or David Meyer and David Kieras's EPIC model (Executive-Process/Interactive Control; 1997) as well as theories specifically interested in capturing response times (e.g., Luce, 1991; Townsend & Ashby, 1983; Ratcliff & McKoon, 2008), come with their own proprietary list of components and their own architecture to bring these components in contact with each other.

This necessitates a choice. For my analyses, I decided to use Card, Moran, and Newell's *Model Human Processor* (1983) as my guide. The Model Human Processor is an information-processing simulator built explicitly to calculate how much time a given cognitive task will take. It consists of a set of operations and a number of sensory and short-term memory stores of fixed capacity and with fixed decay times. The assumption in this model is that there is a perceptual or sensory system, a cognitive system, and a motor system, each tapped by different sets of tasks, and each comprised of different subsystems, which are described by specific parameters. In this model, information processing proceeds in a number of discrete steps, chained in serial fashion.

There are a number of reasons why the Model Human Processor is particularly interesting for the present purposes. One is that the Model Human Processor model is mostly empirical and descriptive in nature: The exact values taken by its parameters—latencies, capacities, and decay times—are derived through experimentation. These parameters are for the most part easily traceable—processes are identified with latencies observed in or derived from specific experimental paradigms, most of which are quite common. This characteristic makes the meta-analytic study of elementary processes quite feasible. The model also imposes what seem rather minimal theoretical demands on the architecture and flow of information in the system, apart from those almost every cognitive psychologist would agree on (e.g., the existence of separate sensory stores for each sensory modality; the existence of a short-term store; the flow of information from the sensory store to short-term memory). The model has also proven to be practically useful—it was specifically designed for implementation in the context of human-computer interaction, and has been quite successful in that field.

I should note that a very similar enterprise—the examination of age differences in the Model Human Processor—was recently undertaken by Jastrzembski and Charness (2007). These authors conducted a meta-analysis of older adults' performance on the major tasks that tap the different components of the Model Human Processor. One difference between the Jastrzembski and Charness study and the meta-analyses reported here is that Jastrzembski and Charness simply took the Card et al. (1983) values for younger adults at face value; they did not empirically re-estimate them. This is somewhat suboptimal, given that the Card et al. values were derived from a very small number of empirical studies (sometimes even a single data point). In contrast, I will re-estimate the model parameters for both younger and older adults from all age-comparative studies I was able to locate. Jastrzembski and Charness also did not conduct allometric analyses, because their main interest was in modeling the aging Model Human Processor, and not in aging theory per se. I, on the other hand, will conduct them. This difference in purpose also makes for a difference in data sets: I excluded studies that tested only older adults, because my main focus is on the age group comparison. I also decided to go into more detail than Jastrzembski and Charness (and Card et al.) did with regard to the cycle time of cognitive processes. Jastrzembski and Charness estimate a single cognitive processor cycle time. (Card et al. assume that processing occurs in discrete bouts, cycles, the duration of which can vary with the domain—perceptual, cognitive, or motor—and the specific task.) Card et al. provide estimates for memory search times, subitizing rates (i.e., the speed at which four or fewer objects can be counted), silent counting rate, perceptual matching, and choice reaction time. I will conduct separate analyses on each of these tasks and will add cycle times for visual search and mental rotation as well. Finally, I will include one oft-studied ERP (event-related potential) measure of processing speed, namely the P300. Card et al. consider learning rates—increases in performance over the course of extended practice—a fundamental aspect of the system as well; therefore I will include these in this chapter, too.

More specifically, then, I will estimate age differences in the speed of *perceptual* processes (viz., fixation duration, the decay time of the visual sensory store, the cycle time of the visual perceptual processor as measured by flicker fusion thresholds, the cycle time of the auditory perceptual processor as measured by auditory gap detection), *motor* processes (the cycle time of the motor processor as measured by tapping speed and movement time toward a target [Fitts's law]), and *cognitive* processes (cycle times for short-term memory scanning, the enumeration process of subitizing and counting, mental rotation, and visual search [feature and conjunction search]; simple and choice reaction time; P300; decay time of the verbal short-term store; and lexical decision), as well as age differences in *practice* effects. In the next chapter, I will try to amalgamate these data into a smaller number of distinct age-related slowing factors, using both a top-down and a bottom-up approach.

4.2. Perceptual Processes

4.2.1. Fixation Times

Much of a human's ability to extract useful information from the visual environment depends on the use of rapid eye movements called saccades. In rapidly shifting environments or in environments where information is dispersed widely across the visual field, saccades typically occur at a rate of two or three per second, each taking about 200 ms to program. (For a review of this literature, see e.g., Pierrot-Deseilligny, Rivaud, Gaymar, Muri, & Vermersch, 1995.) Card et al. consider the time for eye movements an essential parameter of the visual system, but remain relatively vague as to its measurement: They refer to the "dwell time" on any location in a series of "automatic" eye movements. Here, like Jastrzembski and Charness, I examined two types of tasks. The first is saccadic reaction time. In this paradigm, subjects are asked to move their eyes toward some stimulus (typically a light) that turns on in peripheral vision. The dependent measure is the delay, that is, reaction time from the onset of the light to the time the eye starts moving, as measured by an electro-oculogram or by eye tracker technology. These visually guided saccades (sometimes called prosaccades—saccades toward some goal) are assumed to be under exogenous (i.e., environmental) control and are typically executed quite quickly, thus likely falling under Card et al.'s criterion of automatic eye movements. (Antisaccades—saccades away from some goal—are also possible. These will be considered in Chapter 6, which deals with cognitive control: Antisaccades are supposed to be under endogenous control [i.e., controlled by the individual], and are typically executed more slowly than prosaccades.) The second type of measure concerns fixation duration on targets and distractors during a visual search task. In keeping with Card et al.'s criterion of automaticity, I tried to exclude fixation durations that were heavily loaded with cognitive processing. For instance, Kemper, Crow and Kemtes (2004) measured fixation durations while subjects were reading complex sentences; these times likely (and are, in fact, assumed to) reflect comprehension processes much more than purely sensory uptake.

I collected 27 independent studies contained in 25 articles (Abel & Douglas, 2007; Abrams, Pratt, & Chasteen, 1998; Bono et al., 1996; Cassavaugh, Kramer, & Irwin, 2003; Cassavaugh, Kramer, & Peterson, 2004; Crawford et al., 2005; Eenshuistra, Ridderinkhof, & van der Molen, 2004; Gottlob, 2006; Gottlob, Fillmore, & Abroms, 2007; Kaneko, Kuba, Sakata, & Kuchinomachi, 2004; Kramer et al., 2006; Maltz & Shinar, 1999; Moschner & Baloh, 1994; Munoz, Broughton, Goldring, & Armstrong, 1998; Nieuwenhuis, Ridderinkhof, de Jong, Kok, & van der Molen, 2000; Olincy, Ross, Youngd, & Freedman, 1997; Pratt, Welsh, & Dodd, 2006; Raemaekers, Vink, van den Heuvel, Kahn, & Ramsey, 2006; Rambold, Neumann, Sander, & Helmchen, 2006; Rösler et al., 2000; Ryan, Shen, & Reingold, 2006; Scialfa, Hamaluk, Skaloud, & Pratt, 1999; Scialfa & Joffe, 1997; Yang, Kapoula, Debay, Coubard, Orssaud, & Samson, 2006).

The average fixation time for younger adults across these studies (weighted for sample size) was 242 ms; older adults were at least nominally slower: They took 280 ms. The value for younger adults does not deviate much from the original Model Human Processor value; Card et al. (1983) estimate a mean value of 230 ms, with an acceptable range of 70 to 700 ms, "depending on conditions of measurement, task variables, or subject variables" (p. 28).

Figure 4.1 shows the Brinley plot for this data set (101 data points). I first estimated a model that included a task parameter to test for intercept differences between fixation durations in saccadic RT tasks and visual search tasks (dummy coded; saccadic RT = 0 and visual search = 1) as well as the interaction between this task dummy and fixation duration, in order to test for slope differences between fixation durations in saccadic RT and visual search:

$$\text{Fixation duration}_{older} = 48\ (34) + 0.99\ (0.12)\ \text{Fixation duration}_{younger}$$
$$+ 56\ (67)\ \text{Task} - 0.33\ (0.23)$$
$$\text{Task by Fixation duration}_{younger}.$$

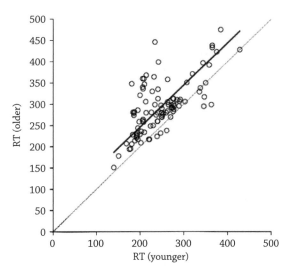

Figure 4.1 Brinley plot of fixation duration data (k = 101). Final regression line is indicated as a solid line; the dotted line is the equality diagonal.

Neither the task parameter nor the interaction term proved significant, ΔLR χ^2 (2) = 4.21, suggesting that age differences are identical across both types of tasks. The simplified equation relating fixation duration of older adults to that of younger adults is:

Fixation duration$_{older}$ = 52 (25) + 0.96 (0.12) Fixation duration$_{younger}$.

The mean and *SE* for the slope parameter suggest that the slope might be fixed at unity without affecting the model significantly. This turned out to be the case, ΔLR χ^2 (1) = 0.09:

Fixation duration$_{older}$ = 45 (7) + 1.00 (0.00) Fixation duration$_{younger}$.

The interpretation is, first, that fixation durations of older adults are reliably longer than those of younger adults. Second, this age-related slowing effect is additive: Older adults fixate on average 45 ms longer than younger adults, regardless of the duration of younger adults' fixation times (within the bounds of the studies here, which is 140 to 428 ms). Compared with the empty model, the equation explains 66% of the variance in older adults' mean fixation duration.

4.2.2. Decay Time of the Visual Sensory Store

Sensory memory refers to the literal, modality-specific representation of sensory stimuli that serves as input to subsequent stages of perception and cognition (e.g., Lu, Neuse, Madigan & Dosher, 2005). The classic demonstration of the existence of a visual sensory store (often called the iconic store) is the partial-report superiority effect (Sperling, 1960). When subjects are presented briefly with an array of

3×3 or 3×4 letters, they are rarely able to recall more than four or five items. If the offset of the display, however, is quickly followed by a cue to recall only a particular row, often all letters within a row can be reported. This effect is attributed to the workings of the iconic store, which simply last too briefly to be accessible after more than four or five items are reported. Results from the partial-report technique suggest that this store can hold at least 9 to 12 items. The memory representations ("icons") decay rapidly and are destroyed by poststimulus masking. Using the partial-report superiority effect with varying stimulus-cue intervals, the duration of iconic memory has been estimated to be 300–500 ms for young adults (Lu et al.).

The typical measure of the speed of decay in iconic memory is an icon's half-life. This half-life can be determined by calculating the time needed for accuracy to decline from its maximum (at a zero ms stimulus-cue interval) to a point halfway to its minimum (at a stimulus-cue interval of, theoretically, infinity). In practice, this is done by fitting the data (stimulus-cue interval on the X-axis, accuracy on the Y-axis) to a 3-parameter exponential decay function (Sperling, 1960):

$$Y = Y_0 + a\, Exp(-b\, X).$$

In this equation, Y_0 stands for the minimum accuracy at long intervals (this is assumed to be the amount of information that gets reliably transferred into the next store in the information-processing sequence, short-term memory or working memory), a reflects the additional amount of information that can be held in iconic memory at a zero ms stimulus-cue interval, and b reflects the exponential decay of that information. The half-life is calculated based on what the empirical halfway point is for each data set; this point may differ from study to study, and it varies across individuals or groups of individuals, such as younger and older adults. Card et al. estimate the half-life of the iconic store at about 200 ms in younger adults, with lower and upper bounds of 90 and 1,000 ms, respectively.

The literature on age-related effects in iconic memory decay is sparse; I was only able to locate three studies (Abel, 1972, cited in Botwinick, 1978; Lu, Neuse, Madigan, & Dosher, 2005; Walsh & Thompson, 1978). (One additional study, Gilmore, Allan & Royer, 1986, was not included because the three-parameter function failed to fit the data for the older adult group and the fit for the younger-adult group suggested an impossibly short half-life of 36 ms.) Note that because a three-parameter function is fitted to the data, each study needs to contain at least four data points to fit the function with at least one degree of freedom. In all three studies, the iconic store was observed to be less stable in older adults compared with younger adults. First, half-life of the icon was considerably shorter in older than in younger adults—214 ms versus 326 ms. Thus, older adults' icons' half-life is about 66% shorter than that of younger adults, or, conversely, the half-life of younger adults' icons is 1.52 times longer. Second, the decay parameter b as estimated from the functions is larger, indicating faster decay in older adults than in younger adults—0.0030 versus 0.0021. Older adults decay rates are thus, on average, 1.45 faster than those of younger adults.

A final note is that I was unable to locate relevant data for the corresponding auditory store, the echoic store.

4.2.3. Cycle Time of the Visual Perceptual Processor: Flicker Fusion Threshold

Card et al. define the cycle time of the visual perceptual processor as the amount of time that passes between the onset of a stimulus and the time at which the information contained in the stimulus becomes available in the iconic store. They measure this cycle time using the stimulus fusion technique—when two stimuli are similar enough (e.g., identical) and occur in rapid succession, a single, fused percept is often formed. If the stimuli are separated in space, apparent motion is the result; if the stimuli occur in the same location and are identical, the percept is a single, stable stimulus.

Card et al. point out that the cycle time varies inversely with stimulus intensity. Other determinants have been identified as well. For instance, Culham and Kline (2002) used sinusoidal gratings and manipulated spatial frequency and contrast of these gratings; both of these influenced the estimate of the cycle time. On the one hand, these findings make a point estimate of cycle time a rather quixotic enterprise; on the other hand, this result assures variability across studies, which, in turn, allows for a broad sweep across Brinley space, making conclusions about the nature of the age difference (additive, multiplicative, or both) easier to draw.

For the purpose of this meta-analysis, I concentrated on a single measure of fusion, the one used most often in aging research, namely flicker fusion threshold. An individual's flicker fusion threshold is the frequency at which she perceives an intermittent (i.e., flickering) light stimulus, always presented at the same location with the same intensity, as a steady light. The minimum number of cycles per second necessary to produce the illusion of fusion is called the critical flicker frequency, or CFF. Card et al. call the CFF the "basic quantum of experience"; they consider it is a measure the duration of the present. Considered in this light, people with lower CFFs live in a longer present; their "now" is prolonged compared with that of people with higher CFFs.

The data again are relatively sparse; I was able to locate 22 independent studies contained in 18 papers (Botwinick & Brinley, 1963; Cronin-Golomb et al., 1991; Csank & Lehmann, 1958; Culham & Kline, 2002; De Corte & Lavergne, 1969; Eisenbarth, MacKeben, Poggel, & Strasburger, 2008; Falk & Kline, 1978; Giaquinto & Nolfe, 1984; Gilburt, Fairweather, Kerr, & Hindmarch, 1992; Hammond & Wooten, 2005; Huntington & Simonson, 1965; Lachenmayr et al., 1994; McFarland, Warren, & Karis, 1958; Misiak, 1951; Schmidtke, 1951; Swift & Tiplady, 1988; Weekers, & Roussel, 1946; Wolf & Schraffa, 1964).

For younger adults, average weighted CFF was 34.13; for older adults, it was 27.78. Note that CFF is scored as frequency per second, and thus as the inverse of speed: Lower values indicate that fewer cycles are necessary to produce fusion and thus signal a slower perceptual system. CFF can be converted into a speed measure, cycle time, by taking its inverse (which I multiplied by 1000, to yield a measurement in ms/cycle). The above result then implies that, on average, younger adults need 29 ms per cycle for fusion to occur, while older adults need 36 ms per cycle for a fused percept. Note that the average younger-adult values are much lower, that is, faster, than the Card et al. estimate, which is 100 ms with a range of 50 to 200 ms. The range in the present 22 studies is much narrower, too: The minimum value for younger adults in the data set is 20 ms, the maximum 72 ms. (For older adults, these values are 22 ms and 98 ms, respectively.)

To keep results in line with all other results in this book, I used cycle time rather than CFF in the Brinley analyses, so that the slopes can be interpreted directly as slowing factors. The data are presented in Figure 4.2; there are a total of 80 data points, nested within the 22 studies. The results are straightforward:

$$\textbf{Cycle time flicker fusion}_{\text{older}} = \textbf{-0.70 (3.0) + 1.25 (0.09)}$$
$$\textbf{Cycle time flicker fusion}_{\text{younger}}$$

The value of the intercept parameter and its *SE* suggest that the intercept might be fixed at zero without affecting the model significantly. This turned out to be the case, ΔLR χ^2 (1) = 0.06, and the final Brinley equation is:

$$\textbf{Cycle time flicker fusion}_{\text{older}} = \textbf{1.23 (0.03) Cycle time flicker fusion}_{\text{younger}}.$$

Thus, the data conform to a purely proportional or multiplicative model, with an age-related slowing factor of about 1.2. This model explained 55% of the variance in older adults' mean cycle time flicker fusion compared with the empty model.

4.2.4. Cycle Time of the Auditory Perceptual Processor: Gap Detection

The cycle time of the auditory perceptual processor is estimated using a close auditory analogue to the critical flicker fusion frequency, namely the gap detection threshold. In the gap detection threshold paradigm, listeners are presented with a continuous sound, interrupted by a brief gap. The gap threshold is defined as the maximum length of the gap that still produces the illusion of fusion. As with flicker fusion studies, many parameters

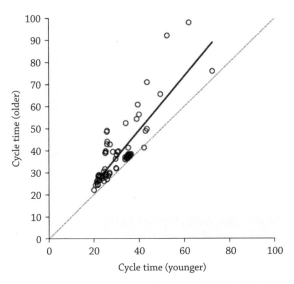

Figure 4.2 Brinley plot of cycle times needed for critical flicker fusion ($k = 80$). Final regression line is indicated as a solid line; the dotted line is the equality diagonal.

can be manipulated, each influencing the perception of the gap—pure tone versus noise, frequency of the tones, the presence/absence of fall/rise times before and after a gap, whether or not the sounds before and after the gap differ in spectral properties, etc.

My harvest of gap detection studies is extremely modest. I was able to collect 10 papers, each reporting a single study (He, Horwitz, Dubno, & Mills, 1999; Heinrich & Schneider, 2006; Humes, Busey, Craig, & Kewley-Port, 2009; Schneider & Hamstra, 1999; Schneider, Pichora-Fuller, Kowalchuk, & Lamb, 1994; Snell, 1997; Snell, & Frisina, 2000; Snell & Hu, 1999; Strouse, Ashmead, Ohde, & Grantham, 1998).

The weighted average shows that younger adults can, on average, detect a gap lasting 4.4 ms; older adults need 8.1 ms. One of the studies (Strouse et al.) showed an extraordinarily large age effect—5.1 ms on average for younger adults, 18.2 ms for older adults. Deleting this study from the pool changed the results somewhat, with gap thresholds of 4.1 ms and 7.3 ms, respectively.

The results from the Brinley analysis are straightforward. Figure 4.3, left-hand panel, shows all data; one outlier is clearly identifiable—the (8 ms, 36 ms) pair from the Strouse et al. paper. After deleting all three data points associated with this study, 46 data points remained, shown in the right-hand panel of Figure 4.3. They are described by the following equation:

$$\text{Gap Threshold}_{older} = -0.06\ (0.71) + 1.33\ (0.08)\ \text{Gap Threshold}_{younger}.$$

This equation could be pruned at no significant cost to fit, $\Delta \text{LR}\ \chi^2\ (1) = 0.66$, by setting the intercept to zero, to:

$$\text{Gap Threshold}_{older} = 1.32\ (0.03)\ \text{Gap Threshold}_{younger}.$$

The results are quite similar to those obtained for the visual processing cycle: Older adults are slowed multiplicatively, and with a comparable slowing factor, 1.3 here,

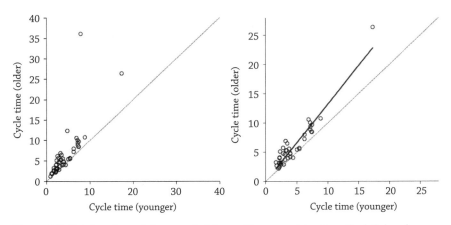

Figure 4.3 Brinley plots of time needed for auditory gap detection; the left-hand panel shows all available data ($k = 49$); the right-hand panel shows the same data with one outlying study removed ($k = 46$; note the change in scale). Final regression line is indicated as a solid line; the dotted line is the equality diagonal.

1.2 in the visual system, and with overlapping confidence intervals. This equation explained 92% of the variance in older adults' mean gap threshold compared with the empty model.

4.3. Motor Processes

4.3.1. Cycle Time of the Motor Processor: Tapping Speed

Card et al. contend that movement is not continuous, but occurs in discrete bursts of micromovements. To measure the movement quantum, they have the subject move a pen back and forth between two lines as fast as she can, and count the number of reversals within a given time period. This task has not been adopted widely in the literature, and I was unable to find any aging studies that implemented it. There is, however, one repetitive motor task that has been reported with some frequency in the aging literature, and that is maximum tapping speed. There are many variations on this paradigm. For instance, Salthouse (1984) had subjects tap the f and j key on a computer keyboard alternatingly for 15 s; Teixeira (2008) had subjects tap down 30 times on a wooden pad with a stylus; Swift and Tiplady (1988) had subjects tap a Morse key for 90 s. Variations, then, exist in the amount of time subjects were tapping, or whether tapping involves one or both hands. Again, this variability might produce paradigm-specific variability that could produce a wider sweep in the Brinley plot.

I was able to locate 20 independent estimates, contained in 15 articles (Bodwell, Mahurin, Waddle, Price, & Cramer, 2003; Cousins, Corrow, Finn, & Salamone, 1998; Crossley & Hiscock, 1992; Elias, Podraza, Pierce, & Robbins, 1990; Jones, Sahakian, Levy, Warburton, & Gray, 1992; Kauranen & Vanharanta, 1996; Ketcham, Seidler, Van Gemmert, & Stelmach, 2002; Kraus, Przuntek, Kegelmann, & Klotz, 2000; McAuley, Jones, Holub, Johnston, & Miller, 2006; Metter, Schrager, Ferrucci, & Talbot, 2005; Nagasaki, Itoh, Maruyama, & Hashizume, 1988; Ruff & Parker, 1993; Salthouse, 1984; Swift & Tiplady, 1988; Teixeira, 2008). (Note that whenever researchers reported data from both the dominant and nondominant hand, I used only the data for the dominant hand, which would presumably yield the faster tapping rate.)

Mean maximum tapping rate, weighted for sample size, was 4.79 taps/s for younger adults and 4.12 taps/s for older adults. To bring the results in line with the other results reported in this book, I converted the tapping rate into a tapping speed, that is, 1000/tapping rate. Thus, the average tapping rate of 4.79 taps/second in younger adults is converted to a tapping speed of 209 ms/tap; the average tapping speed of older adults implies 243 ms/tap. A tap in a series of repeated taps is a dual movement—a stroke up and a stroke down—and so the estimated cycle time of the motor processor is half the tapping speed: 105 ms for younger adults and 121 ms for older adults. My estimate for younger adults is situated at the slow end of the estimate proposed by Card et al.—70 ms, with a range between 30 ms and 100 ms. (Card et al. based their estimate on four studies.) Figure 4.4 reports the data.

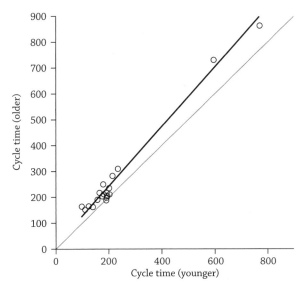

Figure 4.4 Brinley plot of tapping speed data (cycle times) (k = 20). Final regression line is indicated as a solid line; the dotted line is the equality diagonal.

The Brinley equation (20 data points) for tapping speed is:

$$\text{Tapping speed}_{\text{older}} = 4.42\ (10.36) + 1.16\ (0.04)\ \text{Tapping speed}_{\text{younger}}.$$

The intercept could be fixed to zero at no significant cost to fit, ΔLR χ^2 (1) = 0.14. The resulting equation was:

$$\text{Tapping speed}_{\text{older}} = 1.18\ (0.02)\ \text{Tapping speed}_{\text{younger}}.$$

The age-related slowing factor in tapping, 1.18, is relatively modest, but significantly larger than 1. The equation explains 99% of the variance in older adults' mean tapping speed compared with the empty model.

Figure 4.4 suggests that there are two outlying data points, with extremely slow tapping rates of 500 ms/tap or longer (Crossley & Hiscock, 1992; Ketcham et al., 2002). Deleting these from the data set did not, however, meaningfully change the result:

$$\text{Tapping speed}_{\text{older}} = 1.19\ (0.03)\ \text{Tapping speed}_{\text{younger}}.$$

The conclusion then is that tapping speed appears to be slowed purely proportionally with age, with a slowing factor of about 1.2.

4.3.2. Movement Toward a Target: Fitts's Law

A second aspect of motor performance that has received some attention in the aging literature concerns pointing movements, more specifically the time needed to move a limb (typically a hand or its extensions, such as a computer mouse) to a prespecified target. Fitts (1954) discovered that the time needed to do so is directly proportional to the distance D from the starting point to the center of the target and inversely proportional to the target's width W. That is, subjects are fastest when moving a short distance to a large target, and slowest moving a long distance to a small target. Fitts's Law (as this regularity became known) can also be seen as a description of the trade-off between speed and accuracy in motor behavior: With fine-tuning of the accuracy of movement (in other words, shrinking the target) comes a slow-down of movement time.

There are a few variations on the exact equations used to describe Fitts's Law (or Fitts' Law; there's variation in its naming, too). Fitts himself formulated the following equation, taking Shannon's channel capacity theorem as his inspiration:

$$\text{Movement Time} = a + b \log_2 (2D/W).$$

A version that is more popular these days is MacKenzie's (1989) reformulation:

$$\text{Movement Time} = a + b \log_2 (1 + D/W).$$

MacKenzie's version is also known as the Shannon formulation of Fitts's Law, because it is closer in form to the original Shannon-Hartley channel capacity theorem than Fitts's version. MacKenzie's equation also approximates empirical data better, especially for targets that are very wide compared with the distance (MacKenzie, 1992). Therefore, MacKenzie's version is the one I will use.

The unit on the X-axis of this linear function, that is, $\log_2 (1 + D/W)$, is often labeled the index of difficulty, or ID, measured in bits. Movement time is a linear function of the index of difficulty, which is effectively a measure of relative precision needed, being directly proportional to the ratio of distance over size. From this description, it is clear that the b parameter is the parameter of interest, because it describes the increase in movement time with growing task difficulty. The a parameter is often regarded as an error term, mainly because it has escaped explanation. From Shannon's theory, it follows it should be zero; that is, it would take 0 ms to complete a task of zero difficulty (Soukoreff & MacKenzie, 2004), but empirical work often finds positive intercepts. Multiple explanations for this result have been advanced, such as dwell time in the motor system (Fitts & Radford, 1966), muscle activity at the beginning or end of the movement task (MacKenzie, 1992), sensory reaction time (Fitts & Peterson, 1964), the time needed for button presses (MacKenzie, 1992), or even modeling errors (Welford, 1961). One of the main problems for any of these explanations is that negative intercepts are also often observed. (See Soukoreff & MacKenzie, 2004, for a review.) To wit, three out of the nine studies gathered here show a negative intercept for the younger adult subject groups.

The equation for Fitts's Law provides us with an interesting way of analyzing age differences: We can directly fit the equation to average data for younger and older adults as reported in the literature, which allows us to directly compare parameter values between age groups. I was able to locate nine studies from eight papers that allowed for an evaluation of age-related differences in the parameters of Fitts's law; they contained 47 young-old data pairs, or 94 data points total (Chaparro, Bohan, Fernandez,

Choi, & Kattell, 1999; Goggin & Stelmach, 1990; Ketcham, Seidler, Van Gemmert, & Stelmach, 2002; Liao, Jagacinski, & Greenberg, 1997; Rogers, Fisk, McLaughlin, & Pak, 2005; Walker, Philbin, & Fisk, 1997; Welford, 1952, cited in Welford, 1958; Worden, Walker, Bharat, & Hudson, 1997).

The fitted parameters for Fitts's Law, including the age effects on slope and intercept, yielded the following equation:

$$RT = 54 \ (45) + 124 \ (20) \ ID + 24 \ (76) \ \text{dummy (age group)}$$
$$+ \ 66 \ (7) \ \text{dummy (age group) by } ID.$$

This can be rewritten more intelligibly as the following set of two equations:

$$RT_{younger} = 54 + 124 \ ID$$

$$RT_{older} = 78 + 179 \ ID$$

In the equation above, the *SE* of the intercept, as well as the main effect of age, are large compared with their estimates. These variables could indeed be deleted without any significant cost to fit, $\Delta LR \ \chi^2 \ (2) = 2.24$. This reduces the equation to Shannon's form, that is, without an intercept. This final equation is:

$$RT = 123 \ (18) \ ID + 66 \ (7) \ \text{dummy (age group) by } ID.$$

This can be rewritten as:

$$RT_{younger} = 123 \ ID$$

$$RT_{older} = 189 \ ID.$$

Thus, the slope of the function relating response time to the index of difficulty is reliably larger in older adults (189 ms/*ID* unit) than in younger adults (123 ms/*ID* unit); the age-related slowing factor in the slope is 1.54. Card et al. report values between 27 ms and 122 ms for the slope; my estimate for younger adults is virtually identical to the upper bound.

I also performed a Brinley analysis on the 47 data-points from these studies (left-hand panel of Figure 4.5), which yielded a comparable age-related slowing factor:

$$RT_{older} = -40 \ (36) + 1.63 \ (0.09) \ RT_{younger}.$$

This equation could be simplified at no cost to fit, $\Delta LR \ \chi^2 \ (1) = 1.14$, by omitting the intercept:

$$RT_{older} = 1.65 \ (0.09) \ RT_{younger}.$$

This final equation indicates that aging slows deliberate movements toward a target in a purely proportional fashion, with an age-related slowing factor of about 1.6.

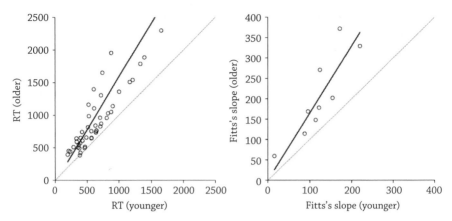

Figure 4.5 Brinley plots of movement time data (Fitts's Law); the left-hand panel plots latency data (k = 47); the right-hand panel plots the slopes of the Fitts functions (k = 9). Final regression lines are indicated as a solid line; the dotted lines are the equality diagonals.

Compared with the empty model, the equation explains 99% of the variance in older adults' mean RT.

I also conducted Brinley analysis on the slopes of the Fitts functions—nine studies, so nine data points. The resulting equation (right-hand panel of Figure 4.5) is:

$$\textbf{Fitts slope}_{\textbf{older}} = \textbf{16 (39)} + \textbf{1.54 (0.29) Fitts slope}_{\textbf{younger}}$$

Fixing the intercept to zero did not reduce fit reliably, ΔLR χ^2 (1) = 0.17:

$$\textbf{Fitts slope}_{\textbf{older}} = \textbf{1.65 (0.12) Fitts slope}_{\textbf{younger}}.$$

These analyses all point to the same conclusion: A purely proportional age deficit in movement times, with a slowing factor around 1.6.

4.4. Speed of the Cognitive System

Although Card et al. (like Jastrzembski and Charness) offer a single-point estimate of cognitive cycle times (70 ms, ranging from 25 to 170 ms), they also note that cycle times do differ between tasks—from around 50 ms/cycle for short-term memory scanning to about 170 ms/cycle for silent counting. These differences between tasks seem meaningful, and therefore I decided to carve up tasks in as much detail as I felt was supported by the literature. I will report on iterative tasks first (iterative tasks are tasks in which multiple identical steps are performed in a sequence, viz., memory search or scanning; mental enumeration, that is, subitizing and counting; mental rotation; and visual search), then I will examine tasks that involve simple decisions (simple vs. choice reaction times, including an examination of age differences in Hick's

Law). Next I will report on age differences in one ERP component, the P300, that has received some attention in the aging literature, ending with an analysis of decay rates in verbal short-term memory.

4.4.1. Cycle Times for Iterative Cognitive Tasks

One way of measuring cognitive cycle times, analogous to the way motor-processor cycle times are assessed, is by having subjects perform a fixed number of presumably identical operations in quick succession and calculating the time needed for a single operation. Here, I examined four such iterative tasks: short-term memory search (sometimes called memory scanning; Sternberg, 1966), enumeration, mental rotation, and visual search. In memory search, the number of steps is determined by the size of the memory set (search for one item among a memory set of two items, among a set of three items, or four, etc.). In enumeration tasks, the number of steps is determined by the number of objects in the display. In mental rotation tasks, the angle of rotation away from the comparison object represents a metaphorical step. (The step here is more metaphorical than real: It is unlikely that mental rotation really occurs according to steps in any measurable quantum.) In visual search, the steps are set by the number of objects to be searched.

Iterative tasks are characterized by a so-called information-processing function—the line that plots response time as a function of the number of "steps." It is easy to see that the slope of this line can be understood as a direct measure of the processing cycle time. For instance, in a memory search task, the slope of the line describing response time as a function of memory-set size tells us what the consequence is of adding one more element to the set-to-be-searched—precisely the definition of cycle time. The slope of the information-processing function is a process-pure measure of cycle time: It only reflects the time needed to query a single item and move to the next; all other processes (sensory uptake, stimulus matching, decision making, motor output, and the like) are included in the intercept of the response time by set-size line. Similarly, the slope of the response time by numerosity line in enumeration tasks directly reflects the rate of enumeration; the slope of RT by angle of rotation equals the rate of mental rotation; and the slope of RT by set size in visual search is a direct measurement of the visual search rate.

There is one extant meta-analysis on age-related effects in iterative tasks (Sliwinski & Hall, 1998; this data set was reanalyzed by Myerson et al., 2003). Sliwinski and Hall examined memory search, mental rotation, and one aspect of visual search (conjunction search; see below). I updated the Sliwinski and Hall data set with additional studies, and added one more aspect of visual search (feature search), as well as enumeration tasks. As recommended by Sliwinski and Hall, I averaged the data across all manipulations except for the iterative dimension prior to applying multilevel regression.

One interesting property of iterative tasks is that the slope of the Brinley lines for each of these tasks corresponds perfectly to the ratio of the information-processing slope of the old over the processing slope of the young. This can be easily derived algebraically; Myerson et al. (2003) provide an empirical example of this conjecture as well. Consider the following set of two equations, which only presupposes that response time (RT) is a linear function of the number of processing steps (NoPS):

$$RT_{younger} = a_{younger} + b_{younger}\, NoPS$$

$$RT_{older} = a_{older} + b_{older}\, NoPS.$$

Isolating NoPs from the first equation gives us:

$$NoPS = (RT_{younger} - a_{younger})/b_{younger}.$$

Inserting this expression into the second equation results in:

$$RT_{older} = a_{older} + b_{older}\, (RT_{younger} - a_{younger})/b_{younger}$$

This can be rearranged to:

$$RT_{older} = (a_{older} - (a_{younger}\, b_{older})/b_{younger}) + (b_{older}/b_{younger})\, RT_{younger}.$$

The latter equation is the Brinley equation. (It describes RT of older adults as a function of RT of younger adults.) The slope of the Brinley equation for iterative tasks is then equal to $b_{older}/b_{younger}$, or the ratio of the information-processing slope of older adults over the information-processing slope of younger adults. Therefore, the Brinley slope for iterative tasks is process-pure, reflecting nothing but the age-related effect in the iterative process—the memory search process, the enumeration process, the mental rotation process, and the visual search process, respectively, in the present data set—at the exclusion of all other processes. One advantage of this property is that it makes iterative tasks ideally suited to put general or dissociated slowing to the test: If all cognitive processes were subject to distinct age-related slowing factors, only task-specific slowing factors would emerge from the data. If, however, slowing factors for tasks within a given task domain (such as the linguistic and spatial domains proofed in Chapter 2) were to coincide, this would be a clear indication that the age-related slowing factor can be identical even for tasks that tap clearly distinct processes.

   In the graphs for the remainder of this section, I will present the data for each of the tasks in three panels. The first of these panels shows the Brinley plot of the raw latencies. The second and third represent Brinley plots of the slopes and intercepts of the information-processing functions. I will explain the usefulness of the two latter graphs in the next subsection—it is easier to work through an example than to derive the results in the abstract.

4.4.1.1. Short-term Memory Scanning Rate

The memory-scanning paradigm was first introduced by Sternberg in 1966. In Sternberg's procedure, a short list of items (the memory set) is presented, one at a time, at a relatively fast clip (typically about one or two items/s), followed by one or more recognition probes. Participants indicate whether or not the probe item was present in the study list and their decision latency and accuracy is recorded.

The basic finding from the Sternberg procedure is that decision latencies increase as a linear function of the size of the list. Sternberg (1966, 1975) interpreted this finding as indicative of an exhaustive serial scanning process—subjects search through the whole list, examining one item at a time and emitting their response only at the end of this process. A finding that supports this conjecture is that slopes for trials where the probe is an item that is indeed in the memory set ("target-present" trials) are typically not shallower than slopes for trials where the probe is not part of the memory set ("target-absent" trials). If search is terminated when the probe matches an item in the memory set, the search process in target-present trials should on average be completed in half the time needed for target-absent trials, where perforce the whole list needs to be scanned. The search is serial, because parallel search should give rise to flat serial position curves in target-present trials: It would take as much time to answer "yes" to the first item in a four-item list as to the fourth. As often in cognitive psychology, things are not that clear-cut, and the debate over the exact search mechanism is still ongoing (e.g., Townsend & Wenger, 2004, who propose a parallel mechanism).

Fortunately, the exact nature of the search mechanism is of lesser concern to us here—our focus of interest is in quantifying the existing age differences in this mechanism. Even if the mechanism is unknown, age-related differences in it can still be investigated, on the condition that a linear information-processing function is obtained and that younger and older adults use the same search mechanism. The former is typically the case; there is no reason to doubt the latter. (See Lange & Verhaeghen, 2009, for a direct comparison of search mechanisms in younger and older adults.)

I was able to locate 15 relevant papers (Sliwinski & Hall included nine), each reporting data from one set of younger-older subjects, for a total of 58 data pairs (Allen, Sliwinski, & Bowie, & Madden, 2002; Cerella, DiCara, Williams, & Bowles, 1986; Coyne, Allen, & Wickens, 1986; Fisk, Rogers, Cooper, & Gilbert, 1997; Fisk, Rogers, & Giambra, 1990; Hertzog, Cooper, & Fisk, 1996; Madden, 1982; Madden et al., 2003; Menich & Baron, 1990; Puglisi, 1986; Rypma, Prabhakaran, Desmond, & Gabrieli, 2001; Salthouse, 1994; Salthouse & Somberg, 1982a; Strayer & Kramer, 1994; Van Gerven, Paas, Van Merriënboer & Schmidt, 2003). The data are plotted in Figure 4.6.

Fitting the data to a model that included dummy terms to evaluate the age effects on the intercept (the dummy [age group] term) and slope (the set-size by dummy [age group] term), I obtained the following equation (in units of milliseconds):

RT = 518 (34) + 60 (8) set-size + 291 (56) dummy (age group)
+ 12 (9) set-size by dummy (age group).

This equation can be rewritten as a set of two equations, one for younger adults and one for older adults:

$$RT_{younger} = 518 + 60 \text{ set-size; and}$$

$$RT_{older} = 809 + 72 \text{ set-size.}$$

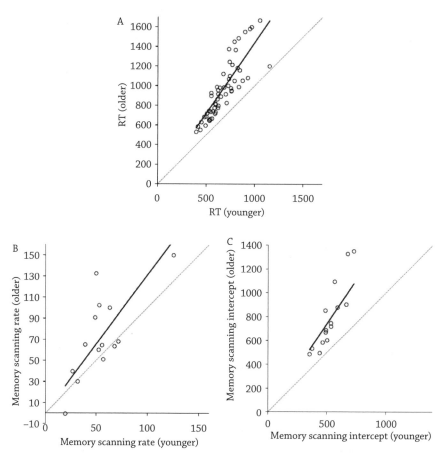

Figure 4.6 Brinley plots of memory scanning data. Panel A shows latency data (k = 58); Panel B shows the Brinley plot of the memory scanning rates obtained in each study (k = 15); Panel C plots the corresponding memory scanning intercepts (k = 15). Final regression lines are indicated as solid lines; the dotted lines are the equality diagonals.

From this, it follows that short-term memory scanning rates in older adults (72 ms/item) are 1.20 times slower than those of younger adults (60 ms/item).

The Brinley analysis (58 data points) likewise shows a significant age-related effect:

$$RT_{older} = 85\ (67) + 1.33\ (0.10)\ RT_{younger}.$$

The slope of this function is reliably different from unity. The size of standard error of the intercept suggests that the intercept of the Brinley function is not significantly different from zero. Fixing the intercept to zero indeed did not significantly impact fit, $\Delta LR\ \chi^2\ (1) = 1.47$. The final equation is then:

$$RT_{older} = 1.44\ (0.06)\ RT_{younger}.$$

The slope of this function is again larger than 1. Compared with the empty model, this equation explains 93% of the variance in older adults' mean RT.

As hinted at above, the Brinley function can tell us a few other things. Let us start again with the two standard equations for memory scanning:

$$RT_{younger} = a_{younger} + b_{younger} \text{ set-size; and}$$

$$RT_{older} = a_{older} + b_{older} \text{ set-size.}$$

A few simplifying assumptions can be made. Assume, for instance, that both the scanning intercept (a_{older}) and the scanning rate (b_{older}) of older adults are simply proportional to those of younger adults; that is, assume that aging slows scanning intercepts and scanning slopes by a certain factor. In that case:

$$a_{older} = A\, a_{younger} \text{ and } b_{older} = B\, b_{younger};$$

with A and B representing the age-related slowing factors for the intercept and scanning rate, respectively.

This gives rise to:

$$RT_{older} = A\, a_{younger} + B\, b_{younger} \text{ set-size.}$$

Given that $RT_{younger} = a_{younger} + b_{younger}$ set-size, we can derive:

$$b_{younger} \text{ set-size} = RT_{younger} - a_{younger};$$

substituting this result in the previous equation yields:

$$RT_{older} = A\, a_{younger} + B\, (RT_{younger} - a_{younger}),$$

or:

$$RT_{older} = A\, a_{younger} - B\, a_{younger} + B\, RT_{younger},$$

which reorganizes to:

$$RT_{older} = (A - B)\, a_{younger} + B\, RT_{younger}.$$

This again shows that RT of older adults is a linear function of RT of younger adults. The slope of this Brinley function is the age-related slowing factor B of the short-term memory (STM) scanning rate (within the bounds of measurement error). This is not new—I already derived this result above. What is new is that the intercept turns out to be of interest as well. If the assumption of simple proportional slowing in the intercept of the information processing function is correct, the intercept of the Brinley equation will be zero if, and only if, A = B. (Technically, it will also be zero if the intercept of the information processing function for the younger adults equals zero, but this is an unrealistic scenario—input/output processes should take at least some measurable amount of time, and they do in this sample.) Thus, if we find a zero intercept in the Brinley function (as is the case for memory scanning), we can conclude (within the statistical power of the comparison) that the age-related slowing factors governing the processing rate (i.e., the slope of the information-processing function) and the age-related slowing rate governing the intercept of the information-processing function are identical.

Note that in the present context there is no need to blindly trust the simplifying assumptions concerning the relationships between intercepts and scanning rates of younger and older adults: They can easily be verified empirically by regressing scanning intercepts and scanning rates of older adults on scanning intercepts and scanning rates of younger adults. To do this, I calculated scanning rates and scanning intercepts for all 15 studies included here and then conducted Brinley analyses on those; the Brinley plots—one for scanning intercepts, one for scanning slopes—are represented in Figure 4.6, Panels B and C.

Turning to slopes (i.e., memory scanning rates) first, I find that the assumption of proportional slowing is indeed warranted. The full Brinley equation is:

STM Scanning rate$_{older}$ = 6 (15) + 1.22 (0.24) STM scanning rate$_{younger}$.

Both of the parameters here are within the bounds of the null hypothesis, zero for the intercept, unity for the slope. Fixing the intercept to zero (the logical choice for theoretical reasons, as well as for reasons of empirical convergence with the analyses on scanning rates reported earlier in this section) yielded no significant decrease in fit, ΔLR χ^2 (1) = 0.08. The slope is now larger than unity:

STM Scanning rate$_{older}$ = 1.31 (0.10) STM scanning rate$_{younger}$.

Likewise, I found the intercept of older adults' information-processing function to be proportional to that of younger adults. The full Brinley model is:

STM scanning intercept$_{older}$ = –440 (166) + 2.34 (0.30)
STM scanning intercept$_{younger}$.

This is quite an ugly result—a very large negative intercept and a very steep slope. Fortunately, even though the *SE* of the intercept suggests that the intercept is smaller than zero, the intercept can be deleted at no significant cost to model fit, ΔLR χ^2 (1) = 2.46. Now the slope estimate is much more reasonable:

STM scanning intercept$_{older}$ = 1.48 (0.07) STM scanning intercept$_{younger}$.

This final ancillary result suggests that we may interpret the nonsignificant intercept of the RT$_{older}$ by RT$_{younger}$ Brinley as indicating equivalent age-related slowing in short-term memory scanning rate and short-term memory intercept, with a slowing factor of about 1.3 or 1.4.

4.4.1.2. *Speed of Enumeration Processes: Subitizing and Silent Counting*

Enumeration tasks are straightforward: Participants are presented with a number of identical items on a computer screen, and they report how many there are. Typically, the number of items is limited to 10, and the display stays on until the subject records her answer; eye movements are allowed.

Research suggests that enumeration is a relatively slow process; Card et al. offer an estimate of 167 ms per object; later research has revised that estimate to be closer to 300 ms/object (e.g., Trick & Pylyshyn, 1993, 1994). There is, however, a notable exception for small numbers: When the display contains four or fewer items, the response time by number-of-objects slope is much shallower—Card et al. estimate it at 46 ms/object—and accuracy is typically perfect. This fast enumeration process for small number of items has been labeled subitizing (Kaufman, Lord, Reese, & Volkmann, 1949), from the Latin "subitus," meaning "sudden." This term reflects the subjective feeling that one simply and immediately knows that there are one, two, three, or four items in the display, without needing to count. This feeling is not quite correct: Even Card et al.'s estimate suggests that subitizing is as slow or un-immediate as memory scanning, and the Card et al. estimate has been criticized for likely being on the low side (e.g., Trick & Pylyshyn, 1993, 1994, situate it around 100 ms/object). Even if subitizing is not immediate, the subitizing rate is about three times faster than the enumeration rate for larger numbers of objects, typically called counting (or silent counting). Given these distinct enumeration slopes, some researchers have proposed that subitizing and counting are supported by different mechanisms: Subjects might be able to tag about four items in parallel (e.g., Gallistel & Gelman, 1992; Mandler & Shebo, 1982; Sagi & Julesz, 1986; Trick & Pylyshyn, 1993, 1994), but displays that are in excess of four items are spatially and serially scanned (e.g., Trick & Pylyshyn, 1994). Recent neuroimaging evidence suggests that subitizing and counting rely on the same brain circuitry, but with different biases in what part of the network is active (e.g., Piazza, Mechelli, Butterworth, & Price, 2002; Vetter, Butterworth, & Bahrami, 2011).

Again, the precise mechanism is less of concern here than the age difference in the two processes. Given that correspondence (see Section 1.3.2.4.1) is needed to draw valid conclusions about Brinley slopes, an important additional question is whether there are age-related differences in subitizing span (i.e., in the number of items that can be enumerated using the subitizing mechanism). Overestimation of the number of objects that can be subitized by older adults would most likely inflate the estimate of the subitizing slope in a Brinley plot. That is, if younger subjects can subitize up four items, but older adults can only subitize up to three items, and we would construct a Brinley plot using one to four items, the slope will be contaminated with the slow counting process. Only two published studies have assessed younger-older adult differences in subitizing spans by pinpointing the inflection point in the curve relating response time to the number of objects in the display. One study (Basak & Verhaeghen, 2003) found that older adults had smaller subitizing spans than younger adults. (Older adults were able to subitize about 2.1 items; younger adults' span reached 2.8 items.) The other study (Watson, Maylor, & Bruce, 2005a) found identical spans of 3.3 items for younger and older adults. A third study (Watson, Maylor, & Muller, 2005) did not include younger adults, but found a span of 3.5 for older adults (and 2.3 for individuals with likely Alzheimer's disease). On the one hand, the Basak and Verhaeghen subitizing span estimates seem atypically low; on the other hand, the span of four items that is typically assumed in the literature is above all ranges estimated in these four studies. In the meta-analysis, I decided to use the range of one to three items as the subitizing range, and four to nine items as the counting range (a decision echoing the one made by Watson et al., 2005).

I was able to locate seven articles that contained sufficient information to allow for the calculation of RT by numerosity slopes and intercepts for both younger and older adults (Basak & Verhaeghen, 2003; Nebes, Brady, & Reynolds, 1992; Trick, Enns, & Brodeur, 1996; Watson, Maylor, Allen, & Bruce, 2007; Watson, Maylor, & Bruce, 2005b, 2005c; Watson, Maylor, & Manson, 2002). These studies contained eight independent sets of subjects for subitizing and eight for counting, for a total of 124 data points. I should note here that, as is usual in this line of research, the data from the largest numerosity tested within a study were discarded from the analyses. This is done to avoid end effects—when subjects are aware that there are, say, at most 10 elements in a display, they don't need to count the final one if they reach 9: They can simply infer that the answer has to be 10 and sidestep the final counting operation. Including the largest numerosity would likely depress the counting slope estimate.

To test for differential age-related effects within the subitizing and counting ranges, I set up the model with a dummy variable for the type of enumeration process, which I will label the "counting" dummy (set at 0 for the subitizing range, one to three items, and at 1 for the counting range, four or more items; no study included here had subjects count beyond nine), as well as the product of this dummy with numerosity. The former term allows me to estimate separate intercepts for the subitizing and counting ranges; the latter to estimate separate slopes for the subitizing and counting ranges. I further included (a) the age group dummy, to estimate the age-related effect in the intercept within the subitizing range; (b) the product of this dummy and the counting dummy, which allows us to estimate the size of the age effect in the intercept within the counting range; (c) the age group by numerosity interaction, to examine the effect of age on the subitizing slope; and (d) the age group by counting by numerosity slope, to examine the effect of age on the counting slope.

The full model is as follows:

RT = 408 (91) – 1024 (82) dummy (counting) + 138 (88) dummy (age group) + 83 (106) dummy (age group) by dummy (counting) + 40 (26) numerosity + 290 (27) dummy (counting) by numerosity + 21 (32) dummy (age group) by numerosity – 16 (34) dummy (age group) by dummy (counting) by numerosity.

This equation can be rewritten more intelligibly as the following set of four equations:

$$RT_{younger, subitizing} = 408 + 40 \text{ numerosity};$$

$$RT_{younger, counting} = -616 + 330 \text{ numerosity};$$

$$RT_{older, subitizing} = 546 + 61 \text{ numerosity};$$

$$RT_{older, counting} = -395 + 335 \text{ numerosity}.$$

Thus, older adults' subitizing rate is nominally 1.52 times slower than that of younger adults; their counting speed is almost identical to that of younger adults—a slowing factor of 1.02. The standard errors around the age by numerosity slope interaction and the age by counting by numerosity interaction are larger than the value of the parameters, suggesting that there is no significant age difference in either the subitizing or the counting rate. Note that the intercept for the counting process is negative for unsubstantive reasons: It is evaluated when numerosity equals zero, which is a nonsensical value. Estimating it at numerosity 4 makes more sense; the intercept is then 723 ms for younger adults and 1000 ms for older adults. Note that both the subitizing rate and the counting rate are eerily close to the Card et al. estimates for these processes (around 40 ms/object for subitizing and around 330 ms/object for counting).

The full Brinley equation on the enumeration data is:

$$RT_{older} = 146 \ (66) + 59 \ (46) \ \textbf{dummy (counting)} + 1.11 \ (0.10) \ RT_{younger}$$
$$- \ 0.08 \ (0.08) \ \textbf{dummy (counting) by} \ RT_{younger}.$$

Neither the estimates for dummy (counting), which compares the intercept for counting with the intercept for subitizing, nor the estimate for dummy (counting) by $RT_{younger}$, which compares the slope for counting with that for subitizing, were much larger than their *SE*. The model could indeed be pruned to a single line by dropping those two terms, with no significant loss to fit, $\Delta LR \ \chi^2 \ (2) = 1.66$:

$$RT_{older} = 183 \ (56) + 1.05 \ (0.06) \ RT_{younger}$$

The standard error of the slope estimate suggests that this slope is not significantly different from unity. Formal analysis bore this out, $\Delta LR \ \chi^2 \ (1) = 0.77$. The final model (Figure 4.7) is then:

$$RT_{older} = 206 \ (48) + RT_{younger}.$$

The conclusion is that there are no significant age differences in either the subitizing rate or the counting rate. Older adults are, however, slower than younger adults on enumeration tasks, but this is an additive effect, that is, it is situated in the intercepts of the information-processing functions. Compared with the empty model, this equation explains 99% of the variance in older adults' mean enumeration RT.

The lack of age effect in both enumeration rates is also confirmed in a direct Brinley analysis on the enumeration rates as derived from the slopes of the information-processing functions of each of the studies (15 data points; 8 for subitizing, 7 for counting). Given the small number of data points and given the lack of significance of the type of enumeration processes, I did not test for differential effects of subitizing and counting. The full model is:

$$\textbf{Enumeration rate}_{older} = -21 \ (19) + 1.04 \ (0.06) \ \textbf{Enumeration rate}_{younger}.$$

This equation can be simplified at no significant loss of fit, $\Delta LR \ \chi^2 \ (2) = 4.65$ to

$$\textbf{Enumeration rate}_{older} = \textbf{Enumeration rate}_{younger}$$

One possible objection to this result—a complete absence of age-related effects—might be that there could be true age differences in the enumeration process after all, but that these are masked by a slow, rate-limiting process. An obvious candidate would be subvocalization rate. The reasoning is as follows: If the time needed to

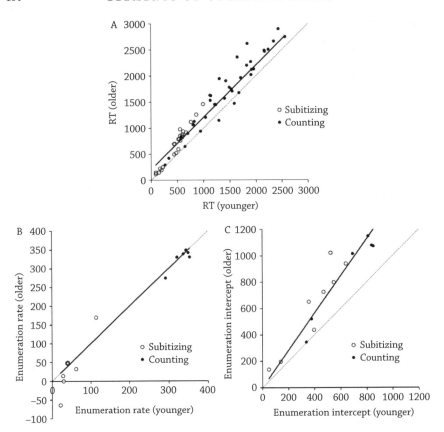

Figure 4.7 Brinley plots of enumeration data. Panel A shows latency data ($k = 124$); Panel B shows the Brinley plot of the enumeration rates obtained in each study ($k = 15$); Panel C plots the corresponding enumeration intercepts ($k = 15$). Final regression lines are indicated as solid lines; the dotted lines are the equality diagonals. Data are separated by subitizing (enumerating one–three items) and counting (enumerating four–nine items); analyses showed that a single Brinley function sufficed to capture both tasks in all three plots.

"count" n objects is really just the time needed to subvocally go through the digits 1 to n, then the absence of age difference might just reflect the absence of age differences in the speed of subvocalization, not the speed of enumeration. This possibility was explored by Watson et al. (2005a). They found that subvocalization occurred at a speed of about 175 ms/digit for both younger and older adults, about half of the observed counting rate in their study (330 ms/object, also identical for younger and older adults), suggesting that there is more to counting than simple subvocalization.

For the Brinley analysis of the intercept, I used the intercept at zero for subitizing and at 4 for counting. This analysis yielded the following equation (15 data points):

$$\text{Enumeration intercept}_{older} = -1\ (0) + 1.41\ (0.02)$$
$$\text{Enumeration intercept}_{younger}.$$

Thus, as already suggested by the Brinley analysis of the raw data points, there is significant age-related slowing in the intercept of the enumeration processes. This isn't surprising, given that these intercepts are assumed to reflect all processes except for the enumeration processes themselves—notably sensory uptake and response processes, which we found to be age-sensitive in Chapter 2. The slowing factor seems to be well within the normal range for sensorimotor slowing—a factor of about 1.4.

4.4.1.3. Mental Rotation

In mental rotation tasks, subjects are typically presented with two stimuli that are either identical to each other or mirror images of each other; one is rotated away from the other at a given angle. Subjects decide whether the stimuli are identical or mirror images. (One variation of this task presents subjects with rotated letters or mirror images of letters; they have to indicate which is which.) The stimuli can be two-dimensional or three-dimensional objects. In the latter case, rotation can be within depth, that is, 2-D rotation within the plane of the display, or in depth, that is, 3-D rotation, typically in a plane orthogonal to the display. Rotation rate turns out to be a linear function of the angle of rotation, regardless of the plane of rotation (within depth or in depth); this discovery was first made by Shepard and Metzler (1971).

I was able to locate eight age-comparative studies in eight papers (two more than Sliwinski & Hall, 1998), for a total of 37 younger-older adult data pairs (Band & Kok, 2000; Berg, Hertzog, & Hunt, 1982; Cerella, Poon, & Fozard, 1981; Dror & Kosslyn, 1994; Dror, Schmitz-Williams, & Smith, 2005; Hale, Lima, & Myerson, 1991; Hale, Myerson, Faust, & Fristoe, 1995; Hertzog, Vernon, & Rypma, 1993).

Fitting a model to extract the rotation intercept and rotation speed as well as the age-related effect in both yielded:

RT = 968 (204) + 4.8 (1.1) rotation angle + 580 (327) dummy (age group) + 3.8 (1.6) age group by rotation angle.

This equation can be rewritten as a set of two:

$$\text{RT}_{\text{younger}} = 968 + 4.8 \text{ rotation angle}$$

$$\text{RT}_{\text{older}} = 1548 + 8.6 \text{ rotation angle.}$$

The age-related slowing factor in mental rotation is sizeable—a ratio of 1.78. It is also significantly different from 1, as shown in the Brinley analysis:

$$\text{RT}_{\text{older}} = -169 \ (89) + 1.86 \ (0.12) \ \text{RT}_{\text{younger}}.$$

The intercept of this function, although large, is not significantly smaller than zero, $\Delta \text{LR } \chi^2 \ (1) = 2.10$. Fixing it to zero yields the following equation:

$$\text{RT}_{\text{older}} = 1.67 \ (0.04) \ \text{RT}_{\text{younger}}.$$

This equation (Figure 4.8, Panel A) explains 98% of the variance in older adults' mean mental rotation RT.

To check whether the assumption of proportional slowing in mental rotation rates was indeed met, a Brinley analysis on these rates was conducted. (Only seven studies were included because slopes could not be calculated for Cerella et al.—angles of rotation were not reported.) The data are represented in Figure 4.8.

The full Brinley model is:

Mental rotation rate$_{older}$ = 0.6 (0.7) + 1.72 (0.28) mental rotation rate$_{younger}$.

This function could indeed be simplified without loss of fit, $\Delta LR \ \chi^2 \ (1) = 2.5$, to a purely proportional function:

Mental rotation rate$_{older}$ = 2.02 (0.05) mental rotation rate$_{younger}$.

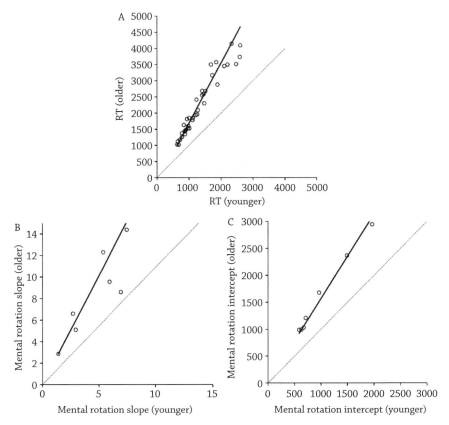

Figure 4.8 Brinley plots of mental rotation data. Panel A shows latency data ($k = 37$); Panel B shows the Brinley plot of the memory scanning rates obtained in each study ($k = 8$); Panel C plots the corresponding memory scanning intercepts ($k = 8$). Final regression lines are indicated as solid lines; the dotted lines are the equality diagonals.

Fitting the intercepts of the mental rotation information-processing function to a Brinley function yielded the following parameters:

$$\text{Mental rotation intercept}_{older} = 134 \ (64) + 1.46 \ (0.06)$$
$$\text{Mental rotation intercept}_{younger}$$

This equation, too, could be reduced, at no cost to fit, $\Delta LR \ \chi^2 \ (1) = 3.43$, to a purely proportional model:

$$\text{Mental rotation intercept}_{older} = 1.57 \ (0.03) \ \text{Mental rotation intercept}_{younger}$$

Thus, mental rotation rate slows down considerably with age: The slowing factor, depending on the measure, is situated somewhere between 1.6 and 2.0. The intercept of the mental rotation function shows significantly smaller, but still substantial, age-related slowing, by a factor of about 1.6.

4.4.1.4. Visual Search Rate

In a visual search task, the participant searches a display of objects for one particular item (the "target") that matches a given description. The task is to indicate whether or not the target is present, and/or where it is located; the display remains on until the participant logs her answer, allowing her to make eye movements as needed or desired.

One consistent finding in visual search paradigms is that reaction time to the target is a linear (sometimes flat, see below) function of the number of distractor items (i.e., the items in the display that are not the target). The slope of this information-processing function tends to be about twice as large for target-absent displays as for target-present displays, indicating that search is serial and self-terminating rather than parallel or exhaustive. (The assumption is that if the target is present and the subject searches the display in n steps, or n shifts of attention, the subject will, on average, find it on the $(n/2)$th step; if the target is absent, all n steps need to be completed before the subject can conclude that the display is targetless.)

One crucial distinction is that between efficient and nonefficient search, often investigated using the feature search and conjunction search paradigm, respectively. (The latter terms suggest allegiance to one specific theory about search, viz. feature integration theory, Treisman & Gelade, 1980, but I don't mean to imply such allegiance here). In feature search, the target is distinct from the distractors in one unique visual feature. This makes the target stand out (like a red wine stain on a white carpet; Madden, 2007)—the term used in the literature is pop-out. This pop-out allows search to be independent of the number of distractors, as testified by a flat or nearly flat information-processing function. In conjunction search, in contrast, targets and distractors share multiple features (e.g., the subject might be looking for a red circle among red squares and green circles; or might be looking for a particular brand of red wine in the store, where all bottles and labels look more or less alike). In that case, search is quite inefficient, and the number of distractors does matter, giving rise to a slope in the information-processing function. The high efficiency of feature search is typically ascribed to preattentive, bottom-up processes; conjunction search requires top-down attentional control. It is sometimes claimed that the former is spared in aging while the latter is not, and that this dissociation is reflected in visual search data—no age deficit in feature search, coupled with a deficit in conjunction search (e.g., Trick & Enns, 1998). This, in turn, has led to the conclusion that the process of integrating visual features, the process of inhibiting distractors, or the serial search process itself is defective in older adults (e.g., Connelly & Hasher, 1993; Trick & Enns, 1998).

I was able to locate 13 independent samples for feature search from 10 papers, with a total of 39 (young, old) pairs (Burton-Danner, Owlsey, & Jackson, 2001; Foster, Berhmann, & Stuss, 1995; Hommel, Li, & Li, 2004; Humphrey and Kramer, 1997; Madden, Whiting, Spaniol, & Bucur, 2005; Plude & Doussard-Roosevelt, 1989; Scialfa, Esau, & Joffe, 1998; Scialfa, Jenkins, Hamaluk, & Skaloud, 2000; Watson et al., 2005b; Watson et al., 2007). I also located 30 independent samples for conjunction search from 28 papers, with a total of 162 (young, old) pairs (Allen et al., 2002; Anandam & Scialfa, 1999; Ferraro & Balota, 1999; Foster et al., 1995; Gorman & Fisher, 1998; Gottlob, 2006; Graf & Uttl, 1995; Hahn, Carlson, Singer, & Gronlund, 2006; Hale, Myerson, Faust, & Fristoe, 1995; Ho & Scialfa, 2002, Hommel et al., 2004; Humphrey & Kramer, 1997; Jenkins, Myerson, Joerding, & Hale, 2000; Lawrence, Myerson, & Hale, 1998; Madden, 1986; Madden et al., 2003; Madden, Pierce, & Allen, 1996; Madden et al., 2004; Maylor & Lavie, 1998; Plude & Doussard-Roosevelt, 1989; Plude & Hoyer, 1986; Plude et al., 1983; Scialfa et al., 1998; Scialfa et al., 2000; Verhaeghen et al., 2002; Watson et al., 2005b; Zacks & Zacks, 1993). Sliwinski and Hall included only seven studies, all on conjunction search. The data are provided in Figure 4.9.

I stress here that the information-processing model really only makes sense to evaluate age-related differences: It is unlikely there would be a fixed rate of visual search independent of the different tweaks and peculiarities of the experimental paradigms. I included data from correct RTs from target-present displays only.

As was done for the subitizing/counting distinction in enumeration, I used a full model to simultaneously estimate parameter values for intercepts and slopes for feature search and conjunction search and the age effects therein. To that aim, I constructed a dummy for conjunction search, taking the value 0 for feature search and 1 for conjunction search. The following equation was obtained:

RT = 513 (85) + 157 (93) dummy (conjunction) + 501 (159) dummy (age group) − 264 (149) dummy (age by conjunction) + 4 (6) set-size + 24 (7) dummy (conjunction by set-size) + 2 (10) dummy (age group) by set-size + 25 (11) dummy (age group) by dummy (conjunction) by set-size.

This equation boils down to the following set of four equations:

$$RT_{younger, feature search} = 513 + 4 \text{ set-size};$$

$$RT_{younger, conjunction search} = 670 + 28 \text{ set-size};$$

$$RT_{older, feauture search} = 1014 + 6 \text{ set-size};$$

$$RT_{older, conjunction search} = 907 + 55 \text{ set-size}.$$

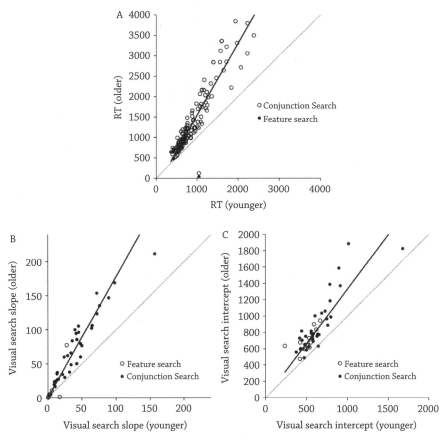

Figure 4.9 Brinley plots of visual search data. Panel A shows latency data (*k* = 162); Panel B shows the Brinley plot of the visual search rates obtained in each study (*k* = 43); Panel C plots the corresponding visual search intercepts (*k* = 43). Final regression lines are indicated as solid lines; the dotted lines are the equality diagonals. Data are separated by feature search and conjunction search; analyses showed that a single Brinley function sufficed to capture both tasks in all three plots.

Feature search yields a rate that is indeed very fast (a nonsignificant 4 ms/item), and not significantly different from zero. The age-related slowing factor is 1.47, but this is not significant, because the age by set-size interaction is not significant. The conjunction search rate shows a larger age effect, 1.96, which does reach significance.

This conclusion diverges from that of the Brinley analysis. Brinley analysis shows that both search rates are significantly larger than unity, but also that they do not differ statistically from each other. The full Brinley model (162 data points) is:

$$\text{RT}_{older} = -222 \ (107) + 1.76 \ (0.18) \ \text{RT}_{younger} - 52 \ (102) \ \text{dummy(conjunction)} + 0.04 \ (0.17) \ \text{dummy(conjunction) by RT}_{younger}.$$

This model could be trimmed at no cost to fit, $\Delta LR\ \chi^2\ (2) = 2.43$, to:

$$RT_{older} = -220\ (48) + 1.76\ (0.08)\ RT_{younger}$$

Thus, the Brinley model suggests that the observed age deficits in visual search can be explained through a single slowing factor of about 1.8, with no need to differentiate between feature search and conjunction search. Compared with the empty model, this equation explains 99% of the variance in older adults' mean RT in visual search tasks.

This interpretation of the Brinley result rests on the assumption of proportional age differences in search slopes. I estimated a full model. This model included a dummy variable for conjunction search (feature search = 0; conjunction search = 1), to test for differential Brinley slopes for feature and conjunction search; it also included the conjunction search by age interaction, to test for differential Brinley slopes for feature and conjunction search. The fitted model was:

$$\text{Visual search rate}_{older} = -1.47\ (0.83) + 1.80\ (0.35)\ \text{Visual search rate}_{younger}$$
$$+ 8.14\ (3.57)\ \text{dummy (conjunction)}$$
$$- 0.18\ (0.37)\ \text{dummy (conjunction) by}$$
$$\text{Visual search rate}_{younger}.$$

This model could indeed be trimmed to a single, proportional line at no significant cost to fit, $\Delta LR\ \chi^2\ (3) = 5.54$:

$$\text{Visual search rate}_{older} = 1.78\ (0.07)\ \text{Visual search rate}_{younger}.$$

This indicates that the interpretation of the Brinley slope for the raw data is correct: There is a significant, purely proportional effect of age on the rate of visual search, and this effect is identical for feature and conjunction search. The effect is quite large, with a slowing factor of about 1.8.

Here is the Brinley model for the intercepts:

$$\text{Visual search intercept}_{older} = -31\ (214) + 1.36\ (0.40)\ \text{Visual search}$$
$$\text{intercept}_{younger} + 75\ (239)\ \text{dummy}$$
$$\text{(conjunction)} - 0.09\ (0.45)\ \text{dummy}$$
$$\text{(conjunction) by Visual search intercept}_{younger}.$$

This model could be trimmed to a single, proportional line at no significant cost to fit, $\Delta LR\ \chi^2\ (3) = 0.75$:

$$\text{Visual search intercept}_{older} = 1.33\ (0.03)\ \text{Visual search intercept}_{younger}.$$

The intercept of the information-processing function for visual search, which is supposed to contain sensorimotor processing that is not part of the search rate per se, is slowed proportionally, with a slowing factor of about 1.3—a value very much in line with the expectation for age-related differences in sensorimotor processing.

A final note: Earlier in this chapter, I examined age-related differences in fixation duration, including fixations on targets and distractors in visual search tasks. The conclusion there was that older adults are slower than younger adults, but the slowing took an additive form: Older adults were, on average, 45 ms slower than younger adults. Eye movements are important for visual search: Larger displays, as well as displays with a larger number of distractors, typically necessitate more eye movements, which, in turn, increase search time. The additive age-related effect in fixation duration translates into a multiplicative effect in search rate once more than a single step is taken—when n steps are necessary, the constant is added n times. It is unlikely, however, that this is the sole mechanism to explain the rather large effect in search rate. Assume, for instance, that the experimental set-up is such that ten items can be purveyed with a single glance. Ten items would then be scanned in about 240 ms for younger adults, and 285 ms for older adults (the numbers are taken from Section 4.2.1); twenty items would take 480 ms for the young and 570 ms for the old; thirty items would take 720 ms in the young and 855 ms in the old. The slowing factor is identical for all three set sizes, but low (1.19). Making this more realistic by adding the overhead or intercept cost we found above (670 ms for younger adults, 907 ms for older adults), we obtain slowing factors around 1.3— still short of 1.8. The additional mechanism might be the number of fixations. It is quite possible that older adults need to perform more fixations to scan the same set, perhaps due to a smaller effective foveal field of vision or to problems with marking or remembering previously visited locations. Two of the fixation-duration studies cited above used visual search tasks; both indeed found that older adults perform a larger number of fixations than younger adults at the same set size: 18.8 fixations vs. 15.7 in Gottlob (2006) and 87 versus 56 in Maltz and Shinar (2006), or ratios between 1.2 and 1.6. The double age-related deficit, one in the number of fixations and the second in their duration, might be compounded to yield the observed deficit in search rate.

4.4.1.5. *Aging and Cognitive Processing Rates in Iterative Tasks: An Interim Summary*

Some more general conclusions can be drawn from the analyses of age-related differences in iterative tasks.

First, within each of the families of processing rates I was able to simplify the number of age-related slowing factors to one—within enumeration, both the subitizing rate and the counting rate shared an identical slowing factor, and within visual search both the rate of feature search and the rate of conjunction search shared an identical slowing factor.

Second, looking across tasks, it is hard not to notice some regularities. For instance, both spatial tasks—mental rotation and visual search—show age-related slowing factors that are close to each other, around 1.8. This opens up the intriguing possibility that the number of slowing factors in the set of iterative tasks might be reduced even further. To investigate this possibility, I set up a Brinley model with all 319 data points, with dummies for enumeration, mental rotation, and visual search, as well as the interaction of each of these dummies with $RT_{younger}$. This model yielded the following equation:

$$RT_{older} = 24 \ (77) + 142 \ (88) \text{ dummy (enumeration)} - 209 \ (106) \text{ dummy} \\ \text{(mental rotation)} - 246 \ (84) \text{ dummy (visual search)} \\ + 1.42 \ (0.12) \ RT_{younger} - 0.57 \ (0.13) \text{ enumeration by } RT_{younger} \\ + 0.42 \ (0.15) \text{ mental rotation by } RT_{younger} + 0.41 \ (0.12) \text{ visual} \\ \text{search by } RT_{younger}.$$

The parameter estimates associated with mental rotation and visual search (both the dummies and their interaction terms with $RT_{younger}$) are very similar and fall squarely within each other's confidence intervals. Simplifying the equation by combining visual search and mental rotation into a single dummy did indeed fail to significantly affect fit, $\Delta LR \ \chi^2 \ (4) = 1.46$. This model also yielded a nonsignificant intercept term for enumeration, $\Delta LR \ \chi^2 \ (1) = 2.40$. The final model, then, is:

$$RT_{older} = 130 \ (37) - 357 \ (39) \text{ dummy (mental rotation/visual search)} \\ + 1.28 \ (0.07) \ RT_{younger} - 0.39 \ (0.06) \text{ enumeration) by } RT_{younger} \\ + 0.56 \ (0.07) \text{ mental rotation/visual search by } RT_{younger}.$$

Thus, we need a set of three equations, not four, to adequately describe the data. In order of increasing age-related slowing factors, these are:

$$RT_{older, \ enumeration} = 130 + 0.89 \ RT_{younger, \ enumeration};$$

$$RT_{older, \ memory \ search} = 130 + 1.28 \ RT_{younger, \ memory \ search};$$

$$RT_{older, \ mental \ rotation/visual \ search} = -227 + 1.84 \ RT_{younger, \ mental \ rotation/visual \ search}.$$

What happens when we directly compare age effects in the cycle times of these tasks—the slopes of the information processing functions? From the analyses above, we know that the Brinley plots of these cycle times yield lines that are purely multiplicative. Graphically, this implies a fan originating in the Cartesian origin. Here is the model:

$$Slope_{older} = 1.31 \ (0.31) \ Slope_{younger} - 0.61 \ (0.43) \text{ enumeration by } Slope_{younger} \\ + 0.24 \ (0.35) \text{ visual search by } Slope_{younger} + 0.58 \ (0.54) \\ \text{mental rotation by } Slope_{younger}.$$

Simplifying the equation by combining visual search and mental rotation did indeed not significantly affect fit, $\Delta LR \ \chi^2 \ (1) = 0.51$:

$$Slope_{older} = 1.31 \ (0.31) \ Slope_{younger} - 0.61 \ (0.43) \text{ enumeration by } Slope_{younger} \\ + 0.28 \ (0.35) \text{ mental rotation/visual search by } Slope_{younger}.$$

The standard errors of the parameters are large, probably too large to take the values seriously as point estimates, but we again have evidence for the existence of three, not four age-related slowing factors: One for enumeration, 0.70 (signifying age-related speed-up, but statistically not different from 1); one for memory scanning, 1.31; and one for visual search/mental rotation, 1.59.

Here is the corresponding analysis on the intercepts (again evaluating the intercept of counting at numerosity 4 rather then numerosity 0):

$$\text{Intercept}_{older} = 1.44 \ (0.08) \ \text{intercept}_{younger} + 0.25 \ (0.13) \ \text{subitizing by}$$
$$\text{intercept}_{younger} - 0.48 \ (0.14) \ \text{counting by intercept}_{younger}$$
$$- 0.03 \ (0.09) \ \text{visual search by intercept}_{younger}$$
$$+ 0.18 \ (0.14) \ \text{mental rotation by intercept}_{younger}.$$

Deleting the three terms with large *SE*s compared with the parameter estimate comes at no cost, ΔLR χ^2 (3) = 7.68, and leads to:

$$\text{Intercept}_{older} = 1.46 \ (0.04) \ \text{intercept}_{younger} - 0.50 \ (0.13) \ \text{counting by}$$
$$\text{intercept}_{younger}.$$

We thus obtain two distinct age-related slowing factors for the intercepts of the information-processing functions: One factor suggesting no slowing, for counting (0.96), and one suggesting moderate slowing, for the three other iterative tasks (1.46). The finding that memory scanning, mental rotation, and visual search all share the same age effects in their intercepts makes sense. Recall that the intercepts of the information-processing functions reflect the time needed for all processes that are not involved in the iterative cycles. Presumably, most of those would be sensorimotor in nature—perceiving the stimulus and outputting the decision. The sensory demands for enumeration are typically minimal—registering the presence of a dot multiple times—while memory search, mental rotation, and visual search all require more complex item recognition or item identification processes. In addition, memory scanning, mental rotation, and visual search, unlike enumeration, also involve comparison processes, matching a physical stimulus with a memorized or imagined stimulus (i.e., matching the memory probe against the item just recovered from STM in the memory scanning task, matching the rotated mental image against the probe in mental rotation, or comparing the probe held in memory with the elements in the display in visual search). Furthermore, memory scanning, mental rotation, and visual search, again unlike enumeration, all involve making yes/no decisions. Given these similarities, it is perhaps not surprising, then, that memory search, mental rotation, and visual search show similar age-related effects in the processes that are tapped by the information-processing intercept—these are processes that are largely shared between the tasks. It is possible (but far from certain) that enumeration shows age-constancy because it does not involve stimulus identification, stimulus-to-memory matching, and binary decision-making, at least one of which would then be age-sensitive.

One final point to make here is that these results demonstrate (as if there was any doubt) that the mind is not governed by a single cognitive processing speed. First, cycle times vary considerably from task to task. In the present sample of tasks, processing times per item range from 4 ms/item (feature visual search), over 27 ms/item (conjunction visual search), 47 ms/item (subitizing) and 54 ms/item (memory scanning) to 326 ms/item (silent counting). (Mental rotation does not have "item" as its independent variable, but rather angle of rotation, and its rate thus cannot be directly compared with the other values.) Second, there are reliable age-associated dissociations within these rates—enumeration shows no age-related slowing; memory scanning shows a moderate slowing of 1.3; and the spatial tasks, visual search and mental rotation, show a more pronounced slowing factor of about 1.8. This suggests that at least these three types of cognitive cycling operations are functionally distinct. I should also point out that the size of the age effect does not correlate positively with the "complexity" of the task as derived from its cycle speed (in fact, the correlation is negative), indicating that this age-related dissociation does not at all fit with a simple task complexity hypothesis (i.e., the idea that tasks that take longer would yield larger age deficits).

4.4.2. Simple Decisions: Simple and Choice Reaction Time

The previous section indirectly revealed that binary decision-making processes might be age-sensitive. This assertion can be tested more directly. The simplest task used to assess decision-making is choice reaction time (CRT). One often-used paradigm involves visual CRT, where the decision is typically spatial in nature. In this task, subjects are presented with an item shown in one of n possible locations; they indicate that location with a press of one of n keys. If the task contains two alternatives, it is called a two-choice RT task (2CRT); if there are three alternatives, it is a three-choice task (3CRT), and so on. Variations exist; for instance, the subject can be asked to press a button for each of n possible stimulus colors. Performance on a choice-reaction-time task is either contrasted with performance on simple reaction time (SRT) tasks—where a single stimulus is shown, and the subject indicates its mere presence with a key press or vocalization—or it is mapped as a function of n. Both types of data will be examined here.

Originally (e.g., Donders, 1868), research into SRT and CRT was motivated by the desire to isolate the timing of the decision-making and response selection components. The assumption was of pure insertion: All the processes in RT tasks were assumed to chain additively, so that the difference in latency between CRT and SRT indexes the time needed for processes involved in CRT but not SRT—presumably decision making and response selection. Such additive relationships do not always hold (for an overview, see, e.g., Jensen, 2006), but subsequent research has suggested that the insertion logic work holds up remarkably well in the case of SRT and CRT (Gottsdanker & Shragg, 1985; Ulrich, Mattes, & Miller, 1999).

I note that Card et al. did not include SRT or CRT in their list of cognitive primitives.

4.4.2.1. Simple/Single versus Choice Reaction Time

I was able to locate 20 papers examining SRT, including a total of 26 independent samples of younger and older adult subjects. Average weighted SRT was 246 ms for younger adults and 310 ms for older adults. For two-choice RT, I was able to locate 16 papers with a total of 20 independent samples of younger and older adult subjects. Average weighted two-choice RT was 283 ms for younger adults and 351 ms for older adults. For four-choice RT, I located 14 papers with a total of 22 independent samples. Average weighted four-choice RT was 532 ms for younger adults and 713 ms for older adults. (Additionally, I was able to locate one study each for five-choice, seven-choice, and nine-choice RT, as well as four studies for eight-choice RT. Given the small number of studies, I did not compute averages.)

4.4.2.1.1. Brinley Analysis

By their very nature, reaction time measures are fast. One of the consequences is that method variance matters. More specifically, RT is very sensitive to stimulus characteristics such as stimulus domain (auditory RT is faster than visual RT; e.g., Sanders, 1998) and stimulus intensity (e.g., Luce, 1991); it is also very sensitive to practice (Sanders & Sanders, 1998). To keep noise due to method variance at a minimum, my Brinley analysis only included studies that included both SRT and CRT measures; I located 18 such studies, contained in 13 papers (Anstey, Dear, Christensen, & Jorm, 2005; Clarkson & Kroll, 1978; Der & Deary, 2006; Emery, Huppert, & Schein, 1995; Fisk, Rogers, Cooper, & Gilbert, 1997; Goldfarb, 1941; Hertzog et al., 1996; Jolles, Houx, Van Boxtel, & Ponds, 1995; Kauranen Vanharanta, 1996; Podlesny & Dustman, 1982; Tun, O'Kane & Wingfield, 2002; Uttl, Graf, & Consentino, 2000; Walker, Philbin, & Fisk, 1997). I used a dummy variable to code for type of RT measure (0 = simple RT; 1 = choice RT). The data set included 45 data points (Figure 4.10, Panel A), 18 data points associated with simple RT and 27 associated with choice RT, namely 12 for two-choice, 2 for three-choice, 9 for four-choice, 1 for five-choice, 1 for seven-choice, and 2 for eight-choice. The resulting Brinley equation was:

$$RT_{older} = -35 \ (73) - 49 \ (62) \ \text{dummy (choice RT)} + 1.40 \ (0.28) \ RT_{younger} + 0.20 \ (0.20) \ \text{choice by } RT_{younger}.$$

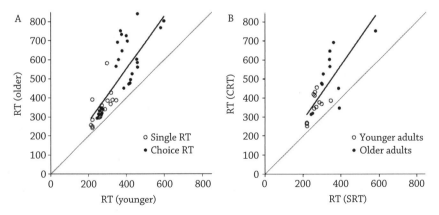

Figure 4.10 Brinley plot (Panel A) and state-trace plot (Panel B) of reaction time data (*k* = 45 and 24, respectively.). Final regression lines are indicated as solid lines; the dotted lines are the equality diagonals. A single Brinley function and state trace, respectively, sufficed to capture the data.

The standard errors suggest that a single line would fit the data well. Omitting the variables associated with the added effects of choice RT did indeed not significantly decrease fit, ΔLR χ^2 (2) = 1.23. The resulting equation was:

$$RT_{older} = -59 \ (57) + 1.58 \ (0.16) \ RT_{younger}.$$

Note that the intercept is not significant, ΔLR χ^2 (1) = 1.04; refitting the equation yielded:

$$RT_{older} = 1.42 \ (0.04) \ RT_{younger}.$$

Compared with the empty model, this equation explains 54% of the variance in mean RT of older adults.

My reason for grouping all levels of choice RT together in one analysis was to include as many studies in the CRT category as possible while keeping the number of parameters manageable. It seemed to me that this approach would increase the chances of finding a non-null result, if one makes the assumption that the complexity effect (and hence potentially the age-related slowing factor) is likely to be monotonic with the number of choices in the task. Conversely, it can also be argued that this was a poor choice, and that collapsing all levels of CRT into a single dummy variable is likely to inflate standard error for the CRT slope and intercept. Therefore, I conducted a new Brinley analysis, now contrasting simple RT with two-choice RT only, only including studies that measured both. The resulting fitted equation (24 data points) was as follows:

$$RT_{older} = 3 \ (213) + 79 \ (264) \ \text{dummy (choice RT)} + 1.30 \ (0.80) \ RT_{younger}$$
$$- 0.10 \ (0.91) \ \text{choice by } RT_{younger}.$$

This equation could again be reduced to a single line at no significant cost to fit, ΔLR χ^2 (2) = 0.87:

$$RT_{older} = -27 \ (89) + 1.46 \ (0.28) \ RT_{younger}.$$

This equation could be trimmed further by removing the intercept, at no significant cost to fit, ΔLR χ^2 (1) = 0.09:

$$RT_{older} = 1.38 \ (0.06) \ RT_{younger}.$$

Thus, a single age-related slowing factor explains the data for SRT and CRT equally well; this slowing factor is about 1.4 or 1.5, depending on whether one wants the added precision of the intercept estimate. This equation explains 52% of the variance in older adults' mean RT.

The implication of both analyses is that the processes associated with simple binary decision-making and response selection as they appear in a choice-reaction-time task are not slowed differentially than the processes involved in detecting the mere presence of a stimulus and pressing a single key to indicate that detection.

4.4.2.1.2. State-Trace Analysis

The design of (most) two-choice RT studies, with their single RT control condition, allows me to construct a state trace, plotting two-choice reaction time as a function of simple reaction time (Figure 4.10, Panel B). The analysis (24 data points) confirms the presence of a single line. The full equation is:

Two-choice RT = 74 (187) + 80 (213) dummy (age group) + 1.09 simple RT
− 0.05 (0.76) age by simple RT.

This can be reduced to a single line, with no significant loss of fit, ΔLR χ^2 (2) = 2.63:

Two-choice RT = 47 (74) + 1.28 (0.24) simple RT.

Fixing the intercept to zero did not significantly affect fit, ΔLR χ^2 (2) = 0.39. The resulting equation is:

Two-choice RT = 1.43 (0.06) simple RT.

This final model explains 54% of the variance in mean two-choice RT compared with the empty model.

This finding confirms the result obtained from the Brinley analysis: The equation relating 2CRT to SRT is identical for younger and older adults, suggesting that the additional decision processes involved in 2CRT are not differentially age-sensitive. The relationship between 2CRT and SRT is multiplicative. This is an indication that the insertion logic is flawed: Under pure-insertion logic, the decision-making and response selection stages inherent in 2CRT should be independent of the processes involved in SRT. This is not the case here: Whatever it is that drives latency differences between SRT tasks in the present sample also leads to proportional increases in 2CRT.

4.4.2.2. Multiple Choices: The Hick-Hyman Law

Choice RT takes longer than simple RT. Within choice RT tasks, the number of choices is monotonically related to response latency—an observation already made by Donders (1868). Hick (1952) and Hyman (1953) noted a strong regularity in this relation, which has since become known as the Hick-Hyman Law (or Hick's Law, for those who value primacy). RT turns out to be a logarithmic function of the number of alternatives, and is typically well-described by the following equation (n is the number of response alternatives):

$$RT = a + b \log_2 (n + 1).$$

One caveat to make is that both Hick and Hyman fitted their functions to data from single subjects (Hick used himself as the subject in his Expt. 1), and those subjects were extremely well-practiced. Both studies also included a large range of response alternatives (typically: 1 through 10). In the studies gathered here, these conditions are not necessarily met, and the accuracy of the fit of this logarithmic function may therefore suffer.

What is the interpretation of the slope and intercept of the Hick-Hyman equation? The intercept is the value of the function at $\log_2 (n + 1) = 0$, that is, at $n = 0$. This is not a readily psychologically interpretable quantity. Much more intuitive for our purposes is the intercept at $\log_2 (n + 1) = 1$, that is, the predicted response time when there is only a single option. This is an alternative and model-derived estimate of simple RT, the measure of the speed of the sensorimotor components of reaction time when no decision is involved. Hyman's original study yielded a mean $(n = 1)$-intercept of 179 ms (ranging from 160 ms to 212 ms). The slope of the Hick-Hyman equation directly reflects the rate of decision-making and response selection, measured in units of bits of information (as $\log_2 [n + 1]$ is often described). Note that the scale is logarithmic, implying that a one-bit increase in information is, in fact, a doubling of the number of alternatives. In Hyman's original study, this slope was 215 ms/bit.

I was able to locate 20 relevant papers (Anstey et al., 2005; Bunce, 2001; Clarkson & Kroll, 1978; Der & Deary, 2006; Emery et al., 1995; Fisk et al., 1997; Goldfarb, 1941; Griew, 1958, cited in Welford, 1961; Hertzog et al., 1996; Jolles et al., 1995; Kauranen & Vanharanta, 1996; Podlesny & Dustman, 1982; Rabbitt, 1964, 1979; Suci et al., cited in Welford, 1961; Tun et al., 2002; Uttl et al., 2000; Walker et al., 1997), yielding a total of 24 independent samples of younger and older adults. Of those, 14 used two response alternatives, six used three response alternatives, and only four used four—not the most dense of data sets. Fitting the Hick-Hyman law to the total of 124 data points yielded the following equation (with the intercept evaluated at $n = 0$):

$$RT = 169 \ (31) + 115 \ (16) \log_2 (n + 1) + 24 \ (50) \ \text{dummy (age group)}$$
$$+ 59 \ (24) \ \text{dummy (age group) by} \ \log_2 (n + 1).$$

This equation can be more intelligibly presented as the following set of two equations:

$$RT_{younger} = 169 + 115 \log_2 (n + 1);$$

$$RT_{older} = 193 + 174 \log_2 (n + 1).$$

Thus, the age-related slowing factor in the slope of the Hick-Hyman equation is 1.60. As noted above, the intercept at $(n = 1)$ is a more readily interpretable variable than the intercept at zero. Younger adults' $(n = 1)$-intercept is 289; older adults' $(n = 1)$-intercept equals 372. The age-related slowing factor in intercepts is then 1.29. For the younger adults, the intercept is considerably higher and the slope considerably more shallow than was the case in Hyman's data. It is not immediately clear why this would be the case. One possibility is that the higher intercept could be due to the likely circumstance that the younger adults in the current set of studies are less well-practiced than those in the Hyman paper. The faster rate of responding over increasing numbers of bits could be due to practice effects as well, if we assume that practice with the task has a larger impact on the easier versions with fewer response alternatives.

I fitted a Brinley function to the data (62 data pairs; Figure 4.11 shows a simplified Brinley plot, in which I collapsed all data for three or more choices, for reasons of legibility). To test for the influence of task complexity on the Brinley function, I added bits, that is, $\log_2 (n + 1)$, as well as the interaction between bits and younger adults'

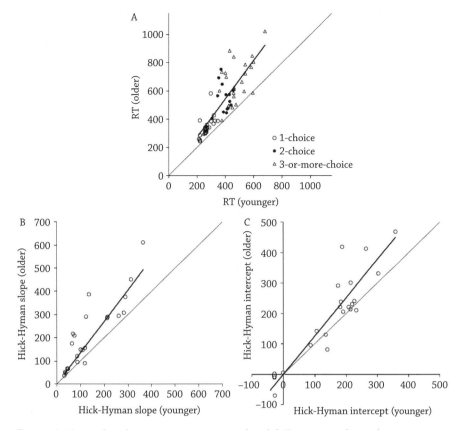

Figure 4.11 Brinley plots to investigate age-related differences in the Hick-Hyman Law. Panel A shows the Brinley plot ($k = 62$) of reaction time as a function of the number of choices (for legibility, three or more choices were collapsed for data presentation reasons only, not for analysis); a single line fit the data best. Panel B and C show Brinley plots of the Hick-Hyman slopes and intercepts, respectively ($k = 24$). Final regression lines are indicated as solid lines; the dotted lines are the equality diagonals.

reaction time to the equation. This equation allows me to estimate a Hicks-Hyman Brinley "intercept" and a Hicks-Hyman Brinley "slope" for each value of $\log_2 (n + 1)$. When n equals zero, $\log_2 (n + 1)$ equals zero as well, and thus the coefficient associated with $RT_{younger}$ (i.e., when both the dummy and its interaction with $RT_{younger}$ are zero) estimates the Brinley slope when there is zero information. If the dummy and/or its interaction turn out to be significant, this would signify that the Brinley intercept and/or slopes, respectively, are a linear function of the number of bits of information, showing that the age-related effect is a function of information load or task complexity.

The resulting Brinley equation was:

$$RT_{older} = -139\ (140) + 116\ (76) \log_2 (n + 1) + 1.54\ (0.41)\ RT_{younger}$$
$$- 0.19\ (0.19) \log_2 (n + 1)\ \text{by}\ RT_{younger}.$$

The standard errors suggest that only a single line is present in the data. Omitting the variables associated with the added effects of choice RT indeed did not significantly decrease fit, $\Delta LR \chi^2 (2) = 3.84$. The resulting equation was:

$$RT_{older} = 0 \, (46) + 1.36 \, (0.12) \, RT_{younger}.$$

The intercept is not significantly different from zero, $\Delta LR \chi^2 (1) = 0.00$. Refitting led to the following equation:

$$RT_{older} = 1.36 \, (0.03) \, RT_{younger}.$$

Compared with the empty model, this equation explains 68% of the variance in mean RT of older adults. One of the implications of this model, in line with the analysis in the previous section on SRT and CRT, is that the added processes in the CRT version of the task, when n is larger than 1, are not more age-sensitive than the processes already present in the single RT version of the task. This, in turn, suggests that binary decision-making and response selection are not more age-sensitive than the processes involved in mere stimulus detection.

The Hicks-Hyman equation defines an information-processing function. Brinley analysis on the slopes from the Hick-Hyman equations (24 data points; Figure 4.11, Panel B) yields the following equation:

$$\text{Hick-Hyman slope}_{older} = 20 \, (25) + 1.35 \, (0.15) \, \text{Hick-Hyman slope}_{younger}$$

This model could indeed be trimmed to a simple proportional model at no significant cost to fit, $\Delta LR \chi^2 (1) = 0.66$:

$$\text{Hick-Hyman slope}_{older} = 1.45 \, (0.09) \, \text{Hick-Hyman slope}_{younger}.$$

This, in turn, suggests (as did the analysis on RT) that there is purely multiplicative age-related slowing in the processes associated with decision-making and response selection in multiple-choice reaction times. The slowing factor is about 1.4.

The full Brinley equation for the $(n + 1)$-intercepts is:

$$\text{Hick-Hyman } (n + 1)\text{-intercept}_{older} = -35 \, (70) + 1.38 \, (0.24) \, \text{Hick-Hyman}$$
$$(n + 1)\text{-intercept}_{younger}.$$

This model could be trimmed to a simple proportional model at no significant cost to fit, $\Delta LR \chi^2 (1) = 0.15$:

$$\text{Hick-Hyman } (n + 1)\text{-intercept}_{older} = 1.26 \, (0.05) \, \text{Hick-Hyman}$$
$$(n + 1)\text{-intercept}_{younger}.$$

The intercepts, too, then, show purely proportional age-related slowing, with a slowing factor of about 1.3 (Figure 4.11, Panel C).

Summarized, the age-related slowing factor in the Hick-Hyman slope, as measured directly and through Brinley plotting of the raw data and of the slopes, lies somewhere between 1.4 and 1.6. This estimate for age-related slowing in the decision-making component of RT is quite compatible with the results for CRT as reported in the previous section—there I observed an age-related slowing factor of 1.4 or 1.5. The results for the intercepts at $(n + 1)$, which presumably measure simple RT, are relatively close to those obtained for actual simple RT: The Hick-Hyman equations yield estimates of 289 ms for younger adults and 372 for older adults; the values for actual SRT studies (reviewed in the previous section) are 246 ms and 310 ms, respectively. The young/old ratios are close as well: 1.29 for Hick-Hyman estimates, 1.29 for SRT data. The slowing factor derived from the Hick-Hyman estimates is around 1.3, which is somewhat (though not drastically) smaller than the joint slowing factor for SRT and CRT, 1.4 to 1.5.

4.4.3. Decomposing Response Time using Event-related Potentials: The P300

The processes underlying measures of RT, even simple RT, are still quite complicated. Some researchers in the field have resorted to electrophysiological measures, notably event-related potentials (ERP), to examine the timing of relatively early components of RT. In ERP studies, a stimulus display is presented and the subject performs some task while electrical activity at the scalp is measured using a dense electrode array (this measurement is called an electroencephalogram, or EEG). When the resulting EEG is locked to the stimulus onset (and many trials are combined), a series of predictable waveforms (often called "components") typically emerges, each associated with specific aspects of processing, often dependent on the task and/or stimulus.

One component that has been studied quite often in an aging context (including a few meta-analyses; Bashore, Osman, & Heffley, 1989; Polich, 1996)—is the P300. The P300 is a positive inflection in the ERP signal, typically occurring at around 300 ms, which is most often observed when a novel or unpredicted stimulus is presented. (For an extensive review, see Polich, 2007.) A typical paradigm to elicit the P300 is the oddball paradigm. In this paradigm, subjects are presented with a series of stimuli to be identified or counted. If one type of stimulus occurs much more rarely than any other, a P300 response is often emitted when that stimulus is presented. The P300 is only elicited when the novel stimulus is crucial for the task, and it is independent of the type of stimulus—visual, tactile, auditory, olfactory, and gustatory stimuli are all capable of producing reliable P300 components. These findings suggest that the P300 component is not driven by sensory processes, but rather reflects a more general, cognitive response to unexpected and/or cognitively salient stimuli.

The question is: What does this response signify? Standard theory (e.g., Donchin, 1981; Fabiani & Friedman, 1995) considers the P300 as indicative of an updating mechanism—that is, when a stable stimulus representation suddenly changes, the contents of working memory need to be revised. Working memory involvement is inferred from subsequent memory effects: Memory for items that elicit a P300 is larger than for items that do not elicit a P300 (Paller, McCarthy, & Wood, 1988; Rushby et al., 2002). The P300 is also sensitive to task demands—when the task is easy, the P300 will occur earlier and its amplitude will be larger. Later research has shown that the P300 has at least two subcomponents with specific scalp distributions, labeled P3a and P3b. One current hypothesis (Polich, 2007) is that the P300 reflects an early attention process starting with frontally located working memory updating (which produces the P3a), likely associated with rapid neural inhibition, which then allows for the transmission of stimulus and/or task information to temporal and parietal structures (which produces the P3b). For this meta-analysis, I unfortunately did not have the luxury of separating out the P3a and P3b, primarily because many of the primary studies do not indicate which of the two is being measured.

One intriguing finding to emerge out of the first meta-analysis on age-related differences in the latency of the P300 component (Bashore, Osman, & Heffley, 1989) was that the age-related effect is additive, not multiplicative: Older adults' P300 was slowed by a constant 80 ms compared with younger adults' P300. A subset of the studies included in Bashore's data set also provided data on latency as measured behaviorally. In these latency measures, a multiplicative relationship emerged, with a slowing factor of 1.29, very much like the result obtained in the previous section. In the present meta-analysis, I aimed for direct comparison, and therefore I included only studies that measured both the P300 and response time. This resulted in the exclusion of a few studies that used the counting version of the oddball paradigm, because this paradigm does not collect RT on a trial-by-trial basis. As is usual in this type of research, P300 latency is measured at peak amplitude (as opposed to measuring its onset).

I was able to locate 34 papers, each contributing one independent set of younger and older adults to the data pool (Aine et al., 2005; Alain & Woods, 1999; Bahramali, 1999; Bashore, Heffley, & Donchin, 1989; Bashore, Martinerie, Weiser, Greenspon, & Heffley, 1988; Coyle, Gordon, Howson, & Meares, 1991; Czigler, Pato, Poszet, & Balazs, 2006; Dodt, Sarnighausen, Pietrowski, Fehm, & Born, 1996; Dujardin, Derambure, Bourriez, Jacquesson, & Guieu, 1993; Fabiani & Friedman, 1995; Fabiani, Friedman, & Cheng, 1998; Ford, Duncan-Johnson, et al., 1982; Ford, Pfefferbaum, Tinklenberg, & Kopell, 1982; Ford, Roth, Mohs, Hopkins, & Kopell, 1979; Friedman, Simpson, & Hamberger, 1993; Gaàl, Csuhaj, & Molnàr, 2007; Geal-Dor, Goldstein, Kamenir, & Babkoff, 2006; Harbin, Marsh, & Harvey, 1984; Iragui, Kutas, Mitchiner, & Hillyard, 1993; Knott et al., 2003; Knott et al., 2004; Marsh, 1975; McEvoy, Pellouchoud, Smith, & Gevins, 2001; Mullis, Holcomb, Diner, & Dykman, 1985; Pfefferbaum, Ford, Roth, & Kopell, 1980a, 1980b; Picton, Cerri, Champagne, Stuss, & Nelson, 1986; Podlesny & Dustman, 1982; Podlesny, Dustman & Shearer, 1984; Pontifex, Hillman, & Polich, 2009; Strayer, Wickens, & Braune, 1987; Tachibana, Aragane, & Sugita, 1996; Tays, Dywan, Mathewson, & Segalowitz, 2008; Verleger, Neukäter, Kömpf, & Vieregge, 1991).

The data set contains a total of 92 (young, old) pairs for both P300 and response times. This meta-analytic data set, like Bashore's (1985) and Donchin's (1996), included a number of different paradigms—the oddball paradigm, stimulus discrimination, visual search, and memory search. Weighted average P300 peak amplitude occurred at 400 ms for younger adults and 452 ms for older adults; RTs were at 518 ms and 580 ms, respectively. These latencies are quite long, suggesting relatively high task demands. At first blush, there is nothing special here—the absolute age difference is larger in RT than P300, 52 ms versus 62 ms, but the proportional difference is virtually identical, 1.12 versus 1.13.

In the Brinley analysis (see Figure 4.12), I estimated age-related differences in P300 latency and RT, using a dummy variable for RT (0 = P300 measurement; 1 = RT measurement). The resulting Brinley equation (184 data points) is:

$$\text{Latency}_{older} = 65\ (28) - 121\ (24)\ \text{dummy(RT)} + 0.95\ (0.07)\ \text{Latency}_{younger}$$
$$+ 0.29\ (0.05)\ \text{RT by Latency}_{younger}.$$

Fixing the P300-slope of this function (i.e., the parameter associated with Latency$_{younger}$) to one did not affect fit reliably, ΔLR χ^2 (1) = 0.53. The final equation is then:

$$\text{Latency}_{older} = 45\ (5) - 116\ (23)\ \text{dummy(RT)} + \text{Latency}_{younger}$$
$$+ 0.28\ (0.05)\ \text{RT by Latency}_{younger}.$$

This equation explains 96% of the variance in older adults' latencies compared with the empty model. It can be rewritten more intelligibly as a set of two equations:

$$\text{P300}_{older} = 45 + \text{P300}_{younger}$$

$$\text{RT}_{older} = -71 + 1.28\ \text{RT}_{younger}.$$

Summarized, the analysis shows—like Bashore's meta-analysis—that there is significant age-related slowing in the P300, and that the effect is additive: Older adults reach peak latency in the P300 on average 45 ms later than younger adults. In the same set of studies, RT did show the expected near-multiplicative relation, with a small negative intercept and an age-related slowing factor of about 1.3, in line with the analyses presented earlier in this chapter. In other words, the age-related effects on P300 dissociate from those on RT: The complexity effects are of a different nature altogether.

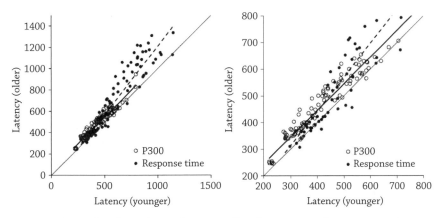

Figure 4.12 Brinley plots of P300 data, as well as the corresponding response times. Panel A shows all latency data (k = 92); Panel B zooms in on the data set, for clarity. The dotted line represents the equality diagonal; the solid line is the regression line for P300; the dashed line is the regression line for the response time data.

One possible interpretation for this dissociation (e.g., Ford, Roth, Mohs, Hopkins, & Kopell, 1979) uses a pure-insertion logic. If the P300 latency reflects the moment in time when the stimulus becomes available in working memory, the difference between P300 and RT indicates all processes that occur within working memory, including response selection and execution. One way to then examine age-related effects in these later processes is to subject the data to a state-trace analysis, predicting RT from peak latency in the P300. The resulting equation (age group was dummy coded (0 = younger; 1 = older) is:

$$RT = 236\ (82) + 0.86\ (0.18)\ P300 - 44\ (122)\ \text{dummy (age group)}$$
$$+ 0.23\ (0.26)\ \text{dummy (age group) by P300.}$$

In this equation, both the dummy associated with age (the age effect on the intercept) and the interaction between age and P300 (the age effect on the slope) are not significant, considering their *SE*. Deleting both, however, made fit plummet, ΔLR χ^2 (2) = 252.51, indicating that there is a significant age effect on either the slope or the intercept of the state trace. Given that the Brinley plot suggested that P300 and RT diverge in slopes, I decided to delete the age group dummy and allow the model to estimate a different slope for younger and older adults. Deleting the age group dummy did not worsen fit significantly, ΔLR χ^2 (1) = 0.13. Here is the resulting equation:

$$RT = 216\ (61) + 0.90\ (0.14)\ P300 + 0.14\ (0.07)\ \text{dummy (age group) by P300.}$$

Fixing the slope of the equation (the term associated with P300) to one did not significantly alter fit, ΔLR χ^2 (1) = 0.50:

$$RT = 176\ (23) + P300 + 0.12\ (0.06)\ \text{dummy (age group) by P300.}$$

This can be rewritten as the following set of two equations:

$$RT_{younger} = 176 + P300_{younger};$$

$$RT_{older} = 176 + 1.12\ P300_{older}.$$

What appears to be happening for younger subjects, then, is that the stages in the processing chain that occur after the P300 are not influenced by the duration of the P300 itself: The absolute difference between P300 peak amplitude and the actual RT remains identical (176 ms on average). Under pure-insertion logic, this makes sense: The time needed to represent information into working memory should have no bearing on how long it would take to process that information. Older adults, however, show a different pattern. For them, longer P300s lead to proportionally longer RTs.

How can this discrepancy be explained?

The most plausible explanation is that the pure-insertion logic is flawed, and that P300 peak latency and RT are simply not part of the same processing chain. One finding that supports this claim is the not uncommon finding that a behavioral RT can be emitted before the P300 climbs to its peak. This is, for instance, the case in the present data set: There are 92 data points for each of the age groups, and 13 of those (14% of the data) yield a faster mean RT than mean P300 peak latency in younger adults; 16 (17% of the data) do so in older adults. Speed-accuracy instructions have an influence on the relative timing: When speed is emphasized, RT is often faster than P300; when accuracy becomes essential, P300 typically precedes the behavioral response (e.g., Strayer et al., 1987). In some studies, the correlation between P300 and RT is rather weak (e.g., a between-subject $r = .26$ in one study on 100 subjects varying between the ages of 18 and 90; Kraiuhin et al., 1990); in others it is larger (e.g., Kutas, Iragui, & Hillyard, 1994, obtained within-individual trial-to-trial correlations between .48 and .66). The correlation tends to be higher when RT is fast, that is, in tasks that have relatively low task demands and are likely to be performed in a bottom-up, stimulus-driven manner (e.g., Verleger, 1997). One interpretation that ties all these results together (Verleger, Jaskowksi, & Wascher, 2005) is that the P300 reflects a coarse decision-making and/or monitoring process that occurs in parallel with the more purely stimulus-driven decisions that tend to drive RT. If we accept this viewpoint, P300 and RT simply measure different aspects of processing, which make differential aging effects possible. The larger proportional differences between RT and P300 in older adults with increasing P300 (and increasing RT) could be explained by the age-related shift toward more conservative speed-accuracy trade-offs—thus withholding RT just a little longer—that we already encountered when decomposing RT using the EZ diffusion model (Section 3.1.3).

4.4.4. Decay Rate of Verbal Short-term Memory

Verbal short-term memory holds representations of verbal stimuli, typically in some form of acoustic code, in a highly active, immediately accessible state (e.g., Atkinson & Shiffrin, 1968). If not rehearsed or refreshed, its contents are available for a few seconds or tens of seconds at most. The decay rate of verbal short-term memory, one of Card et al.'s elementary parameters, is typically measured using the Brown-Peterson paradigm (Brown, 1958; Peterson & Peterson, 1959). In the typical Brown-Peterson task, subjects are presented with consonant trigrams (e.g., "KGS" or "GSB"), followed by a brief episode of simple arithmetic operations (typically counting backwards by 3s from a three-digit number). Performance suffers as the bout of intermittent processing lengthens.

The literature on aging and decay in verbal short-term memory is sparse; I was only able to collect data from six relevant studies contained in five papers (Floden, Stuss, & Craik, 2000; Inman & Parkinson, 1983; Pucket and Stockburger, 1988; Pucket & Lawson, 1989; Parkinson, Inman, & Dannenbaum, 1985). (A few additional studies included fewer than the four stimulus-recall intervals needed to fit the decay curve.) I fitted the data (expressed as percent correct) to the same 3-parameter exponential decay function I used for fitting iconic-memory decay rates:

$$Y = Y_0 + a \, \text{Exp}(-b \, X).$$

Here, Y_0 stands for the minimum accuracy at long intervals (this is assumed to be the amount of information that gets reliably transferred into long-term memory), a

reflects the additional amount of information that can be held in short-term memory at a zero stimulus-cue interval (with consonant trigrams, $a + Y_0$, that is, the amount of information retrieved at a zero stimulus-cue interval, is almost always three items, or 100% correct), and b reflects the exponential decay of that information.

In all six studies, the short-term memory store was observed to be less stable in older adults compared with younger adults. First, half-life of the memory representation was considerably shorter in older than in younger adults—5.9 s versus 7.7 s. Thus, older adults' short-term memory representations' half-life is about 70% shorter than that of younger adults, or, conversely, the half-life of younger adults' short-term memory representations is 1.42 times longer. Second, the decay parameter b as estimated from the functions is larger (indicating faster decay) in older adults than in younger adults—0.25 versus 0.15. Measured by this parameter, older adults decay rates are thus, on average, 1.43 times faster than those of younger adults.

An additional finding is that although young and older adults do not differ in their initial level of performance (younger adults' mean is at 95.1%; older adults' at 97.5%), older adults do seem to channel less information into long-term memory than younger adults, as estimated from the Y_0 parameter—63.3% ultimate retention versus 51.5%.

4.4.5. Speed of Linguistic Operations: Lexical Decision

Many tasks in daily life require access to lexical information—the meaning of words. Speed of access to this information is typically measured using lexical decision tasks. (Other lexical-access tasks include picture naming or word naming.) In a lexical decision task, subjects are presented with a series of words and nonwords (i.e., letter strings that are not words but, in most studies, are orthographically and phonologically similar to words, e.g., "flirp"), interspersed randomly. They are asked to make a decision whether each stimulus is a word or a nonword; only response times to words are counted as lexical decision times. Speed on a lexical decision task is only a proxy for lexical access time—lexical decision tasks also contain perceptual and motor processes, and, given the typically fast speed at which such tasks are executed, may even be dominated by them (an argument also made by, among others, Balota & Chumbley, 1984; Balota & Spieler, 1999).

In an attempt to keep the measures of lexical decision speed as process-pure as possible, I included only tasks that were solely about lexical decision, discarding tasks that included distractors (including double-lexical decision tasks, where subjects make decisions about the presence of two words in a display) or negative priming or semantic priming manipulations. I did include lexical decision data from semantic priming experiments where the word was preceded by a "neutral" prime (such as a series of Xs), or by an unrelated prime.

I was able to extract relevant data from 26 papers, yielding a total of 33 independent samples (Allen, Madden, & Crozier, 1991; Allen, Madden, Weber, & Groth, 1993; Allen, Mei-Ching, Murphy, Sanders, Judge, & McCann, 2002; Allen, Murphy, Kaufman, Groth, & Begovic, 2004; Allen, Smith, Groth, Pickle, Grabbe, & Madden, 2002; Balota & Ferraro, 1996; Bennett & McEvoy, 1999; Bowles & Poon, 1981, 1985; Caza & Moscovitch, 2005; Cerella & Fozard, 1994; Ferraro, King, Ronning, Pekarski, & Risan, 2003; Fisk, Cooper, Hertzog, Batsakes, & Mead, 1996; Gold, Andersen, Jicha, & Smith,

2009; James & MacKay, 2007; Jenkins et al., 2000; Joyce, Paller, McIsaac, & Kutas, 1998; Lawrence et al., 1998; Madden & Greene, 1987; Madden, Welsh-Bohmer, & Tupler, 1999; Ratcliff et al., 2004; Ratcliff, Thapar, & McKoon, 2010; Stern, Prather, Swinney, & Zurif, 1991; Tainturier, Tremblay, & Lecours, 1989; Verhaeghen et al., 2002; Wurm, Labouvie-Vief, Aycock, Rebucal, & Koch, 2004). The weighted average lexical decision time for younger adults was 679 ms; for older adults, it was 863 ms.

Results from the Brinley analysis (121 younger-older pairs; Figure 4.13) were straightforward. The full model was:

Lexical Decision$_{older}$ = –47 (87) + 1.36 (0.14) lexical decision$_{younger}$.

This equation could be simplified at no cost to fit, $\Delta LR \; \chi^2 \; (1) = 0.28$, by fixing the intercept to zero:

Lexical Decision$_{older}$ = 1.28 (0.02) lexical decision$_{younger}$.

The equation explained 91% of the variance in older adults' mean lexical decision times compared with the empty model.

One noteworthy result here is that the age-relayed slowing factor is much larger than the one obtained in Chapter 2 for what I labeled there as linguistic tasks. The reader may recall that linguistic tasks effectively showed an age-related speed-up (the Brinley slope was 0.8). One tempting potential explanation for the discrepancy is that the linguistic tasks examined in the previous chapter are, by definition, more varied than the lexical decision tasks examined here—besides lexical decision tasks, the linguistic category also contained tasks of letter reading, word naming, picture naming, semantic category judgment, semantic matching, semanticity judgment,

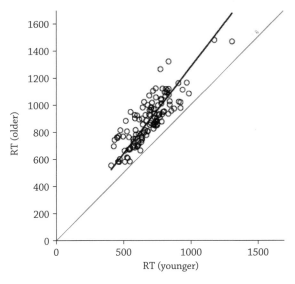

Figure 4.13 Brinley plot of lexical decision data ($k = 121$). Final regression line is indicated as a solid line; the dotted line is the equality diagonal.

synonym matching, synonym-antonym production, reading rate, speech discrimination, spoken word identification, grammatical judgment, and generating an appropriate verb for a noun. Some of those tasks, it seems, capture what some have called the
"pragmatics" of cognition (Baltes, Dittmann-Kohli, & Dixon, 1984; Sperber & Wilson,
1986)—the superbly tuned use of language as honed over a lifetime of use. If such
pragmatic tasks (maybe semantic category judgment, semantic matching, synonym
matching, synonym-antonym production, and generating an appropriate verb for a
noun would all fall under that category) show an age-related advantage rather than
a deficit, and if they take on average longer to complete than lexical decision tasks
do, their inclusion in the Chapter 1 data set might have brought the Brinley slope
down compared with the current data set, which only contains lexical decision tasks.
To test this hypothesis, I returned to the data set from Chapter 2, and identified 62
data points that seem to fall into the "pragmatics" category, and 75 that fall into the
lexical decision category. The data are presented in Figure 4.14. I fitted OLS regression to each of the two subsets. (The reader may recall that multilevel models failed to
converge on the linguistic data set.) The pragmatics line had a steeper, not shallower,
slope than the lexical decision line, 1.60 vs. 1.04, suggesting that there is no merit to
the hypothesis that slow pragmatics tasks drive the age-related speed-up observed in
the Chapter 2 data set.

The conclusion then remains that Chapter 2's model simply misspecified the equation governing linguistic tasks. The failure to converge suggests that this data set
plainly has a lower signal-to-noise ratio than desired.

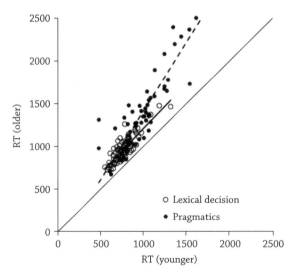

Figure 4.14 Brinley plot contrasting lexical decision data ($k = 75$) with data on the
"pragmatic" use of language (i.e., semantic category judgment, semantic matching,
synonym matching, synonym-antonym production, and generating an appropriate verb
for a noun; $k = 62$); all data were sourced from Chapter 2. The dotted line is the equality
diagonal; the solid line is the OLS regression line for lexical decision tasks; the dashed
line is the OLS regression line for the pragmatic tasks.

4.5. Practice Effects and Disuse

The final aspect of the Model Human Processor examined here is the effect of practice. Card et al. consider the effectiveness of practice (they label it the "learning principle," p. 57) an elementary aspect of the cognitive system—one among its nine principles of organization.

In its bare-bones formulation, the learning principle is extremely simple: The time needed to perform a task decreases with increasing practice. It was probably Snoddy (1926) who first observed that this benefit over practice can be well-approximated by a power function. Given that the practice effect is such a fundamental aspect of the cognitive system, a description of age-related differences within the Model Human Processor would be incomplete without its inclusion.

There is another reason to study age differences in practice effects. As mentioned in the introduction to Chapter 3, it has been argued quite often that the comparison between the typical younger-adult and older-adult samples in the literature may be flawed because the older adults typically tested in cognitive psychology labs might be suffering from the ill effects of "disuse" (Thorndike, Bregman, Tilton, & Woodyard, 1928). The concern is that the typical younger-adult subject used as the comparison group in cognitive aging studies (usually an undergraduate student) dwells in an environment that continually supports and exercises the type of skills needed for high performance on the type of cognitive tasks characteristically included in our experiments. Compared with younger adults, older adults might come to the response box with a less readily available and/or accessible skill-set, and are then likely to underperform on the basis of this impediment alone. A straightforward test for the assertion that older adults' lack of practice with the task is the root cause of age-related slowing would be to provide both age groups with ample practice and examine changes in age-related differences over the course of the experiment (e.g., Baron & Cerella, 1993; Kausler, 1982). If disuse plays a role, we would expect shrinkage of the age-related difference (ideally measured by the age-related slowing factor) over the course of practice. A more extreme version of the disuse hypothesis, one that claims that all observed age differences are due to disuse, would predict that all age differences disappear with extended practice.

4.5.1. Modeling Learning Effects: The Power Law of Practice

Practice effects are most often captured in so-called learning curves, which plot performance (here: response times) as a function of the number of practice trials. Learning curves are nonlinear: The fastest rate of learning occurs early in practice; after that, gains turn smoothly to almost-zero. One function that captures this curve very well is the power function (e.g., Mazur & Hastie, 1978; Newell & Rosenbloom, 1981; Snoddy, 1926). Its success in describing practice-related behavior is hard to overstate: It applies to such diverse tasks as pressing buttons, reading inverted text, rolling cigars, generating geometry proofs, manufacturing machine tools (all examples cited in Newell and Rosenbloom, 1981), performing mental arithmetic on both large and small numbers (Delaney, Reder, Staszewski, & Ritter, 1998), performing a scheduling task (Nerb, Ritter, & Krems, 1999), and even writing books (Ohlsson, 1992). Given the ubiquitousness of the phenomenon, it is often simply known as the power law of practice. There are serious doubts as to whether the power law applies at the level of individuals (e.g., Heathcote, Brown, & Mewhort, 2000; Myung, Kim, & Pitt, 2000), but the general consensus is that at the group level—which is the level considered here—the power law holds quite well. At its simplest, the learning curve can be described as a two-parameter function:

$$RT = b\,N^{-a}.$$

In this equation, RT stands for response time on a given trial or block N; b represents the initial level of performance, that is, response time at (the nonexistent) trial or block zero; and a is the learning rate. Larger values of a denote faster learning, that is, steeper learning curves. (Contrary to common parlance, steep learning curves indicate that practice progresses at a fast clip.) One handy property of this equation is that it linearizes after logarithmic transformation, as derived here:

$$\log(RT) = \log\,(b\,N^{-a})$$

becomes:

$$\log(RT) = \log\,(b) + \log(N^{-a}),$$

which, in turn, becomes:

$$\log(RT) = \log\,(b) - a\,\log(N).$$

In other words, log(RT) is a linear function of log(N); the intercept of this function is the logarithm of the initial response time and the slope of this function is the learning rate. This transformation then allows us to investigate and compare learning rates of groups of younger and older adults using linear regression techniques, including multilevel modeling.

There is one drawback to this specific equation: The model does not incorporate an asymptote for learning. The assumption is that after an endless stretch of practice, performance will approach a response time of zero—an unrealistic scenario. The model easily can be extended to include an asymptote, but these extensions do not have the advantage that they linearize after a simple transformation. In principle, one could first estimate the asymptote for each study and then subtract it from all available data points to fit the log of this remainder to the log of the number of trials. This is problematic in practice, however—Newell and Rosenbloom, for instance, posit that the asymptote might be visible only after 1,000 or so practice trials. Therefore, in the next subsections, I will fit the simpler two-parameter form of the power law.

4.5.2. Fitting the Power Law to Data of Younger and Older Adults

Baron and Cerella (1993) were the first researchers to conduct a meta-analysis on age-related differences in practice data; they reported data from 18 studies.

Jastrzembski and Charness collected 14 studies, largely nonoverlapping with those gathered in Baron and Cerella. I was able to collect a total of 33 studies, about double the amount of studies in either of the two previous data sets. Inclusion criteria were simple. First, I included only studies that did not involve instruction, but merely repeated presentation of the same task. Second, I used only studies that reported data over at least four blocks or trials of practice. Third, I excluded studies where the change in RT over trials was predicated on a change in strategy. This excluded, for instance, studies on instance learning (e.g., Jenkins et al., 2000; Touron et al., 2001; Touron & Hertzog, 2004). For the same reason, I excluded studies on digit-symbol substitution: Early in practice, a substitution task is likely to be performed using the lookup table; later on, retrieval from memory becomes increasingly likely. If there are age differences in the time point at which the shift in strategy occurs, age differences in the learning rate will be confounded with the strategy shift. Likewise, I excluded studies on implicit sequence or pattern learning. In these studies (for an overview see, e.g., D. Howard, 2001) participants typically perform a serial choice-reaction-time task. For instance, dots appear one after the other in different locations on a screen, and the participant indicates with a mouse click or a key press where the dot is located. Unbeknownst to the participant, at least part of the sequence is predictable. Over the course of a session, participants typically become faster and more accurate for the predictable part of the sequence, even though they are typically unaware of the existence of the pattern. In these studies, then, the task shifts from a pure reaction time measure to a measure of implicit memory retrieval. I did include baseline conditions from implicit memory studies in the data set. In these conditions stimulus sequences are random, and the speed-up over consecutive blocks is effectively a practice-related speed-up in serial CRT. Finally, I excluded studies where subjects were trained to perform sequences of rather complex behavior that took multiple seconds to perform (e.g., squaring operations, Charness & Campbell, 1988; an ATM sequence learning in Jamieson & Rogers, 2000). In that case, the locus of the practice effect is unclear: Any of the constituent processes could be the source of the effect. I should additionally note that I, as everywhere in this book, restricted myself to studies that compared performance of a group of older adults to that of a group of younger adults. This excluded, most notably, one large-scale clinical trial, the ACTIVE study (Ball et al., 2002) and its many spin-offs—those studies only tested older adults, not younger adults (and, in addition, typically provide only a two-point assessment of the practice effects.)

The tasks represented in the data set are diverse, including, among others, choice reaction time, serial choice reaction time (SCRT, in which participants perform multiple CRT trials in a series), counting, digit tracing, card sorting, perceptual identification, visual search, memory search, mental rotation, and the Stroop task. Some papers offer detailed trial-by-trial data; others group trials together in blocks, and what constitutes a block is not consistent between studies. For all these reasons, the actual estimate of the learning rate is not a useful measure; rather, the focus is on the age differences in learning rates as indicated by significant $\log(N)$ by age group interactions. (Recall that the analyses are multilevel, which takes the nested nature of the data into account. This is helpful in the context of testing interactions when the slope of the function is expected to vary widely due to different definitions of the units on the X-axis.)

Figure 4.15 shows the data. The top panels show all the available data; the left-hand panel presents them in raw coordinates and the right-hand panel after log-log transformation; the center panels shows averaged data for the first four blocks, in both raw coordinates and after log-log transformation. The transformed plots strongly suggest

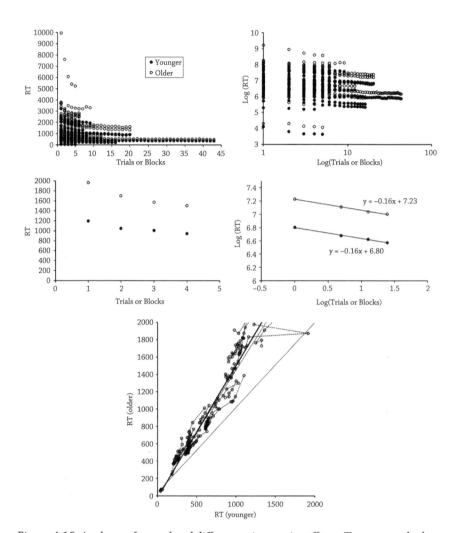

Figure 4.15 Analyses of age-related differences in practice effects. The top panels show the data, in raw RT by trial or block coordinates and after logarithmic transformation of both RT and trial or block. The center panels show averaged data for the first four blocks/trials of practice, in raw and in log-log coordinates. The plots indicate that older adults learn just as fast as younger adults. The bottom panel shows the Brinley plot (data from the same study are linked) with the average Brinley function (RT_{older} = 1.46 $RT_{younger}$) superimposed as a solid line; the dotted line is the equality diagonal. The data suggest that practice implies sliding down the preexisting Brinley function for the task.

that the power law provides a good fit to the data. They also suggest that the learning rates are identical across age groups, as evidenced by parallel lines.

The first model tested included all available data—622 data points, 311 for each age group, 33 independent subject groups from 31 papers (Anandam & Scialfa, 1999; Baron & Mattila, 1989; Berg, Hertzog, & Hunt, 1982; Bherer et al., 2005; Botwinick & Thompson, 1967; Charness & Campbell, 1988; Curran, 1997; Davidson, Zacks, & Williams, 2003; Dennis, Howard, & Howard, 2006; Falduto & Baron, 1986; Fisk, Cooper, Hertzog, Anderson-Garlach, & Lee, 1995; Grant, Storandt, & Botwinick, 1978; Hertzog, Cooper, & Fisk, 1996; Hertzog, Williams, & Walsh, 1976; Howard & Howard, 1992, 1997, 2001; Howard, Howard, Dennis et al., 2004; Howard, Howard, Japiske et al., 2004; Hoyer, Hoyer, Treat, & Baltes, 1978; Jenkins et al., 2000; Jordan & Rabbitt, 1977; Kramer & Weber, 1999; Madden, 1983; Madden & Nebes, 1980; McDowd, 1986; Negash, Howard, Japiske, & Howard, 2003; Noble, Baker, & Jones, 1964; Salthouse & Somberg, 1982b; Strayer & Kramer, 1994; Welford, 1977). I used log(block) (as defined by the authors of the original articles), as the independent variable. Age group was entered as a dummy variable to test for age effects on the intercept of the function (initial RT); age differences in slope (learning rate) were tested using the age group by log(block) interaction term. The full equation was:

$$\log(RT) = 6.44\ (0.07) + 0.40\ (0.10)\ \text{dummy (age group)} - 0.078\ (0.033)$$
$$\log(\text{block}) - 0.016\ (0.046)\ \text{dummy (age group) by } \log(\text{block})$$

The age effect on slope is small compared with its standard error. Deleting this term yielded no significant cost to fit, $\Delta LR^2\ (1) = 0.11$, and the resulting equation was:

$$\log(RT) = 6.46\ (0.06) + 0.38\ (0.05)\ \text{dummy (age group)}$$
$$- 0.086\ (0.023)\ \log(\text{block}).$$

This result can be rewritten as a set of two power functions, one for younger adults and one for older adults:

$$RT_{younger} = 639\ N^{-0.086};$$

$$RT_{older} = 934\ N^{-0.086}.$$

The conclusion is simple: Older adults benefit, on average, as much (or as little) from repeated practice as younger adults do—there are no age differences in learning rate.

An important qualification is that equality of learning rates does not mean that the absolute age difference in RT is identical across the number of practice trials; it means that the proportional age difference remains identical over practice. This can be demonstrated algebraically. We have two equations, one describing log(RT) of younger adults as a function of blocks:

$$\log(RT_{younger}) = \log(b) - a\ \log(\text{block}).$$

The other equation describes log(RT) of older adults. The analysis above demonstrated that the latter function is identical to that of younger adults, except for an intercept difference, which I shall label c:

$$\log(RT_{older}) = \log(b) - a \log(block) + c.$$

After substitution:

$$\log(RT_{older}) = \log(RT_{younger}) + c$$

this is equivalent to:

$$\log(RT_{older}) - \log(RT_{younger}) = c.$$

Taking the exponent of each side:

$$\exp(\log(RT_{older}) - \log(RT_{younger})) = \exp(c),$$

this can be simplified to:

$$\exp(\log(RT_{older}))/\exp(\log(RT_{younger})) = \exp(c),$$

which finally leads us to:

$$RT_{older}/RT_{younger} = \exp(c).$$

Note that the block (or trial) variable does not figure in this equation. This implies that the age difference, expressed as an older-over-younger ratio, that is, as a slowing factor, is independent of the amount of practice received: The slowing factor is identical across all levels of practice. Note, however, that a constant slowing factor implies that absolute age differences are smaller when RT is shorter. Given that RT decreases with practice, this finding then implies that over the course of practice the absolute age difference (i.e., $RT_{older} - RT_{younger}$) will grow smaller.

The model allows us to calculate the age-related slowing ratio directly from the intercept-difference parameter c associated with age group: $\exp(0.38)$ (or $e^{0.38}$) equals 1.46. This slowing factor is close to the average age-related slowing factor derived in Chapter 2 and earlier in this chapter. Figure 4.15, bottom panel, shows a Brinley plot of the practice data (zooming in on the 0~2000 ms interval for detail). The data are indeed described reasonably well by a slowing factor of 1.46 (the solid line). As younger and older adults get more practice with the task, the data points simply slide down the Brinley function. This plot also illustrates clearly that what stays constant over practice is the age-related slowing *factor*, not the absolute age difference, which shrinks considerably in magnitude over the course of practice.

4.5.3. Fitting the Power Law of Practice to Individual Tasks: Choice Reaction Time, Serial Reaction Time, Memory Search, and Visual Search

Null effects are always hard to assess. One obvious question is whether the null effect for age in practice studies is independent of the task (i.e., all tasks show identical practice effects for younger and older adults), or whether there are differential task effects, but they simply sum to zero—some tasks show slower learning in older adults compared with younger adults, others show faster learning. The most direct way to test this moderation hypothesis would be to include the different tasks as explicit variables in the equation. In practice, the number of predictors would be unwieldy. As an alternative, I conducted four separate analyses on each of the four tasks that were included five times or more in the data set, namely choice RT (Botwinick & Thompson, 1967; Jordan & Rabbitt, 1977; McDowd, 1986; Noble et al., 1964), serial RT (Curran, 1997; Dennis, Howard, & Howard, 2003; Howard & Howard, 1991, 1997, 2001; Howard, Howard, Dennis et al., 2004; Howard, Howard, Japiske et al., 2004; Negash, Howard, Japiske, & Howard, 2003), memory scanning (Baron & Mattila, 1989; Fisk et al., 1995; Hertzog, Williams, & Walsh, 1976; Salthouse & Somberg, 1982b; Strayer & Kramer, 1994), and visual search (Anandam & Scialfa, 1999; Kramer & Weber, 1999; Madden, 1983; Madden & Nebes, 1980).

Turning to **choice RT** first (92 data points from five studies), I get the following equation:

$$\log(CRT) = 6.12\ (0.11) + 0.44\ (0.15)\ \text{dummy (age group)} - 0.25\ (0.06)$$
$$\log(\text{block}) + 0.03\ (0.08)\ \text{dummy (age group) by } \log(\text{block}).$$

The age effect on slope is positive but small, and small compared with its standard error. Deleting this term came at no significant cost to fit, $\Delta LR\ \chi^2\ (1) = 0.16$, and the resulting equation was:

$$\log(CRT) = 6.10\ (0.09) + 0.50\ (0.07)\ \text{dummy (age group)}$$
$$- 0.23\ (0.04)\ \log(\text{block}).$$

This can be rewritten as a set of two power functions, one for younger adults and one for older adults:

$$CRT_{\text{younger}} = 444\ N^{-0.23};$$

$$CRT_{\text{older}} = 728\ N^{-0.23}.$$

The conclusion is the same as for the full data set: Older adults are slower than younger adults, but the practice effect as measured by the learning rate is identical for the two age groups.

The second data set concerns **serial RT** as culled from the control conditions or control trials of implicit learning paradigms (148 data points from 11 studies). (Recall that these are serial RTs for the "random" conditions, in which no predictable sequence was present.) Here is the equation:

$$\log(\text{serial RT}) = 6.32 \ (0.16) + 0.34 \ (0.23) \ \text{dummy (age group)} - 0.11 \ (0.12)$$
$$\log(\text{block}) - 0.06 \ (0.17) \ \text{dummy (age group) by } \log(\text{block}).$$

The age effect on slope is negative and quite large compared with the slope for the young, but it is very small compared with its standard error. Deleting this term came at no significant cost to fit, ΔLR χ^2 (1) = 0.10, and the resulting equation was:

$$\log(\text{serial RT}) = 6.36 \ (0.13) + 0.28 \ (0.11) \ \text{dummy (age group)}$$
$$- 0.14 \ (0.09) \ \log(\text{block}).$$

This can be rewritten as a set of two power functions, one for younger adults and one for older adults:

$$\text{Serial RT}_{\text{younger}} = 578 \ N^{-0.14};$$

$$\text{Serial RT}_{\text{older}} = 765 \ N^{-0.14}.$$

Again the conclusion is that older adults are slower than younger adults, but the practice effect, as measured by the learning rate, is identical across the two age groups.

The third data set contains **memory search** data (252 data points from five studies):

$$\log(\text{memory scanning RT}) = 6.39 \ (0.07) + 0.48 \ (0.11) \ \text{dummy (age group)}$$
$$- 0.03 \ (0.03) \ \log(\text{block}) - 0.04 \ (0.04) \ \text{dummy (age group) by } \log(\text{block})$$

The age effect on slope is negative, but not significant, ΔLR χ^2 (1) = 1.42. After deleting the interaction term, the equation becomes:

$$\log(\text{memory scanning RT}) = 6.45 \ (0.06) + 0.36 \ (0.04) \ \text{dummy (age group)}$$
$$- 0.06 \ (0.02) \ \log(\text{block}).$$

The equation above can be rewritten as a set of two power functions, one for younger adults and one for older adults:

$$\text{Memory scanning RT}_{\text{younger}} = 634 \ N^{-0.06};$$

$$\text{Memory scanning RT}_{\text{older}} = 912 \ N^{-0.06}.$$

Again, older adults are slower than younger adults, but learning rate does not differ between groups.

The final data set concerns **visual search** (56 data points from five studies):

$$\log(\text{visual search RT}) = 6.53 \ (0.08) + 0.29 \ (0.12) \ \text{dummy (age group)}$$
$$- 0.07 \ (0.07) \ \log(\text{block}) + 0.04 \ (0.09) \ \text{dummy (age group) by } \log(\text{block}).$$

The age effect on slope is positive and not at all significant, $\Delta LR\ \chi^2$ (1) = 0.16. After deleting the interaction term, the resulting equation was:

log(visual search RT) = 6.51 (0.07) + 0.33 (0.06) dummy (age group) − 0.05 (0.05) log(block).

This can be rewritten as a set of two power functions, one for younger adults and one for older adults:

$$\text{Visual search RT}_{younger} = 672\ N^{-0.05};$$

$$\text{Visual search RT}_{older} = 931\ N^{-0.05}.$$

We again find that older adults are slower than younger adults, but the practice effect, as measured by the learning rate, is identical for the two age groups.

4.5.4. Practice in Speed of Processing and Transfer Effects

One additional aspect of plasticity of response times concerns transfer of practice effects: Does practice on one speeded task lead to improvement in other speeded tasks? Does the change, in other words, remain restricted to the level of skill—increased efficiency in performing all or specific components of a specific task and/or increased efficiency in assembling these components—or does the repeated execution of a particular task result in changes at a deeper level?

Relatively few studies have examined transfer effects of speed-of-processing training in older adults; I am not aware of any studies that looked at age differences in the effect (except Hoyer, Hoyer, Treat, & Baltes, 1978, which was, however, not included here because the data did not allow for the computation of effect sizes). I obtained data from four studies (Ball et al., 2002; Edwards, Wadley, Vance, Wood, Roenker, & Ball, 2005; Roenker, Cissell, Ball, Wadley, & Edwards, 2003; Vance et al., 2007); Figure 4.16 summarizes the results. All of these studies use variants of the speed-of-processing training component of the ACTIVE clinical trial (Ball et al., 2002). This regimen is essentially repeated exposure to a visual identification task, with the target presented in the visual periphery; training is extensive and entails ten 1-hour sessions. The control conditions concern computer/Internet training, training in memory or reasoning tasks, or practice in driving simulator tasks.

In the analysis, I distinguished three types of tasks. Target tasks are the tasks used in the practice sessions; near-transfer tasks are tasks of processing speed not included in the practice sessions (SRT, CRT, Stroop, Trail Making, Digit Symbol Substitution, letter or pattern comparison tests, the Speed subtest from the Everyday Problem Solving battery); far-transfer tasks are other cognitive tasks (tests for memory, reasoning, Instrumental Activities of Daily Living [IADL], driving ability, and the like). Effect sizes were calculated as the mean standardized difference between the posttest and the pretest; I averaged effect first within study, and then across studies, weighting for sample size. As can be seen in Figure 4.16, there is clear evidence for practice effects on the target measures (*MSD* = 1.64 for experimental subjects vs. 0.04 for

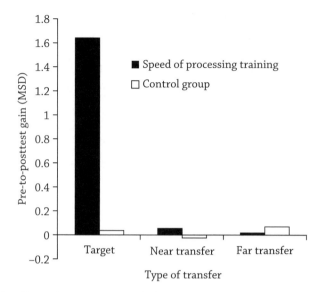

Figure 4.16 Effects of training in speed-of-processing tasks and control treatments (expressed as mean standardized difference between posttest performance and pretest performance) on target abilities, as well as on near-transfer tasks and far-transfer tasks. Data are averaged over four studies. The only notable effect is the effect of the trained skill on the target skill itself.

control subjects), but the evidence for transfer effects is slight, to say the least—all the effects are small (comprised within 0.07 *MSD* of the mean), regardless of whether subjects were practiced on speed of processing or not. (One additional study examining transfer, namely, Hoyer, Hoyer, Treat, & Baltes, 1978, did not provide enough data for a calculation of effect sizes, but none of the treatment main effects were significant, suggesting a lack of transfer effects in this study as well.)

The end conclusion from this small sample of studies is then that the effects of practice in speed of processing in older adults are very local—restricted to the particular task trained, and not extending into any other type of task. This is, then, the training of a skill, not the enhancement of ability.

4.5.5. Practice Effects and Aging: Summary and Conclusion

I examined age-related differences in practice effects for two reasons. One is purely descriptive, driven by my interest in the Model Human Processor. The other, although based on the answer to the first question, has more theoretical relevance. It concerns the question whether or not some (or even all) of the age differences in speed observed in the literature might be due to disuse, that is, lack of recent and/or relevant practice in older adults compared with younger adults. The results are quite clear: Younger and older adults show identical learning rates as measured by the exponent in the power law of practice. This also implies that proportional age differences remain stable over the course of practice. This was true both when I considered the full data set and when I zoomed in to examine the four tasks included most often in the literature. It was also true for implicit sequence learning. Again, I note that parallel lines in log(RT) – log(block) space imply that the age differences as expressed in units that matter most for the actual participants—real time—do grow smaller over increasing amounts of practice. Studies that investigated transfer effects of speed-of-processing practice found no evidence for the existence of such transfer, suggesting that practice effects are limited to increased efficiency in the specific components of the task, and/or the efficiency of their assemblage.

4.6. The Aging Model Human Processor: Conclusions

At the end of this long set of analyses of age-related differences in elementary tasks, what have we learned?

One result is that we now have a good idea of what the *Aging Model Human Processor* looks like, both in terms of average time needed for the specific tasks and processes investigated here, and in terms of the (linear) slowing models that fit each of these tasks and processes to the Young-Adult Model Human Processor. Table 4.1 provides the parameter estimates for both younger and older adults for each of the 15 elementary tasks/processes investigated in this chapter (fixation duration, flicker fusion threshold, gap detection threshold, tapping speed, movement time toward a target, memory scanning, subitizing, counting, mental rotation, feature visual search, conjunction visual search, simple reaction time, choice reaction time, P300, and lexical decision times), as well as the half-life of the iconic and short-term memory store, and the Hicks-Hyman Law. Table 4.1 also reproduces Card et al.'s original estimates, which were often based on a very small set of studies; this allows us to compare the values calculated in this chapter with the 1982 estimates.

My estimates are derived from more sources than Card et al.'s, which might be one reason to trust them better. They are also derived from studies that included older adults, and that might be a reason for mistrust—perhaps there are some subtle sampling biases at work. Most of the studies do use undergraduates as the population of choice, and given that latencies tend to correlate negatively with general intelligence, and college students tend to have IQs above 100 (the population mean), we might expect that the estimates will be faster than those for a true average Human Processor. The same goes true for Card et al.'s estimates.

There are clear convergences between the two data sets—fixation duration, Fitt's law, memory scanning, subitizing, simple RT, movement time, and the half-life of short-term memory all provide estimates that are within a reasonable distance of each other. Other estimates diverge notably: The flicker fusion thresholds I collected are faster by a factor of three compared with Card et al.'s estimates; silent counting is slower by a factor of two; tapping speed is about 50% slower, and the half-life of the iconic store is about 75% longer. I also provided estimates of tasks and processes not included in Card et al.—auditory gap detection, mental rotation speed, visual search rates, two-choice RT, P300, and lexical decision times.

Table 4.2 provides a second type of summary: The results of the Brinley analysis for the 15 elementary tasks. This table and the underlying data form the basis for the analyses in the next chapter, where I will attempt to find regularities in this data set.

Table 4.1 **Mean parameter estimates for cognitive, perceptual, and motor tasks for younger and older adults, as based on the meta-analyses presented in Chapter 4. Original estimates by Card et al. for the Model Human Processor are also provided. Age ratio is always computed so that higher numbers indicate a disadvantage for older adults. STM = Short-term memory; RT = reaction time; *k* is the number of studies included in each estimate.**

Task or process	Model Human Processor, younger	Observed younger	Observed older	k	Age ratio
Fixation duration	230 ms	242 ms	280 ms	27	1.16
Half-life iconic store	200 ms	326 ms	214 ms	3	1.52
Flicker fusion threshold	100 ms/cycle	29 ms/cycle	36 ms/cycle	22	1.24
Auditory gap detection	NA	4.4 ms	8.1 ms	10	1.84
Tapping speed	70 ms/cycle	105 ms/cycle	121 ms/cycle	20	1.15
Fitts's Law	100 ms/ID	124 ms/ID	179 ms/ID	9	1.44
Memory scanning	50 ms/item	60 ms/item	72 ms/item	9	1.2
Subitizing	46 ms/item	40 ms/item	61 ms/item	8	1.53
Counting	167 ms/item	330 ms/item	335 ms/item	8	1.02
Mental rotation	NA	4.8 ms/degree	8.6 ms/degree	8	1.79
Feature search	NA	4 ms/item	6 ms/item	39	1.5
Conjunction search	NA	28 ms/item	55 ms/item	30	1.96
Simple RT	240 ms	246 ms	310 ms	26	1.26
Two-choice RT	NA	283 ms	351 ms	20	1.24
Hick-Hyman Law	150 ms/bit	115 ms/bit	174 ms/bit	24	1.51
P300	NA	400 ms	452 ms	38	1.13
Half-life STM	7 s	7.7 s	5.9 s	6	1.31
Lexical Decision	NA	679 ms	863 ms	33	1.27

A second main result concerns practice effects. I found here that these effects are largely identical across age groups, regardless of the task. This result has theoretical implications, especially for the idea that disuse is a major determinant of cognitive aging—at least for the types of elementary tasks included here, disuse seems to play no discernible role. Another, more descriptive implication is that the equations relating performance of older adults to those of younger adults are largely impervious to training or practice as well. Consequently, human factor psychologists interested in describing latencies of older adults after practice can just extrapolate from data obtained on practiced younger adults, using the equations provided in Table 4.2.

Table 4.2 **Summary of age-related effects on 15 elementary tasks, formulated as Brinley equations. Equations are presented both in their full, unconstrained form and in their final form as derived in the text, with parameters fixed to 0 or 1, or bound to those of similar tasks. Asterisks denote parameters that were fixed at the given value. Parameter values sharing a superscript letter were fixed to be equal to each other.**

	Full model		Final model	
Task	*Slope (SE)*	*Intercept (SE)*	*Slope (SE)*	*Intercept (SE)*
Fixation duration	0.96 (0.12)	52 (25)	1*	45 (7)
Flicker fusion cycle time	1.25 (0.09)	−0.70 (3.0)	1.23 (0.03)	0*
Gap detection threshold	1.33 (0.08)	−0.06 (0.71)	1.32 (0.03)	0*
Tapping speed	1.16 (0.04)	4.42 (10.36)	1.18 (0.02)	0*
Movement time	1.63 (0.09)	−40 (36)	1.65 (0.09)	0*
Memory scanning	1.33 (0.10)	85 (67)	1.44 (0.06)	0*
Subitizing	1.11 (0.10)	146 (66)	1	206[a] (48)
Counting	1.03 (0.08)	205 (46)	1	206[a] (48)
Mental rotation	1.86 (0.12)	−169 (89)	1.67 (0.04)	0*
Feature search	1.76 (0.18)	−222 (107)	1.76[b] (0.80)	−220[c] (48)
Conjunction search	1.80 (0.17)	1274 (102)	1.76[b] (0.80)	−220[c] (48)
Single RT	1.40 (0.28)	−35 (73)	1.42[d] (0.04)	0*
Choice RT	1.60 (0.20)	−84 (62)	1.42[d] (0.04)	0*
P300	0.95 (0.07)	65 (28)	1*	45 (5)
Lexical decision	1.36 (0.14)	−47 (87)	1.28 (0.02)	0*

5

Toward a Sparse Ontology of Age Effects in Elementary Processes

The Dimensionality of the Aging Model Human Processor

The previous chapter collected data on age-related differences in the speed of executing a large number of elementary tasks, as well as memory decay rates and practice effects. The aim of the current chapter is to detect regularities in the age-related effects observed in these tasks. Given that the decay-rate data are quite different in nature from the response time data, and given that the practice data showed no interesting added effects to the examination of Brinley slopes or curves (practice merely results in a slide down the preexisting, so to speak, Brinley line), these two types of data will not be considered here, and I limit myself to the 15 response time tasks. The main goal here is to reduce the set of 15 tasks to a smaller number of clusters or dimensions. First, I will examine how well the one-dimensional, general slowing model fares compared with the full 15-dimensional model. Next, I will investigate a few alternative models that yield a dimensionality somewhere in-between 1 and 15, namely, between 2 and 6.

5.1. Full-dimensionality and Single-dimension Accounts of Age-related Slowing in Elementary Processes

The Brinley plot for all 15 tasks (1,014 data points) is provided in Figure 5.1; Figure 5.2 zooms in on the [0~1,400 ms] range. Figures 5.3 and 5.4 show the regression lines obtained in Chapter 4. Figure 5.3 shows the unconstrained models; Figure 5.4 shows the final models. (The regression parameters are provided in Table 4.2.)

Equipped with these data, we can now start answering the question: What is the dimensionality of the age-related effects in this data set? Fifteen dimensions, of course, would completely describe the present data set, at least when task (rather than study) is the unit of analysis. A formal analysis confirms this: Compared with the empty model, the full model with separate slopes and intercepts for each of the

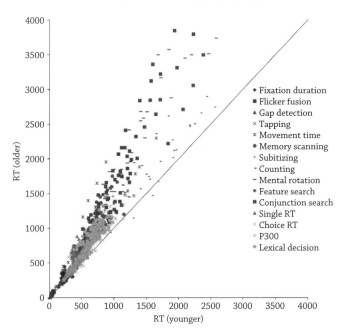

Figure 5.1 Brinley plot of all data analyzed in Chapter 5, grouped by task (*k* = 1,014). The equality diagonal is represented by a dotted line. See plate section for color version of this figure.

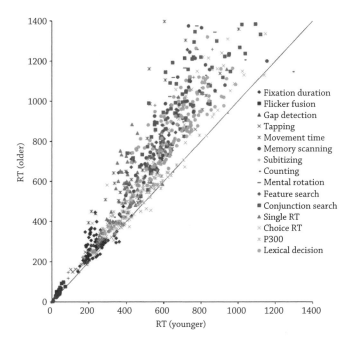

Figure 5.2 Brinley plot of all data analyzed in Chapter 5, grouped by task (*k* = 1,014). This plot is identical to Figure 5.1, now zooming in on the [0~1,400 ms] range. The equality diagonal is represented by a dotted line. See plate section for color version of this figure.

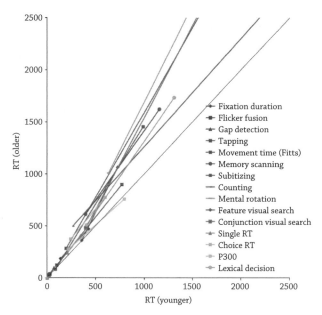

Figure 5.3 Results of the regression analyses presented in Chapter 4. Multilevel regression lines are plotted in Brinley space, using the appropriate data range for each task; the models are the original full models, with a separate slope and intercept estimated for each task. The equality diagonal is represented by a dotted line. See plate section for color version of this figure.

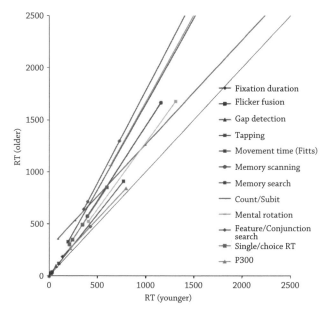

Figure 5.4 Results of the regression analyses presented in Chapter 4. Multilevel regression lines are plotted in Brinley space, using the appropriate data range for each task; the models are the final, constrained, models for each task. The equality diagonal is represented by a dotted line. See plate section for color version of this figure.

15 tasks explains 98.49% of the variance. Adjusting R^2 for the number of predictors did not substantially reduce the fit: The model now explains 98.45% of the variance.

How does the 15-D model compare to the general slowing model? Despite the clear fan in the Brinley plot, a single dimension does fit impressively, with 95.97% of the variance in older adults' RT accounted for in the multilevel model (91.04% in a standard OLS analysis; 95.97% when adjusted for the number of predictors). The difference in fit between the 15-D and the general slowing model is not large (the difference in R^2 is 0.52% for the unadjusted estimate and 2.48% for the adjusted estimate), but it is highly significant, ΔLR χ^2 (28) = 731.76, p <.001. This, then, shows again that the general slowing model is both a powerful approximation of the data (explaining 96% of the variance is no mean feat), and blatantly imperfect: It falls statistically far short of providing a complete explanation. The equation for the single-line model is:

$$RT_{older} = -44 \ (12) + 1.40 \ (0.03) \ RT_{younger}.$$

This equation does not differ all that much from the equation derived from the (partially independent) data set examined in Chapter 2 ($RT_{older} = -52$ (26) ms + 1.44 (0.04) $RT_{younger}$), or from the one obtained in the very first published meta-analytic Brinley plot ($RT_{older} = -70 + 1.36 \ RT_{younger}$; Cerella et al., 1980). This convergence across different data sets strongly suggests that a straight line with an intercept of about –50 ms and a slope of around 1.4 captures age-related slowing across a variety of tasks pretty well. Thus, if a researcher or designer needs a quick estimate of older adults' expected latency in a task for which latency of younger adults is known, this would be the equation to use.

One corollary of this finding is that it should be quite easy to reduce the number of dimensions from 15 to, say, 3 or 4, without giving up too much detail compared with the full model. The next sections provide such reductions.

5.2. Reduced-dimensionality Accounts of Age-related Slowing in Elementary Processes

Starting from the overall Brinley plot of all 15 tasks, one could imagine any number of strategies to reduce the data's dimensionality. I tried four. The first approach is to simply reproduce the Card et al. Model Human Processor groupings, checking for differential age-related effects in the sensory cycle time, the motor cycle time, and the cognitive cycle time. For the second model, I eyeballed the Brinley plot for functions that showed overlap in location (the spatial-configuration model). The third approach was a more formal cluster analysis, grouping statistically identical lines together and iterating this process until no further clustering was possible. The final strategy based its identification of the basic dimensions on a factor-analysis of the brain structures that supposedly underlie the 15 tasks (the anatomy-driven model). I'll describe each model in turn and then present a few conclusions, including one attempt at a convergence or compromise model.

5.2.1. The Model Human Processor Model

Card et al.'s original formulation makes a main distinction between sensory processes, motor processes, and cognitive processes, and posits a distinct cycle time for each. The analyses above have shown that assigning a single cycling time to each of those processors would be quite naïve. One could, however, still imagine that the effects of age fall along these broad fault lines. To test this, I set up a model in which I grouped fixation duration, flicker fusion threshold, and gap detection threshold into a sensory factor; tapping time and movement time in a motor factor; and memory scanning, subitizing, counting, mental rotation, feature visual search, conjunction visual search, simple reaction time, choice reaction time, P300, and lexical decision times into a cognitive factor. The initial model fit the data quite well, with 95.97% the variance accounted for (95.95% when adjusted for the number of predictors), but it could be pruned at no cost to fit, ΔLR χ^2 (2) = 2.33, by collapsing the age-related effects on the motor processor with the age-related effects on the cognitive processor, with 95.98% of the variance accounted for (95.97% when adjusted for the number of predictors). This model then explains 2.48 % less of the variance than the full 15-dimensional model (adjusted for the number of predictors), and offers just the slightest of increments compared with the single-line model (0.04% of the variance). Fit was reliably lower than that of the full model, ΔLR χ^2 (26) = 721.51, but better than that of the single-line model, ΔLR χ^2 (2) = 10.25.

The end result of this analysis is a set of two equations, one describing age-related effects on sensory processing, the other on cognitive and motor processing. Figure 5.5 shows the data as two clouds along with the multilevel regression lines (zooming in on the 0~2,000 range, for presentational clarity). The sensory dimension yields only a small age-related effect, with a slope that is statistically not distinguishable from 1 and an intercept that is statistically not distinguishable from zero:

$$RT_{older} = 15\ (23) + 1.08\ (0.11)\ RT_{younger}.$$

The cognitive/motor dimension yields significant age-related effects in both intercept and slope:

$$RT_{older} = -57\ (27) + 1.43\ (0.11)\ RT_{younger}.$$

5.2.2. The Spatial-configuration Model

The second reduced-dimensionality model is based on careful eyeballing of the spatial layout of the different tasks in the Brinley plot, augmented by information from the unconstrained estimates for slopes and intercepts for each of the tasks. (The unconstrained estimates were used because these contain the largest amount of information.) Figure 5.6 represents the four dimensions that resulted from this admittedly subjective exercise.

A first dimension is comprised of fixation duration, flicker fusion, gap detection, and P300. This dimension yields only a small age-related effect, with a slope that is statistically not distinguishable from 1:

$$RT_{older} = 32\ (13) + 1.05\ (0.04)\ RT_{younger}.$$

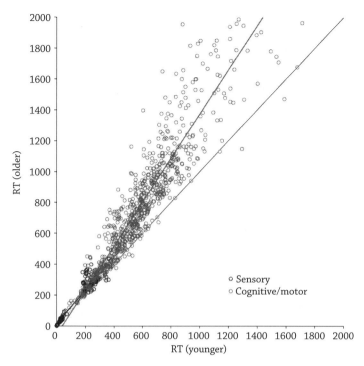

Figure 5.5 Data reduction model using Card et al.'s Human Information Processor. Two factors are distinguished, sensory and cognitive/motor, explaining 96% of the variance. All data points within the 0~2,000 range are plotted, as well as the multilevel regression lines for each of the factors.

The second dimension includes counting and tapping, as well as single and choice reaction time, with a small but significant age-related effect:

$$RT_{older} = 40\ (17) + 1.13\ (0.04)\ RT_{younger}.$$

The third dimension yields a larger age-related effect, and consists of memory search and lexical decision:

$$RT_{older} = 30\ (42) + 1.29\ (0.07)\ RT_{younger}.$$

Finally, the fourth dimension yields a much larger age-related effect. It consists of subitizing, movement time, feature and conjunction visual search, and mental rotation:

$$RT_{older} = -274\ (21) + 1.83\ (0.04)\ RT_{younger}.$$

One possible interpretation of the pattern is as follows: The first dimension arguably consists of low-level sensory tasks, the second of rhythm production and reaction time, the third of tasks operating on linguistic stimuli, and the fourth of tasks of spatial processing—if one considers subitizing a spatial task, as some have (e.g., Trick &

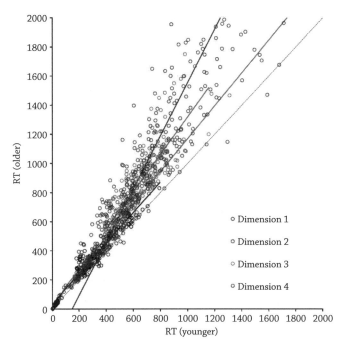

Figure 5.6 Data reduction model guided by the spatial layout of the data. Four dimensions are distinguished (Dimension 1: fixation duration, flicker fusion, gap detection, and P300; Dimension 2: counting, tapping, single, and choice RT; Dimension 3: memory search and lexical decision; Dimension 4: subitizing, movement time, feature and conjunction visual search, and mental rotation), explaining 98% of the variance. All data points within the 0~2,000 range are plotted, as well as the multilevel regression lines for each of the factors. See plate section for color version of this figure.

Pylyshyn, 1993). This four-pronged model explains 97.54% of the variance (97.52% adjusted), 1.55% (adjusted) more than the single-line model and 0.93% (adjusted) less than the full model. The differences in model fit are significant in both directions: The spatial configuration model fits reliably less well than the full model, ΔLR χ^2 (22) = 238.08, but better than the single-line model, ΔLR χ^2 (8) = 493.67. Like the single-line model, then, this model can serve as useful shorthand for the age-related effects, but it does not capture the full complexity of the data.

There is a glass-half-full, glass-half-empty feeling to this analysis: Although the dimensions are separable, and the model fits less well than the full-dimensional model, the reader can also, I hope, appreciate from the graph that there is considerable overlap in the data clouds for the different dimensions, to the point where it is nearly impossible to predict any given point's membership to any given dimension.

5.2.3. The Cluster Analysis model

The regression analyses in this chapter demonstrated that there are certain equivalences in the age-related effects (e.g., SRT = CRT, subitizing = counting, etc.) that could be useful in reducing the data set's complexity. I conducted a more formal cluster analysis by comparing each of the 15 regression lines with each of the other 14. This analysis led to the identification of seven distinct clusters, that is, seven groupings within which all members shared the same age-related effect (two of the seven were singletons). This exercise was repeated with the regression lines for clusters as the unit until no further clusterings were obtained. This exercise proved relatively fruitless: Only two of the clusters combined.

The end result is then a set of six regression lines. This set only partially overlapped with the groupings derived from the spatial-configuration analysis. Fit was excellent, with 97.98% of the variance explained (97.96% when adjusted for the number of predictors). It is perhaps not surprising that this model fits somewhat better (numerically; a formal test is not possible) than the spatial-configuration model, given that it was explicitly guided by statistical analysis aimed at creating distinct clusters. Fit was still reliably lower than that of the full model, $\Delta LR \ \chi^2 \ (18) = 65.56$, but much better than that of the single-line model, $\Delta LR \ \chi^2 \ (10) = 666.195$. The lower part of Figure 5.7 again shows considerable overlap in the data clouds. I order the dimensions here by increasing size of the Brinley slope.

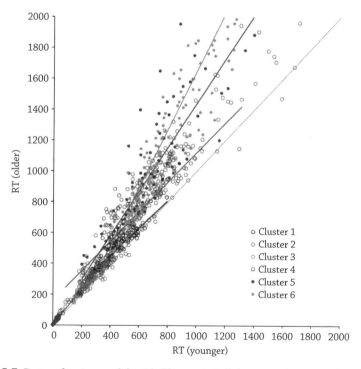

Figure 5.7 Data reduction model guided by statistical cluster analysis. Six clusters are distinguished (Cluster 1: P300; Cluster 2: counting, subitizing, lexical decision, and choice reaction time; Cluster 3: fixation duration; Cluster 4: tapping rate, flicker fusion threshold, gap detection threshold, and simple reaction time; Cluster 5: memory scanning and movement time; Cluster 6: feature search, conjunction search, and mental rotation), explaining 98% of the variance. All data points within the 0~2,000 range are plotted, as well as the multilevel regression lines for each of the factors. See plate section for color version of this figure.

The first cluster is comprised of a single task, P300:

$$RT_{older} = 103 \ (32) + 0.88 \ (0.08) \ RT_{younger}.$$

The second cluster consists of counting, subitizing, lexical decision, and choice reaction time:

$$RT_{older} = 161 \ (17) + 0.96 \ (0.04) \ RT_{younger}.$$

The third is again a single task, fixation duration:

$$RT_{older} = 47 \ (41) + 0.99 \ (0.15) \ RT_{younger}.$$

The fourth cluster contains tapping rate, flicker fusion threshold, gap detection threshold, and simple reaction time:

$$RT_{older} = 2 \ (20) + 1.16 \ (0.05) \ RT_{younger}.$$

The fifth cluster consists of memory scanning and movement time:

$$RT_{older} = 11 \ (34) + 1.43 \ (0.06) \ RT_{younger}.$$

The final cluster includes both types of visual search, as well as mental rotation:

$$RT_{older} = -240 \ (23) + 1.89 \ (0.03) \ RT_{younger}.$$

Here, the groupings are less intuitive than those for the first model, with the exception of the sixth dimension, which is all comprised of spatial tasks. One potential added generality is that the first three clusters all have slopes statistically equal to one, but different intercepts; the other three clusters all have slopes larger than one, and those are all are distinct from one another. Interpreting this result within the Cerella (Cerella et al., 1980) framework outlined in Chapter 1, one could suggest that there is no "central" or "computational" slowing in the first three clusters, but merely different degrees of "peripheral," or sensorimotor slowing; the final three clusters show distinct degrees of slowing in central processing.

5.2.4. The Anatomy-driven Model

The fourth model I fitted to the data aimed for anatomical plausibility. Cognitive tasks obviously have their substrate in the brain; my reasoning was that age-related effects might perhaps follow the furcations observed in the substrate. To trace these furcations, I first performed a crude meta-analysis on the substrate of each of the 15 different tasks, employing factor analysis to reduce the number of dimensions in the brain data to a manageable level.

The meta-analysis was performed with the help of PubBrain (*pubbrain.org*), a database that collects abstracts of neuroscience articles. PubBrain notes both the tasks used in these papers, as well as the brain regions associated with them. Typing in a search term (e.g., "simple reaction time") then yields a heat map (and a text file) representing the number of times each of 38 prespecified brain regions is mentioned in an abstract that contains the search term. This is an admittedly crude system—association of a task with a brain region within the context of an abstract is not the same thing as a brain region univocally being identified as the substrate of that task—but I would submit that the technique is sufficient for the present purpose. The 15 tasks, as well as the brain structures tapped by PubBrain, are shown in Table 5.1. (I used the search term "Sternberg task" instead of "memory scanning," "auditory gap" for "gap detection," and "saccade" for "fixation duration," because these seemed to yield more precise results. I kept the term "movement time" instead of "Fitts," because the latter generated almost no hits.)

In the next step, I entered the data from the heat map into an exploratory factor analysis (viz., principal component analysis with oblimin rotation). In this analysis, the tasks constitute the factors; the brain regions have loadings on these factors. (Another way to think of this is to consider the brain regions as the entities whose involvement, or lack thereof, contributes to the scores on each of these tasks—a not unreasonable assumption.) I extracted five factors. Cumulatively, these explained 94% of the total variance (39% for the first factor, 24% for the second, 15% for the third, 8% for the fourth, and 7% for the fifth; extracting a sixth would have added an additional 3%). All Eigen values for the first five factors were larger than 1; the sixth factor had an Eigen value of 0.46. The scree plot likewise suggested that five factors were sufficient. The loadings of the brain regions on these five factors are shown in Table 5.2; the correlation matrix of the five factors is reported in Table 5.3. Finally, Table 5.4 shows the component score coefficient matrix, that is, the loadings of the 15 tasks on the five factors.

It appears that the five factors track gross anatomical structure quite nicely. The first factor contains mostly frontal structures (the five highest loadings are for the precentral gyrus, the middle frontal gyrus, the inferior and superior frontal gyrus, and the supplementary motor cortex); the second consists mostly of parietal structures (the five highest loadings are for the superior parietal lobule, the precuneus cortex, the angular gyrus, the supramarginal gyrus, and the postcentral gyrus); the third consists mostly of occipital regions (the four highest loadings are for the cuneal cortex, the lingual gyrus, the occipital pole, and the lateral occipital cortex); the fourth mainly taps the brainstem (perhaps more as a conduit rather than an originating structure), with a small additional loading from the hippocampus; the fifth factor taps mainly temporal regions (the five highest loadings are for the inferior frontal gyrus, the middle temporal gyrus, the superior temporal gyrus, the temporal fusiform cortex, and the inferior temporal gyrus).

For the multilevel analysis, I constructed five task dimensions from these factors. To simplify the analysis, each task was classified into only one of the five factors; this was done on the basis of its strongest loading (indicated in boldface in Table 5.4). Fit of the model was excellent, with 97.64% of the variance explained, about as good as the fit of the spatial-configuration model (97.62% when adjusted for the number of predictors). Like both previous dimension-reduction models, the anatomical model fits reliably less well than the full model, ΔLR χ^2 (20) = 228.19, but better than the single-line model, ΔLR χ^2 (9) = 503.56.

Table 5.1 Heat map of brain regions associated with citations for the 15 tasks of interest, as retrieved from PubBrain.org. The number in each cell indicates the number of Abstracts that cite both the particular brain region and the particular task.

Brain region	Fixation duration	Flicker fusion	Gap detection	Tapping rate	Movement time	Memory scanning	Subitizing	Counting	Mental rotation	Feature visual search	Conjunction visual search	Simple reaction time	Choice reaction time	P300	Lexical decision
Amygdala	19	9	11	4	1,231	5	0	205	7	1	0	75	89	56	24
Angular gyrus	30	18	17	14	1,819	11	5	270	118	30	27	171	169	171	51
Brainstem	301	71	111	34	9,744	25	0	1,081	76	4	7	620	201	187	9
Caudate	27	14	12	16	4,168	11	0	449	25	1	4	201	282	80	34
Cerebellum	51	1	10	25	1,573	11	0	224	21	2	1	168	28	34	8
Cingulate gyrus	43	25	26	6	3,063	21	0	604	33	5	7	228	335	228	85
Cuneal cortex	39	127	17	5	1,469	8	1	238	38	48	25	241	122	109	51
Frontal medial cortex	31	21	13	33	3,255	19	1	324	69	16	9	368	448	270	86
Frontal orbital cortex	31	21	13	33	3,255	19	1	326	69	16	9	368	449	270	87
Frontal pole	32	21	13	33	3,258	19	1	324	69	16	9	369	449	272	86
Heschl's gyrus	28	20	56	11	1,204	12	2	274	33	14	7	165	124	211	106
Hippocampus	45	23	34	4	4,319	6	0	845	25	7	2	208	280	194	43
Inferior frontal gyrus	40	25	15	35	3,762	47	3	401	101	27	14	467	614	353	141
Inferior temporal gyrus	30	20	44	10	1,204	13	2	275	37	15	7	160	128	208	115

Table 5.1 (continued)

Brain region	Fixation duration	Flicker fusion	Gap detection	Tapping rate	Movement time	Memory scanning	Subitizing	Counting	Mental rotation	Feature visual search	Conjunction visual search	Simple reaction time	Choice reaction time	P300	Lexical decision
Insular cortex	12	8	9	5	929	2	0	184	13	2	0	61	72	50	26
Lateral occipital cortex	37	120	17	5	1,420	7	1	229	33	40	20	209	118	104	48
Lingual gyrus	39	127	17	5	1,465	8	1	236	41	48	25	240	120	108	54
Middle frontal gyrus	40	25	15	35	3,745	47	2	390	96	26	14	466	613	350	104
Middle temporal gyrus	28	20	44	10	1,200	13	2	278	34	15	7	156	126	209	124
Nucleus accumbens	14	8	9	4	1,412	0	0	194	7	1	0	63	96	40	21
Occipital pole	37	121	17	5	1,421	7	1	229	33	40	20	209	122	104	49
Opercular cortex	34	21	14	33	3,261	20	1	325	70	18	11	367	424	269	88
Pallidum	24	14	12	15	4,182	12	0	432	23	1	3	209	272	77	32
Parahippocampal gyrus	30	21	44	10	1,245	12	2	290	34	15	7	166	131	214	108
Planum temporale	28	20	44	10	1,195	12	2	273	33	14	7	156	124	209	107
Postcentral gyrus	30	18	18	15	1,889	11	5	270	115	29	26	176	167	175	48
Precentral gyrus	37	26	13	60	4,794	21	1	351	100	17	10	526	515	279	94
Precuneus cortex	30	19	18	14	1,833	13	5	270	120	30	27	171	172	176	55

(Continued)

Table 5.1 (continued)

Brain region	Fixation duration	Flicker fusion	Gap detection	Tapping rate	Movement time	Memory scanning	Subitizing	Counting	Mental rotation	Feature visual search	Conjunction visual search	Simple reaction time	Choice reaction time	P300	Lexical decision
Putamen	26	14	12	17	4,176	12	0	446	22	2	3	202	276	77	35
Subcallosal cortex	12	8	9	4	890	0	0	173	6	1	0	55	65	40	21
Superior frontal gyrus	40	25	15	35	3,742	46	2	389	98	24	15	459	609	351	106
Superior parietal lobule	30	18	17	14	1,831	11	5	268	128	31	30	169	170	171	48
Superior temporal gyrus	30	20	44	10	1,218	12	2	276	36	17	9	160	130	231	118
Supplementary motor cortex	32	21	13	42	3,500	22	1	333	74	16	9	386	438	268	89
Supramarginal gyrus	30	18	18	15	1,825	11	5	269	115	30	26	170	167	175	53
Temporal fusiform cortex	29	21	44	10	1,205	14	2	276	38	16	8	162	125	208	118
Temporal pole	28	20	44	10	1,195	12	2	274	33	14	7	155	127	207	107
Thalamus	35	89	10	9	2,758	3	0	351	11	3	1	193	125	70	7

Table 5.2 **Factor score matrix for the 38 brain regions on each of five factors derived from a principal component analysis on the data from Table 5.1.**

Brain region	Factor 1 "Frontal"	Factor 2 "Parietal"	Factor 3 "Occipital"	Factor 4 "Brainstem"	Factor 5 Temporal'
Amygdala	−1.00	−1.12	−0.83	−0.65	−0.86
Angular gyrus	−0.38	2.11	−0.13	−0.31	−0.38
Brainstem	1.31	−0.37	0.62	5.68	−1.81
Caudate	0.13	−0.98	−0.71	−0.02	−1.21
Cerebellum	−0.39	−0.85	−0.94	−0.49	−1.48
Cingulate gyrus	0.24	−0.89	−0.33	0.24	0.38
Cuneal cortex	−0.59	0.22	2.91	−0.50	−0.38
Frontal medial cortex	1.10	−0.07	−0.23	−0.20	0.29
Frontal orbital cortex	1.10	−0.07	−0.23	−0.19	0.31
Frontal pole	1.10	−0.07	−0.23	−0.19	0.30
Heschl's gyrus	−0.81	−0.16	−0.41	0.27	1.27
Hippocampus	0.00	−1.11	−0.46	0.71	−0.68
Inferior frontal gyrus	1.96	0.83	0.04	0.13	1.67
Inferior temporal gyrus	−0.76	−0.13	−0.39	0.13	1.33
Insular cortex	−1.08	−1.04	−0.85	−0.73	−0.88
Lateral occipital cortex	−0.67	−0.03	2.46	−0.51	−0.43
Lingual gyrus	−0.59	0.24	2.90	−0.50	−0.34
Middle frontal gyrus	2.03	0.59	0.12	0.05	1.08
Middle temporal gyrus	−0.79	−0.17	−0.38	0.14	1.48
Nucleus accumbens	−1.06	−1.11	−0.86	−0.70	−1.06
Occipital pole	−0.66	−0.04	2.47	−0.51	−0.41
Opercular cortex	1.07	0.02	−0.14	−0.19	0.33
Pallidum	0.12	−1.03	−0.71	−0.05	−1.21
Parahippocampal gyrus	−0.76	−0.16	−0.36	0.16	1.24
Planum temporale	−0.79	−0.17	−0.41	0.11	1.21
Postcentral gyrus	−0.35	2.05	−0.17	−0.29	−0.41
Precentral gyrus	2.13	0.18	−0.22	−0.07	−0.03
Precuneus cortex	−0.34	2.13	−0.12	−0.29	−0.29
Putamen	0.15	−1.03	−0.70	−0.05	−1.18

(Continued)

Table 5.2 (continued)

Brain region	Factor 1 "Frontal"	Factor 2 "Parietal"	Factor 3 "Occipital"	Factor 4 "Brainstem"	Factor 5 Temporal'
Subcallosal cortex	−1.17	−1.10	−0.86	−0.76	−0.99
Superior frontal gyrus	2.00	0.62	0.07	0.05	1.07
Superior parietal lobule	−0.35	2.31	−0.07	−0.33	−0.48
Superior temporal gyrus	−0.76	−0.05	−0.29	0.14	1.45
Supplementary motor cortex	1.33	−0.02	−0.28	−0.17	0.26
Supramarginal gyrus	−0.37	2.06	−0.15	−0.31	−0.33
Temporal fusiform cortex	−0.75	−0.09	−0.32	0.12	1.38
Temporal pole	−0.79	−0.17	−0.41	0.11	1.20
Thalamus	−0.54	−1.32	0.62	−0.02	−1.42

Figure 5.8 shows the model. The figure again shows considerable overlap in the data clouds. All five lines were, however, distinct. I tested them pair by pair: Collapsing any of two pairs of lines yielded a significant decrease in fit.

The first dimension, associated with the "brainstem" factor, is comprised of fixation duration, counting, gap detection, and movement time. It shows only a small age-related effect (its slope is not statistically different from 1, its intercept rather small):

$$RT_{older} = 46\ (19) + 1.07\ (0.04)\ RT_{younger}.$$

Table 5.3 **Correlation matrix of the five factors derived from the data in Table 5.2.**

	Factor 1 "Frontal"	Factor 2 "Parietal"	Factor 3 "Occipital"	Factor 4 "Brainstem"	Factor 5 Temporal'
Factor 1	1.00				
Factor 2	0.15	1.00			
Factor 3	−0.04	0.19	1.00		
Factor 4	0.29	−0.08	0.02	1.00	
Factor 5	0.15	0.24	−0.07	−0.11	1.00

Table 5.4 **Component score coefficient matrix for the factor analysis performed on the data in Table 5.2. The highest loading for each cognitive task is boldfaced.**

	Factor 1 "Frontal"	Factor 2 "Parietal"	Factor 3 "Occipital"	Factor 4 "Brainstem"	Factor 5 Temporal'
Fixation duration	0.04	0.06	0.06	**0.27**	−0.13
Flicker fusion	0.00	−0.12	**0.58**	0.02	−0.01
Gap detection	−0.16	0.02	−0.02	**0.44**	0.21
Tapping	**0.23**	0.02	−0.08	−0.06	−0.09
Movement time	0.15	−0.02	−0.02	**0.15**	−0.21
Memory scanning	0.16	0.00	0.01	0.01	**0.16**
Subitizing	−0.09	**0.37**	−0.16	0.05	0.06
Counting	0.03	−0.04	−0.02	**0.26**	−0.07
Mental rotation	0.09	**0.33**	−0.11	0.00	−0.11
Feature search	0.00	0.14	**0.38**	−0.06	0.08
Conjunction search	−0.01	**0.28**	0.18	−0.03	−0.08
Single RT	**0.20**	−0.04	0.13	0.05	−0.02
Choice RT	**0.26**	−0.05	−0.01	−0.14	0.00
P300	0.08	0.03	−0.02	0.05	**0.34**
Lexical decision	−0.04	−0.04	0.01	0.04	**0.57**

The second dimension, associated with the "temporal" factor, includes P300, memory search, and lexical decision. This dimension yields a moderate age effect:

$$RT_{older} = 6\ (25) + 1.24\ (0.05)\ RT_{younger}.$$

The third dimension, associated with the "frontal" factor, consists of tapping and single and choice reaction time. This dimension yields an intermediate age effect:

$$RT_{older} = -26\ (14) + 1.34\ (0.04)\ RT_{younger}.$$

The fourth dimension, associated with the "occipital" factor, consists of flicker fusion and feature visual search, showing a more pronounced age-related effect:

$$RT_{older} = -15\ (22) + 1.48\ (0.05)\ RT_{younger}.$$

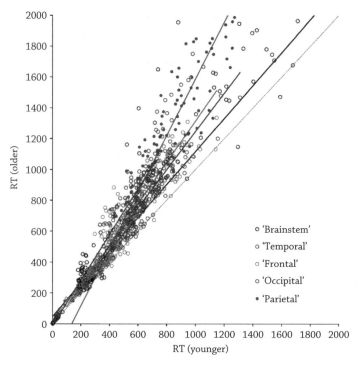

Figure 5.8 Data reduction model guided by the anatomical model derived from the data in Table 5.2. Five factors are distinguished ("Brainstem": fixation duration, counting, gap detection, and movement time; "temporal": P300, memory scanning, and lexical decision; "frontal": tapping, single RT, and choice RT; "occipital": flicker fusion threshold and feature visual search; "parietal": subitizing, conjunction visual search, and mental rotation), explaining 98% of the variance. All data points within the 0~2,000 range are plotted, as well as the multilevel regression lines for each of the factors. See plate section for color version of this figure.

Finally, the fifth dimension is associated with the "parietal" factor. It consists of subitizing, conjunction visual search, and mental rotation, and shows a large age-related effect:

$$RT_{older} = -253\ (23) + 1.84\ (0.04)\ RT_{younger}.$$

Clearly, then, observed age-related slowing differs across the tasks associated with the five main brain regions. Allow me to emphasize that this was not a foregone conclusion. I compiled a list of 15 tasks that seemed interesting to investigate, guided by the human-factors literature rather than the cognitive-aging literature. I then factor-analyzed the 15 tasks using a large body of neuroscience literature (most of it conducted on college-age adults) to find commonalities and differences in the substrate. The five factors describing the 15 tasks fell out along anatomical lines, its contributors delineating the main large-scale subdivisions in the cortex, plus the brainstem. Only in a last step did aging enter into the picture: Brinley intercepts and slopes were calculated for each of these five factors, and five distinct lines were found. Nothing in the previous steps of this exercise was likely to bias the results toward this conclusion. For instance, if general slowing were the correct hypothesis, a single line still could have emerged. Likewise, there is no reason to assume that the five task factors could not have collapsed into a smaller number of age-related effects.

5.2.5. Dimensionality-reduction Models: Empirical Conclusions

The four dimensionality-reduction exercises lead to three major conclusions.

First, a single-line model (often labeled the "general slowing" model) fits the data extremely well by any criterion (it explains 96% of the variance), but it also fits reliably less well than any of models with (I hope) reasonable furcations that I explored here. This implies that the general slowing model, tempting as it is and fitting as well as it does, also has been unequivocally falsified. It does not provide a full account of the data.

Second, a full (or almost full, 99% of the variance explained) account of the data needs to take all different tasks into account: Each of the reduced models tested explained less of the variance than the full 15-D model did.

Neither of these two conclusions is particularly novel or stunning, although I admit being surprised at how much explanatory power the general slowing model does hold, especially given the large and diverse array of tasks included in the present data set.

A third conclusion (only seemingly contradicting the second) is that reasonable carve-ups of Brinley space can be achieved at a relatively small (but significant) cost to fit. I provided and tested four alternative carve-ups here; many more are obviously possible. There really is no a priori reason to prefer one of the alternatives over any of the others. All four models explained a large and about equal amount of variance: The best-fitting model explained only 2% more of the variance than the worst-fitting model; taking out the worst-fitting model left the remaining three models within a 0.5% range of each other. Simple reasoning does not help either: There are good reasons to trust the rationale behind each of the four. This, in my mind, makes each of the reduced models equally defensible or indefensible. This is both good news and bad news—bad news for those who wish to see strong, univocal theory in this field, good news for those who favor empirical generalizations and prefer to work with malleable models or frameworks.

It is possible, however, to deduce some generalities from the models fitted here, particularly if we concentrate on the latter three.

One is that spatial tasks reliably separate from linguistic tasks, as I already concluded in Chapter 2 (e.g., Lima et al., 1991). Spatial tasks are represented in the current sample by mental rotation, the two types of visual search, and possibly by subitizing and/or movement time. In all three analyses, these tasks yielded (or tended to yield) the larger of the age-related effects, with Brinley slopes around 1.6 to 1.8. The one linguistic task—lexical decision—showed a markedly smaller age effect, yielding a Brinley slope between 1.0 and 1.3. Interestingly, the anatomical model notes a further bifurcation within spatial tasks. First, spatial tasks that mainly originate in occipital structures—flicker fusion and feature visual search—show a smaller age-related effect (Brinley slope of 1.5) than tasks mainly tapping parietal structures—subitizing, conjunction visual search, and mental rotation (Brinley slope of 1.8). In (neuro)psychological terms, one generality here might be that tasks that primarily tap lower-level spatial processes (as they occur in the occipital regions) show smaller age-related differences than spatial tasks that requite integration of sensory information and active manipulation of this information (a task often ascribed to parietal structures; the so-called dorsal stream of vision; Mishkin & Ungerleider, 1982). These "smaller" age-related slowing factors for more passive spatial tasks are still, however, larger than those for all other nonspatial tasks.

It might be tempting to ascribe the dissociation between spatial and lexical decision tasks at least partially to brain asymmetry—perhaps aging spares the left, "lingual" hemisphere more than the right, "spatial" hemisphere. Is this so? The number of relevant studies is very small—I found four. In concordance with the right hemi-aging model (the term is likely to have been coined by Dolcos, Rice, & Cabeza, 2002), Li, Moore, Tyner, and Hu (2009) found that older adults' functional connectivity as measured in the resting state was more reduced in the right than the left hemisphere. One other study, however, using a different dependent measure, found the exact opposite pattern: Age differences in white matter abnormalities were more pronounced in the left than in the right hemisphere (Pfefferbaum, Adalsteinsson, & Sullivan, 2005). Raz et al. (2005), in a volumetric study, found no age differences in hemispheric asymmetry; neither did Leenders et al. (1990) in a study looking at a small host of perfusion measures. This pattern is what one would expect if there were no differential hemi-aging of the brain: Mostly null results, and the remaining results split evenly over the two possibilities. Therefore, the prudent course of action would be to look for an alternative explanation for the lexical-spatial dissociation.

The literature also often posits that peripheral, sensorimotor tasks show smaller age differences than other, more "cognitive" or "central" tasks. (This assertion has its roots in Cerella et al., 1980.) In Chapter 4, I logged single reaction times, choice reaction times, saccadic reaction times, digit-digit reaction times, vocal reaction times, initiation time for single reaction times, preparation times for target detection, attentional capture, and mouse movement times under this rubric. The end conclusion was that the sensorimotor tasks showed smaller age-related effects than the spatial tasks, larger effects than the linguistic tasks, and the same age-related slowing factor as the unclassified cognitive tasks.

The analyses in the current chapter do not lead to equivocal results. The former three models do seem to offer some convergence. In the Model Human Processor and the spatial configuration models, the two motor tasks (tapping rate and movement time) showed consistently larger age-related effects than any of the perceptual tasks (fixation duration, flicker fusion threshold, and gap detection threshold). In the cluster analysis, movement time but not tapping rate showed a larger effect than the perceptual tasks; perceptual tasks tended to show the smallest age-related effects, with Brinley slopes between 1.0 and 1.2. One possible and admittedly post hoc interpretation of this pattern is that sensorimotor tasks show small age-related effects when there is no decision component involved; age differences increase when decisions need to be made. Flicker fusion, gap detection, tapping, and even eye movements toward a target can be argued to be rather involuntary tasks, happening outside conscious control, and with no need for actual decisions. These tasks show small age-related effects. Simple and choice reaction time seem to both involve the need to make at least a conscious decision (presence/absence, and location1/location2, respectively) and tend to show larger age-related effects; movement time—another task that yields larger age-related effects—includes making a decision about the trajectory needed to hit the target. The decision component would then drive age-related differences in these tasks into "cognitive" territory, with the associated larger age-related effects. (Note that this schematic necessitates a rather minimal definition of decision-making, different from the one I used in Chapter 4, which involved a selection among alternatives.)

The situation is more complicated, however, when one considers the anatomy-driven model. Although two of the sensory tasks (fixation duration and gap detection) are included in a factor that shows a very modest age-related slowing factor (a Brinley slope of 1.1, an intercept of about 46 ms), the third (flicker fusion) is included in a factor with a reliably larger age-related effect (Brinley slope of about 1.5). For the motor processes, we find a flip in the estimated age-related effects: Movement time is now included in the "brainstem" factor, which shows a Brinley slope of 1.1; tapping is included in the "frontal" factor, with a slope of 1.3, and it clusters with both types of reaction time tasks. The anatomy-driven model has the advantage that it comes with its own inbuilt explanation of the discrepancy: Sensorimotor tasks with different slowing factors originate from parts of the substrate that show differential age-related slowing. This isn't entirely circular reasoning, as I noted above, because the task factors were derived without any input about the degree of their age-sensitivity. The anatomy-driven model seemingly reinforces the psychological point made above: When sensorimotor tasks do not involve the type of decision making typically associated with frontal-lobe functioning, age differences are small; when they do (single RT, choice RT) age differences are larger. Additionally, when sensorimotor tasks originate in brain regions that are associated with a particular slowing factor, they tend to show that slowing factor—tapping rate ("frontal") and flicker fusion ("parietal") being cases in point.

5.2.6. Dimensionality-reduction Models and the Promise of a Structural, Brain-based Explanation

Although all four dimensionality-reduction models explain the data about equally well, the anatomy-driven model seems particularly intriguing, precisely for the reason mentioned in the previous paragraph: It comes with a plausible built-in explanatory mechanism—changes in brain structure, brain efficiency, or both. Some satisfaction can be found in the idea that age-related effects seemingly coincide with gross brain anatomy. Of course, we still run the risk of tautology: It is one thing to state that age-related slowing effects originate in the brain (and, again, where else would they originate?); it is another to understand what actually drives the age-related slowing effects in the different brain structures. That additional step toward true explanation needs to be taken. Here, I speculatively examine two types of hypotheses—one tied to age-related differences in structural brain integrity (most notably: volume changes with age), the other tied to age-related differences in cerebral blood flow.

5.2.6.1. Differential Age-related Slowing and Differences in Structural Brain Integrity

One possibility is that the differential age-related slowing factors for tasks originating in different brain regions indicate structural differences in the integrity of gray matter, white matter, or both. If this were the case, we would expect a strong correlation between the age-related slowing effects observed in our data and age-related differences in volume or integrity in the specific brain structures underlying them— brain structures that are more vulnerable to aging should yield larger slowing factors in the tasks associated with them. The available evidence is still relatively sparse, but not very encouraging. Raz (2004) provides perhaps the largest meta-analytic overview of volumetric brain aging data. Table 5.5 reproduces his data, that is, the average

Table 5.5 **Review of the literature on region-specific age-related changes in cerebral volume and cerebral blood flow. The aim is to compare the rank ordering of changes to the Brinley slopes obtained in this chapter, also included in the table. Voluminometric data do not track the Brinley slopes well; regional blood flow seems to offer a closer match to the data.**

	Dependent measure	Temporal lobe	Frontal lobe	Occipital lobe	Parietal lobe
Brinley slope (Section 3.6.2.4)	*Brinley slope*	1.24	1.34	1.48	1.84
Meta-analytic data on regional volume					
Cross-sectional gray matter volume (Raz, 2005)	Age-volume correlation	−0.37	−0.56	−0.19	−0.20
Cross-sectional white matter volume (Raz, 2005)	Age-volume correlation	(NA)	−0.36	(NA)	−0.24
Longitudinal (Raz, 2005)	Yearly % volume change	−0.49	−1.11	−0.27	−0.81
Primary data on regional blood flow					
Akiyama (1997)	Age-perfusion correlation	−0.32	−0.30	−0.38	−0.49
Chen et al. (2011)	Age-perfusion correlation	−0.71	−0.84	−0.56	−1.04
Leenders et al. (1990), cerebral blood flow	Age-perfusion correlation	−0.55	−0.52	−0.27	−0.11
Leenders et al. (1990), oxygen metabolic rate	Age-perfusion correlation	−0.22	−0.54	−0.20	−0.22
Leenders et al. (1990), oxygen extraction fraction	Age-perfusion correlation	0.27	0.21	0.28	0.11
Leenders et al. (1990), cerebral blood volume	Age-perfusion correlation	0.34	−0.43	−0.39	−0.26

correlation between age and volume in gray and white matter for the four main brain lobes, averaged across eight cross-sectional studies, as well as the yearly percent volume change in these four lobes obtained from the three longitudinal studies that investigated all four.

The table shows that the observed age-related slowing effects do not track the volumetric data very well. The Brinley slopes are ordered, from smaller to larger age-related effects, as follows: temporal-frontal-occipital-parietal; the cross-sectional volumetric data are ordered, from smaller to larger age-related effects: occipital-parietal-temporal-frontal for gray matter, and parietal-occipital-temporal-frontal for total volume; the longitudinal data are ordered: occipital-temporal-parietal-frontal. (The brain data roughly follow a pattern that is often described as "last in, first out," that is, brain regions that mature last during development tend to decline first during aging; Raz, 2000; Kochunov et al., 2007.) The correlation between the Brinley slopes and the cross-sectional age-related volumetric decline (four data pairs) is large and in the opposite direction as would be predicted from a volumetric theory, $r = .61$. (The correlation should be negative: Larger Brinley slopes should be associated with larger negative age-colume correlations.) The correlation between Brinley slopes and yearly longitudinal change (four data pairs) is in the expected direction, but small: $-.11$.

The situation is not better when brain volume is considered as a mediator between age and speed of processing in individual studies. Salthouse (2011b) assessed the literature; seven of the papers in his review (Brickman et al., 2006; Chee et al., 2009; Chen et al., 2010, Muller-Oehring et al., 2007; Rabbitt et al., 2006; Tisserand et al., 2000; and Walhovd & Fjell, 2007) measured volume of white or gray matter or both in different regions of interest in subjects of different adult ages, and included one or the other aspect of processing speed as the dependent variable. (One later study, Kerchner et al., 2012, reported an absence of significant mediation between age and perceptual speed through white matter volume, but did not allow for the calculation of the percentage of age-related variance explained.) Based on the correlations provided, I calculated that, on average (and averaging within study first), the volumetric data explain 27% of the age-related variance in the speed measures. This is a respectable number, but (regional) brain volume is clearly not the only determinant of speed of processing.

The pattern does not change for more specific measures of conductivity or connectivity. For instance, in a recent study, Davis et al. (2009) applied diffusion tensor imaging (DTI) to examine white matter tracts in younger and older adults. The assumption is that intact white matter tracts expedite information transfer; age-related decline in white matter integrity would then slow down information transfer. Davis et al. applied tractography analysis to the data, allowing them to examine the intactness of very specific fiber tracts. In addition, the authors were interested in long white matter tracts, that is, tracts spanning across cortical lobes rather than staying within a lobe or region of interest. The main finding of this study was a posterior-to-anterior gradient in integrity within lobes: White matter deficits increased gradually from occipital to frontal cortex. This was, however, only true for fiber tracts traversing the parietal cortex, not for those traversing the temporal lobe. Davis et al. found particular age-sensitivity for radial diffusion, less so for axial diffusivity, indicating that aging is associated with myelodegeneration, that is, deterioration of the myelin sheath around the neural axons, which then leads to slower and/or noisier transmission of the neural signal (e.g., Song et al., 2002). Davis et al. also looked at correlations between white matter measures and cognitive performance. Curiously, significant correlations between radial diffusivity and performance were only obtained for measures of episodic and working memory, but not for the two elementary tasks that were included— movement time and reaction time—nor for the Rapid Visual Information Processing subtest of the CANTAB.

Similar results were obtained by Charlton et al. (2006), and Ryan et al. (2011), who found that DTI parameters did not correlate with executive functioning and processing speed (at least for non-APOE ε4 carriers; Ryan et al.; APOE ε4 is an allele that is associated with increased risk for, among others, Alzheimer's disease), although it correlated with working memory performance (Charlton et al.) and episodic memory performance (Ryan et al.). Cook et al. (2002) did find a white matter hyperintensity-speed correlation, but it did not mediate much of the age-related variance (viz., 13%). Three other studies, in contrast, obtained strong evidence for mediation of age-related differences in processing speed through white matter abnormalities. Ystad et al. (2009), found strong correlations within a group of older adults between integrity in specific white matter tracts (all originating in the thalamus or putamen) and measures of visual processing speed (color naming) and executive functioning, but no correlation with memory performance. (This study did not statistically control for age or APOE ε4 status when investigating these correlations.) Rabbitt et al. (2007; the raw correlations were reported in Salthouse, 2011b) found, within a group of older adults, that white matter lesions were a strong mediator of age-related differences in measures of perceptual speed and visual search (64% of age-related variance accounted for). Finally, Kerchner et al. (2012) found that all of the age-related variance in perceptual speed (but not episodic memory) within a group of older adults was accounted for by white matter integrity (their paper did not provide sufficient detail to allow for the computation of the actual percent of age-related variance accounted for). Other studies report significant correlations between different measures of white matter integrity and speed-of-processing, but do not allow for an assessment of the meditational effect (e.g., Bendlin et al., 2010). One study, Sullivan, Rohlfing, and Pfefferbaum (2010), reports independent contributions of age and white matter integrity on measures of perceptual speed, again without enough information to calculate possible mediation effects.

Combined over these studies, it seems that there is modest evidence that white matter abnormalities associated with age are correlated with declines in processing speed. The findings run from zero to 64% (and potentially 100%, Kerchner et al.) mediation, suggesting that the white matter abnormalities hypothesis does hold some explanatory power, but that white matter abnormalities are unlikely to be the only determinant.

One more possibility to connect the differential Brinley slopes to age-related differences in brain integrity considers not the type of processing or the specific area of cortex, but the length of the pathway the signal has to traverse. If one assumes that in old age the conductivity of a neural signal through brain tissue is slowed by a fixed proportion, differential age-related slowing effects might reflect the length of processing pathways rather than the specific age-related differences in the brain regions associated with most of the task processing (a proposal perhaps first formulated by Cerella

& Hale, 1994). For instance, one main vision pathway in the brain goes from occipital structures to parietal structures (the dorsal stream); if processing demands allow for an early output to the motor cortex, that is, from the occipital cortex rather than the parietal cortex, one might expect that, all else being equal, age differences would be smaller than if processing continues along the pathway to the parietal cortex. This proposal indeed appears to have merit: "Occipital" spatial tasks (flicker fusion, feature visual search) yield smaller age effects than "parietal" spatial tasks (mental rotation, conjunction visual search). Likewise, processing that can be output from early sensorimotor structures (fixation duration, counting, gap detection, movement time) lead to smaller age differences than sensorimotor processes that require additional involvement from the frontal cortex because of the additional decision-making component (SRT, CRT, tapping). This explanation seems still quite a bit more speculative than the volumetric or white-matter-integrity based explanations, and a more principled investigation into the merits of the path-length argument would be very welcome.

5.2.6.2. *Differential Age-related Slowing and Differences in Cerebral Blood Flow: The Oxygenation Hypothesis*

An alternative explanation for the differential Brinley slopes is that they reflect not the anatomical integrity of the substrate, but differential vascular (or other oxygenation-related) effects in the underlying brain structures. One relevant measure is regional cerebral blood flow. Cerebral blood flow is determined by a number of factors, including the state of dilation of the blood vessels and cerebral perfusion pressure, which is a function of both the body's blood pressure and intracranial pressure. Cerebral blood flow is directly coupled to cerebral metabolic oxygen consumption (e.g., Hoge, Atkinson, Gill, Crelier, Marrett, & Pike, 1999; Uludag et al., 2004), and this provides an obvious plausible reason for its connection to cognition. There is some evidence that regional cerebral blood flow and regional brain atrophy (in either gray or white matter volume, or both) are independent of each other (e.g., Akiyama et al., 1997; Chen, Rosas, & Salat, 2011), suggesting that my quest here will not simply duplicate the conclusions I reached above concerning the (non-)link between Brinley slopes and structural differences.

I was able to find three studies that compared cerebral blood flow in younger and older adults over both the whole brain and at a scale small enough to be useful for deriving correlations with the Brinley slopes derived in this chapter. The results are summarized in Table 5.5. I describe the studies here in some detail, to highlight convergence and divergence in methods and dependent variables.

Leenders et al. (1990) obtained PET scans from 34 subjects between the ages of 22 and 89. Three planes were scanned, 2, 4 and 6 cm, respectively, above the orbitomeatal line, using a steady-state inhalation technique with oxygen-15 as the tracer. (By today's standards, and even by 1990s standards, as the authors admit, these are low-resolution data.) The scans were then processed to yield four different measures: blood flow, oxygen metabolic rate, oxygen extraction, and blood volume. For regional blood flow and oxygen extraction, the correlations with age follow largely the same pattern as those from the volumetric data described above, resulting in a positive correlation between Brinley slopes and the blood parameters (remember that a negative correlation would be expected if slopes and oxygenation were causally related). The regional oxygen extraction ratio and cerebral blood volume parameters do, however, correlate negatively with the Brinley slopes. The average correlation over the four dependent measures is still positive, but small, $r = .14$.

In the second study, Akiyama et al. (1997) examined 79 individuals between the ages of 22 and 89. Computed tomography (CT) scans were used to provide measures of cerebral atrophy, tissue density, and cerebral perfusion (a proxy for blood flow). One important finding was that perfusion data and density data diverged. The correlations between age and tissue density were ordered largely as they appear in the Raz (2004) volumetric meta-analysis: The frontal cortex shows the larger effect ($r = -.31$), occipital cortex the smallest effect ($r = .10$, ns), with the temporal cortex situated in-between ($r = -.25$); an exception to the pattern was the parietal cortex, which showed larger relative effects than usual ($r = -.32$). For perfusion, the ordering, from larger to smaller effect, was: parietal, occipital, temporal, and frontal. The second important finding emerges from the latter ordering: There is a strong correlation in the expected direction between this set of correlations and the Brinley slopes found in the anatomy-driven model (four data points), $r = -.97$.

The third and final study (Chen et al., 2011) allows for a more stringent test. In this study, 11 younger and 37 older adults were scanned. An interesting feature of this data set is that blood flow data were reported at the level of cortical parcellations, rather than at the level of brain lobes—the level at which PubBrain (from which I derived the anatomy-driven model) aggregates its data. From this study, then, it is possible to derive effect sizes for the effect of age on perfusion in each of the four brain factors I derived above, now using perfusion measures for each of the cortical parcellations. The correlation between the effect of age on regional blood flow and the Brinley slopes is $-.65$.

Thus, two out of three studies show the expected negative correlation between regional blood flow and regional Brinley slope (and in both cases, the correlation is strongly negative); in the one divergent study, the size and direction of the correlation depends on the measure; this study is also relatively dated in its methods. I would cautiously conclude that there is some evidence for a blood flow/oxygenation hypothesis, although it could admittedly be stronger.

The oxygenation hypothesis gets some additional support from cognitive aging studies that show a rather strong relationship between cognitive performance and aerobic fitness, with increased blood flow as the likely mediator mechanism (for an excellent review, see Hillman, Erickson, & Kramer, 2008). Note that this evidence is situated at the between-subject or within-subject level rather than at the brain-region level. That is, the evidence shows that subjects with higher blood flow do better cognitively, rather than showing that (within-subject) regions that show higher blood flow show better cognitive performance. It isn't clear if this change in level of analysis makes a difference.

5.2.6.3. Brinley Slopes and the Brain: Conclusion

Although the anatomically derived model is quite seductive, the current state of knowledge about differential aging in the brain and differential effects of aging on cognition does not suggest as strong a convergence as one would intuitively assume. More specifically, both volumetric and connectivity data turn out to be quite discouraging with regard to an explanation of Brinley slopes. First, the deterioration in both volume and connectivity (basically: worse from the back of the brain to the front) does not map onto the relative slowing effects observed in tasks typically associated with these different regions. Second, intriguing bits of the brain-behavior puzzle are missing. For instance, it has not been unequivocally established that white matter integrity is essential for high performance on the elementary tasks considered in the present chapter (or even, perhaps, for the executive control tasks considered in the next chapter). At least in the present state of scientific affairs, it seems rather unlikely that the differential age-related slowing observed in the elementary tasks included in the anatomy-driven model are caused by differential structural changes in gray matter within the lobes of the brain per se. (I feel it is still too soon for a full verdict on white matter changes—the effect appears to be present, but the available data suggest it is also relatively modest.) Other mechanisms, such as path length, look more promising, but relevant data are simply lacking. Finally, an explanation in terms of blood flow and/or oxygenation does receive some support from the literature, but the support is not unequivocal, and the differential effects of regional blood flow on different aspects of sensorimotor and cognitive processing have largely gone uninvestigated.

5.3. Age-related Slowing in Elementary Tasks: Conclusions and Outlook

The major question in this chapter concerned the dimensionality of the processing-speed data gathered in Chapter 4. Is it possible to reduce the dimensionality of the data from the number of tasks and processes (15 in total) to a more manageable number? I tested a few models that seemed reasonable to me—a single-line model, the model suggested by the Model Human Processor, a model driven by the geography in Brinley space, a model driven by cluster analysis, and a model driven by anatomical considerations. The bottom-line is that although predictability as measured by proportion of variance explained suffers from such reductions, the drop in predictability is not catastrophic at all. The largest drop, obviously, is from a full 15-dimensional model to a single-line model—from 98.45% to 95.97%, or a drop of 2.48%. Empirically, the end result of even the simplest model is quite satisfying: No researcher who can explain 95% of the relevant variance or more has any reason to complain.

For those interested in description, the bigger message is that the single-line, or "general slowing," model—although explicitly falsified—still captures the data exceedingly well, certainly given that the tasks included here span a wide range of the spectrum of response time tasks. Likewise, the Model Human Processor, boiled down here to merely two age-related effects, one for sensory processing, the other for motor and cognitive processing, falsified as it is, still provides an excellent description of the data. One corollary of this result is that either or both of these models would work well as a baseline, that is, a null hypothesis, for researchers investigating age-related dissociations or interactions. A model for age-related differences would then be interesting only if it cannot be reduced to a model that presupposes either a general effect (a single line), or a dissociation between sensory processing and motor/cognitive processing. The former case is in principle (Faust et al., 1999) easy to test; for the latter, a more elaborate research design is needed, with appropriate control conditions to capture the perceptual and cognitive/motor components of the task.

Turning to the slightly higher-dimensional models, the end conclusion must be that "Everybody has won and all must have prizes" (Carroll, 1865). All four models, although reliably less precise than the 15-D model, all also fit reliably better than the single-line model. Moreover, they all explain just about the same amount of variance. The conclusion then appears to be that any reasonable carve-up of the data will work, a conclusion that is both empirically reassuring and empirically and theoretically vexing. Can we derive further, deeper truth from these four models?

Examining the four models more closely, it does appear that some general conclusions emerge. More specifically, I noted three generalities that fit most, but not all of the models. The goal of these generalities is to provide predictability for new tasks; it is not to replace the existing set of 30 parameters for the tasks and processes examined here. For instance, if a researcher is interested in predicting what would be the minimum size of icons on a computer tablet such that people can navigate between them at a specified rate, Fitts's law and its parameters (as estimated by Card et al., or as estimated here) will help her build a model for younger adults, and the movement time Brinley equation will help her transform this model for older adults; alternatively, she can rely directly on the parameters for older adults extracted here. If the task is new, however, some guideline might be helpful in deciding what equation to apply.

Here are the three generalities that, I hope, could build a consensus model:

1. Spatial tasks yield larger age-related effects than linguistic tasks and, more generally, tasks involving manipulations of lexical items (such as memory search) as well.
2. Within spatial tasks, lower-level or "early" tasks, likely involving occipital structures (such as flicker fusion threshold and feature visual search), generally yield smaller age-related effects than more integrative, "later" spatial tasks, likely driven more by parietal structures (such as subitizing, conjunction visual search, and mental rotation).
3. When no decision component is involved, sensorimotor tasks yield small or no age-related effects; when a decision component is involved, a more moderate age-related slowing factor is observed (flicker fusion threshold and tapping rate vs. movement time, simple RT, and choice RT).

This conclusion is slightly more detailed than the conclusion about furcations reached in Chapter 2. One point of gain is that the sensorimotor slowing factor has been broken into two; the other dissociation-related conclusions from Chapter 2 largely remain unchanged.

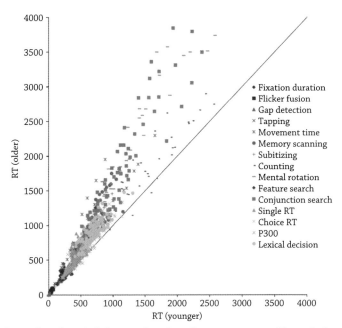

Figure 5.1 Brinley plot of all data analyzed in Chapter 5, grouped by task (*k* = 1,014). The equality diagonal is represented by a dotted line.

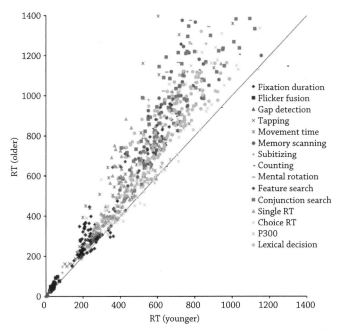

Figure 5.2 Brinley plot of all data analyzed in Chapter 5, grouped by task (*k* = 1,014). This plot is identical to Figure 5.1, now zooming in on the [0~1,400 ms] range. The equality diagonal is represented by a dotted line.

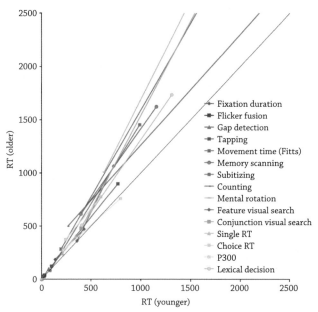

Figure 5.3 Results of the regression analyses presented in Chapter 4. Multilevel regression lines are plotted in Brinley space, using the appropriate data range for each task; the models are the original full models, with a separate slope and intercept estimated for each task. The equality diagonal is represented by a dotted line.

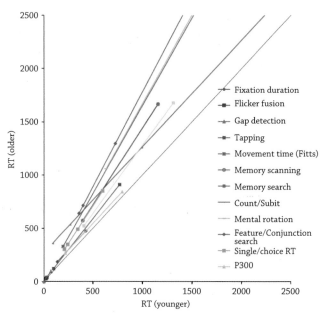

Figure 5.4 Results of the regression analyses presented in Chapter 4. Multilevel regression lines are plotted in Brinley space, using the appropriate data range for each task; the models are the final, constrained, models for each task. The equality diagonal is represented by a dotted line.

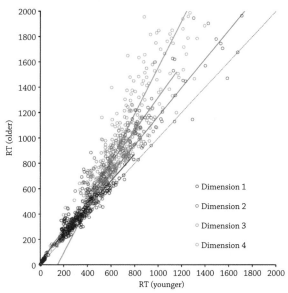

Figure 5.6 Data reduction model guided by the spatial layout of the data. Four dimensions are distinguished (Dimension 1: fixation duration, flicker fusion, gap detection, and P300; Dimension 2: counting, tapping, single, and choice RT; Dimension 3: memory search and lexical decision; Dimension 4: subitizing, movement time, feature and conjunction visual search, and mental rotation), explaining 98% of the variance. All data points within the 0~2,000 range are plotted, as well as the multilevel regression lines for each of the factors.

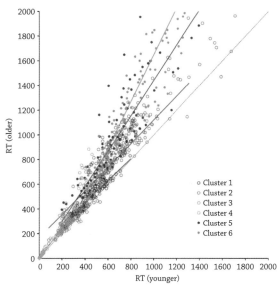

Figure 5.7 Data reduction model guided by statistical cluster analysis. Six clusters are distinguished (Cluster 1: P300; Cluster 2: counting, subitizing, lexical decision, and choice reaction time; Cluster 3: fixation duration; Cluster 4: tapping rate, flicker fusion threshold, gap detection threshold, and simple reaction time; Cluster 5: memory scanning and movement time; Cluster 6: feature search, conjunction search, and mental rotation), explaining 98% of the variance. All data points within the 0~2,000 range are plotted, as well as the multilevel regression lines for each of the factors.

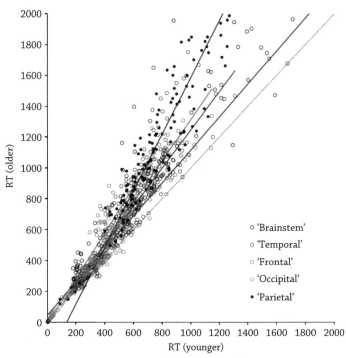

Figure 5.8 Data reduction model guided by the anatomical model derived from the data in Table 5.2. Five factors are distinguished ("Brainstem": fixation duration, counting, gap detection, and movement time; "temporal": P300, memory scanning, and lexical decision; "frontal": tapping, single RT, and choice RT; "occipital": flicker fusion threshold and feature visual search; "parietal": subitizing, conjunction visual search, and mental rotation), explaining 98% of the variance. All data points within the 0~2,000 range are plotted, as well as the multilevel regression lines for each of the factors.

6

Age-related Differences in the Speed of Executive Control

In Chapter 4, I collected data from a large number of studies that examined elementary processes of the mind. The human cognitive system, of course, rarely performs such tasks in isolation—typically, there is a task context (internally set or externally prescribed) that determines which tasks are to be performed on what specific subset of the stimuli that present themselves to the sensory apparatus. The processes that help the cognitive system engage in such (we hope) coherent, goal-directed behaviors are often labeled executive control processes or cognitive control processes. I will use the terms executive control and cognitive control interchangeably throughout this chapter.

6.1. Elementary Processes of Cognitive/Executive Control: A Brief Overview

Broadly speaking, the term cognitive control refers to the general-purpose mechanisms that modulate the operation of various cognitive processes and regulate the dynamics of human cognition. (I lifted this definition from Miyake, Friedman, Emerson, Witzki, & Howerter, 2002, p. 50, although I would argue that the most insightful definition is probably still Rabbitt's—"Clearly, only the central executive can sin," 1997, p. 2.)

For the purpose of a meta-analysis, high-level conceptual definitions matter less than a viable operational definition and a potentially fruitful classification scheme, just like the scheme provided by Card, Moran, and Newell's taxonomy of elementary processes helped set the stage for the analyses in Chapter 4. Ideally, like Card et al.'s, this classification scheme should deal with (at least presumed) *elementary* aspects of cognitive control, preferably at the process level rather than at the level of task or paradigm.

One taxonomy has been advanced by Smith and Jonides (1999), who claim (without attribution) that there is "some agreement" that there are five such elementary control processes: (a) attention and inhibition, that is, processes implicated in narrowly focusing attention on relevant information while blocking out irrelevant information; (b) task management, that is, sequencing of processes in complex tasks; (c) planning the assorted steps needed to reach a goal; (d) monitoring and updating the contents of working memory in the service of sequential tasks; and (e) the coding of timing and location of stimuli in working memory. Smith and Jonides deem inhibition/attention and task management the most elementary of these processes. Generally, those processes are considered to be driven by the prefrontal cortex (e.g., Rabbitt, 1997; Smith & Jonides; Miller & Cohen, 2001).

A more empirical stance—derived from a confirmatory factor analysis of a broad set of measures purported to measure elementary facets of executive control—was taken by Miyake, Friedman, and colleagues (Friedman et al., 2006; Miyake et al., 2000; for similar attempts, see Oberauer, Süß, Schulze, Wilhelm, & Wittmann, 2000; and Süß, Oberauer, Wittmann, Wilhelm, & Schulze, 2002). Their classification lists three distinct, but related concepts: (a) inhibition of prepotent responses (indexed by tasks such as Stroop, the antisaccade task, and the stop-signal task); (b) shifting of mental sets (indexed by costs when switching between two tasks); and (c) updating of the contents of working memory (indexed by running-span tasks, the keep-track task, and the N-Back task). The correlation between the latent factors representing inhibiting and shifting was .42 in Miyake et al. and .64 in Friedman et al.; the correlation between inhibiting and updating was .63 in Miyake et al., and .62 in Friedman et al; and the correlation between shifting and updating was .56 in Miyake et al. and .39 in Friedman et al.

The Miyake/Friedman conclusion that the three types of control behavior are related but distinct has received support from findings from the functional brain imaging literature. For instance, in a literature review of functional magnetic resonance imaging (fMRI) studies on executive control using the Miyake et al. study as their guide, Collette and Van der Linden (2002) argue that although there is specificity in the relationship between brain and executive control function (i.e., specific, distinct brain regions are related to each of the different specific executive functions), executive control processes also seem to be implemented in shared brain regions, notably many areas of the prefrontal dorsolateral cortex (particularly BA 9/46 and the anterior cingulate gyrus). These results underscore both the unity and diversity of executive functions. The same broader point is made in Kane and Engle's (2002) overview of the neuroimaging literature concerning working memory functioning. The source of the commonality is unclear; Miyake et al. suggest that all executive tasks share crucial common processes, namely goal-maintenance, context information, and inhibitory requirements; Kane and Engle hypothesize that the shared process is the need to maintain information in the presence of interference (p. 639; the interference originates from intervening tasks or intervening items that enter into the focus of attention but have to be discarded later).

The validity of these purportedly elementary measures of cognitive control can be assessed by investigating their correlations with performance on standard neuropsychological tests of executive control (often called 'frontal functioning' in this literature). The available evidence suggests the presence of at least moderate correlations. Performance on the Wisconsin Card Sorting Test is related to shifting (a standardized coefficient in a path model, comparable to a beta weight in linear regression analysis, of 0.33; Miyake et al., 2000). The total number of moves required on the Tower of Hanoi taps into inhibition (a standardized coefficient of 0.37; ibidem). The number of stereotyped sequences produced in a random number generation task

(Baddeley, 1996) correlates with inhibition (standardized coefficient of –0.39; ibidem), while the amount to which the random numbers are spread equally across all possible numbers correlates with updating (standardized coefficient of 0.33; ibidem). Operation span (Turner & Engle, 1989)—a general test for verbal working memory capacity—is related to updating (standardized coefficient of 0.61; ibidem). Fluid intelligence as measured by Raven's Progressive Matrices and the WAIS Block Design subtest correlates with updating only (standardized coefficient of 0.74; Friedman et al., 2006). Finally, dual-task performance (maze tracing combined with word generation) was not found to correlate with any of the three executive control factors (Miyake et al.), perhaps indicating that it is, as Smith and Jonides (1999) claim, a separate factor.

In this chapter, then, I will investigate age-related differences in elementary control processes. The literature review above suggests that there are at least three (Miyake/Friedman and colleagues) and potentially five (Smith/Jonides) relevant factors. Three factors are shared between these frameworks, and two of those—inhibition and shifting—have been extensively researched in the context of cognitive aging. The third—updating—has only recently received more notice, and the amount of data available does not appear to warrant a meta-analysis. (Although there are numerous studies looking at aging and updating tasks, most notably the N-Back task, the issue is that updating tasks are most often considered under the aspect of efficacy, i.e., accuracy, rather than efficiency, i.e., speed. This places this literature firmly outside the scope of this book, although the oft-observed decline in memory accuracy after an updating operation might very well turn out to be a cognitive primitive with excellent predictive power for more complex aspects of cognition; Kane, Conway, Miura, & Colflesh, 2007; Verhaeghen, 2011). Of the two factors specific to the Smith/Jonides framework—planning/coordination, and coding of timing/sequence in working memory—only the first is measured in the speed domain. This then leaves us in practice with meta-analyses of age-related differences in tasks measuring inhibition, shifting, and coordination. Additionally, I will report on age differences in one often-used neuropsychological task of executive control that uses latency as its dependent variable, namely the Trail Making Test.

On a final note, like all well-laid plans, this one might turn out to falter. As we will see, many of the tasks included in this chapter are controversial in the sense that they have been challenged on their status as measures of executive control.

6.2. Age-related Deficits in Executive Control: Brinley Plots and State Trace Plots

The literature on aging and cognitive control seems to have come to some consensus (a) that older adults have particular problems with executive control; and (b) that these problems lead to (or at least contribute to) age-related differences in more complex, assembled aspects of cognition (for overviews, see, e.g., Braver & West, 2008; Raz, 2000; West, 1996). The former assertion is examined in the present chapter; the latter will be tackled in Chapter 9. To foreshadow, I will find both assertions lacking.

The first observation to make with regard to age-related differences in cognitive control is that it is, in effect, not surprising that age differences are observed in tasks requiring cognitive control. After all, just about any study in cognitive aging shows that age-related differences are the rule, not the exception. The previous chapters bear ample testimony to this fact. From the viewpoint of theory, the interesting question is not: "Are there age-related differences in executive control?", but rather: "Are there *unique* (i.e., *specific*) age-related deficits in executive control?"

One way to investigate whether the age-related differences observed in cognitive control are unique or specific to cognitive control is to assess whether these age-related differences are larger than expected on the basis of the age-related differences observed in the same tasks but with the cognitive control requirement removed. This is the method used in the present chapter. (Another method is to examine whether age-related differences in more basic cognitive abilities [e.g., speed-of-processing] completely [or mostly] mediate age-related differences in cognitive control. This method will be used in Chapter 9.) Fortuitously, most paradigms used for tapping executive control have the no-control (or low-control) versus high-control comparison purposely built in. A good example is the Stroop color-word task. In the typical version of this task, subjects see words or letter strings printed or projected in color; the ink or screen color of each stimulus needs to be reported. In the executive-control version of the task (the "interference" condition), the words-to-be-read are color words incompatible with the ink color in which they are printed (e.g., the word "red" shown in green); in the baseline version, the stimuli are "neutral," typically strings of colored Xs or non-color words. If the age-related differences are larger in the executive-control version than the neutral version, we may conclude that there is a specific age-related deficit in executive control.

The previous chapters have already demonstrated that the latter part is not simply a matter of comparing the absolute difference in latency. In Chapter 1, I advanced this point on theoretical/methodological grounds; Chapters 2 and 4 reaffirmed this point empirically—aging typically does not lead to an additive rescaling of latencies; that is, older adults are not a constant X ms slower than younger adults. Rather, latencies of older adults are typically much better (yet not perfectly) described as a multiplicative, or proportional function of those of younger adults (i.e., older adults are X times slower than younger adults). As explained in Chapter 1, this near-ratio relationship between latencies of younger and older adults complicates the interpretation of absolute age differences across different tasks (including interactions in analysis of variance), especially in cases such as the one considered here, where one of the tasks (the high-control task) is likely to consistently yield much longer response times than the other (the low-control task). Thus, as in the previous chapters, I will use Brinley plots as a way to test the dimensionality of the data. Here, the contrast is very principled and within task: For each task, I will examine whether the two Brinley functions (one for the executive-control version, one for the baseline version) are reliably different from each other or whether they coincide. If they coincide, the conclusion would be that there are no specific age differences in the aspect of executive control tapped by the particular tasks; if they are distinct, the conclusion is of a specific, unique age-related deficit (or benefit, as the case may be) in the aspect of executive control under study. As explained in Chapter 1, in tasks like these, that is, with two clearly delineated conditions, the inverse plot can be constructed as well: high-control response time as a function of baseline response time in each of the two groups. The regression lines in these state-trace plots—one for younger adults, one for older adults—indicate what the relationship is (if any) between the high-control version of the task and the low-control version: additive, multiplicative, or both.

6.3. Age-related Differences in Inhibitory Functioning

The first aspect of executive control examined here is inhibition. Inhibition (some-times also referred to as resistance to interference, but this concept also has a more narrow meaning, see below) can be generally defined as the ability to down-regulate or inhibit the processing of information that is external to the task at hand (e.g., Hasher & Zacks, 1988; Hasher, Zacks, & May, 1999). This ability seems so basic to the opera-tions of the cognitive speed—both to its efficiency and its efficacy—that it has been proposed as a central mechanism that underlies age differences in a wide variety of complex cognitive tasks such as working memory, episodic memory, speed of process-ing, and abstract reasoning (e.g., Darowski et al., 2008). The assertion is that resis-tance to inference from irrelevant stimuli or tasks breaks down with advancing age, and that this breakdown, in turn, leads to mental clutter in working memory, thereby limiting its functional capacity and likely also its speed of operation. This hypothesis is still situated at a high level of abstraction—different subtypes of inhibitory processing have been posited. In the following sections, I will first explicate these divisions, and then examine age-related differences in each of the aspects of inhibition separately.

6.3.1. Subtypes of Inhibition

Quite a number of researchers have claimed, some from a priori conceptualizations (e.g., Dempster & Corkill, 1999; Harnishfeger, 1995; Hasher et al., 1999; Nigg, 2000), some from latent-variable analysis (Friedman & Miyake, 2004), that the concept of inhibition or resistance to interference should be further broken down into different components or functions.

The most basic distinction posited in the literature is between *intentional* and *unin-tentional* forms of inhibition (the terminology is Harnishfeger's, 1995; Nigg, 2000, uses the terms "executive" and "automatic" inhibition; Andrés, Guerrini, Phillips, & Perfect, 2008, label the latter as "reactive" inhibition). Intentional inhibition requires the ability to deliberately (and effortfully) suppress irrelevant stimuli or responses in the light of the goals set by the task. The Stroop task would be a good example of an intentional inhibition task. Unintentional inhibition, by contrast, occurs prior to con-scious awareness. Inhibition of return and negative priming fall under this category. (I describe these tasks in more detail below.)

Within intentional inhibition, distinctions have been made among different com-ponents or functions that roughly correspond to different stages in the informa-tion processing chain. These were perhaps labeled most intuitively by Hasher et al. (1999): Inhibition (a) limits access to the focus of attention to relevant information only; (b) deletes information that is no longer relevant for the present goals from the focus of attention; and (c) restrains the system from producing strongly activated but incorrect responses (for a recent review, see Hasher, Lustig, & Zacks, 2007).

The concept of *access* refers to early control, that is, control over perceptual processing and stimulus selection (Nigg's, 2000, interference control; Harnishfeger's, 1995, resistance to interference; Dempster's, 1993, control of perceptual interference; and Friedman & Miyake's, 2004, resistance to distractor interference are similar constructs). The access function determines which activated representations will enter the focus of attention and will be acted upon; it suppresses information that is not relevant for the task. The relevant paradigms used most often in the aging literature include reading with and without interspersed distractor words (Connelly, Hasher, & Zacks, 1991); and the Eriksen flanker task (both described in more detail below).

The second function of inhibitory control is to *delete* irrelevant contents from working memory. These irrelevant contents could be information that intruded past the access gate (thus making the deletion function a second line of defense of the cognitive system), or information that was previously task-relevant, but now no longer is. The concept is closely related to Nigg's and Harnishfeger's concepts of cognitive inhibition, Dempster's control of verbal-linguistic interference, and Friedman and Miyake's resistance to proactive interference. Hasher, Zacks, and colleagues have measured the deletion function with a host of paradigms, including directed-forgetting tasks (e.g., Zacks, Radvansky, & Hasher, 1996), updating tasks (e.g., De Beni & Palladino, 2004), text comprehension that requires meaning revision (e.g., Hamm & Hasher, 1992), and memory for alternative sentence completion (e.g., Hartman & Hasher, 1991; Hasher, Quig, & May, 1997; Charlot & Feyereisen, 2004). It is hard not to notice that quite a few of those measures come close to or overlap with the measures used for the concept of updating as defined by Miyake et al. (2000). Performance on all these tasks is measured in accuracy rather than speed, and thus an analysis of the deletion function of inhibition falls outside the scope of this book.

The third function of inhibition is to suppress or *restrain* highly activated responses that are inappropriate given the task goal. This function is akin to Nigg's and Harnishfeger's concept of behavioral inhibition, Dempster's control of motor interference, and Friedman and Miyake's prepotent response inhibition. Hasher, Zacks, and colleagues measure this aspect of inhibition with the Stroop task and the stop-signal task. (Hasher et al., 2007, also list inhibition of return under this heading. Like Andrés et al., 2008, and Feyereisen & Charlot, 2008, I classify this task as a test of unintentional inhibition.) Friedman and Miyake additionally tap this function using the antisaccade task (Hallett, 1978). Performance in the stop-signal task is measured in the accuracy domain; therefore, only data on the Stroop task and the antisaccade task will be included here.

6.3.2. Age Differences in Unintentional Inhibitory Control

6.3.2.1. *Inhibition of Return*

Inhibition of return is an involuntary phenomenon of covert attention first reported by Posner and Cohen (1984; for a review, see Klein, 2000). Many variations exist, but in Posner and Cohen's original paradigm, participants are asked to detect a target—a small, bright square—presented in one of two peripheral locations indicated by empty boxes, one to the left and one to the right of a centrally located fixation box. Prior to the appearance of the target, one of the two peripheral boxes is brightened for 150 ms. This brightening is called cueing (although it is not indicative of any specific event within the trial); the brightened location is called the cued location. This cueing is believed to create an attention shift toward the cued location. This shift is covert rather than overt—eye movements are not allowed. After a brief delay—Posner and Cohen used 0, 50, 100, 200, 300, and 500 ms delays—the target appears. Crucially, the target is presented in the center box with high probability (80%), but it can also appear in the periphery. Thus, on 10% of the trials the cued location is tapped, while on 10% of the trials the target appears in the contralateral, "uncued" location. The expectation in the paradigm is that although attention is initially drawn to the cued location, it will return to the center location, because that is where the target appears most often. Posner and Cohen were originally interested in capturing the dynamics of this shift. They used the latency difference between the cued and uncued location as their index of the attention shift: Initially, the cued location should yield the fastest response, but this advantage should disappear as soon as attention becomes firmly attached to the center box. Typical results with the paradigm indeed show an initial facilitation of the cued location, followed after about 300 ms by a reversal, where latency becomes much longer when the target appears at the cued location—the phenomenon now known as inhibition of return. Posner and Cohen speculate that an initial facilitation and subsequent inhibition work hand in hand to produce the data pattern. Facilitation obviously serves to improve the efficiency of target detection—selecting out an area of import in the visual/attentional field. The subsequent inhibition might serve to maximize sampling of the visual environment: Once attention moves away from a particular location, this location gets inhibited, effectively creating a bias toward attentional/visual exploration of the environment. This makes inhibition of return one possible key ingredient of efficient visual search in a static environment (e.g., Faust & Balota, 1997; Kramer et al, 2006): It creates an implicit (and automatic) memory of locations visited, thus preventing unnecessary re-examination of stimuli—an excellent foraging facilitator (MacInnes & Klein, 2003).

I was able to collect inhibition-of-return data from 14 papers, yielding a total of 21 experiments (Bao, Zhou, & Fu, 2004; Castel et al, 2003; Connelly & Hasher, 1993; Faust & Balota, 1997; Hartley & Kieley, 1995; Kramer et al., 2006; Langley, Fuentes, Hochhalter, Brandt, & Overmier, 2001; Langley, Fuentes, Vivas, & Saville, 2007; Langley, Vivas, Fuentes, & Bagne, 2005; McAuliffe, Chasteen, & Pratt, 2006; McCrae & Abrams, 2001; Poliakoff, Coward, Lowe, & O'Boyle, 2007; Pratt & Chasteen, 2007; Tsuchida, 2005).

Figure 6.1 represents the results both as a Brinley plot (left-hand panel) and a state-trace plot (right-hand panel). Within the Brinley plot, an insert shows the average latency for younger and older adults for both versions of the task. The comparison is always between latency for the cued location versus latency for the uncued location(s). Given the relatively small number of data points, I decided not to analyze different paradigmatic variations separately; I also averaged latencies for younger and older adults across all manipulations to yield single estimates for cued and non-cued locations, as recommended by Sliwinski and Hall (1998). In practice, this meant averaging across cue-target intervals (Bao et al., Castel et al.); cue-target versus target-target

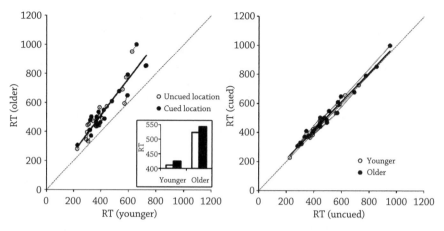

Figure 6.1 Inhibition of return: Results from meta-analyses (left-hand panel: Brinley plot, with average latencies in both conditions for both age groups in inset; right-hand panel: state-trace plot) of 21 studies. Data from the same study are connected by dotted lines. A single multilevel regression line (represented by the solid line) sufficed to capture the data in both instances, indicating that there is no age-related deficit in inhibition of return. The dotted line represents the equality diagonal.

conditions (Poliakoff et al.); single versus double cueing (Hartley & Kieley, Expts. 1 and 2); and detection versus categorization conditions (Langley et al, 2001).

   If there were an age-related deficit in inhibition of return, we would expect age effects to be smaller for the cued location than the uncued location(s). This is not the case when raw latencies are considered: The average age effect is 102 ms at the cued location and 100 ms at the uncued location (or, conversely, the inhibition of return effect is 14 ms in younger adults, and 17 ms in older adults; all four values are weighted for sample size). These raw latency differences, however, are not corrected for age-related slowing as observed in the baseline condition, that is, the uncued location. The data clouds in the Brinley and state-trace plots suggest that a single line might suffice to capture the data in both plots, indicating that the observed age-related slowing effect at the cued location is indeed as large as that at the uncued location. A formal analysis confirms this observation.

   For the Brinley analysis (42 data points), the full model, with dummy terms for location (cued vs. uncued) to test for intercept differences, and the location by RT interaction term to test for slope differences, yielded the following equation (*SE* of the parameters between parentheses):

$$RT_{older} = 9.68\ (8.47) + 1.25\ (0.09)\ RT_{younger} + 5.83\ (12.89)\ \text{location}$$
$$- 0.01\ (0.03)\ \text{location by RT}_{younger}.$$

The *SE*s suggest that both the location parameter and the location by RT parameter could be set to zero without affecting the model significantly. This turned out to be the case, $\Delta LR\ \chi^2\ (2) = 0.50$, and the final Brinley equation is:

$$RT_{older} = 7.04\ (28.07) + 1.26\ (0.09)\ RT_{younger}.$$

This mode explains 74% of the variance in older adults' average RT compared with the empty model.

Likewise, the full model for the state-trace analysis,

$$RT_{cued} = 19.38\ (15.61) + 0.99\ (0.04)\ RT_{uncued} + 9.50\ (21.68)\ \text{age group}$$
$$- 0.00\ (0.05)\ \text{age group by } RT_{uncued},$$

could be trimmed at no significant loss to fit, $\Delta LR\ \chi^2\ (2) = 1.30$, to a single line:

$$RT_{cued} = 20.08\ (10.24) + 0.99\ (0.02)\ RT_{uncued}.$$

The slope of this state trace was not significantly different from 1, $\Delta LR\ \chi^2\ (1) = 0.09$. It explained 95% of the variance.

Taken together, the results again show that older adults are overall slower than younger adults (the slowing factor is about 1.3). More importantly, there is no specific age-related deficit in inhibition of return—access to the cued, that is, inhibited location, and the uncued, that is, non-inhibited location(s), is slowed by an identical rate. Accessing the inhibited location leads to an additive cost, suggesting that the type of inhibition required by this task simply adds a new stage to processing, as predicted by Posner's model.

In this particular task, we can examine age-related slowing under one more aspect, namely its dynamics, or time course. Figure 6.2 plots all available data (63 data points per age group) as a function of the delay between the peripheral cue and the target.

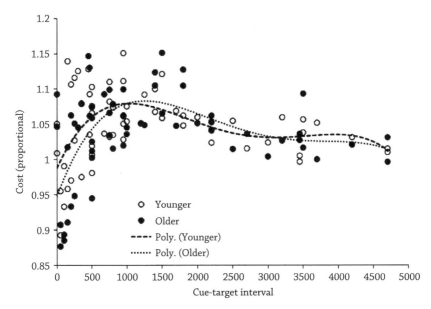

Figure 6.2 The inhibition of return effect in younger and older adults ($k = 63$ per age group) as a function of delay between cue and stimulus. The data are modeled by a fourth-order polynomial, overlaid in the figure.

The plot shows the inhibition of return cost as the ratio of RT for the cued location and the RT for the uncued location; it ignores the nested structure of the data (the data are difference scores and therefore quite noisy; connecting data from individual study makes the graph effectively unreadable). For illustrative purposes, I captured this relation, again ignoring the nested structure of the data, with two fourth-order polynomials, one for each age group, overlaid in the figure. (A ratio score was used to control for age-related baseline slowing: The Brinley plot revealed near-multiplicative data.)

The relationship between delay and inhibition of return is curvilinear, as expected. At very short delays, there is facilitation for the cued location, shown by a location effect smaller than 1. At delays of about 50 ms (younger adults) and 220 ms (older adults) inhibition starts to build up, reaching a peak at around 1,000 ms for the younger adults and 1,200 ms for the older adults, followed by slow decay to what may be an asymptotic value at around 3,000 ms. The amplitude of the peak seems to not differ much between age groups; this is expected if a multiplicative aging model holds (as the equation above demonstrated). The age-related delay in the peak (1,200 ms vs. 1,000 ms) roughly corresponds to the slowing factor we found in that equation (viz., 1.26). One unexplained finding is the time point at which facilitation turns into inhibition, which shows a ratio of about 4 (220 ms/50 ms). Further research is necessary to determine whether this estimate for the facilitation/inhibition cross-over is correct. It might very well not be. After all, the data are sparse: Only 13 out of 63 data points represent delays of 300 ms or less. Moreover, two of the studies included here have examined the dynamics of the effect over a large range and with multiple delays, and they yield mutually inconsistent results. Bao et al. (2004) included 11 different delays, between 150 ms and 4,200 ms; they observed facilitation in neither age group. Castel et al. (2003) included 11 different delays between 50 ms and 3,000 ms; they found age differences in facilitation that were disproportionate (difference scores of −67 ms vs. −20 ms for older and younger adults at 50 ms), and cross-over values at about 100 ms versus about 500 ms. For now, the conclusion appears to be that the time course of the emergence of the inhibition of return effect might be disproportionately delayed in older adults, but its magnitude and the timing of its peak can be explained perfectly by "general" or baseline slowing, that is, by slowing as observed in latency to the uncued location.

6.3.2.2. Negative Priming

6.3.2.2.1. Meta-analysis

A second paradigm often used to test age differences in automatic inhibitory functioning is negative priming. Psychologists use the term priming to refer to the influence of previous processing of a stimulus on subsequent processing of the same stimulus or similar stimuli. Typically, priming is positive—re-encountering a stimulus tends to speed up response time. Priming can, however, incur a cost—"negative" priming—when the type of processing required in the first episode hampers fast processing of the stimulus in the second episode. In the typical negative priming paradigm, subjects are shown a series of pairs of stimuli. One of the members of the pair is the target to-be-responded-to, the other (the distractor) is to be ignored. Both are easily perceptually identified—for instance, stimuli might be line drawing of objects and the task might be to name the object; targets might be depicted in red, distractors in blue. If the distractor on one trial (the prime trial) becomes the target on the next trial (the test trial), performance is usually hampered. In the example, if the object shown in blue becomes the target—the object in red—in the next trial, naming latency is typically increased.

Traditionally, the negative priming cost is calculated by subtracting reaction time on test trials in a condition in which the target was a distractor on the prime trial (the negative priming condition) from reaction time on test trials in a condition in which targets and distractors are never repeated (the control condition). The modal explanation for this negative priming effect is that an attentional mechanism blocks the representation of the distractor stimulus on the prime trial from access to the response systems (e.g., Hasher & Zacks, 1988; McDowd, Oseas-Kreger, & Filion, 1995; Tipper, 1985). If that same stimulus is then presented as a target on the test trial, additional processing time is required to overcome the response inhibition generated on the previous trial, resulting in longer latency for the response (and sometimes in more errors).

Note that the hypothesized age-related effects will be counterintuitive. This is because participants with a less efficiently functioning inhibitory apparatus— presumably older adults—should in effect be hampered less when responding to a target that was a distractor on the previous trial, and thus show a smaller negative priming effect. If there were a complete breakdown of inhibitory mechanisms in later adulthood, one would even expect older adults not to be slowed at all in negative priming conditions compared with baseline. This seems to have been the implicit expectation in the field: Early reviewers of the phenomenon have focused almost exclusively on the presence or absence of negative priming effects in older adults (e.g., May, Kane, & Hasher, 1995; McDowd et al., 1995). Strictly speaking, however, the real question is whether older adults, after controlling for age-related slowing in the baseline condition, show smaller negative priming effects than younger adults. This is a different question altogether: This age by condition interaction might be observed in either the presence or absence of a reliable negative priming effect in older adults; it is also possible that negative priming effects are statistically significant in younger adults and not in older adults (the pattern May et al. and McDowd et al. were investigating) even when the age by condition interaction is not significant.

In the present meta-analysis, I restricted myself to tasks of identity negative priming, given that almost all of the work on negative priming in aging has used this paradigm. Identity priming refers to negative priming in tasks in which the response is related to the identity of a stimulus, as in the examples above (naming a pictured object). This stands in opposition to location priming, in which the response is related to the location of a stimulus (e.g., pressing a key on the keyboard corresponding to the location of a particular stimulus). I note here that it has been claimed that identity negative priming should be vulnerable to the effects of aging, whereas location negative priming may stay intact (May et al., 1995). It should also be noted that two meta-analyses have preceded the current one—the first by Verhaeghen and De Meersman (1998a; 21 independent studies), updated by Gamboz, Russo, & Fox in 2002 (37 independent studies). I simply built on those by adding six new studies, leading to a new total of 43 independent studies (Anderson, Sekuler, & Middlebrook, 1994; Connelly & Hasher, 1993; Earles et al., 1997; Ferraro, Sturgill, & Bohlman, 1996; Gamboz, 2000; Gamboz, Russo, & Fox, 2000; Grant & Dagenbach, 2000; Hasher, Stoltzfus, Zacks, & Rypma, 1991; Hasher & Zacks, 1988; Hogge, Salmon, & Collette, 2008; Intons-Peterson, Rocchi, West, McLellan, & Hackney, 1998; Kane, Hasher, Stoltzfus, Zacks, & Connelly, 1994; Kane, May, Hasher, Rahhal, & Stoltzfus, 1997; Kieley & Hartley, 1997; Kramer, Humphrey, Larish, Logan, & Strayer, 1994; Kramer & Strayer, 2001; Langley, Overmier, Knopman, & Prod'Homme, 1998; Little & Hartley, 2000; McArthur, Lahar, & Isaak, 1996; McDowd, Fillion, & Bowman, 1996; McDowd & Oseas-Kreger, 1991; Pesta & Sanders, 2000; Schooler et al., 1997; Stoltzfus, Hasher, Zacks, Ulivi, & Goldstein, 1993; Sullivan & Faust, 1993; Sullivan, Faust, & Balota, 1994; Sullivan, Faust, & Balota, 1995; Tipper, 1991; Titz, Behrendt, Menge, & Hasselhorn, 2008; Troche, Gibbons, & Rammsayer, 2008; West, Ball, Edwards, & Cissell, 1994; Witthöft, Sander, Süß, & Wittmann, 2009).

Mean latency (weighted for sample size) in the baseline condition was 618 ms for younger adults and 733 ms for older adults; weighted mean latency in the negative priming condition was 638 ms for younger adults and 751 ms for older adults. The mean negative priming effect was thus 21 ms for younger adults and 18 ms for older adults. These effects are relatively small, and the average age difference—exactly 2.11 ms—is even smaller, but it is in the direction predicted by inhibition theory.

For the Brinley analysis (86 data points; Figure 6.3), the full model, with dummy terms for type of condition (baseline vs. negative priming) to test for intercept differences, and the condition by RT interaction term to test for slope differences, yielded the following equation:

$$RT_{older} = 18.07\ (39.82) + 1.16\ (0.06)\ RT_{younger} + 0.42\ (55.55)\ \text{condition}$$
$$-\ 0.01\ (0.08)\ \text{condition by}\ RT_{younger}.$$

The standard errors suggest that the intercept, the condition parameter, and the condition by RT parameter could all be set to zero without affecting the model significantly. This turned out to be the case, $\Delta LR\ \chi^2\ (3) = 0.54$, pseudo-$R^2 = .82$, and the final Brinley equation is:

$$RT_{older} = 1.18\ (0.01)\ RT_{younger}.$$

The available evidence from these 43 studies, then, suggests that the age-related slowing factor observed in negative priming conditions is equal to, not smaller than, the one observed in baseline conditions. This, in turn, suggests that older adults do not have a deficient automatic inhibition mechanism as measured by the negative priming effect, or at least not more deficient than that of younger adults.

Results from the state-trace analysis are equally unambiguous. The full model fits as follows:

$$RT_{negative\ priming} = -8.42\ (4.34) + 1.05\ (0.01)\ RT_{baseline} - 3.27\ (6.88)\ \text{age group}$$
$$-\ 0.00\ (0.01)\ \text{age group by}\ RT_{baseline}.$$

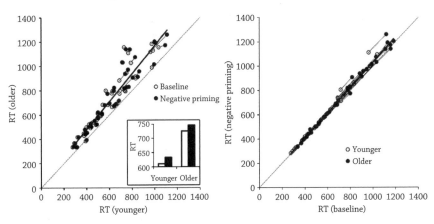

Figure 6.3 Negative priming: Results from meta-analyses (left-hand panel: Brinley plot, with average latencies in both conditions for both age groups in inset; right-hand panel: state-trace plot) of 43 studies. Data from the same study are connected by dotted lines. A single multilevel regression line (represented by the solid line) sufficed to capture the data in both instances, indicating that there is no age-related deficit in the negative priming effect. The dotted line represents the equality diagonal.

Neither of the parameters associated with age are significant, suggesting that a single line suffices to explain the data. A single-line model indeed did not fit significantly less well than the full model, ΔLR χ^2 (2) = 5.83:

$$RT_{negative\ priming} = -8.54\ (2.93) + 1.04\ (0.01)\ RT_{baseline}.$$

The presence of a single line in the state-trace plot again strongly suggests that there is no age-related deficit in inhibitory processing as measured through the negative priming task. The model fits the data well, explaining 99% of the variance.

Note that the slope, although modest, is indeed larger than unity; fixing it to be equal to 1 yields a significant drop in fit, ΔLR χ^2 (2) = 6.40. Thus, the negative priming effect is near-multiplicative compared with baseline latencies. This suggests that, unlike inhibition of return, the mechanism responsible for the negative priming effect does interfere with central processing.

6.3.2.2.2. Complications: Reliability, Statistical Power, and Retrieval Effects

There are some important caveats to make concerning these conclusions. One concerns the reliability of the negative priming task; the second concerns the confirmation of null results in the face of small effect sizes; the third concerns the mechanism that produces negative priming. I address each of those in turn.

Recent studies have cast some serious doubt on the reliability of the measurement of negative priming. Low reliability would make it much more difficult to reliably assess individual or group differences, and may contribute to the null result observed with regard to aging. Four studies directly estimated the reliability of the negative priming effect. Borrella, Varretti, & De Beni et al. (2009) estimated the reliability of the negative priming effect as .12 (for a version in which the two stimuli are presented with both vertical separation and a 100 ms stimulus onset asynchrony (SOA)) and .33 (for a version in which the stimuli overlap in both space and time); Kieley and Hartley (1997) obtained a reliability coefficient of .32. Troche, et al. (2008) obtained test-retest estimates of −.12 (sic) for younger adults and .45 for older adults, and split-half reliabilities of .14 and .70, respectively. Witthöft et al. (2009), using Cronbach's alpha, estimated the reliability at .51 for younger adults and .66 for older adults. The average reliability coefficient, weighted for sample size, is .34. This value is within the range that is typically considered unacceptable (i.e., internal consistency lower than .5; Cronbach & Shavelson, 2004).

The lack of reliability of the measure also underscores a weakness with the reasoning that null findings in older adults signify a breakdown in inhibition. The effect may simply be too small to be easily detectable in primary studies with the small sample sizes typically used in aging research. An effect size analysis (mean standardized difference) on all 42 studies that allowed for the computation of effect sizes resulted in a negative priming effect size in younger adults of 0.24; the effect size is 0.18 in older adults. (The difference between the two is not significant; χ^2 (1) = 0.85.) With the typical sample sizes in aging research (in the present set of data, 28 younger and 30 older adults), power is low, even if a one-tailed test is conducted: 35% for the typical younger-adults effect, 26% for the typical older-adult effect. Thus, it is quite unsurprising that many researchers fail to find significant negative priming effects, especially in older adults. In order to obtain a power of .80, which is usually considered respectable (Cohen, 1988), the sample size for studies with younger adults should be 107 or more; for older adults, it should be 191 or more.

The third caveat is that since the mid-1990s the field of negative priming has wandered away from accepting the inhibition account as the (sole) explanation for the negative priming effect. At least three competing mechanisms have been offered (for a more extensive, and excellent, review, see Mayr & Buchner, 2007): episodic retrieval, feature mismatch, and temporal discrimination. The former has received some empirical support; empirical evidence for the latter two is scant.

The episodic-retrieval account of negative priming (e.g., Milliken, Joordens, Merikle, & Seiffert, 1998; Neill, Valdes, Terry, & Gorfein, 1992) borrows an assumption from Logan's (1988) instance theory of automaticity, namely that every instance of a stimulus will automatically trigger the retrieval of previous encounters with that stimulus. If one adds the assumption that response information is part of the retrieved episode, then negative priming can easily be explained by the incompatibility between the current task requirement for the target (e.g., "name this stimulus") and the tag stemming from the retrieved episode when the target was the distractor ("do not respond to this stimulus"). This incompatibility needs to be resolved, and this takes time—a negative priming cost. The episodic retrieval account can explain effects that are difficult to reconcile with the inhibition account, such as timing effects (e.g., when the prime is preceded by pre-prime, negative priming covaries with the temporal discriminability of prime and pre-prime, Neill et al., 1992; and negative priming effects have been observed with an interval of one month between prime and prove; DeSchepper & Treisman, 1996). Conversely, proponents of the inhibition account point at the existence of semantic negative priming effects (a to-be-ignored picture of a dog creates negative priming for the picture of a cat; Tipper, 1985), which is hard to explain in a framework that assumes instance retrieval.

Two proposals have been made to reconcile the two points of view. May, Kane, Hasher and colleagues (Kane, May, Hasher, Rahhal, & Stolzfus, 1997; May, Kane, & Hasher, 1995) propose that inhibition is the default modus operandi, but that retrieval can take its place when demanded by the experimental context. For instance, if the perceptual quality of the stimulus is low or if exposure time is brief, episodic retrieval might help determine the stimulus's identity. Another context variable claimed to enhance retrieval occurs when stimuli are repeated with unchanged roles across repetitions. In that case, the stimulus's identity is diagnostic of the response, and memory retrieval becomes useful. Thus, if a significant proportion of the trials are repeated targets, repeated distractors, or both, subjects might rely more on episodic memories of the trials, thus speeding up on repeated target trials, and slowing down even more than usual on negative priming trials. May et al. argue that older adults would only show an absence of negative priming when episodic retrieval demands are low, that is, when inhibition processes are the sole determinant of the task. In contrast, when the task demands or encourages retrieval, older adults should show negative priming effects, presumably (although May et al. do not make this assumption explicit) because encoding and retrieval processes in what is effectively an implicit memory task operate as efficiently in older adults as in younger adults.

One straightforward next step in the Brinley analysis, then, is to purify the data set and restrict the analysis to "standard" negative priming studies that are assumed to tap only inhibitory processes, not retrieval processes—that is, studies without perceptual degradation, with sufficiently long stimulus durations (Kane et al., 1997, consider an exposure of 300 ms "standard," and 150 ms "brief"), and without repeated targets and/or distractors. This excluded Kane et al. (1997) due to stimulus degradation; and Kane et al. (1994), Kieley and Hartley (1997, Expt. 1), Pesta and Sanders (2000), Schooler et al. (1997, Expt 1), Sullivan and Faust (1993), Sullivan et al. (1995; Expts. 1 and 2), and Witthöft et al. (2008) due to target and/or distractor repetitions. This purification did not change the results in any meaningful way: The average negative priming effect, weighted for sample size, was 20 ms for younger adults and 19 ms for older adults, with an age difference of 1.45 ms in the predicted direction. For the Brinley analysis (68 data points), the full model with dummy terms for type of condition (baseline vs. negative priming) to test for intercept differences and the condition by RT interaction term to test for slope differences, yielded the following equation:

$$RT_{older} = 17.72\ (37.31) + 1.16\ (0.06)\ RT_{younger} + 4.31\ (51.93)\ \text{condition}$$
$$- 0.02\ (0.08)\ \text{condition by RT}_{younger}.$$

The standard errors suggest that both the condition parameter and the condition by RT parameter could be set to zero without affecting the model significantly. This turned out to be the case, $\Delta LR\ \chi^2\ (2) = 0.11$, and the final Brinley equation is:

$$RT_{older} = 20.46\ (25.93) + 1.15\ (0.04)\ RT_{younger}.$$

Likewise, the full model for the state-trace analysis,

$$RT_{negative\ priming} = -9.64\ (4.38) + 1.05\ (0.01)\ RT_{baseline} + 0.76\ (6.48)\ age\ group$$
$$- 0.01\ (0.01)\ age\ group\ by\ RT_{baseline},$$

suggests that the two lines for younger and older adults coincide (both the age group and the age group by RT parameters have standard errors that are equal to or larger than the parameters). The model with those two variables omitted, however, failed to converge, so this assertion could not be tested directly.

An alternative way to investigate the Kane et al. hypothesis is to rerun the multi-level regression analysis on the full 86-data-point data set, now including a dummy for purported memory retrieval and all its interactions. This likewise did not change the results of the Brinley analysis: The model, including a memory retrieval parameter as well as a condition parameter and all interactions, did not fit the data better than a single-line model, $\Delta LR\ \chi^2$ (6) = 0.24. This was also true for the state-trace analysis; the full model did not fit better than the single-line model, $\Delta LR\ \chi^2$ (6) = 11.18.

A second proposal to reconcile the memory account and the inhibition account is Tipper's (2001) suggestion that inhibition and retrieval do not operate as mutually exclusive mechanisms, but rather that they operate in concert. In this view, inhibition is a forward-operating process, a lingering activation history inherited from the attentional processing in the prime display (i.e., selecting the target from the distractor); retrieval is a backward-operating process, triggered by the processes necessary to analyze the probe (such as object identification). Both processes are necessary, just like memory needs both encoding (a forward process) and retrieval (a backward process); which one comes to the fore in experimental results depends on the paradigm. Under his account, then, my analyses yield a double conclusion: The absence of age differences in the negative priming task suggests that older adults are as proficient as younger adults in both types of processes.

6.3.3. Age Differences in Intentional Inhibitory Control

In this section, I will examine age-related differences in intentional inhibitory control. Data on latencies for the "delete" function are scarce and will not be included here. I therefore limit myself to meta-analyses on assumed age-related deficits in the "access" function, with the Eriksen flanker task and the reading with distractors task as indicators, and age-related deficits in the "restraint" function, with the Stroop task and the antisaccade task as indicators.

6.3.3.1. The Access Function of Inhibition

6.3.3.1.1. The Eriksen Flanker Task

In the flanker task (Eriksen, & Eriksen, 1974), one of two responses has to be emitted. A single target is presented in the middle of the screen; this target is associated with one of the responses. The target is surrounded by distractors—flankers—which can either be associated with the same response as the target (compatible condition), or with the other response (incompatible condition). A simple example would be an arrow paradigm where the subject presses a key with the right hand if a central target arrow faces right and a key with the left hand if the arrow faces left. The subject is typically faster when the target arrow is flanked by arrows pointing in the same direction (compatible condition) and slower when the arrow is flanked with arrows pointing in the opposite direction (incompatible condition). Note that efficiency of inhibitory processing enters twice in this difference score: Inefficient filtering will lead not just to slower responses in the incompatible condition but also to facilitation in the compatible condition. To disentangle facilitation from inhibition, an alternative measure of inhibition is necessary. Instead of comparing the incompatible condition with a compatible condition, one compares it with a neutral condition. A neutral condition would either contain no flankers (but this introduces a perceptual confound: the target stimulus no longer needs to be detected among distractors), or flankers that evoke no response (such as a set of asterisks surrounding the central arrow). This more purified measurement is used less often in aging research: I located 14 studies examining the flanker effect in younger and older adults; all 14 included compatible and incompatible conditions; only seven also included a neutral condition. Therefore, my analysis concentrated on compatible and incompatible conditions only. In the present context, the Brinley analysis is of limited usefulness. What it tells us is whether the age effect on incompatible trials is as large as the age effect on compatible trials. This is not indicative of the presence or absence of an age-related problem with filtering out the flanking distractors; all it denotes is whether the filtering effects are symmetrical, that is, whether the age difference in facilitation is equal to the age difference in interference.

The 14 studies were contained within 12 papers (Collette, Germain, Hogge, & Van der Linden, 2009; Collette, Schmidt, Scherrer, Adam, & Salmon, 2009; Fernandez-Duque & Black, 2006; Jennings, Dagenbach, Engle, & Funke, 2007; Kramer et al., 1994; Madden & Gottlob, 1997; Nieuwenhuis et al., 2002; Shaw, 1991; Sullivan, 1999; Wild-Wall, Falkenstein, & Hohnsbein, 2008; Zeef & Kok, 1993; Zeef, Sonke, Kok, Buiten, & Kenemans, 1996). Half of the studies (7 out of 14) used a letter identification paradigm, four used the arrow task, and three used a word categorization task. Average response time in the compatible condition, weighted for sample size, was 568 ms for younger adults, and 702 ms for older adults; RT in the incompatible condition was 617 ms and 762 ms, respectively. Thus, the average flanker effect was nominally larger for older adults than for younger adults: 61 ms versus 48 ms, a difference of 13 ms.

The full Brinley model (28 data points; Figure 6.4) included a dummy term for type of condition (compatible vs. incompatible) to test for intercept differences, and the condition by RT interaction term to test for slope differences. It yielded the following equation:

$$RT_{older} = 61 \ (55) + 1.11 \ (0.10) \ RT_{younger} - 27 \ (84) \ \text{condition}$$
$$+ \ 0.05 \ (0.14) \ \text{condition by } RT_{younger}.$$

The standard errors suggest that the intercept, the condition parameter, and the condition by RT parameter can all be set to zero without affecting the model significantly. This turned out to be the case, $\Delta LR \ \chi^2 \ (3) = 1.49$, yielding:

$$RT_{older} = 1.22 \ (0.02) \ RT_{younger}.$$

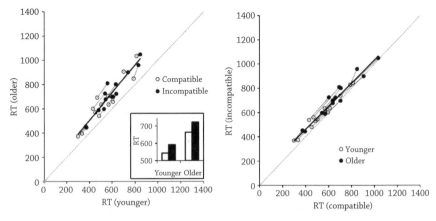

Figure 6.4 Eriksen flanker task: Results from meta-analyses (left-hand panel: Brinley plot, with average latencies in both conditions for both age groups in inset; right-hand panel: state-trace plot) of 14 studies. Data from the same study are connected by dotted lines. A single multilevel regression line (represented by the solid line) sufficed to capture the data in both instances, indicating that there is no age-related deficit in the flanker effect. The dotted line represents the equality diagonal.

The Brinley model thus suggests that the age-related effects in inhibition are symmetrical; that is, the age difference in the facilitation effect elicited by compatible flankers is as large as the age difference in the interference effect elicited by incompatible flankers. The model explained 88% of the variance.

The state-trace analysis is the real test for the inhibition hypothesis: The difference between the compatible and incompatible condition is a strong indicator of the efficiency to filter out distractors, given that it includes both the facilitation and interference effects associated with defective filtering.

The full model for the state-trace analysis,

$$\mathbf{RT}_{incompatible} = \mathbf{88\ (34) + 0.93\ (0.06)\ RT}_{compatible} + \mathbf{11\ (49)\ age\ group} \\ + \mathbf{0.01\ (0.08)\ age\ group\ by\ RT}_{compatible},$$

could be trimmed at no significant loss to fit, $\Delta LR\ \chi^2\ (2) = 1.86$, to

$$\mathbf{RT}_{incompatible} = \mathbf{82\ (24) + 0.95\ (0.04)\ RT}_{compatible}.$$

The standard error around the slope of the equation suggests that this slope is statistically indistinguishable from unity. The slope could indeed be fixed to equal 1 at no significant loss to fit, $\Delta LR\ \chi^2\ (1) = 1.46$, and the final model explained 96% of the variance:

$$\mathbf{RT}_{incompatible} = \mathbf{54\ (7) + 1.00\ (0.00)\ RT}_{compatible}.$$

The state-trace analysis then supports two conclusions. The first is that the flanker effect is additive to the baseline latency: The incompatible condition is slowed by a fixed amount (on average 54 ms) compared with the compatible condition. The second conclusion is that this cost does not reliably covary with age, suggesting that there is no specific age-related deficit in flanker processing.

6.3.3.1.2. Reading with Distractors

The reading with distractors task (pioneered by Connelly, Hasher, & Zacks, 1991) is very straightforward: Participants read a passage of prose that is either interspersed with distractor words (the distractor condition), or is not (the baseline condition). Texts are typically short (in the studies reviewed here the texts vary between 100 and 136 words), and words are interspersed quite frequently (e.g., the first sentence of the sample passage in Connelly & Hasher, with the passage to be read in italics and the distractors in standard font, is: '*The car ride* river *was getting bumpy* jeep *now that* reli-gious *George had* religious *left the main* digging tools *road to use the* religious *dirt road*'). Two dependent measures are typically used: Time needed to read the passage out loud and accuracy in a recall or recognition task. The task was designed explicitly to measure "inhibitory attentional mechanisms" (Connelly & Hasher, p. 533). Most of the primary studies conclude that reading times of older adults are slowed down much more by the presence of distractors than those of younger adults, indicating an age-related inhibition deficit. Variations on the basic paradigm include the type of distractor (in ascending order of likely interference with the text: blocks of *X*s, words unrelated to the passage, or words related to the passage) and their distinctiveness (distractors can be marked by using a different font or font type or font color, or by presenting them in columns).

The number of studies is again quite modest; I was able to collect data from 10 independent studies included in six papers (Connelley et al, 1991; Carlson, Hasher, Connelly, & Zacks, 1995; Duchek, Balota, & Thessing, 1998; Dywan & Murphy, 1996; Feyereisen & Charlot, 2008; Li, Hasher, Jonas, Rahhal, & May, 1998). Figure 6.5 reproduces the data. Because the times reflect reading times for a whole passage, the units are seconds rather than milliseconds. On average (and weighted for sample size), younger adults needed 45.4 seconds for control passages, and 71.2 seconds for passages with distractors; older adults took 59.8 seconds and 94.4 seconds, respectively. Thus, the distractor effect is 25.7 s for younger adults and 34.6 s for older adults. Clearly, older adults are slowed down by the presence of distractors to a much larger extent than younger adults are.

The full Brinley model (condition is a dummy, with 0 indicating that no distractors were present, and 1 indicating distractor presence; 20 data points) is:

$$RT_{older} = 2 \ (13) + 1.28 \ (0.28) \ RT_{younger} + 31 \ (15) \ \text{condition}$$
$$- \ 0.41 \ (0.29) \ \text{condition by} \ RT_{younger}.$$

This equation could be trimmed, at no significant cost to fit, $\Delta LR \ \chi^2 \ (2) = 4.83$, to a single-line model:

$$RT_{older} = 22 \ (6) + 0.95 \ (0.10) \ RT_{younger}.$$

This model, in turn, could be simplified, $\Delta LR \ \chi^2 \ (1) = 0.34$, to a straightforward additive model that explained 70% of the variance:

$$RT_{older} = 20 \ (4) + 1.00 \ (0.00) \ RT_{younger}.$$

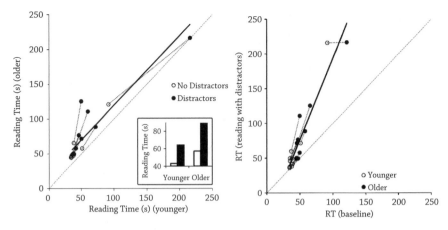

Figure 6.5 Reading with distractors: Results from meta-analyses (left-hand panel: Brinley plot, with average latencies in both conditions for both age groups in inset; right-hand panel: state-trace plot) of 10 studies. Data from the same study are connected by dotted lines. A single multilevel regression line (represented by the solid line) sufficed to capture the data in both instances, indicating that there is no age-related deficit in the ability to suppress distractors while reading. The dotted line represents the equality diagonal.

The full model for the state-trace analysis,

$$RT_{distractors} = -40\ (9) + 2.42\ (0.18)\ RT_{baseline} - 17\ (14)\ \text{age group} + 0.14\ (0.19)\ \text{age group by } RT_{baseline},$$

likewise could be trimmed at no cost to fit, $\Delta LR\ \chi^2\ (2) = 1.81$, to a single-line model with a somewhat disappointing fit (pseudo-$R^2 = 47$):

$$RT_{distractors} = -41\ (10) + 2.35\ (0.18)\ RT_{baseline}.$$

Taken together, the Brinley and state-trace analysis suggest that there is no specific age-related deficit in reading with distractors: The age-related difference in the distractor condition is statistically equivalent to that in the baseline condition, and the relationship between reading with and without distractors is identical in younger and older adults.

Note that the state-trace plot suggests that the effect is not completely multiplicative. For both younger and older adults, the cost becomes larger with longer baseline reading time, suggesting that there is some form of build-up of an additional cost—maybe fatigue?—for passages that are longer, more complex, or both. The graph also shows why the initial studies reported disproportional age-related effects: Older adults are much slower in their baseline performance, and this inflates condition differences. Failure to take age-related differences in baseline performance into account, therefore, is very likely to be the source of the false positive conclusions regarding this task.

As was the case with the negative priming studies, it is possible to purify the present data set to maximize the chances of finding age-related differences in the distractor-inhibition process, if any exist. If one assumes that there is such an age-related deficit, one would expect that this difference would emerge first and/or foremost in the condition theoretically requiring the largest amount of inhibitory processing, that is, when the distractor words are semantically related to the text in which they are embedded. Only seven studies used related distractors. Essentially, the results remain the same. The full Brinley model was:

$$RT_{older} = 3\ (18) + 1.30\ (0.38)\ RT_{younger} + 42\ (22)\ \text{condition}$$
$$- 0.46\ (0.40)\ \text{condition by } RT_{younger}.$$

This equation could be trimmed, at no significant cost to fit, $\Delta LR\ \chi^2\ (2) = 4.23$, to a single-line model:

$$RT_{older} = 28\ (10) + 0.95\ (0.13)\ RT_{younger}.$$

This model, in turn, could be simplified, $\Delta LR\ \chi^2\ (1) = 0.34$, to a straightforward additive model:

$$RT_{older} = 20\ (4) + 1.00\ (0.00)\ RT_{younger}.$$

The full model for the state-trace analysis,

$$RT_{distractors} = -65\ (21) + 3.05\ (0.42)\ RT_{baseline} + 53\ (30)\ \text{age group}$$
$$- 1.12\ (0.53)\ \text{age group by } RT_{baseline},$$

likewise could be trimmed at no cost to fit, $\Delta LR\ \chi^2\ (2) = 4.03$, to a single-line model:

$$RT_{distractors} = -33\ (16) + 2.30\ (0.28)\ RT_{baseline}.$$

Low statistical power might be an issue here, both in the selected data set and the full data set—the sample of studies is very small. Eyeball examination of the Brinley and state-trace plot in Figure 6.5 does suggest that the two data clouds (baseline/distractors in the Brinley; young/old in the state trace) indeed overlap.

We can dig a little deeper into the available evidence. At least three studies have tried to unravel the mechanism behind the distractor effect and its (lack of) age-related differences.

First, Dywan and Murphy (1996) interspersed 136-word texts in standard roman font with four different italicized distractor words that were related to the passage (each repeated 10 times)—a procedure almost identical to that of Connelly et al. (2001). The presence of distractors interfered with reading: Both groups made more reading stumbles in the distractor condition, but older adults more so than the younger adults. Comprehension was tested using a six-choice multiple-choice format; one of the wrong responses was one of the distractor words. Older adults were much more likely than younger adults to circle this intruder. Both of these results can be explained through age-related differences in efficiency of filtering, that is, inhibition. A third result, however, cannot be explained by this mechanism: After all stories were presented, participants were again given the six alternatives presented for the earlier comprehension test, but now the question was to indicate which of the six had been presented as a distractor. On this task, the younger adults outperformed the older adults: They recognized 32% of the distractors, older adults recognized 25%. This result strongly suggests that younger adults were not better than older adults in suppressing entry of the irrelevant information into the memory system—otherwise they would not have recognized the distractors. Dywan and Murphy interpreted their results as indicative of a source-monitoring deficit: Whereas younger adults were more likely to endorse distractor items in the recognition test than in the comprehension test, as the task requires (32% vs. 8%), older adults were about equally likely to endorse the distractor items in either condition (25% vs. 20%). This suggests that older adults are more likely to base their answer on familiarity, whereas younger adults seem to monitor the source of the information more closely. Source-monitoring deficits are quite large in older adults (for a meta-analysis, see Old & Naveh-Benjamin, 2008).

Two other studies attempted to obtain more direct, online measures of access, and both cast serious doubt on the access interpretation for the reading-with-distractor results.

First, Phillips and Lesperance (2003) recorded EEG signals while participants were processing sentences that contained distractor words semantically related to each other, but not to other words in the sentences—a sentence like "The train oak is maple never on pine time." Each sentence was followed by a probe. This probe could be either related to the sentence (e.g., late), to the distractors (e.g., tree), or to neither (e.g., table). The measure of interest is a particular ERP component, the N400 (Kutas & Hillyard, 1980) exhibited during display of the probe. The N400 is a negative deflection (topologically distributed over central-parietal sites on the scalp), peaking approximately 400 ms (300–500 ms) after the presentation of the stimulus. It is assumed to indicate to what extent the stimulus word is expected, given the semantic context; when the stimulus is preceded by a semantically appropriate context, its amplitude is reduced. In the present context, the N400 then measures to what extent both target information (i.e., the sentence) and distractor information are represented in working memory—a direct measure of access. Younger adults showed clear reductions in N400 to both the target-related and distractor-related probes, indicating that both the words in the sentence and the distractors are processed to the level of meaning. Older adults showed no such reduction, indicating—or so Phillips and Lesperance claim—that the presence of distractors interrupts online processing of the sentence, which remains unresolved within the time frame of the sentence-probe sequence (about 700 ms). In other words, younger adults process the distractors and the sentence well within 700 ms, to the point where they have both meanings readily available in mind; older adults likewise process both distractors and sentence within 700 ms, but the conflicting information does not lead to the emergence of two separate streams of meaning within that time frame. Further work where the sentence-probe interval is lengthened is necessary to determine the time course of semantic activation for older adults. (I note here that comprehension questions did show that older adults were able to extract the meaning of the sentences, so the problem may be one of time resolution rather than an indication that older adults process the two streams in a qualitatively different way than do younger adults.) At the very least, the results do not indicate that older adults are less able to filter out irrelevant distractors than are younger adults.

In a second study using online measures, Kemper, McDowd, and Kramer (2006) examined eye movements while participants were reading sentences interspersed with distractors. Distractors were either made visually very distinct (red font) or much less distinct (italics) and were either related ("The postman opened the package to inspect its *enclose* contents before sending it.") to the sentence or not ("The postman opened the package to inspect its *taxpayer* contents before sending it."). Predictability of the targets was either high ("The postman opened the package to inspect its contents before sending it.") or low ("The postman opened the package to inspect its packing before sending it.").

The only age difference that emerged in sentence processing was that younger adults were sensitive to target predictability (they spent more time on unpredictable targets and made more regressions to them), but older adults were not. Kemper and McDowd reasoned that if older adults had a specific deficit with inhibiting irrelevant information they would (a) fixate distractors more often and/or longer; (b) regress more often to distractors (i.e., make more leftwards fixations to distractors after a first pass over the sentence); and (c) have disrupted sentence processing as indicated by different patterns of first-pass fixation times. None of these expectations bore out. Older and younger adults had statistically identical probabilities of fixating the distractor, and statistically indistinguishable distractor fixation durations. Both age groups were equally sensitive to distractor type: Both fixated the italic distractors longer than the red distractors, indicating that each group was equally sensitive to distractor discriminability. Older adults did not make more regressions to the distractor than younger adults. Finally, both age groups were equally sensitive to distractor characteristics: Both age groups regressed more often to the italic distractor than to the red distractor, and both age groups regressed more often to the semantically related distractor than the unrelated distractor. The results suggest (as did those of Phillips and Lesperance) that older adults have more trouble extracting the meaning of these distractor-loaded sentences on the fly, or at least within the same time frame as younger adults.

In sum, neither the meta-analysis reported here, nor the more mechanistic studies looking at mechanisms underlying the distractor costs suggest a deficit in the access function of inhibitory processing in older adults in the reading-with-distractors task.

6.3.3.2. *The Restraint Function of Inhibition*

The restraint function of inhibition refers to control over the last step before overt behavior is emitted: When information is represented in working memory (e.g., because the access and delete function of inhibition have failed), the restraint function serves to stop the implementation of the actual behavior. I examined two tasks of restraint: the Stroop task and the antisaccade task.

6.3.3.2.1. The Stroop Task
The Stroop task (1935) is one of the most often used tests to measure failures in inhibition. In its simplest form, the task compares response times for naming the ink color

of neutral stimuli (e.g., Xs; this is the baseline condition) with response times for naming the ink color of incompatible color words (e.g., the word "green" printed in blue; this is the interference condition). The standard assumption is that there is a conflict between the dominant response of reading the word and the nondominant response of naming the color; the response time cost, or Stroop effect, stems from this conflict.

I was able to locate 49 studies contained in 31 papers (Anandam & Scialfa, 1999; Andrés, Guerrini, Phillips, & Perfect, 2008; Berardi, Parasuraman, & Haxby, 2001; Brink & McDowd, 1999; Cohn, Dustman, & Bradford, 1984; Comalli, Wapner, & Werner, 1962; Davidson, Zacks, & Williams, 2003; Dulaney & Rogers, 1994; Earles et al., 1997; Kemper, Herman, & Lian, 2003; Kieley & Hartley, 1997; Kwong See & Ryan, 1995; Li & Bosman, 1996; Little & Hartley, 2000; Panek, Rush, & Slade, 1984; Park et al., 1996; Rodríguez-Aranda & Sundet, 2006; Rush, Barch, & Braver, 2006; Salthouse, 1996a; Salthouse, Atkinson, & Berish., 2003; Salthouse & Meinz, 1995; Sommers & Danielson, 1999; Sommers & Huff, 2003; Spieler, Balota, & Faust, 1996; Thornton & Raz, 2006; Uttl & Graf, 1997; Van der Elst, Van Boxtel, Van Breukelen, & Jolles, 2006; Weir, Bruun, & Barber, 1997; West, 1999; West & Alain, 2000; West & Baylis, 1998). Twenty of those were included in the one earlier meta-analysis on the topic (Verhaeghen & De Meersman, 1998b).

The average time needed to name colors in the baseline condition is 579 ms in younger adults and 741 ms in older adults; the average time needed for the interference condition is 833 ms and 1,220 ms, respectively. Thus, older adults show a Stroop effect that is nominally (much) larger than that of younger adults: 479 ms versus 254 ms.

A Brinley analysis on the data (see Figure 6.6) reveals, however, that the age-related effect in Stroop score is an artifact of baseline slowing: A single line suffices to capture the data. The full model, including a dummy for condition (neutral vs. interference) as well as the condition by age interaction,

$$RT_{older} = -330\ (177) + 1.85\ (0.30)\ RT_{younger} - 44\ (237)\ \text{condition} + 0.06\ (0.36)\ \text{condition by}\ RT_{younger}$$

could be fruitfully pruned to a single line, $\Delta LR\ \chi^2\ (2) = 0.04$, explaining 77% of the variance:

$$RT_{older} = -354\ (74) + 1.89\ (0.10)\ RT_{younger}.$$

State-trace analysis proved more complicated. The full model,

$$RT_{colorword} = 489\ (228) + 0.59\ (0.39)\ RT_{color\ naming} + 250\ (257)\ \text{age group} + 0.06\ (0.42)\ \text{age group by}\ RT_{color\ naming},$$

is odd, to say the least, with a slope smaller than unity. Visual inspection of Figure 6.6 suggests that this model is misspecified. More particularly, it appears that there is a bifurcation, with some studies showing a smaller interference over neutral ratio than others. Informally, a ratio of 1.4 seems to constitute a nice dividing line between the two elongated clouds that appear in the graph. (Studies with a small ratio are Anandam & Scialfa, 1999; Davidson et al., 2003; Little & Hartley, 2000; Rush et al.,

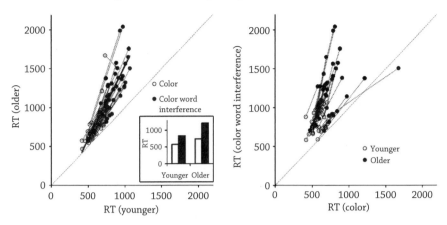

Figure 6.6 Stroop interference: Results from meta-analyses (left-hand panel: Brinley plot, with average latencies in both conditions for both age groups in inset; right-hand panel: state-trace plot) of 49 studies. Data from the same study are connected by dotted lines. A single multilevel regression line (represented by the solid line) sufficed to capture the data in the Brinley plot (the state-trace analysis was problematic, see text), indicating that there is no age-related deficit in the Stroop effect. The dotted line represents the equality diagonal.

2006; Thornton & Raz, 2006; Sommers & Danielson, 1999; and Spieler et al., 1996). Given the apparent misspecification, it seems prudent not to take the state-trace analysis at face value; I left it further unanalyzed. I do note that the standard errors for the age-related parameters (slope and intercept) exceed the parameter values themselves, suggesting a null effect for age in this model.

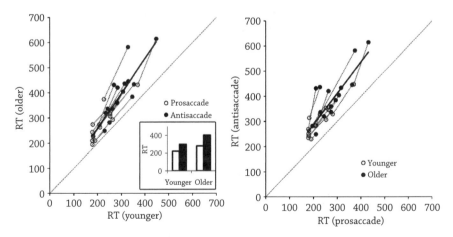

Figure 6.7 Antisaccade task: Results from meta-analyses (left-hand panel: Brinley plot, with average latencies in both conditions for both age groups in inset; right-hand panel: state-trace plot) of 15 studies. Data from the same study are connected by dotted lines. A single multilevel regression line (represented by the solid line) sufficed to capture the data in both plots, indicating that there is no age-related deficit in the antisaccade effect. The dotted line represents the equality diagonal.

In sum, the Brinley analysis shows that, after controlling for baseline slowing, there is no specific age-related deficit in the Stroop interference effect. The state-trace analysis appears to confirm this, but the state-trace data are also profoundly noisy.

6.3.3.2.2. Antisaccade

In the antisaccade task, the participant fixates a central location on the screen. After a brief period, a cue flashes in the periphery, typically to the left or to the right. Next, a target is presented on the side opposite to where the cue was flashed, far enough away that a saccade is required to bring the target into focus. The subject's task is to iden-tify that target. Latency and accuracy in this antisaccade condition are compared with latency and accuracy in a prosaccade version of the task, that is, a version where cue and target appear in the same location. The assumption is that the default response is to make a saccade in the direction of an abrupt-onset cue; in the antisaccade condi-tion, this response needs to be inhibited in favor of the alternative response. This typi-cally leads to a robust cost in both latency and accuracy. A variation steers the glance with arrows pointing at the peripheral location instead of a flashed cue; the cue-target interval can be manipulated as well.

I was able to locate 15 studies, published in 13 papers, that compared latency data for younger and older adults on an antisaccade and a prosaccade task (Bialystok, Craik, & Ryan, 2006; Bojko, Kramer, & Peterson, 2004; Butler & Zacks, 2006; Butler, Zacks, & Henderson, 1999; Fischer, Biscaldi, & Gezeck, 1997; Klein, Fischer, Hartnegg, Heiss, & Roth, 2000; Munoz, Broughton, Goldring, & Armstrong, 1998; Nieuwenhuis, Ridderinkhof, de Jong, Kok, & van der Molen, 2000; Olincy, Ross, Young, & Freedman, 1997; Olk & Kingstone, 2009; Raemaekers, Vink, van den Heuvel, Kahn, & Ramsey, 2006; Sweeney, Rosano, Berman, & Luna, 2001). On aver-age, younger adults had a 207 ms prosaccade latency and a 292 antisaccade latency; older adults needed 279 ms and 402 ms, respectively. Thus, the average antisaccade cost is nominally larger in older adults—123 ms—than in younger adults—75 ms, with the usual pattern that the larger costs resides with the group with the larger baseline response time.

A Brinley analysis on the data (see Figure 6.7) showed that a single line suffices to capture the data. The full model, including a dummy for condition (prosaccade vs. antisaccade) as well as the condition by age interaction,

$$RT_{older} = 34\ (49) + 1.11\ (0.24)\ RT_{younger} - 61\ (78)\ \text{condition}$$
$$+ 0.33\ (0.29)\ \text{condition by}\ RT_{younger},$$

could be fruitfully pruned to a single line, $\Delta LR\ \chi^2\ (2) = 2.61$, pseudo-$R^2 = .77$:

$$RT_{older} = -20\ (34) + 1.39\ (0.13)\ RT_{younger}.$$

Likewise, the state-trace analysis reduced the data to a single line. The full model,

$$RT_{antisaccade} = 83\ (35) + 0.97\ (0.15)\ RT_{prosaccade} - 15\ (48)\ \text{age group}$$
$$+ 0.22\ (0.20)\ \text{age group by}\ RT_{prosaccade},$$

could be trimmed at no significant loss to fit, ΔLR χ^2 (2) = 1.51, pseudo-R^2 = .70, to

$$\text{RT}_{\text{antisaccade}} = 40\ (33) + 1.24\ (0.13)\ \text{RT}_{\text{prosaccade}}.$$

Thus, the nominally larger latency cost in older adults in the antisaccade task is simply an artifact of baseline slowing: The age difference obtained in antisaccade trials is perfectly in line with the age difference obtained in prosaccade trials.

The situation is different—and a tad more complicated—for accuracy (see Figure 6.8). We should bear in mind here that, generally speaking, accuracy data tend to be noisier than latency data (see Verhaeghen, 2000; the best example is perhaps still the original Brinley paper, 1965, with very linear Brinley plots for RT, but a much noisier function for accuracy). For younger adults, error rate on antisaccade trials was 17.1% on average, compared with 4.6% on prosaccade trials; older adults showed an average error rate of 24.5% on antisaccade trials versus 6.7% on prosaccade trials. The accuracy cost is then 12.5% for younger adults, and 17.8% for older adults. These data are difficult to evaluate, especially given that the error rates are so low for the prosaccade task: Any possible interaction in the presence of such a large ceiling effect should be interpreted with caution.

If we discard that warning for now, we can note that at first glance the Brinley data look inconclusive: The scatter in error rates is large, especially in the older adults, and a single outlier is clearly visible. The state-trace plot, while no less noisy, does suggest that the error rates for older adults in antisaccade trials are larger than those for younger adults: The two data clouds separate out; older adults' data are more vertically elevated in the plot. This conclusion is strengthened by the horizontal overlap in the

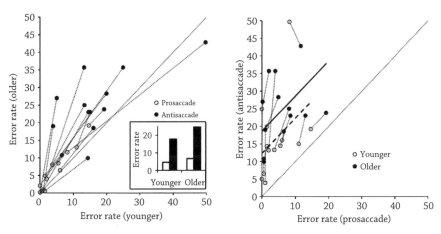

Figure 6.8 Error rates in the antisaccade task: Results from meta-analyses (left-hand panel: Brinley plot, with average latencies in both conditions for both age groups in inset; right-hand panel: state-trace plot) of 15 studies. Data from the same study are connected by dotted lines. The Brinley plot seemed too noisy to warrant interpretation; the state-trace analysis yielded two separate lines, indicating that older adults (solid line) show a larger antisaccade effect than younger adults (dashed line).

plots—again, with the cautionary remark that error rates are close to the measurement floor. Formal analysis bears this out. The full model,

$$\text{Error}_{\text{antisaccade}} = 11.7\ (3.6) + 1.14\ (0.58)\ \text{Error}_{\text{prosaccade}} + 10.6\ (3.1)\ \text{age group}$$
$$- 0.73\ (0.45)\ \text{age group by RT}_{\text{prosaccade}},$$

could be pared down to a model without the interaction and with a slope fixed at unity at no significant cost to fit, $\Delta\text{LR } \chi^2\ (2) = 3.30$:

$$\text{Error}_{\text{antisaccade}} = 12.3\ (2.7) + 1.00\ (0.00)\ \text{Error}_{\text{prosaccade}} + 6.3\ (2.4)\ \text{age group}.$$

This is a purely additive model, with an extra 6.3% error rate penalty for being an older adult. Deleting the age group variable results in a significant decrease in fit, ΔLR $\chi^2\ (1) = 8.80$.

Thus, in the accuracy domain, there appears to be an additive cost of making antisaccades, and this cost is larger in older adults than in younger adults.

As with a few of the other tasks considered here, doubts have been raised about the nature of the processes tapped by the antisaccade task. Specifically, it has been argued that antisaccade tasks rely heavily on goal maintenance and response selection, and not on the restraint function aspect of inhibition (Abel & Douglas, 2007; Olk & Kingstone, 2009; Raemaekers et al., 2006).

In summary, it seems that there is little evidence that older adults are particularly slower in executing antisaccades; there is evidence, however, that older adults commit considerably more antisaccade errors than younger adults. This finding is complicated by the presence of a floor effect in error rates on prosaccade tasks, as well as by rival accounts of such data—some have argued that these errors indicate goal neglect rather than the lack of inhibition of a prepotent response.

6.4. Age-related Differences in Task Shifting

The second aspect of executive control examined here concerns the planning and execution of switches between different tasks (e.g., Allport, Styles, & Hsieh, 1994; Monsell, 1996). This task switching ability is measured in the way one would expect: Subjects perform multiple (usually two) tasks in succession, and the cost of switching is quantified. Most often, the tasks involve forced-choice timed decisions, with response time as the main dependent measure. Sometimes, but not always, the tasks are performed on the same class of stimuli, so that the stimuli themselves do not give any indication as to which of the tasks has to be performed. For example, a series of digits may be shown: If the number is printed in red, the participant must make an odd/even judgment; if the number is printed in blue, the participant must report whether or not the number is larger than 5. This example involves cueing, that is, the color of the digit indicates which task has to be performed. Cueing can be made more explicit still by providing a word cue ("odd/even"; "size"), and the cue-stimulus interval can be lengthened to enhance the participant's readiness for the task. The place of the switch in the sequence of events can be predictable (typically in some form of alternating runs, i.e., an ABAB or AABBAABB design), most often it is not. Unpredictable switches obviously need to be cued; predictable switch paradigms sometimes use no cueing, relying instead on the participant to keep track of the task sequence herself. Some paradigms also include "pure-task," that is, single-task blocks (as opposed to the mixed-task blocks just described), in which each of the tasks is performed by itself.

A full design, then, contains three types of trials: pure-task trials (which are by definition non-switch), non-switch trials in mixed-task blocks (i.e., trials on which the task to be performed is identical to the task performed on the preceding trial), and switch trials (i.e., trials on which the task to be performed is different from the task performed on the preceding trial). Two types of switch costs can be computed. The first involves the comparison, within a mixed block, between switch and non-switch trials. Various names have been used for this cost, such as local switch cost, specific switch cost, Type 1 switch cost, and switching cost. I will use the latter term, given that it is the most descriptive, and given that it is this switching cost that is typically implied when researchers consider task switching as an executive process or an individual differences variable (e.g., Miyake et al., 2000). The second type of cost involves the comparison between (by necessity non-switch) trials in the pure-task blocks with the non-switch trials in the mixed-task blocks, or (sometimes) between the pure-task trials and the mean of the mixed-task trials. This cost has been labeled the global switch cost, general switch cost, Type 2 switch cost, and mixing cost. I will adopt the latter term. Note that the analyses on age differences in these two types of costs as described in the next section were reported earlier in Wasylyshyn, Verhaeghen, and Sliwinski (2010). The analyses on the dynamics of the switching cost are new.

6.4.1. Age Differences in Switching Cost

Research has shown that task switching is not a unitary process. Early conceptualizations of the switching cost saw two steps—disengaging the previous, now irrelevant task set and activating the new task set. More recent work has pointed at additional processes that might contribute to the switch cost. For instance, if the general class of stimuli remains constant throughout a trial, there will be a build-up of proactive interference or negative priming stemming from previous processing of similar items (Allport & Wylie, 1999), and/or from inhibiting the response tendencies inherited from the previous task set (Monsell, 2003). If the cues used to indicate which task to perform remain the same throughout a trial, the switch cost may include (or even reduce to) a repetition priming benefit for the non-switch trials—when the task switches, so does the cue; when the task remains the same, so will the cue, and the cue will then be processed faster because it is repeated, making non-switch trials faster for this reason alone (e.g., Logan & Bundesen, 2003). Finally, it has been noted that a switching cost remains even after very long cue-stimulus intervals, suggesting that full task preparation is delayed, either by necessity (Rogers & Monsell, 1995) or choice (De Jong, 2000) until the actual presentation of the stimulus.

It is difficult to assess age differences in each of these alleged components in a meta-analysis, because of the small sample sizes available. Therefore, I restrict my analysis to the switching cost per se. We (Wasylyshyn et al., 2011) were able to locate 34 experiments that allowed for an assessment of the task switching cost

(Bojko et al., 2004; Buchler, Hoyer, & Cerella, 2008; Cepeda, Kramer, & Gonzalez de Sather, 2001; de Jong, 2001; DiGirolamo et al., 2001; Eppinger, Kray, Mecklinger, & John, 2007; Friedman, Nessler, Johnson, Ritter, & Bersick, 2008; Gamboz, Borella, & Brandimonte, 2009; Goffaux, Phillips, Sinai, & Pushkar, 2008; Hahn, Andersen, & Kramer, 2004; Kramer, Hahn, & Gopher, 1999; Kray, 2006; Kray, Eber, & Lindenberger, 2004; Kray & Eppinger, 2006; Kray, Li, & Lindenberger, 2002; Kray & Lindenberger, 2000; Lien, Ruthruff, & Kuhns, 2008; Mayr, 2001; Mayr & Liebscher, 2001; Meiran, Gotler, & Perlman, 2001; Ravizza & Ciranni, 2002; Salthouse, Fristoe, McGuthry, & Hambrick, 1998; Spieler, Mayr, & LaGrone, 2006; van Asselen & Ridderinkhof, 2000; West & Travers, 2008; Witt et al., 2006).

Tasks and procedure varied widely; average RT (weighted for sample size) for younger adults on switch trials was 954 ms, compared with 730 ms on non-switch trials; for older adults, these numbers are 1498 ms and 1105 ms, respectively. Thus, the average task-switching cost is nominally larger for older adults (394 ms) than for younger adults (223 ms).

However, the Brinley analysis (68 data points; Figure 6.9) indicated that a single line sufficed to explain the data:

$$RT_{older} = 104\ (124) + 1.47\ (0.14)\ RT_{younger}$$

We also analyzed the effects of selected moderator variables. The first variable is whether a cue to switch was present or absent. Having to switch rapidly between task sets without the aid of external cues is thought to be highly reliant on internal action control. Consistent with this idea, cueing paradigms generally result in smaller switch costs (Kray & Lindenberger, 2000; Kray et al., 2002). The second moderating

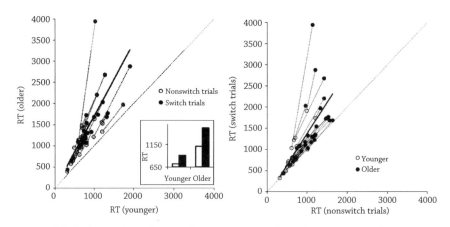

Figure 6.9 Task switching (i.e., performance on switch trials vs. non-switch trials): Results from meta-analyses (left-hand panel: Brinley plot, with average latencies in both conditions for both age groups in inset; right-hand panel: state-trace plot) of 34 studies. Data from the same study are connected by dotted lines. A single multilevel regression line (represented by the solid line) sufficed to capture the data in both plots, indicating that there is no age-related deficit in task switching. The dotted line represents the equality diagonal.

variable is whether the sequence of tasks is predictable (i.e., participants are aware of a pre-specified task sequence) or not (i.e., the task sequence is presented in a random fashion). Some previous research has suggested that paradigms employing unpredictable task sequences generally yield larger task switching costs (Rogers & Monsell, 1995; but see Tornay & Milán, 2001). We found no effects.

The state-trace analysis likewise suggested that a single line is sufficient to fit the data:

$$RT_{\text{switch trials}} = -94\ (145) + 1.43\ (0.15)\ RT_{\text{non-switch trials}}.$$

The conclusion is then that a single line suffices to explain the data in both the Brinley and state-trace analysis. Older adults are slower than younger adults, but once baseline slowing is taken into account, older adults switch between tasks as efficiently as younger adults.

Additionally, the state-trace analysis reveals that the switching requirement has a multiplicative effect on RT, with a slowing factor of about 1.5. This implies that task switching costs increase with time needed for the non-switch versions of the task, and therefore with presumed task difficulty.

6.4.2. Age Differences in the Dynamics of Task Preparation

I mentioned above that part of the switching cost is assumed to be due to insufficient preparedness for the upcoming task. Task preparedness is assumed to be a monotonic function of the cue-stimulus interval (CSI): When more time is available between the presentation of the cue and the actual stimulus, subjects have more time to prepare the implementation of the next task set.

To examine age differences in the efficiency of preparation, I examined switching costs as a function of CSI. I included all CSIs reported separately in any of the studies. In a preliminary analysis (performed to examine whether an analysis of switch costs is warranted), I compared the influence of CSI on switch trials and non-switch trials separately (including age group and the age group by CSI parameters as well). If the preparation hypothesis is correct, CSI should have an impact on switch trials only, and not for non-switch trials, because the latter do not need a reconfiguration of the task set. This turned out to be true—the model indicated a nonsignificant slope of 0.02 for the non-switch trials, and a significant slope of -0.18 for switch trials; the age effect turned out to be purely additive (Figure 6.10, top panel). This result indicates that an analysis of the switching cost as a function of CSI is warranted. I calculated switching costs as the ratio of switch and non-switch trials, which, as suggested by the state-trace analysis above, is the more appropriate measure. Switch cost as a function of CSI is shown in Figure 6.10, bottom panel.

In a first step, I analyzed cost as a function of CSI and CSI-squared (the latter term was included to test for any non-linearity in the data). Age group, age group by CSI and age group by CSI-squared parameters were included as well. Nonlinearity is suggested in the hypothesis that there is a residual switch cost, that is, a cost that remains even after very long CSI. Neither of the nonlinear components (i.e., the effect of CSI-squared and its interaction with age) turned out to be significant. There

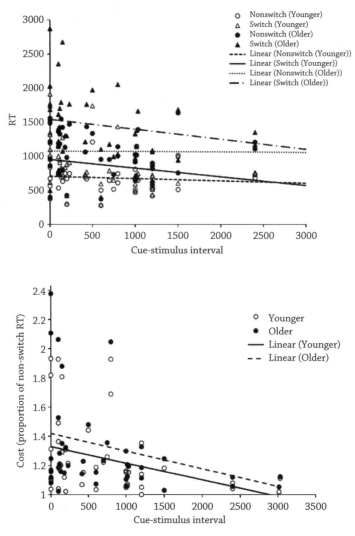

Figure 6.10 The dynamics of task switching in younger and older adults. Top panel shows response time (RT) for switch and non-switch trials as a function of age and cue-stimulus interval (CSI). RT for switch trials becomes faster with longer preparation time; there is no age difference in this dynamic. Bottom panel shows proportional switch cost as a function of CSI. This analysis likewise indicates that the dynamics of preparedness do not change with age.

was no indication for an age-related difference in the dynamics of preparedness. The intercept, which indicates the ratio of switch over non-switch trials at 0 ms CSI, was 1.33 for younger adults, and 1.42 for older adults, the common slope was –0.00012. Given that CSIs are expressed in ms, this means that the ratio goes down by 0.12 for every second the CSI is lengthened, converging on unity—no cost—at 2,892 ms for younger and 3,468 ms for older adults. I note here that two studies (Meiran et al.,

2001, Expts. 2 and 3) used CSIs that come close to this mark—3,016 ms and 3,032 ms, respectively—and still observed switching costs, ranging from 13 ms to 181 ms. This suggests that the estimates are somewhat unrealistic. The bottom-line, however, is that the dynamics of task-set preparation are very similar for younger and older adults. There is, put simply, no age deficit in task switch preparation.

6.4.3. Age Differences in Mixing Costs

The second type of cost, mixing cost, is typically taken to indicate the set-up cost associated with maintaining and scheduling two (or more, as the case may be) mental task sets. (A mental task set is the set of subtasks and processes necessary to perform a task.) Like the switching cost, the mixing cost may have multiple origins. An early review (Los, 1996) distinguishes between stimulus-driven, likely passive (or bottom-up), and strategic, more active (or top-down) accounts for the mixing cost. Stimulus-driven mechanisms include a lack of repetition priming and an increase in negative priming (e.g., Los, 1996; Monsell, 2003); both of these would impose a de facto penalty on mixed-task blocks. It seems more likely, however, that the main mechanism is top-down rather than bottom-up, given that mixing costs (unlike switching costs) disappear entirely with sufficient practice with mixed-task blocks (Minear & Shah, 2008).

Multiple strategic, top-down mechanisms have been proposed. For instance, de Jong (2001) has argued that one of the requirements for efficient switching is the active disengagement from the no-longer-relevant task set. De Jong assumes that participants can, however, opt to not fully disengage. This would have the effect that they can reinstate the task set more readily when it is needed again. This lack of disengagement would then lead to slowing on all mixed-block trials, switch and non-switch, because the non-relevant task set is always kept active and interferes with the current task set. In this view, a higher mixing cost would then (at least partially) reflect the setting of a more conservative control strategy; de Jong claims (not unreasonably) that older adults might be more prone to use this conservative strategy. (A similar observation has been made by Meiran, Gotler, & Perlman, 2001.) A different view, often encountered in aging research, is that pure-task blocks and mixed-task blocks differ in effective memory requirements (Kray et al., 2002; Strayer & Kramer, 1994) and/or the need to coordinate the multiple task sets involved (Verhaeghen & Cerella, 2002), particularly to resolve task-set conflicts (Kray & Lindenberger, 2002; Mayr, 2001), and that this might be the mechanism driving the age differences in mixing costs (if any).

We (Wasylyshyn et al., 2011) were able to locate 16 experiments that allowed for a comparison of pure-task trials with non-switch trials in mixed blocks (Buchler, Hoyer, & Cerella, 2008; Cepeda, Kramer, & Gonzalez de Sather, 2001; de Jong, 2001; Friedman, Nessler, Johnson, Ritter, & Bersick, 2008; Gamboz, Borella, & Brandimonte, 2009; Goffaux, Phillips, Sinai, & Pushkar, 2008; Kray, Li, & Lindenberger, 2002; Kray & Lindenberger, 2000; Lien, Ruthruff, & Kuhns, 2008; Mayr, 2001; Mayr & Liebscher, 2001; Meiran, Gotler, & Perlman, 2001; Spieler, Mayr, & LaGrone, 2006; van Asselen & Ridderinkhof, 2000; West & Travers, 2008). (There are additional papers that compare pure-task trials with either switch trials or the average of mixed-task blocks; Brinley, 1965; Hartley & Kieley, 1995; Mayr & Kliegl, 2000; Verhaeghen &

Basak, 2002; Verhaeghen & Hoyer, 2007. These are not considered here.) Average response times on pure-block trials was 279 ms for younger adults and 431 ms for older adults; response times on non-switch trials in mixed blocks in the same studies was 371 ms and 642 ms, respectively. The mixing cost was 91 ms for younger adults and 210 ms for older adults. The data are shown in Figure 6.11.

The Brinley analysis (24 data points) with dummy terms for trial type (pure-task vs. non-switch) to test for intercept differences, and the trial type by RT interaction term to test for slope differences, yielded the following equation:

$$RT_{older} = 67\ (113) + 1.25\ (0.19)\ RT_{younger} + 121\ (154)\ \textbf{trial type}$$
$$+ 0.02\ (0.24)\ \textbf{trial type by RT}_{younger}.$$

The standard errors suggest that both the trial type parameter and its interaction with younger adults' latency can be set to zero without affecting the model significantly. This, however, turned out not to be the case, $\Delta LR\ \chi^2\ (2) = 7.61$. Only the interaction parameter could be dropped at no cost to significance, $\Delta LR\ \chi^2\ (1) = 0.01$. The final Brinley equation is:

$$RT_{older} = 58\ (71) + 1.26\ (0.11)\ RT_{younger} + 134\ (45)\ \textbf{trial type}.$$

Thus, two lines are needed to describe the data: One for non-switch trials, one for switch trials. This, in turn, suggests that older adults show a larger task mixing cost than do younger adults.

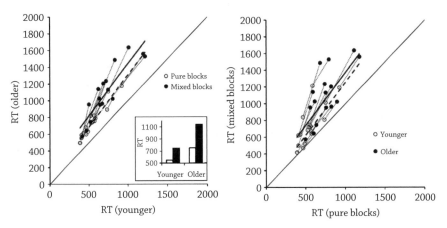

Figure 6.11 Task mixing (i.e., performance on non-switch trials in mixed blocks and trials in pure, non-switch blocks): Results from meta-analyses (left-hand panel: Brinley plot, with average latencies in both conditions for both age groups in inset; right-hand panel: state-trace plot) of 16 studies. Data from the same study are connected by dotted lines. Two multilevel regression lines are needed to capture the data in both plots, indicating an age-related deficit in task mixing. The dotted line represents the equality diagonal; in the Brinley plot, the solid line represents mixed blocks, the dashed line pure blocks; in the state-trace plot, the solid line represents older adults, the dashed line younger adults.

State-trace analysis confirms this pattern, or almost. From the Brinley analysis, we would expect two parallel lines, one for younger adults, one for older adults. The equation is:

$$RT_{\text{non-switch trials}} = -23\ (141) + 1.28\ (0.24)\ RT_{\text{pure-task trials}} + 149\ (204)\ \text{age}$$
$$\text{group} - 0.05\ (0.30)\ \text{age group by } RT_{\text{pure-task trials}},$$

which could be trimmed, at virtually no cost to fit, $\Delta LR\ \chi^2\ (1) = 0.03$, to:

$$RT_{\text{non-switch trials}} = -6\ (91) + 1.26\ (0.14)\ RT_{\text{pure-task trials}} + 118\ (61)\ \text{age group.}$$

Deleting the age group term resulted in only a marginally significant decrease in fit, $\Delta LR\ \chi^2\ (1) = 3.51$, $p = .061$. I will risk a Type-I error, however, and proclaim that the two lines are, indeed, distinct.

The end conclusion is that older adults show reliably larger task mixing costs than younger adults.

6.5. Age-related Differences Task Coordination/ planning: Dual-task Performance

The final basic aspect of cognitive control I will examine is the ability to control or plan behavior. I will focus on the ability to perform two tasks at once, often called dual-task performance. In a dual-task paradigm, performance on a single task is compared with performance on the same task when a second task is performed concurrently (e.g., a visual reaction time task with or without a concurrent auditory reaction time task). Rabbitt (1997) considers dual-task performance the "test bed for the exploration of the functions of planning and control" (p. 5), as do Baddeley and Della Sala (1996). Note that Miyake et al. (2000) did not obtain significant correlations between dual-task performance and three other aspects of executive control (i.e., inhibition, shifting, and updating), suggesting that this construct is quite distinct from the other executive control mechanisms examined here.

Here, I will simply review the results from our previous meta-analysis (Verhaeghen et al., 2003), which collected data from 33 dual-task studies (Anderson, 1999; Anderson et al., 2000; Baddeley, Logie, Bressi, Della Sala, & Spinnler, 1986; Broadbent & Heron, 1962; Chen et al., 1996; Craik & McDowd, 1987; Gick, Craik, & Morris, 1988; Greenwood & Parasuraman, 1991; Guttentag & Madden, 1987; Hartley & Little, 1999; Hawkins, Kramer & Capaldi, 1992; Isingrini, Vazou, & Leroy, 1995; Kramer, Larish, & Strayer, 1995; Li, 1999; Li, Lindenberger, Freund, & Baltes, 2001; Light, Kennison, Prull, La Voie, & Zuellig, 1996; Light & Prull, 1995; Light, Prull, & Kennison, 2000; Lindenberger, Marsiske, & Baltes, 2000; Lorsbach & Simpson, 1988; Madden, 1986; McDowd & Craik, 1988; Morris, Gick, & Craik, 1988; Park, Puglisi, & Smith, 1986; Park, Smith, Dudley, & Lafronza, 1989; Ponds, Brouwer, & van Wolffelaar, 1988; Rogers, Bertus, & Gilbert, 1994; Salthouse, Fristoe, Lineweaver, & Coon, 1995; Salthouse & Somberg, 1982a; Somberg & Salthouse, 1982; Tecce, Cattanach, Yrchik,

Meinbresse, & Dessonville, 1982; Tsang & Shaner, 1998; Tun & Wingfield, 1994; Tun, Wingfield, & Stine, 1991; Tun, Wingfield, Stine, & Mecsas, 1992; Wright, 1981).

Figure 6.12 shows the data. Average single-task response time was 947 ms in younger adults and 1,253 ms in older adults; dual-task response times were 1,084 ms and 1,482 ms, respectively. Thus, dual-task cost was on average 137 ms in younger adults and 229 ms in older adults.

In the Brinley analysis, two lines emerged, one for single-task performance, one for dual-task performance:

$$\mathrm{RT}_{older} = -200\ (46) + 1.63\ (0.08)\ \mathrm{RT}_{younger} + 36\ (12)\ \text{trial type.}$$

This suggests that older adults have a specific deficit in dual-task performance, and need on average 36 ms longer than younger adults do. The model accounts for 96% of the variance compared with the empty model.

In our paper, we also investigated the influence of selected moderator variables— whether the task relied primarily on sensorimotor or central processes, whether the primary and secondary tasks were verbal or spatial, whether or not the input modality (visual vs. authority) matched between primary and secondary task, and whether output was manual or vocal. As expected, the slope for verbal tasks (1.78, SE = .12) was significantly steeper than that for verbal tasks (1.18, SE = .15). The verbal-nonverbal contrast, however, did not influence the dual-task effects. The only other moderator variable to influence age-related slowing (but not dual-task cost) was one that coded for whether the input modalities for the primary and secondary tasks matched (e.g.,

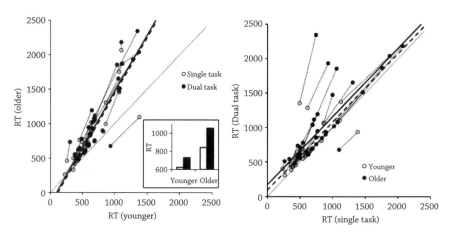

Figure 6.12 Dual-task performance: Results from meta-analyses (left-hand panel: Brinley plot, with average latencies in both conditions for both age groups in inset; right-hand panel: state-trace plot) of 33 studies. Data from the same study are connected by dotted lines. Two multilevel regression lines are needed to capture the data in both plots, indicating an age-related deficit in dual-task costs. The dotted line represents the equality diagonal; in the Brinley plot, the solid line represents dual-task blocks, the dashed line single-task blocks; in the state-trace plot, the solid line represents older adults, the dashed line younger adults.

both were visual or both were auditory). Older adults exhibited less slowing on tasks in which the input modality matched compared with studies in which input modalities did not match (–134, *SE* = 33). Modality match did not interact with either dual-task cost or the Brinley slope. In sum, none of moderator variables investigated produced a differential age-related effect.

The state-trace analysis confirmed the presence of two lines, one for younger adults, another for older adults:

$$\text{RT}_{\text{dual-task}} = 92 \ (25) + 0.99 \ (0.06) \ \text{RT}_{\text{single-task}} + 78 \ (12) \ \textbf{age group.}$$

This equation suggests that the dual-task cost is independent of latency in the single-task conditions, but differs between age groups. Younger adults are, on average, 92 ms slower in dual-task conditions than in single-task conditions; older adults are, on average, 170 ms slower. The model accounts for 96% of the variance compared with the empty model.

In the state-trace analysis, we found that the additive cost was significantly higher for verbal (271.1, *SE* = 65.1) than nonverbal (99.3, *SE* = 49.6) primary tasks. The average slope for verbal tasks (0.75, *SE* = 0.13) was significantly lower than for nonverbal tasks (1.08, *SE* = 0.10), although both slopes did not differ significantly from 1.0. The verbal-nonverbal contrast did not modify any other effect. The additive cost was also larger for studies in which the input modality matched (127.7, *SE* = 29.6) compared with studies in which input modalities did not match (80.1, *SE* = 11.5). Vocal-output tasks were associated with reduced and nonsignificant additive dual-task costs and with reduced and nonsignificant age effects: the intercept for younger adults in vocal RT was 38 ms (*SE* = 36) versus 106 ms in manual RT (*SE* = 26); in older adults, these values were increased by 30 ms (*SE* = 22) versus 96 (*SE* = 13), respectively. Most moderator variables, then, did not reliably influence the effects of age, except that age effects in dual-task costs were absent in tasks using vocal response times.

Overall, the pattern can be easily interpreted. The state traces, one for younger adults, one for older adults, have positive intercepts and slopes of one, showing an additive effect. This indicates that dual-tasking involves a set-up cost that does not permeate the computational processes involved in the baseline task. Second, the lines for single and dual tasks separate out in the Brinley plot, indicating that there is a specific age-related deficit in the coordination processes associated with dual-task performance. Note, however, that the age effect in dual tasking is relatively modest. The slowing factor in the baseline task was 1.6 (this is the slope of the baseline Brinley function). The degree of slowing in the dual-task effect can be estimated by the old/young ratio of the difference in intercepts. This factor had a value of 1.8, an increase of 20% over baseline slowing (80%–60%).

6.6. Age Differences in One Neuropsychological Test of Executive Control: The Trail Making Test

The Trail Making Test (TMT), originally part of the Army Individual Test Battery (1944) is a popular test in neuropsychological practice, perhaps because it is fast and easy to administer. It also tends to correlates well with severity of cognitive impairment after neurological damage (e.g., Corrigan & Hinkeldey, 1987). Trail Making is a connect-the-dot test, performed in two versions, A and B. In Part A, 25 circles, each containing a different number from the set 1 to 25, have to be connected in numerical order (1-2-3 and so on). In Part B, the subject alternates between numbers and letters (1-A-2-B-3-C and so on). Subjects are instructed to be fast. Both parts of the test require the same set of basic abilities—attention, visual scanning, and motor speed; Part B is additionally assumed to involve a new component, labeled "cognitive flexibility" (e.g., Korrte et al., 2002) or "set-switching"/"set-shifting" (e.g., Arbuthnott & Frank, 2000). Typically, the difference score between Part B and Part A is used to isolate this component (e.g., Heaton, Nelson, Thompson, Burks, & Franklin, 1985); some researchers have—as I will—advocated the use of ratio scores (Arbuthnott & Frank, 2000; Corrigan & Hinkeldey, 1987; Golden, Osmon, Moses, & Berg, 1981).

I was able to locate 19 relevant studies contained in 15 papers (Berardi, Parasuraman, & Haxby, 2001; Bornstein, 1985; Davies, 1968; Botwinick & Storandt, 1974; Drane, Yuseph, Huthwaite, & Klingler, 2002; Elias, Robbins, Walter, & Schultz, 1993; Goul & Brown, 1970; Kennedy, 1981; Periáñez et al., 2007; Salthouse et al., 1997; Salthouse & Fristoe, 1995; Stuss, Stethem, & Poirier, 1987; Tombaugh, 2004; Yeudall, Reddon, Gill, & Stefanyk, 1987).

Figure 6.13 shows the data. Part B is indeed performed much slower, on average, than Part A. In younger adults, Part A takes on average 1,033 ms/element, Part B takes 2,271 ms/element; in older adults, these numbers are 1,801 ms/element and 4,392 ms/element, respectively. There are nominally strong age effects: The difference

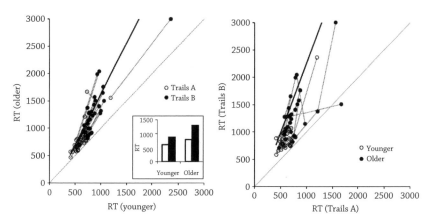

Figure 6.13 Trail Making test: Results from meta-analyses (left-hand panel: Brinley plot, with average latencies in both conditions for both age groups in inset; right-hand panel: state-trace plot) of 19 studies. Data from the same study are connected by dotted lines. A single multilevel regression line (represented by the solid line) sufficed to capture the data in both plots, indicating that there is no age-related deficit in the processes specifically measured by Trail Making B, compared with Trail Making A. The dotted line represents the equality diagonal.

between Part A and Part B is 1,237 ms/element in younger adults, and 2,591 ms/element in older adults.

The full Brinley model for these data,

$$RT_{older} = -14\ (593) + 1.64\ (0.59)\ RT_{younger} - 466\ (817)\ part$$
$$+\ 0.32\ (0.64)\ part\ by\ RT_{younger,}$$

could be reduced to a single-line model without any significant cost to fit, $\Delta LR\ \chi^2$ (2) = 0.33, pseudo-R^2 = .87:

$$RT_{older} = -243\ (201) + 1.86\ (0.12)\ RT_{younger}.$$

This, then, suggests that older adults are not differentially slowed on Part B compared with Part A: Both parts show the same age-related slowing factor. This age-related slowing factor is large—1.86—and in line with the expected slowing factor for spatial tasks. (The intercept is not significant, but seems simply too large for me to leave it out of the equation.)

The state-trace analysis likewise yielded a single line. The full model,

$$RT_{Part\ B} = 102\ (445) + 2.11\ (0.44)\ RT_{Part\ A} - 302\ (568)\ age\ group$$
$$+\ 0.39\ (0.49)\ age\ group\ by\ RT_{Part\ A,}$$

reduced to a single-line model, $\Delta LR\ \chi^2$ (2) = 1.22. pseudo-R^2 = .89:

$$RT_{Part\ B} = -281\ (190) + 2.54\ (0.14)\ RT_{Part\ A}.$$

This model reinforces the results from the Brinley analysis that there is no age-related deficit in Trail Making once baseline slowing is taken into account.

At first blush, the multiplicative result obtained from the state-trace model is unexpected. The Trail Making Test is sometimes billed as a test for task switching or flexibility; given that it compares response time in a switching block with response time in a pure-task block, it would primarily measure mixing costs. We observed above, however, that mixing costs are additive. A second discrepancy to note is that there are no significant age-related effects specific to Part B, the mixed-trial part, compared with Part A, the pure-trial part. We observed above that task mixing leads to large age-related costs. Perhaps the explanation is simple: What is being mixed in Part B is not the task (the task remains essentially the same: Visit the circles in order), but rather the stimulus set. This switching between sets necessitates continuous updating and retrieval of a memory of the last item completed in the previous set (aided, in Trail Making, by the physical presence of the trail as completed so far on the page). Task A thus effectively becomes a 1-Back task; Task B a 2-Back task. It seems, then, that the test might be better characterized as a test of focus-switching (e.g., Garavan, 1998; Verhaeghen & Basak, 2005) in which elements stored in working memory need to be brought into the focus of attention for processing and then updated. Multiple studies have demonstrated age equivalence in focus-switching costs in latency measures (but not accuracy) once baseline slowing has been taken into account (e.g., Vaughan, Basak, Hartman, & Verhaeghen, 2008; Verhaeghen & Basak, 2005).

The state-trace model also suggests that a difference score between Part B and Part A is a dramatically suboptimal metric, especially for groups or individuals much slower than the mean of the comparison group. Difference scores will easily lead to false positives, given the very large slope of the state-trace function. The ratio of Part B over Part A is a better approximation of the function found in the state-trace analysis, because it provides a better correction for baseline slowing. It is not perfect, however, given the negative intercept of the function.

6.7. Age Differences in Executive Control: Summary and Outlook

The meta-analyses presented in this chapter lead to two empirical conclusions, each at a different level of observation. First, at the level of absolute age differences—the level older adults deal with in their daily lives, and also the level human-factor psychologists are most interested in—near-universal deficits in executive control are to be noted: Absolute age differences are typically larger for task versions requiring executive control than for versions with minimal control demands. This finding, however, stands in stark contrast to the second conclusion, as revealed by Brinley plots and state traces. Table 6.1 (quite dramatically) summarizes those results, providing the Brinley and state-trace equations for each of the aspects of executive control analyzed here. Clearly, most executive-control tasks do not show age-related deficits over and beyond those already present in their low-control or no-control baseline version. The only exceptions are dual-task performance and task mixing. Perhaps most surprising given the attention this explanation has received in the literature, none of the tasks involving inhibition or resistance to interference showed age-sensitivity in the control process. Neither did task switching, the aspect of task shifting typically considered to be the best measure of task shifting, nor Trail Making, a purported measure of planning and set-shifting. At a very global level, then, this chapter demonstrates that the oft-asserted (or assumed) decline in executive control with advancing age (at least in the latency domain) is true only at the shallowest level, that of direct observation, that is, when slowing in the baseline version of the executive-demand task is not taken into account. When it is, the story is one of remarkable age-constancy, with very few exceptions. In other words, the rumors of the age-related demise of cognitive/executive control are greatly exaggerated.

What to make of the exceptions? We can impose a slightly grander scheme on the results (see also Verhaeghen & Cerella, 2002). Inhibition and task switching, both age-insensitive, involve selective attention; that is, they involve opting into the one relevant stream of information and/or the one relevant task set from the multitudes that are available to the subject. Tasks that are age-sensitive, in contrast (task mixing and dual tasking), seem to tap into divided attention—two or more streams of information are simultaneously active and both are (presumably) represented in attention and/or awareness. Both task-mixing costs and dual-task performance have in common that performance on a block of dual-task trials is compared with performance on a block of single-task trials. The two paradigms differ mainly in their

Table 6.1 **Summary of results from the meta-analyses on aging and speed of executive control conducted in Chapter 6. Brinley functions and state traces separated by construct and task.**

Task	Brinley equation: $RT_{older} =$		State-trace equation: $RT_{executive\ control} =$	
	Baseline condition	*Executive control condition*	*Younger adults*	*Older adults*
Unintentional inhibition				
Inhibition of return	$7 + 1.26$ $RT_{younger}$	(same as baseline)	$20 + 0.99$ $RT_{baseline}$	(same as young)
Negative priming	$19 + 1.15$ $RT_{younger}$	(same as baseline)	$-9 + 1.04$ $RT_{baseline}$	(same as young)
Intentional inhibition: Access				
Eriksen flanker	$48 + 1.14$ $RT_{younger}$	(same as baseline)	$82 + 0.95$ $RT_{baseline}$	(same as young)
Reading with distractors	$22 + 0.95$ $RT_{younger}$	(same as baseline)	$-41 + 2.35$ $RT_{baseline}$	(same as young)
Intentional inhibition: Restraint				
Stroop	$-354 + 1.89$ $RT_{younger}$	(same as baseline)	(unspecified)	(unspecified)
Antisaccade	$-20 + 1.39$ $RT_{younger}$	(same as baseline)	$40 + 1.24$ $RT_{baseline}$	(same as young)
Task shifting				
Switching	$104 + 1.47$ $RT_{younger}$	(same as baseline)	$-110 + 1.48$ $RT_{baseline}$	(same as young)
Mixing	$58 + 1.26$ $RT_{younger}$	$192 + 1.26\ RT_{younger}$	$-6 + 1.26$ $RT_{baseline}$	$112 + 1.26$ $RT_{baseline}$
Coordination/planning				
Dual-task performance	$-200 + 1.63$ $RT_{younger}$	$-164 + 1.63\ RT_{younger}$	$92 + 0.99$ $RT_{baseline}$	$170 + 1.63$ $RT_{baseline-243\ +}$ $_{1.86\ RT}$
Neurological tests				
Trail Making	$-243 + 1.86$ $RT_{younger}$	(same as baseline)	$-281 + 2.54$ $RT_{baseline}$	(same as young)

temporal dynamics: In task-mixing studies, task A and task B are performed in succession; in dual tasking, they are performed concurrently. One potential deeper commonality could then be situated in age-related differences in working memory capacity as mediated by frontal-lobe functioning.

Several researchers (Bopp & Verhaeghen, 2007; Kramer et al., 1999; Kray and Lindenberger, 2000) have stressed that aging comes with impairments in the organization of cognitive processing within working memory. Thus, older adults can seemingly efficiently activate and deactivate the cognitive system to perform task switches efficiently (i.e., there are no age-related differences in task-switching costs), but they are impaired when maintaining and coordinating multiple task sets. Even ostensibly contradictory results might fit this pattern.

For instance, Kray and Lindenberger (2000) originally found that age differences in mixing were significantly greater than in switching, but later found the opposite results when they increased the number of potentially relevant task sets from two to four (Kray et al., 2002). In the latter case, the increased working memory demands might have caused an age deficit to emerge in a process that is normally age-insensitive. A second possibility is the view taken by de Jong (2001, see Section 6.4.3), namely that older adults strategically overprepare by keeping all task sets highly active in working memory, perhaps in the service of selective attention. This state of high alert might then come at the cost of continuous and time-consuming refreshing (Barrouillet & Camos, 2007; Johnson, 1992). Such refreshing would be extraneous to the task processing per se and thus likely lead to an additive cost, as was found here. More research is needed to disentangle these different proposals and judge them on their relative merits. Whatever the precise mechanism, at a broad level of generalization, one could conclude that tasks of selective attention are mostly age-insensitive and that reliable age differences in response time only emerge in tasks that involve divided attention and/or the maintenance of two distinct mental task sets.

I should also point out, on a less important note, that the slowing factors obtained in the Brinley plots for the baseline tasks are largely in line with what one would expect given the results from the Chapters 2 and 4—shallow slopes for mostly linguistic tasks (picture naming in negative priming tasks, and reading in reading with distractors), intermediate slopes for reaction time tasks (prosaccade in antisaccade, no-return in inhibition of return, and neutral RT in the flanker task), and steep slopes for spatial tasks (color naming in Stroop, and visual search in Trail Making). Tasks that form a mixture (like dual-task, or task mixing and task switching, where different studies use very different baseline tasks) show the standard "general" or average Brinley slope, between 1.3 to 1.6. These findings can serve either as further corroboration (if any were needed) of the furcations found in Chapters 2 and 4, or as an additional validity check on the present set of data.

Finally, I would like to point out two (relatively) blind spots in the literature. One is the relative dearth of studies concerned with the deletion or filtering aspect of inhibition. Much research in the field has covered access and restraint; filtering has been comparatively understudied, and no paradigm has emerged that has led to a body of literature large enough to be included here. The same is true for the executive control process of updating the contents of working memory, which has largely gone unnoticed in theoretical accounts of cognitive aging, and has not yielded a literature large enough to warrant meta-analysis.

7

Lifespan Trajectories

In Chapters 1 through 6, I examined different cognitive tasks and how age affects the speed of performance on these tasks. In each of these cases, age was operationalized as a dichotomy: Younger adults (age 18–25, typically) versus older adults (age 65 and up, typically). This obviously sidesteps one of the more interesting questions about aging, namely how one goes from that first slice through the lifespan to the second. What are the dynamics of adult development? For the tasks that decline, when does decline begin and what shape does it take? Is decline, for instance, gradual or discontinuous, linear or nonlinear? Additionally, we may wonder whether the differences we observed between our age slices are really age differences: To what extent do generational and historical influences play a role in cognitive "aging" of the sort I have investigated here?

These questions appear to be surprisingly far from settled. As recent as 2009, Salthouse published an article with the title "When does age-related cognitive decline begin?", seemingly indicating the need to find such a starting point. Quite a number of researchers have been willing to claim that there is a specific inflection point in the cognition by age curve, but there is little agreement on where this point is situated. Some see stability until the fifties—"relatively little decline in performance occurs until people are about 50 years old." (Albert & Heaton, 1988); "no or little drop in performance before age 55"(Rönnlund, Nyberg, Bäckman, & Nilsson, 2005). Others see the sixties as the age when decline occurs—"cognitive abilities generally remain stable throughout adult life until around age sixty." (Plassman et al., 1995); "most abilities tend to peak in early midlife, plateau until the late fifties or sixties, and then show decline, initially at a slow pace, but accelerating as the late seventies are reached." (Schaie, 1989a). Yet others don't see decline until very late in life—"Cognitive decline may begin after midlife, but most often occurs at higher ages (70 or higher)" (Aartsen et al., 2002).

One source of confusion is that age-related decline in any cognitive measure is likely to be gradual rather than stepped. (See Cerella, 1990, and Cerella & Hale, 1994, for perhaps the most thorough treatment of this question in the domain of processing speed.) If we accept this assumption (I will investigate it empirically later in this chapter), the question "At what age does decline begin?" can then refer to at least two time points. First, one could argue that the beginning of decline is situated at the age at which the pinnacle of performance is reached, because this is a true turning point; second, one could argue that decline starts when it first becomes noticeable, statistically or otherwise. The turning point is relatively easy to determine, as long as some form of lifespan curve can be overlaid on the data, for instance by fitting the data to a mathematical model (as I will do here). The location of the point of noticeable decline is more problematic. Even if we use a technical definition—such as the point where decline becomes statistically significant compared with some standard age—the problem is still that statistical significance is a function of the standard error of measurement, and the standard error of measurement varies with sample size and measurement reliability.

Another possible confound is the task under consideration. It has long been known (e.g., Horn & Cattell, 1966) that tasks of crystallized cognition—that is, tasks relying primarily on skills, knowledge, and expertise—tend to peak later and decline less rapidly than tasks of fluid intelligence—that is, tasks relying on the ability to solve novel problems or on the active manipulation of information during the course of the test itself. Most of the tasks tackled in this book are of the fluid variety, but some (notably lexical decision) are arguably measures of crystallized intelligence. The domain that is being studied is then an important determinant of the inflection point. Worse, even within domain, inflection points might differ. Within the domain of fluid intelligence, for instance, there is a venerable tradition that assigns earlier peaks and/or faster declines to fluid tasks that are more difficult or more complex, as determined by objective task parameters or by young-adult response times (e.g., Birren, Allen, & Landau, 1954; Welford, 1959). Accordingly, in this chapter I will take these task and difficulty/complexity effects into account as much as possible when modeling the data.

A third aspect to consider is the difference between aging at the group level and aging at the level of the individual. At the group level (which is by necessity the level I will model here), we are concerned with the mean level of performance as a function of age. This change in mean level can arise from at least two sources: a gradual, more or less identical decline in every individual, or a wide variety of individual aging trajectories (some conceivably even positive) with an average downward trend. If the latter is true, the group trend is quite uninformative about the individual; at best, the group trend can then serve as a norm. Longitudinal studies (where individual trajectories can be observed directly) strongly suggest that the latter pattern—interindividual variability—is the rule. For instance, one unequivocal result from the Seattle Longitudinal Study (see Schaie, 2005, for an overview) is that universal patterns of change simply do not exist. The cross-sectional analyses from this study (i.e., the analysis of different age groups, all assessed at the same approximate moment in time) show clear downward trends for all four fluid abilities examined (inductive reasoning, perceptual speed, spatial orientation, and verbal memory), starting at age 25 or earlier. The two crystallized abilities (verbal ability and numeric ability) show mostly stability. The longitudinal results, however, reveal large variability in patterns. For instance, around age 50, only about half of the participants effectively experienced a decrease on at least two abilities. Although at age 88 almost all participants experienced decline on at least two abilities, the identity of these two (or more) abilities differed widely across participants, underscoring that there is no preordained pattern. Moreover, even at age 88, hardly any participants showed decline on all six measures. Group curves simply do not generalize to the level of the individual. The same study also shows that decline is not a universal given. Although the number of participants whose scores increase declines over the course of adulthood (from 12% to 0%), and the number of participants whose scores decline increases over the course of adulthood (from 20% to 50%), it is quite striking that the majority of subjects (50% to 60%) show no significant change in tests scores at all. Amazingly, the percentage of non-changers does not covary with age. In other words, even most 80-year-olds experience stability in their test scores, not decline.

7.1. Lifespan Curves: The Interplay of Growth and Decline

If we want to investigate age-related differences in speed of processing over age, the first question is how to characterize these curves.

There are essentially two possibilities. One is to describe the curves as they apply to the adult lifespan (college-age subjects and older); the other is to extend them over the full lifespan, starting (technically, but not in practice) at age zero. At the group level, childhood and adolescence are typically periods of cognitive growth; the period after young adulthood is increasingly characterized by decline. This generalization appears to hold across a wide variety of domains, such as sports (e.g., Baker & Tang, 2010; Baker, Tang, & Turner, 2003; Berthelot et al., 2011; Tanaka & Seals, 2003), chess playing (e.g., Charness & Bosman, 1990; Fair, 2007), scientific and artistic output (e.g., Lehman, 1953; Simonton, 1988), the sales price commanded by modern American painters (Galenson & Weinberg, 2000), as well as different aspects of physiological functioning (e.g., Fotenos, Snyder, Girton, Morris, & Buckner, 2005; Kühnert & Nieschlag, 2004; Van Disseldorp et al., 2008). The standard pattern in all these domains is one of humped curves, with an initial rise in performance to either an inflection point or a high-performance plateau, which is then followed by a steady decline. Figure 7.1 provides just a few sample data sets from a wide variety of domains—marathon running, chess playing, motor vehicle crash rates, and number of publications by academic psychologists. The curves differ in the sharpness of the peaks, the age at which the peak is situated, and the severity of the decline, but they all show the humped or scalloped pattern—decelerating growth followed by accelerated decline.

Cognition is no exception to the pattern of accelerated decline. To illustrate, Table 7.1 reproduces a secondary analysis of data from Tim Salthouse's lab as performed by Verhaeghen and Salthouse (1997). This is a large-sample analysis, involving more than 2,200 subjects for each of the measures. To test for acceleration patterns, Verhaeghen and Salthouse simply split the samples by age, using age 50 (about the median age in these studies) as the cut-off, and then examined the age-cognition correlations for five aspects of cognition: perceptual speed, short-term memory/working memory, episodic memory, reasoning ability, and spatial ability. For all five abilities, correlations between age and performance were nominally larger for the older half of the sample than for the younger half—correlations before age 50 varied between $-.14$ and $-.27$; correlations past age 50 varied between $-.23$ and $-.37$. The difference was significant for three of the five constructs, namely speed, episodic memory, and

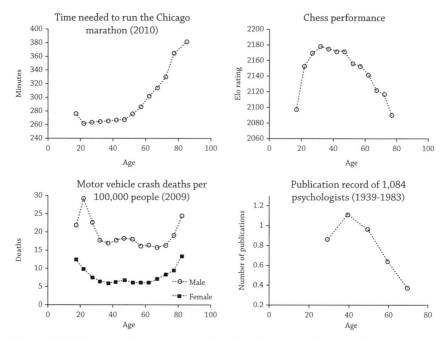

Figure 7.1 Lifespan performance curves based on large-sample data in four domains: Running (26.2 miles, all participants in the 2010 Chicago Marathon, data from TriRun.com), chess (Elo ratings of all FIDE-World Chess Federation members, January 2006; data reported by Salthouse, 2006), driving (motor vehicle crash deaths in 2009, data from census.gov), and publication record of male academic psychologists (*n* = 1,084, data from Horner, Rushton, & Vernon, 1986).

Table 7.1 **Correlations between age and five cognitive constructs as found in samples of studies by Salthouse and colleagues, split for samples under and over the age of 50 (data from Verhaeghen & Salthouse, 1997). N is the number of participants involved, k the number of studies; correlation is the averaged correlation weighted for sample size. STM/WM concerns tasks of short-term memory, working memory, or both.**

		Under 50 years of age		Over 50 years of age	
Type of correlation	*k*	*N*	Correlation	*N*	Correlation
Age-speed	28	2,892	−.27	2,393	−.37
Age-STM/WM	14	1,370	−.19	1,158	−.24
Age-episodic memory	14	1,439	−.15	1,298	−.23
Age-reasoning	10	1,284	−.14	1,132	−.28
Age-space	12	1,297	−.18	1,068	−.25

reasoning. An additional analysis considered the whole span of ages, and fitted a quadratic polynomial to test for nonlinear effects. All quadratic coefficients turned out to be negative, indicating accelerated decline (cognition was scored such that higher scores indicate better performance); in three of the five cases (speed, primary memory/working memory, and reasoning) the quadratic component was statistically significant.

7.2. Modeling Lifespan Curves: Quadratic Polynomials and Exponential Functions

The results summarized in the previous section suggest a curvilinear trend in the speed by age relation. In our 1997 meta-analysis, Salthouse and I modeled this trend as atheoretically as possible—we simply assessed the presence or absence of curvature by including a quadratic term. This approach can be used for multilevel meta-analysis as well; I will use it here for a first pass over the data.

An alternative is to adopt one or the other exponential growth model as they are implemented, for instance, in biology. Such models were originally introduced by Von Bertalanffy (1938) to model the body size of sharks as a function of age, from birth to maturity. The assumption was that the rate of growth declines with size. The rate of change in length (Von Bertalanffy's original area of interest) can be modeled as:

$$dl/dt = K\,(L_\infty - l).$$

In this equation, t stands for time (or age), l for length, and K for the rate of growth. L_∞ stands for the asymptotic length. The equation simply states that growth rate is a constant proportion of the difference between maximum length and current length, resulting in a decrease in growth rate as the organism approaches its full-grown status.

Integrating this equation to obtain length at a given time t gets us a growth curve:

$$l_t = L_\infty\,(1 - e^{-K(t-t_0)})$$

The parameter t_0 is defined as the time (or age) at which the organism would have zero length. Often this time is estimated as zero, the age at birth. An alternative formulation gets rid of t_0 and replaces it with length at birth, L_0:

$$l_t = L_\infty - (L_\infty - L_0)e^{-Kt}$$

In nonmathematical language, this version of the Von Bertalanffy growth function (affectionately known as VBGF) characterizes length (which, in our case, could stand in for response time) by three parameters: Onset value (or: response time at birth), end value (or: response time at maturity), and the rate of growth, which is a function of age. The relationship between length and age in this equation is exponential. Just like the quadratic polynomial, the VBGF can be adapted for multilevel linear modeling, in this case by fitting the logarithm of performance (i.e., processing speed) to age. (For more details on the actual models used, see below.)

The Von Bertalanffy equation has served as inspiration to quite a number of developmental researchers in many different fields. Most importantly, it has been shown to work well to characterize the development (i.e., speed-up) of response times over the course of childhood. Figure 7.2 shows such data (from Kail, 1991b) modeled by a VBGF exponential. The fits are remarkably good (88% and more of the variance explained) for four out of the six abilities, and not obviously wrong for the other two (i.e., although the data are quite noisy, it looks as if the function captures the overall trend very well). Kail (1991a) has also successfully (84.1% of the variance explained) fitted this function to meta-analytically derived Brinley slopes, comparing groups of children and adolescents between the ages of 5 and 14 to groups of young adults, with a separate slope for each successive year of age (1,519 pairs of response times from 72 studies; tasks included choice RT, semantic judgment, visual search, and mental rotation, among others).

VBGF modeling can also be applied to aging: Mathematically, growth can be mirrored to become decline or decay simply by reversing the arrow of time. Figure 7.3 shows aging data modeled this way by Cerella and Hale (1994); an accelerated exponential (i.e., a VBGF) was fitted to adult lifespan data from seven studies. The fits,

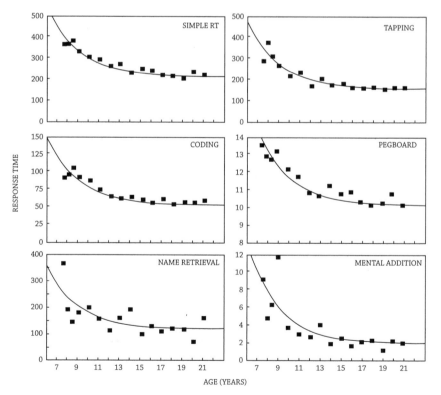

Figure 7.2 Response time in six tasks as a function of age, with exponential functions overlaid. Reproduced from Kail (1991b).

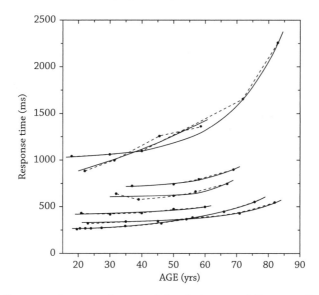

Figure 7.3 Response times on select speeded tasks in seven different studies, as first collected by Cerella (1990) and then fitted to exponential curves (overlaid) by Cerella and Hale (1994). Reproduced from Cerella and Hale (1994).

again, are remarkably good; median variance accounted for over the seven data sets was 99%. It should be noted, however, that the data set was carefully selected—a hand-picked subset of 23 potentially relevant data sets collected earlier by Cerella (1990), specifically selected because they looked like they might fit an exponential curve. In the present chapter, I will apply no such censorship to the data, except for the usual restriction that response times for younger adults do not exceed 2,000 ms.

Both VBGF functions—growth and decline—can be combined by mere summation (with an adjustment factor, see below) to form a humped function to fit true lifespan data. Such curves fit physicological data quite well. For instance, Berthelot et al. (2011) successfully fit summed VBGF functions to world record times for different ages in two swimming events and one track event, explaining, on average, 99% of the variance. The VBGF fits cognitive data quite well, too. For instance, Li and colleagues (2004) tested 356 subjects between the ages of 6 and 89, tested on 15 different cognitive tasks, and fit the double-VBGF model to the data. The proportion of variance accounted for ranged from .73 to .97, with a mean of .89, and there were no systematic deviations from the pattern described by the exponential curves.

The conclusion here is then that such exponential models are excellent candidate curves for modeling lifespan and adult lifespan data for both theoretical and empirical reasons.

7.1.2. Modeling Lifespan Curves: Possible Mechanisms

Before attempting the actual modeling, it makes sense to investigate the plausibility of these models for modeling processing speed. The curves might fit response times well, but is there a mechanism that can explain the increase and then decrease in speed over the lifespan?

At a very high level of abstraction, most theoreticians agree that changes in connectivity are the key to aging (and conversely perhaps to development). Cerella and Hale (with precedents in Cerella, 1990, and Myerson et al., 1990) modeled their aging data using a very simplified neural network, starting from the assumption that the size of the population of active elements in the network (they call these "synaptic vesicles, or dendritic branches, or neural connections," p. 169) drives performance. The analogy Cerella and Hale put forward is that of a net of links, forming multiple paths from input to output. If more links are active, the path from input to output will be very direct, and hence the path can be traveled quickly. Deleting links makes detours necessary, thereby delaying the response.

To model decline in as simple a fashion as possible, Cerella and Hale implemented a single constant hazard rate; that is, every element in their network had an equal probability of being deactivated over any given time interval. Mathematically, this model solves exactly to the VBGF decline model. Cerella and Hale take care to point out that the exact implementation of the model does not matter, as long as the hazard function is constant. In other words, what is damaged over time does not need to be actual connections between elements; anything that fosters or hinders transmission, including chemical signals, would yield equivalent results. Ultimately, the Cerella and Hale model boils down to a simple entropy model, "the accumulation of random, irreparable losses in molecular fidelity [which] accumulates to slowly overwhelm maintenance systems" (Hayflick, 2007, p. 2351). The net effect of entropy is a global decrease in functioning, neatly described by a VBGF curve.

An entropic model does not necessarily suppose that slowing occurs in a general, one-dimensional fashion. Hayflick gives the example of entropy in cars—certain car components are more vulnerable to defects than others, and this may depend on make, model, and year of manufacture. It is unlikely that "the whole car" will break down; it is much more likely that a particular subsystem will fail, and that this will be the common weakest link for a given make, model, and year. In humans in developed countries, Hayflick argues, the typical weakest links in the biological make-up are the vascular system and the cells susceptible to cancer. The increasing molecular instability that is the consequence of entropy will then first become visible in those systems, making them the leading causes of death. Something similar might be happening in cognitive aging. For instance, Cerella and Hale explain differential aging by the degree of connectivity necessary to perform the task. They argue, for instance, that spatial processing might require denser connections; networks with denser connections indeed turn out to be more vulnerable to the effects of entropy than sparser networks.

A similar model has been proposed by Shu-Chen Li and colleagues (e.g., Li, Lindenberger, & Sikström, 2001). Their vehicle for aging is chemical—neuromodulation of the synaptic transmission. The point of departure is the observation that aging is associated with increasing deficiencies in the dopamine system. This defect is implemented in neural networks not by lesioning the connections (as in the Cerella and Hale model), but by changing the gain of transmission from one neuron to the next. (Gain is a parameter that maps weighted inputs from other cells onto an output "firing rate" in the postsynaptic cell via a monotonically increasing, typically sigmoid activation function; Servan-Schreiber, Printz, & Cohen, 1990.) Lower gain leads to a decrease in the signal-to-noise ratio of information transmission in the brain; the net result of a steady decrease in average gain over the lifespan is thus an increase in neural noise. This neuromodulation model of cognitive aging has been wildly successful. Implemented in specific neural networks, it has been found to explain adult age differences in learning rate, asymptotic performance, interference susceptibility, complexity cost, associative binding, intra and interindividual variability, and ability dedifferentiation. Linear decreases in the gain parameter (similar to Cerella and Hale's hazard function) give rise to nonlinear and accelerated effects over age, although it is not clear at present whether these would fit the VBGF model. (This would likely depend on the task implementation in the model; Li, personal communication, 2011.)

Both of these models—Cerella and Hale's entropy model and Li's neuromodulation account—provide excellent proof of concept that a simple linear progression of a single underlying mechanism can give rise to curvilinearity in the performance by age curve, as well as age-related dissociations between tasks. Both also predict an increase in the noise of internal representations, either concomitant with the decline in performance (Cerella/Hale) or as the root cause of the decline (Li). There is indeed empirical evidence that aging gives rise to increased noise, at least at the level of behavior. This can be seen perhaps most clearly in the study of intraindividual variability, that is, of inconsistency in response time (see Hultsch & MacDonald, 2004, for an early review). Inconsistency, even after controlling for mean performance, follows the same U-shaped trajectory over the lifespan as mean RT (Li, Huxhold, & Schmiedek, 2004; Williams, Hultsch, Strauss, Hunter, & Tannock, 2005), and shows an accelerated pattern within the older-adult portion of the lifespan (e.g., 75–92 years, Bielak, Hultsch, Strauss, MacDonald, & Hunter, 2010; 70–102 years, Lövdén, Li, Shing, & Lindenberger, 2007; 75–89 years, MacDonald, Hultsch, & Dixon, 2003). Inconsistency is also longitudinally predictive of cognitive outcomes (Bielak et al., 2010)—people who are more inconsistent tend to show larger decline—suggesting that noise and performance are intimately coupled, an outcome compatible with both the entropy and neuromodulation models.

Both models are, however, difficult to confirm or falsify at the level at which they are posited. With regard to Li's dopamine model, there is little doubt that there are strong age effects on dopamine receptor availability (e.g., Kaasinen et al., 2000; Karlsson et al., 2009). Figure 7.4 shows results from one lifespan study (including an adolescent age range in addition to an adult age range) using a receptor-binding imaging technique to investigate the efficiency of the dopamine system. The results suggest a monotonic lifespan function rather than the humped functions collected in Figure 7.1. Of course, this should not detract from the plausibility of this theory as an explanation of *aging* effects: It is possible and plausible that different mechanisms operate at different ends of the lifespan. For instance, the increase in processing speed in children might be driven primarily by neuroanatomical changes, while the decline in old age might at least partially be mediated by changes in neurotransmitter availability. Indeed, there are indications that dopamine receptor binding explains almost all of the age-related variance in diverse aspects of cognition within the adult age range. (The caveat is the extremely small number of subjects in these studies, which can easily inflate correlations.) Bäckman et al. (2000) examined 11 subjects; dopamine

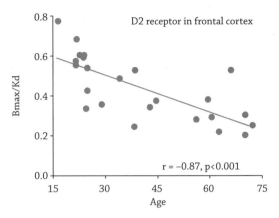

Figure 7.4 D2 (dopamine) receptor density in extrastriatal regions over a large part of the lifespan. The function is clearly monotonic from age 15 on, not humped. From Kaasinen et al. (2000).

D2 receptor binding explained between 94% and 98% (median: 96%) of the variance in tests of perceptual speed and episodic memory. Erixon-Lindroth et al. (2005) examined 12 subjects; striatal dopamine transporter binding explained between 71% and 96% (median: 90%) of variance in tasks of executive control and episodic memory.

The connectivity model likewise appears biologically plausible, at least when viewed at the large scale. Figure 7.5 reproduces data from two relatively recent studies (one a primary study, the other a meta-analysis) examining age-related differences in brain connectivity. Dosenbach et al. (top panel of Figure 7.5) assessed functional connectivity (i.e., the patterns of correlations between brain regions during rest) in 238 subjects between the ages of 7 and 30. Activity was measured in 160 regions of interest, allowing for the computation of 12,720 correlations per subject. Out of those 12,720, the researchers selected the 200 correlations that were most reliably different between children and adults. A functional connectivity maturation index was then computed from those. This maturation index—shown in the figure as a function of age—thus represents a 200-dimensional weighted index of an individual's overall functional brain maturity. The figure also shows two growth curve models overlaid, one of them the VBGF. The data conform quite nicely to the model, strongly suggesting that brain connectivity follows a VBGF pattern. What is missing from this picture, however, is some indication that this maturation index is related to changes in cognition, and that the connectivity index fits data beyond age 30.

The lower part of Figure 7.5 reproduces part of the Walhovd et al. (2011) data set, consisting of 883 subjects between the ages of 18 and 94 aggregated from six independent samples. The graph reproduces volume of cerebral white matter (controlled for intracranial volume), an indirect measure of connectivity. White matter consists mainly of myelinated nerve fibers that connect different regions of the brain. It is therefore an indirect measure of connectivity between different brain structures (e.g., O'Sullivan et al., 2001). The lines in the graph provide linear or quadratic fits to each of the six samples; median proportion of variance explained varied between 5% and 56%, with a median of 26%. The curvilinearity is clearly visible in the data.

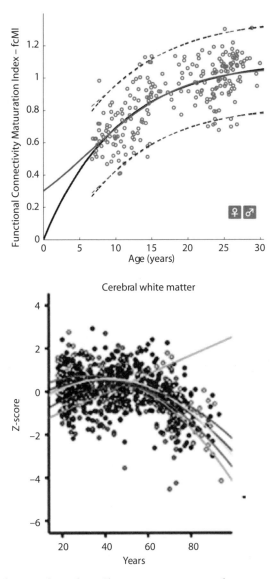

Figure 7.5 Two large-scale studies of brain connectivity over large parts of the lifespan. Top panel: Functional connectivity maturation index; data from Dosenbach et al. (2010); bottom panel: volume of cerebral white matter, from Walhovd et al. (2011).

Both of the graphs reproduced in Figure 7.5 suggest a VBGF-like pattern of growth for the first half of the lifespan and a VBGF-like pattern of decline in the latter half of the lifespan. Both, however, also suggest that the hump in the function occurs later than the hump shown in the Cerella and Hale data (and the data I will describe later in this chapter), that is, at around age 40. Again, the failure of the brain-parameter peak to coincide with that of behavioral data does not disqualify the brain parameter as a determinant of behavioral change—multiple influences, each with its own time course, may conspire to give the behavioral curve its particular shape. In fact, the combination of a steady-decline mechanism, such as dopamine binding, and a later-peaking mechanism, such as connectivity, would by necessity yield a humped curve with a peak that occurs earlier than that of the later-peaking mechanism. This is illustrated in Figure 7.6: The same humped VBGF can be modeled as the sum of a steadily declining and a steadily increasing function (top panel), or as the sum of a steadily decreasing and a humped function (bottom panel).

I am not arguing here that these two mechanisms—connectivity and dopamine— are the major determinants of the double-VBGF curve that appears to characterize

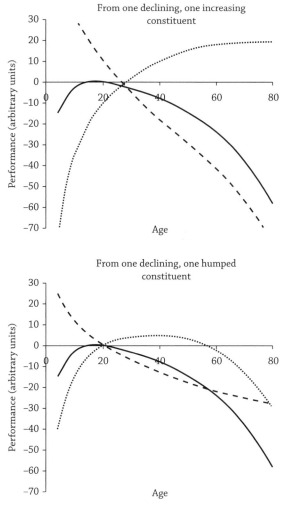

Figure 7.6 Proof of concept that a humped Von Bertalanffy growth function (depicted in each of the graphs as a solid line) can be described as the sum of either a steadily declining and a steadily increasing function (top panel), or of a steadily decreasing and a humped function (bottom panel).

processing speed over the lifespan (meditational analyses are needed before this conclusion can be reached); I am merely offering a proof of concept and making the case that this is a plausible explanation. The truth-value of this explanation falls outside the realm of currently available data.

7.1.3.3. *Models for Fitting Lifespan Data: Conclusions*

The data reviewed in this section suggest that a curvilinear model (U-shaped over the entire lifespan, a positively accelerated decay function when only the adult portion of the lifespan is considered) should fit the data well. Theoretical considerations, as well as actual fitting of data suggest that an exponential model, representing a Von Bertalanffy growth function, should fit particularly well. In the next section, I investigate this assumption empirically.

In this section, I also reviewed large-scale models that suggest that such a curvilinear function might come about by a loss of connectivity. The literature review on the biological mechanisms that underlie the curvilinearity—a rise and fall in (functional) connectivity and loss of dopamine receptors—suggests that, in practice, neither mechanism alone can explain the data. Functional connectivity peaks later in life than the data it is supposed to explain, and dopamine receptor density declines from childhood on. One possibility is that both mechanisms operate in concert, with a build-up of (functional) connectivity dominating childhood and adolescence, until the decline in the efficiency of the dopamine system starts dominating in young adulthood, causing the system to slow down even as (functional) connectivity is still increasing.

7.2. The Meta-analysis on Lifespan Trajectories in Processing Speed: Data Set and Scaling Issues

7.2.1. The Data Set

In my literature search, I cast as wide a web as I thought permissible. The only criteria for inclusion in the meta-analysis were that data should be available for at least four age groups past the age of 18, with at least one of those falling within the 18–30 range, and that response times were reported, with the younger adults' average RT below 2,000 ms. I enforced the four-data-point requirement so that I could fit linearized nonlinear multilevel models and still have a degree of freedom left. The age requirement allows me to produce a reasonable estimate of the culminating point for speeded processing. The response-time requirement was introduced to make the analyses compatible with those from Chapters 2 and 4, where the same constraint was imposed. (I did relax the latter criterion when examining the age trajectories of individual tasks, as I will explain below.)

I was able to collect data from 50 studies contained within 33 publications (Bedard et al., 2002; Botwinick & Storandt, 1974; Cepeda, Kramer, & Gonzalez de Sather, 2001; Clement, 1962; Cohn, Dustman, & Bradford, 1984; Davies, 1968; Der & Deary, 2006; Drane, Yuseph, Huthwaite, & Klingler, 2002; Elias, Robbins, Walter, & Schultz, 1993;

Fozard, Vercruyssen, Reynolds, Hancock, & Quilter, 1994; Fromm-Auch & Yeudall, 1983; Giambra & Quilter, 1988; Goldfarb, 1941; Goul & Brown, 1970; Graf & Uttl, 1995; Hommel et al., 2004; Houx & Jolles, 1993; Kennedy, 1981; Koga & Morant, 1923; Lawrence, Myerson, & Hale, 1998; Madden, 1992; Miles, 1931; Pontón et al., 1996; Reimers & Maylor, 2005; Salthouse, 1994b; Stuss et al., 1987; Tombaugh, 2004; Treitz, Heyder, & Daum, 2007; Uttl & Graf, 1997; Uttl, Graf, & Consetino, 2000; Van der Elst et al., 2006; Williams et al., 2005). Although the harvest seems modest, this is still a large data set compared with previous efforts: The previously largest formal meta-analysis of this kind (Cerella & Hale, 1994) contained only seven studies of middle-aged and older adults, as well as 21 studies including only children and/or adolescents. One informal review of lifespan curves (Cerella, 1990) contained 23 studies.

The tasks included in the set of studies varied rather widely—SRT, CRT, go/nogo RT, a cancellation task, a clock test, abstract matching, digit symbol substitution, different category membership classification tasks, lexical decision, memory search, visual search, mental rotation, Stroop, task switching, and Trail Making. In a first set of analyses, I pooled all tasks; in the next section, I will provide breakdowns for the four tasks most frequently reported, that is, simple reaction time and choice reaction time, the Stroop task, and the Trail Making test. In total, 149 different age-by-RT curves were reported in these 49 studies, with a total of 1,292 data points, 1,132 of which pertained to subject groups age 18 or older. Figure 7.7 (top panel) shows the data; data points that were derived from the same measure within the same study are joined by dotted lines.

7.2.2. Scaling Issues: How to Best Represent the Data

Figure 7.8 (top panel) suggests that tasks that are performed more slowly, as indexed by higher young-adult RTs, show stronger age-related effects, that is, steeper slopes and/ or stronger upward curvature. As mentioned above, I am hardly the first researcher to note this pattern—its first appearance dates from at least 1954 (Birren et al.).

Obviously, this pattern is real. It is thus tempting to cast this as a substantive finding (as Birren and colleagues did)—indicating, for instance, that tasks that require more complex manipulation of information or a multitude of stages yield larger age effects than simpler tasks. I would, however, argue that at least part of this pattern reflects a scaling issue, rather than a substantive interaction between age and task characteristics. This argument follows directly from the Brinley analyses presented throughout this book. These analyses showed that, in most cases, RT of older adults is a near-constant proportion of that of younger adults. If this is the case, then the age effect on response time measured in absolute terms (i.e., seconds or milliseconds) will be larger in tasks requiring more time.

One potential way to correct this scaling issue is to log-transform the data. Here is the reasoning: If

$$RT_{older} = b * RT_{younger},$$

then

$$\log(RT_{older}) = \log(b * RT_{younger}).$$

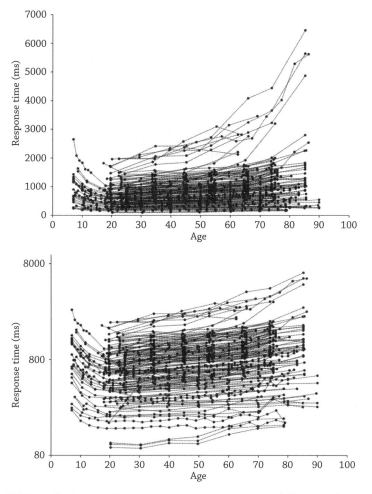

Figure 7.7 Data from 50 studies examining response times in different tasks over a large portion of the lifespan (at least young adulthood to older adulthood). Top panel: raw data; bottom panel: Y-axis rescaled logarithmically. Data from the same study and task are connected by dotted lines.

Given that $\log(x * y) = \log(x) + \log(y)$, this implies that

$$\log(RT_{older}) = \log(b) + \log(RT_{younger}),$$

or, in terms of the age difference:

$$\log(RT_{older}) - \log(RT_{younger}) = \log(b).$$

What this implies is that, no matter how long it takes for younger adults to perform the task, after logarithmic transformation the age difference will always be a constant, namely $\log(b)$ (i.e., the log of the age-related slowing factor). This, in turn, means that

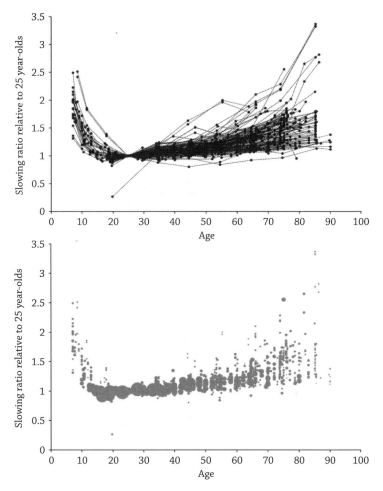

Figure 7.8 Lifespan data shown as slowing ratios relative to speed at age 25 within each task within each study. Top panel: all data, with points within the same task within the same study joined by dotted lines; bottom panel: bubble plot of the same data, with the size of the bubbles proportional to sample size.

the fan effect observed in the top panel of Figure 7.7 should disappear after logarithmic transformation, giving way to sets of parallel lines.

At the risk of being redundant, here is another way to look at this same phenomenon. Consider two tasks, X and Y. Assuming identical proportional age-related effects, we get

$$RT_{X,older} = b * RT_{X,younger}$$

and

$$RT_{Y,older} = b * RT_{Y,younger}.$$

The difference between the two tasks in older adults is a proportion of the difference between the two tasks in younger adults:

$$RT_{X,older} - RT_{Y,older} = b * (RT_{X,younger} - RT_{Y,younger}).$$

When the task difference in younger adults grows larger, it thus grows larger by a proportional factor in older adults, causing fanning-out. After log-transform of RT, we get

$$\log(RT_{X,older}) = \log(b) + \log(RT_{X,younger}),$$

and

$$\log(RT_{Y,older}) = \log(b) + \log(RT_{Y,younger}).$$

The task difference in older adults is now

$$\log(RT_{X,older}) - \log(RT_{Y,older}) = \log(RT_{X,younger}) - \log(RT_{Y,younger}).$$

In other words, if the assumption of proportional slowing holds, the differences between tasks should remain constant over age after logarithmic transformation, and different tasks should simply show parallel lifespan trajectories on this transformed measure.

Is this true? The bottom panel of Figure 7.7 recasts the top panel on a logarithmic scale. Clearly, the fan has abated, and the curves look much more parallel. Do note, however, that this model does not fully explain the data: The fan has not completely disappeared. This result, too, might ultimately be reducible to a result from the Brinley analyses: Age-related slowing is not perfectly proportional. This deviation leads to a fan effect even in log-transformed data. Take the Brinley equation that best described the data set from Chapter 2:

$$RT_{younger} = 1.44 \, RT_{older} - 52.$$

If we apply this equation to two tasks, one taking younger adults 250 ms to perform, the other 2,000 ms, we get 308 ms and 2,828 as the expected response times for older adults. The time difference between the two tasks is 1750 ms for younger adults and 2,520 for older adults. This represents the fan effect in raw RT: Differences between conditions get magnified with advancing age. There is still a fan, but subtler, in log-transformed data: The transformed scores are 5.52 and 7.60 for younger, and 5.73 and 7.95 for older adults; the difference is now 2.08 for younger and 2.22 for older adults. Thus, under the "real" Brinley equation (i.e., one with a significant negative intercept), a fan effect remains in the age-by-RT plots even after logarithmic transformation. The fan effect in log-transformed data will be larger the more the age relation differs from a purely multiplicative relationship. In practice, that means that spatial tasks will be particularly vulnerable to this effect.

How, then, to analyze these data? One lesson to be gleaned from the analyses above is that modeling the data as they are (i.e., as raw RT) is likely to be highly problematic.

Most of the age by complexity interactions of interest (e.g., age-related effects in the Stroop interference condition vs. age-related differences in the Stroop baseline condition; or age-related effects in Trail Making Part B vs. Trail Making Part A) are confounded with RT in younger adults. Given the fan effect, it is likely we would obtain false positives for the analysis of such interactions.

One possible solution is to standardize the data. One popular way of standardizing is to set performance of younger adults at zero and express deviations from this point in other age groups as a *mean standardized difference* (also known as Cohen's *d*; Cohen, 1992), that is, the difference between the two means divided by either the pooled standard deviation or the standard deviation of the younger-adult group (e.g., Salthouse, 1991c, 2010). A similar method is to express performance of all age groups as a *z*-score or a transformation thereof (such as a *T*-score, with a mean of 50 and a standard deviation of 10) (e.g., Schaie, 2005). One drawback of both methods is that these measures do not translate into terms that are immediately useful for, say, design or engineering purposes—knowing that a task at age 70 has a mean standardized difference of −0.94 isn't as directly functional a piece of knowledge as knowing that it is slowed by a factor of 2.0. Another potential problem is that standardized curves are subject to two sources of measurement error, that is, measurement error in the means and measurement error in the standard deviation(s), making the curves potentially noisy. For these reasons, I refrained from standardization.

Another possibility is to calculate an $RT_{older}/RT_{younger}$ *ratio score* for each group for any given task in a given study. This measure has the advantage that it requires no knowledge of RT variability in either age group, and that its meaning is intuitively graspable—a ratio of 2.0 at age 70 quite simply means a 70-year-old will need on average twice the amount of time for the task as a younger adult. The drawback is that the ratio scores can still deliver spurious dissociations between tasks, as explained above: Only if the slowing in response time follows a perfectly proportional pattern will age trajectories be identical for tasks with identical age-related effects—and for most tasks the perfect proportional slowing model has been falsified, as testified in Chapters 2, 4, and 6 of this book.

There is a mathematical solution to this problem, however. Starting from the Brinley equation,

$$RT_{older} = a + b\,RT_{younger},$$

the $RT_{older}/RT_{younger}$ ratio can be expressed as:

$$RT_{older}/RT_{younger} = (a + b\,RT_{younger})/RT_{younger} = b + a/RT_{younger}.$$

This equation implies that the older/younger ratio is a function of the inverse of the response time of younger adults, and this is a known quantity, which can be included in the equations used to model lifespan trajectories. This equation will describe a three-dimensional surface with slowing ratio predicted from both the subject's age and the inverse of the young-adult response time for the particular task in the particular study in which it was assessed. (For more details, see the next section.)

A third possibility for a common metric, less intuitive and therefore more of interest to the theoretician than the practitioner, is to plot and analyze *Brinley slopes* as a function of the mean age of the subjects they are derived from (Cerella & Hale, 1994). The drawback here is that the Brinley plots themselves are typically an amalgam of different tasks, and so the curves are not task-pure (let alone process-pure). The advantage is that the age-related slowing factors are now entered into the analysis directly, and so no correction for young-adult baseline speed is necessary.

In this chapter, then, I will model the lifespan trajectories of the data presented in Figure 7.7 in two ways. The first (Section 7.2.5.1 and 7.2.5.2) is to use all available data points and find a satisfactory general description of the age trajectories of interest. (I will derive trajectories for adults, for the lifespan, and I will additionally derive different curves for different tasks.) To do this, I will use the ratio measure. This function, then, is one step removed from the actual data. The second (Section 7.2.5.3) is to plot Brinley slopes as a function of age (again plotting the two portions of the life span separately). This analysis is two steps removed from the data—Brinley plots are constructed, and the slopes are then entered into the final analysis.

Before I turn to the modeling of the full lifespan, however, I will first zoom in on the adult age range (Section 7.2.3 and 7.2.4). This magnification will allow me to descend a little deeper, namely to the level of dissociations between task domains and within tasks. (This cannot be done with the full lifespan data because the data for children and adolescents are too sparse.) I will restrict this analysis to ratio scores, because there are not enough data points to comfortably permit the calculation of Brinley slopes at the task level.

7.2.3 Adult Lifespan Trajectories: Ratio Scores, Reference Age, and Reference RT

In my first modeling of adult lifespan trajectories, I used the ratio score, $RT_{older}/RT_{younger}$, as the dependent variable.

One decision concerns the denominator to be used for the ratio. (As I explain below, this denominator will also serve to set a reference time for all analyses.) One possibility (ultimately discarded) would be to simply pick a specific young adult data point from each study (e.g., the data point closest to age 18). This technique has the drawback that it introduces horizontal jitter in the data—some studies would use 16-year-olds as reference points, others 30-year-olds. Instead, I fixed the reference age at age 25 and calculated the corresponding response time for each study. There is nothing magical about this age—it is simply a round number, and in this pool of studies it typically (viz., in 45 out of 50 studies) was either an age included in the study (six cases) or fell in-between two observed age ranges (39) cases. It is also, coincidentally, the flexing point in the Cerella and Hale meta-analysis. For the 39 studies in which 25 years of age fell in-between two observed data points, I used linear extrapolation to calculate expected response time at age 25 from the two flanking ages; for the five studies where the youngest group was older than 25 years of age, I used linear extrapolation from the two nearest older-age data points. By definition, then, the slowing ratio is equal to 1 at age 25. This does not imply that the fastest response time for each study is constrained to be at 25—the ratio can go below 1, indicating faster response times than those imputed at age 25.

Figure 7.8 shows the ratio scores. The top panel presents the data, connecting data that were derived from the same measure within the same study by dotted lines, to highlight the dependencies within the data set. The plot suggests that the decline in speed over the lifespan is positively accelerated: The trajectories curve upwards, so that decline becomes progressively larger with advancing age. The figure also suggests that the minimum of the function—the apex of speeded processing—is situated in the early twenties. The bottom panel recasts the data as a bubble plot; the size of the bubbles is proportional to the number of subjects in each age group. This figure illustrates that sample size, on average, is a negative function of age. This is unfortunate, because it implies that the precision of measurement declines with advancing age. Do note that even if only the studies with the largest sample sizes are considered, a steady, monotonic increase in relative latency is noticeable even in the young-to-middle-aged adult range.

One additional point to note is the high variability at either end of the lifespan, suggesting quite diverse paths with respect to different tasks, different subject groups, or both. As explained above, part of this fanning effect is likely an artifact of the time taken by younger adults to perform the task (ratio scores are susceptible to the same bias as log-transformed scores). This young-adult baseline time, then—I will label it reference time or reference RT—needs to be taken into account for a full description of the data. (Note that this reference time would be typically related to task difficulty.) Given that age 25 is used as the reference age in all subsequent analyses, I will use RT at age 25 for a given task in a given study as the reference RT for the lifespan curve described by that task within that study. Figure 7.9 shows the 3-D plot, predicting ratio scores (on the Z-axis) from age (on the X-axis) and reference time (on the Y-axis). The two panels in the figure show the same data observed from different vantage points, so that the three-dimensionality can be better appreciated. The figure indeed suggests that slowing ratios increase with reference time, as predicted; this can be seen by the increasing 3-D curvature in the figure as age increases. This, in turn, suggests that at least part of the fan is due to the influence of reference RT on ratio scores—a consequence of the not-quite-multiplicative nature of age differences. A more formal analysis of this figure is obviously in order. I will provide such analyses in the next few sections.

7.2.3.1. Adult Lifespan Trajectories: Polynomials

As a first pass over the age trajectories within the adult age range, I fitted a quadratic polynomial—an equation that includes both a linear and a quadratic component—to the data, using multilevel regression, with task nested within study. The quadratic polynomial model serves to determine whether or not significant curvature is present in the data.

The mathematical analysis of ratio scores above yielded clear expectations for older/younger RT ratio as a function of reference time:

$$RT_{older}/RT_{younger} = b + a/RT_{younger}.$$

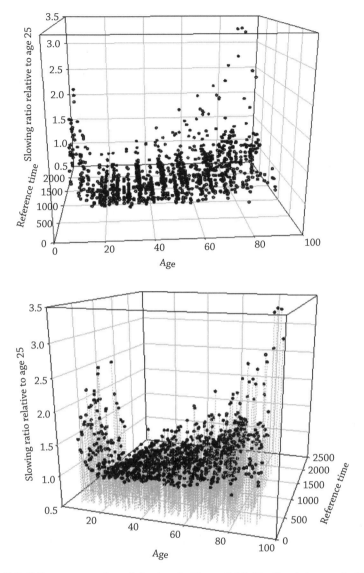

Figure 7.9 3-D representation of the data in Figure 5.10. The X-axis is age; the Y-axis represents slowing ratios relative to speed at age 25 within each task within each study; the Z-axis is the reference time, that is, RT for the task at age 25. The two panels show the same data from a different vantage point.

The ratio is thus a linear function of the inverse of reference time, that is, response time at age 25 ($1/RT_{age25}$). Building the reference time into the model will allow us to test whether a 3-D representation (as in Figure 7.9) is de facto necessary. For the actual estimation, I multiplied the inverse of reference time by 1,000; this keeps the numbers within an estimable range. Also note, given that a is usually negative, the curve, when reverted back to reference time, will be negatively accelerated with a positive overall slope: The ratio goes up with increasing reference time and moves toward a horizontal asymptote, namely b. For the actual estimation, I subtracted 25 from the actual age, to force the intercept of the function to be equal to 1. (This simply reflects the regularity that I built into this data set, namely that the age-related slowing ratio is scaled relative to response time at age 25, so that the older/younger speed ratio at age 25 is, by definition, equal to 1.)

The final model included three predictors: (Age − 25), (Age − 25)^2, and 1,000 (Age − 25)/(RT$_{age25}$). The latter term reflects the interaction between age and reference time, that is, the increasing 3-D curvature over increasing age. If this term were zero, a 2-D representation of the data—ratio scores as a function of age—would suffice. The reference time is not entered as a main effect because its effect is zero at age 25 (i.e., the proportion RT$_{age25}$/ RT$_{age25}$ is by definition equal to 1 across all values of RT$_{age25}$).

I fitted this function to the data using HLM, nesting data points within studies. (Age − 25) and the interaction between age and reference time were entered as random effects, (Age − 25)^2 as a fixed effect. The final equation (Panel A of Figure 7.10) is:

Slowing ratio = 1 (0) + 0.0066 (0.001) (Age − 25) + 0.00015 (0.00001)
(Age − 25)^2 − 0.0029 (0.0005) ∗ 1,000 ∗ (Age − 25)/(RT$_{age25}$)

The standard errors of the estimated parameters show that all parameters are significantly different from zero. This indicates that the ratio scores increase with age (i.e., individuals become slower as they age), that the increase is accelerated (i.e., the effect of age on response time becomes progressively larger with advancing age), and that reference time is needed to paint a full picture. The equation explains a rather respectable 70.71% of the variance compared with the empty model.

Embarrassingly, a model including the interaction of (Age − 25) with the reference time rather than the inverse of the reference time fits the data just as well—even better, nominally, with 74.49% of the variance explained compared with the empty model. This model is a "flat" model, that is, the influence of reference time is linear. The equation (panel B of Figure 7.10) is:

Slowing ratio = 1 (0) − 0.0029 (0.0012) (Age − 25) + 0.00015 (0.00001)
(Age − 25)^2 + 0.0000068 (0.0000014) ∗ 1,000(Age − 25)
∗ RT$_{age25}$

The percent variance explained can be increased to 77.22% by adding a term that includes the product of (Age − 25) and the square of reference time, thus letting the model empirically determine what curvature to chose for the Y-slice through the data (the associated coefficient can be positive—upward curvature—or negative—downward curvature). The equation obtained (Panel C of Figure 7.10) is:

Slowing ratio = 1 (0) − 0.0053 (0.0020) (Age − 25) + 0.00015 (0.00001)
(Age − 25)^2 + 0.000015 (0.000003) (Age − 25) ∗ RT$_{age25}$
+ 0.00000001 (0.00000000) (Age − 25) ∗ RT$_{age25}$^{2}

Sliced along the Y-axis (i.e., looking at a particular age), this is a model with upwards curvature but an initial dip—like a scoop. Although the model fits the data well, it is

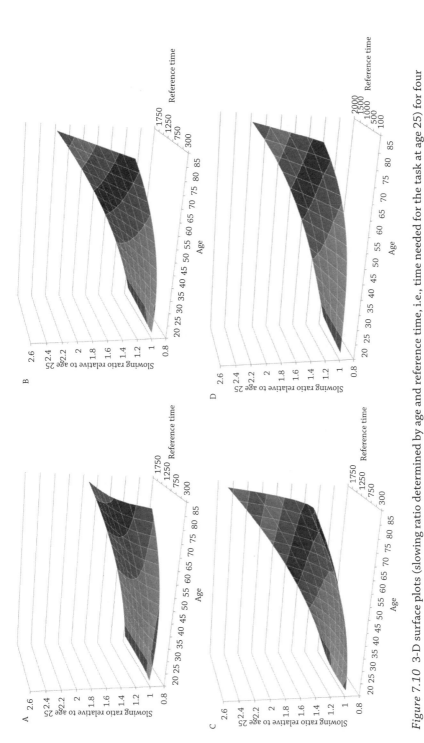

Figure 7.10 3-D surface plots (slowing ratio determined by age and reference time, i.e., time needed for the task at age 25) for four models tested in the text. Data and model are restricted to the adult portion of the lifespan (from age 18 on). Panel A: quadratic age trend with monotonically decelerating effect of reference time, $R^2 = 0.70$; Panel B: quadratic age trend with linear effect of reference time, $R^2 = 0.75$; Panel C: quadratic age trend with monotonically accelerating effect of reference time, $R^2 = 0.77$; Panel D: third-order polynomial for age with linear effect of reference time, $R^2 = 0.76$.

also hard to understand why aging should lead to this behavior. This strange curvature might then be a first signal that domain-specific or task-specific analyses might be in order. I will present such analyses later in this chapter.

Figure 7.10 illustrates quite strikingly that under each of these models, age-related slowing starts early in adulthood, perhaps even before age 25. The models all agree that there is a positive acceleration of slowing over the adult lifespan. The models disagree over the role of reference time, but it appears that, empirically, a model that predicts positive curvature describes the data best. Upward curvature was also part of the models proposed by Birren et al. (1954) and Welford (1959); Cerella and Hale (1994), on the other hand, proposed a flat model like the second model fitted here. In the remainder of this chapter, I fitted the flat model, for two reasons. First, the flat model is the more neutral model of the three, simply implying influence of the reference time, rather than a specific shape of that influence (much in the same way that correlation applies linearity but is often used to merely test the existence of covariance). It also fits the data quite well, and explains only 2.73% less of the variance than the best-fitting model considered here, the scoop model, which may be contaminated with domain or task effects. Second, the flat model is also the simplest model, containing one parameter less than the curved model. This is helpful when constructing interactions involving the reference time, as I will do later in this chapter.

One additional question is whether these models describe the lifespan curvature in the data adequately. More specifically, higher-order (cubic, quadric, and so on) trends might be present, perhaps implying later points of flexion or longer periods of stability, as suggested by some longitudinal studies (e.g., Schaie, 1989b). To test for this possibility, I fit a polynomial model with a linear, quadratic, cubic, and quintic age term (as above, age was always entered as calendar Age − 25 years), as well as a constant, fixed at 1, and a linear age by reference time interaction. (I also used as a starting point a model where only age and the reference time interaction term were random; this did not change the final result.) The model was pruned by deleting nonsignificant terms, one at a time, starting with the highest power of age. The final model was:

$$\text{Slowing ratio} = 1\ (0) + 0.0000022\ (0.0000003)\ (\text{Age} - 25)^3$$
$$+ 0.0000059\ (0.0000008)\ (\text{Age} - 25) * \text{RT}_{age25}.$$

This model (depicted in Panel D of Figure 7.10) shows neither a new flexing point, nor a period of stability past age 25. Rather, it shows steeper slowing over age than the previous models, now a function of the cube of age rather than its square. This model explains 75.85% of the variance compared with the empty model, which does not seem to be critically larger than the 74.49% explained by the quadratic polynomial with the same reference time interaction term.

7.2.3.2. Adult Lifespan Trajectories: Exponential Models

The result from the previous section suggests rather strong lifespan curvature and a peak at or before age 25. This emboldened me to fit a VBGF, which models slowing as an exponential function of age. The exponential model is mathematically simpler than the quadratic model, because only a single parameter associated with age is estimated, rather than two. The exponential model does assume a peak at age 25 or earlier. For the age-related part of the model, I assumed:

$$\text{Slowing ratio} = e^{a*(\text{Age} - 25)}.$$

(In this equation, e is the basis of the natural logarithm, approximately equal to 2.72.) This model predicts a slowing factor of 1 when age equals 25 (i.e., $e^0 = 1$.)

To linearize the equation, I took the natural logarithm of both sides, obtaining:

$$\text{Ln(slowing ratio)} = \ln(e^{a*(\text{Age} - 25)}) = a\,(\text{Age} - 25).$$

Thus, after logarithmic transformation of the older/younger slowing ratio, the exponential model reduces to a linear equation with a single parameter, a. As in the previous section, I added a term representing reference time, to check on its influence and partial it out of the estimation of the lifespan-related coefficient:

$$\text{Ln(slowing ratio)} = a\,(\text{Age} - 25) + b\,(\text{Age} - 25) * (\text{RT}_{\text{age25}})$$

Note that the logarithmic transformation makes the relationship between ln(slowing ratio) and reference time nonlinear and thus not directly comparable with the terms in the previous equations. I decided to leave the term in; estimating it "incorrectly" seemed better than not estimating it at all.

$$\text{Ln(slowing ratio)} = 0.0033\,(0.0008)\,(\text{Age} - 25)$$
$$+ 0.0000050\,(0.0000010)\,(\text{Age} - 25) * (\text{RT}_{\text{age25}})$$

This model explains 74.08% of the variance compared with the empty model, comparable to the amount of variance explained in the quadratic and cubic models estimated above (i.e., 74.49% and 75.85%, resp.). Another way to compare the models is to look only at the age-related portion of the equation, that is, to drop the reference time by age interaction terms. Without these terms, the quadratic model explained 65.51% of the variance, the cubic model 64.56%, and the exponential model 67.86%. Given the small differences in amount of variance explained, it is probably fair to conclude that all nonlinear models tested here fit about equally well.

7.2.3.3. Adult Lifespan Trajectories: Conclusions

The results from all analyses point at three conclusions. The first is that the data show significant upwards curvature—the rate of slowing increases with age. The second is that the low point of the curve, that is, the age at which participants are on average fastest is situated at age 25 or younger. Fitting more complex polynomials (I went up until fourth-order) did not yield any evidence for either a humped U-shaped function within the adult age range, or for a plateau of stability. The third conclusion is more technical, namely that reference time plays a significant role—when describing age-related differences in response speed using ratio scores, the time required for the task by younger adults needs to be included for a complete description of the data.

7.2.4. Adult Lifespan Trajectories: Dissociations between Tasks and Task Domains

Previous chapters were, among other things, very much concerned with the testing of age-related dissociations. We found merit in some but not in others. The adult lifespan data gathered here allow us to revisit some of these earlier dissociations and nondissociations, both between broad task domains and within particular tasks. Given the composition of the data set, the latter is restricted to the contrasts between simple reaction time and choice reaction time, the neutral and interference conditions in the Stroop task, and Part A and Part B of the Trail Making Test. Exponential models were fitted.

7.2.4.1. Adult Lifespan Trajectory Dissociations between Task Domains

Chapters 2 and 4 revealed an essential age-related dissociation between spatial tasks on the one hand (large slowing factor, around 1.8) and linguistic tasks on the other (smaller slowing factor, around 1.3). The situation is less clear for sensorimotor slowing. In Chapters 2 and 4, I obtained an average slowing factor for sensorimotor tasks between 1.0 and 1.4, depending on the task.

 For the present analyses, I sorted the available tasks into these three categories, using the same classification scheme I applied in Chapter 2. The linguistic tasks included lexical decision, double lexical decision, and synonym-antonym tasks; the sensorimotor tasks included RT tasks (simple RT and choice RT), copying tasks, cancellation tasks, as well as Part A of different versions of the Trail Making test; the spatial tasks included visual search and shape classification.

 The final data set (615 data-points) contained 16 curves for linguistic tasks, with a total of 127 data points; 35 curves for sensorimotor tasks, 388 data points, and 15 curves for spatial tasks, 110 data points. I fit a simple exponential model, using ln(Age − 25) as the age term, the age term by reference time interaction, and the interaction between the age term and a dummy code for sensorimotor tasks, and between age and a dummy code for spatial tasks, as the predictors. The latter two interaction terms test whether lexical processing, sensorimotor processing, and spatial processing show different exponential age trajectories once the effect of reference time on the age trajectory for the ratio scores is taken into account. The choice of dummy variables makes linguistic processing (with the expected smallest age effect) the default or baseline cognitive measure for this analysis. The fitted equation is:

$$\text{Ln(slowing ratio)} = -0.00096 \ (0.00099) \ (\text{Age} - 25) + 0.0000067$$
$$(0.0000006) \ (\text{Age} - 25) * (\text{RT}_{age25})$$
$$+ \ 0.0035 \ (0.0008) \ (\text{Age} - 25) * \text{dummy(Sensorimotor)}$$
$$+ \ 0.0032 \ (0.0005) \ (\text{Age} - 25) * \text{dummy(Spatial)}.$$

 This equation shows not a trifurcation, but a bifurcation, with a large age effect shared between spatial processing and sensorimotor processing, and a zero age effect for linguistic processing. Compiling the effects of spatial processing and sensorimotor processing into a single dummy variable and fixing the age effect for linguistic tasks to zero did not affect fit significantly, ΔLR χ^2 (2) = 0.68:

$$\textbf{Ln(slowing ratio) = 0 (0) (Age – 25) + 0.0000064 (0.0000004) (Age}$$
$$\textbf{– 25)} * \textbf{(RT}_{age25}\textbf{) + 0.0030 (0.0004) (Age – 25)}$$
$$* \textbf{dummy(Sensorimotor or Spatial).}$$

This equation, which explained 71.91% of the variance, can be rewritten as a set of two equations:

$$\textbf{Ln(linguistic slowing ratio) = 0.0000064 (Age – 25)} * \textbf{(RT}_{age25}\textbf{);}$$

$$\textbf{Ln(spatial/sensorimotor slowing ratio) = 0.0030 (Age – 25)} * \textbf{(RT}_{age25}\textbf{).}$$

This data set, then, confirms again the bifurcation between lexical tasks and spatial tasks. The age effect in lexical tasks was not significant—more in line with the findings from Chapter 2 than those from Chapter 4. The sensorimotor tasks did show an age-related effect, which, in this analysis, was identical to that of the spatial tasks. This result reaffirms the conclusion that age-related slowing in sensorimotor tasks is real and, at least in this analysis, quite large.

7.2.4.2. *Adult Lifespan Trajectory Dissociations within Tasks: Reaction Time, Stroop, and Trail Making*

In the current set of studies, three of the within-task contrasts examined in Chapters 4 and 6 were well-represented: single and/or choice RT (16 studies, 312 data points in total over the two conditions, single and choice), the Stroop Color Word test (10 studies, 176 data points in total over the two conditions, neutral and interference), and the Trail Making Test (10 studies, 122 data points in total over the two conditions, Trails A and Trails B). To increase statistical power, I relaxed the requirement that reference times be smaller than 2,000 ms—keeping this requirement would have cut most of the Trail Making B conditions.

To examine the possible dissociations, I fitted a simple exponential model, including ln(Age – 25) as the age term, the age term by reference time interaction, and the interaction between the age term and a dummy code representing the within-task conditions (the dummy was set at 0 for the simplest of the two conditions, and 1 for the more complex of the two conditions). The latter term tests whether the two conditions within each task show different exponential age trajectories once the effect of reference time on the age trajectory for the ratio scores is taken into account. The results from Chapters 4 and 6 would raise the expectation that they would not—a single factor sufficed to capture both conditions within each task in the Brinley plots or, where applicable, state traces.

Figure 7.11 shows the data for each of two conditions for each of the three tasks. It is clear that within each task, the trajectories for each of the conditions diverge—on average, the slowing ratio becomes increasingly larger with advancing age for CRT compared with SRT, for the Stroop interference condition compared with the neutral condition, and for Trail Making B compared with Trail Making A. This is fully

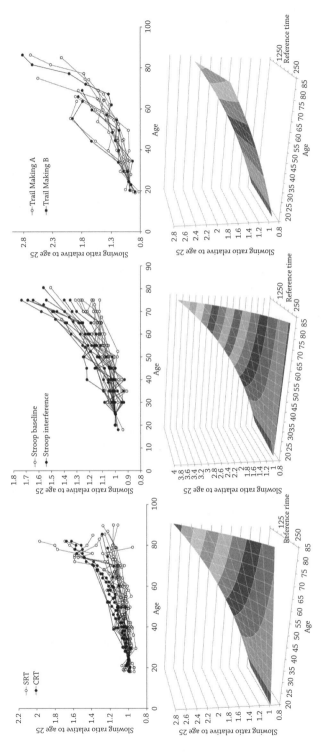

Figure 7.11 Adult lifespan data for reaction time (simple *vs.* choice), the Stroop task (baseline *vs.* interference), and the Trail Making test (version A *vs.* version B). Top panels show the data in 2-D; bottom panels show the fitted 3-D surfaces (exponential models). In none of the 3-D surfaces was a dissociation between the two versions of interest obtained.

expected, given the difference in reference time between conditions. The real question is: Do they diverge more than expected on the basis of the baseline, young-adult difference in response time between conditions?

For SRT/CRT, the equation was:

$$\text{Ln(slowing ratio)} = 0.0056 \, (0.0024) \, (\text{Age} - 25) - 0.0000033 \, (0.0000088)$$
$$(\text{Age} - 25) * (\text{RT}_{\text{age25}}) + 0.0015 \, (0.0012) \, (\text{Age} - 25)$$
$$* (\text{SRT vs. CRT}).$$

The condition by age interaction term was not significant, suggesting that the age trajectory for SRT and CRT was identical. Dropping the term led to the final equation:

$$\text{Ln(slowing ratio)} = 0.0017 \, (0.0005) \, (\text{Age} - 25) + 0.0000076$$
$$(0.0000009) \, (\text{Age} - 25) * (\text{RT}_{\text{age25}}).$$

For Stroop, the equation was:

$$\text{Ln(slowing ratio)} = -0.00000061 \, (0.001900) \, (\text{Age} - 25)$$
$$+ 0.0000059 \, (0.0000035) \, (\text{Age} - 25) * (\text{RT}_{\text{age25}})$$
$$+ 0.0019 \, (0.001) \, (\text{Age} - 25) * (\text{neutral vs. interference}).$$

The condition by age interaction term was not significant. Dropping the term led to the final equation:

$$\text{Ln(slowing ratio)} = -0.0039 \, (0.0007) \, (\text{Age} - 25)$$
$$+ 0.000013 \, (0.000001) \, (\text{Age} - 25) * (\text{RT}_{\text{age25}}).$$

Note that this final equation looks puzzling at first blush. The negative coefficient associated with the age term suggests that the age effect is negative, that is, an age-related speed-up. The figure (center panels) shows what is really happening: The negative age trend is only there for very fast responses, for more realistic "slower" responses (certainly from a reference time of about 500 ms onwards), the age trend is positive, as expected.

For Trail Making, the equation was:

$$\text{Ln(slowing ratio)} = 0.012 \, (0.003) \, (\text{Age} - 25) - 0.00000004 \, (0.0000024)$$
$$(\text{Age} - 25) * (\text{RT}_{\text{age25}}) + 0.0012 \, (0.0030) \, (\text{Age} - 25)$$
$$* (\text{A vs. B}).$$

The condition by age interaction term was not significant. Dropping the term led to the final equation:

$$\text{Ln(slowing ratio)} = 0.011 \, (0.001) \, (\text{Age} - 25) + 0.0000015$$
$$(0.000007) \, (\text{Age} - 25) * (\text{RT}_{\text{age25}})$$

The 3-D surfaces for the three tasks (slowing ratios as a function of age and reference time at age 25) are depicted in the bottom row of Figure 7.11. The end conclusion is that the lifespan trajectory analyses confirm what we found in the Brinley analyses for these tasks in the previous chapters: There is no age-related dissociation between SRT and CRT, between Stroop baseline and Stroop interference, and between Part A and B of the Trail Making Test.

Thus, the divergent trajectories within the three tasks shown in the top panels in Figure 7.11 is an artifact due to not taking actual response times of younger adults into account. If nothing else, these data demonstrate quite dramatically that even ratio scores are a potentially misleading way to cast young-old differences—conclusions of specific age-related deficits can be predicated on age by condition interactions that are quite spurious, based on nothing but a difference in the average time needed by younger adults to complete the tasks under study.

The three data plots also illustrate another important point, namely that there are quite striking differences in slowing surfaces between these tasks. This implies that the general slowing surface derived above (even if it explains an impressive amount of variance) can only be seen as a first approximation. For a full picture of age-related effects, even at the level of proportions, the individual tasks need to be taken into account. The result also indicates that the differences between tasks are not reducible to 2-D effects. Rather, they seem to operate both along the age axis and the reference time axis; that is, they are a joint function of age and task difficulty. The Stroop data, for instance, show particularly strong curvature along both the age axis and the reference time axis, whereas Trail Making hardly exhibits any. The curvature comes from the Brinley functions, as I explained earlier in this chapter.

The point here is not to contend that one representation of age-related differences in a task is better than the other, but simply that different representations serve different purposes. I would argue, as I have done throughout this book, that Brinley plots are very well-suited to inform us about the truth-value of observed age-related dissociations. I would also contend that if the goal is to predict actual response times at any given moment in the lifespan, lifespan curves or surfaces are the more precise tool.

7.2.5. Full Lifespan Trajectories

The intent of this chapter was to model age trajectories over the adult lifespan. However, in the set of studies I collected here, quite a few also reported data on children or adolescents. This is fortuitous, because it allows us to estimate a full lifespan curve from early childhood to late adulthood. I will fit these data using two methods. The first is the method used for the adult range, that is, fitting ratio scores to a 3-D lifespan surface. (I will start this exercise by fitting the childhood/adolescence data first, then adding the adulthood data.) The second is to use Brinley slopes as our estimate of age-related slowing.

7.2.5.1. Fitting the Early Part of the Lifespan: Ratio Scores

Data from children and adolescents can be treated in much the same way as those of adults—we can fit slowing factors expressed as ratios, comparing different age groups to a common reference age. To make the analyses between the earlier and the later part of the lifespan comparable, I used the same reference age as for the adult data, that is, age 25. Consequently, my analyses include all data points where the mean age was

25 or younger (this creates some overlap with the adult-age data set)—a total of 269 data points, culled from 41 lifespan curves (thus, this is a subset of the data shown in Figure 7.9). As in the previous sections, I fitted two classes of models, a quadratic polynomial and an exponential model. The age terms in the model were centered on age 25, that is, (25 – Age), to mirror the adult-age data, and, as in the adult-age analyses, reference time (i.e., response time needed at age 25 as calculated through interpolation or extrapolation) was included in the model as an interaction term.

The quadratic polynomial explained 89.09% of the variance compared with the empty model:

Slowing ratio = 1 (0) – 0.034 (0.004) (25 – Age) + 0.0043 (0.0002)
$$(25 - Age)^2 + 0.000015 \ (0.000008) \ 1000(25 - Age) * RT_{age25}.$$

A simple exponential model clearly captured less of the variance, 62.14%:

Ln(slowing ratio) = –0.0067 (0.0038) (25 – Age) + 0.0000066
$$(0.0000038) \ (25 - Age) * (RT_{age25})$$

When examining the shape of the surface, it became clear that the exponential model was misspecified mainly because it assumes that the reference age (or older) is the fastest point in the curve. The data suggest that this is not the case. To fix this, I introduced a quadratic correction term in this equation (this adds curvature to the data and thus allows the function to find the age where performance is fastest). This increased the variance explained to 74.86%:

Ln(slowing ratio) = –0.024 (0.004) (25 – Age) + 0.0028 (0.0002)
$$(25 - Age)^2 + 0.0000083 \ (0.0000031) \ (25 - Age)$$
$$* (RT_{age25}).$$

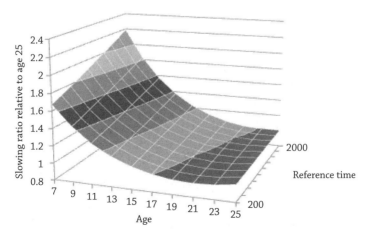

Figure 7.12 3-D surface plot (slowing ratio determined by age and reference time, i.e., time needed for the task at age 25) for the childhood and adolescence portion of the lifespan (the cut-off is at age 25); the model depicted is an exponential model with quadratic adjustment with a linear effect of reference time, $R^2 = .75$.

The quadratic model clearly wins, but the exponential model with a quadratic adjustment does not compare too unfavorably. I depict this model in Figure 7.12.

These two models have at least three aspects in common. First, both models show significant curvature over age, mirroring what was observed in the older-adult data: The further away from age 25, that is, the younger the subjects, the larger the impact of age.

Second, both models show a positive interaction of age and reference time, marginally significant for the quadratic polynomial, significant for the adjusted exponential model. This implies a fan of ratios, again mirroring what we observed in the adult-age data: The further away from age 25, that is, the younger subjects are, the wider the spread in slowing ratios as a function of reference time. The reason for this is likely the same as in the older adults—the fan derives from the geometry of children's and adolescents' Brinley plots.

Third, both models predict that the minimum in the slowing ratios (the fastest point in this portion of the lifespan) occurs earlier than age 25—a finding in agreement with my conclusions from the adult-age data. The exact minimum varies with reference time (be it not by much). If we take 1,000 ms as the reference time, the quadratic polynomial places the minimum at age 23 (where the slowing ratio is 0.98); the adjusted exponential model yields its minimum at age 22 (with a slowing ratio of 0.98).

7.2.5.2. *Fitting the Full Lifespan Model: Welded Exponential Models on Ratio Scores*

The two data sets—the adults and the subject groups younger than age 25—can be merged, or rather welded together. The reference age of 25, where the slowing ratio is by definition equal to 1, provides a suitable seam for welding. There are multiple options for what models to weld. For reasons of symmetry and in deference to Cerella and Hale (1992; see also the next section) I opted to simply link the exponential model

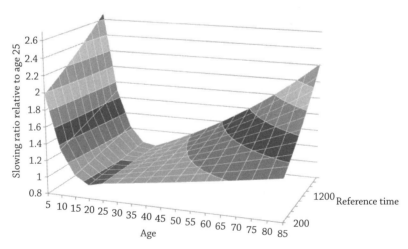

Figure 7.13 3-D surface plot for the full lifespan (slowing ratio determined by age and reference time, i.e., time needed for the task at age 25), obtained by welding the adjusted exponential model for childhood/adolescence (Fig. 7.12) to the exponential model for adulthood.

for the adult data to the adjusted exponential model for the child/adolescent data. The result is shown in Figure 7.13. One new insight from this figure is that the fanning of slowing ratios is larger in adulthood than in childhood/adolescence. For instance, when the reference time for the task is 1,000 ms, slowing relative to a 25-year-old is just about the same in a ten-year-old and a seventy-five-year-old (slowing ratios of 1.53 and 1.51, respectively). The spread of slowing ratios, however, is larger for the seventy-five-year-olds than for the ten-year-olds (from 1.24 at 200 ms to 1.94 at 2,000 ms vs. 1.38 and 1.68, respectively). I am not aware of a theoretical explanation for this finding, but it suggests that researchers interested in fault lines in speeded aspects of the human mind might be better off studying older adults than children, simply because the wider spread of slowing factors leaves more room for dissociations. The data also imply that a purely proportional age-related slowing model would fit data from children and adolescents better than those of middle-aged and older adults.

7.2.5.3. Fitting the Full Lifespan: Double-Exponential Models for Brinley Slopes

A second way to model the lifespan data is to directly fit Brinley slopes (a method pioneered by Cerella & Hale, 1994). The principle is simple: A Brinley plot is constructed for each age group (the group of on-average-7-year-olds, the group of on-average-8-year-olds, etc.) with performance of that age group on the Y-axis, and performance of the reference group (25-year-olds in our case) on the X-axis.

This procedure has its advantages and drawbacks.

One advantage is that we are now fitting actual age-related slowing factors, instead of an approximation (at least, if we consider the reasoning behind calling the slopes of Brinley functions age-related slowing factors valid). This eliminates the need for the inclusion of a reference response time in the equation and allows for the direct fitting of a 2-D response time by curve. Another advantage (which is also a disadvantage) is that the data are no longer nested within studies. This means that multilevel modeling cannot be applied to these data, which, in turn, gives us more freedom in the choice of curves to fit—we are no longer limited to functions that can be linearized. The model I will use here is the double-exponential model espoused by Cerella and Hale (1994), which models development and aging simultaneously. The previous sections already demonstrated that such a model should be viable—both parts of the lifespan can be fit to a simple exponential function.

The procedure does have a major drawback. In order to estimate reliable Brinley slopes, we need as many data points per age group as possible. The only practical way to do this is by combining tasks. This, then, means that the estimated slope will, by necessity, be heterogeneous, that is, made up of different tasks that may (and likely do) yield distinct age-related effects, as amply demonstrated in previous chapters. Additionally, the mixture of these tasks will in practice differ from age group to age group, introducing additional noise. The expectation is that ultimately the different task-driven biases in each age group will cancel each other out, so that an average slowing function can be drawn through these slope estimates and be meaningful.

My goal was to estimate a Brinley slope for each discrete year of age. It became immediately clear that not all ages have a sufficient number of points to justify an estimate of the slope. My ad hoc criterion for the minimum number of points to estimate a Brinley slope was 4. If an age group did not have a sufficient number of data points (this was the case for age 14, for instance), I simply lumped them with the next age group (or age groups, as necessary) and used the mean age of this amalgam as the age estimate. For instance, given that there were not enough data points to compute a slope estimate for age 14, I grouped the data with those for age 15, and the resulting Brinley slope was considered to be an estimate of the slope at age 14.5. The X-data for the Brinley plots were the reference response times used in the previous sections. Thus, all Brinley slopes are evaluated against the observed or interpolated/extrapolated speed of the task at age 25. Figure 7.14 shows the fit of the 67 thus estimated Brinley functions as a function of age. Fit is very good—the lowest R^2 value is .79; the average is .97. The figure does reveal an important caveat: The Brinley lines are estimated less well at either end of the lifespan, as testified by a reliable quadratic correlation ($r = .41$) between age and fit. This effect is likely due to two factors: (a) Sample sizes are smaller for the child and older-adult samples compared with the younger-adult samples (see the bubble plot in the bottom panel of Figure 7.8); and (b) there is increasing variability in task slopes as individuals are further away from young-adulthood (see, e.g., Figure 7.10 and Figure 7.13). This means we should expect that the estimates at either end of the lifespan are less reliable than those in young adulthood and middle age.

Figure 7.15 presents the Brinley slopes as a function of age. The data show a lop-sided U-shaped function, just like the ratio score data did. I fitted Cerella and Hale's double-exponential model to the data, using the CNLR procedure in SPSS. This model fits the data simultaneously to a growth curve and a decay curve:

$$\text{Brinley slope} = a\, e^{-b\,\text{Age}} + c\,(e^{\,d\,\text{Age}} - 1) + 1.$$

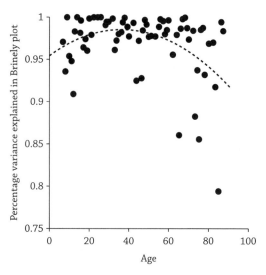

Figure 7.14 Fit (R^2) of Brinley functions fitted to the lifespan data at each year of age, as a function of age. The data show a curvilinear relationship, such that fit is worse at either end of the lifespan. The dotted line indicates the best-fitting quadratic function ($R^2 = .17$).

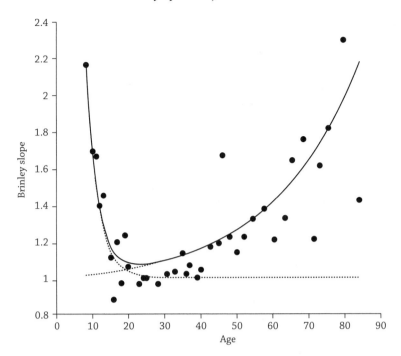

Figure 7.15 Lifespan trajectory of Brinley slopes, relative to 25-year-olds. The dotted lines represent the exponential growth and decay functions, the solid line the double-exponential lifespan trajectory (R^2 = .73).

The first term in this equation (viz., a $e^{-b \, \text{Age}}$) describes a speed-up of response time as a function of age, that is, growth or development; the second term (viz. c ($e^{d \, \text{Age}}$ – 1) + 1) describes slowing as a function of age, that is, decay or aging. The two terms are summed to yield the U-shaped lifespan trajectory, adding 1 as a correction term. The b and d parameters are rates (of growth and decay, respectively); parameter a denotes the starting value (i.e., age-related slowing at age zero); and parameter c modulates the first and second derivative of the function at age zero. The model fits the data quite well, explaining 72.7% of the variance (by comparison, a fourth-order polynomial explained 66.0% of the variance):

$$\text{Brinley slope} = 12.44 \, e^{-0.297 \, \text{Age}} + 0.039 \, (e^{0.041 \, \text{Age}} - 1) + 1.$$

This curve is overlaid on the data in Figure 7.15 as a solid line. The dotted lines represent the underlying growth and decay functions. Although the lifespan curve is the sum of these two underlying curves, the story of the lifetime of cognitive speed is predominantly one of decline overtaking growth—the growth curve asymptotes in early adulthood (ducking under the 1.01 mark at age 24); after that age, in practice only decline is noticeable.

What does this curve teach us about the starting point of cognitive aging? First, the minimum of this function is at age 23, the same age estimated by the exponential functions fitted to the speed ratios. Thus, if we define the starting point of aging as the point of inflection of the lifespan curve (i.e., the point were the pinnacle of processing speed is reached), cognitive aging starts at age 23. Second, note the two underlying curves, the growth curve and the decay curve, depicted as dotted lines in the figure. The decay curve dominates the growth curve from age 19 on. This, of course, would imply that we truly believe these are the underlying curves generating the overall trajectory. As I explained in Section 7.1.2, multiple sets of curves can generate the humped pattern, and there is no way to falsify any of them, unless the precise mechanism is known.

One caveat: Although the double-exponential curve fits the data well, considerable variability is present as well, as one would expect given the diversity in tasks. I tried to decrease this variability by separating out the three task domains examined earlier in this chapter (i.e., linguistic, sensorimotor, and spatial), calculating Brinley slopes for each. Figure 7.16 shows the lifespan trajectory of these three types of tasks, with the best-fitting curves overlaid. The reliability of these slope estimates is somewhat uncertain—some of the Brinley plots contain very few points. This may have influenced the fit for the early part of the lifespan especially (it is unlikely that the minimum of the curve is truly situated at age 11), and there are no data points for linguistic tasks in the child/adolescent range. The curves do converge on the same conclusions with regard to the between-task-domain effects in adulthood as the ratio analysis did: The curve for lexical tasks shows a lifespan trajectory that indicates much more modest age-related slowing than the trajectories describing slowing in sensorimotor tasks and spatial tasks. The latter two curves are indistinguishable, at least in the adult portion of the graph, as was the case for ratio scores. The plot also

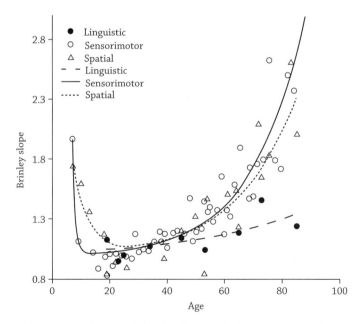

Figure 7.16 Lifespan trajectory of Brinley slopes, relative to 25-year-olds, separated by task family (linguistic, sensorimotor, and spatial) with the best-fitting double-exponential model for each overlaid on the data.

suggests that the linguistic lifespan trajectory starts diverging from the other two at around age 35.

7.3. Lifespan Trajectories: Conclusions

In this chapter, I fitted full lifespan and adult lifespan data. Accelerated curvilinear models described the data best; these models were U-shaped over the entire lifespan, and showed accelerated decline when only the adult portion of the lifespan was considered. The peak of the function appeared to be situated in early adulthood, at around age 23.

At least two large-scale biologically inspired models could explain such a curvilinear function. Both have in common that they place the locus of age-related differences in adulthood in a loss of connectivity—either through a direct loss of (functional) connectivity or indirectly through changes in the dopamine system. Neither mechanism in separation is able to account for the lifespan speed-of-processing data, because each mechanism has its own lifespan trajectory, which does not coincide with the speed data. Specifically, loss of functional connectivity occurs later in life than the hump in the processing speed function (the peak in functional connectivity is situated around age 40 or so, vs. the early twenties for processing speed), and data for dopamine receptor binding suggest a monotonically decreasing lifespan function rather than a humped function. One possibility is that both mechanisms operate in concert to determine the system's processing speed, with a build-up of (functional and anatomical) connectivity dominating childhood and adolescence, until the steady decline in the efficiency of the dopamine system takes over in young adulthood, causing the system to slow down even as (functional and anatomical) connectivity is still increasing.

When I investigated domain or task-related dissociations within the lifespan trajectories, the analyses confirmed the linguistic/spatial breakdowns obtained earlier in this book. As in Chapters 4 and 6, I found no evidence for within-task dissociations between the neutral and the interference condition in Stroop, between the baseline and task-switching version of the Trail Making test, and between simple and choice reaction time.

8

The Role of Generational Differences

All of the curves reported in Chapter 7 are estimated from cross-sectional studies, that is, studies that test individuals of a range of ages at roughly the same point in time. One criticism often leveled at this research design is that the age variable is confounded with many other variables. The most salient of these is cohort or generation. (See Schaie, 1965, for perhaps the earliest treatment of this topic.) That is, the older individuals tested in cross-sectional studies may perform cognitive tasks more slowly not because they have grown slower over the course of their lifetime, but simply because they are a few generations older than the younger adults. If successive generations get progressively faster at the types of tasks included here, cross-sectional data will—likely by a large amount—overestimate the amount of slowing due to the aging process per se. (One disrespectful analogy is the personal computer: Older computers are slower not because they slow down [much] as they age, but because successive generations of computers have grown faster and faster; Salthouse, 2010.)

8.1. Generational Differences in Time-lag Studies: The Flynn Effect

Perhaps the most convincing way to examine generational differences is through time-lag studies. In time-lag studies, subjects of the same age are tested at different points in time. (Think, for instance, of SAT scores gathered in different years—the subjects are all roughly the same age, 18 or so, and generational differences would show up as a non-flat trajectory when these scores are plotted as a function of calendar year.) Most of the research on this topic has focused on higher-order forms of cognition, mostly tests of fluid intelligence. The seminal research on the topic was performed by James Flynn (e.g., 1987); the generational increase in fluid IQ scores he uncovered has since been labeled the Flynn effect. Flynn gathered data from extremely large samples in 14 nations. The data concern either norming samples for IQ tests or selection data of military recruits in countries with compulsory military service (viz., the Netherlands, Belgium, France, and Norway; the military system in these countries required testing of every male of military age in the population). The time period covered varied widely across studies, but was typically around 25 years. The conclusions were astounding, pointing at a median gain of five IQ points, or one third of a standard deviation, per decade. (All IQ tests set the mean at 100; most set the standard deviation at 15, and so a gain of five IQ points equals a gain of one third of a standard deviation.)

The largest effects involved tests designed to measure nonverbal reasoning and abstract problem-solving, such as Raven's progressive matrices and the Performance subtest from the Wechsler scales; gains were much smaller for tests of crystallized intelligence. (More recent reports suggest that at least in Northern Europe (Denmark and Norway) the effect may have reached an asymptote in the 1990s, or may even have reversed (Sundet, Barlaug, & Torjussen, 2004; Teasdale & Owen, 2005), but this finding would not affect the studies considered here.) Many explanations for the Flynn effect have been advanced, including improved physical health, enhanced nutrition, and increasing well-being, as well as the extensive educational and technological changes that have occurred within the Western world over the course of the 20th century (e.g., Neisser, 1998).

The data are very clear with regard to fluid intelligence. One question is whether the Flynn effect also applies to tests of processing speed. Seven studies seem to be relevant here. Flynn and Weiss (2007) examined the standardization samples of the Wechsler Intelligence Scale for Children (WISC); the two subtests that tap processing speed, namely Coding and Symbol Search, showed substantial gains (equivalent to 4.75 IQ points, or 3.7 points per decade) in the brief period from 1989 to 2002. Must, Must, and Raudik (2003) examined gains in Symbol-Digit Substitution over a 60-year period in samples of over 300 school children each, and found gains equivalent to about 18 IQ points, or about three IQ points per decade. Wichters et al. (2004) found a 0.28 SD difference per decade (or 4.2 IQ points) in Digits Symbol Substitution performance over a 31-year time lag in Dutch adults. Dickinson and Hiscock (2010) examined norming samples for the WAIS (WAIS vs. WAIS-R, with a time delay of 24.5 years), and obtained a Flynn effect of 3.7 IQ points per decade for the Digit Symbol Substitution subtest. A second study by Dickinson and Hiscock (2011) examined norming samples for different neuropsychological tests, and found gains of six IQ points per decade for the Trail Making Test (the norming samples spanned a time lag of 36 years), nonsignificant gain for the written version of the Symbol Digit Modalities (a substitution test; the norming samples spanned 12 years), but a six IQ points per decade gain in an oral version, and no significant gain for Finger Tapping (a test for motor speed). In a small-sample time-lag study spanning 20 years, Nettelbeck and Wilson (2004) found no evidence (gain = 0.7 IQ points per decade) for generational differences in inspection time, even though they replicated the small Flynn effect for verbal IQ (a finding that suggests the data have some validity). Finally, Hoyer, Stawski, Wasylyshyn, and Verhaeghen (2004) examined younger and older adults' raw Digit Symbol Substitution scores as reported in 141 studies published in *Psychology and Aging* and the *Journals of Gerontology* between 1986 and 2002. Regressing raw scores on year of publication (a proxy of when the study was conducted) yielded an absolute null result (the beta coefficient was 0.00), suggesting no Flynn effect at all in these data. (The data are reproduced in Figure 8.1.) This result should be highlighted because the data are not obtained from a random sample (as in the other studies summarized here), but from exactly the type of sample used most often in this book (and, in fact, this is a subset of the sample investigated in Chapter 2): Experimental studies, typically with an extreme

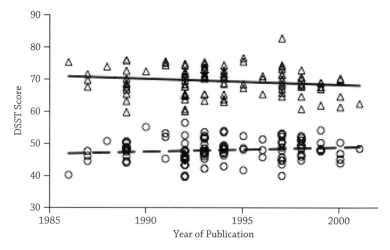

Figure 8.1 Average performance on the WAIS Digit Symbol Substitution Test in 141 studies as a function of year of publication and age (triangles: younger adults; circles: older adults). No historic/cohort effect appears to be visible in the data. Figure reproduced from Hoyer, Stawski, Wasylyshyn, & Verhaeghen (2004).

age groups design, and reported in gerontology journals. Thus, this meta-analysis has low ecological validity compared with most Flynn-effect studies when considering its generalizability to the real world, but high ecological validity for the type of samples included in this book.

Overall, the data suggest a Flynn effect in tests of processing speed of a magnitude of 2.9 IQ point per decade (or 0.19 SD per decade). This estimate is somewhat lower than the estimate obtained for more complex tests of fluid intelligence. It is worth noting that within speeded measures two of the tests that assess the sensorimotor system (inspection time and tapping speed) show no Flynn effect; Trail Making, however, which also seems to be mostly a test of sensorimotor functioning, does show a substantial Flynn effect. Substitution tests show a Flynn effect of, per average, 3.2 IQ points, or 0.21 SD, per decade, except in the Hoyer et al. meta-analysis.

The available evidence then clearly suggests that age-related differences in cognition reported in the literature consist of a mixture of at least two influences: "true" age effects and generational effects, which additionally reduce performance of the older cohorts (see also Flynn, 1998). The generational effect is substantial. One study (Dickinson & Hiscock, 2010) statistically subtracted the Flynn effect from the age results reported in the WAIS norming samples; it estimated the pure age effect to be about half the size of the observed age-related effect. A second study estimated the pure age effect to be about 68% of the observed effect (Lee, Gorsuch, Saklofske, & Patterson, 2008).

By way of a "what if?" analysis, Figure 8.2, panel A reproduces all adult-age speed ratios reported in Chapter 7, corrected for the average Flynn effect in speed as calculated above (0.19 SD per decade, or 0.019 SD per year). To apply this correction, I simply subtracted 0.019 times (Age – 25) times the standard deviation of the reference speed from each observed response time prior to dividing them by the 25-year-olds'

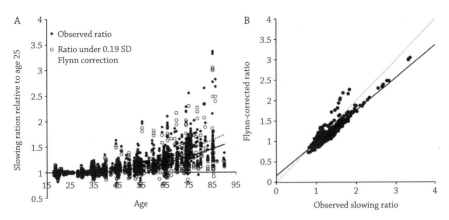

Figure 8.2 Panel A: Slowing ratios relative to performance at age 25 as a function of age; the original ratios are shown (the dotted line is best-fitting second-order polynomial to these data), as well as the Flynn-corrected ratios (with the solid line as the best-fitting second-order polynomial). The data suggest that the Flynn effect affects both the ratios as well as the estimate of the age at which performance peaks. Panel B: Flynn-corrected ratios as a function of observed ratios, again showing how the observed data might overestimate the aging effect under the assumption that the Flynn effect is operative in these data. Best fitting regression line indicated by the solid line; the equality diagonal by the dotted line.

reference time. The standard deviation of the reference response time is not always reported; when it was missing, I estimated it using the best-fitting equation relating SD to the mean as obtained in Chapter 3 (i.e., $SD = -80$ ms $+ 0.33$ *Mean*). To allow for a quick comparison between the two data sets (i.e., the corrected and the original data), I superimposed simple OLS second-order polynomials fitted to each data set in the figure.

There are at least two things worth noting here. First, the Flynn-corrected data indeed yield a smaller age-related effect than the original data. To assess the size of the effect, I regressed the Flynn-corrected ratio scores on the observed scores using OLS (the scatterplot is provided in panel B of Figure 8.2). The resulting equation ($R^2 = .87$) was:

$$\text{Ratio}_{\text{Flynn-corrected}} = 0.16 + 0.80 \ \text{Ratio}_{\text{uncorrected.}}$$

Forcing the equation through the origin decreased R^2 slightly, to .85:

$$\text{Ratio}_{\text{Flynn-corrected}} = 0.93 \ \text{Ratio}_{\text{uncorrected.}}$$

Thus, the "true" age effect in ratio scores is, on average, between 80% and 93% of the observed speed ratio (depending on whether or not an intercept is taken into account). Observed scores thus overestimate the true age effect, on average, by 8% to 25% (i.e., the inverse of .93 and .80). This is not a negligible amount, but the consequence of the

Flynn effect for the measurement of age-related differences in speed appears to be less dramatic than it is for intelligence tests.

Second, the minimum of this function, or the peak of processing speed, has now moved upwards about 5 years, to age 28. The corrected curve is also much flatter than the observed curve, making it is reasonable to speak of a plateau in speeded processing for much of middle age. The curve remains quite close to 1 until at least age 40.

One big caveat needs to be mentioned here. All of the studies in this section, especially the ones that "correct" age-related studies for the Flynn effect (including the correction in Figure 8.2), make the assumption that the Flynn effect is purely a cohort effect, without any age by cohort interaction. That is, the assumption is that the Flynn effect serves to speed up younger cohorts, without influencing older cohorts at all. Time-lag studies, however, do not just measure cohort or generational differences; the observed differences between individuals are also conflated with historical time. The assumption in most interpretations of the Flynn effect is then that of the analogy touched on above, namely that the speeding up over successive generations is like the speeding up of computers over historical time—a generation-driven obsolescence (Salthouse, 2010). It is, however, also possible, that the time-lag differences reflect historical differences that benefit middle-aged and older adults as well, maybe as much as they do younger adults. Salthouse (2010) uses a salary-inflation analogy here: Salaries go up with generation, but also with career age, thus benefitting adults of all ages. If this were the case, longitudinal trajectories would underestimate the true age effect (because the historical drift works against the aging process), and cross-sectional comparisons would present a more accurate picture of the real aging effects than generally assumed. To assess these rival explanations, we need to turn to yet another design: longitudinal panel studies.

8.2. Generational Differences in Longitudinal Studies

A second way to assess generational influences is through longitudinal panel studies. In longitudinal studies, a set of subjects is followed over a period of time; panel studies sample subjects of different ages (and therefore, different cohorts). Longitudinal panel designs combine both, repeatedly testing subjects of different ages. When panels of cohorts are followed over time, it becomes possible to examine whether the longitudinal differences are smaller than, equal to, or larger than the corresponding cross-sectional differences at the first (or any subsequent) time of measurement.

The basic reasoning here is that cross-sectional differences conflate age differences and cohort differences, and that longitudinal differences are a function of time of measurement and age (e.g., Baltes, 1968; Schaie, 1965). If cross-sectional differences and longitudinal differences coincide, this would suggest that cohort differences are equal to zero, and cross-sectional and longitudinal differences are both excellent estimates of true age differences. (The alternative, namely that cohort differences and time of measurement effects cancel each other out is typically considered too esoteric to be taken seriously.) Alternatively, if cross-sectional differences are larger than longitudinal differences (the modal result in the field), the interpretation is typically that part of the cross-sectional age-related differences are due to cohort or generational differences. For instance, the Seattle Longitudinal Study Schaie (summarized in Schaie, 2005) found that for almost all abilities, participants born earlier scored lower, independent of age. This suggests that a large part of the age-related decline observed in cross-sectional studies is not due to age at all, but rather to cohort differences—the observed "decline" in cross-sectional studies is a case of a worse starting point rather than an actual decline.

Not everyone, however, agrees with these conclusions. Salthouse (1991), for instance, observes that in the Seattle Longitudinal Study (and most other longitudinal work), cohort effects are taken into account, but period effects (i.e., effects related to time of measurement) are not. Salthouse reanalyzed Schaie's data and found that when time of measurement is taken into account, longitudinal results do not differ much from cross-sectional results: Only verbal ability increases with age, all other variables decline markedly and do so from early adulthood on. Part of Schaie's conclusions may also be tied to selection effects. Singer, Verhaeghen, Ghisletta, Lindenberger, and Baltes (2003) analyzed data from the Berlin Aging Study and obtained the typical result that cross-sectional age effects were larger than longitudinal age effects. When only the data from those participants who returned for a second and third round of testing were considered, however, cross-sectional and longitudinal results overlapped quite nicely. This finding suggests that selection effects might be a major (and largely neglected) problem in longitudinal research—only the fittest return, and this leads us to underestimate age effects. Finally, some researchers (e.g., Ghisletta & de Ribaupierre, 2005; Salthouse, 2009, 2010) have argued that retest effects might be more important to explain longitudinal results than previously thought.

We can take the discussion out of the abstract realm by investigating actual data sets. A search of the PsycInfo database, using the keywords "longitudinal," "speed," and "response time," yielded eight studies that allowed for the plotting of actual trajectories (Christensen et al., 2000; 2004; Deary & Der, 2005; Fozard, Vercruyssen, Reynolds, & Hancock, 1990; Huppert & Whittington, 1993; Salthouse, 2005; Schaie, 1989b; Zelinski & Lewis, 2003). Together, these eight studies yielded 10 trajectories for different types of reaction time, and five for perceptual speed.

The data are plotted in Figure 8.3. The connected dots in the figure represent longitudinal data; unconnected dots represent different cohorts. (Note that RT data and perceptual speed data are scaled in opposite directions; slower is up for RT, but down for perceptual speed.) Figure 8.4 (top panel) presents the same data in a different light, namely as change per year as observed in both the longitudinal and the cross-sectional trajectories. (Note that the data are scaled in the original metric reported in each study [RT and complex RT measured in ms/year; change in raw or standardized test scores for the perceptual speed tasks], except that scores were all scaled in the same direction, such that positive scores indicate that subjects slow down with advancing age.) Figure 8.3 also contains three additional studies that did not provide enough information to allow for the plotting of the trajectories, but did allow for the calculation of slopes (MacDonald et al., 2003; Sliwinski & Buschke, 1999; Zimprich, 2002). The cross-sectional slope was calculated at the first time of measurement; the longitudinal slope over as many measurement points as were available. Figure 8.4 (bottom panel) provides the ratio of the cross-sectional slope over the longitudinal slope as a common metric for all studies. For the latter analysis, two data points (from Deary

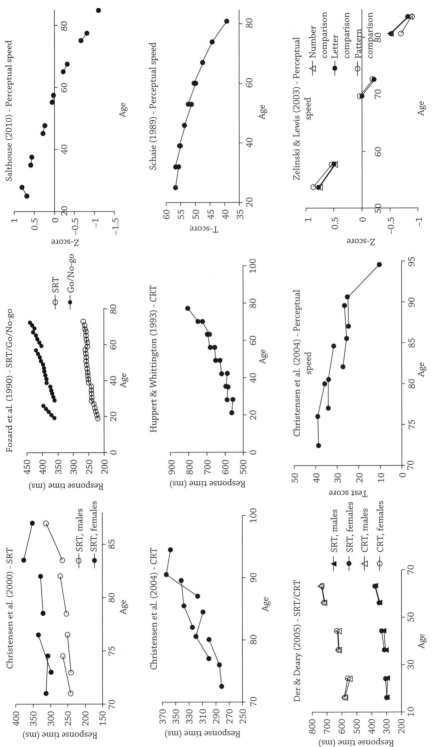

Figure 8.3 Data from nine studies examining speed in a longitudinal (i.e., repeated) measurements of the same sample; unconnected dots represent different cohorts.

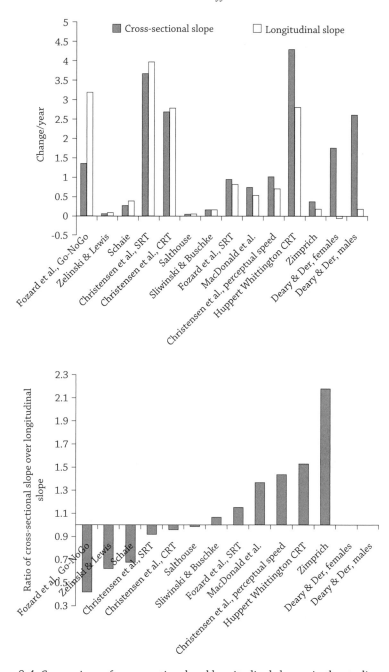

Figure 8.4 Comparison of cross-sectional and longitudinal change in the studies depicted in Figure 5.21, as well as three additional studies. The top panel shows cross-sectional and longitudinal slopes (i.e., change per year); the bottom panel shows the ratios, indicating whether cross-sectional estimates and longitudinal estimates are comparable. Average ratio was 1.11, indicating that cross-sectional differences overestimate longitudinal change.

& Der, 2005) were censored because they were excessively large, namely –35.96 and 13.87, due to a very small longitudinal effect. This censorship poignantly illustrates the main methodological caveat about these data, namely the extremely small number of studies—adding or deleting one or a few might have a big impact on the conclusions. Another caveat is that capturing all these data into a slope measurement is an oversimplification—we already know that cross-sectional age-related differences are not linear with age (and this is likely also the case with longitudinal change). Given that the age effect is likely to be larger in older cohorts (if the lifespan trajectories reported in the previous sections hold longitudinally), differences in the mean age in these studies will drive the estimate of the age effect. It is also possible that the divergence (if any) between cross-sectional and longitudinal data is in itself a function of differences in mean age and/or cohort.

What do the data tell us? The easiest way to read the trajectory data (Figure 8.3) is to examine whether or not the longitudinal trajectories and the cross-sectional trajectories coincide, that is, whether they form a single curve. If they do, longitudinal and cross-sectional data yield the same conclusions. This seems to be more or less the case for the SRT and CRT Christensen et al. data, for the SRT portion of the Deary and Der and the Fozard data, and for most of the Salthouse data. Misalignments, when they occur, seem to happen in both directions. The Deary and Der CRT data, the Christensen perceptual speed data, and the Huppert and Whittington data all show positive cohort effects; that is, younger cohorts are faster than older cohorts, and if the longitudinal trajectories are projected through, they overestimate the speed for the next-older cohort. These results point in the direction of a Flynn effect that operates solely on successive cohorts. In contrast, the Fozard et al. CRT data, the Schaie data, and the Zelinski and Lewis data all show negative cohort effects; that is, the longitudinal projections underestimate the speed of the next-older cohort—an anti-Flynn effect. A simple tally would then lead to the conclusion that the cross-sectional data and longitudinal data paint the same picture. This conclusion is somewhat strengthened by the observation that there is no obvious difference in the studies finding negative cohort and positive cohort effect in terms of either population (e.g., mean age or gender composition) or task. This suggests that the outcome in any given study may be a matter of random variation around a null result.

The direct comparison of slopes, and especially of the ratio of slopes, only partially confirms this suspicion. (Note that these are the same data from the trajectory analysis, with the addition of a few studies that provide direct slope estimates.) There seems to be a difference between tasks—choice RT shows a nice balance between longitudinal and cross-sectional slope estimates (average ratio of 0.97), SRT an underestimation (average ratio of 0.85), and cross-sectional perceptual speed data overestimate the longitudinal effect (average ratio of 1.19). Again, the number of studies is too small to tell us whether the difference in ratio for the three different tasks is a true difference (perhaps signaling that "simpler" response time tasks show no Flynn effect, but more complex perceptual speed measures do; a conclusion in line with that from the previous section), or whether it is a random variation around a null effect. When I average the data by averaging across all studies (allowing one data point per study, averaging across tasks), the ratio is 1.11, indicating that cross-sectional differences overestimate longitudinal change on average by 11%. Thus, an observed cross-sectional slowing ratio of 1.5 would become 1.34 if measured longitudinally. When I average across the three task-specific ratios, however, I obtain an estimated mean ratio of 1.00, leading to the conclusion that cross-sectional age differences, on average, predict longitudinal change perfectly. If the task-related results are not due to random fluctuations around a mean (be it 1 or 1.11), but reflect true task-related cohort differences, then all Brinley-related estimates, and perhaps even dissociations become more or less suspect. Again, the small number of data sets does not allow us to reach a firm conclusion.

8.3. Generational Effects in Brinley Slopes and Ratio Scores

The previous section dealt with the influence of generational differences on the estimation of the effects of aging. Time-lag and longitudinal panel studies are designed to (partially) answer the question as to the origin of observed age-related differences observed in cross-sectional research. These studies rightfully attack the implicit assumption that cross-sectionally observed age differences are due to aging alone. When the goal, however, is to describe age-related differences (e.g., for human-factors purposes), the cross-sectional question isn't meaningless at all. Imagine, for instance, that we need to calculate the average response time of older adults from the moment a traffic light turns orange to the moment the brake pedal is pushed; assume also that we have collected data from younger adults performing this task. The best research practice, obviously, would be to test a group of older adults; the next best option is to turn to calculations of age-related slowing factors. These, in turn, need to be derived from current data; that is, we need to know what age effects we might expect at the current moment in time. From this perspective, the question is not what mechanisms are at the root of observed age differences, or what mechanisms cause age effects to diverge between tasks, but rather whether these curves remain stable over historical time; that is, whether the conclusions we reach today will still hold reasonably well 50 years from now.

The answer here turns out to be cautiously affirmative.

First, and more informally, it seems that the results from past Brinley analyses coincide quite well with those from more recent times. The very first meta-analytic Brinley study, three decades ago (Cerella et al., 1980), reported an average Brinley slope (calculated using OLS) of 1.36; the Cerella (1985) "central processing" slope (again, using OLS) was 1.46; my independent analysis of seven years' worth of data points gathered from studies exclusively published after Cerella's analysis (viz., 1997–2004), presented in Chapter 2, obtained an OLS slope of 1.46 and a multilevel slope of 1.44; the data collected in Chapter 5 yielded a multilevel slope of 1.40. In the two data sets that are exclusive to this book, standard error around the slope was 0.04 and 0.03, respectively, suggesting that all of these estimates are squarely within each other's margin of error. This result suggests that within the historical (and geographical) time frame of these studies, age differences remain remarkably stable over time. Thus, applied research that builds on these average age differences should be quite robust over historical time.

Do the dissociations found here hold up over historical time as well? Lima et al. (1991) obtained a slope of 1.47 for linguistic tasks and 2.02 for nonlinguistic tasks (i.e., reaction time tasks and spatial tasks); mine were 1.36 (SE = 0.14) and 1.83 (SE = 0.05). The data do not exactly coincide, but the general pattern has remained stable over twenty years.

A more formal analysis involves a direct examination of the stability of age-related differences within the sample of studies gathered in Chapter 7. I compared the ratio of response time at age 60 over response time at age 25 within each of the lifespan cross-sectional studies. For studies that did not test a group of subjects exactly 60 years old, I linearly interpolated the data point from the two data points nearest in age. These data can then be arranged by date of publication as a proxy for the date the study was conducted, which, in turn, is a proxy for cohort or generation. Figure 8.5 shows the results. I obtained a linear correlation of 0.17 between slowing ratio and year of publication (as shown in the top panel of the figure), implying that date of publication explains 2.79% of the variance. With 140 data points, this correlation is significant, indicating that age-related differences in speed as measured by ratio scores have grown larger over historical time. Fitting a second-order polynomial revealed a significant quadratic component. The (nonlinear) correlation increased to r = 0.31, explaining 9.79% of the variance. Inspection of the figure suggests an inverted U-shaped function. After an initial rise, cross-sectional age differences have started to decline from the 1970s on. It is clear from the figure that age differences measured before 1960 appear to be rather small, generally with slowing ratios of 1.2 or smaller. Those data all, without exception, refer to reaction time measurements, mostly simple RT, and are thus a clearly nonrepresentative sample of speeded measures. To correct for this potential bias, I redid the analysis after restricting the data to studies published since 1960 (in effect, since 1962; 130 data points; bottom panel of Figure 8.5). The correlation is now −0.12, with 1.36% of the variance explained; this correlation is just shy of two-tailed significance (p = .06). If we take the regression estimate at face value, the conclusion is that the old/young ratio in speeded measures as estimated from cross-sectional studies decreases over historical time at a rate of about 0.02 per decade. (Again, that would be an anti-Flynn effect.) I do admit that the evidence is weak—the data are simply too noisy to draw strong conclusions.

The tentative conclusion is that age differences are relatively stable over historical time, at least within the historical and geographical confines of the studies considered here.

8.4. Generational Effects: Conclusion

I examined generational differences in response time under three guises.

First, I examined time-lag studies, that is, studies where subjects of similar age are compared across different time points. The main conclusion from this literature review was that there is a steady increase in processing speed over cohorts or generations, equivalent to about three IQ points, or 0.2 SD, per decade. A what-if analysis correcting slowing ratios for the Flynn effect suggests that the Flynn effect (if estimated at 0.2 SD) indeed has a substantial impact, with observed speed ratios overestimating

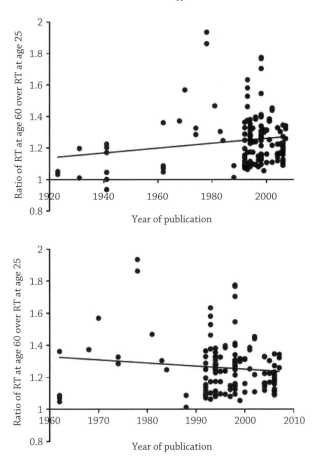

Figure 8.5 Age-related slowing ratios (RT at age 60/RT at age 25) as a function of year of publication. Top panel: All data; bottom panel, data published after 1960.

the "true" age effect by about 10% to 25%. When generational effects were removed from speed ratios, performance peak moved to age 28, five years later than observed in the cross-sectional data, and early middle age showed a plateau rather than decline. Time-lag effects appear to be smaller or even nonexistent for simple sensorimotor measures, but it appears to be robust for substitution measures. The latter result has one important caveat: One meta-analysis suggests that although this effect in substitution tests may be operating in the general population, it does not appear to do so in a large sample of extreme age-group studies from the literature. Given that this is the type of study extensively sampled in this book, the results presented in the previous chapters might be somewhat immune to such time-lag effects.

The second line of inquiry concerned time-lag differences in longitudinal panel studies, that is, studies that follow subjects of different cohorts over time. Perhaps surprisingly, about one third of the studies showed no cohort effects, one third showed negative cohort effects, and one third showed positive cohort effects. The average ratio of cross-sectional over longitudinal slopes was 1.11, suggesting that cross-sectional age differences generally overestimate longitudinal age differences by about 10%. When I broke down the results by task, reaction time tasks showed a ratio that was essentially 1, and perceptual speed measures showed an average ratio of 1.2. The latter result is in accordance with those from the time-lag analyses. The tentative conclusion is then that simpler measures of processing speed are less (the data suggest: not) amenable to cohort or time-of-measurement effects than more complex measures such as perceptual speed.

The third result concerns the evolution of age differences over historical time. Brinley slopes and dissociations in Brinley slopes have remained rather stable over the 30-year period that is available, and age differences expressed as slowing ratios have remained mostly stable over the second half of the 20th century. Thus, although speed of processing does show time-lag and/or historical effects, observed age differences in speed of processing are rather stable across time.

9

Age-related Slowing and Its Relationship to Complex Abilities

In the previous chapters, the focus was on description—how age affects speed in elementary processes and in tasks of executive control, and what shape these differences take. I also discussed a few explanatory mechanisms. The description was, if not thorough or exhaustive, then at least exhausting (100,000 words, give or take, so far). Now, then, is the moment for the question every writer dreads: What does this all amount to? When people age, performance in a multitude of tasks of processing speed declines. (I have added plenty of detail to this description, but that is the major conclusion.) So what? Does this matter?

This is precisely the question I take up in this chapter—does the age-related decline in processing speed have consequences outside the narrow realm of processing speed? Before I answer this question, I would like to start with three observations.

The first observation is the one I started this chapter with: With advancing age, speed in most tasks declines considerably.

The second observation is that these age-related differences show relatively low dimensionality. The data presented throughout this book suggest that the age-related differences in response times (and, as we have seen in Chapter 2, likely in accuracy as well) are governed by surprisingly few parameters—at the group level, response times of older adults can be predicted from response times of younger adults with relatively high accuracy without much need for information about the task at all. In other words, there appears to be a large communality in age-related effects in a large variety of response-time tasks. This suggests (but does not prove) that age-related changes in speeded processing might be governed by a limited number of likely very basic mechanisms. (I have reviewed a few such proposals throughout this book.)

The third observation is that, at least in younger adults, speed of processing and fluid intelligence are at least moderately correlated, suggesting some basic aspect of processing that is either speed of processing itself, or else is important for high functioning in complex tasks of cognition (for reviews, see Jensen, 2006; Sheppard & Vernon, 2008). For instance, the correlation between inspection time (the minimum presentation time needed before a given stimulus becomes identifiable, a very basic measure of processing speed) and fluid intelligence ranges from about .30 to .50 (Deary & Stough, 1996; Grudnik & Kranzler, 2001); the correlation between reaction time and fluid intelligence typically ranges from about .20 to .30 (Jensen, 1998, 2006). One meta-analysis on the subject (which included both age-homogenous and age-heterogeneous samples) estimates the average inspection time-fluid intelligence correlation at .36, and the average reaction time-fluid intelligence correlation at .26 (Sheppard & Vernon, 2008).

If we combine these three observations—speed of processing is associated, maybe causally, maybe through a third factor, with fluid intelligence, speed of processing declines with age, and this is likely tied to very basic processing mechanisms—and the suspicion arises that age-related differences in speed of processing might be a fundamental aspect of aging that indeed has consequences for more complex aspects of fluid cognition. It is this suspicion that will drive the meta-analyses in the present chapter.

9.1. Speed-cognition Correlations: Theories and Models

The idea that individual (and hence, perhaps, age-related) differences in more complex aspects of cognition can be tied to individual (and hence, perhaps, age-related) differences in more basic aspects of cognition has a long history, going back at least to Francis Galton (Jensen, 2006). Galton considered intelligence to be a low-level property of the nervous system. Therefore, he claimed it should manifest itself in the efficiency of operation of even the simplest tasks, such as the speed of sensory discrimination and speed of response to external stimuli. This is, of course, an extremely reductionist view, and Galton's work was subsequently mostly ignored until the 1980s. Since then, however, the individual-differences literature has returned to this hypothesis, and—as indicated above—found quite a bit of support for the existence of a positive correlation between measures of fluid intelligence and measures of basic speed of processing. This, in turn, has given rise to theories that posit that there might then be a relationship between age-related slowing and the observed decline in more complex aspects of cognition. At least two sets of such theories have gained some traction in the literature—mediational models and common-factor models.

9.1.1. Mediational Models of Processing Speed and Aging

Mediational models of the age-speed-cognition relation assign a special role to speed of processing. The claim is that part of the age-related variance in higher-order cognition—typically tests of episodic memory or aspects of fluid intelligence such as reasoning or spatial ability (e.g., Salthouse, 1996b; Verhaeghen & Salthouse, 1997)—is mediated by age-related declines in speed of processing. Note that this view doesn't necessarily imply that speed is the only mediating mechanism; researchers working in this tradition often posit that a limited number of other basic cognitive mechanisms such as working memory capacity (e.g., Verhaeghen, 2011), and/or selected aspects of executive control (e.g., Hasher & Zacks, 1988) might function as mediators as well, independent of, or in concert with, basic declines in speed.

The most bare-bone versions of this model are variance-partitioning models—through the use of partial correlations or other mediational techniques (such as path analysis), the proportion of age-related variance in complex aspects of cognition that is associated with one or more basic aspects of cognition (such as speed) is calculated and assessed. Variance-partitioning models have been quite successful. Summarizing 55 comparisons from seven different studies, Salthouse (1993) found that perceptual speed measures were on average associated with 74% of the age-related variance in different aspects of fluid cognition. The proportion of age-related variance associated with working memory seems to be somewhat smaller but still substantial (around 50%; Salthouse, 1992b). (As far as I know, nobody has investigated the proportion of age-related variance explained by executive control processes in a meta-analysis. I will do this later in this chapter, in an analysis also reported in Verhaeghen, 2011.) One other outcome of variance-partitioning studies is that age-related effects in the basic aspects of cognition are not independent. For instance, it has been long known that the proportion of age-related variance in cognitive performance that is related to working memory capacity is also shared to a large extent with processing-speed measures (Hultsch, Hertzog, & Dixon, 1990; Park et al., 1996; Salthouse, 1991b, 1992a, 1996b; Salthouse & Meinz, 1995).

Less descriptive is a set of models that I will call cascade models (the term appears to have been coined by Fry & Hale, 1996, 2000, in the context of development in the early part of the lifespan). Cascade models start from the observation that age-related deficits in basic aspects of processing are interrelated, and posit a flow of directionality of effects (and thus a hierarchy) within those basic aspects. For instance, in the model proposed by Fry and Hale, age-related changes in processing speed (due to development or aging), in turn influence working memory performance, which, in turn, affects performance on different tests of fluid ability.

In its most extreme version, the cascade model is also a causal model. The causal version of the cascade model reifies the meditational variable(s); that is, it truly considers a decline in speed of processing (and/or working memory and/or executive control and/or any other mediator in the model) as the proximal cause of age-related differences, in the same way that a slower computer processor will influence software performance. It is of course possible that speed of processing indeed physically limits the efficiency and/or effectiveness of information processing. The Fry and Hale model appears to imply this. So do the limited-time and simultaneity mechanisms of aging proposed by Salthouse (1996b): When less time is available for processing, performance might suffer either directly because an external deadline expires (the limited-time mechanism) or indirectly because the intermediate results of processing, stored in working memory, might have decayed by the time they are needed (the simultaneity mechanism). Note here that the argument for direct causality applies essentially to the clock speed of the mind as a whole, and not to specific tasks. We saw earlier, in Section 8.4, that speed-of-processing training does not transfer to other aspects of the system. This would contradict a causal hypothesis only if we would truly believe that this training affects the speed of the cognitive system as a whole, as opposed to the speed of a circumscribed task. As things stand, there is no reason to believe that this is the case—if it were, we should at least obtain near-transfer, and this is not the case. Causality should, however, still apply in a local sense: If one increases the speed of a specific task, subjects should be able to circumvent either or both the limited-time or the simultaneity mechanism when this mechanism is implicated in the task. As far as I know, this conjecture has never been tested.

A second possibility, perhaps closest to Galton's hypothesis, is that speed is not causal, but a biomarker or proxy par excellence. That is, speed might be the most sensitive (in the case of individual differences) or earliest (in the case of age-related differences) behavioral indicator that a more general, low-level underlying suboptimality is creeping into in the substrate (see Anstey, 2008, for a review on biomarkers of aging). Speed then acts as the canary, so to speak, in the coal mine of the aging mind. For instance, age-related slowing has been associated with a loss of brain connectivity (e.g., Cerella & Hale, 1994; see also Chapter 5), with changes in neurotransmitter systems (e.g., Bäckman et al., 2000), with changes in brain glucose metabolic rate or intracellular pH levels (e.g., S. Hoyer, 2002), or with the degree of neural myelinization (e.g., Anderson & Reid, 2005). High cognitive speed is then an indicator of a well-functioning substrate at the apex of its integrity; decreases in speed are indicative of insults to the system. Under this scenario, measures of speed might mediate age-related variance simply because measures of speed are closer indicators of such a general mechanism.

A third possibility is that the measures used to tap processing speed are, in fact, indicative of a yet deeper underlying set of basic abilities that are shared with the more complex tasks of higher-order cognition. For instance, Nettelbeck (2001) has argued that tasks of response time, even simple ones like inspection time, measure "focused attentional capacities to detect organization and change under severe time constraints [as well as] decision processes [...] that monitor responding" (p. 459). It is these attentional capacities and decision-making processes that the tasks have in common with higher-order aspects of cognition. Another example is van Ravenzwaaij, Brown, and Wagenmakers's (2010) explanation of the speed-fluid intelligence correlation in terms of Ratcliff's diffusion model. These researchers hypothesized that differences in drift rate in the diffusion model are associated with differences in intelligence; they were able to model quite a few phenomena in the field that had previously eluded a unitary explanation—the finding that RT distributions tend to be right-skewed, the finding that slower response time quartiles correlate more highly with intelligence than faster response time quartiles, the fact that fluid intelligence correlates more strongly with the dispersion in RT than with its mean, the linear relation between the mean and the standard deviation of RT, linear Brinley plots between groups differing in drift rate, and the stronger correlation between fluid intelligence and inspection time than between intelligence and reaction time. The effort seems to be viable beyond the modeling stage: There is some empirical evidence that drift rate acts as the link between different aspects of cognition. For instance, Schmiedek, Oberauer, Wilhelm, Süß, and Wittmann (2007) showed that drift rate is a strong predictor not just of psychometric speed, but also of working memory and reasoning ability. Likewise, Ratcliff et al. (2010) found that a common factor for drift rate explains a large proportion of the variance across subjects in two IQ measures, matrix reasoning and vocabulary. Speed is then not causal, but an indicator of a system with an excellent drift rate, which also leads to high performance on other tasks. Because simple speeded tasks are determined to a larger extent by this basic parameter, they might give the appearance of being causal variables.

I note here that scenarios two and three—speed as a biomarker or an excellent predictor of basic aspects of the processing system—are hard to distinguish from another set of models, namely common-factor models. I turn to those next.

9.1.2. Common-factor Models of Processing Speed and Aging

A second set of theories emphasizes the proposed joint movement over time of a host of cognitive (and other) variables (e.g., Lindenberger & Baltes, 1997; Salthouse, 1996b; Verhaeghen & Salthouse, 1997). This set of theories was inspired by a proposal originally formulated by Kliegl and Mayr (1992). Kliegl and Mayr observed that many, possibly even all of the age-related influences on a wide range of cognitive variables are shared, and postulated that a single common factor might mediate age-related influences on all cognitive variables. Hence, these models are often referred to as common-factor models, sometimes common-cause models. In more relaxed versions of these models—perhaps best described as shared-influence models—direct relations from age to individual cognitive variables are allowed in addition to the relationship mediated by the common factor (e.g., Salthouse & Ferrer-Caja, 2003). Although single common-factor models may seem overly simplistic, they have been found to provide moderately good fits to the data in several projects (e.g., Lindenberger, Mayr, & Kliegl, 1993; Salthouse, 1996a, 1996b; Salthouse, Hancock, et al., 1996). One aspect of the common-factor model that is particularly intriguing is that it stretches rather widely. Investigation of large-scale correlation matrices has shown that the same general determinant is linked to age-related declines in a variety of different cognitive variables, as well as age-related differences in sensorimotor variables such as visual and auditory acuity, balance, and grip strength (Anstey & Smith, 1999; Baltes & Lindenberger, 1997; Christensen, Mackinnon, Korten, & Jorm, 2001; Lindenberger & Baltes, 1994). One reason for this broad reach may be that all these measures "are an expression of the physiological architecture of the aging brain" (Baltes & Lindenberger, 1997, p. 13).

Note that because the magnitude of the relations between the common factor and the individual variables and between age and the individual variables can vary, the common factor model does not imply that all variables should exhibit equivalent age-related differences. However, it does suggest that there is considerable overlap between the age-related influences that occur on one variable and the age-related influences on other variables.

9.2. Speed-cognition Correlations: Meta-analytic Data

This, then, is the main idea I will explore in this chapter—that the speed-cognition correlation may reflect common variance due to either an amorphous common factor reflecting a general resource, or to more direct mediational effects of speed. I will explore this core idea by fitting these models to a correlation matrix derived through meta-analysis—an update of the Verhaeghen and Salthouse (1997) data set and analyses. The models I will fit will increase in the number of underlying theoretical assumptions, starting with the raw correlation matrix, over a model that assumes that the effects of age on all cognitive variables are independent, to a model that proposes a precise cascade of age-related effects. (For more on the progression of such models, see Salthouse & Czaja, 2000; Schmiedek & Li, 2004; Verhaeghen & Salthouse, 1997.)

The data used as input for this analysis are a correlation matrix of age and various measures of cognitive performance. These correlations were culled from studies that used a continuous age range from about age 18 to about age 80. (I opted to concentrate on studies including a continuous age range rather than the more usual young-old group design to avoid the inflation of correlations that typically results from extreme-groups designs.) In the 1997 meta-analysis that served as my inspiration, Salthouse and I assigned the dependent variables as we found them in the various individual studies to one of five primary categories: speed, short-term memory/working memory, episodic memory, reasoning, and spatial abilities; we collected data from 91 studies. For the present analysis, I decided to additionally include measures of executive control. I located an additional 28 studies; these also allowed me enough detail to split the short-term/memory-working memory construct into two separate constructs, short-term memory and working memory. The final sample consisted of studies that (a) included a continuous-age sample of normal adults (i.e., free from known psychological or organic pathology as indicated by self-report), with the youngest participant 30 years of age or younger and the oldest 60 years of age or older; (b) assessed performance on at least one of the seven target cognitive variables (speed, short-term memory, working memory, executive control, episodic memory, reasoning, and spatial ability); and (c) reported correlation coefficients between at least two of the variables of interest. Sample size was not a criterion; the smallest sample in the set was 35, and most studies tested 100 participants or more. In the reference list, the 119 studies included in these analyses are preceded by a "#" symbol.

The speed measures consisted largely of measures of reaction time or paper-and-pencil tests of perceptual speed (e.g., tasks requiring matching, search, and substitution). Because reaction time and perceptual speed are scored in opposite directions (higher reaction times denote slower speed; higher perceptual speed scores denote faster speed), I flipped the sign for any correlations involving reaction time, so that all tasks were scored as speed (higher scores denote faster speed).

Tasks of immediate memory were considered to be short-term memory tasks if the presentation of the to-be-remembered items was not interspersed with intervening tasks; immediate memory tasks were considered working memory tasks if intervening tasks were used. Thus, digit span and digit span backward were categorized as short-term memory tasks; reading span, listening span, operation span, and the like were categorized as working memory tasks. Note that there is some controversy as to whether reordering tasks such as digit span backward are working memory tasks or short-term memory tasks (Craik, 1986; Grégoire & Van der Linden, 1997; Myerson, Emery, White, & Hale, 2003). I grouped reordering tasks with the short-term memory tasks, given that at least one meta-analysis found that age-related differences on backward span tasks were closer to those observed for forward span tasks than to those observed for working memory span tasks (Bopp & Verhaeghen, 2005). This then potentially contaminates the estimation of the short-term memory construct with working memory, and overly purifies the working memory construct; the likely net effect is that the age-short-term-memory correlation might be slightly inflated and the age-working-memory correlation slightly underestimated.

Two types of executive control tasks were included in the samples; this was a fall-out of the natural composition of the measures rather than a decision on my part to censor any tasks. The first of these was resistance to interference, measured by tasks such as Stroop, reading with distractors, the antisaccade task, and the Hayling Sentence Completion test (Burgess & Shallice, 1997). One reservation about these measures as applied here is that some studies report interference scores controlled for baseline speed, while others do not. This means that the resistance to interference measures are to varying degrees controlled for their relationship with speed, potentially underestimating their correlation not only with speed, but with any other variable correlated with speed, including age. The second was task shifting, measured by Trail Making B, the Wisconsin Card Sorting Test, and experimental tasks of task switching.

Episodic memory measures were derived from free recall tasks, paired-associate recall tasks, and prose recall tasks. Reasoning measures were obtained from matrices, series completions, analogies, figural relations, and category tests or experimental tasks. Finally, spatial ability measures were derived from psychometric tests and experimental tasks of closure, cube assembly, surface development, paper folding, block design, and integration-synthesis.

Note that differential correlations between age and cognition and among cognitive variables are at least in part influenced by (un)reliability of the measures. To explore the influence of unreliability, Verhaeghen and Salthouse (1997) computed split-half reliability coefficients from a subsample of the studies gathered in their meta-analysis (viz., data gathered by Salthouse), using the Spearman-Brown formula wherever possible. Mean weighted reliabilities for the five cognitive variables included in this analysis proved satisfactory: For speed, mean weighted reliability (weighted for sample size) was $r = .90$; for short-term memory/working memory, $r = .85$; for episodic memory, $r = .77$; for reasoning, $r = .87$, and for spatial abilities, $r = .90$. Reliability was also assessed separately for the younger and older half of the sample, splitting at age 50; there was no evidence of differential reliability in the two samples, and r still ranged from .77 to .90. (I have no data for short-term memory and working memory separated, or for the executive control measures.)

9.2.1. The Meta-analysis: The Correlation Matrix

Correlation coefficients between pairs of the 10 variables (i.e., age and the nine cognitive variables) were combined over studies using the procedure advocated by Hedges and Olkin (1985). In a number of cases, more than one measure for each construct was included within a single study; in that case, I averaged correlations between measures representing the same pairs of constructs to yield a single estimate of each relevant correlation per study. The averaging of the correlations consisted of first transforming the relevant correlations to Fisher z scores, averaging those, and then converting the average Fisher z value back to a single correlation coefficient. Finally, a mean weighted correlation coefficient (r_+) was computed for each pair of variables, with differential weight given to each correlation coefficient as a function of sample size (Hedges & Olkin, 1982). Confidence intervals around r_+ allow for statistical testing.

The mean weighted correlations are presented in Table 9.1. All correlations were significantly different from zero, with the exception of the short-term memory-resistance to interference correlation (but this correlation was derived from a single study, so statistical power was low). All age-cognition correlations were reliably different from –1; they varied from $r_+ = -.53$ (for speed) to $r_+ = -.12$ (for short-term memory). The average age-cognition correlation was –.39; age thus, on average, explained about 15% of individual differences in cognitive functioning among adults. All cognition-cognition correlations were reliably different from 1; ranging from $r_+ = .19$ (short-term memory and resistance to interference) to $r_+ = .64$ (speed and reasoning), with an average cognition-cognition correlation of .41, indicating that cognitive measures share, on average, 17% of their variance. Thus, age had a reliable negative influence on all cognitive variables, which were all (with one exception) interconnected positively.

The average correlation between short-term memory and the other cognitive measures was .32; short-term memory thus shared, on average, 10% of its variance with the other cognitive measures. Working memory had an average correlation of .41 with the other cognitive measures, sharing, on average, 17% of its variance with the other cognitive measures. Resistance to interference had an average correlation of .41 with the other cognitive measures, sharing, on average, 17% of its variance with the other cognitive measures. Task shifting had an average correlation of .42 with the other cognitive measures, sharing, on average, 18% of its variance with the other cognitive measures. Finally, executive control had an average correlation of .39 with the other cognitive measures, sharing, on average, 16% of its variance with the other cognitive measures. As noted above, the average cognition-cognition correlation was .41. Thus, speed stands out, at least somewhat, as a better predictor of other measures of cognition than most; short-term memory stands out as a poorer predictor than most.

All these correlations are derived from age-heterogeneous samples. This implies that the correlations between cognitive variables also contain shared age-related variance, and are thus likely to be inflated as a consequence (e.g., Hofer & Sliwinski, 2001)—I will expand on this point a little further below. Therefore, Table 9.1 also presents the correlations between the cognitive variables after controlling for age (shown in italics). (Partialling out age amounts to taking the correlation at the average age of the sample; Lord, 1963. In this meta-analysis, that is about 50 years of age.) This procedure decreases the correlations among cognitive variables, which now range between $r_+ = .10$ (episodic memory and task shifting) and $r_+ = .57$ (space and reasoning), with an average cognition-cognition correlation of $r_+ = .31$, indicating that cognitive measures share, on average, 10% of their variance. Comparing this number with the percent of shared variance above, we can conclude that most of the shared variance in cognition observed in age-heterogeneous samples of adults is due to cognition per se, but that a sizeable portion of that shared variance, 41% (i.e., (17 – 10)/17), appears to be due to age-related influences (e.g., correlated and uncorrelated change in cognition; see below) rather than what is usually referred to as "individual differences."

Table 9.1 The meta-analytically derived correlation matrix (based on data culled from a total of 119 studies), with age-partialled correlations added in italics; the number of studies used to calculate the average correlation is indicated within parentheses underneath each correlation.

	Age	Speed	Short-term memory	Working memory	Episodic memory	Reasoning	Spatial ability	Resistance to interference
Speed	–.53							
	—							
	(73)							
Short-term memory	–.12	.27						
	—	*.25*						
	(25)	(16)						
Working memory	–.42	.41	.40					
	—	*.25*	*.39*					
	(17)	(15)	(2)					
Episodic memory	–.38	.41	.24	.31				
	—	*.27*	*.21*	*.18*				
	(47)	(44)	(11)	(7)				
Reasoning	–.45	.64	0.49	.62	.55			
	—	*.53*	*.50*	*.54*	*.46*			
	(53)	(31)	(5)	(8)	(21)			
Spatial ability	–.41	.54	.35	.45	.52	.64		
	—	*.42*	*.34*	*.34*	*.43*	*.57*		
	(50)	(34)	(8)	(9)	(20)	(18)		
Resistance to interference	–.45	.58	.19	.33	.30	.43	.37	
	—	*.46*	*.15*	*.17*	*.16*	*.29*	*.23*	
	(11)	(11)	(1)	(4)	(4)	(4)	(3)	
Task shifting	–.35	.37	.26	.29	.22	.57	.25	.28
	—	*.24*	*.24*	*.17*	*.10*	*.50*	*.13*	*.15*
	(10)	(10)	(3)	(3)	(6)	(3)	(4)	(2)

When age is partialled out, the correlations between the more basic (speed, short-term memory, working memory, and executive control) and the more complex cognitive measures (episodic memory, spatial ability, and reasoning) generally decrease as well. The correlations with speed especially are considerably reduced. It is still nominally the best predictor, but not by much, with an average correlation with the other measures of .35, explaining 12% of the variance. Working memory, short-term memory, and resistance to interference all have an average correlation with other cognitive measures of .32, explaining 10% of the variance. Task shifting and executive control both have an average correlation with cognition of .27, explaining 7% of the variance. The surprise here is the predictive power of short-term memory, which is on par with that of most other variables, although short-term memory was a poor predictor when the raw correlation matrix was used. This suggests that short-term memory is an important part of cognition, but only in an individual-differences context, not an aging context.

One end conclusion from these analyses is that speed, as an individual-differences variable, shares a reasonably large amount of variance with other measures of cognition. Looking at the raw correlations, which include shared age-related variance, speed is a better predictor than any other "basic" cognitive variable (short-term memory, working memory, resistance to interference, task shifting, and executive control). It is still a strong predictor when age is partialled out, but the difference in predictive power compared with the other basic variables is now much smaller. This suggests that speed might be particularly sensitive to the effects of age or aging (as already suggested by its large correlation with age). It is likely that the underlying cause of this sensitivity is to some extent shared with the other cognitive variables, but that the other variables share less of the cause of their sensitivity to age with each other than they do with speed.

Another conclusion is that all measures of cognition included here share a good amount of variance, whether or not the correlation matrix is controlled for age. This suggests that a common-factor model is likely to fit the data well—the issue I turn to next.

9.2.2. Common-factor Models

Estimating a common-factor model—as the name suggests—entails constructing a single factor out of all cognitive variables; age then loads onto this common factor. Variants of the model differ in how strict the assumptions for additional paths are (see Salthouse & Czaja, 2000; Schmiedek & Li, 2004).

I note here that the meta-analytic correlation matrix is already at a higher level of abstraction than is typically used in primary research. Ideally, one would build models using the data from individual tests to construct latent factors (e.g., Raven's Progressive Matrices and the Culture Fair would both load on a latent Reasoning factor), but this level of detail is impossible with the data at hand. One unfortunate consequence of the meta-analytic approach is that what is arguably the strongest model—Schmiedek and Li's nested-factors model—cannot be fitted, because it requires access to the test level.

9.2.2.1. Baseline: The Independent-constructs Model

The first model I fitted, the independent-constructs model (Salthouse & Czaja, 2000), is not a common factor model at all, but a baseline against which to evaluate the common-factor model. The underlying assumption in the independent-constructs model is that all age-related differences on each of the cognitive factors or constructs are independent. Such a model would be compatible with the view that age-related differences associated with the different cognitive variables are qualitatively distinct, likely implying that the causes of these age-related differences are distinct as well (e.g., each construct relies on different brain structures, which all show distinct age-related differences). It deserves mention that this model is fated to disappoint. It assumes that the correlations between cognitive variables are all due to age, and, as we have seen in the previous section, this is an untenable assumption: Even after age is controlled for, the correlations between cognitive variables are positive and generally sizeable.

I fitted the independent-constructs model by setting up paths from age to each of the constructs, with no other paths allowed. (There is no need to illustrate this model; the path coefficients are simply equal to the correlation coefficients between age and each of the variables). The *chi*-square statistic for this model was quite high, indicating unsatisfactory fit, χ^2 (28, N = 4,220) = 13,586.34, p <.001, that is, a large discrepancy between the actual correlation matrix and the matrix reconstructed on the basis of the model. (Note that N here refers to the average number of subjects implicated in each of the cells of the correlation matrix.) *Chi*-square statistics for structural models are based on the number of participants, with larger numbers leading to higher power in the test and thus to an easy rejection of the model. In this case, a simple rule of thumb (e.g., Bollen, 1989) is that the χ^2 value should not exceed 2 *df*. It is clear that the model fails by this standard. It fails by any other standard as well (i.e., GFI = .58, AGFI = .33, NFI = .64, RMSEA = 0.34; RMR = 0.22). What this shows us is that the assumption that age has independent effects on each of the variables is wrong; there must be more structure to the data.

9.2.2.2. The Common-factor Model

Figure 9.1 shows the data considered under a strict common-factor model, that is, a model in which age influences a common factor comprised of all cognitive variables, with no additional paths from age to the individual variables allowed. This model fits the data better than the independent-constructs model, but fit is not excellent, χ^2 (27, N = 4,220) = 2,589.57, p <.001, GFI = .88, AGFI = .80, NFI = .91, RMSEA = .15; RMR = 0.07. The common-factor model and the independent-constructs model are nested; that is, the common-factor model is a less constrained version of the independent-constructs model. The χ^2 test for the difference, with 1 *df*, is highly significant, χ^2 = 10,996.77, suggesting that the common-factor model fits the data much better.

In this model, the correlation between age and the common factor is relatively high, –.56, thus suggesting that age explains 32% of the variance in this common factor. The individual factor loadings of the constructs seem to be quite acceptable,

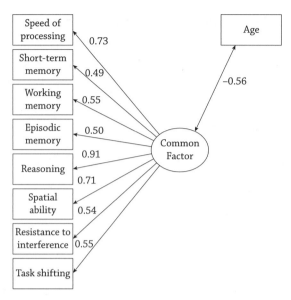

Figure 9.1 Meta-analytic data fitted to a strict common-factor model; χ^2 (27, N = 4,220) = 2,589.57, p <.001, GFI = .88; RMR = 0.066. All paths are significant.

and range from 0.49 (short-term memory) to 0.91 (Reasoning). The loadings are not uniform (χ^2 (7) = 547.45) and thus this common-factor model does not imply that the effect of age is identical across all variables. What it does suggest is that the constructs have considerable overlap in their age-related influences, through the common factor.

9.2.2.3. A Common-factor Model with Construct-specific Effects Added

Figure 9.2 presents a less strict variant of the common-factor model. This model is identical to the previous one, except that additional paths from age to each of the cognitive constructs are estimated; those that were significant at p <.05 were retained, the others eliminated. (The path from the common factor to reasoning was fixed to unity to anchor the factor and allow the model to converge. Fixing the value at .91—the value for the common-factor model—did not alter the results substantially.) This model still fits far from well, χ^2 (19, N = 4,220) = 1,781.05, p <.001, GFI = .91, AGFI = .79, NFI = .93, RMSEA = .15, RMR = .06, but it does fit the data significantly and appreciably better than the common-factor model, $\Delta\chi^2$ (8) = 808.52.

In this model, the correlation between age and the common factor is –.47, with age thus explaining 22% of the variance in the common factor. With the exception of the direct path from age to reasoning, all other paths were significant, indicating that these variables' relationship to age through the common factor was either overestimated or underestimated. Six of the misspecifications were negative, namely those for speed, working memory, episodic memory, spatial ability, and resistance to interference, indicating that the common-factor influence underestimated the

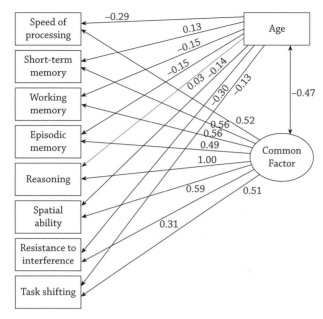

Figure 9.2 Meta-analytic data fitted to a common-factor model with construct-specific loadings allowed;, χ^2 (19, N = 4,220) = 1,781.05, p <.001, GFI = .91, RMR = .06. The path from Age to Reasoning (dotted line) is not significant; all other paths are.

negative impact of age on these four constructs. One path, from age to short-term memory, was positive, indicating that the common-factor model overestimated the negative impact of age on this construct. This analysis then demonstrates that we cannot claim that a single common factor would explain all of the age-related variance on cognitive tasks.

9.2.2.4. Common-factor Models: An Appreciation

The key finding from this section is that the age-related influences on different cognitive variables are not independent of one another: Common-factor models fit the data much better than the independent-constructs model. Additionally, one could make the case that only if most of the age-related effects can be modeled with direct paths from age to the individual variables one should conclude that age-related effects on the different cognitive variables are largely independent of each other (Verhaeghen & Salthouse, 1997, p. 245). By this standard, too, the independence hypothesis has failed: In the common-factor model with construct-specific paths, the direct paths from age to the variables were all smaller in magnitude than the paths through the common factor, thus giving larger weight to their common influence. The presence of significant direct paths from age to some of the cognitive variables does, however, indicate that the simplest, and most extreme, version of the common-factor model is inadequate.

9.2.3. Mediational Models

The second family of models is based on the assumption that basic aspects of cognitive processing—speed, short-term memory, working memory, and executive control—partially mediate the influences of age on measures of higher-order cognition—episodic memory, reasoning, and spatial ability. Here, too, models can be more restrictive in the theoretical assumptions they make (cascade models fall into that category), or more relaxed (such as models based on variance partitioning).

9.2.3.1. Variance Partitioning

The most neutral mediational model would be one that does not make any (or at least, no strong) assumptions about any a priori structure within the set of basic variables. Table 9.2 presents results from the simplest of mediational analysis—the table shows the partial correlation between age and each cognitive construct after partialling out the influence of each of the "basic" constructs, one at a time. This table allows us to evaluate the mediating effect of each basic cognitive construct Y on the relationship between age and higher-order construct X. The percent attenuation in the age-X relationship due to Y is illustrated in Figure 9.3. This percentage is calculated by dividing the R^2 for the partial correlation between age and X (partialling out Y) by the R^2 for the age-X correlation, multiplying this ratio by 100, and then subtracting it from 100 (Salthouse, 1991). The latter R^2 value indicates the total amount of age-related variance in variable X; the former indicates the amount of age-related variance that is not

Table 9.2 **Meta-analytically derived age-ability correlations, before and after partialling out the influence of specific basic abilities.**

Ability	Age-ability correlation	Age-ability correlation after partialling out				
		Speed	Short-term memory	Working memory	Resistance to interference	Task shifting
Speed	−.53	—	−.52	−.39	−.37	−.46
Short-term memory	−.12	−.03	—	−.06	−.04	−.03
Working memory	−.42	−.26	−.41	—	−.32	−.35
Episodic memory	−.38	−.21	−.37	−.26	−.29	−.33
Reasoning	−.45	−.17	−.45	−.24	−.31	−.32
Spatial ability	−.41	−.18	−.40	−.25	−.30	−.36
Resistance to interference	−.45	−.20	−.44	−.33	—	−.39
Task shifting	−.35	−.19	−.33	−.24	−.26	—

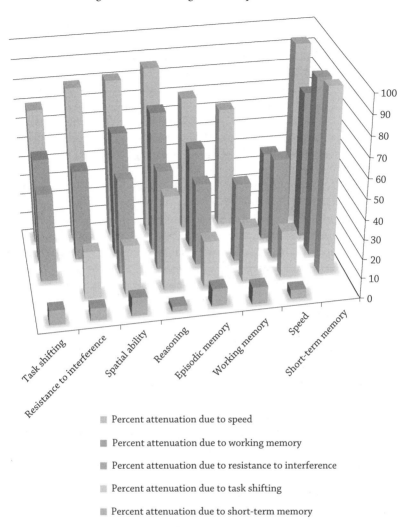

Figure 9.3 Amount of age-related variance in cognitive abilities mediated by select basic abilities, as calculated from the meta-analytic data set.

due to variable Y. Simply put: high bars in the figure indicate that the mediating variable is a very powerful mediator for that particular variable.

It is important here to clarify what exactly is implied in the attenuation statistic. The percentage reduction in the age-related variance in X after controlling for Y is commonly interpreted as the percentage of the age-related variance in X that is predicted by *age differences* in Y, but this is incorrect. It can be shown (Lindenberger & Pötter, 1998) that the effect of age on X mediated through Y depends partially on the age-partialled correlation between X and Y. This means that the attenuation statistic in reality indicates how much of the age-related variance in X is predicted by *individual differences* in Y (i.e., by differences between individuals that are associated with age, as well as differences that are orthogonal to age). This interpretation is somewhat counterintuitive—in effect, individual differences that are independent of age are used to predict age-related differences. This limits the usefulness of the statistic somewhat: The finding of a significant reduction in the amount of age-related variance in X after partialling out Y may be consistent with a causal model (i.e., a model that claims that age causes a decline in Y which, in turn, causes a decline in X), but it does not necessarily imply that the causal model is correct. This, of course, is true of any meditational model in any field. It is also hard to see how it could be otherwise: If we want to predict, say, age-related differences in reasoning from age-related differences in processing speed, a true underlying speed-reasoning correlation is a necessity to make that causal claim.

One potential concern with regard to differential predictability (i.e., some of the basic variables explain a larger amount of the age-related variance) is that the variable that produces the largest decrease in the amount of age-related variance in X might simply be the one with the highest individual-differences correlation with X. The issue does not appear to be pressing in the present data set: The age-partialled correlations between basic measures and more complex measures are all of the same magnitude— correlations around .3 (as a reminder: speed has an average r_+ = .35; working memory, short-term memory, and resistance to interference yielded r_+ = .32; and task shifting and executive control r_+ = .27).

Lindenberger and Pötter (1998) suggest two intriguing remedies. One is to rely on theory for interpretations of causality. This remedy runs the risk of being circular, especially given that the field is no longer naïve to the relevant data. That is, there may be perfectly good reasons why we might be able, a priori, to produce reasonable explanations as to why speed would be linked to age-related differences in memory functioning, and perfectly good reasons why we might think it would not. Once data have been collected and a correlation observed, we might then be tempted to emphasize the reasoning consistent with the observed outcome, and downregulate the losing proposition. A second remedy, which I will implement later in this chapter, is to actively hunt for converging evidence using other methods; in the case of age-related differences, one such piece of evidence could be found in interindividual differences in intraindividual change in a longitudinal design.

Turning to the data at hand, an examination of Table 9.2 and Figure 9.3 supports three intriguing conclusions. First, one variable in particular—speed-of-processing— appears to be quite successful as a mediator. Individual differences in speed are associated with 62% to 93% (on average: 78%) of the age-related variance in other aspects of cognition.

Second, most other basic variables do quite well as mediators, too: Working memory is associated with on average 58% of the age-related variance in cognition, resistance to interference with 53%, and task shifting with 38%.

Third, one variable, short-term memory, does not appear to be a successful mediator at all: On average, only 7% of the age-related variance in other aspects of cognition is associated with individual differences in short-term memory. That does not mean that short-term memory is not associated with the other variables: In fact, short-term memory is the cognitive construct that has the largest amount of age-related variance explained by the other basic variables—87% on average. Taken together, these two findings suggest that short-term memory is not a particularly interesting variable in the context of causal explanations for aging in higher-order cognition: It shows little decline (the raw correlation with age as calculated above was –.12; see also Bopp & Verhaeghen, 2005), it explains little age-related variance in other constructs, and the small amount of age-related variance in short-term memory is almost entirely reducible to individual differences in other constructs.

9.2.3.2. The Cascade Model

The second mediational model fit to the data is the cascade model. Cascade models are more theory-driven than variance-partitioning models, in that they impose a clear flow of influence. I distinguished five categories within the variables, each represented as a latent construct whenever more than a single measure was used to define it, with successive stages in this categorization scheme representing the hypothesized flow of influence. That is, the first category is hypothesized to influence all others; the second category to influence the third, fourth, and fifth; the third to influence the fourth and the fifth; and the fourth to influence the fourth. The categories are: (a) age (measured by age); (b) speed (measured by speed); (c) executive control (measured by task shifting and resistance to interference); (d) working memory/short-term memory (measured by working memory and short-term memory); and (e) higher-order cognition (measured by episodic memory, reasoning, and spatial ability). Alternative schedules of influence can be imagined—I set up the model in (largely) the same way Hale and Fry (1996) and Verhaeghen and Salthouse (1997) set up their versions of the cascade.

New in this model, compared with Verhaeghen and Salthouse (1997) is the addition of the executive control construct. I added it as a tier between speed and working memory; this is the level where a number of other researchers have placed this construct. For instance, many researchers outside the field of aging (e.g., Nelson, Yoash-Gantz, Pickett, Campbell, 2009; Rose, Feldman, & Jankowski, 2011) place speed prior to executive control in the flow of influence; theories stressing the importance of resistance to interference as an explanation for cognitive aging (e.g., Hasher & Zacks, 1988) expect resistance to interference to influence working memory rather than the other way around. The grouping of all three aspects of higher-order cognition into a single latent construct seemed desirable because of the relatively high intercorrelations between these variables (>.52); keeping them in separate constructs would have necessitated choices of flow of influence that seemed quite arbitrary to me.

In the structural equation modeling analysis to test the cascade model, I first estimated all possible paths from an earlier category to a later category (i.e., from age to speed, executive control, working memory/short-term memory, and higher-order cognition; from speed to executive control, working memory/short-term memory, and higher-order cognition; from executive control to working memory/short-term memory, and higher-order cognition; and from working memory/short-term memory to higher-order cognition). The model was then trimmed by deleting all nonsignificant paths. The resulting cascade model is presented in Figure 9.4. (The paths shown in the figure as being equal to 1 were fixed as such to anchor the respective factors.)

The first observation to make is that the model is not a very compelling fit to the data, χ^2 (22, $N = 4{,}220$) = 1,686.53, $p < .001$, GFI = .92, AGFI = .84, NFI = .94, RMSEA = 0.13, RMR = .05. Its fit is quite comparable to that of the common-factor model with

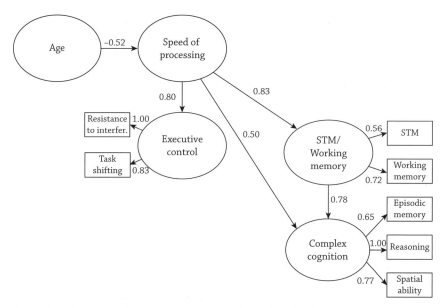

Figure 9.4 Meta-analytic data fitted to a cascade model, χ^2 (22, *N* = 4,220) = 1,686.53, *p* <.001, GFI = .92, RMR = .05. All paths are significant.

construct-specific effects added (the AGFI statistic is slightly higher), suggesting that this might be as good a fit as the correlation matrix will allow.

A first conclusion is that speed functions as an important mediator, mediating age-related variance to all other cognitive constructs (executive control, working memory/short-term memory, higher-order cognition). It mediates all of the effects of age on working memory/short-term memory, executive control, and higher-order cognition (as indexed by the lack of a significant direct path from age to these variables).

A second conclusion is that executive control does not function as a mediator at all—all of the age-related variance in executive control is explained by speed, and executive control itself transmits no variance further down the line, neither to working memory/short-term memory, nor to higher-order cognition. There might be multiple reasons for this. The most interesting would be that executive control is indeed not a mediator between age and higher-order cognition (or, for that matter, between speed and higher-order cognition). In that case, high levels of resistance to interference and/ or fast task shifting capabilities are end results of a quick mind rather than precursors to a smart mind. A second, less interesting, reason could be low reliability in the component measures of executive control, which depressed the correlations below the significance threshold. I am aware of one study (Salthouse et al., 2003) that investigated reliability of executive control measures in a large age-heterogeneous sample (261 adults). Reliability (measured as internal consistency) ranged from acceptable to quite high for almost all executive control measures included (e.g., Trail Making A: .90; Trail Making B: .70; Stroop: .90 for neutral, .92 for incongruent, .77 for the difference score; Reading with distractors: .93 without and .89 with distractors, .81 for the difference score; anti-saccade: .82 for congruent accuracy, .84 for incongruent accuracy,

.71 for the difference; stop signal RT: .89), suggesting that unreliability is unlikely to be the culprit. A third potential reason for the lack of mediating power could be that the executive control construct and its subconstructs are not well-measured by the tasks included here. More specifically, if the component tasks of the general control construct, or those of resistance to interference or task shifting, have low intercorrelations among themselves, a coherent factor may fail to emerge. Additionally, if one or more of these component tasks do not correlate with higher-order cognition, the correlation at the aggregate level will be diluted. These potential issues are difficult to assess in the present data set; there simply are not enough within-construct correlations to meta-analyze. Individual-differences research (e.g., Friedman & Miyake, 2004; Friedman et al., 2006; Miyake et al., 2000) suggests that factor loadings from latent constructs in the executive-control realm tend to be relatively modest. The resistance to interference construct in particular may have measurement problems. Thus, we should be careful to ascribe the failure of the executive control measures to mediate age-related variance to executive control processes per se—the problem might lie with the purity with which the construct can be, or has been, measured.

A third conclusion from the final model is that working memory/short-term memory is a mediator of age-related differences. As was the case for executive control, working memory/short-term memory's age-related variance is completely mediated by speed, but, contrary to executive control, working memory/short-term memory does mediate a substantial portion of the age-related variance in higher-order cognition. Working memory/short-term memory is not a complete mediator of the speed-higher-order cognition relationship (there is still a direct path from speed to higher-order cognition), but its mediating power is still quite high. The direct effect of speed on higher-order cognition is .61; the mediated effect through working memory/short-term memory is .48 (i.e., .62 x .78). Working memory/short-term memory thus mediates 44% of the effects of speed on higher-order cognition.

9.2.2.3. *Speed-cognition Correlations: Conclusions from the Meta-analyses*

At the most abstract level, the question driving the meta-analyses presented here was whether the effects of age on different aspects of cognition—speed, working memory, short-term memory, task shifting, resistance to interference, executive control, episodic memory, reasoning, and spatial ability—were independent or not. The correlation matrix clearly showed that the cognitive variables formed a positive manifold: All variables were positively and reliably (with one exception) correlated with each other. They were also all negatively correlated with age. A common-factor model, in which age influences a common factor measured by all the cognitive variables, fits the data much better than an independent-constructs model in which age influences all cognitive variables independently. This clearly indicates that there is shared age-related variance in the set of cognitive variables. A common-factor model with added independent effects, however, fits the data better still. This indicates that a single common factor is not sufficient to explain all of the age-related effects: Corrections for individual constructs are necessary. Neither result is hardly surprising—almost all constructs in cognitive psychology are both separate and interconnected (e.g., Carroll, 1993); it makes intuitive sense that their age effects are as well.

At a slightly deeper level, the question was whether age-related differences in higher-order cognition (episodic memory, reasoning, and spatial ability) might be traced to the effects of age on more basic aspects of cognition (speed, working memory, short-term memory, task shifting, resistance to interference, and executive control). Given the theme of this book, I was particularly interested in the role of speed.

Variance partitioning suggests that speed is indeed a powerful mediator, explaining a rather whopping 78% of the age-related variance in the other aspects of cognition, more so than working memory, executive control, resistance to interference, or task shifting, which all explain 58% or less. Short-term memory, in this analysis, turned out not to mediate any variance, and the age-related variance in it was almost completely explained by the other basic variables. Mediational analysis using a cascade model likewise suggests that speed is a powerful mediator between age and executive control (effectively explaining all of the age-related variance), between age and working memory/short-term memory (again explaining all of the age-related variance), and between age and higher-order cognition (again explaining all of the age-related variance).

One additional stark conclusion from the cascade model was that the executive control measures did not function as mediators of age-related variance at all, transmitting no variance to either working memory/short-term memory or higher-order cognition. This may be due to measurement problems, or it might signify that age-related differences in executive control are not the cause of age-related differences in memory, spatial ability, or reasoning ability.

It is important to reemphasize that none of the results I obtained here are consistent with interpretations based on a single, monolithic determinant of the age-related effects on cognitive functioning. Direct paths from age to several cognitive variables were found in both the single common factor and mediational models, indicating that independent influences of age (i.e., influences not mediated by other variables in the model) can be detected in many aspects of cognition, even in models that make very limited assumptions about the structure of the cognitive system.

Finally, I would like to reiterate that the meta-analysis avoids some common pitfalls—I included only studies with a continuous age range (extreme-group designs can notoriously inflate correlations), and for the measures for which reliability could be calculated, reliability proved satisfactory. The meta-analysis has one major shortcoming, however: Not all correlates were available from every study, and so unknown amounts of between-sample variability are introduced in each of the correlations. This should be potentially bothersome, especially for those correlations that are derived from a small number of studies, such as the executive-control measures.

9.3. Speed-cognition Correlations: The Longitudinal Perspective

It is important to note that all the results presented so far in this chapter, strong as they are, are based on cross-sectional data. This is potentially problematic. (For a more extensive and more technical treatment of this topic, see Sliwinski & Hofer, 2000a, 2000b.) What cross-sectional data can ultimately tell us is that individual differences in processing speed are correlated with and predict individual differences in more complex cognition abilities, and—the crucial piece of information—that individual differences in speed mediate some of the individual differences in cognition that are due to age.

But what is contained in this "age" term? One important thing to keep in mind is that the age variable here contains everything that distinguishes people of different ages as they are assessed in the lab, which is much more than merely the aging processes. The problem isn't just that cross-sectional studies have cohort differences built into them, as discussed in the previous chapter, but also that the broad range of ages in itself introduces a new confound, leading to what has been termed "fictitious associations" (Yule, 1903, p. 134) or, more incisively, mean-induced association (Hofer, Flaherty, & Hoffman, 2006). The problem is the use of mixed groups (in our case, people of different ages) to make inferences about the association between two variables, A and B, that are both associated with group status. If, for instance, A and B are not correlated with each other in younger adults, but A declines with age, and so does B, but independently of the changes in A, a correlation between A and B will emerge in the full sample of younger and older adults. A standard example pertaining to cognitive aging is the so-called white-hair problem: The proportion of white hairs on the scalp is rumored to be a good predictor of memory ability. (I note that I am not aware of research that actually demonstrates this.) This could lead one, perhaps, to infer that follicular atrophy is the root of memory problems, or even to the fallacy that hair follicles are the seat of memory. It is easy to see why the correlation is there, and why it is spurious: The proportion of white hairs on the scalp typically goes up with age while memory performance typically goes down, but there is no direct relationship between memory functioning and hair color. The solution to the white-hair problem is easy—the common assumption is that partialling out age will reduce the correlation to zero (assuming perfect measurement). (Experimental psychologists can helpfully point out here that there is another simple method to check on the association, and that is to manipulate hair color, and see if it changes memory performance. Hair dye may fool the eye of the beholder, but is unlikely to fool the California Verbal Learning Test.)

Partialling out age lies at the heart of many of the procedures used for determining the proportion of age-related variance accounted for by speed in more complex cognition, including the procedures I used above (sections 9.2.3.1–9.2.3.2). This procedure is, however, still likely to yield biased results. Sliwinski and Hofer derive the equation for the covariation between A and B in what they call a narrow-age cohort study, that is, subjects of (approximately) the same age. Importantly, partialling age out of a typical age-heterogeneous sample (as I did in Table 9.1) is equivalent to creating a fictitious narrow-age cohort study with the average age of the subjects as the "age" of the simulated narrow-age cohort (Lord, 1963). The equation shows that the covariation between the two measures A and B is a function of three types of covariance: (a) the covariation between levels (L) (i.e., the individual difference correlation at young-adult age); (b) the covariation between the slope (S) of one and the level of the other variable (i.e., how initial levels in A influence the change in B, and vice versa); and (c) the covariation between the slopes (i.e., coupled change between the two measures):

$$\text{Cov } (A,B) = \text{Cov } (L_{Ai}L_{Bi}) + [\text{Age}]\text{Cov } (L_{Ai}S_{Bi}) + [\text{Age}]\text{Cov } (S_{Ai}L_{Bi}) + [\text{Age}^2]\text{Cov } (S_{Ai}S_{Bi}).$$

This equation shows why the white-hair example works: If none of the covariances is larger than zero (i.e., there is no correlation between initial hair color and initial level of cognition; initial hair color does not drive a change in cognition; initial levels of cognition do not influence change in hair color; changes in hair color and changes in cognition are independent), then taking age out of the correlation between white-hair proportion and cognition (either through testing subjects of the same age or by partialling out age) will reveal the true null effect.

Sliwinski and Hofer argue that it is the third type of covariation—coupled change—that cognitive aging researchers should be really interested in. Coupled change reflects the interdependency of process: How much are changes in, say, speed and changes in, say, reasoning correlated? (Not everyone agrees with this assertion; see below for studies that focus on the second type of covariation. Additionally, as I will explicate below, there are two more types of slope-slope covariation one could be interested in as well—correlations at the between-subject level and correlations at the within-subject level.) The equation shows that when coupled change is the case, our estimate of the covariance (or correlation) between A and B in a narrow-age cohort, or in a cross-sectional sample with age partialled out, will be inflated. One interesting aspect of the equation is that the covariance associated with coupled change increases by a factor of age-squared, whereas the other covariations either do not increase or increase by a factor of age. This implies that as age advances, coupled change will come to dominate the covariation between measures. Researchers interested in this particular type of covariation can use this property to their advantage, and elect to sample older cohorts, or groups with higher mean ages, rather than younger cohorts.

The Sliwinski and Hofer analysis leaves us with two options to examine the effects of speed on higher-order cognition in old age. The first is to examine the correlation within narrow-age cohorts; the second is to take recourse to longitudinal data, where coupled change (or other aspects of the covariation between speed and cognition) can be examined directly. Note also that the problem is relevant to any theory of aging based on correlational results, including theories built on factor analyses that yield a common factor. Do note, however, that studies where the covariates of age are used as mere indicators or biomarkers of functional or biological age are not subject to this criticism, because these studies remain at the level of the observed correlation (Anstey, 2008). To return to the white-hair example: Although the proportion of white hairs of the scalp is not causally related to cognition, it can still be a useful biomarker.

9.3.1. The Speed-cognition Correlation: Narrow-cohort Analysis

Narrow-cohort analysis is relatively rare in aging research: Most of our efforts, for very good reason, concern correlations with continuous samples (as in the meta-analysis conducted earlier in this chapter), or with a broad range of ages in the older-adult group. At least one large-scale meta-analysis has focused on speed-cognition correlations (Sheppard & Vernon, 2008) and could be helpful here. Not all studies included in this meta-analysis used a narrow-cohort design, but many do; the sample includes 172 studies, totaling more than 50,000 participants. Sheppard and Vernon report the following mean correlations between speed measures and measures of general intelligence: for RT, $r = .26$; for general speed of processing (examples given for this category of tests are arithmetic and trail making), $r = .29$; for memory-scanning speed, $r = .25$, and for inspection time, $r = .36$. Across all the different studies and measures that were reviewed in this paper (a total of 1,146 correlations), mean r (scaled so that a positive correlation indicates that faster speed is associated with higher intelligence) was .24. These correlations are all reliably larger than zero, and indeed smaller than expected on the basis of the full-age-range meta-analysis reported above, which yielded an average r of .47. They also appear to be smaller than expected on the basis of the age-partialled correlations reported above, which yielded a mean r of .35.

To examine what happens to these correlations when only narrow-cohort studies are included, I did a convenience sampling of Sheppard and Vernon's references—I retrieved all studies published since 2000 that included a narrow cohort. My definition of narrow cohort is ad hoc—I am not aware of any precise definition of this concept in the literature. When the studies focused on younger adults, I included studies that tested subjects with an age span of 20 years or less (the largest range I used was age 18–38). The reason for this relatively large span is that young adulthood is a period of relative stability in speed of processing (see, e.g., Figure 7.8). Studies using older adults were included if the span was 5 years or smaller; old age is a period of more rapid change. For the same reason, developmental studies were included if the age span was 5 years or smaller. Some studies did not report age spans; I included those that described their population as "undergraduate students" or "military recruits," unless the study reported a suspiciously large SD for participant age (in practice, the smallest SD in the discarded studies was 6). Sheppard and Vernon list 42 studies published since 2000; 13 of those fit my selection criteria (Ackerman, Beier, & Boyle, 2002; Colom, Rebollo, Palacios, Juan-Espinosa, & Kyllonen, 2004; Danthiir et al., 2005; Fink & Neubauer, 2001; Hertzog & Bleckley, 2001; Hitch, Towse, & Hutton., 2001; Lemke & Zimprich, 2005; Luciano et al., 2005; McCrory & Cooper, 2005; Rindermann & Neubauer, 2004; Schweizer, 2001; Vigil-Colet & Codorniu-Raga, 2002; Wickett & Vernon, 2000). I also added three relevant studies (with, in practice, a smaller than 4-year age range) from the samples of longitudinal studies that I will use later in this chapter (Deary, Allerhand, & Der, 2009; Deary, Johnson, & Starr, 2010; Witt & Cunningham, 1979). In sum, then, 16 studies were included, representing 19 independent subject groups and yielding a total of 332 speed-cognition correlations. Multiple correlations obtained from the same sample were pooled before averaging (e.g., Lemke & Zimprich, 2005, speed and memory, and Zimprich & Martin, 2002, speed and intelligence reported data from the same study).

The average weighted speed-cognition correlation in this sample of studies (first averaged within study, to avoid statistical dependency, then weighted for sample size) was .33 (95% confidence interval between .30 and .36), which is (as expected) smaller than the average speed-cognition correlation in the full-age-range meta-analysis

I reported above in my full-age-range analysis, $r_+ = .47$, but is not reliably different from (and almost identical to) the average age-partialled speed-cognition correlation, $r_+ = 35$. To make a somewhat fairer comparison, I recalculated the weighted average of the narrow-cohort studies, restricting the analysis to correlations between speed and the different aspects of cognition included in the full-age-range meta-analysis. (In practice, this discarded mostly tests of verbal ability and of numerical ability.) This did not change the average correlation, $r_+ = .33$.

The average weighted speed-WM correlation, based on 48 correlations in six studies, was .28 (95% confidence interval between .22 and .33), compared with $r_+ = .42$ in the full-age-range meta-analysis and $r_+ = .25$ in the age-partialled meta-analysis. The average weighted speed-spatial correlation, based on 105 correlations in nine studies, was .23 (95% confidence interval between .19 and .26), compared with .54 in the full-age-range meta-analysis and $r_+ = .42$ in the age-partialled meta-analysis. (Note that the age-partialled correlation lies well outside the 95% CI of the narrow-cohort correlation.) The average weighted speed-reasoning correlation, based on 131 correlations in 10 studies, was .30 (95% confidence interval between .26 and .34), compared with.64 in the full-age-range meta-analysis and $r_+ = .53$ in the age-partialled meta-analysis. (Again, the age-partialled correlation lies well outside the 95% CI of the narrow-cohort correlation.) Only one study investigated episodic memory; its mean correlation was .21, compared with .41 in the full-age-range meta-analysis and $r_+ = .27$ in the age-partialled meta-analysis.

The conclusion, then, is that narrow-cohort studies do indeed, as expected, yield speed-cognition correlations that are quite a bit smaller than the speed-cognition correlations reported in full-age-range studies. For two of the four variables—reasoning and spatial ability—the age-partialled correlations obtained from the full-age-range samples also overestimated the speed-cognition correlations as observed in the narrow-cohort samples. This is likely due to the fact that age-partialling is equivalent to measuring the cross-sectional correlation at the mean age of the sample. In practice, the mean age of the age-heterogeneous studies in my meta-analysis is higher (around age 50) than the mean age of the narrow-cohort samples included here (the modal study examined college-age students). As we saw in the previous section, the correlation matrix of (even narrow) older cohorts is contaminated with other sources of covariance (Hofer & Sliwinski, 2001). This assertion can be examined directly here: Two of the three longitudinal studies included allow for a comparison across two measurement points. The results are indeed in agreement with the Sliwinski and Hofer contention: Speed-cognition correlations tend to get tighter with advancing age. Deary et al. report an average correlation of .35 at the first measurement point, and an r of .43 thirteen years later; Witt and Cunningham report $r = .56$ at the first measurement point and $r = .63$ nineteen and a half years later.

A crucial point to make is that although the narrow-cohort correlations are smaller than expected on the basis of the full-age-range analyses, age-partialled or not (and perhaps smaller than quite a few researchers in the aging field would be hoping for), they do not shrink to zero—the lower limit if the confidence intervals around the average speed-cognition correlations is around .20 or higher, and speed is associated, on average, with 10% of the variance in the cognitive variables. Quite telling is that even at the within-study level, speed-cognition correlations (after averaging within constructs) range between .13 and .59. The clear end conclusion is that not all of the covariation between measures of speed and cognition as obtained in age-heterogeneous samples is due to changes in mean level.

This analysis then yields reassuring results, at least to some degree, for both the common-factor and speed-mediation hypothesis: Both of these hypotheses require that speed and cognition be correlated regardless of the age of the subjects. Whether causation applies can only be assessed in longitudinal research. Longitudinal research, then, is where I turn next.

9.3.2. The Speed-cognition Correlation: Longitudinal Analyses

Longitudinal analysis has rightfully been advertized as the only method to truly evaluate claims of causality for relationships between variables that cannot be manipulated in isolation, such as the cognitive abilities examined here (e.g., Hofer et al., 2006; Lindenberger, Von Oertzen, Ghisletta, & Hertzog, 2011).

As we have seen earlier in this chapter, in cross-sectional research the conclusions regarding the relation between speed and complex cognition are relatively clear: Speed correlates quite strongly with most cognitive abilities, although there is disagreement about what this correlation means. This is not the case for longitudinal research, where the field does not seem to have converged on a clear conclusion. There are at least three reasons for this lack of agreement.

First, although the literature on speed mediation in a longitudinal context is growing, it is also still relative sparse, due in large part to the cost and effort associated with such studies. When I reviewed the literature for the meta-analysis that is about to follow, I was able to find a total of 19 studies—a small number compared with the 72 studies included in the full-age-range cross-sectional meta-analysis.

Second, initial results from longitudinal studies were not exactly good news for the common-cause or speed-mediation hypothesis. Several of the pioneering studies conducted and published in the 1990s and early 2000s claimed a much more tenuous role for speed as an explanatory variable than cross-sectional results had led the field to expect (Hultsch, Hertzog, Small, McDonald-Miszczak, & Dixon, 1992; MacDonald, Hultsch, Strauss, & Dixon, 2003; Sliwinski & Buschke, 1999; Taylor, Miller, & Tinklenberg, 1992; Zimprich, 2002; Zimprich & Martin, 2002). The situation was such that in a 1999 paper, Sliwinski and Hofer went on record to state that the meditational hypothesis of cognitive aging (by which they meant mediation by speed, executive processes, or a common cause) was "not supported by longitudinal studies" (p. 351). This conclusion was, at that time, correct: Sliwinski and Hofer reviewed the only two extant studies that fell within their definition of mediation (viz., coupled change within individuals), and both of these studies yielded close-to-null results. The general perception that longitudinal research has long disproved the meditational hypothesis seems to have stuck with the field.

A third problem concerns the question as to what exactly comprises satisfactory evidence for a common cause model or a speed mediation model in a longitudinal context. The problem is dual: There is no common method, and there is no common metric. This complicates matters for both narrative and quantitative reviewers. In a longitudinal study investigating speed-cognition correlations, there are at least four data points: speed at Time 1, cognition at Time 1, speed at Time 2, and cognition at Time 2. This allows for three types of comparisons: (a) Speed at Time 1 can be correlated with cognition at Time 2, and vice versa (*cross-lagged correlations*); (b) speed at Time 1 can be correlated with change in cognition from Time 1 to Time 2, and vice versa (*level-change correlations*, sometimes used to test the *cognitive reserve* hypothesis); and (c) change in speed from Time 1 to Time 2 can be correlated with change in cognition from Time 1 and Time 2 (*coupled change*). These analyses are not interchangeable, and neither are the conclusions that can be drawn from them. To make matters worse, at different points in time different investigators have endorsed each of those methods as the single correct way to analyze meditational effects. There appears to be roughly a historical progression through this sequence, in the sense that studies advocating (a) appeared before those advocating (b), which appeared before studies advocating (c), and that the introduction of each successive method appears to have cooled enthusiasm for the method previously in vogue. Quite recently, two new analytical methods, extensions of (c) and (b), respectively, have been proposed—*coupled change within individuals* (in which measurement-to-measurement changes in speed within an individual are correlated with measurement-to-measurement changes in cognition within the same individual) and *lead-lag analysis* (in which change in each variable is modeled as a function of both the auto-regression effect and the coupling effect of the previous score of the other variable).

I will examine data concerning each of these types of analyses in turn. My literature search was complicated by the question of what constitutes a "study." The issue is data duplication or near-data duplication: By definition, longitudinal research includes multiple points or waves of measurement; often each of these waves, or successive accumulations of data, is published separately. Additionally, some studies focus on one aspect of the data in one article and on another in a second. The number of participants or the exact measures can then vary from paper to paper. In the meta-analyses, I always opted for including either the most recent or what I considered the most pertinent data set from a particular longitudinal study. This was particularly the case for the Seattle Longitudinal Study by Schaie and colleagues; the Victoria Longitudinal Study by Dixon, Hultsch, Hertzog, and colleagues; and the Swedish Adoption/Twin study, by Finkel and colleagues.

9.3.2.1. Cross-lagged Correlations

The first type of longitudinal analysis concerns cross-lagged correlations (sometimes also called cross-lag, or time-lagged correlations; probably originating in Campbell & Stanley, 1963), that is, correlations between speed at Time 1 and cognition at Time 2, as well as the inverse. The reasoning is that a deterministic relationship presupposes that the correlation between the antecedent at Time 1 and the consequent at Time 2 is larger than the correlation between the consequent at Time 1 and the antecedent at Time 2. Under this assumption, then, the Time 1 speed to Time 2 cognition correlation should be larger than the Time 1 cognition to Time 2 speed correlation.

Cross-lagged correlations were quite popular in the 1980s, but their popularity waned considerably after the publication of an extensive critique of the method in which Rogosa (1980) describes their use as "a dead end" (p. 257). Rogosa's critique boils down to two main points. One is that causality is never a closed system—third variables might be responsible for cross-lagged correlations between two variables. Part of the remedy, Rogosa suggests, is to formulate explicit mechanistic explanations, that is, plausible mechanisms that link the two variables. In the context of the speed-cognition correlations, as I mentioned above, attempts at such mechanistic explanations have clearly been made. The second problem is technical. Rogosa shows mathematically that the difference in size between the two cross-lagged correlations is not at all informative about the reciprocal causation between the two variables— differences, or a lack of difference, between correlations do not correspond directly to the presence or absence of a causal effect. This second problem is not remediable in the typical cross-lagged correlation context (i.e., a context of two measurement points and two variables), although the issue can be addressed in lead-lag analysis (see Section 9.3.2.5). As a result, cross-lagged correlations are rarely reported in post-1982 papers, except as corroborating evidence in the context of other types of analyses (e.g., Ghisletta & Lindenberger, 2003).

The message is clear: Differences between cross-lagged correlations should not be used to make causal inferences. Investigating cross-lagged correlations is, however, still important, because it is one way to determine that the two variables are indeed related. That is, although the relative size of the cross-lagged correlations is not informative, an absence of cross-lagged correlation would be a source of worry about any kind of causal or mediational model.

I was able to collect six studies investigating cross-lagged speed-cognition correlations (Christensen et al., 2000, 2004; Deary, Allerhand, & Der, 2009; Ghisletta & Lindenberger, 2003; Schaie, 1989b; Witt & Cunningham, 1979); these studies followed subjects over an average weighted span of 7.4 years. Note that in this and all further analyses in this section on longitudinal research speed, I scaled speed such that higher levels of speed indicate that subjects are faster. Thus, a positive speed-cognition correlation indicates that faster individuals have higher levels of cognition, and vice versa. I will use → symbols to indicate cross-lagged correlations. Thus, the speed → cognition correlation is the correlation between speed at Time 1 and cognition at Time 2; the cognition → speed correlation is the correlation between cognition at Time 1 and speed at Time 2.

Two results are important here. The first one is that the weighted average cross-lagged correlations are both reliably larger than zero. The average speed → cognition cross-lagged correlation is .34 (95% confidence interval from .31 to .36), the average cognition → speed correlation is .32 (95% confidence interval from .29 to .35). This result indicates that speed and cognition are clearly correlated over the time lags investigated in these studies. Again, a significant cross-lag correlation does not imply causation, but it is a prerequisite—without this correlation, any causal or mediational hypothesis would fail.

The absolute value of a correlation is informative, but perhaps more informative in the present context is the comparison between the size of the cross-lagged correlation and the size of the autocorrelations of speed and cognition. Arguably, the speed → cognition and cognition → speed correlations are limited by the size of the speed → speed and cognition → cognition correlations. The average weighted speed-speed autocorrelation in the five studies that present this information is .50 over an average span of 7.5 years (95% confidence interval from .48 to .53); the average weighted cognition-cognition autocorrelation in these same studies is .66 (95% confidence interval from .64 to .69). The upper bound for the cross-correlations is the product of those two autocorrelations, which is .33. In this subsample, the average speed → cognition cross-lagged correlation is .23 (95% confidence interval between .20 and .27) the average cognition → speed correlation is .27 (95% confidence interval between .24 and .31). This then implies that speed at Time 1 explains about 49% of the reliable variance in cognition at Time 2 (i.e.,.23^2/.33^2), and cognition at Time 1 explains about 67% of the reliable variance in speed at Time 2 (i.e.,.27^2/.33^2). These are quite strong numbers, indicating that speed and cognition are indeed fellow travelers over the adult life span.

The second conclusion is that the two correlations are quite symmetrical. They are, in fact, contained within each others' confidence interval, indicating that, at the aggregate level, they are not statistically different from each other. This does not mean, however, that every study yields identical speed → cognition and cognition → speed correlations. All patterns are present, sometimes even within studies. Christensen et al. (2002) obtained stronger cognition → speed correlations than speed → cognition correlations in three out of 12 measures, the opposite pattern in six measures, and essentially identical correlations in the three other measures. Deary et al. obtained stronger cognition → speed correlations than speed → cognition correlations in three out of four measures, and the opposite pattern in the fourth. Schaie (1989) found that correlations between speed at Time 1 and cognition at Time 2 were about as large as those between cognition at Time 1 and speed at Time 2. Importantly, in Schaie's study, the age-cognition correlations were attenuated considerably when speed was partialled out at either of the two time points. What this means is that even when the cross-sectional results replicate the usual speed mediation result, the cross-lagged correlations may not show strong asymmetries. Schaie took this as strong evidence against a causal link from speed to cognition, but the finding could also be taken to merely reinforce Rogosa's critique of the asymmetries between correlations. Two other studies did obtain larger speed → cognition correlations than cognition → speed correlations. Witt and Cunningham, in a small young-adult narrow age cohort, but with a long time between the two measurement points, found very high correlations (.65 on average) between speed at Time 1 and cognition at Time 2, with much more modest correlations going in the other direction (.24 on average). Ghisletta and Lindenberger obtained, on average, a speed → cognition correlation of .49, compared with a cognition → speed correlation of .33.

In sum, the data indicate that the cross-lag correlations between speed and cognition are symmetrical, with .33 being a good point estimate. These correlations appear modest, but correcting them for unreliability by using the product of the autocorrelations as the expected value for the cross-correlation ceiling indicates that they explain about one half to two thirds of the variance. The end conclusion is that speed and cognition do move together over the adult life span, as required for any common-factor or cascade model to hold.

9.3.2.2. *Correlations between Levels and Change: Speed as a Cognitive Reserve?*

A second type of longitudinal analysis concerns the correlation between levels of speed at Time 1 and change in cognition from Time 1 to subsequent measurement points. (Change is typically measured as the linear slope over time, that is, as change per year.) This correlation is then often compared with the correlation between levels of cognition at Time 1 and subsequent changes in speed. The rationale for this comparison is that if speed is a necessary resource for cognition, then high levels of speed should protect against cognitive decline, but the reverse would not necessarily be true—a conjecture also known as the cognitive reserve hypothesis (Stern, 2002, 2009; Tucker-Drob, Johnson, & Jones, 2009), or the hypothesis of differential preservation (Salthouse, 2006; Salthouse, Babcock, Skovronek, Mitchell, & Palmon, 1990).

An alternative to the cognitive reserve hypothesis, sometimes labeled the preserved differentiation hypothesis (Salthouse, 2006; Salthouse et al., 1990), states that decline might well be independent of initial level of performance. Thus, although high- and low-reserve people (in this case: faster and slower individuals) differ in their levels of cognitive performance, their rates of decline in performance might be comparable (e.g., Tucker-Drob et al., 2009). The preserved-differentiation phenomenon— disparity in initial level of performance coupled with parallel rates of decline—is quite common in longitudinal research that investigates the stability of individual differences of many kinds. For instance, within the Berlin Aging study (BASE), preserved differentiation has been noted for gender differences (in cross-sectional comparisons, females scored higher than males on memory, fluency, and the intelligence composite, but the longitudinal slopes for the two genders were not significantly different) as well as differences in socioeconomic status (e.g., cross-sectionally, participants scoring 1 *SD* above the mean on a socioeconomic status composite scored higher on all intelligence variables than participants scoring 1 *SD* below the mean on the SES composite, but the longitudinal trajectories for the two groups were statistically parallel) (Singer et al., 2003; see Carmelli, Swan, LaRue, & Eslinger, 1997; Gribbin, Schaie, & Parham, 1980; and Hultsch, Hertzog, Dixon, & Small, 1998, for similar results).

It should be noted that, as fascinating as the discussion surrounding the cognitive-reserve concept may be, it also falls somewhat outside the scope of this chapter. In fact, the common-factor model and the cascade model are both indifferent to the cognitive-reserve hypothesis; nothing in either model's logic predicts either cognitive reserve or preserved differentiation, nor would either model be embarrassed by the validation of either hypothesis. My analysis is, then, informative about the reserve versus preservation debate, but not necessarily about speed-cognition mediation.

I was only able to collect four relevant studies (Christensen et al., 2000, 2004; Finkel, Reynolds, McArdle, & Pedersen, 2005; Tucker-Drob et al., 2009); three of these report both the correlation between level of speed and slope of cognition and the correlation between level of cognition and slope of speed correlation; one study only reports the former. All correlations are scaled such that higher values of speed indicate subjects being better, that is, faster. Support for the reserve hypothesis would then consist of a negative correlation between level and slope: Higher initial levels of ability would lead to shallower slopes, that is, less decline.

The studies present rather inconclusive evidence. At the level of the aggregate, the data support neither hypothesis: The mean weighted correlation between levels of speed and the slope of cognition is small, but reliably positive (i.e., the confidence interval does not include zero), $r_+ = .08$ (95% confidence interval from .05 to .12); the mean weighted correlation between levels of cognition and the slope of speed is zero,

r_+ = .00 (95% confidence interval between –.04 and .04). The difference between the correlations is significant (the 95% confidence intervals do not overlap). (Note that the level of speed-slope of cognition correlation goes up to .10, 95% confidence interval between .06 and .14, if we include only the three studies that provide both types of correlation; this also lifts the difference between the two correlations to significance.) The cognitive-reserve hypothesis would have predicted a negative correlation between levels of speed and slope of cognition, the preserved-differentiation hypothesis a zero correlation. Instead, we find that higher levels of speed are associated with faster declines in cognition (and lower levels of speed with slower decline).

There is plenty of reason to be cautious about this conclusion. The correlation is modest, of course, and it may be due in whole or in part to regression to the mean; it is also obtained from an extremely small number of studies. Equally striking is the large variability between studies. Notably, the Christensen et al. (2004) study shows strong positive correlations overall; the Tucker-Drob et al. study shows essentially a zero correlation for level of speed and change in cognition but a strong negative correlation for level of cognition and change in speed; Finkel et al. show a small overall negative correlation between level of speed and change in cognition and a moderate positive correlation between level of cognition and change in speed. The Finkel et al. study, however, had one added characteristic: Finkel et al. did not only examine linear change over time, they also measured quadratic change, that is, the potential acceleration or deceleration in decline over time. This quadratic correlation revealed moderate to strong relationships: The average quadratic correlation between level of speed and change in cognition was –.33; the average quadratic correlation between level of cognition and change in speed correlation was –.61. If we include the quadratic "slope" into the calculations for the average correlations, the average correlation between level of speed and change in cognition decreases to .08 (95% confidence interval from .05 to .12, or .10 if only the studies with both types of correlations are included), and the correlation between level of cognition and decline in speed becomes reliably negative, r_+ = –.12 (95% confidence interval from –.13 to –.06).

The guarded but simple conclusion is that there is at present little evidence for the reserve hypothesis view. In my judgment, the correlations between levels and slopes are small enough to be negligible; a slightly less guarded conclusion may then be that the data are more compatible with the preserved differentiation hypothesis if only the linear decline component is considered, although no firm conclusions can be reached at this stage due to the small sample of studies and the divergence of results obtained from individual studies.

9.3.2.3. Coupled Change

A third type of longitudinal analysis concerns coupled change—how change in speed correlates with change in cognition. Such couplings are assessed most simply by investigating the correlation between the slope of speed over time and the slope of other aspects of cognition over time. (When there are only two measurement points, the slope is often operationalized as the difference score; the regression over actual time can be used as well.) This analysis is crucial for both the common-factor and the cascade model: Whether speed and cognition are fellow travelers, or whether speed effects cascade down the system, subjects who slow down more between measurement points should also experience a larger decline in cognitive performance. It can be argued that evidence for coupled change is all that is required for the weaker version of the common-factor model, the version which merely states that there is common variance in change. It is, however, clearly only a necessary, not a sufficient condition for acceptance of the cascade model. That is, the cascade model presupposes coupled change, but coupled change does not imply mediation or causation. I was able to locate 11 relevant studies with a total of 37 correlations (Christensen et al., 2000, 2004; Finkel et al., 2005; Hertzog, Dixon, Hultsch, & MacDonald, 2003; Lemke & Zimprich, 2005; Salthouse, 2011a; Taylor et al., 1992; Tucker-Drob, 2011a, 2011b; Sliwinski & Buschke, 2004; Wilson et al., 2002).

Taken together, the data show clear support for the coupled-change hypothesis.

First, the average correlation, weighted for sample size, between slopes in speed and slopes in other aspects of cognition is rather large, $r = .59$ (95% confidence interval between .58 and .61).

Second, none of the 37 reported correlations between slopes in speed and slopes in other aspects of cognition were negative. At the study level, correlations tended to be quite respectable. Only two studies had correlations below .25; one of those was .19, and the one study that found a near-zero correlation (Taylor et al., 1992, $r = .04$) had a very small sample size, $n = 30$. Thus, a large majority of the studies in this analysis provided direct support for the existence of coupled change.

Third, the correlation compares quite favorably to the cross-sectional correlation (i.e., the correlation between levels of speed and levels of cognition at the first time of measurement). Nine of the 11 studies included this correlation, which had a weighted average of .47 (95% confidence interval between .45 and .49), not statistically different from the weighted average coupled-change correlation in these same nine studies, which was .50 (95% confidence interval between .49 and .52). The cross-sectional correlation in this sample was thus clearly not an overestimate of the coupled-change correlation.

Interestingly, there is also coupling between the cross-sectional and the longitudinal correlations. Figure 9.5 plots the correlation between change in speed and change in cognition as a function of the correlation between level in speed and level in cognition; the left-hand panel shows all correlations, the right-hand panel shows the correlations after within-study averaging. In both cases, the correlation between the correlations is relatively high (.56 in the former, .57 in the latter), indicating that studies and/or cognitive measures that show large cross-sectional intercorrelations also show large longitudinal intercorrelations. Thus, cross-sectional speed-cognition correlations are somewhat predictive of longitudinal correlations, indicating that what drives couplings in individual differences at a particular slice in time is also likely to drive coupled change over time. (I do note here that some of these mechanisms might be trivial; it is, for instance, possible that reliability issues limit both the cross-sectional and coupled-change correlations for some studies and that other studies use more reliable measures.)

Fourth, the coupled-change correlation is substantially different for measures of crystallized intelligence and those of fluid abilities. Four studies (Christensen et al., 2002, 2004; Hertzog et al., 2003; and Wilson et al., 2002) included measures

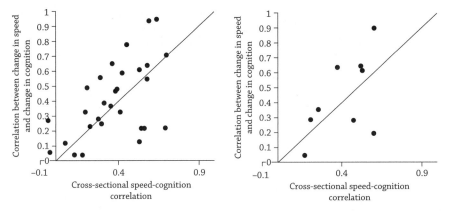

Figure 9.5. Plot of the correlation between longitudinal change in speed and longitudinal change in cognition as a function of the cross-sectional correlation between speed and cognition in the same study. The left-hand panel shows all pairs of correlations (29 data points); the right-hand panel shows them after within-study averaging (k = 9). The dotted line is the equality diagonal.

of crystallized intelligence (a Gc factor, verbal intelligence, and a vocabulary measure, respectively.); the average coupled-change correlation with speed, weighted for sample size, was .28. All studies included measures of fluid cognition; the average weighted speed-cognition coupled-change correlation for those was .55; this correlation was significantly larger than the speed-crystallized intelligence coupling. This result is what should be expected if one assumes (as many researchers do, e.g., Salthouse, 1996) that speed should be closely related to fluid intelligence, and not, or less so, to crystallized intelligence. This is also the result found in the meta-analysis on cross-sectional correlations between intelligence and speed (Sheppard & Vernon, 2008), where speed was found to generally correlate stronger with fluid intelligence than with crystallized intelligence. In that meta-analysis, as in the current analysis, the correlation with crystallized intelligence was still generally larger than zero. Thus, the finding of a stronger speed-fluid cognition coupling than speed-crystallized intelligence coupling adds credence to the conclusion that speed and cognition are coupled.

One important question: Exactly how coupled is coupled change? That is, is it reasonable to assume that a single change factor would suffice to explain the coupling? One issue to consider here is the composition of the correlation matrix—which variables are included. If a larger number of measures and/or more diverse measures are included, a conclusion of coupled change would carry more weight than if the measures all converge on a narrow construct. Five studies have explicitly modeled change as a single latent factor across a rather wide variety of cognitive (and other) constructs. Hertzog et al. (2003) included measures of working memory, reasoning, word knowledge, episodic memory, and speed in their test battery and found that a single-factor model of change fit their data very well. This single factor accounted for between 45% and 68% of the change in any of these five measures, with an average of 54%. Lindenberger and Ghisletta (2009) incorporated perceptual speed, episodic memory, fluency, verbal knowledge, as well as measures of close visual acuity, distant visual acuity, and hearing in a single latent change factor that explained 60% of the variance. Reynolds, Gatz, and Pedersen (2002) factor-analyzed change measures from nine tests in the Swedish Adoption/ Twin Study of Aging (Information, Synonyms, Block Design, Figure Logic, Digits Forward, Digits Backward, Thurstone's Picture Memory, Symbol Digit, and Figure ID). When change was measured as change per year, a single-factor model sufficed to explain the data; on average, this single factor captured 10% of the variance in each of the measures. Wilson et al. (2002) applied principal-components factor analysis to seven abilities (story retention, word retention, word generation, word knowledge, working memory, perceptual speed, and spatial ability) and found that a single factor fit the data well, with 62% of the variance accounted for. Finally, in what is arguably the most detailed study on this issue, Tucker-Drob (2011a) built a hierarchical factor model of latent change, setting up three indicators for each of four cognitive constructs (reasoning, spatial visualization, episodic memory, and processing speed), which, in turn, loaded on a global change factor. On average, 39% of the variance in change in any given test was due to the global factor, 33% was due to change specific to each of the four constructs, and 28% was test-specific.

Taken together, these studies all point to the conclusion that cognitive aging is a domain-general, domain-specific, and likely task-specific process. Summarized over these five studies, the domain-general portion, that is, a single-factor solution, explained between 10% and 62% of the variance in cognitive change over time (but note that in some studies, this unit was a score on a specific cognitive test or task, in others it was a construct derived from multiple tests); the weighted average was 43%.

Summarized, there is ample evidence for strongly coupled change between speed and other aspects of cognition, with an average correlation between slopes of.59. Cross-sectional correlations did not overestimate coupled change and were moderately correlated with coupled change, suggesting that models derived from cross-sectional correlations may have some validity as predictors for coupled change as well. (Or, in other words, patterns of age-related differences appear to have some validity to explain patterns of aging-related changes.) The coupling is stronger for fluid aspects than for crystallized aspects of cognition. Models that posit a single factor structure of change (a.k.a. "It all goes together when it goes"; Rabbitt, 1999) capture a rather large amount of variance.

9.3.2.4. Coupled Change within Individuals

The previous section investigated coupled change at the between-subject or individual-differences level. The question that can be answered with these data is the question whether individuals who decline more on speed also show larger declines in cognition. Recently, Hofer and Sliwinski and colleagues (e.g., Hofer & Sliwinski, 2001) have argued that coupled change should also be investigated at the within-subject or intraindividual level. The intraindividual-change perspective asks a different question: *Within* individuals, are changes in speed related to concomitant changes in cognition? More simply stated: The coupled-change perspective compares two or more people, and assumes that if person *A* declines more on speed than person *B* does, *A* should also decline more on cognition; the intraindividual-change perspective compares person *A* with herself, and asserts that on days when *A* is slower, she should also perform less well on cognitive tasks. These are related, but distinct questions.

To my knowledge, three papers, from two studies, have investigated coupled change between speed and cognition at the within-individual level (Sliwinski & Buschke, 1999, 2004; Zimprich, 2002). These studies apply latent growth curve models to the data to predict cognition at time t from age, speed intercepts, and speed slopes. The model has two levels, with level 1 describing intraindividual change, and the second level including between-person differences (see Sliwinski and Buschke, 2004, for more details). This allows the researchers to estimate how well occasion-to-occasion changes in cognition are predicted by occasion-to-occasion changes in speed within an individual after adjusting for average decline. One advantage of this methodology is that it yields a metric that is directly comparable to one traditional cross-sectional metric: the percentage of age-related variance explained.

The earliest of these three studies, Sliwinski and Buschke (1999), was very instrumental in sowing serious doubt about longitudinal meditational claims. In this paper, fluctuations in speed explained on average 13% of the age-related variance in cognition—a much more modest amount than predicted from cross-sectional analyses, 86% in this study. This paper has been superseded by a 2004 paper by the same authors, examining the same data set (the Einstein Aging Study), but with one more measurement occasion and an additional sample of participants included. The message is about the same: 18% of the age-related variance in within-individual variations in cognition is due to within-individual variations in speed. Finally, the Zimprich (2002) study obtained an even more modest estimate—4% of the age-related variance in cognition is coupled with changes in speed. This again stands in stark contrast to estimates of the age-related variance accounted for cross-sectionally at the first point of measurement. These range from 56% (comprehension) to 98% (block design and picture arrangement), with an average value of 86%. Clearly, the cross-sectional between-subject estimates of speed mediation are much larger than the longitudinal within-subject estimates. The weighted average of the amount of age-related variance explained by within-individual changes in speed in the latter two studies is 16%. The estimate goes up by only 0.5% when deleting tests of crystallized intelligence (WAIS-verbal tests).

The conclusion is then that within-person slowing does correlate with within-person declines in cognition, but to a much smaller extent than expected from cross-sectional, between-subject studies. Within-person slowing clearly does not account for all or even most of the within-person age effects in cognition. The reason for the discrepancy between the size of the effects of between-subject and within-individual coupling isn't immediately clear. Sliwinski and Buschke (2004) point out that between-person age differences and within-person age change may reflect different processes (age differences are confounded with cohort; within-person change with period). The time frame of measurement might also be important. It is possible that within an individual speed and cognition covary over the long term, but not in the short-term, where other sources of day-to-day variance (e.g., life stressors or fluctuations in health) might obscure the relationship. If the other sources of variance are more salient in the time frames typically used (the data waves in Sliwinski and Buschke were spread one year apart), the magnitude of the within-person speed-cognition relationship may be underestimated. There is indeed evidence that within-subject variability in cognitive tests is quite large, which may make such underestimations of coupled change likely. For instance, Salthouse (2007) tested a total of more than 1,500 adults across a wide age range on a battery of 16 cognitive tests in three sessions within an interval of approximately 2 weeks and found that within-person variability across the three assessments was equivalent in magnitude to the cross-sectional age differences expected over an interval of 15–25 years. The presence of such large fluctuations may make it particularly hard to detect the signal of true coupling. How we are to evaluate the numbers might also depend on the deeper theory we wish to espouse. If explanations involve functional brain changes, coupling on shorter time scales might be expected; if they revolve around structural changes, one might expect that the coupling arising from, say, slow erosions in white matter tracts would not be observable in the short-term compared with much more salient day-to-day influences.

This is clearly an area where more research is needed, and short-burst longitudinal studies (where subjects are tested at the intervals usual in longitudinal research, every year or every couple of years, but with intensive repeated testing at each time point) are needed to help disentangle short-term and long-term coupling effects. Such studies are now underway (e.g., Salthouse, 2010; Sliwinski, Hoffman, & Hofer, 2010).

9.3.2.5. *Lead-lag Analysis*

The final (and most recent) type of longitudinal mediational analysis is lead-lag analysis, first proposed by McArdle and colleagues (McArdle, 2001; McArdle & Hamagami, 2003; McArdle, Hamagami, Meredith, & Bradway, 2000). It models longitudinal data using a so-called bivariate dual-change score model (BDCSM, a variation on latent growth curve models) to test dynamic hypotheses about pairs of variables. In order to run this analysis, longitudinal studies with multiple measurement points are needed; the dynamic relationship of the two variables of interest is modeled simultaneously by modeling change as a function of both the auto-regression or self-feedback effect (i.e., the influence on a variable exerted by its own previous score), and the coupling effect of the previous score of the other variable. This allows for statistical testing of the following questions: Does variable *A* (or *B*) influence subsequent change in variable *A* (or *B*); (b) Does variable *A* (or *B*) influence subsequent change in variable *B* (or *A*); and (c) Does the effect of variable *A* on subsequent change in variable *B* differ reliably from the effect of variable *B* on subsequent change in variable *A*? This, in turn, allows one to assess whether one of the variables effectively drives change in the other, thus acting like a leader; the variable whose change is predicted by the leader is called the lagger.

This is a very new method, and the literature is consequently sparse. I was able to collect four relevant studies, which report a total of eight different analyses (Ghisletta & De Ribaupierre, 2005; Ghisletta & Lindenberger, 2003; Finkel, Reynolds, McArdle, Hamagami, & Pedersen, 2009; McArdle et al., 2000). The data are reported as standardized regression coefficients, not correlations. Four findings are noteworthy, and they strongly suggest that speed has either a causal relationship with more complex aspects of cognition, or is an early and very sensitive biomarker.

First, at the level of the aggregate, speed clearly leads cognition, and not the other way around. The average weighted regression coefficient for speed leading cognition is 0.39; the average weighted regression coefficient for cognition leading speed is 0.01 (arguably close to zero). This result is clearly at odds with a common-cause or common-factor account, at least as commonly understood. If a common mechanism were operating, both coefficients should be positive, indicating that speed and other aspects of cognition travel together.

Second, seven out of the eight analyses reported show larger effects for speed leading cognition than for cognition leading speed (the exception is McArdle et al., 2001, where one out of four measures, Digit Span, leads speed rather than speed leading the measure). At the level of the individual studies, all four studies show the speed-lead effect, with regression coefficients ranging from 0.10 to 0.51. Given that this is a small sample of studies, consistency across studies inspires some faith in the conclusions.

Third, both at the level of individual analyses and at the level of studies, all speed-lead effects are positive (effects ranged from 0.00 to 0.65). This suggests that the overall positive effect is not a mere artifact of averaging across measures. This stands in sharp contrast to the cognition-leader effects: Negative effects were observed in three out of eight analyses and one out of the four studies.

Fourth, as was the case in the coupled-change analysis, measures of crystallized abilities (knowledge, verbal ability, and vocabulary) yielded smaller lead-lag coefficients than measures of fluid cognition (fluency, spatial ability, memory, digit span, and block design)—the regressions coefficients were 0.17 versus 0.31, respectively. Thus, the analyses strongly suggest that, consistent with the speed-mediation model (e.g., Salthouse, 1996a), processing speed is a stronger leading indicator of age changes in measures of fluid ability than those of crystallized ability.

In sum, lead-lag analysis leads strong support for models that posit a structure in the mediation effects. More specifically, speed influences change in other aspects of cognition reliably, but other aspects of cognition exert, on average, only a negligible influence on changes in speed.

9.3.3. Longitudinal Speed-cognition Correlations: Conclusions

I investigated data from five different types of longitudinal analyses. The main question was whether the general conclusions derived from cross-sectional analyses—namely that a considerable amount of the age-related variance in cognition is shared with speed, potentially even in a causal way, with speed driving cognition—hold in a longitudinal context. As noted, one complication with longitudinal analyses is that each type of analysis is designed to answer a different question. Although some analyses can answer the question whether or not change in speed and change in cognition are correlated, none is equipped with the tools to answer whether or not a complicated cascade model fits the longitudinal data. Table 9.3 summarizes the data.

The central conclusion from this review of the longitudinal literature is that speed and higher-order cognition are indeed coupled (individuals who decline more on one also decline more on the other)—a conclusion that is in concordance with the cross-sectional analyses reported in the first main section of this chapter. The main evidence for this conclusion comes from the examination of cross-correlations (which explain on average 58% of the relevant variance) and from the study of coupled change (a single change factor explains on average 43% of the variance).

Table 9.3 **Summary of the findings concerning longitudinal correlations between speed and other aspects of fluid cognition, with 95% confidence interval (when available) indicated within brackets. Time 1 and Time 2 refer to successive measurement points; level is performance at a measurement point; *k* is the number of studies used to calculate the average correlation.**

Type of correlation	k	Speed to cognition	Cognition to speed
Cross-lagged (level at Time 1 to level at Time 2)	6	34 (.31–.36)	32 (.29–.35)
Speed-as-reserve (Level Time 1 to change from Time 1 to Time 2)	4	.08 (.05–.12)	.00 (−.04–.04)
Coupled change (change from Time 1 to Time 2)	11	.59 (.58–.61)	
Within-person coupling	3	16% of age-related variance explained	(NA)
Lead-lag analysis	4	0.39* (NA)	0.01* (NA)

* This result is expressed as a regression coefficient rather than a correlation.

One extremely important caveat is that this conclusion only holds well when differences between subjects are considered. It fares significantly less well when coupled change is studied at the within-subject level—declines in speed explain only 16% of the variance in higher-order cognition, on average, in two independent samples. There is a glass-half-filled, glass-half-empty aspect to this number: Explaining 16% of the relevant variance is clearly not nothing (within-person slowing does correlate with within-person declines in cognition); but 16% is also much less than is predicted at the between-subject level in either longitudinal or cross-sectional data sets. I also argued that the modesty of the coupling might be due to the relatively short time scale over which such coupled fluctuations have been observed.

A second important conclusion is that structure is apparent within this between-subject coupling: Speed appears to push or drive higher-order cognition; the inverse is not true. This finding, consistently obtained in four independent data sets, indicates that a cascade model, with speed leading other indicators, is indeed feasible. As explained above, this does not imply that mental speed itself is the causal mechanism; speed could still be a proxy or biomarker for deeper underlying psychological and/or physiological phenomena.

A third conclusion is that longitudinal research offers little support for the hypothesis that speed works as a cognitive reserve: Initial levels of speed do not protect against decline in more complex aspects of cognition.

At a slightly higher level of abstraction, one important deduction is that the conclusions from these longitudinal analyses do not stand in contrast or contradiction to those from cross-sectional research. This may be somewhat surprising, given the long and venerable tradition of distrust in cross-sectional variance-partitioning research, founded on methodological concerns (e.g., Lindenberger & Pötter, 1998; Hofer & Sliwinski, 2001; Hertzog, Lindenberger, Ghisletta, & Von Oertzen, 2006). Methodological comments obviously should not be dismissed (and I have done my fair share of math-driven complaining, e.g., Verhaeghen, 2000), but it is also useful to investigate the actual impact of such methodological flaws on empirically derived conclusions, an aspect often missing in such critiques. When examined with real data sets, as I did in this chapter, the conclusions from cross-sectional and longitudinal do not appear to diverge all that much. This does not imply that cross-sectional research will always act as a good proxy or substitute for longitudinal work, but it does imply that cross-sectional data are de facto not as problematic as is often thought.

9.4. The Interplay Between Speed and More Complex Aspects of Cognition: Conclusions

In this chapter, I investigated the relationship between age-related differences in speed of processing and age-related differences in more complex aspects of cognition. More specifically, I investigated evidence for two sets of theories, the common-factor view and the mediational model. Both theories suppose that age-related differences or changes in cognition are not independent, but that a portion of the age-related variance in these measures is shared. Common-factor theories postulate that a single common factor mediates a substantial portion of age-related influences on all cognitive variables. This model assigns no special role to speed—it is a variable that, like and with other aspects of cognition, goes down with age without playing a causal or otherwise special role. Mediational models, on the other hand, claim that speed mediates age-related differences in other aspects of cognitive performance, often under the form of a cascade—age decreases speed, which, in turn, decreases working memory performance, which, in turn, decreases performance on aspects of higher-order cognition such as episodic memory, reasoning ability, or spatial ability. I gathered meta-analytic data from a large number of studies that suggested that both types of models have some merit indeed.

Turning to the cross-sectional evidence first, there is ample evidence that age-related differences in different aspects of cognition are not independent. The correlation matrix clearly shows that the cognitive variables form a positive manifold: All cognitive variables are positively and reliably (with one exception) correlated with each other, and negatively correlated with age. A common-factor model fits the data much better than an independent-constructs model, clearly indicating that there is shared age-related variance in the set of cognitive variables. There is, however, also ample evidence that a common-factor model does not suffice: Corrections for individual constructs were necessary to get a complete picture. Mediational models also fit the data quite well. Speed explains 78% of the age-related variance in the other aspects of cognition, more so than working memory, executive control, resistance to interference, or task shifting, each of which explains less than 60% of the age-related variance. Short-term memory, in this analysis, turned out not to mediate any variance, and the age-related variance in it was almost completely explained by the other basic variables. Fitting a cascade model again suggested that speed is a powerful mediator between age and executive control (effectively explaining all of the age-related variance), between age and working memory/short-term memory (again explaining all of the age-related variance), and between age and higher-order cognition (with again complete mediation). The cascade model, however, provides no evidence for a mediational role of executive control, at least as measured here (i.e., by resistance to interference and task shifting).

The available longitudinal evidence confirms the interdependence of different aspects of cognition over the adult lifespan. Changes in speed and changes in other aspects of cognition are correlated (a single change factor explains on average 43% of the variance), and within-individual changes in speed are correlated with within-individual changes in higher-order cognition (explaining on average 16% of the within-subject age-related variance). These findings fit well with both common-factor models and mediational models of the relation between speed and cognition. Moreover, in lead-lag analyses, speed appears to drive changes in higher-order cognition, but higher-order cognition has no leading role for changes in speed—a finding that fits better with a mediational hypothesis than with a common-factor view.

Thus, the analyses I presented here all converge on the conclusion that age-related changes in speed (and/or other basic aspects of processing associated with it) drive age-related changes in more complex aspects of cognition.

Finally, I would like to reiterate that the leading and mediational role of speed does not necessarily imply direct causation. Some researchers indeed assume that a decline in speed causes age-related differences, in much the same way that a slower computer processor influences software performance. The Fry and Hale (1996) model appears to imply this; so do the limited-time and simultaneity mechanisms of aging proposed by Salthouse (1996b). Others see speed not as causal, but as a biomarker or proxy, that is, the most sensitive (in the case of individual differences) or earliest (in the case of age-related differences) indicator of a more general, low-level underlying age-related decline in functioning (e.g., Anstey, 2008). Yet other researchers assume that processing speed measures are, in fact, indicative of a deeper underlying set of basic abilities, such as focused attention, speed of evidence accumulation, or decision-making processes, that are shared with the more complex tasks of higher-order cognition. The models presented here are compatible with any of those explanations.

10

The Elements of Cognitive
Aging: Conclusions

At the end of a long and somewhat gnarly volume such as this, a quick summary of the main findings might provide some relief.

Before I do so, I would like to point out that in summarizing the literature, this book also exposed the existence of a few noticeable gaps in our knowledge. Some of those are minor, because they can be easily remedied: For instance, we have no data on age-related effects in the half-life of the auditory sensory store. It would take one study to rectify this oversight. Some lacunae are more vexing. For instance, although the hypothesis of an age-related decline in inhibitory functioning has been around for quite a while (e.g., Hasher & Zacks, 1988), there is still a relative dearth of studies concerned with age-related effects in the deletion or filtering aspect of inhibition. The same is true for the executive control process of updating the contents of working memory, which has largely gone unnoticed in theoretical accounts of cognitive aging (one counterexample is Verhaeghen, 2012), and has not yielded a literature large enough to warrant meta-analysis.

It is relatively easy to provide a summary of the data, numerous as they are: The main results are captured straightforwardly in the key figures and tables of this book—chief among them Figure 2.2 (dissociations in the quasirandom sample of studies); Table 4.2 (summarizing the Brinley slopes and intercepts for elementary tasks); Table 4.1 (reporting the parameters for the aging Model Human Processor); Table 6.1 (summarizing the results of the analyses of age-specific effects in cognitive control); Figure 7.15 (showing the lifespan trajectory of Brinley slopes); Table 9.3 (summarizing longitudinal correlations between speed and cognition); and Figure 9.4 (presenting the cascade model of age-related effects in cognition). The challenge is to lift the insights gained from these findings beyond the level of the mere equation or the illustrative graph.

The reader may have noticed that I tend to be reluctant about theory; that is, I tend to refrain from making grand pronouncements regarding the precise mechanisms behind each of the findings. One reason for my reticence is that I firmly believe that empirical data have a value of their own; imposing an interpretative framework prematurely might restrict our reading of the findings and/or stifle additional attempts at explanation. Another reason is that reviews of the present kind are by nature ill-suited to create theory or even to test it. They can still be useful, however, in constraining efforts at theory or explanation—the data summaries might rule out particular theories or suggest that some explanations fit the pattern of results better than others. Throughout this book I have often paused to point at theories that seem to fall short in explaining the data (e.g., a theory that would state that aging leads to a general deficit in executive control, or even just in inhibition; Section 6.7). I have also, once or twice, hinted at explanations that do seem to provide good fits to the phenomena at hand (e.g., how an oxygenation hypothesis might explain some of the observed age-related dissociations in elementary tasks; Section 5.2.6.2).

There are, however, some abstractions I feel can be taken away safely from this all too lengthy review. In the remainder of this chapter (and this book), I will highlight some of the substantive findings, grouped by theme: The reality of age-related slowing, its dimensionality, its evolution over the lifespan, its causes, its consequences, and its modifiability. I will also briefly reiterate a few methodological conclusions.

10.1. Is Age-related Slowing Truly Age-related Slowing, or Are There Alternative Explanations?

Conclusion 1: Age-related slowing is real. One important conclusion from this book is that age-related slowing is real (Chapter 3; Chapter 8); that is, older adults' slower response times reflect slower processing, and the slowdown is largely due to aging. Alternatives to this conclusion have been proposed, none of which, at least as investigated here, could explain all of the age-related variance. Some of those alternatives, however, do explain some of the variance. Conclusions 2 and 3 expand on this.

Conclusion 2: Some of the alternative explanations for age-related cognitive slowing carry little weight, at least as operationalized here. These include:

a. *Increased interindividual variability* or *differential sample heterogeneity*: Older-adult samples are no more variable than younger-adult samples once age-related slowing is taken into account (Section 3.2). Potential heterogeneity might have signaled that the samples of older adults examined in our studies include more individuals who are cognitively compromised.

b. *Nonlinear effects*, which might influence the estimation of dimensionality in Brinley plots: There is no evidence for nonlinearity in young-old plots (section 3.3).

c. *Measurement (un)reliability*, which would limit our ability to find dissociations by increasing extraneous measurement noise: Although there is direct evidence that the variability in Brinley slopes is indeed, and unsurprisingly, associated with study characteristics that influence reliability, this unreliability does not appear to bias the estimate of the mean of the age-related slowing factors (Section 3.4).

d. *Sampling characteristics*: Observable characteristics of the samples; that is, mean age and mean level of education do not appear to influence the estimate of Brinley slopes or intercepts (Section 3.5).

e. *Disuse,* that is, lack of recent and/or relevant practice in older adults compared with younger adults: Younger and older adults show identical learning rates as measured by the exponent in the power law of practice. This was true both when the full data set was considered and when the tasks most often investigated were analyzed separately (serial RT, choice RT, memory search, visual search, and implicit sequence learning) (Section 4.5).

Conclusion 3: Some of the alternative explanations for age-related cognitive slowing do account for some of the variance typically ascribed to aging:

a. Part of age-related slowing might be a result of *increased caution* associated with advancing age. There is some evidence that older adults give higher priority to accuracy over speed of responding than do younger adults. Evidence for this position comes from a decomposition of response times and accuracy into con-stituent parameters using the EZ diffusion model (Section 3.1.3). This analy-sis demonstrated that older adults set more conservative criteria than younger adults.

   This mechanism, however, cannot explain all of the age-related variance:

   • First, the EZ diffusion analysis also showed that older adults have slower drift rates as well as slower nondecision times, indicating the presence of "real" age-related slowing independent of the setting of a more conservative response criterion (Section 3.1.3).
   • Second, there is independent evidence that older adults do not simply set a higher criterion while being situated on the same speed-accuracy trade-off curve—the brunt of the evidence indicates (a) that speed-accuracy curves are less efficient in older adults than in younger adults (Section 3.1.1); and (b) that tasks that yield larger age-related slowing also yield larger age-related declines in accuracy, contrary to what would be expected from a straightforward speed-accuracy trade-off (Section 3.1.2).

b. Part of age-related slowing might be a due to *cohort, that is, generational differ-ences*: More recent generations perform at a higher speed than older generations (Section 8.1). Specifically, an analysis of data on perceptual speed suggests a rise of about 0.2 *SD*/decade. One implication would be that cross-sectional research underestimates the age of peak functioning; the other that cross-sectional research possibly overestimates the age-related decline (my best estimate is an overestima-tion in slowing factors by, on average, 8% to 25%; Section 8.1).

   Here, too, a few caveats must be raised:

• First, it isn't clear whether these generational effects only benefit the young, or whether these effects spread across individuals of all ages (or differentially across ages), in which case cross-sectional estimates of the lifespan might still be close to the truth (Section 5.3.1).
• Second, the impact of cohort effects seems to be larger for perceptual speed than for reaction time tasks, which show essentially no cohort effects (Section 8.1).
• Third, age differences in measures of processing speed as measured by Brinley slopes appear to be relatively stable over the thirty-odd years of recorded history (Section 8.3).

10.2. What Is the Dimensionality of Age-related Cognitive Slowing? Can different types of slowing be distinguished?

An important motivator for the analyses in this book was the question of the dimensionality of age-related slowing. How many distinct types or domains of slowing can be distinguished?

Conclusion 4: The hypothesis of general age-related slowing is roundly refuted. This finding was obtained in independent analyses of two separate data sets: A single-line model, although fitting very well (e.g., 83% of the within-study variance explained in a random sample of studies), simply does not do the data full justice (Section 2.2.2 and 5.1).

Conclusion 5: The hypothesis of a general age-related deficit in executive functioning or cognitive control is roundly refuted. The summary table of empirical results on age-related differences in executive control tasks (Table 6.1) clearly shows that very few age-related dissociations were found. Tasks of inhibition (whether unintentional inhibition, inhibition of access, or restraint) showed no specific age-related deficits; neither did task switching. In contrast, a specific age-related deficit was noted for tasks that require the maintenance of two or more task sets and/or the coordination of divided attention, namely task mixing and dual-task performance. There are, however, two reasons to think the ground is shakier here than for Conclusion 4:

a. Acceptance of this conclusion hinges on acceptance of the null hypothesis for quite a number of tasks—inhibition of return, negative priming, the Eriksen flanker task, reading with distractors, Stroop, the antisaccade task, task switching, and Trail Making. (The reader can make up her own mind as to whether such repeated lack of disconfirmation of the null hypothesis implies converging evidence for a null effect or an accumulation of mere chance events. I lean toward the former.)
b. Some of the effects of executive control might be more tangible in the accuracy domain than the response time domain (I showed this in the antisaccade effect, Section 6.3.3.2.2), and the accuracy domain went largely uninvestigated here.

Conclusion 6: A full description of age-related effects requires about the same dimensionality as the set of tasks included (Section 5.1). This conclusion is somewhat disheartening for theorists dreaming of strong explanations and clear phase transitions in aging effects. I also immediately need to qualify the statement: When zooming in on pairs of related tasks, I found that some failed to yield dissociations. Specifically, simple RT and choice RT (Section 4.4.2.1.1), subitizing and counting (Section 4.4.1.2), feature search, and conjunction search (Section 4.4.1.4) all yield identical age-related effects.

Conclusion 7: Conclusion 6 notwithstanding, age-related slowing effects can be meaningfully decomposed into a smaller number of effects than there are tasks—about three to six dimensions (Section 5.3)—with a small, but significant cost to fit. This is in concordance with the idea that age-related slowing can be captured in a limited number of major dissociations. The question how these dimensions should be interpreted, however, remains. Throughout Chapter 5, I described a few such models, concluding in Section 5.3 that each of these models (based on cluster analysis, anatomical plausibility, and the geometry of the Brinley plot, respectively) is viable, but still fails to provide a full picture of age-related slowing effects. I observed the following generalities, which may be useful to help build a consensus model (Section 5.3; Section 6.7):

a. *Spatial tasks yield larger age-related effects than linguistic tasks* and, more generally, tasks involving manipulations of linguistic information.

b. *Within spatial tasks, lower-level or "early" tasks, likely involving occipital structures* (such as flicker fusion threshold and feature visual search),*generally yield smaller age-related effects than more integrative, "later" spatial tasks, likely driven more by parietal structures* (such as subitizing, conjunction visual search, and mental rotation).

c. *Sensorimotor tasks yield small or no age-related effects but only when no decision component is involved; when a decision component is involved, a more moderate age-related slowing factor is observed* (flicker fusion threshold and tapping rate vs. movement time, simple RT, and choice RT).

d. *An additional age-related impairment arises when the task requires maintaining and coordinating multiple task sets in working memory. This impairment takes the form of an additive cost; that is, it is independent of the processes involved in the individual/single tasks.*

10.3. How Does Speed of Processing Develop and Decay Over the Lifespan?

Conclusion 8: Speed of processing follows a U-shaped trajectory over the lifespan. For the adult lifespan portion of the curve, the curve implies accelerated decline. When checkable, the dissociations and similarities observed in extreme group designs (Conclusion 7) appear to replicate in the adult lifespan curves (Section 7.2.4).

Conclusion 9: Age-related decline in speed of processing starts early. The minimum of the lifespan curve for processing speed is at age 23 (Section 7.2.5.3). The empirical function is quite peaked—the sometimes-assumed plateau of high functioning is absent. It is possible, however, that both the sharpness of the peak and its placement are exaggerated in cross-sectional research; statistically canceling out the Flynn effect (i.e., the effect that drives increased performance over successive generations) places the peak at age 28, with an effective plateau of high functioning until about age 40.

10.4. How Can Age-related Slowing Be Explained?

Conclusion 10: The likely underlying causes for the age-related decline in processing speed are multiple, and include:

a. *General mechanisms,* which would serve to slow or moderate the slowing of performance across a wide variety of tasks. Such mechanisms could be:

- The physiological mechanisms of:
  i. *Decreased dopamine receptor efficiency* (Section 7.1.2)
  ii. *Decreased connectivity* (Section 7.1.2)
- Possibly, the psychological mechanism of increased *cautiousness* (Section 3.1.3). It is important to note here that this mechanism is modulated by task domain—tasks that yield larger slowing also yield more conservative boundary settings, suggesting that caution may be a consequence of (i.e., a psychological reaction to) more fundamental changes rather than a cause.
  - The potentially buffering effect of *knowledge*, as seen in the preservation or near-preservation of linguistic functioning (Section 2.2.2; Section 7.2.4.1).
b. *Specific mechanisms* to explain the major dissociations observed around the general decline. For instance, in Section 5.2.4, I described what appear to be five region-specific slowing factors: little slowing in tasks associated with the brainstem; a slowing factor of about 1.2 for tasks associated with the temporal lobe; a slowing factor of about 1.3 for tasks associated with the frontal lobes; a slowing factor of about 1.5 for tasks associated with the occipital lobes; and a slowing factor of about 1.8 for tasks associated with the parietal lobes. These could be the result of region-specific changes in *vascularity* and the concomitant changes in oxygenation, changes in anatomical and/or functional *connectivity* between specific regions, or differential *path lengths* necessary for the performance of these tasks (Section 5.2.6.1; Section 5.2.6.2).

Figure 10.1 illustrates my thinking about these mechanisms and how they interact over the lifespan; the scheme is lacking in detail and likely to be proven wrong, but I hope it might provide some insight. In this schematic, a decline in a general efficiency mechanism (e.g., a steady age-related decline in the efficiency of the dopamine system) is combined with more specific mechanisms, which I suspect take the form of a set of late-peaking U-shaped curves, described by an initial developmental buildup (e.g., of functional connectivity as subserved by white-matter changes) followed by a downturn (e.g., by regional changes in functional connectivity as caused by changes in white matter structure and/or vascular efficiency); the task or domain-specificity lies in the regional variations around the average U-shaped curve. Combined, these two mechanisms lead to the lopsided U-shape of the general lifespan trajectory, which, in turn, in cross-section, yields the different observed Brinley functions. This schematic is not a theory, of course, but merely an empirical generalization based on, still, a small number of (read: too few) studies investigating these fundamental mechanisms.

10.5. Does the Decline in Processing Speed over the Adult Lifespan Have Consequences for Other Aspects of Cognition?

Conclusion 11: Age-related changes in diverse cognitive functions are intricately interrelated. I offer two converging pieces of evidence for this position.

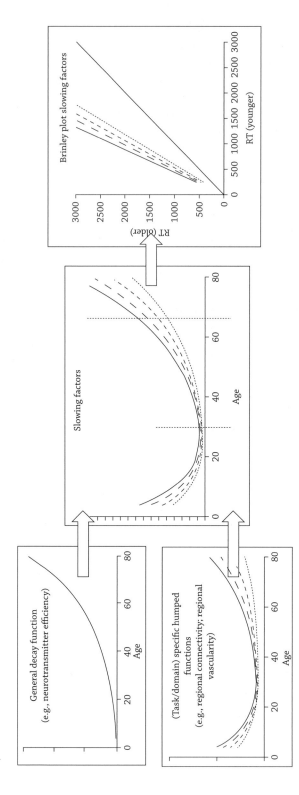

Figure 10.1 A broad-stroke framework to understand age-related slowing as the confluence of a general decay function and more task or domain-specific influences on functional connectivity; this confluence produces a set of lifespan functions, which lead to specific age-related slowing factors in a Brinley plot.

a. *Cross-sectional correlations*: All "fluid" cognitive variables (I examined speed, short-term memory, working memory, executive control, episodic memory, reasoning ability, and spatial ability) are positively and reliably correlated with one another and negatively correlated with age. A common-factor model in which age loaded on a single cognitive factor fits the correlation matrix much better than a model that presupposes that the age effects on all constructs are independent. This clearly indicates that there is shared age-related variance in the set of cognitive variables (Section 9.2.2.2).

b. *Longitudinal correlations*: Changes in speed are correlated with changes in higher-order cognition (a single change factor explains on average 43% of the variance; Section 9.3.2.3), and within-individual changes in speed are correlated with within-individual changes in higher-order cognition (explaining on average 16% of the within-subject age-related variance; Section 9.3.2.4).

Conclusion 12: Within the interwovenness of cognitive decline, speed of processing has privileged status.

a. In *cross-sectional studies*, mediational models with speed of processing as the driving variable fit the data quite well. Speed explains 78% of the age-related variance in the other aspects of cognition, more so than working memory, executive control, resistance to interference, or task shifting, which all explain 58% or less (Section 9.2.3.1).

b. *Longitudinally*, lead-lag analyses show that speed drives changes in higher-order cognition, but higher-order cognition has no such leading role for changes in speed (Section 9.3.2.5).

It is important to note that the leading and mediational roles of speed do not necessarily imply direct causation; that is, this does not necessarily mean that slowing of the clock speed of the mind (if there is such a thing) drives a decline in performance on episodic memory tasks, shrinks reasoning ability, and so on. Speed's role could very well be to serve as a biomarker or proxy, that is, the most sensitive and/or earliest indicator of a more general, low-level underlying age-related decline in intactness of the substrate. A third possibility is that processing speed measures are indicative of a deeper underlying set of basic abilities that are shared with the more complex tasks of higher-order cognition, such as focused attention, speed of evidence accumulation, or speed of decision-making processes (Section 9.11).

10.6. Can Age-related Slowing be Remediated or Reversed?

For those of us who are aging (which will be almost all of us—see Conclusion 9), one possibly pressing question concerns if and how age-related declines in cognitive speed can be remediated. I have somewhat underplayed this question throughout the book, but the following conclusion can be drawn:

Conclusion 13: Speed of processing can be improved, even in old age. There are at least two ways to increase speed of processing:

a. First, performance can be improved with *repeated exposure to the task* (Section 4.5). There are, however, two clear limitations to be noted here. The first is that learning rates of older adults as measured by the exponent in the power law of practice are identical to those of younger adults (Section 4.5.2; Section 4.5.3). This suggests that the effect is not one of remediation or reversal of age-related slowing, but simply one of increased efficiency of the processes involved in the particular task and/or the assemblage of these processes in the service of the task. The second limitation is that there is no indication whatsoever that the effects of repeated practice generalize beyond the task at hand (Section 4.5.4).

b. Second, performance can be improved with *aerobic fitness training* (see Hertzog et al., 2009, for an overview). The effects of fitness training appear to be rather large; they spread throughout the cognitive system. These effects are already visible after relatively short training regimens (3 months or even shorter), but they are restricted to aerobic fitness training—strength or flexibility training do not yield the same benefits.

10.7. What are the Implications of the Findings for Research Praxis?

At least two important methodological lessons can be drawn from the analyses contained in this book. The first is not new, but it bears repeating.

Conclusion 14: The use of raw, untransformed latencies as input for ANOVA or the use of difference scores to investigate differential age-specificity of tasks or processes is almost never warranted. The reason is that the relationship between younger and older adults' response times within many (if not most) tasks or task domains is better described by a multiplicative function ($RT_{older} = a\ RT_{younger}$) than an additive function ($RT_{older} = a + RT_{younger}$) (e.g., Section 2.2.2; Table 4.2; Table 6.1). The multiplicative function implies that age differences will grow larger as time needed for the task increases, which typically means that age differences grow with task complexity, and an ANOVA will then often flag an interaction—a false positive.

There are at least three solutions to this problem:

a. The first solution is suboptimal, and it entails a *logarithmic transformation* of the data; this transformation makes the relationship additive (Section 2.2.3). This solution works perfectly when the young-old relationship is multiplicative (e.g., inhibition of return); it works well when the relationship is near-multiplicative (e.g., antisaccade); but it falls short when the relationship has a large negative intercept, in which case it is likely to yield false positives (e.g., Stroop, task switching, Trail Making) (Section 6.7).

b. A more optimal solution is to include as *many conditions* in the experiment as feasible, so that the actual young-old relationship can be determined and a priori contrasts between tasks can be evaluated. This probably works best with iterative tasks (Section 4.4.1; Section 4.6).

c. A third solution is to take advantage of the method of *state traces* (Section 1.3.3). One could—as I have done throughout this book—regress the critical condition on the baseline condition (now with the subject as the unit of analysis), adding a term for age and the interaction between age and baseline time to test for the additive and multiplicative effects of age. One more model-agnostic variant of this method (Zhang, Han, Verhaeghen, & Nillson, 2007; see also Cronbach & Furby, 1970, and Embretson, 1987) encompasses regressing the critical condition onto the baseline condition (again with the subject as the unit of analysis), and then subjecting the residuals to a test for the main effect of age. The latter test evaluates whether or not older adults' response times are larger than expected on the basis of the baseline condition.

Conclusion 15: The age-related slowing factor in sensorimotor processes is large enough to warrant including a sensorimotor control condition in experimental studies relying on measurement of relatively fast latencies. There are two bodies of evidence for the importance of sensorimotor processes. The first is the slowing factor associated with these tasks, around 1.4 to 1.5 (Section 2.2.2; Section 2.2.3; Section 5.2.1). The second is the significant age effect in nondecision times as obtained from the EZ diffusion model (a slowing factor of 1.3; Section 3.1.3). These nondecision times (i.e., sensorimotor processes) make up the brunt of the response times in the relatively fast tasks considered here (on average, two thirds of the total latency). Thus, slowing in sensorimotor tasks may play a larger role in cognitive experiments than usually assumed. The inclusion of sensorimotor control conditions in aging studies is necessary to ascertain that the deficits obtained (if any) are due to the cognitive components of the task rather than to sensorimotor and simple response decision processes.

10.9. Final Words: Aging and the Need for Middle-way Theories

One clear theory-related conclusion of the present review—a conclusion that is not exactly breaking news—is that single-parameter models of aging (e.g., Hasher & Zacks, 1988; Li et al., 2001; Salthouse, 1996;, Park, Polk, Mikels, Taylor, & Marshuetz, 2001, for an attempt at a unifying multifactor approach). Given that the age-related dissociations are relatively large-scale and few, my hope is that their number is finite enough to make a unifying approach viable. I attempted one here (Section 7.2.5.2; Conclusion 11/12), a model based on a particular configuration of general factors, modulated by more local mechanisms; see Figure 10.1.

My final lament is that there is a clear shortage of and lack of interest in these types of theories, that is, models that are situated at a middle level of abstraction. Perhaps all of us are captured by the karma of our methodological biases: Experimentalists and neuroimagers are trained to favor local approaches; they then prefer precise explanations for relatively minute phenomena; individual-differences psychologists have a keen eye for commonalities and are easily seduced by the positive manifold of age-related changes.

The field, I would argue, needs middle-way theories, a level of explanation that is one floor up from the hustle and bustle of local explanations and one floor down from the "it-all-goes-together-when-it-goes." This, after all, is the level older adults themselves ultimately care most about: What broad changes can be expected with advancing age, and how can they be explained? I hope this book has provided one step in the direction of a fuller description, as well as one step toward a fuller understanding.

REFERENCES

Note: Studies preceded by a "*" symbol are included in the quasirandom sample of studies examined in Chapter 2; studies preceded by a "#" symbol are included in the correlation matrix built in Chapter 9.

Aartsen, M. J., Smiths, C. H. M., van Tilburg, T., Knopscheer, K. C. P. M., & Deeg, D. J. H. (2002). Activity in older adults: Cause or consequence of cognitive functioning? A longitudinal study on everyday activities and cognitive performance in older adults. *Journals of Gerontology: Psychological Sciences*, 75, 153–162.

Abel, L. A., & Douglas, J. (2007). Effects of age on latency and error generation in internally mediated saccades. *Neurobiology of Aging*, 28, 627–637.

Abrams, R. A., Pratt, J., & Chasteen, A. L. (1998). Aging and movement: Variability of force pulses for saccadic eye movements. *Psychology and Aging*, 13, 387–395.

Ackerman, P. L., Beier, M. E., & Boyle, M. O. (2002). Individual differences in working memory within a nomological network of cognitive and perceptual speed abilities. *Journal of Experimental Psychology: General*, 131, 567–589.

Ackerman, P. L., Beier, M. E., & Boyle, M. O. (2005). Working memory and intelligence: The same or different constructs? *Psychological Bulletin*, 131, 30–60.

#Aftanas, M. S., & Royce, J. R. (1969). Analysis of brain damage tests administered to normal subjects with factor score comparisons across age. *Multivariate Behavioral Research*, 4, 459–481.

Aine, C. J., Adair, J. C., Knoefel, J. E., Hudson, D., Qualls, C., Kovacevic, S., . . . Stephen, J. M. (2005). Temporal dynamics of age-related differences in auditory incidental verbal learning. *Cognitive Brain Research*, 24, 1–18.

Akiyama, H., Meyer, J. S., Mortel, K. F., Terayama, Y., Thornby, J. I., & Konno, S. (1997). Normal human aging: Factors contributing to cerebral atrophy. *Journal of the Neurological Sciences*, 152, 39–49.

Alain, C., & Woods, D. L. (1999). Age-related changes in processing auditory stimuli during visual attention: Evidence for deficits in inhibitory control and sensory memory. *Psychology and Aging*, 14, 507–519.

Albert, M. S., & Heaton, R. K. (1988). Intelligence testing. In M.S. Albert, & M.B. Moss (Eds), *Geriatric neuropsychology* (pp. 10–32). New York, NY: Guilford.

#Albert, M. S., Heller, H. S., & Milberg, W. (1988). Change in naming ability with age. *Psychology and Aging*, 3, 173–178.

Allen, P. A., Madden, D. J., & Crozier, L. C. (1991). Adult age differences in letter-level and word-level processing. *Psychology and Aging*, 6, 261–271.

Allen, P. A., Madden, D. J., Weber, T. A., & Groth, K. E. (1993). Influence of age and processing stage on visual word recognition. *Psychology and Aging*, 8, 274–282.

*Allen, P. A., Mei-Ching, L., Murphy, M. D., Sanders, R. E., Judge, K. S., & McCann, R. S. (2002). Age differences in overlapping-task performance: Evidence for efficient parallel processing in older adults. *Psychology and Aging*, 17, 505–519.

*Allen, P. A., Murphy, M. D., Kaufman, M., Groth, K. E., & Begovic, A. (2004). Age differences in central (semantic) and peripheral processing: The importance of considering both response times and errors. *Journals of Gerontology: Psychological Sciences*, 59, 210–219.

Allen, P. A., Sliwinski, M., Bowie, T., & Madden, D. J. (2002). Differential age effects in semantic and episodic memory. *Journals of Gerontology: Psychological Sciences*, 57, 173–186.

*Allen, P. A., Smith, A. F., Groth, K. E., Pickle, J. L., Grabbe, J. W., & Madden, D. J. (2002). Differential age effects for case and hue mixing in visual word recognition. *Psychology and Aging*, 17, 622–635.

*Allen, P. A., Smith, A. F., Jerge, K. A., & Vires-Collins, H. (1997). Age differences in mental multiplication: Evidence for peripheral but not central decrements. *Journals of Gerontology: Psychological Sciences*, 52, 81–90.

*Allen, P. A., Smith, A. F., Vires-Collins, H., & Sperry, S. (1998). The psychological refractory period: Evidence for age differences in attentional time-sharing. *Psychology and Aging*, 13, 218–229.

*Allen, P. A., Stadtlander, L. M., Groth, K. E., Pickle, J. L., & Madden, D. J. (2000). Adult age invariance in sentence utilization. *Aging, Neuropsychology, and Cognition*, 7, 54–67.

Allport, A., Styles, E., & Hsieh, S. (1994). Shifting intentional set: Exploring the dynamic control of tasks. In C. Umiltà & M. Moscovitch (Eds.), *Attention and performance XV: Conscious and nonconscious information processing* (pp. 421–452). Cambridge, MA: MIT Press, Bradford Books.

Allport, D. A., & Wylie, G. (1999). Task-switching: Positive and negative priming of task-set. In G. W. Humphreys, J. Duncan, & A. M. Treisman (Eds.), *Attention, space and action: Studies in cognitive neuroscience* (pp. 273–296). Oxford, UK: Oxford University Press.

*Anandam, B. T., & Scialfa, C. T. (1999). Aging and the development of automaticity in feature search. *Aging, Neuropsychology, and Cognition*, 6, 117–140.

Anderson, J. R. (1983). *The architecture of cognition*. Cambridge, MA: Harvard University Press.

Anderson, M., & Reid, C. (2005). Intelligence. In M. Hewstone, F. D. Fincham, & J. Foster (Eds.), *Psychology* (pp. 268–290). Oxford, UK: Blackwell.

*Anderson, N. D. (1999). The attentional demands of encoding and retrieval in younger and older adults: 2. evidence from secondary task reaction time distributions. *Psychology and Aging*, 14, 645–655.

Anderson, N. D., Iidaka, T., Cabeza, R., Kapur, S., McIntosh, A. R., & Craik, F. I. M. (2000). The effect of divided attention on encoding and retrieval-related brain activity: A PET study of younger and older adults. *Journal of Cognitive Neuroscience*, 12, 775–792.

Anderson, N. D., Sekuler, A. B., & Middlebrook, J. (1994, April). *Age related differences in an identity negative priming task*. Paper presented at the Cognitive Aging Conference, Atlanta, GA.

Andrés, P., Guerrini, C., Phillips, L. H., & Perfect, T. J. (2008). Differential effects of aging on executive and automatic inhibition. *Developmental Neuropsychology*, 33, 101–123.

Anstey, K. J. (2008). Biomarkers and cognitive ageing: What do we know and where to from here? In S. M. Hofer & D. Alwin (Eds.), *Handbook of cognitive aging* (pp. 327–339). Thousand Oaks, CA: Sage.

Anstey, K. J., Dear, K., Christensen, H., & Jorm, A. F. (2005). Biomarkers, health, lifestyle, and demographic variables as correlates of reaction time performance in early, middle, and late adulthood. *The Quarterly Journal of Experimental Psychology*, 58A, 5–21.

Anstey, K. J., & Smith, G. A. (1999). Interrelationships among biological markers of aging, health, activity, acculturation, and cognitive performance in late adulthood. *Psychology and Aging*, 14, 605–618.

Arbuthnott, K., & Frank, J. (2000). Trail making test, part B as a measure of executive control: Validation using a set-switching paradigm. *Journal of Clinical and Experimental Neuropsychology*, 22, 518–528.

#Arenberg, D. (1988). Analysis and synthesis in problem solving and aging. In M. L. Howe & C. J. Brainerd (Eds.), *Cognitive development in adulthood* (pp. 161–183). New York, NY: Springer-Verlag.

*Atchley, P., & Kramer, A. F. (1998). Spatial cuing in a stereoscopic display: Attention remains "depth-aware" with age. *Journals of Gerontology: Psychological Sciences*, 53, 318–323.

*Atchley, P., & Kramer, A. F. (2000). Age related changes in the control of attention in depth. *Psychology and Aging*, 15, 78–87.

Atkinson, R. C., & Shiffrin, R. M. (1968). Human memory: A proposed system and its control processes. In K. W. Spence & J. T. Spence (Eds.) *The psychology of learning and motivation: Advances in research and theory,Vol. 2* (pp. 89–195). New York, NY: Academic.

Bäckman, L., Ginovart, N., Dixon, R. A., Wahlin, T. B. R., Halldin, C., & Farde, L. (2000). Age-related cognitive deficits mediated by changes in the striatal dopamine system. *American Journal of Psychiatry*, 157, 635–637.

Baddeley, A. (1996). The fractionation of working memory. *Proceedings of the National Academy of Sciences*, 93, 13468–13472.

Baddeley, A.D., & Della Sala, S. (1996). Working memory and executive control. *Proceedings of the Royal Society, B*, 351, 1397–1484.

Baddeley, A., Logie, R., Bressi, S., Della Sala, S., & Spinnler, H. (1986). Dementia and working memory. *The Quarterly Journal of Experimental Psychology*, 38A, 603–618.

Bahramali, H. (1999). The effects of age on late components of the ERP and reaction time. *Experimental Aging Research*, 25, 69–80.

Baker, A. B., & Tang, Y. Q. (2010). Aging performance for masters records in athletics, swimming, rowing, cycling, triathlon, and weightlifting. *Experimental Aging Research*, 36, 453–477.

Baker, A. B., Tang, Y. Q., & Turner, M. J. (2003). Percentage decline in masters superathlete track and field performance with aging. *Experimental Aging Research*, 29, 47–65.

Ball, K., Berch, D. B., Helmers, K. F., Jobe, J. B., Leveck, M. D., Marsiske, M.,...Willis, S. L. (2002). Effects of cognitive training interventions with older adults. *JAMA: the Journal of the American Medical Association*, 288, 2271–2281.

Balota, D. A., & Chumbley, J. I. (1984). Are lexical decisions a good measure of lexical access? The role of word frequency in the neglected decision stage. *Journal of Experimental Psychology: Human perception and performance*, 10, 340.

Balota, D. A., & Ferraro, F. R. (1996). Lexical, sublexical, and implicit memory processes in healthy young, healthy older adults, and in individuals with dementia of the Alzheimer's type. *Neuropsychology*, 10, 82–95.

Balota, D. A., & Spieler, D. H. (1999). Word frequency, repetition, and lexicality effects in word recognition tasks: Beyond measures of central tendency. *Journal of Experimental Psychology: General*, 128, 32–55.

Baltes, P. B. (1968). Longitudinal and cross-sectional sequences in the study of age and generation effects. *Human Development*, 11, 145–171.

Baltes, P. B., Dittmann-Kohli, F., & Dixon, R. A. (1984). New perspectives on the development of intelligence in adulthood: Toward a dual-process conception and a model of selective optimization with compensation. *Life-span Development and Behavior*, 6, 33–76.

#Baltes, P. B., & Lindenberger, U. (1997). Emergence of a powerful connection between sensory and cognitive functions across the adult life span: A new window to the study of cognitive aging? *Psychology and Aging*, 12, 12–21.

Bamber, D. (1979). State-trace analysis: A method of testing simple theories of causation. *Journal of Mathematical Psychology*, 19, 137–181.

Band, G. P., & Kok, A. (2000). Age effects on response monitoring in a mental-rotation task. *Biological Psychology*, 51, 201–221.

Bao, Y., Zhou, J., & Fu, L. (2004). Aging and the time course of inhibition of return in a static environment. *Acta Neurobiologiae Experimentalis*, 64, 403–414.

Baron, A., & Cerella, J. (1993). Laboratory tests of the disuse account of cognitive decline. In J. Cerella, W. Hoyer, J Rybash, & M. Commons (Eds.), *Adult information processing: Limits on loss* (pp. 175–203). San Diego, CA: Academic Press.

Baron, A., & Mattila, W. R. (1989). Response slowing of older adults: Effects of time-limit contingencies on single-and dual-task performances. *Psychology and Aging*, 4, 66–72.

#Barr, R. A., & Giambra, L. M. (1990). Age-related decrement in auditory selective attention. *Psychology and Aging*, 5, 597–599.

#Barrett, G. V., Mihal, W. L., Panek, P. E., Stems, H. L., & Alexander, R.A. (1977). Information processing skills predictive of accident involvement for younger and older commercial drivers. *Industrial Gerontology*, 4, 173–182.

Barrouillet, P., & Camos, V. (2007). The time-based resource-sharing model of working memory. In N. Osaka, R. Logie, & M. D'Esposito (Eds.), *The cognitive neuroscience of working memory* (pp. 59–80). Oxford, UK: Oxford University Press.

*Basak, C., & Verhaeghen, P. (2003). Subitizing speed, subitizing range, counting speed, the Stroop effect, and aging: Capacity differences and speed equivalence. *Psychology and Aging*, 18, 240–249.

Bashore, T. R., Heffley, E. E., & Donchin, E. (1989). [Age effects on stimulus and response processing]. *Unpublished raw data.*

Bashore, T. R., Martinerie, J. M., Weiser, P. C., Greenspon, L. C., & Heffley, E. F. (1988). Preservation of mental processing speed in aerobically fit older men. *Psychophysiology*, 25, 433–434.

Bashore, T. R., Osman, A., & Heffley, E. F. (1989). Mental slowing in elderly persons: A cognitive psychophysiological analysis. *Psychology and Aging*, 4, 235–244.

*Batsakes, P. J., & Fisk, A. D. (2000). Age-related differences in dual-task visual search: Are performance gains retained? *Journals of Gerontology: Psychological Sciences*, 55, 332–342.

Bedard, A. C., Nichols, S., Barbosa, J. A., Schachar, R., Logan, G. D., & Tannock, R. (2002). The development of selective inhibitory control across the life span. *Developmental Neuropsychology*, 21, 93–111.

Bendlin, B. B., Fitzgerald, M. E., Ries, M. L., Xu, G., Kastman, E. K., Thiel, B. W., . . . Johnson, S. C. (2010). White matter in aging and cognition: A cross-sectional study of microstructure in adults aged eighteen to eighty-three. *Developmental neuropsychology*, 35, 257–277.

Bennett, D. J., & McEvoy, C. L. (1999). Mediated priming in younger and older adults. *Experimental Aging Research*, 25, 141–159.

Berardi, A. M., Parasuraman, R., & Haxby, J. V. (2001). Overall vigilance and sustained attention decrements in healthy aging. *Experimental Aging Research*, 27(1), 19–39.

Berardi, A. M., Parasuraman, R., & Haxby, J. V. (2005). Sustained attention in mild Alzheimer's disease. *Developmental Neuropsychology*, 28, 507–537.

Berg, C., Hertzog, C., & Hunt, E. (1982). Age differences in the speed of mental rotation. *Developmental Psychology*, 18, 95.

Berthelot, G., Len, S., Hellard, P., Tafflet, M., Guillaume, M., Vollmer, J. C., . . . Toussaint, J. F. (2011). Exponential growth combined with exponential decline explains lifetime performance evolution in individual and human species. *Age*, 34, 1001–1009.

*Bherer, L., & Belleville, S. (2004). Age-related differences in response preparation: The role of time uncertainty. *Journals of Gerontology: Psychological Sciences*, 59, 66–74.

*Bherer, L., & Belleville, S. (2004). The effect of training on preparatory attention in older adults: Evidence for the role of uncertainty in age-related preparatory deficits. *Aging, Neuropsychology, and Cognition*, 11, 37–50.

Bherer, L., Kramer, A. F., Peterson, M., Colcombe, S. J., Erickson, K. I., & Becic, E. (2005). Training effects on dual-task performance: Are there age-related differences in plasticity of attentional control? *Psychology and Aging*, 20, 695–709.

Bialystok, E., Craik, F.I.M., & Ryan, J. (2006) Executive control in a modified anti-saccade task: Effects of aging and bilingualism. *Journal of Experimental Psychology: Learning, Memory, and Cognition*, 32, 1341–1354.

Bielak, A. A., Hultsch, D. F., Strauss, E., MacDonald, S. W., & Hunter, M. A. (2010). Intraindividual variability is related to cognitive change in older adults: Evidence for within-person coupling. *Psychology and Aging*, 25, 575–586.

Birren, J. E. (1960). Psychological aspects of aging. *Annual Review of Psychology*, 11, 161–198.

Birren, J. E., Allen, W. R.,& Landau, H. G. (1954). The relation of problem length in simple addition to time required, probability of success, and age. *Journal of Gerontology*, 9, 150–161.

#Birren, J. E., & Morrison, D. E (1961). Analysis of the WAIS subtests in relation to age and education. *Journal of Gerontology*, 16, 363–369.

Blazer, D. G., Hays, J. C., Fillenbaum, G. G., & Gold, D. T. (1997). Memory complaint as a predictor of cognitive decline. *Journal of Aging and Health*, 9, 171–184.

Bodwell, J. A., Mahurin, R. K., Waddle, S., Price, R., & Cramer, S. C. (2003). Age and features of movement influence motor overflow. *Journal of the American Geriatric Society*, 51, 1735–1739.

*Bojko, A., Kramer, A. F., & Peterson, M. S. (2004). Age equivalence in switch costs for prosaccade and antisaccade tasks. *Psychology and Aging*, 19, 226–234.

Bollen, K.A. (1989). *Structural equations with latent variables*. New York, NY: Wiley.

Bonnesen, J. L., & Burgess, E. O. (2004). Senior moments: The acceptability of an ageist phrase. *Journal of Aging Studies*, 18, 123–142.

Bono, F., Oliveri, R. L., Zappia, M., Aguglia U., Puccio, G., & Quattrone, A. (1996). Computerized analysis of eye movements as a function of age. *Archives in Gerontology and Geriatrics*, 22, 261–269.

Bopp, K. L., & Verhaeghen, P. (2005). Aging and verbal memory span: A meta-analysis. *Journals of Gerontology: Psychological Sciences*, 60, 223–233.

Bopp, K. L., & Verhaeghen, P. (2007). Age-related differences in control processes in verbal and visuospatial working memory: Storage, transformation, supervision, and coordination. *Journals of Gerontology: Psychological Sciences*, 62, 239–246.

Borella, E., Carretti, B., & De Beni, R. (2008). Working memory and inhibition across the adult life-span. *Acta Psychologica*, 128, 33–44.

Bornstein, R. A. (1985). Normative data on selected neuropsychological measures from a nonclinical sample. *Journal of Clinical Psychology*, 42, 651–659.

#Bors, D.A., & Forrin, B. (1995). Age, speed of information processing, recall, and fluid intelligence. *Intelligence*, 20, 229–248.

Botwinick, J. (1978). *Aging and behavior* (2nd ed.). New York, NY: Springer-Verlag.

Botwinick, J., & Brinley, J. F. (1963). Age differences in relations between CFF and apparent motion. *Journal of Genetic Psychology*, 102, 189–194.

#Botwinick, J., & Storandt, M. (1974). *Memory, related functions and age*. Springfield, IL: Charles Thomas.

Botwinick, J., & Thompson, L.W. (1967) Practice of speeded response in relation to age, sex, and set. *Journal of Gerontology*, 22, 72–76.

Bowles, N. L., & Poon, L. W. (1981). The effect of age on speed of lexical access. *Experimental Aging Research*, 7, 417–425.

Bowles, N. L., & Poon, L. W. (1985). Aging and retrieval of words in semantic memory. *Journal of Gerontology*, 40, 71–77.

Braver, T. S. & West, R. L. (2008). Working memory, executive processes, and aging. In F.I. Craik & T.L. Salthouse (Eds.), *Handbook of aging and cognition* (3rd ed., pp. 311–372). New York, NY: Erlbaum.

Brébion, G. (2001). Language processing, slowing, and speed=accuracy trade-off in the elderly. *Experimental Aging Research*, 27, 137–150.

*Brébion, G., Smith, M. J., & Ehrlich, M. (1997). Working memory and aging: Deficit or strategy differences. *Aging, Neuropsychology, and Cognition*, 4, 58–73.

Brickman, A. M., Zimmerman, M. E., Paul, R. H., Grieve, S. M., Tate, D. F., Cohen, R. A.,...Gordon, E. (2006). Regional white matter and neuropsychological functioning across the adult lifespan. *Biological Psychiatry*, 60, 444–453.

#Briggs, S.D., Raz, N., & Marks, W. (1999). Age-related deficits in generation and manipulation of mental images: I. The role of sensorimotor speed and working memory. *Psychology and Aging*, 14, 427–435.

*Brink, J. M., & McDowd, J. M. (1999). Aging and selective attention: An issue of complexity or multiple mechanisms? *Journals of Gerontology: Psychological Sciences*, 54, 30–33.

Brinley, J. F. (1965). Cognitive sets, speed and accuracy of performance in the elderly. In A. T. Welford & J. E. Birren (Eds.), *Behavior, aging and the nervous system* (pp. 114–149). Springfield, IL: Thomas.

Broadbent, D. E., & Heron, A. (1962). Effects of a subsidiary task on performance involving immediate memory by younger and older men. *British Journal of Psychology*, 53, 189–198.

#Bromley, D. B. (1991). Aspects of written language production over adult life. *Psychology and Aging*, 6, 296–308.

Brown, J. (1958). Some tests of the decay theory of immediate memory. *Quarterly Journal of Experimental Psychology*, 10, 12–21.

Buchler, N. G., Hoyer, W. J., & Cerella, J. (2008). Rules and more rules: The effects of multiple tasks, extensive training, and aging on task-switching performance. *Memory & Cognition*, 36, 735–748.

Buddha (ND). *Jara Sutta* (SN 4.6). Available at: http://www.accesstoinsight.org/tipitaka/kn/snp/snp.4.06.than.html

#Bugg, J. M., DeLosh, E. L., Davalos, D. B., & Davis, H. P. (2007). Age differences in Stroop interference: Contributions of general slowing and task-specific deficits. *Aging, Neuropsychology, and Cognition*, 14, 155–167.

#Bugg, J. M., Zook, N. A., DeLosh, E. L., Davalos, D. B., & Davis, H. P. (2006). Age differences in fluid intelligence: Contributions of general slowing and frontal decline. *Brain and Cognition*, 62, 9–16.

Bunce, D. (2001). The locus of age× health-related physical fitness interactions in serial choice responding as a function of task complexity: Central processing or motor function? *Experimental Aging Research*, 27, 103–122.

#Bunce, D. J., Barrowclough, A., & Morris, I. (1996). The moderating influence of physical fitness on age gradients in vigilance and serial choice responding tasks. *Psychology and Aging*, 11, 671–682.

#Bunce, D. J., Warr, P. B., & Cochrane, T. (1993). Blocks in choice responding as a function of age and physical fitness. *Psychology and Aging*, 8, 26–33.

Burgess, P. W., & Shallice, T. (1997). *The Hayling and Brixton tests*. Oxford, UK: Harcourt Assessment.

#Burke, H. R. (1972). Raven's Progressive Matrices: Validity, reliability, and norms. *Journal of Psychology*, 82, 253–257.

Burton-Danner, K., Owsley, C., & Jackson, G. R. (2001). Aging and feature search: The effect of search area. *Experimental Aging Research*, 27, 1–18.

Butler, K. M., & Zacks, R. T. (2006). Age deficits in the control of prepotent responses: Evidence for an inhibitory decline. *Psychology and Aging*, 21, 638–643.

Butler, K. M., Zacks, R. T., & Henderson, J. M. (1999). Suppression of reflexive saccades in younger and older adults: Age comparisons on an antisaccade task. *Memory & Cognition*, 27, 584–591.

Campbell, D. T., & Stanley, J. C. (1963). *Experimental and quasi-experimental designs for generalized causal inference*. Boston, MA: Houghton Mifflin.

Card, S. K., Moran, T. P., & Newell, A. (1983). *The psychology of human–computer interaction*. Hillsdale, NJ: Erlbaum.

Carlson, M. C., Hasher, L., Connelly, S. L., & Zacks, R. T. (1995). Aging, distraction, and the benefits of predictable location. *Psychology and Aging*, 10, 427–436.

Carmelli, D., Swan, G. E., LaRue, A., & Eslinger, P. J. (1997). Correlates of change in cognitive function in survivors from the Western Collaborative Group Study. *Neuroepidemiology*, 16, 285–295.

Carroll, J.B. (1993). *Human cognitive abilities: A survey of factor-analytic studies*. Cambridge, UK: Cambridge University Press.

Carroll, L. (1865). *Alice's adventures in Wonderland*. London: MacMillan.

Carstensen, L.L. (2011). *A long bright future: Happiness, health and financial security in an age of increased longevity*. New York, NY: Public Affairs.

*Cassavaugh, N. D., Kramer, A. F., & Irwin, D. E. (2003). Influence of task-irrelevant onset distractors on the visual search performance of young and old adults. *Aging, Neuropsychology, and Cognition*, 10, 44–60.

Cassavaugh, N. D., Kramer, A. F., & Peterson, M. S. (2004). Aging and the strategic control of the fixation offset effect. *Psychology and Aging*, 19, 357–361.

*Castel, A. D., Chasteen, A. L., Scialfa, C. T., & Pratt, J. (2003). Adult age differences in the time course of inhibition of return. *Journals of Gerontology: Psychological Sciences*, 58, 256–259.

Caza, N., & Moscovitch, M. (2005). Effects of cumulative frequency, but not of frequency trajectory, in lexical decision times of older adults and patients with Alzheimer's disease. *Journal of Memory and Language*, 53, 456–471.

Cepeda, N. J., Kramer, A. F., & Gonzalez de Sather, J. C. M. (2001). Changes in executive control across the lifespan: Examination of task-switching performance. *Developmental Psychology*, 37, 715–730.

Cerella, J. (1985). Information processing rates in the elderly. *Psychological Bulletin*, 98, 67–83.

Cerella, J. (1990). Aging and information processing rate. In J. E. Birren & K. W. Schaie (Eds.), *Handbook of the psychology of aging* (3rd ed., pp. 201–221). San Diego, CA: Academic Press.

Cerella, J. (1994). Generalized slowing in Brinley plots. *Journal of Gerontology: Psychological Sciences*, 49, 65–71.

Cerella, J., DiCara, R., Williams, D., & Bowles, N. (1986). Relations between information processing and intelligence in elderly adults. *Intelligence*, 10, 75–91.

Cerella, J., & Fozard, J. L. (1984). Lexical access and age. *Developmental Psychology*, 20, 235–243.

Cerella, J., & Hale, S. (1994). The rise and fall in information-processing rates over the life span. *Acta Psychologica*, 86, 109–197.

Cerella, J., Poon, L. W., & Fozard, J. L. (1981). Mental rotation and age reconsidered. *Journal of Gerontology*, 36, 620–624.

Cerella, J., Poon, L. W., & Williams, D. H. (1980). Age and the complexity hypothesis. In L. W. Poon (Ed.), *Aging in the 1980s* (pp. 332–340). Washington, DC: American Psychological Association.

Chaparro, A., Bohan, M., Fernandez, J., Choi, S. D., & Kattel, B. (1999). The impact of age on computer input device use: Psychophysical and physiological measures. *International Journal of Industrial Ergonomics*, 24, 503–513.

*Charlot, V., & Feyereisen, P. (2004). Aging and the deletion function of inhibition. *Aging, Neuropsychology, and Cognition*, 11, 12–24.

Charlton, R. A., Barrick, T. R., McIntyre, D. J., Shen, Y., O'Sullivan, M., Howe, F. A., . . . Markus, H. S. (2006). White matter damage on diffusion tensor imaging correlates with age-related cognitive decline. *Neurology*, 66, 217–222.

#Charness, N. (1987). Component processes in bridge bidding and novel problem-solving tasks. *Canadian Journal of Psychology*, 41, 223–243.

Charness, N., and Bosman, E. A. (1990). Expertise and aging: Life in the lab. In T.M. Hess (Ed.), *Aging and cognition: Knowledge organization and utilization* (pp. 343–385). Amsterdam, Netherlands: Elsevier.

Charness, N., & Campbell, J. I. (1988). Acquiring skill at mental calculation in adulthood: A task decomposition. *Journal of Experimental Psychology: General*, 117, 115.

Chee, M. W. L., Chen, K. H. M., Zheng, H., Chan, K. P. L., Isaac, V., Sim, S. K. Y., . . . Pin Ng, T. (2009). Cognitive function and brain structure correlations in healthy elderly East Asians. *NeuroImage*, 46, 257–269.

Chen, H., Schultz, A. B., Ashton-Miller, J. A., Giordani, B., Alexander, N. B., & Guire, K. E. (1996). Stepping over obstacles: Dividing attention impairs performance of old more than young adults. *Journals of Gerontology: Medical Sciences*, 51, 116–122.

Chen, J., Hale, S., & Myerson, J. (2007). Predicting the size of individual and group differences on speeded tasks. *Psychonomic Bulletin & Review*, 14, 534–541.

Chen, J. J., Rosas, H. D., & Salat, D. H. (2011). Age-associated reductions in cerebral blood flow are independent from regional atrophy. *NeuroImage*, 55, 468–478.

Chen, K. H. M., Chuah, L. Y. M., Sim, S. K. Y., & Chee, M. W. L. (2010). Hippocampal region-specific contributions to memory performance in normal elderly. *Brain and Cognition*, 72, 400–407.

#Chen, T., & Li, D. (2007). The roles of working memory updating and processing speed in mediating age-related differences in fluid intelligence. *Aging, Neuropsychology, and Cognition*, 14, 631–646.

#Chown, S. M. (1961). Age and the rigidities. *Journal of Gerontology*, 16, 353–362.

Christensen, H., Korten, A. E., Mackinnon, A. J., Jorm, A. F., Henderson, A. S., & Rodgers, B. (2000). Are changes in sensory disability, reaction time, and grip strength associated with changes in memory and crystallized intelligence? A longitudinal analysis in an elderly community sample. *Gerontology*, 46, 276.

Christensen, H., Mackinnon, A. J., Korten, A., & Jorm, A. F. (2001). The "common cause hypothesis" of cognitive aging: Evidence for not only a common factor but also specific associations of age with vision and grip strength in a cross-sectional analysis. *Psychology and Aging*, 16, 588–599.

Christensen, H., Mackinnon, A., Jorm, A. F., Korten, A., Jacomb, P., Hofer, S. M., & Henderson, S. (2004). The Canberra longitudinal study: Design, aims, methodology, outcomes and recent empirical investigations. *Aging Neuropsychology and Cognition*, 11, 169–195.

Cicero, M. T. De senectute. In M. T. Cicero (trans. 1923). *On old age, on friendship, on divination* (Loeb Classical Library, Vol 154). Cambridge, MA: Harvard University Press.

#Clark, J. W. (1960). The aging dimension: A factorial analysis of individual differences with age on psychological and physiological measurements. *Journal of Gerontology*, 15, 183–187.

Clarkson, P. M., & Kroll, W. (1978). Practice effects on fractionated response time related to age and activity level. *Journal of Motor Behavior*, 10, 275.

Clement, F. (1962). Modifications du temps de reaction simple en function de l'age et de quelques autres facteurs [Modifactions of simple reaction time as a function of age and some other factors]. *Revue de Psychologie Appliquee*, 12, 163–188.

Cohen, J. (1988). *Statistical power analysis for the behavioral sciences*. Hillsdale, NJ: Erlbaum.

Cohen, J. (1992). Statistical power analysis. *Current Directions in Psychological Science*, 1, 98–101.

#Cohn, N. B., Dustman, R. E., & Bradford, D. C. (1984). Age-related decrements in Stroop color test performance. *Journal of Clinical Psychology*, 40, 1244–1250.

Collette, F., Germain, S., Hogge, M., & Van der Linden, M. (2009). Inhibitory control of memory in normal ageing: Dissociation between impaired intentional and preserved unintentional processes. *Memory*, 17, 104–122.

Collette, F., Schmidt, C., Scherrer, C., Adam, S., & Salmon, E. (2009). Specificity of inhibitory deficits in normal aging and Alzheimer's disease. *Neurobiology of Aging*, 30, 875–889.

Collette, F., & Van der Linden, M. (2002). Brain imaging of the central executive component of working memory. *Neuroscience & Biobehavioral Reviews*, 26, 105–125.

Colom, R., Rebollo, I., Palacios, A., Juan-Espinosa, M., & Kyllonen, P. C. (2004). Working memory is (almost) perfectly predicted by g. *Intelligence*, 32, 277–296.

Comalli, P. E., Jr., Wapner, S., & Werner, H. (1962). Interference effects of Stroop color-word test in childhood, adulthood, and aging. *The Journal of Genetic Psychology*, 100, 47–53.

#Compton, R. J., Banich, M. T., Mohanty, A., Milham, M. P., Herrington, J., Miller, . . . Heller, W. (2003). Paying attention to emotion: An fMRI investigation of cognitive and emotional Stroop tasks. *Cognitive, Affective, and Behavioral Neuroscience*, 3, 81–96.

Connelly, S. L., & Hasher, L. (1993). Aging and the inhibition of spatial location. *Journal of Experimental Psychology: Human Perception and Performance*, 19, 1238.

Connelly, S. L., Hasher, L., & Zacks, R. T. (1991). Age and reading: The impact of distraction. *Psychology and Aging*, 6, 533–541.

Cook, I. A., Leuchter, A. F., Morgan, M. L., Conlee, E. W., David, S., Lufkin, R., . . . Rosenberg-Thompson, S. (2002). Cognitive and physiologic correlates of subclinical structural brain disease in elderly healthy control subjects. *Archives of Neurology*, 59, 1612–1620.

#Cornelius, S.W. (1984). Classic pattern of intellectual aging: Test familiarity, difficulty and performance. *Journal of Gerontology*, 39, 201–206.

Corrigan, J. D., & Hinkeldey, N. S. (1987). Relationships between parts A and B of the Trail Making Test. *Journal of Clinical Psychology*, 43, 402–409.

Cousins, M. S., Corrow, C., Finn, M., & Salamone, J. D. (1998). Temporal measures of human finger tapping: Effects of age. *Pharmacology Biochemistry and Behavior*, 59, 445–449.

Coyle, S., Gordon, E., Howson, A., & Meares, R. (1991). The effects of age on auditory event-related potentials. *Experimental Aging Research*, 17, 103–111.

Coyne, A. C., Allen, P. A., & Wickens, D. D. (1986). Influence of adult age on primary and secondary memory search. *Psychology and Aging*, 1, 187.

Craik, F. I. M. (1986). A functional account of age differences in memory. In F. Klix and H. Hagendorf (Eds.), *Human memory and cognitive capabilities: Mechanisms and performances* (pp. 409–422). Amsterdam, Netherlands: Elsevier.

Craik, F. I. M., & McDowd, J. M. (1987). Age differences in recall and recognition. *Journal of Experimental Psychology: Learning, Memory, and Cognition*, 13, 474–479.

Crawford, T. J., Higham, S., Renvoize, T., Patel, J., Dale, M., Suriya, A., Tetley, S. (2005). Inhibitory control of saccadic eye movements and cognitive impairment in Alzheimer's disease. *Biological Psychiatry*, 57, 1052–1060.

Cronbach, L. J., & Furby, L. (1970). How we should measure" change": Or should we? *Psychological Bulletin*, 74, 68–80.

Cronbach, L. J., & Shavelson, R. J. (2004). My current thoughts on coefficient alpha and successor procedures. *Educational and Psychological Measurement*, 64, 391–418.

Cronin-Golomb, A., Corkin, S., Rizzo, J. E., Cohen, J., Growdon, J. H., & Banks, K. S. (1991). Visual dysfunction in Alzheimer's disease: Relation to normal aging. *Annals of Neurology*, 29, 41–52.

#Crook, T. H., & West, R. L. (1990). Name recall performance across the adult life-span. *British Journal of Psychology*, 81, 335–349.

Crossley, M., & Hiscock, M. (1992). Age-related differences in concurrent task performance of normal adults: Evidence for a decline in processing resources. *Psychology and Aging*, 7, 499–506.

#Crosson, C. W. (1984). Age and field independence among women. *Experimental Aging Research*, 10, 165–170.

Csank, J. Z., & Lehmann, H. E. (1958). Developmental norms on four psychophysiological measures for use in the evaluation of psychotic disorders. *Canadian Journal of Psychology*, 12, 127–133.

Culham, J. C., & Kline, D. (2002). The age deficit on photopic counterphase flicker: contrast, spatial frequency and luminance effects. *Canadian Journal of Experimental Psychology*, 56, 177–186.

Curran, T. (1997). Effects of aging on implicit sequence learning: Accounting for sequence structure and explicit knowledge. *Psychological Research*, 60, 24–41.

Cutler, S. J., & Grams, A. E. (1988). Correlates of self-reported everyday memory problems. *Journal of Gerontology: Social Sciences*, 43, 82–90.

Czigler, I., Pató, L., Poszet, E., & Balázs, L. (2006). Age and novelty: Event-related potentials to visual stimuli within an auditory oddball—visual detection task. *International Journal of Psychophysiology*, 62, 290–299.

Danthiir, V., Wilhelm, O., Schulze, R., & Roberts, R. D. (2005). Factor structure and validity of paper-and-pencil measures of mental speed: Evidence for a higher-order model? *Intelligence*, 33, 491–514.

#Darowski, E. S., Helder, E., Zacks, R. T., Hasher, L. & Hambrick, D. Z. (2008). Age-related differences in cognition: The role of distraction control. *Neuropsychology*, 22, 638–644.

*Davidson, D. J., Zacks, R. T., & Williams, C. C. (2003). Stroop interference, practice, and aging. *Aging, Neuropsychology, and Cognition*, 10, 85–98.

Davies, A. (1968). The influence of age on trail making test performance. *Journal of Clinical Psychology*, 24, 96–98.

#Davies, A. D., & Leytham, G. W. (1964). Perception of verticality in adult life. *British Journal of Psychology*, 55, 315–320.

Davis, S. W., Dennis, N. A., Buchler, N. G., White, L. E., Madden, D. J., & Cabeza, R. (2009). Assessing the effects of age on long white matter tracts using diffusion tensor tractography. *NeuroImage*, 46, 530–541.

Deary, I. J., Allerhand, M., & Der, G. (2009). Smarter in middle age, faster in old age: A cross-lagged panel analysis of reaction time and cognitive ability over 13 years in the West of Scotland Twenty-07 Study. *Psychology and Aging*, 24, 40–47.

Deary, I. J., & Der, G. (2005). Reaction time, age, and cognitive ability: Longitudinal findings from age 16 to 63 years in representative population samples. *Aging, Neuropsychology, and Cognition*, 12, 187–215.

Deary, I. J., Johnson, W., & Starr, J. M. (2010). Are processing speed tasks biomarkers of cognitive aging? *Psychology and Aging*, 25, 219–228.

Deary, I. J., & Stough, C. (1996). Intelligence and inspection time: Achievements, prospects, and problems. *American Psychologist*, 51, 599–608.

De Beni, R., & Palladino, P. (2004). Decline in working memory updating through ageing: Intrusion error analyses. *Memory*, 12, 75–89.

De Corte, M. T., & Lavergne, G. (1969). La mesure de la frequence critique de fusion, methode d'exploration du champ visuel. *Archives of International Physiology*, 77, 231–244.

De Jong, R. (2000). An intention-activation account of residual switch costs. In S. Monsell & J. Driver (Eds.), *Control of cognitive processes: Attention and performance XVIII* (pp. 357–376). Cambridge, MA: MIT Press.

De Jong, R. (2001). Adult age differences in goal activation and goal maintenance. *European Journal of Cognitive Psychology*, 13, 71–89.

Delaney, P. F., Reder, L. M., Staszewski, J. J., & Ritter, F. E. (1998). The strategy-specific nature of improvement: The power law applies by strategy within task. *Psychological Science*, 9, 1–7.

Dempster, F. N. (1993). Resistance to interference: Developmental changes in a basic processing mechanism. In M. L. Howe and R. Pasnak (Eds.), *Emerging themes in cognitive development, Vol. 1: Foundations* (pp. 3–27). New York, NY: Springer.

Dempster, F. N., & Corkill, A. J. (1999). Individual differences in susceptibility to interference and general cognitive ability. *Acta Psychologica*, 101, 395–416.

*Dennis, N. A., Howard, J. H., & Howard, D. V. (2003). Age deficits in learning sequences of spoken words. *Journals of Gerontology: Psychological Sciences*, 58, 224–227.

Dennis, N. A., Howard, J. H., Jr., & Howard, D. V. (2006). Implicit sequence learning without motor sequencing in young and old adults. *Experimental Brain Research*, 175, 153–164.

Department of Health and Human Services (2006). *National vital statistics reposts (Vol. 54)*. Washington, DC: Author.

Der, G., & Deary, I. J. (2006). Age and sex differences in reaction time in adulthood: Results from the United Kingdom Health and Lifestyle Survey. *Psychology and Aging*, 21, 62.

Dickinson, M. D., & Hiscock, M. (2010). Age-related IQ decline is reduced markedly after adjustment for the Flynn effect. *Journal of Clinical and Experimental Neuropsychology*, 32, 865–870.

Dickinson, M. D., & Hiscock, M. (2011). The Flynn effect in neuropsychological assessment. *Applied Neuropsychology*, 18, 136–142.

DiGirolamo, G. J., Kramer, A. F., Barad, V., Cepeda, N. J., Weissman, D. H., Milham, M. P., . . . McAuley, E. (2001). General and task-specific frontal lobe recruitment in older adults during executive processes: A fMRI investigation of task-switching. *Neuroreport*, 12, 2065–2071.

*Dijkstra, K., Yaxley, R. H., Madden, C. J., & Zwaan, R. A. (2004). The role of age and perceptual symbols in language comprehension. *Psychology and Aging*, 19, 352–356.

#Dirken, J. M. (1972). *Functional age of industrial workers*. Groningen, The Netherlands: Wolters-Noordhoff.

Dolcos, F., Rice, H. J., & Cabeza, R. (2002). Hemispheric asymmetry and aging: Right hemisphere decline or asymmetry reduction. *Neuroscience and Biobehavioral Reviews*, 26, 819–826.

Donchin, E. (1981). Surprise! . . . Surprise? *Psychophysiology*, 18, 493–515.

Donders, F. C. (1868). Over de snelheid van psychische processen. [On the speed of mental processes.] *Onderzoekingen gedaan in het Physiologisch Laboratorium der Utrechtsche Hoogeschool, 1868–69*, 92–120.

*Doose, G., & Feyereisen, P. (2001). Task specificity in age-related slowing: Word production versus conceptual comparison. *Journals of Gerontology: Psychological Sciences*, 56, 85–87.

Dodt, C., Sarnighausen, H. E., Pietrowsky, R., Fehm, H. L., & Born, J. (1996). Ceruletide improves event-related potential indicators of cognitive processing in young but not in elderly humans. *Journal of Clinical Psychopharmacology*, 16, 440–445.

Dosenbach, N. U., Nardos, B., Cohen, A. L., Fair, D. A., Power, J. D., Church, J. A., . . . Schlaggar, B. L. (2010). Prediction of individual brain maturity using fMRI. *Science*, 329, 1358–1361.

Drane, D. L., Yuspeh, R. L., Huthwaite, J. S., & Klingler, L. K. (2002). Demographic characteristics and normative observations for derived-trail making test indices. *Neuropsychiatry, Neuropsychology and Behavioral Neurology*, 15, 39–43.

Dror, I. E., & Kosslyn, S. M. (1994). Mental imagery and aging. *Psychology and Aging*, 9, 90.

Dror, I. E., Schmitz-Williams, I. C., & Smith, W. (2005). Older adults use mental representations that reduce cognitive load: Mental rotation utilizes holistic representations and processing. *Experimental Aging Research*, 31, 409–420.

Duchek, J. M., Balota, D. A., & Thessing, V. C. (1998). Inhibition of visual and conceptual information during reading in healthy aging and Alzheimer's disease. *Aging, Neuropsychology, and Cognition*, 5, 169–181.

Dujardin, K., Derambure, P., Bourriez, J. L., Jacquesson, J. M., & Guieu, J. D. (1993). P300 component of the event-related potentials (ERP) during an attention task: Effects of age, stimulus modality and event probability. *International Journal of Psychophysiology*, 14, 255–267.

Dulaney, C. L., & Rogers, W. A. (1994). Mechanisms underlying reduction in Stroop interference with practice for young and old adults. *Journal of Experimental Psychology: Learning, Memory, and Cognition*, 20, 470–484.

Dunn, J. C., & Kirsner, K. (1988). Discovering functionally independent mental processes: The principle of reversed association. *Psychological Review*, 95, 91–101.

*Duverne, S., & Lemaire, P. (2004). Age-related differences in arithmetic problem-verification strategies. *Journals of Gerontology: Psychological Sciences*, 59, 135–142.

Dye, M. W. G., Green, C. S., Bavelier, D. (2009). Increasing speed of processing with action video games. *Current Directions in Psychological Science*, 18, 321–326.

Dywan, J., & Murphy, W. E. (1996). Aging and inhibitory control in text comprehension. *Psychology and Aging*, 11, 199–206.

*Earles, J. L., Connor, L. T., Frieske, D., Park, D. C., et al. (1997). Age differences in inhibition: Possible causes and consequences. *Aging, Neuropsychology, and Cognition*, 4, 45–57.

Edwards, J. D., Wadley, V. G., Vance, D. E., Wood, K., Roenker, D. L., & Ball, K. K. (2005). The impact of speed of processing training on cognitive and everyday performance. *Aging and Mental Health*, 9, 262–271.

#Edwards, A. E., & Wine, D. B. (1963). Personality changes with age: Their dependency on concomitant intellectual decline. *Journal of Gerontology*, 18, 182–184.

Eenshuistra, R. M., Ridderinkhof, K. R., & van der Molen, M. W. (2004). Age changes in antisaccade task performance: Inhibitory control or working-memory engagement? *Brain and Cognition*, 56, 177–188.

Eisenbarth, W., MacKeben, M., Poggel, D. A., & Strasburger, H. (2008). Characteristics of dynamic processing in the visual field of patients with age-related maculopathy. *Graefe's Archive for Clinical and Experimental Ophthalmology*, 246, 27–37.

Elias, M. F., Podraza, A. M., Pierce, T. W., & Robbins, M. A. (1990). Determining neuropsychological cut scores for older, healthy adults. *Experimental Aging Research*, 16, 209–220.

Elias, M. F., Robbins, M. A., Walter, L. J., & Schultz, N. R. (1993). The influence of gender and age on Halstead-Reitan neuropsychological test performance. *Journals of Gerontology: Psychological Sciences*, 48, 278–281.

Emery, C. F., Huppert, F. A., & Schein, R. L. (1995). Relationships among age, exercise, health, and cognitive function in a British sample. *The Gerontologist*, 35, 378–385.

Eppinger, B., Kray, J., Mecklinger, A., & John, O. (2007). Age differences in response monitoring: Evidence from ERPs. *Biological Psychology*, 75, 52–67.

Eriksen, B. A., & Eriksen, C. W. (1974). Effects of noise letters upon the identification of a target letter in a nonsearch task. *Attention, Perception, & Psychophysics*, 16, 143–149.

Erixon-Lindroth, N., Farde, L., Robins-Wahlin, T.-B., Sovago, J., Halldin, C., and Bäckman, L. (2005). The role of the striatal dopamine transporter in cognitive aging. *Psychiatry Research: Neuroimaging*, 138, 1–12.

Fabiani, M., & Friedman, D. (1995). Changes in brain activity patterns in aging: The novelty oddball. *Psychophysiology*, 32, 579–594.

Fabiani, M., Friedman, D., & Cheng, J. C. (1998). Individual differences in P3 scalp distribution in older adults, and their relationship to frontal lobe function. *Psychophysiology*, 35, 698–708.

Fair, R. C. (2007). Estimated age effects in athletic events and chess. *Experimental Aging Research*, 33, 37–57.

Falduto, L. L., & Baron, A. (1986). Age-related effects of practice and task complexity on card sorting. *Journal of Gerontology*, 41, 659–661.

Falk, J. L., & Kline, D. W. (1978). Stimulus persistence in CFF: Overarousal or underactivation?. *Experimental Aging Research*, 4, 109–123.

#Fastenau, P. S., Denburg, N. L., & Abeles, N. (1996). Age differences in retrieval: Further support for the resource-reduction hypothesis. *Psychology and Aging*, 11, 140–146.

Faust, M. E., & Balota, D. A. (1997). Inhibition of return and visuospatial attention in healthy older adults and individuals with dementia of the Alzheimer type. *Neuropsychology*, 11, 13–29.

Faust, M. E., Balota, D. A., Spieler, D. H., & Ferraro, F. R. (1999). Individual differences in information-processing rate and amount: Implications for group differences in response latency. *Psychological Bulletin*, 125, 777–799.

Feyereisen, P., & Charlot, V. (2008). Are there uniform age-related changes across tasks involving inhibitory control through access, deletion, and restraint functions? A preliminary investigation. *Experimental Aging Research*, 34, 392–418.

*Fernandes, M. A., & Moscovitch, M. (2003). Interference effects from divided attention during retrieval in younger and older adults. *Psychology and Aging*, 18, 219–230.

Fernandez-Duque, D., & Black, S. E. (2006). Attentional networks in normal aging and Alzheimer's disease. *Neuropsychology*, 20, 133–143.

*Ferraro, F. R., & Balota, D. A. (1999). Memory scanning performance in healthy young adults, healthy older adults, and individuals with dementia of the alzheimer type. *Aging, Neuropsychology, and Cognition*, 6, 260–272.

Ferraro, F. R., King, B., Ronning, B., Pekarski, K., & Risan, J. (2003). Effects of induced emotional state on lexical processing in younger and older adults. *The Journal of Psychology*, 137, 262–272.

Ferraro, F. R., Sturgill, D. S., & Bohlman, D. (1996, April). *Aging and the inhibition of letter case and number quality information*. Paper presented at the Cognitive Aging Conference, Atlanta, GA.

Fink, A., & Neubauer, A. C. (2001). Speed of information processing, psychometric intelligence: And time estimation as an index of cognitive load. *Personality and Individual Differences*, 30, 1009–1021.

Fink, A., & Neubauer, A. C. (2005). Individual differences in time estimation related to cognitive ability, speed of information processing and working memory. *Intelligence*, 33, 5–26.

Finkel, D., Reynolds, C. A., McArdle, J. J., Hamagami, F., & Pedersen, N. L. (2009). Genetic variance in processing speed drives variation in aging of spatial and memory abilities. *Developmental Psychology*, 45, 820–834.

Finkel, D., Reynolds, C. A., McArdle, J. J., & Pedersen, N. L. (2005). The longitudinal relationship between processing speed and cognitive ability: Genetic and environmental influences. *Behavior Genetics*, 35, 535–549.

Fischer, B., Biscaldi, M., & Gezeck, S. (1997). On the development of voluntary and reflexive components in human saccade generation. *Brain Research*, 754, 285–297

Fisk, A. D., Cooper, B. P., Hertzog, C., Anderson-Garlach, M. M., & Lee, M. D. (1995). Understanding performance and learning in consistent memory search: An age-related perspective. *Psychology and Aging*, 10, 255–268.

Fisk, A. D., Cooper, B. P., Hertzog, C., Batsakes, P. J., and Mead, S. E. (1996). Aging and automaticity: Evaluation of instance-based and strength-based mechanisms. *Aging, Neuropsychology, and Cognition*, 3, 1–22.

Fisk, A. D., & Fisher, D. L. (1994). Brinley plots and theories of aging: The explicit, muddled, and implicit debates. *Journal of Gerontology: Psychological Sciences*, 49, 81–89.

Fisk, A. D., Fisher, D. L., & Rogers, W. A. (1992). General slowing alone cannot explain age-related search effects: Reply to Cerella (1991). *Journal of Experimental Psychology: General*, 121, 73–78.

*Fisk, A. D., Rogers, W. A., Cooper, B. P., & Gilbert, D. K. (1997). Automatic category search and its transfer: Aging, type of search, and level of learning. *Journals of Gerontology: Psychological Sciences*, 52, 91–102.

Fisk, A. D., Rogers, W. A., & Giambra, L. M. (1990). Consistent and varied memory/visual search: Is there an interaction between age and response-set effects. *Journals of Gerontology: Psychological Sciences*, 45, 81–87.

#Fisk, J. E. & Sharp, C. A. (2004). Age-related impairment in executive functioning: Updating, inhibition, shifting, and access. *Journal of Clinical and Experimental Neuropsychology*, 26, 874–890.

Fitts, P. M. (1954). The information capacity of the human motor system in controlling the amplitude of movement. *Journal of Experimental Psychology*, 47, 381–391.

Fitts, P. M., & Peterson, J. R. (1964). Information capacity of discrete motor responses. *Journal of Experimental Psychology*, 67, 103–112.

Fitts, P. M., & Radford, B. K. (1966). Information capacity of discrete motor responses under different cognitive sets. *Journal of Experimental Psychology*, 71, 475.

Floden, D., Stuss, D. T., & Craik, F. I. (2000). Age differences in performance on two versions of the Brown-Peterson Task. *Aging, Neuropsychology, and Cognition*, 7, 245–259.

Flynn, J. R. (1987). Massive IQ Gains in 14 Nations: What IQ Tests Really Measure. *Psychological Bulletin*, 101, 171–191.

Flynn, J. R. (1998). IQ gains over time: Toward finding causes. In U. Neisser (Ed.), *The rising curve: Long-term gains in IQ and related measures* (pp. 25–66). Washington, DC: American Psychological Association.

Flynn, J. R., & Weiss, L. G. (2007). American IQ gains from 1932 to 2002: The WISC subtests and educational progress. *International Journal of Testing*, 7, 209–224.

Ford, J. M., Duncan-Johnson, C. C., Pfefferbaum, A., & Kopell, B. S. (1982). Expectancy for events in old age: Stimulus sequence effects on P300 and reaction time. *Journal of Gerontology*, 37, 696–704.

Ford, J. M., Pfefferbaum, A., Tinklenberg, J. R., & Kopell, B. S. (1982). Effects of perceptual and cognitive difficulty on P3 and RT in young and old adults. *Electroencephalography and Clinical Neurophysiology*, 54, 311–321.

Ford, J. M., Roth, W. T., Mohs, R. C., Hopkins, W. F., & Kopell, B. S. (1979). Event-related potentials recorded from young and old adults during a memory retrieval task. *Electroencephalography and Clinical Neurophysiology*, 47, 450–459.

Forstmann, B. U., Tittgemeyer, M., Wagenmakers, E.-J., Derrfuss, J., Imperati, D., & Brown. S. (2011). The speed-accuracy tradeoff in the elderly brain: A structural model-based approach. *Journal of Neuroscience*, 31, 177242–177249.

Foster, J. K., Behrmann, M., & Stuss, D. T. (1995). Aging and visual search: Generalized cognitive slowing or selective deficit in attention? *Aging, Neuropsychology, and Cognition*, 2, 279–299.

Fotenos, A. F., Snyder, A. Z., Girton, L. E., Morris, J. C., & Buckner, R. L. (2005). Normative estimates of cross-sectional and longitudinal brain volume decline in aging and AD. *Neurology*, 64, 1032–1039.

Fozard, J.L., Vercruyssen, M., Reynolds, S.L., & Hancock, P.A. (1990), Longitudinal analysis of age-related slowing: BLSA reaction time data, *Proceedings of the Human Factors Society 34th Annual Meeting*, 163–167.

Fozard, J. L., Vercruyssen, M., Reynolds, S. L., Hancock, P. A., & Quilter, R. E. (1994). Age differences and changes in reaction time: The Baltimore Longitudinal Study of Aging. *Journals of Gerontology: Psychological Sciences*, 49, 179–189.

Friedman, D., Nessler, D., Johnson, R., Ritter, W., & Bersick, M. (2008). Age-related changes in executive function: An event-related potential (ERP) investigation of task-switching. *Aging, Neuropsychology, and Cognition*, 15, 1–34.

Friedman, D., Simpson, G., & Hamberger, M. (1993). Age-related changes in scalp topography to novel and target stimuli. *Psychophysiology*, 30, 383–396.

Friedman, N. P., & Miyake, A. (2004). The relations among inhibition and interference cognitive functions: A latent variable analysis. *Journal of Experimental Psychology: General*, 133, 101–135.

Friedman, N. P., Miyake, A., Corley, R. P., Young, S. E., DeFries, J. C., & Hewitt, J. K. (2006). Not all executive functions are related to intelligence. *Psychological Science*, 17, 172–179.

Fromm-Auch, D., & Yeudall, L. T. (1983). Normative data for the Halstead-Reitan neuropsychological tests. *Journal of Clinical and Experimental Neuropsychology*, 5, 221–238.

Fry, A. F., & Hale, S. (1996). Processing speed, working memory, and fluid intelligence: Evidence for a developmental cascade. *Psychological Science*, 7, 237–241.

Fry, A. F., & Hale, S. (2000). Relationships among processing speed, working memory, and fluid intelligence in children. *Biological Psychology*, 54, 1–34.

Gaál, Z. A., Csuhaj, R., & Molnár, M. (2007). Age-dependent changes of auditory evoked potentials—effect of task difficulty. *Biological Psychology*, 76, 196–208.

*Gaeta, H., Friedman, D., Ritter, W., & Cheng, J. (2001). An event-related potential evaluation of involuntary attentional shifts in young and older adults. *Psychology and Aging*, 16, 55–68.

Galenson, D.W., and Weinberg, B.A. 2000. Age and quality of work: The case of modern American painters. *Journal of Political Economy*, 108, 761–777.

Gallistel, C. R., & Gelman, R. (1992). Preverbal and verbal counting and computation. *Cognition*, 44, 43–74.

Gamboz, N. (2000). *Evaluation of inhibitory processes in cognitive aging*. (Unpublished doctoral dissertation). University of Essex, UK.

Gamboz, N., Borella, E., & Brandimonte, M. A. (2009). The role of switching, inhibition and working memory in older adults' performance in the Wisconsin Card Sorting Test. *Aging, Neuropsychology, and Cognition*, 16, 260–284.

*Gamboz, N., Russo, R., & Fox, E. (2000). Target selection difficulty, negative priming, and aging. *Psychology and Aging*, 15, 542–550.

Gamboz, N., Russo, R., & Fox, E. (2002). Age differences and the identity negative priming effect: An updated meta-analysis. *Psychology and Aging*, 17, 525–531.

Garavan, H. (1998). Serial attention within working memory. *Memory & Cognition*, 26, 263–276.

Geal-Dor, M., Goldstein, A., Kamenir, Y., & Babkoff, H. (2006). The effect of aging on event-related potentials and behavioral responses: Comparison of tonal, phonologic and semantic targets. *Clinical Neurophysiology*, 117, 1974–1989.

*Geldmacher, D. S., Fritsch, T., & Riedel, T. M. (2000). Effects of stimulus properties and age on random-array letter cancellation tasks. *Aging, Neuropsychology, and Cognition*, 7, 194–204.

Ghisletta, P., & de Ribaupierre, A. (2005). A dynamic investigation of cognitive dedifferentiation with control for retest: Evidence from the Swiss interdisciplinary longitudinal study on the oldest old. *Psychology and Aging*, 20, 671–682.

Ghisletta, P., & Lindenberger, U. (2003). Age-based structural dynamics between perceptual speed and knowledge in the Berlin Aging Study: Direct evidence for ability dedifferentiation in old age. *Psychology and Aging*, 18, 696–713.

Giaquinto, S., & Nolfe, G. (1984). Central processing in the aged. *Monographs in Neural Sciences*, 11, 169–175.

Giaquinto, S., & Nolfe, G. (1986). The EEG in the normal elderly: A contribution to the interpretation of aging and dementia. *Electroencephalography and Clinical Neurophysiology*, 63, 540–546.

Giambra, L. M., & Quilter, R. E. (1988). Sustained attention in adulthood: A unique, large-sample, longitudinal and multicohort analysis using the Mackworth Clock-Test. *Psychology and Aging*, 3, 75–83.

Gick, M. L., Craik, F. I. M., & Morris, R. G. (1988). Task complexity and age differences in working memory. *Memory & Cognition*, 16, 353–361.

Gilburt, S. J. A., Fairweather, D. B., Kerr, J. S., & Hindmarch, I. (1992). The effects of acute and repeated doses of suriclone on subjective sleep, psychomotor performance and cognitive function in young and elderly volunteers. *Fundamental and Clinical Pharmacology*, 6, 251–258.

Gilmore, G. C., Allan, T. M., & Royer, F. L. (1986). Iconic memory and aging. *Journal of Gerontology*, 41, 183–190.

Goffaux, P., Phillips, N. A., Sinai, M., & Pushkar, D. (2008). Neurophysiological measures of task-set switching: Effects of working memory and aging. *Journals of Gerontology: Psychological Sciences*, 63, 57–66.

Goggin, N. L., & Stelmach, G. E. (1990). Age-related differences in a kinematic analysis of precued movements. *Canadian Journal on Aging*, 9, 371–385.

Gold, B. T., Andersen, A. H., Jicha, G. A., & Smith, C. D. (2009). Aging influences the neural correlates of lexical decision but not automatic semantic priming. *Cerebral Cortex*, 19, 2671–2679.

Golden, C. J., Osmon, D. C., Moses, J. A., & Berg, R. A. (1981). *Interpretation of the Halstead-Reitan neuropsychological test battery: A casebook approach*. New York, NY: Grune & Stratton.

#Goldfarb, W. (1941). *An investigation of reaction time in older adults* (Contributions to Education No. 831). New York, NY: Teachers College, Columbia University Press.

*Gorman, M. F., & Fisher, D. L. (1998). Visual search tasks: Slowing of strategic and nonstrategic processes in the nonlexical domain. *Journals of Gerontology: Psychological Sciences*, 53, 189–200.

Gottsdanker, R., & Shragg, G. P. (1985). Verification of Donders' subtraction method. *Journal of Experimental Psychology: Human Perception and Performance*, 11, 765–776.

Gottlob, L. R. (2006). Age-related deficits in guided search using cues. *Psychology and Aging*, 21, 526–534.

Gottlob, L. R., Fillmore, M. T., & Abroms, B. D. (2007). Age-group differences in inhibiting an oculomotor response. *Aging, Neuropsychology, and Cognition*, 14, 586–593.

*Gottlob, L. R., & Madden, D. J. (1999). Age differences in the strategic allocation of visual attention. *Journals of Gerontology: Psychological Sciences*, 54, 165–172.

Goul, W. R., & Brown, M. (1970). Effects of age and intelligence on Trail Making Test performance and validity. *Perceptual and Motor Skills*, 30, 319–326.

*Grady, C. L. (2002). Introduction to the special section on aging, cognition, and neuroimaging. *Psychology and Aging*, 17, 3–6.

#Graf, P., & Uttl, B. (1995). Component processes of memory: Changes across the adult lifespan. *Swiss Journal of Psychology*, 54, 113–130.

Grant, E. A., Storandt, M., & Botwinick, J. (1978). Incentive and practice in the psychomotor performance of the elderly. *Journal of Gerontology*, 33, 413–415.

Grant, J. D., & Dagenbach, D. (2000). Further considerations regarding inhibitory processes, working memory, and cognitive aging. *American Journal of Psychology*, 113, 69–94.

Greenwood, P., & Parasuraman, R. (1991). Effects of aging on the speed and attentional cost of cognitive operations. *Developmental Neuropsychology*, 7, 421–434.

Grégoire, J., & Van der Linden, M. (1997). Effect of age on forward and backward digit spans. *Aging, Neuropsychology, and Cognition*, 4, 140–149.

Gribbin, K., Schaie, K. W., & Parham, I. A. (1980). Complexity of life style and maintenance of intellectual abilities. *Journal of Social Issues*, 36, 47–61.

Grudnik, J. L., & Kranzler, J. H. (2001). Meta-analysis of the relationship between intelligence and inspection time. *Intelligence*, 29, 523–535.

Guttentag, R. E., & Madden, D. J. (1987). Adult age differences in the attentional capacity demands of letter matching. *Experimental Aging Research*, 13, 93–99.

Hahn, S., Andersen, G. J., & Kramer, A. F. (2004). Age influences on multi-dimensional set switching. *Aging, Neuropsychology, and Cognition*, 11, 25–36.

Hahn, S., Carlson, C., Singer, S., & Gronlund, S. D. (2006). Aging and visual search: Automatic and controlled attentional bias to threat faces. *Acta Psychologica*, 123, 312–336.

Hale, S., Lima, S. D., & Myerson, J. (1991). General cognitive slowing in the nonlexical domain: An experimental validation. *Psychology and Aging*, 6, 512.

Hale, S., & Myerson, J. (1996). Experimental evidence for differential slowing in the lexical and nonlexical domains. *Aging, Neuropsychology, and Cognition*, 3, 154–165.

Hale, S., Myerson, J., Faust, M., & Fristoe, N. (1995). Converging evidence for domain-specific slowing from multiple nonlexical tasks and multiple analytic methods. *Journals of Gerontology: Psychological Sciences*, 50, 202.

Hale, S., Myerson, J., Smith, G. A., & Poon, L. W. (1988). Age, variability, and speed: Between-subjects diversity. *Psychology and Aging*, 3, 407–410.

Hale, S., Myerson, J., & Wagstaff, D. (1987). General slowing of nonverbal information processing: Evidence for a power law. *Journal of Gerontology*, 42, 131–136.

Hallett, P. E. (1978). Primary and secondary saccades to goals defined by instructions. *Vision Research*, 18, 1279–1296.

Hamm, V. P., & Hasher, L. (1992). Age and the availability of inferences. *Psychology and Aging*, 7, 56–64.

Hammond, B.R., & Wooten, B.R. (2005). CFF Thresholds: Relation to macular pigment optical density. *Ophthalmic and Physiological Optics*, 25, 315–319.

Harbin, T. J., Marsh, G. R., & Harvey, M. T. (1984). Differences in the late components of the event-related potential due to age and to semantic and non-semantic tasks. *Electroencephalography and Clinical Neurophysiology/Evoked Potentials Section*, 59, 489–496.

Harnishfeger, K.K. (1995). The development of cognitive inhibition. In F.N. Dempster & C.J. Brainerd (Eds.), *Interference and inhibition in cognition* (pp. 175–204). New York, NY: Academic Press.

Hartley, A. A., & Kieley, J. M. (1995). Adult age differences in the inhibition of return of visual attention. *Psychology and Aging*, 10, 670–683.

Hartley, A. A., & Little, D. M. (1999). Age-related differences and similarities in dual-task interference. *Journal of Experimental Psychology: General*, 128, 416–449.

Hartman, M., & Hasher, L. (1991). Aging and suppression: Memory for previously relevant information. *Psychology and Aging*, 6, 587–594.

Hasher, L., Lustig, C., & Zacks, R. T. (2007). Inhibitory mechanisms and the control of attention. In A. Conway, C. Jarrold, M. Kane, A. Miyake, & J. Towse (Eds.), *Variation in working memory* (pp. 227–249). New York, NY: Oxford University Press.

Hasher, L., Quig, M. B., & May, C. P. (1997). Inhibitory control over no-longer-relevant information: Adult age differences. *Memory & Cognition*, 25, 286–295.

Hasher, L., Stoltzfus, E. R., Zacks, R. T., & Rypma, B. (1991). Age and inhibition. *Journal of Experimental Psychology: Learning, Memory, and Cognition*, 17, 163–169.

Hasher, L., & Zacks, R. T. (1988). Working memory, comprehension, and aging: A review and a new view. In G. H. Bower (Ed.), *The psychology of learning and motivation* (Vol. 22, pp. 193–225). San Diego, CA: Academic Press.

Hasher, L., Zacks, R. T., & May, C. P. (1999). Inhibitory control, circadian arousal, and age. In D. Gopher & A. Koriat (Eds.), *Attention & Performance, XVII, Cognitive Regulation of Performance: Interaction of Theory and Application* (pp. 653–675). Cambridge, MA: MIT Press.

Hawkins, H. L., Kramer, A. F., & Capaldi, D. (1992). Aging, exercise, and attention. *Psychology and Aging*, 7, 643–653.

Hayflick, L. (2007). Entropy explains aging, genetic determinism explains longevity, and undefined terminology explains misunderstanding both. *PLoS genetics*, 3, e220.

He N.J., Horwitz, A. R., Dubno, J. R., & Mills, J. H. (1999). Psychometric functions for gap detection in noise measured from young and aged subjects. *Journal of the Acoustical Society of America*, 106, 966–978.

Heathcote, A., Brown, S., & Mewhort, D. J. (2000). The power law repealed: The case for an exponential law of practice. *Psychonomic Bulletin & Review*, 7, 185–207.

Heaton, R. K., Nelson, L. M., Thompson, D. S., Burks, J. S., & Franklin, G. M. (1985). Neuropsychological findings in relapsing-remitting and chronic-progressive multiple sclerosis. *Journal of Consulting and Clinical Psychology*, 53, 103–110.

#Hedden, T., Lautenschlager, G. J. & Park, D. C. (2005). Contributions of processing ability and knowledge to verbal memory tasks across the adult lifespan. *Quarterly Journal of Experimental Psychology*, 58A, 169–190.

*Hedden, T., & Park, D. (2001). Aging and interference in verbal working memory. *Psychology and Aging*, 16, 666–681.

Hedges, L. V., & Olkin, I. (1985). *Statistical methods for meta-analysis*. Orlando, FL: Academic Press.

Heinrich A., and Schneider B. (2006). Age-related changes in within- and between-channel gap detection using sinusoidal stimuli. *Journal of the Acoustical Society of America*, 119, 2316–2326.

Henry, J. D., MacLeod, M. S., Phillips, L. H., & Crawford, J. R. (2004). A meta-analytic review of prospective memory and aging. *Psychology and Aging*, 19, 27–39.

*Hernandez, A. E., & Kohnert, K. J. (1999). Aging and language switching in bilinguals. *Aging, Neuropsychology, and Cognition*, 6, 69–83.

Hertzog, C., & Bleckley, M. K. (2001). Age differences in the structure of intelligence: Influences of information processing speed. *Intelligence*, 29, 191–217.

#Heron, A., & Chown, S. (1967). *Age and function*. Boston: Little, Brown.

Hertzog, C., Cooper, B. P., & Fisk, A. D. (1996). Aging and individual differences in the development of skilled memory search performance. *Psychology and Aging*, 11, 497.

Hertzog, C., Dixon, R. A., Hultsch, D. F., & MacDonald, S. W. (2003). Latent change models of adult cognition: Are changes in processing speed and working memory associated with changes in episodic memory? *Psychology and Aging*, 18, 755–763.

Hertzog, C., Kramer, A. F., Wilson, R. S., & Lindenberger, U. (2009). Enrichment effects on adult cognitive development: Can the functional capacity of older adults be preserved and enhanced? *Psychological Science in the Public Interest*, 9, 1–65.

Hertzog, C., Lindenberger, U., Ghisletta, P., & Von Oertzen, T. (2006). On the power of multivariate latent growth curve models to detect correlated change. *Psychological Methods*, 11, 244–252.

Hertzog, C., Vernon, M. C., & Rypma, B. (1993). Age differences in mental rotation task performance: The influence of speed/accuracy tradeoffs. *Journals of Gerontology: Psychological Sciences*, 48, 150–156.

Hertzog, C. K., Williams, M. V., & Walsh, D. A. (1976). The effect of practice on age differences in central perceptual processing. *Journal of Gerontology*, 31, 428–433.

*Hess, T. M., Follett, K. J., & McGee, K. A. (1998). Aging and impression formation: The impact of processing skills and goals. *Journals of Gerontology: Psychological Sciences*, 53, 175–187.

Hick, W. E. (1952). On the rate of gain of information. *Quarterly Journal of Experimental Psychology*, 4, 11–26.

Hillman, C. H., Erickson, K. I., & Kramer, A. F. (2008). Be smart, exercise your heart: Exercise effects on brain and cognition. *Nature Reviews Neuroscience*, 9, 58–65.

Hitch, G. J., Towse, J. N., & Hutton, U. (2001). What limits children's working memory span? Theoretical accounts and applications for scholastic development. *Journal of Experimental Psychology: General*, 130, 184–198.

*Ho, G., & Scialfa, C. T. (2002). Age, skill transfer, and conjunction search. *Journals of Gerontology: Psychological Sciences*, 57, 277–287.

Hofer, S. M., Flaherty, B. P., & Hoffman, L. (2006). Cross-sectional analysis of time-dependent data: Mean-induced association in age-heterogeneous samples and an alternative method based on sequential narrow age-cohort samples. *Multivariate Behavioral Research*, 41, 165–187.

Hofer, S. M., & Sliwinski, M. J. (2001). Understanding ageing. *Gerontology*, 47, 341–352.

Hoge, R. D., Atkinson, J., Gill, B., Crelier, G. R., Marrett, S., & Pike, G. B. (1999). Linear coupling between cerebral blood flow and oxygen consumption in activated human cortex. *Proceedings of the National Academy of Sciences*, 96, 9403–9408.

Hogge, M., Salmon, E., & Collette, F. (2008). Interference and negative priming in normal aging and in mild Alzheimer's disease. *Psychologica Belgica*, 48, 1–23.

Hommel, B., Li, K. Z., & Li, S. C. (2004). Visual search across the life span. *Developmental Psychology*, 40, 545.

#Hooper, E H., Hooper, J.O., & Colbert, K.C. (1984). *Personality and memory correlates of cognitive functioning*. Basel, Switzerland: Karger.

#Horn, J. L., & Cattell, R. B. (1966). Refinement and test of the theory of fluid and crystallized general intelligences. *Journal of Educational Psychology*, 57, 253.

#Horn, J. L., Donaldson, G., & Engstrom, R. (1981). Apprehension, memory, and fluid intelligence decline in adulthood. *Research on Aging*, 3, 33–84.

Houx, P. J., & Jolles, J. (1993). Age-related decline of psychomotor speed: Effects of age, brain health, sex, and education. *Perceptual and Motor Skills*, 76, 195–211.

Howard, D. V. (2001). Implicit memory and learning. In G. Maddox (Ed.), *The encyclopedia of aging*. *3rd ed*. New York, NY: Springer.

Howard, D. V., & Howard, J. H. (1989). Age differences in learning serial patterns: Direct versus indirect measures. *Psychology and Aging*, 4, 357–364.

Howard, D. V., & Howard, J. H., Jr. (1992). Adult age differences in the rate of learning serial patterns: Evidence from direct and indirect tests. *Psychology and Aging*, 7, 232–241.

*Howard, J. H., & Howard, D. V. (1997). Age differences in implicit learning of higher order dependencies in serial patterns. *Psychology and Aging*, 12, 634–656.

Howard, D. V., & Howard, J. H., Jr. (2001). When it does hurt to try: Adult age differences in the effects of instructions on implicit pattern learning. *Psychonomic Bulletin & Review*, 8, 798–805.

*Howard, D. V., Howard, J. H., Japikse, K., DiYanni, C., Thompson, A., & Somberg, R. (2004). Implicit sequence learning: Effects of level of structure, adult age, and extended practice. *Psychology and Aging*, 19, 79–92.

Howard, J.H., Jr., Howard, D.V., Dennis, N.A., Yankovich, H., & Vaidya, C.J. (2004). Implicit spatial contextual learning in healthy aging. *Neuropsychology*, 18, 124–134.

Hoyer, F. W., Hoyer, W. J., Treat, N. J., & Baltes, P. B. (1978). Training response speed in young and elderly women. *The International Journal of Aging and Human Development*, 9, 247–253.

Hoyer, S. (2002). The aging brain: Changes in the neuronal insulin/insulin receptor signal transduction cascade trigger late-onset sporadic Alzheimer disease (SAD): A mini-review. *Journal of Neural Transmission*, 109, 991–1002.

#Hoyer, W. J., Rebok, G. W., & Sved, S. M. (1979). Effects of varying irrelevant information on adult age differences in problem solving. *Journal of Gerontology*, 34, 553–560.

Hoyer, W. J., Stawski, R. S., Wasylyshyn, C., & Verhaeghen, P. (2004). Adult age and digit symbol substitution performance: A meta-analysis. *Psychology and Aging*, 19, 211–214.

Hultsch, D. F., Hertzog, C., & Dixon, R. A. (1990). Ability correlates of memory performance in adulthood and aging. *Psychology and Aging*, 5, 356–368.

Hultsch, D. F., Hertzog, C., Small, B. J., & Dixon, R. A. (1999). Use it or lose it: Engaged lifestyle as a buffer of cognitive decline in aging? *Psychology and Aging*, 14, 245–263.

Hultsch, D. F., Hertzog, C., Small, B. J., McDonald-Miszczak, L., & Dixon, R. A. (1992). Short-term longitudinal change in cognitive performance in later life. *Psychology and Aging*, 7, 571–584.

Humes, L. E., Busey, T. A., Craig, J. C., & Kewley-Port, D. (2009). The effects of age on sensory thresholds and temporal gap detection in hearing, vision, and touch. *Attention and Perceptual Psychophysics*, 71, 860–871.

*Hummert, M. L., Garstka, T. A., O'Brien, L. T., Greenwald, A. G., & Mellott, D. S. (2002). Using the implicit association test to measure age differences in implicit social cognitions. *Psychology and Aging*, 17, 482–495.

*Humphrey, D. G., & Kramer, A. F. (1997). Age differences in visual search for feature, conjunction, and triple-conjunction targets. *Psychology and Aging*, 12, 704–717.

Huppert, F.A., Whittington, J.E. (1993). Changes in cognitive function in a population sample. In B. D. Cox, F. A. Huppert, & M. J. Whichelow (Eds.), *The Health and Lifestyle Survey: Seven years on* (pp. 155–172). Aldershot, UK: Dartmouth.

Hyman, R. (1953). Stimulus information as a determinant of reaction time. *Journal of Experimental Psychology*, 45, 188.

Inman, V. W., & Parkinson, S. R. (1983). Differences in Brown-Peterson recall as a function of age and retention interval. *Journal of Gerontology*, 38, 58–64.

Intons-Peterson, M. J., Rocchi, P., West, T., McLellan, K., & Hackney, A. (1998). Aging, optimal testing time, and negative priming. *Journal of Experimental Psychology: Learning, Memory, and Cognition*, 24, 362–376.

Jaccard, J. J., & Turrisi, R. (2003). *Interaction effects in multiple regression*. Thousand Oaks, CA: Sage Publications.

Hultsch, D. F., and MacDonald, S.W.S. (2004). Intraindividual variability in performance as a theoretical window onto cognitive aging. In R. A. Dixon, L. Backman, and L-G Nilsson (Eds.), *New frontiers in cognitive aging* (pp. 65–88). New York, NY: Oxford University Press.

Huntington, J. M., & Simonson, E. (1965). Critical flicker fusion frequency as a function of exposure time in two different age groups. *Journal of Gerontology*, 20, 527–529.

Iragui, V. J., Kutas, M., Mitchiner, M. R., & Hillyard, S. A. (1993). Effects of aging on event-related brain potentials and reaction times in an auditory oddball task. *Psychophysiology*, 30, 10–22.

Isingrini, M., Vazou, F., & Leroy, P. (1995). Dissociation of implicit and explicit memory tests: Effect of age and divided attention on category exemplar generation and cued recall. *Memory & Cognition*, 23, 462–467.

James, L. E., & MacKay, D. G. (2007). New age-linked asymmetries: Aging and the processing of familiar versus novel language on the input versus output side. *Psychology and Aging*, 22, 94–103.

Jamieson, B. A., & Rogers, W. A. (2000). Age-related effects of blocked and random practice schedules on learning a new technology. *Journals of Gerontology Series: Psychological Sciences*, 55, 343–353.

Jastrzembski, T. S., & Charness, N. (2007). The Model Human Processor and the older adult: Parameter estimation and validation within a mobile phone task. *Journal of Experimental Psychology: Applied*, 13, 224–248.

*Jenkins, L., Myerson, J., Joerding, J. A., & Hale, S. (2000). Converging evidence that visuospatial cognition is more age-sensitive than verbal cognition. *Psychology and Aging*, 15, 157–175.

Jennings, J. M., Dagenbach, D., Engle, C. M., & Funke, L. J. (2007). Age-related changes and the attention network task: An examination of alerting, orienting, and executive function. *Aging, Neuropsychology, and Cognition*, 14, 353–369.

Jensen, A. R. (1998). *The g factor: The science of mental ability*. Westport, CT: Praeger.

Jensen, A. R. (2006). *Clocking the mind: Mental chronometry and individual differences*. Amsterdam, Netherlands: Elsevier.

Jolles, J., Houx, P. J., Van Boxtel, M. P. J., & Ponds, R. W. H. M. (1995). *Maastricht aging study: Determinants of cognitive aging*. Maastricht: Neuropsych Publishers.

Jordan, T. C., & Rabbitt, P. M. A. (1977). Response times to stimuli of increasing complexity as a function of ageing. *British Journal of Psychology*, 68, 189–201.

Joyce, C. A., Paller, K. A., McIsaac, H. K., & Kutas, M. (1998). Memory changes with normal aging: Behavioral and electrophysiological measures. *Psychophysiology*, 35, 669–678.

Jones, G. M. M., Sahakian, B. J., Levy, R., Warburton, D. M., & Gray, J. A. (1992). Effects of acute subcutaneous nicotine on attention, information processing and short-term memory in Alzheimer's disease. *Psychopharmacology*, 108, 485–494.

Johnson, M. K. (1992). MEM: Mechanisms of recollection. *Journal of Cognitive Neuroscience*, 4, 268–280.

Kaasinen, V., Vilkman, H., Hietala, J., Någren, K., Helenius, H., Olsson, H., . . . Rinne, J. O. (2000). Age-related dopamine D2/D3 receptor loss in extrastriatal regions of the human brain. *Neurobiology of Aging*, 21, 683–688.

Kail, R. (1991a). Developmental change in speed of processing during childhood and adolescence. *Psychological Bulletin*, 109, 490–501.

Kail, R. (1991b). Processing time declines exponentially during childhood and adolescence. *Developmental Psychology*, 27, 259.

Kane, M. J., Conway, A. R., Miura, T. K., & Colflesh, G. J. (2007). Working memory, attention control, and the N-back task: A question of construct validity. *Journal of Experimental Psychology: Learning, Memory, and Cognition*, 33, 615–622.

Kane, M. J., & Engle, R. W. (2002). The role of prefrontal cortex in working-memory capacity, executive attention, and general fluid intelligence: An individual-differences perspective. *Psychonomic Bulletin & Review*, 9, 637–671.

Kane, M. J., & Engle, R. W. (2003). Working memory capacity and the control of attention: The contributions of goal neglect, response competition, and task set to Stroop interference. *Journal of Experimental Psychology: General*, 132, 47–70.

Kane, M. J., Hasher, L., Stoltzfus, E. R., Zacks, R. T., & Connelly, S. L. (1994). Inhibitory attentional mechanisms and aging. *Psychology and Aging*, 9, 103–112.

Kane, M. J., May, C. P., Hasher, L., Rahhal, T., & Stoltzfus, E. R. (1997). Dual mechanisms of negative priming. *Journal of Experimental Psychology: Human Perception and Performance*, 23, 632–650.

Kaneko, R., Kuba, Y., Sakata, Y., & Kuchinomachi, Y. (2004). Aging and shifts of visual attention in saccadic eye movements. *Experimental Aging Research*, 30, 149–162.

Karlsson, S., Nyberg, L., Karlsson, P., Fischer, H., Thilers, P., MacDonald, S.W.S., . . . Bäckman, L. (2009). Modulation of striatal dopamine D1 binding by cognitive processing. *Neuroimage* 48, 398–404.

#Kaufman, A. S., Reynolds, C. R., & McLean, J. E. (1989). Age and WAIS-R intelligence in a national sample of adults in the 20-to-74-year age range: A cross-sectional analysis with educational level controlled. *Intelligence*, 13, 235–253.

Kaufman, E. L., Lord, M. W., Reese, T. W., & Volkmann, J. (1949). The discrimination of visual number. *The American Journal of Psychology*, 62, 498–525.

Kauranen, K., & Vanharanta, H. (1996). Influences of aging, gender, and handedness on motor performance of upper and lower extremities. *Perceptual and Motor Skills*, 82, 515–525.

Kausler, D. H. (1982). *Experimental psychology and human aging*. New York, NY: Wiley.

Kausler, D. H. (1991). *Experimental psychology, cognition, and human aging. 2nd ed.* New York, NY: Springer-Verlag.

#Kausler, D. H. (1994). *Learning and memory in normal aging*. San Diego, CA: Academic Press.

Kemper, S., Crow, A., & Kemtes, K. (2004). Eye fixation patterns of high and low span young and older adults: Down the garden path and back again. *Psychology and Aging*, 19, 157–170.

*Kemper, S., Herman, R. E., & Liu, C. (2004). Sentence production by young and older adults in controlled contexts. *Journals of Gerontology: Psychological Sciences*, 59, 220–224.

*Kemper, S., Herman, R., & Lian, C. (2003). Age differences in sentence production. *Journals of Gerontology: Psychological Sciences*, 58, S260–268.

Kemper, S., McDowd, J., & Kramer, A. E. (2006). Eye movements of young and older adults while reading with distraction. *Psychology and Aging*, 21, 32–39.

Kennedy, K. J. (1981). Age effects on trail making test performance. *Perceptual and Motor Skills, 52,* 671–675.

Kerchner, G. A., Racine, C. A., Hale, S., Wilheim, R., Laluz, V., Miller, B. L., & Kramer, J. H. (2012). Cognitive processing speed in older adults: Relationship with white matter integrity. *PloS one,* 7(11), e50425.

Ketcham, C. J., Seidler, R. D., Van Gemmert, A. W. A., & Stelmach, G. E. (2002). Age-related kinematic differences as influenced by task difficulty, target-size, and movement amplitude. *Journals of Gerontology: Psychological Sciences and Social Sciences, 57,* 54–64.

*Kieley, J. M., & Hartley, A. A. (1997). Age-related equivalence of identity suppression in the stroop color-word task. *Psychology and Aging, 12,* 22–29.

#Kirasic, K. C., Allen, G. L., Dobson, S. H., & Binder, K. S. (1996). Aging, cognitive resources, and declarative learning. *Psychology and Aging, 11,* 658–670.

Klein, C., Fischer, B., Hartnegg, K., Heiss, W. H., & Roth, M. (2000). Optomotor and neuropsychological performance in old age. *Experimental Brain Research, 135,* 141–154.

Klein, R. M. (2000). Inhibition of return. *Trends in Cognitive Sciences, 4,* 138–147.

Kliegl, R., & Mayr, U. (1992). Commentary: Shifting levels of explanation in cognitive aging. *Human Development, 35,* 343–349.

Kliegl, R., Mayr, U., & Krampe, R. T. (1994). Time-accuracy functions for determining process and person differences: An application to cognitive aging. *Cognitive Psychology, 26,* 134–164.

Knott, V., Bradford, L., Dulude, L., Millar, A., Alwahabi, F., Lau, T., ... Wiens, A. (2003). Effects of stimulus modality and response mode on the P300 event-related potential differentiation of young and elderly adults. *Clinical Electroencephalography, 34,* 182–190.

Knott, V., Millar, A., Dulude, L., Bradford, L., Alwahhabi, F., Lau, T., ... Wiens, A. (2004). Event-related potentials in young and elderly adults during a visual spatial working memory task. *Clinical Electroencephalography, 35,* 185–192.

Kochunov, P., Thompson, P. M., Lancaster, J. L., Bartzokis, G., Smith, S., Coyle, T., ... Fox, P. T. (2007). Relationship between white matter fractional anisotropy and other indices of cerebral health in normal aging: Tract-based spatial statistics study of aging. *NeuroImage, 35,* 478–487.

Koga, Y., & Morant, G. M. (1923). On the degree of association between reaction times in the case of different senses. *Biometrika, 15,* 346–372.

Korrte, K. B., Horner, M. D., & Windham, W. K. (2002). The trail making test part B: Cognitive flexibility or ability to maintain set? *Applied Neuropsychology, 9,* 106–109.

#Koss, E., Haxby, J. V., DeCarli, C., Shapiro, M. B., Friedland, R. P., & Rapoport, S. I. (1991). Patterns of performance preservation and loss in healthy aging. *Developmental Neuropsychology, 7,* 99–113.

Kraiuhin, C., Gordon, E., Coyle, S., Sara, G., Rennie, C., Howson, A., ... Meares, R. (1990). Normal latency of the P300 event-related potential in mild-to-moderate Alzheimer's disease and depression. *Biological Psychiatry, 28,* 372–386.

*Kramer, A. F., & Atchley, P. (2000). Age-related effects in the marking of old objects in visual search. *Psychology and Aging, 15,* 286–296.

Kramer, A. F., Boot, W. R., McCarley, J. S., Peterson, M. S., Colcombe, A., & Scialfa, C. T. (2006). Aging, memory and visual search. *Acta Psychologica, 122,* 288–304.

Kramer, A. F., Hahn, S., & Gopher, D. (1999). Task coordination and aging: Explorations of executive control processes in the task switching paradigm. *Acta Psychologica, 101,* 339–378.

*Kramer, A. F., Hahn, S., Irwin, D. E., & Theeuwes, J. (1999). Attentional capture and aging: Implications for visual search performance and oculomotor control. *Psychology and Aging, 14,* 135–154.

Kramer, A. F., Humphrey, D. G., Larish, J. F., Logan, G. D., & Strayer, D. L. (1994). Aging and inhibition: Beyond a unitary view of inhibitory processes in attention. *Psychology and Aging, 4,* 491–512.

Kramer, A. F., Larish, J. F., & Strayer, D. L. (1995). Training for attentional control in dual task settings: A comparison of young and old adults. *Journal of Experimental Psychology: Applied, 1,* 50–76.

*Kramer, A. F., & Strayer, D. L. (2001). Influence of stimulus repetition on negative priming. *Psychology and Aging, 16,* 580–587.

*Kramer, A. F., & Weber, T. A. (1999). Object-based attentional selection and aging. *Psychology and Aging*, 14, 99–107.

#Kraus, J., Chalker, S., & Macindoe, I. (1967). Vocabulary and chronological age as predictors of "abstraction" on the Shipley-Hartford Retreat Scale. *Australian Journal of Psychology*, 19, 133–135.

Kraus, P. H., Przuntek, H., Kegelmann, A., & Klotz, P. (2000). Motor performance: Normative data, age dependence and handedness. *Journal of Neural Transmission*, 107, 73–85.

Kray, J. (2006). Task-set switching under cue-based versus memory-based switching conditions in younger and older adults. *Brain Research*, 1105, 83–92.

Kray, J., Eber, J., & Lindenberger, U. (2004). Age differences in executive functioning across the lifespan: The role of verbalization in task preparation. *Acta Psychologica*, 115, 143–165.

Kray, J., & Eppinger, B. (2006). Effects of associate learning on age differences in task-set switching. *Acta Psychologica*, 123, 187–203.

Kray, J., Li, K. Z. H., Lindenberger, U. (2002). Age-related changes in task-switching components: The role of task uncertainty. *Brain & Cognition*, 49, 363–381.

*Kray, J., & Lindenberger, U. (2000). Adult age differences in task switching. *Psychology and Aging*, 15, 126–147.

Kumar, A., Rakitin, B. C., Nambisan, R., Habeck, C., & Stern, Y. (2008). Response-signal methods reveal age-related differences in object working memory. *Psychology and Aging*, 23, 315–329.

Kühnert, B., & Nieschlag, E. (2004). Reproductive functions of the ageing male. *Human Reproduction Update*, 10, 327–339.

Kutas, M., & Hillyard, S. A. (1980). Reading senseless sentences: Brain potentials reflect semantic incongruity. *Science*, 207, 203–205.

Kutas, M., Iragui, V., & Hillyard, S. A. (1994). Effects of aging on event-related brain potentials (ERPs) in a visual detection task. *Electroencephalography and Clinical Neurophysiology/Evoked Potentials Section*, 92, 126–139.

Kwong See, S. T., & Ryan, E. B. (1995). Cognitive mediation of adult age differences in language performance. *Psychology and Aging*, 10, 458–468.

Lachenmayr, B. J., Kojetinsky, S., Ostermaier, N., Angstwurm, K., Vivell, P. M., & Schaumberger, M. (1994). The different effects of aging on normal sensitivity in flicker and light-sense perimetry. *Investigations in Ophthalmology and Vision Science*, 35, 2741–2748.

Lange, E. B., & Verhaeghen, P. (2009). No age differences in complex memory search: Older adults search as efficiently as younger adults. *Psychology and Aging*, 24, 105–115.

Langley, L. K., Fuentes, L. J., Hochhalter, A. K., Brandt, J., & Overmier, J. B. (2001). Inhibition of return in aging and Alzheimers disease: Performance as a function of task demands and stimulus timing. *Journal of Clinical and Experimental Neuropsychology*, 23, 431–446.

Langley, L. K., Fuentes, L. J., Vivas, A. B., & Saville, A. L. (2007). Aging and temporal patterns of inhibition of return. *Journals of Gerontology: Psychological Sciences*, 62, 71–77.

Langley, L. K., Overmier, J. B., Knopman, D. S., & Prod'Homme, M. M. (1998). Inhibition and habituation: Preserved mechanisms of attentional selection in aging and Alzheimer's disease. *Neuropsychology*, 12, 353–366.

Langley, L. K., Vivas, A. B., Fuentes, L. J., & Bagne, A. G. (2005). Differential age effects on attention-based inhibition: Inhibitory tagging and inhibition of return. *Psychology and Aging*, 20, 356–360.

*Lawrence, B., Myerson, J., & Hale, S. (1998). Differential decline of verbal and visuospatial processing speed across the adult life span. *Aging, Neuropsychology, and Cognition*, 5, 129–146.

*Lazzara, M. M., Yonelinas, A. P., & Ober, B. A. (2002). Implicit memory in aging: Normal transfer across semantic decisions and stimulus format. *Aging, Neuropsychology, and Cognition*, 9, 145–156.

Lee, H. F., Gorsuch, R. L., Saklofske, D. H., & Patterson, C. A. (2008). Cognitive differences for ages 16 to 89 years (Canadian WAIS-III) Curvilinear with Flynn and processing speed corrections. *Journal of Psychoeducational Assessment*, 26, 382–394.

#Lee, J. A., & Pollack, R. A. (1978). The effects of age on perceptual problem-solving strategies. *Experimental Aging Research*, 4, 37–54.

Leenders, K. L., Perani, D., Lammertsma, A. A., Heather, J. D., Buckingham, P., Jones, T., ...Frackowiak, R. S. J. (1990). Cerebral blood flow, blood volume and oxygen utilization. Normal values and effect of age. *Brain*, 113, 27–47.

Lehman, H. C. (1953). *Age and achievement*. Princeton, NJ: Princeton University Press.

Lemke, U., & Zimprich, D. (2005). Longitudinal changes in memory performance and processing speed in old age. *Aging, Neuropsychology, and Cognition*, 12, 57–77.

Li, K. Z. H. (1999). Selection from working memory: On the relationship between processing and storage components. *Aging, Neuropsychology, and Cognition*, 6, 99–116.

Li, K. Z., & Bosman, E. A. (1996). Age differences in Stroop-like interference as a function of semantic relatedness. *Aging, Neuropsychology, and Cognition*, 3, 272–284.

Li, K. Z., Hasher, L., Jonas, D., Rahhal, T. A., & May, C. P. (1998). Distractibility, circadian arousal, and aging: A boundary condition? *Psychology and Aging*, 13, 574–583.

Li, K. Z. H., Lindenberger, U., Freund, A. M., & Baltes, P. B. (2001). Walking while memorizing: Age-related differences in compensatory behavior. *Psychological Science*, 12, 230–237.

Li, S.-C., Huxhold, O., & Schmiedek, F. (2004). Aging and attenuated processing robustness: Evidence from cognitive and sensorimotor functioning. *Gerontology*, 50, 28–34.

Li, S. C., Lindenberger, U., & Sikström, S. (2001). Aging cognition: From neuromodulation to representation. *Trends in Cognitive Sciences*, 5, 479–486.

Li, Z., Moore, A. B., Tyner, C., & Hu, X. (2009). Asymmetric connectivity reduction and its relationship to "HAROLD" in aging brain. *Brain Research*, 1295, 149–158.

Liao, M. J., Jagacinski, R. J., & Greenberg, N. (1997). Quantifying the performance limitations of older and younger adults in a target acquisition task. *Journal of Experimental Psychology: Human Perception and Performance*, 23, 1644.

Lien, M., Ruthruff, E., & Kuhns, D. (2008). Age-related differences in switching between cognitive tasks: Does internal control ability decline with age? *Psychology and Aging*, 23, 330–341.

Light, L. L., Kennison, R., Prull, M. W., La Voie, D., & Zuellig, A. (1996). One-trial associative priming of nonwords in young and older adults. *Psychology and Aging*, 11, 417–430.

Light, L. L., & Prull, M. W. (1995). Aging, divided attention, and repetition priming. *Swiss Journal of Psychology*, 54, 87–101.

Light, L. L., Prull, M. W., & Kennison, R. F. (2000). Dividing attention, aging, and priming in exemplar generation and category verification. *Memory and Cognition*, 28, 856–872.

Lima, S. D, Hale, S., & Myerson, J. (1991). How general is general slowing? Evidence from the lexical domain. *Psychology and Aging*, 6, 416–425.

*Lincourt, A. E., Folk, C. L., & Hoyer, W. J. (1997). Effects of aging on voluntary and involuntary shifts of attention. *Aging, Neuropsychology, and Cognition*, 4, 290–303.

Lindenberger, U., & Baltes, P. B. (1994). Sensory functioning and intelligence in old age: A strong connection. *Psychology and Aging*, 9, 339–355.

Lindenberger, U., & Baltes, P. B. (1997). Intellectual functioning in old and very old age: Cross-sectional results from the Berlin Aging Study. *Psychology and Aging*, 12, 410–432.

Lindenberger, U., & Ghisletta, P. (2009). Cognitive and sensory declines in old age: Gauging the evidence for a common cause. *Psychology and Aging*, 24, 1–16.

Lindenberger, U., Marsiske, M., & Baltes, P. B. (2000). Memorizing while walking: Increase in dual-task costs from young adulthood to old age. *Psychology and Aging*, 15, 417–436.

Lindenberger, U., Mayr, U., & Kliegl, R. (1993). Speed and intelligence in old age. *Psychology and Aging*, 8, 207–220.

Lindenberger, U., & Pötter, U. (1998). The complex nature of unique and shared effects in hierarchical linear regression: Implications for developmental psychology. *Psychological Methods*, 3, 218–230.

Lindenberger, U., Von Oertzen, T., Ghisletta, P., & Hertzog, C. (2011). Cross-sectional age variance extraction: What's change got to do with it? *Psychology and Aging*, 26, 34–47.

*Little, D. M., & Hartley, A. A. (2000). Further evidence that negative priming in the Stroop color-word task is equivalent in older and younger adults. *Psychology and Aging*, 15, 9–17.

*Logan, J. M., & Balota, D. A. (2003). Conscious and unconscious lexical retrieval blocking in younger and older adults. *Psychology and Aging*, 18, 537–550.

Logan, G. D., & Bundesen, C. (2003). Clever homunculus: Is there an endogenous act of control in the explicit task-cuing procedure? *Journal of Experimental Psychology: Human Perception and Performance*, 29, 575–599.

Lord, F.M. (1963). Elementary models for measuring change. In C.W. Harris (Ed.), *Problems in measuring change* (pp. 21–38). Madison, WI: The University of Wisconsin Press.

Lorsbach, T.C., & Simpson, G. B. (1988). Dual-task performance as a function of adult age and task complexity. *Psychology and Aging*, 3, 210–212.

Los, S. A. (1996). On the origin of mixing costs: Exploring information processing in pure and mixed blocks of trials. *Acta Psychologica*, 94, 145–188.

#Lövdén, M. (2003). The episodic memory and inhibition accounts of age-related increases in false memories: A consistency check. *Journal of Memory & Language*, 49, 268–283.

Lövdén, M., Li, S-C., Shing, Y-L., & Lindenberger, U. (2007). Within-person trial-to-trial variability precedes and predicts cognitive decline in old age: Longitudinal data from the Berlin aging study. *Neuropsychologia*, 45, 2827–2838.

Lu, Z.-L., Neuse, J., Madigan, S., & Dosher, B., (2005). Decay of iconic memory in observers with mild cognitive impairment, *Proceedings of the National Academy of Science, USA*, 102, 1797–1802.

Luce, R. D. (1991). *Response times: Their role in inferring elementary mental organization*. New York, NY: Oxford University Press.

Luciano, M., Posthuma, D., Wright, M. J., de Geus, E. J. C., Smith, G. A., Geffen, G. M., ... Martin, N.G. (2005). Perceptual speed does not cause intelligence, and intelligence does not cause perceptual speed. *Biological Psychology*, 70, 1–8.

McAuliffe, J., Chasteen, A. L., & Pratt, J. (2006). Object-and location-based inhibition of return in younger and older adults. *Psychology and Aging*, 21, 406–410.

MacDonald, S. W., Hultsch, D. F., & Dixon, R. A. (2003). Performance variability is related to change in cognition: Evidence from the Victoria Longitudinal Study. *Psychology and Aging*, 18, 510–523.

MacDonald, S. W., Hultsch, D. F., Strauss, E., & Dixon, R. A. (2003). Age-related slowing of digit symbol substitution revisited: What do longitudinal age changes reflect? *Journals of Gerontology: Psychological Sciences*, 58, 187–194.

MacInnes, W. J., & Klein, R. M. (2003). Inhibition of return biases orienting during the search of complex scenes. *Scientific World Journal*, 3, 75–86.

MacKenzie, I. S. (1992). Fitts' law as a research and design tool in human–computer interaction. *Human–Computer Interaction*, 7, 91–139.

*MacKay, D. G., & James, L. E. (2004). Sequencing, speech production, and selective effects of aging on phonological and morphological speech errors. *Psychology and Aging*, 19, 93–107.

Madden, D. J. (1982). Age differences and similarities in the improvement of controlled search. *Experimental Aging Research*, 8, 91–98.

Madden, D. J. (1983). Aging and distraction by highly familiar stimuli during visual search. *Developmental Psychology*, 19, 499–507.

Madden, D. J. (1986). Adult age differences in the attentional capacity demands of visual search. *Cognitive Development*, 1, 335–363.

Madden, D. J. (1987). Aging, attention, and the use of meaning during visual search. *Cognitive Development*, 2, 201–216.

Madden, D. J. (1992). Four to ten milliseconds per year: Age-related slowing of visual word identification. *Journals of Gerontology: Psychological Sciences*, 47, 59–68.

Madden, D. J. (2007). Aging and visual attention. *Current Directions in Psychological Science*, 16, 70–74.

*Madden, D. J., & Gottlob, L. R. (1997). Adult age differences in strategic and dynamic components of focusing visual attention. *Aging, Neuropsychology, and Cognition*, 4, 185–210.

Madden, D. J., & Greene, H. A. (1987). From retina to response: Contrast sensitivity and memory retrieval during visual word recognition. *Experimental Aging Research*, 13, 15–21.

*Madden, D. J., & Langley, L. K. (2003). Age-related changes in selective attention and perceptual load during visual search. *Psychology and Aging*, 18, 54–67.

*Madden, D. J., Langley, L. K., Thurston, R. C., Whiting, W. L., & Blumenthal, J. A. (2003). Interaction of blood pressure and adult age in memory search and visual search performance. *Aging, Neuropsychology, and Cognition, 10,* 241–254.

Madden, D. J., & Nebes, R. D. (1980). Aging and the development of automaticity in visual search. *Developmental Psychology, 16,* 377–384.

Madden, D. J., Pierce, T. W., & Allen, P. A. (1996). Adult age differences in the use of distractor homogeneity during visual search. *Psychology and Aging, 11,* 454.

*Madden, D. J., Turkington, T. G., Provenzale, J. M., Denny, L. L., Langley, L. K., Hawk, T. C., & Coleman, R.E. (2002). Aging and attentional guidance during visual search: Functional neuroanatomy by positron emission tomography. *Psychology and Aging, 17,* 24–43.

Madden, D. J., Welsh-Bohmer, K. A., & Tupler, L. A. (1999). Task complexity and signal detection analyses of lexical decision performance in Alzheimer's disease. *Developmental Neuropsychology, 16,* 1–18.

*Madden, D. J., Whiting, W. L., Cabeza, R., & Huettel, S. A. (2004). Age-related preservation of top-down attentional guidance during visual search. *Psychology and Aging, 19,* 304–309.

Madden, D. J., Whiting, W. L., Spaniol, J., & Bucur, B. (2005). Adult age differences in the implicit and explicit components of top-down attentional guidance during visual search. *Psychology and Aging, 20,* 317.

#Maitland, S. B., Intrieri, R. C., Schaie, K. W., & Willis, S. L. (2000). Gender differences in cognitive abilities: Invariance of covariance and latent mean structures. *Aging, Neuropsychology, and Cognition, 7,* 32–53.

Maltz, M., & Shinar, D. (1999). Eye movements of younger and older drivers. *Human Factors, 41,* 15–25.

Mandler, G., & Shebo, B. J. (1982). Subitizing: An analysis of its component processes. *Journal of Experimental Psychology: General, 111,* 1.

*Marczinski, C. A., Milliken, B., & Nelson, S. (2003). Aging and repetition effects: Separate specific and nonspecific influences. *Psychology and Aging, 18,* 780–790.

Marsh, G. R. (1975). Age differences in evoked potential correlates of a memory scanning process. *Experimental Aging Research, 1,* 3–16.

#Mason, C. E, & Ganzler, H. (1964). Adult norms for the Shipley Institute of Living Scale and Hooper Visual Organization Test based on age and education. *Journal of Gerontology, 19,* 419–424.

May, C. P., Kane, M. J., & Hasher, L. (1995). Determinants of negative priming. *Psychological Bulletin, 118,* 35–54.

*May, C. P., Zacks, R. T., Hasher, L., & Multhaup, K. S. (1999). Inhibition in the processing of garden-path sentences. *Psychology and Aging, 14,* 304–313.

*Maylor, E. A., & Lavie, N. (1998). The influence of perceptual load on age differences in selective attention. *Psychology and Aging, 13,* 563–573.

Maylor, E. A., & Rabbitt, P. M. (1994). Applying Brinley plots to individuals: Effects of aging on performance distributions in two speeded tasks. *Psychology and Aging, 9,* 224–230.

Maylor, E. A., Watson, D. G., & Muller, Z. (2005). Effects of Alzheimer's disease on visual enumeration. *Journal of Gerontology: Psychological Sciences, 60,* 129–135.

*Mayr, U. (2001). Age differences in the selection of mental sets: The role of inhibition, stimulus ambiguity, and response-set overlap. *Psychology and Aging, 16,* 96–109.

Mayr, S., & Buchner, A. (2007). Negative priming as a memory phenomenon: A review of 20 years of negative priming research. *Zeitschrift für Psychologie/Journal of Psychology, 215,* 35–51.

Mayr, U., & Kliegl, R. (2000). Task-set switching and long-term memory retrieval. *Journal of Experimental Psychology: Learning, Memory, and Cognition, 26,* 1124–1140.

Mayr, U., Kliegl, R., & Krampe, R. T. (1996). Sequential and coordinative processing dynamics in figural transformations across the life span. *Cognition, 59,* 61–90.

Mayr, U., & Liebscher, T. (2001). Is there an age deficit in the selection of mental sets? *European Journal of Cognitive Psychology, 13,* 47–69.

Mazur, J. E., & Hastie, R. (1978). Learning as accumulation: A reexamination of the learning curve. *Psychological Bulletin, 85,* 1256.

McArdle, J. J. (2001). A latent difference score approach to longitudinal dynamic structure analysis. In R. Cudeck, S. du Toit, & D. Sörbom, (Eds.) *Structural equation modeling: Present and future. A festschrift in honor of Karl Jöreskog* (pp. 1–40). Lincolnwood, IL: Scientific Software International, Inc.

McArdle, J. J., & Hamagami, F. (2003). Structural equation models for evaluating dynamic concepts within longitudinal twin analyses. *Behavior Genetics, 33,* 137–159.

McArdle, J. J., Hamagami, F., Meredith, W., & Bradway, K. P. (2000). Modeling the dynamic hypotheses of Gf-Gc theory using longitudinal life-span data. *Learning and Individual Differences, 12,* 53–79.

#McArdle, J. J., & Prescott, C. A. (1992). Age-based construct validation using structural equation modeling. *Experimental Aging Research, 18,* 87–115.

McArthur, A. D., Lahar, C. J., & Isaak, M. I. (1996, April). *Inhibitory mechanisms, interference, and the attentional blink in younger and older adults.* Paper presented at the Cognitive Aging Conference, Atlanta, GA.

*McCarley, J. S., Kramer, A. F., Colcombe, A. M., & Scialfa, C. T. (2004). Priming of pop-out in visual search: A comparison of young and old adults. *Aging, Neuropsychology, and Cognition, 11,* 80–88.

*McCarley, J. S., Mounts, J. R. W., & Kramer, A. F. (2004). Age-related differences in localized attentional interference. *Psychology and Aging, 19,* 203–210.

*McCrae, C. S., & Abrams, R. A. (2001). Age-related differences in object- and location-based inhibition of return of attention. *Psychology and Aging, 16,* 437–449.

#McCrae, R. R., Arenberg, D., & Costa, P. T. (1987). Declines in divergent thinking with age: Cross-sectional, longitudinal, and cross-sequential analyses. *Psychology and Aging, 2,* 130–137.

McCrory, C., & Cooper, C. (2005). The relationship between three auditory inspection time tasks and general intelligence. *Personality and Individual Differences, 38,* 1835–1845.

McDowd, J. M. (1986). The effects of age and extended practice on divided attention performance. *Journal of Gerontology, 41,* 764–769.

McDowd, J. M., & Craik, F. I. M. (1988). Effects of aging and task difficulty on divided attention performance. *Journal of Experimental Psychology: Human Perception and Performance, 14,* 267–280.

McDowd, J. M., Filion, D., & Bowman, S. D. (1996, April). *Location, location, location: The primacy of spatial location for inhibition in selective attention among older adults.* Paper presented at the Cognitive Aging Conference, Atlanta, GA.

McDowd, J. M., & Oseas-Kreger, D. M. (1991). Aging, inhibitory processes, and negative priming. *Journal of Gerontology: Psychological Sciences, 46,* 340–345.

McDowd, J. M., Oseas-Kreger, D. M., & Filion, D. L. (1995). Inhibitory processes in cognition and aging. In F. N. Dempster & C. J. Brainerd (Eds.), *Interference and inhibition in cognition* (pp. 363–400). San Diego, CA: Academic Press.

McDowd, J. M., & Shaw, R. J. (2000). Attention and aging: A functional perspective. In F. I. M. Craik & T. A. Salthouse (Eds.), *The handbook of aging and cognition* (2nd ed., pp. 221–292). Mahwah, NJ: Erlbaum.

McEvoy, L. K., Pellouchoud, E., Smith, M. E., & Gevins, A. (2001). Neurophysiological signals of working memory in normal aging. *Cognitive Brain Research, 11,* 363–376.

McFarland, R. A., Warren, B., & Karis, C. (1958). Alterations in critical flicker frequency as a function of age and light: Dark ratio. *Journal of Experimental Psychology, 56,* 529–538.

Meinz, E. J., & Salthouse, T. A. (1998). The effects of age and experience on memory for visually presented music. *Journals of Gerontology: Psychological Sciences, 53,* 60–69.

*Meiran, N., Gotler, A., & Perlman, A. (2001). Old age is associated with a pattern of relatively intact and relatively impaired task-set switching abilities. *Journals of Gerontology: Psychological Sciences, 56,* 88–102.

Meiran, N., Levine, J., Meiran, N., & Henik, A. (2000). Task-set switching in schizophrenia. *Neuropsychology, 14,* 471–482.

Menich, S. R., & Baron, A. (1990). Age-related effects of reinforced practice on recognition memory: Consistent versus varied stimulus-response relations. *Journals of Gerontology: Psychological Sciences, 45,* 88–93.

MetLife Foundation (2006). *MetLife Foundation Alzheimer's survey: What America thinks.* New York, NY: Author.

Metter, E. J., Schrager, M., Ferrucci, L., & Talbot, L. A. (2005). Evaluation of movement speed and reaction time as predictors of all-cause mortality in men. *Journals of Gerontology: Medical Sciences*, 60, 840–846.

Meyer, D. E., & Kieras, D. E. (1997). A computational theory of executive control processes and human multiple-task performance: Part 1. Basic Mechanisms. *Psychological Review*, 104, 3–65.

Miles, W. R. (1931). Measures of certain human abilities throughout the life span. *Proceedings of the National Academy of Sciences of the United States of America*, 17, 627–633.

Miller, E. K., & Cohen, J. D. (2001). An integrative theory of prefrontal cortex function. *Annual Review of Neuroscience*, 24, 167–202.

*Miller, L. M. S., & Stine-Morrow, E. A. L. (1998). Aging and the effects of knowledge on on-line reading strategies. *Journals of Gerontology: Psychological Sciences*, 53, 223–233.

Milliken, B., Joordens, S., Merikle, P. M., & Seiffert, A. E. (1998). Selective attention: A reevaluation of the implications of negative priming. *Psychological Review*, 105, 203–229.

Minear, M., & Shah, P. (2008). Training and transfer effects in task switching. *Memory & Cognition*, 36, 1470–1483.

Misiak, H. (1951). The decrease of critical flicker frequency with age. *Science*, 113, 551–552.

Miyake, A., Friedman, N. P., Emerson, M. J., Witzki, A. H., Howerter, A., & Wager, T. D. (2000). The unity and diversity of executive functions and their contributions to complex "frontal lobe" tasks: A latent variable analysis. *Cognitive Psychology*, 41, 49–100.

Monsell, S. (2003). Task switching. *Trends in Cognitive Sciences*, 7, 134–140.

Monsell, S. (1996). Control of mental processes. In V. Bruce (Ed.), *Unsolved mysteries of the mind: Tutorial essays in cognition* (pp. 93–148). Hillsdale, NJ: Erlbaum.

Morris, R. G., Gick, M. L., & Craik, F. I. M. (1988). Processing resources and age differences in working memory. *Memory & Cognition*, 16, 362–366.

*Morrow, D. G., Stine-Morrow, E. A. L., Leirer, V. O., Andrassy, J. M., & Kahn, J. (1997). The role of reader age and focus of attention in creating situation models from narratives. *Journals of Gerontology: Psychological Sciences*, 52, 73–80.

Morse, C. K. (1993). Does variability increase with age? An archival study of cognitive measures. *Psychology and Aging*, 8, 156–164.

Moschner, C., & Baloh, R.W. (1994). Age-related changes in visual tracking. *Journals of Gerontology: Medical Sciences*, 49, 235–238.

Muller-Oehring, E. M., Schulte, T., Raassi, C., Pfefferbaum, A., & Sulli- van, E. V. (2007). Local–global interference is modulated by age, sex and anterior corpus callosum size. *Brain Research*, 1142, 189–205.

Mullis, R. J., Holcomb, P. J., Diner, B. C., & Dykman, R. A. (1985). The effects of aging on the P3 component of the visual event-related potential. *Electroencephalography and Clinical Neurophysiology/Evoked Potentials Section*, 62, 141–149.

Munoz, D. P., Broughton, J. R., Goldring, J. E., & Armstrong, I. T. (1998). Age-related performance of human subjects on saccadic eye movement tasks. *Experimental Brain Research*, 121, 391–400.

Must, O., Must, A., & Raudik, V. (2003). The secular rise in IQs: In Estonia, the Flynn effect is not a Jensen effect. *Intelligence*, 31, 461–471.

Myerson, J., Adams, D. R., Hale, S., & Jenkins, L. (2003). Analysis of group differences in processing speed: Brinley plots, Q–Q plots, and other conspiracies. *Psychonomic Bulletin and Review*, 10, 224–237.

Myerson, J., Emery, L., White, D. A., & Hale, S. (2003). Effects of age, domain, and processing demands on memory span: Evidence for differential decline. *Aging, Neuropsychology, and Cognition*, 10, 20–27.

Myerson J., Ferraro, F. R., Hale, S., & Lima, S. D. (1992). General slowing in semantic priming and word recognition. *Psychology and Aging*, 7, 257–270.

Myerson, J., & Hale, S. (1993). General slowing and age invariance in cognitive processing: The other side of the coin. In J. Cerella, J. Rybash, W. Hoyer, & M. L. Commons (Eds.), *Adult information processing: Limits on loss* (pp. 115–141). San Diego, CA: Academic Press.

Myerson, J., Hale, S., Wagstaff, D., Poon, L. W., & Smith, G. A. (1990). The information-loss model: A mathematical theory of age-related cognitive slowing. *Psychological Review*, 97, 475–487.

Myerson, J., Hale, S., Zheng, Y., Jenkins, L., & Widaman, K. F. (2003). The Difference Engine: A model of individual and group differences in processing speed. *Psychonomic Bulletin & Review*, 10, 262–288.

Myerson, J., Robertson, S., & Hale, S. (2007). Aging and intraindividual variability in performance: Analyses of response time distributions. *Journal of the Experimental Analysis of Behavior*, 88, 319–337.

Myung, I. J., Kim, C., & Pitt, M. A. (2000). Toward an explanation of the power law artifact: Insights from response surface analysis. *Memory & Cognition*, 28, 832–840.

Nagasaki, H., Itoh, H., Maruyama, H., & Hashizume, K. (1988). Characteristic difficulty in rhythmic movement with aging and its relation to Parkinson's disease. *Experimental Aging Research*, 14, 171–176.

Nebes, R. D., Brady, C. B., & Reynolds, C. F. (1992). Cognitive slowing in Alzheimer's disease and geriatric depression. *Journals of Gerontology: Psychological Sciences*, 47, 331–336.

Needham, J., & Lerner, I. M. (1940). The terminology of relative growth rates. *Nature*, 146, 618.

*Negash, S., Howard, D. V., Japikse, K. C., & Howard, J. H. (2003). Age-related differences in implicit learning of non-spatial sequential patterns. *Aging, Neuropsychology, and Cognition*, 10, 108–121.

Neill, W. T., Valdes, L. A., Terry, K. M., & Gorfein, D. S. (1992). Persistence of negative priming: II. Evidence for episodic trace retrieval. *Journal of Experimental Psychology: Learning, Memory, and Cognition*, 18, 993–1000.

Neisser, U. (Ed.) (1998). *The rising curve: Long-term gains in IQ and related measures*. Washington, D.C.: American Psychological Association.

Nelson, L. A., Yoash-Gantz, R. E., Pickett, T. C., & Campbell, T. A. (2009). Relationship between processing speed and executive functioning performance among OEF/OIF veterans: Implications for postdeployment rehabilitation. *The Journal of Head Trauma Rehabilitation*, 24, 32–40.

Nerb, J., Ritter, F. E., & Krems, J. F. (1999). Knowledge level learning and the power law: A Soar model of skill acquisition in scheduling. *Kognitionswissenschaft*, 8, 20–29.

Nettelbeck, T. (2001). Correlation between inspection time and psychometric abilities: A personal interpretation. *Intelligence*, 29, 459–474.

Nettelbeck, T., & Wilson, C. (2004). The Flynn effect: Smarter not faster. *Intelligence*, 32, 85–93.

Newell, A. (1990). *Unified Theories of Cognition*. Cambridge, MA: Harvard University Press.

Newell, A., & Rosenbloom, P. S. (1981). Mechanisms of skill acquisition and the law of practice. In J. R. Anderson (Ed.), *Cognitive skills and their acquisition* (pp. 1–55). Hillsdale, NJ: Erlbaum.

*Nielson, K. A., Langenecker, S. A., & Garavan, H. (2002). Differences in the functional neuroanatomy of inhibitory control across the adult life span. *Psychology and Aging*, 17, 56–71.

Nieuwenhuis, S., Ridderinkhof, K. R., De Jong, R., Kok, A., & Van der Molen, M. W. (2000). Inhibitory inefficiency and failures of intention activation: Age-related decline in the control of saccadic eye movements. *Psychology and Aging*, 15, 635–647.

Nieuwenhuis, S., Ridderinkhof, K. R., Talsma, D., Coles, M. G. H., Holroyd, C. B., Kok, A., & Van der Molen, M. W. (2002). A computational account of altered error processing in older age: Dopamine and the error-related negativity. *Cognitive, Affective & Behavioral Neuroscience*, 2, 19–36.

Nigg, J. T. (2000). On inhibition/disinhibition in developmental psychopathology: Views from cognitive and personality psychology and a working inhibition taxonomy. *Psychological Bulletin*, 126, 220–246.

Noble, C. E., Baker, B.L., & Jones, T.A. (1964). Age and sex parameters in psychomotor learning. *Perceptual and Motor Skills*, 19, 935–945.

Oberauer, K., Süß, H. M., Schulze, R., Wilhelm, O., & Wittmann, W. W. (2000). Working memory capacity—facets of a cognitive ability construct. *Personality and Individual Differences*, 29, 1017–1045.

Ohlsson, S. (1992). The learning curve for writing books: Evidence from Professor Asimov. *Psychological Science*, 3, 380–382.

*Olson, I. R., Zhang, J. X., Mitchell, K. J., Johnson, M. K., Bloise, S. M., & Higgins, J. A. (2004). Preserved spatial memory over brief intervals in older adults. *Psychology and Aging*, 19, 310–317.

Olincy, A., Ross, R. G., Young, D. A., & Freedman, R. (1997). Age diminishes performance on an antisaccade movement task. *Neurobiology of Aging*, 18, 483–489.

Olk, B., & Kingstone, A. (2009). A new look at aging and performance in the antisaccade task: The impact of response selection. *European Journal of Cognitive Psychology*, 21, 406–427.

Paller, K. A., McCarthy, G., & Wood, C. C. (1988). ERPs predictive of subsequent recall and recognition performance. *Biological Psychology*, 26, 269–276.

Panek, P. E., Rush, M. C., & Slade, L. A. (1984). Locus of the age-Stroop interference relationship. *Journal of Genetic Psychology*, 145, 209–216.

Park, D.C., Polk, T., Mikels, J., Taylor, S.F., & Marshuetz, C. (2001). Cerebral aging: Integration of brain and behavioral models of cognitive function. *Dialogues in Clinical Neuroscience*, 3, 151–165.

Park, D. C., Puglisi, J. T., & Smith, A. D. (1986). Memory for pictures: Does an age-related decline exist? *Psychology and Aging*, 1, 11–17.

Park, D. C., Smith, A. D., Dudley, W. N., & Lafronza, V. N. (1989). Effects of age and a divided attention memory task presented during encoding and retrieval on memory. *Journal of Experimental Psychology: Learning, Memory, and Cognition*, 15, 1185–1191.

#Park, D. C., Smith, A. D., Lautenschlager, G., Earles, J., Frieske, D., Zwahr, M., & Gaines, C. (1996). Mediators of long-term memory performance across the life span. *Psychology and Aging*, 11, 621–637.

Parkinson, S. R., Inman, V. W., & Dannenbaum, S. E. (1985). Adult age differences in short-term forgetting. *Acta Psychologica*, 60, 83–101.

Perfect, T. J. (1994). What can Brinley plots tell us about cognitive aging? *Journal of Gerontology: Psychological Sciences*, 49, 60–64.

Periáñez, J. A., Rios-Lago, M., Rodriguez-Sanchez, J. M., Adrover-Roig, D., Sánchez-Cubillo, I., Crespo-Facorro, B.,...Barcelo, F. (2007). Trail Making Test in traumatic brain injury, schizophrenia, and normal ageing: Sample comparisons and normative data. *Archives of Clinical Neuropsychology*, 22, 433–447.

#Perlmutter, M., & Nyquist, L. (1990). Relationships between self-reported physical and mental health and intelligence performance across adulthood. *Journals of Gerontology: Psychological Sciences*, 45, 145–155.

Pesta, B. J., & Sanders, R. E. (2000). Aging and negative priming: Is ignored information inhibited or remembered? *Experimental Aging Research*, 26, 37–56.

Peterson, L., & Peterson, M. J. (1959). Short-term retention of individual verbal items. *Journal of Experimental Psychology*, 58, 193.

Pfefferbaum, A., Adalsteinsson, E., & Sullivan, E. V. (2005). Frontal circuitry degradation marks healthy adult aging: Evidence from diffusion tensor imaging. *NeuroImage*, 26, 891–899.

Pfefferbaum, A., Ford, J. M., Roth, W. T., & Kopell, B. S. (1980a). Age differences in P3-reaction time associations. *Electroencephalography and Clinical Neurophysiology*, 49, 257–265.

Pfefferbaum, A., Ford, J. M., Roth, W. T., & Kopell, B. S. (1980b). Age-related changes in auditory event-related potentials. *Electroencephalography and Clinical Neurophysiology*, 49, 266–276.

*Pfütze, E., Sommer, W., & Schweinberger, S. R. (2002). Age-related slowing in face and name recognition: Evidence from event-related brain potentials. *Psychology and Aging*, 17, 140–160.

Phillips, N. A., & Lesperance, D. (2003). Breaking the waves: Age differences in electrical brain activity when reading text with distractors. *Psychology and Aging*, 18, 126–139.

Piazza, M., Mechelli, A., Butterworth, B., & Price, C. J. (2002). Are subitizing and counting implemented as separate or functionally overlapping processes? *NeuroImage*, 15, 435–446.

Picton, T. W., Cerri, A. M., Champagne, S. C., Stuss, D. T., & Nelson, R. F. (1986). The effects of age and task difficulty on the late positive component of the auditory evoked potential. *Electroencephalography and Clinical Neurophysiology Supplementary*, 38, 130–131.

#Pierce, T. W., Elias, M. W., Keohane, P.J., Podraza, A. M., Robbins, M.A., & Schultz, N.R. (1989). Validity of a short form of the Category test in relation to age, education, and gender. *Experimental Aging Research*, 15, 137–141.

Pierrot-Deseilligny, C., Rivaud, S., Gaymard, B., Muri, R., Vermersch, A. I. (1995). Cortical control of saccades. *Annals of Neurology*, 37, 557–567.

Plassman, B.L., Welsh, K.A., Helms, M., Brandt, J., Page, W.F., Breitner, J.C.S. (1995). Intelligence and education as predictors of cognitive state in late life: A 50-year follow-up. *Neurology*, 45, 1446–1450.

Plude, D. J., & Doussard-Roosevelt, J. A. (1989). Aging, selective attention, and feature integration. *Psychology and Aging*, 4, 98–105.

Plude, D. J., & Hoyer, W. J. (1986). Age and the selectivity of visual information processing. *Psychology and Aging*, 1, 4–10.

Plude, D. J., Kaye, D. B., Hoyer, W. J., Post, T. A., Saynisch, M. J., & Hahn, M. V. (1983). Aging and visual search under consistent and varied mapping. *Developmental Psychology*, 19, 508–512.

Pocklington, B. A., & Maybery, M. T. (2006). Proportional slowing or disinhibition in ADHD? A Brinley plot meta-analysis of Stroop color and word test performance. *International Journal of Disability, Development and Education*, 53, 67–91.

Podlesny, J. A., & Dustman, R. E. (1982). Age effects on heart rate, sustained potential, and P3 responses during reaction-time tasks. *Neurobiology of Aging*, 3, 1–9.

Podlesny, J. A., Dustman, R. E., & Shearer, D. E. (1984). Aging and respond-withhold tasks: Effects on sustained potentials, P3 responses and late activity. *Electroencephalography and clinical neurophysiology*, 58, 130–139.

Poliakoff, E., Coward, R., Lowe, C., & O'Boyle, D. J. (2007). The effect of age on inhibition of return is independent of non-ocular response inhibition. *Neuropsychologia*, 45, 387–396.

Polich, J. (1996). Meta-analysis of P300 normative aging studies. *Psychophysiology*, 33, 334–353.

Polich, J. (2007). Updating P300: An integrative theory of P3a and P3b. *Clinical Neurophysiology: Official Journal of the International Federation of Clinical Neurophysiology*, 118, 2128–2148.

Ponds, R. W. H. M., Brouwer, W. H., & van Wolffelaar, P. C. (1988). Age differences in divided attention in a simulated driving task. *Journals of Gerontology: Psychological Sciences*, 43, 151–156.

Pontifex, M. B., Hillman, C. H., & Polich, J. (2009). Age, physical fitness, and attention: P3a and P3b. *Psychophysiology*, 46, 379–387.

Pontón, M. O., Satz, P., Herrera, L., Ortiz, F. R. E. D. D. Y., Urrutia, C. P., Young, R., . . . Namerow, N. (1996). Normative data stratified by age and education for the Neuropsychological Screening Battery for Hispanics (NeSBHIS): Initial report. *Journal of the International Neuropsychological Society*, 2, 96–104.

Posner, M. I., & Cohen, Y. A. (1984). Components of visual orienting. In H. Bouma & D. G. Bouwhuis (Eds.), *Attention and performance X* (pp. 531–556). Hillsdale, NJ: Erlbaum.

*Pratt, J., Abrams, R. A., & Chasteen, A. L. (1997). Initiation and inhibition of saccadic eye movements in younger and older adults: An analysis of the gap effect. *Journals of Gerontology: Psychological Sciences*, 52, 103–107.

*Pratt, J., & Bellomo, C. N. (1999). Attentional capture in younger and older adults. *Aging, Neuropsychology, and Cognition*, 6, 19–31.

Pratt, J., & Chasteen, A. L. (2007). Examining inhibition of return with multiple sequential cues in younger and older adults. *Psychology and Aging*, 22, 404–409.

Pratt, J., Dodd, M. D., & Welsh, T. N. (2006). Growing older does not always mean moving slower: Examining aging and the saccadic motor system. *Journal of Motor Behavior*, 38, 372–382.

#Prigatano, G. P., & Parsons, O. A. (1976). Relationship of age and education to Halstead test performance in different patient populations. *Journal of Consulting and Clinical Psychology*, 44, 527–533.

Prince, M., Brown, S. D., & Heathcote, A. (2012). The design and analysis of state-trace experiments. *Psychological Methods*, 17, 78–99.

Puckett, J. M., & Lawson, W. M. (1989). Absence of adult age differences in forgetting in the Brown-Peterson task. *Acta Psychologica*, 72, 159–175.

Puckett, J. M., & Stockburger, D. W. (1988). Absence of age-related proneness to short-term retroactive interference in the absence of rehearsal. *Psychology and Aging*, 3, 342.

*Prull, M. W. (2004). Exploring the identification-production hypothesis of repetition priming in young and older adults. *Psychology and Aging*, 19, 108–124.

Puglisi, J. T. (1986). Age-related slowing in memory search for three-dimensional objects. *Journal of Gerontology*, 41, 72–78.

Raabe, S., Höger, R., & Delius, J. D. (2006). Sex differences in mental rotation strategy. *Perceptual and Motor Skills*, 103, 917–930.

Rabbitt, P. (1964). Ignoring irrelevant information. *British Journal of Psychology*, 55, 403–414.

Rabbitt, P. (1979). How old and young subjects monitor and control responses for accuracy and speed. *British Journal of Psychology*, 70, 305–311.

Rabbitt, P. (1997). Introduction: Methodologies and models in the study of executive function. In P. Rabbitt (Ed.), *Methodology of frontal and executive function* (pp. 1–38). Hove, UK: Psychology Press.

Rabbitt, P., Scott, M., Lunn, M., Thacker, N., Lowe, C., Pendleton, N.,...Jackson, A. (2007). White matter lesions account for all age-related declines in speed but not in intelligence. *Neuropsychology*, 21, 363–370.

Rabbitt, P., Scott, M., Thacker, N., Lowe, C., Jackson, A., Horan, M., & Pendleton, N. (2006). Losses in gross brain volume and cerebral blood flow account for age-related differences in speed but not in fluid intelligence. *Neuropsychology*, 20, 549–557.

*Radvansky, G. A., Copeland, D. E., Berish, D. E., & Dijkstra, K. (2003). Aging and situation model updating. *Aging, Neuropsychology, and Cognition*, 10, 158–166.

*Radvansky, G. A., Copeland, D. E., & Zwaan, R. A. (2003). Brief report: Aging and functional spatial relations in comprehension and memory. *Psychology and Aging*, 18, 161–165.

*Radvansky, G. A., & Curiel, J. M. (1998). Narrative comprehension and aging: The fate of completed goal information. *Psychology and Aging*, 13, 69–79.

Raemaekers, M., Vink, M., van den Heuvel, M. P., Kahn, R. S., & Ramsey, N. F. (2006). Effects of aging on BOLD fMRI during prosaccades and antisaccades. *Journal of Cognitive Neuroscience*, 18, 594–603.

Rambold, H., Neumann, G., Sander, T., & Helmchen, C. (2006). Age-related changes of vergence under natural viewing conditions. *Neurobiology of Aging*, 27, 163–172.

Ratcliff, R. (1978). A theory of memory retrieval. *Psychological Review*, 85, 59–108.

Ratcliff, R. (2008). Modeling aging effects on two-choice tasks: Response signal and response time data. *Psychology and Aging*, 23, 900–916.

Ratcliff, R., & McKoon, G. (2008). The diffusion decision model: Theory and data for two-choice decision tasks. *Neural Computation*, 20, 873–922.

Ratcliff, R., Spieler, D., & McKoon, G. (2000). Explicitly modeling the effects of aging on response time. *Psychonomic Bulletin and Review*, 7, 1–25.

*Ratcliff, R., Thapar, A., Gomez, P., & McKoon, G. (2004). A diffusion model analysis of the effects of aging in the lexical-decision task. *Psychology and Aging*, 19, 278–289.

*Ratcliff, R., Thapar, A., & McKoon, G. (2001). The effects of aging on reaction time in a signal detection task. *Psychology and Aging*, 16, 323–341.

Ratcliff, R., Thapar, A., & McKoon, G. (2006a). Aging and individual differences in rapid two-choice decisions. *Psychonomic Bulletin and Review*, 13, 626–635.

Ratcliff, R., Thapar, A., & McKoon, G. (2006b). Aging, practice, and perceptual tasks: A diffusion model analysis. *Psychology and Aging*, 21, 353–371.

Ratcliff, R., Thapar, A., & McKoon, G. (2007). Application of the diffusion model to two-choice tasks for adults 75–90 years old. *Psychology and Aging*, 22, 56–66.

Ratcliff, R., Thapar, A., & McKoon, G. (2010). Individual differences, aging, and IQ in two-choice tasks. *Cognitive Psychology*, 60, 127–157.

Ratcliff, R., & Tuerlinckx, F. (2002). Estimating the parameters of the diffusion model: Approaches to dealing with contaminant reaction times and parameter variability. *Psychonomic Bulletin and Review*, 9, 438–481.

Rauscher, F. H., Shaw, G. L., & Ky, K. N. (1993). Music and spatial task performance. *Nature*, 365, 611.

Ravizza, S. M., & Ciranni, M. A. (2002). Contributions of the prefrontal cortex and basal ganglia to set shifting. *Journal of Cognitive Neuroscience*, 14(3), 472–483.

Raz, N. (2000). Aging of the brain and its impact on cognitive performance: Integration of structural and functional findings. In F.I.M. Craik and T.A. Salthouse (Eds.) *Handbook of aging and cognition, 2nd ed.* (pp. 1–90). Mahwah, NJ: Erlbaum.

Raz, N. (2004). The aging brain: Structural changes and their implications for cognitive aging. In R. Dixon & L. G. Nilsson (Eds.) *New frontiers in cognitive aging (pp. 115–134)*. New York, NY: Oxford University Press.

Raz, N., Lindenberger, U., Rodrigue, K. M., Kennedy, K. M., Head, D., Williamson, A., . . . Acker, J. D. (2005). Regional brain changes in aging healthy adults: General trends, individual differences and modifiers. *Cerebral Cortex*, 15, 1676–1689.

Reimers, S., & Maylor, E. A. (2005). Task switching across the life span: Effects of age on general and specific switch costs. *Developmental Psychology*, 41, 661–671.

Reynolds, C. A., Gatz, M., & Pedersen, N. L. (2002). Individual variation for cognitive decline: Quantitative methods for describing patterns of change. *Psychology and Aging*, 17, 271–287.

#Riege, W. H., & Inman, V. (1981). Age differences in nonverbal memory tasks. *Journal of Gerontology*, 36, 51–58.

Rindermann, H., & Neubauer, A. C. (2004). Processing speed, intelligence, creativity, and school performance: Testing of causal hypotheses using structural equation models. *Intelligence*, 32, 573–589.

#Robertson-Tchabo, E. A., & Arenberg, D. (1976). Age differences in cognition in healthy educated men: A factor analysis of experimental measures. *Experimental Aging Research*, 2, 75–89.

Rodríguez-Aranda, C., & Sundet, K. (2006). The frontal hypothesis of cognitive aging: Factor structure and age effects on four frontal tests among healthy individuals. *Journal of Genetic Psychology*, 167, 269–287.

Roenker, D. L., Cissell, G. M., Ball, K. K., Wadley, V. G., & Edwards, J. D. (2003). Speed-of-processing and driving simulator training result in improved driving performance. *Human Factors*, 45, 218–233.

Rogers, R. D., & Monsell, S. (1995). Costs of a predictable switch between simple cognitive tasks. *Journal of Experimental Psychology: General*, 124, 207–231.

Rogers, W. A., Bertus, E. L., & Gilbert, D. K. (1994). Dual-task assessment of age differences in automatic process development. *Psychology and Aging*, 9, 398–413.

Rogers, W. A., Fisk, A. D., McLaughlin, A. C., & Pak, R. (2005). Touch a screen or turn a knob: Choosing the best device for the job. *Human Factors*, 47, 271–288.

Rogosa, D. (1980). A critique of cross-lagged correlation. *Psychological Bulletin*, 88, 245–258.

Rönnlund, M., Nyberg, L., Bäckman, L., & Nilsson, L. (2005). Stability, growth, and decline in adult life span development of declarative memory: Cross-sectional and longitudinal data from a population-based study. *Psychology and Aging*, 20, 3–18.

Rose, S. A., Feldman, J. F., & Jankowski, J. J. (2011). Modeling a cascade of effects: The role of speed and executive functioning in preterm/full-term differences in academic achievement. *Developmental Science*, 14, 1161–1175.

Rosenthal, R. (1979). The "File Drawer Problem" and the tolerance for null results. *Psychological Bulletin*, 86, 638–641.

Rösler, A., Mapstone, M. E., Hays, A. K., Mesulam, M. M., Rademaker, A., Gitelman, D.R., & Weintraub, S. (2000). Alterations of visual search strategy in Alzheimer's disease and aging. *Neuropsychology*, 14, 398–408.

Ruff, R. M., & Parker, S. B. (1993). Gender- and age-specific changes in motor speed and eye-hand coordination in adults: Normative values for the Finger Tapping and Grooved Pegboard Tests. *Perceptual and Motor Skills*, 76, 1219–1230.

Rush, B. K., Barch, D. M., & Braver, T. S. (2006). Accounting for cognitive aging: Context processing, inhibition or processing speed? *Aging, Neuropsychology, and Cognition*, 13, 588–610.

Rushby, J. A., Barry, R. J., & Johnstone, S. S. (2002). Event-related potential correlates of serial-position effects during an elaborative memory test. *International Journal of Psychophysiology: Official Journal of the International Organization of Psychophysiology*, 46, 13–27.

Ryan, J. D., Shen, J., & Reingold, E. M. (2006). Modulation of distraction in aging. *British Journal of Psychology*, 97, 339–351.

Ryan, L., Walther, K., Bendlin, B. B., Lue, L. F., Walker, D. G., & Glisky, E. L. (2011). Age-related differences in white matter integrity and cognitive function are related to APOE status. *NeuroImage*, 54, 1565–1577.

*Rypma, B., Prabhakaran, V., Desmond, J. E., & Gabrieli, J. D. E. (2001). Age differences in prefrontal cortical activity in working memory. *Psychology and Aging*, 16, 371–384.

Sagi, D., & Julesz, B. (1986). Enhanced detection in the aperture of focal attention during simple discrimination tasks. *Nature*, 321, 693–695.

Salthouse, T.A.(1978*). Age and speed: The nature of the relationship*. (unpublished manuscript).

#Salthouse, T. A. (1991a). Age and experience effects on the interpretation of orthographic drawings of three-dimensional objects. *Psychology and Aging*, 6, 426–433.

#Salthouse, T. A. (1991b). Mediation of adult age differences in cognition by reductions in working memory and speed of processing. *Psychological Science*, 2, 179–183.

Salthouse, T. A. (1991c). *Theoretical perspectives on cognitive aging*. Hillsdale, NJ: Erlbaum.

#Salthouse, T. A. (1992a). Influence of processing speed on adult age differences in working memory. *Acta Psychologica*, 79, 155–170.

Salthouse, T. A. (1992b). Why do adult age differences increase with task complexity? *Developmental Psychology*, 28, 905–918.

#Salthouse, T. A. (1993). Speed mediation of adult age differences in cognition. *Developmental Psychology*, 29, 722–738.

#Salthouse, T. A. (1994a). Aging associations: Influence of speed on adult age differences in associative learning. *Journal of Experimental Psychology: Learning, Memory, and Cognition*, 20, 1486–1503.

#Salthouse, T. A. (1994b). The nature of the influence of speed on adult age differences in cognition. *Developmental Psychology*, 30, 240–259.

#Salthouse, T. A. (1995a). Differential age-related influences on memory for verbal-symbolic information and visual-spatial information. *Journals of Gerontology: Psychological Sciences*, 50, 193–201.

#Salthouse, T. A. (1995b). Influence of processing speed on adult age differences in learning. *Swiss Journal of Psychology*, 54, 102–112.

#Salthouse, T A. (1996a). General and specific speed mediation of adult age differences in memory. *Journals of Gerontology: Psychological Sciences*, 51B, 30–42.

Salthouse, T. A. (1996b). The processing-speed theory of adult age differences in cognition. *Psychological Review*, 103, 403–428.

#Salthouse, T.A. (2001). Structural models of the relations between age and measures of cognitive functioning. *Intelligence*, 29, 93–115.

#Salthouse, T.A. (2004). Localizing age-related individual differences in a hierarchical structure. *Intelligence*, 32, 541–561,

#Salthouse, T.A. (2005). Relations between cognitive abilities and measures of executive functioning. *Neuropsychology*, 19, 532–545.

Salthouse, T. A. (2006). Mental exercise and mental aging: Evaluating the validity of the "use it or lose it" hypothesis. *Perspectives on Psychological Science*, 1, 68–87.

Salthouse, T. A. (2007). Implications of within-person variability in cognitive and neuropsychological functioning on the interpretation of change. *Neuropsychology*, 21, 401–411.

Salthouse, T. A. (2009). When does age-related cognitive decline begin? *Neurobiology of Aging*, 30, 507–514.

Salthouse, T. A. (2010). *Major issues in cognitive aging*. New York, NY: Oxford University Press.

Salthouse, T. A. (2011a). Effects of age on time-dependent cognitive change. *Psychological Science*, 22, 682–688.

Salthouse, T. A. (2011b). Neuroanatomical substrates of age-related cognitive decline. *Psychological Bulletin*, 137, 753–784.

#Salthouse, T. A., Atkinson, T. M., & Berish, D. E. (2003). Executive functioning as a potential mediator of age-related cognitive decline in normal adults. *Journal of Experimental Psychology: General*, 132, 566–594.

#Salthouse, T.A., & Babcock, R.L. (1991). Decomposing adult age differences in working memory. *Developmental Psychology*, 27, 763–776.

Salthouse, T. A., Babcock, R. L., Skovronek, E., Mitchell, D. R., & Palmon, R. (1990). Age and experience effects in spatial visualization. *Developmental Psychology*, 26, 128–136.

#Salthouse, T. A., Berish, D. E., & Siedlecki, K. L. (2004) Construct validity and age sensitivity of prospective memory. *Memory & Cognition*, 32, 1133–1148.

#Salthouse, T. A., & Czaja, S. (2000). Structural constraints on process explanations in cognitive aging. *Psychology and Aging*, 15, 44–55.

#Salthouse, T. A., & Davis, H. P. (2006). Organization of cognitive abilities and neuropsychological variables across the lifespan. *Developmental Review*, 26, 31–54.

Salthouse, T. A., & Ferrer-Caja, E. (2003). What needs to be explained to account for age-related effects on multiple cognitive variables? *Psychology and Aging*, 18, 91–110.

Salthouse, T. A., & Fristoe, N. M. (1995). Process analysis of adult age effects on a computer-administered trail making test. *Neuropsychology*, 9, 518–528.

#Salthouse, T. A., Fristoe, N. M., Lineweaver, T. T., & Coon, V. E. (1995). Aging of attention: Does the ability to divide decline? *Memory & Cognition*, 23, 59–71.

#Salthouse, T. A., Fristoe, N., McGuthry, K. & Hambrick, D. Z. (1998). Relation of task switching to age, speed, and fluid intelligence. *Psychology and Aging*, 13, 445–461.

#Salthouse, T. A., Fristoe, N. M., & Rhee, S. H. (1996). How localized are age-related effects on neuropsychological measures? *Neuropsychology*, 10, 272–285.

#Salthouse, T. A., Hambrick, D. Z., Lukas, K. E., & Dell, T. C. (1996). Determinants of adult age differences in synthetic work performance. *Journal of Experimental Psychology: Applied*, 2, 305–329.

#Salthouse, T. A., & Hancock, H. E. (1995). *Effects of age and speed on memory as a function of stimulus presentation time.* (unpublished manuscript). Georgia Institute of Technology, School of Psychology, Atlanta, GA.

#Salthouse, T. A., Hancock, H. E., Meinz, E. J., & Hambrick, D. Z. (1996). Interrelations of age, visual acuity, and cognitive functioning. *Journals of Gerontology: Psychological Sciences*, 51, 317–330.

#Salthouse, T. A., Kausler, D. H., & Saults, J. S. (1988). Investigation of student status, background variables, and the feasibility of standard tasks in cognitive aging research. *Psychology and Aging*, 3, 29–37.

#Salthouse, T. A., Letz, R., & Hooisma, J. (1994). Causes and consequences of age-related slowing in speeded substitution performance. *Developmental Neuropsychology*, 10, 203–214.

#Salthouse, T. A., & Meinz, E. J. (1995). Aging, inhibition, working memory, and speed. *Journals of Gerontology: Psychological Sciences*, 50, 297–306.

#Salthouse, T. A., & Mitchell, D. R. D. (1990). Effects of age and naturally occurring experience on spatial visualization performance. *Developmental Psychology*, 26, 845–854.

#Salthouse, T. A., Pink, J. E., & Tucker-Drob, E. M. (2008). Contextual analysis of fluid intelligence. *Intelligence*, 36, 464–486.

Salthouse, T. A., Rogan, J. D., & Prill, K. A. (1984). Division of attention: Age differences on a visually presented memory task. *Memory & Cognition*, 12, 613–620.

#Salthouse, T. A., & Siedlecki, K. L. (2007a). Efficiency of route selection as a function of adult age. *Brain and Cognition*, 63, 279–287.

#Salthouse, T. A., & Siedlecki, K. L. (2007b). An individual differences analysis of false recognition. *American Journal of Psychology*, 120, 429–458.

#Salthouse, T. A., Siedlecki, K. L., & Krueger, L. E. (2006). An individual differences analysis of memory control. *Journal of Memory and Language*, 55, 102–125.

Salthouse, T. A., & Somberg, B. L. (1982a). Isolating the age deficit in speeded performance. *Journal of Gerontology*, 37, 59–63.

Salthouse, T. A., & Somberg, B. L. (1982b). Skilled performance: Effects of adult age and experience on elementary processes. *Journal of Experimental Psychology: General*, 111, 176–207.

#Salthouse, T. A., Toth, J., Daniels, K., Parks, C., Pak, R., Wolbrette, M., & Hocking, K. (2000). Effects of aging on the efficiency of task switching in a variant of the Trail Making Test. *Neuropsychology*, 14, 102–111.

*#Salthouse, T. A., Toth, J. P., Hancock, H. E., & Woodard, J. L. (1997). Controlled and automatic forms of memory and attention: Process purity and the uniqueness of age-related influences. *Journals of Gerontology: Psychological Sciences*, 52, 216–228.

Sanders, A. F., & Sanders, A. (1998). *Elements of human performance: Reaction processes and attention in human skill*. Hillsdale, NJ: Lawrence Erlbaum.

Schaie, K. W. (1965). A general model for the study of developmental problems. *Psychological Bulletin*, 64, 92–107.

Schaie, K. W. (1989a). Individual differences in rate of cognitive change in adulthood. In V. L. Bengtson & K. W. Schaie (Eds.), *The course of later life: Research and reflections* (pp. 65–85). New York, NY: Springer.

#Schaie, K. W. (1989b). Perceptual speed in adulthood: Cross-sectional and longitudinal studies. *Psychology and Aging*, 4, 443–453.

Schaie, K. W. (2005). *Developmental influences on adult intellectual development: The Seattle Longitudinal Study*. New York, NY: Oxford University Press.

#Schludermann, E. H., Schludermann, S. M., Merryman, P. W., & Brown, B. W. (1983). Halstead's studies in the neuropsychology of aging. *Archives of Gerontology and Geriatrics*, 2, 49–172.

Schmidtke, H. (1951). Über die Messung der psychischen Ermüdung mit Hilfe des Flimmertests [On the measurement of mental fatigue using the flicker test]. *Psychologische Forschung*, 23, 409–463.

Schmiedek, F., & Li, S. C. (2004). Toward an alternative representation for disentangling age-associated differences in general and specific cognitive abilities. *Psychology and Aging*, 19, 40–56.

Schmiedek, F., Oberauer, K., Wilhelm, O., Süß, H. M., & Wittmann, W. W. (2007). Individual differences in components of reaction time distributions and their relations to working memory and intelligence. *Journal of Experimental Psychology: General*, 136, 414–429.

*Schmitter-Edgecombe, M. (1999). Effects of divided attention and time course on automatic and controlled components of memory in older adults. *Psychology and Aging*, 14, 331–345.

*Schmitter-Edgecombe, M., & Simpson, A. L. (2001). Effects of age and intentionality on content memory and temporal memory for performed activities. *Aging, Neuropsychology, and Cognition*, 8, 81–97.

Schneider, B. A., & Hamstra, S. J. (1999). Gap detection thresholds as a function of tonal duration for younger and older adults. *Journal of the Acoustical Society of America*, 106, 371–380.

Schneider, B. A., Pichora-Fuller, M. K., Kowalchuk, D., & Lamb, M. (1994). Gap detection and the precedence effect in young and old adults. *Journal of the Acoustical Society of America*, 95, 980–991.

*Schooler, C., Neumann, E., Caplan, L. J., & Roberts, B. R. (1997). Continued inhibitory capacity throughout adulthood: Conceptual negative priming in younger and older adults. *Psychology and Aging*, 12, 667–674.

Schweizer, K. (2001). Preattentive processing and cognitive ability. *Intelligence*, 29, 169–186.

Scialfa, C. T., Esau, C. T. S. S. P., & Joffe, K. M. (1998). Age, target-distractor similarity, and visual search. *Experimental Aging Research*, 24, 337–358.

Scialfa, C. T., Hamaluk, E., Pratt, J., & Skaloud, P. (1999). Age differences in saccadic averaging. *Psychology and Aging*, 14, 695–699.

*Scialfa, C. T., Jenkins, L., Hamaluk, E., & Skaloud, P. (2000). Aging and the development of automaticity in conjunction search. *Journals of Gerontology: Psychological Sciences*, 55, 27–46.

*Scialfa, C. T., & Joffe, K. M. (1997). Age differences in feature and conjunction search: Implications for theories of visual search and generalized slowing. *Aging, Neuropsychology, and Cognition*, 4, 227–246.

Servan-Schreiber, D., Printz, H., & Cohen, J. D. (1990). A network model of catecholamine effects: Gain, signal-to-noise ratio, and behavior. *Science*, 249, 892–895.

*Shammi, P., Bosman, E., & Stuss, D. T. (1998). Aging and variability in performance. *Aging, Neuropsychology, and Cognition*, 5, 1–13.

Shaw, R. J. (1991). Age-related increases in the effects of automatic semantic activation. *Psychology and Aging*, 6, 595–604.

Shepard, R. N., & Metzler, J. (1971). Mental rotation of three-dimensional objects. *Science*, 171, 701–703.

Sheppard, L. D., & Vernon, P. A. (2008). Intelligence and speed of information-processing: A review of 50 years of research. *Personality and Individual Differences*, 44, 535–551.

Shingleton, A.W. (2010). Allometry. *Nature Education Knowledge*, 1, 2.

#Siedlecki, K. L., Salthouse, T. A., & Berish, D. E. Is there anything special about the aging of source memory? *Psychology and Aging*, 20, 19–32.

Simonton, D. K. (1988). Age and outstanding achievement: What do we know after a century of research? Psychological Bulletin, 104, 251–267.

Singer, T., Verhaeghen, P., Ghisletta, P., Lindenberger, U., & Baltes, P. B. (2003). The fate of cognition in very old age: Six-year longitudinal findings in the Berlin aging study (BASE). *Psychology and Aging*, 18, 318–331.

*Sliwinski, M. (1997). Aging and counting speed: Evidence for process-specific slowing. *Psychology and Aging*, 12, 38–49.

Sliwinski, M., & Buschke, H. (1999). Cross-sectional and longitudinal relationships among age, cognition, and processing speed. *Psychology and Aging*, 14, 18–33.

Sliwinski, M., & Buschke, H. (2004). Modeling intraindividual cognitive change in aging adults: Results from the Einstein Aging Studies. *Aging Neuropsychology and Cognition*, 11, 196–211.

Sliwinski, M., & Hall, C. B. (1998). Constraints on general slowing: A meta-analysis using hierarchical linear models with random coefficients. *Psychology and Aging*, 13, 164–175.

Sliwinski, M., & Hofer, S. (1999). How strong is the evidence for mediational hypotheses of age-related memory loss? Commentary. *Gerontology*, 45, 351–354.

Sliwinski, M., Hoffman, L., & Hofer, S. M. (2010). Evaluating convergence of within-person change and between-person age differences in age-heterogeneous longitudinal studies. *Research in Human Development*, 7, 45–60.

Sliwinski, M., Lipton, R. B., Buschke, H., & Stewart, W. F. (1996). The effect of pre-clinical dementia on estimates of normal cognitive function in aging. *Journal of Gerontology: Psychological Sciences*, 51, 217–225.

Smith, E. E., & Jonides, J. (1999). Storage and executive processes in the frontal lobes. *Science*, 283, 1657–1661.

Snell, K. B. (1997). Age-related changes in temporal gap detection. *Journal of the Acoustical Society of America*, 101, 2214–2220.

Snell, K. B., & Frisina, D. R. (2000). Relationships among age-related differences in gap detection and word recognition. *Journal of the Acoustical Society of America*, 107, 1615–1626.

Snell, K. B., & Hu, H-L. (1999). The effect of temporal placement on gap detectability. *Journal of the Acoustical Society of America*, 106, 3571–3577.

Snoddy, G. S. (1926). Learning and stability. *Journal of Applied Psychology*, 10, 1–36.

Somberg, B. L., & Salthouse, T. A. (1982). Divided attention abilities in young and old adults. *Journal of Experimental Psychology: Human Perception and Performance*, 8, 651–663.

Sommers, M. S., & Danielson, S. M. (1999). Inhibitory processes and spoken word recognition in young and older adults: The interaction of lexical competition and semantic context. *Psychology and Aging*, 14, 458–472.

*Sommers, M. S., & Huff, L. M. (2003). The effects of age and dementia of the Alzheimer's type on phonological false memories. *Psychology and Aging*, 18, 791–806.

Song, S. K., Sun, S. W., Ramsbottom, M. J., Chang, C., Russell, J., & Cross, A. H. (2002). Dysmyelination revealed through MRI as increased radial (but unchanged axial) diffusion of water. *NeuroImage*, 17, 1429–1436.

Soukoreff, R. W., & MacKenzie, I. S. (2004). Towards a standard for pointing device evaluation, perspectives on 27 years of Fitts' law research in HCI. *International Journal of Human-Computer Studies*, 61, 751–789.

Sperber, D., & Wilson, D. (1986) *Relevance: Communication and Cognition*. Oxford, UK: Blackwell.

Sperling, G. (1960). The information available in brief visual presentations. *Psychological Monographs: General and Applied*, 74, whole issue.

Spieler, D. H., Balota, D. A., & Faust, M. E. (1996). Stroop performance in healthy younger and older adults and in individuals with dementia of the Alzheimer's type. *Journal of Experimental Psychology: Human Perception and Performance*, 22, 461–479.

Spieler, D., Mayr, U., & LaGrone, S. (2006). Outsourcing cognitive control to the environment: Adult-age differences in the use of task cues. *Psychonomic Bulletin & Review*, 5, 787–793.

#Stankov, L. (1988). Aging, attention, and intelligence. *Psychology and Aging*, 3, 59–74.

#Stankov, L. (1994). The complexity effect phenomenon is an epiphenomenon of age-related fluid intelligence decline. *Personality and Individual Differences*, 16, 265–288.

Starns, J.J., & Ratcliff, R. (2010). The effects of aging on the speed-accuracy compromise: Boundary optimality in the diffusion model. *Psychology and Aging*, 25, 377–390.

Steele, K. M., Dalla Bella, S., Peretz, I., Dunlop, T., Dawe, L. A., Humphrey, G. K.,...Olmstead, C. G. (1999). Prelude or requiem for the 'Mozart effect'? *Nature*, 400, 826–827.

Stern, C., Prather, P., Swinney, D., & Zurif, E. (1991). The time course of automatic lexical access and aging. *Brain and Language*, 40, 359–372.

Stern, Y. (2002). What is cognitive reserve? Theory and research application of the reserve concept. *Journal of the International Neuropsychological Society*, 8, 448–460.

Stern, Y. (2009). Cognitive reserve. *Neuropsychologia*, 47, 2015–2028.

Sternberg, S. (1966). High-speed scanning in human memory. *Science*, 153, 652–654.

Sternberg, S. (1975). Memory scanning: New findings and current controversies. *The Quarterly Journal of Experimental Psychology*, 27, 1–32.

#Sterne, D. M. (1973). The Hooper Visual Organization Test and Trail Making Tests as discriminants of brain injury. *Journal of Clinical Psychology*, 29, 212–213.

*Stine-Morrow, E. A. L., Miller, L. M. S., & Nevin, J. A. (1999). The effects of context and feedback on age differences in spoken word recognition. *Journals of Gerontology: Psychological Sciences*, 54, 125–134.

*Stine-Morrow, E. A. L., Soederberg Miller, L. M., & Leno, R. (2001). Patterns of on-line resource allocation to narrative text by younger and older readers. *Aging, Neuropsychology, and Cognition*, 8, 36–53.

Stoltzfus, E. R., Hasher, L., Zacks, R. T., Ulivi, M. S., & Goldstein, D. (1993). Investigations of inhibition and interference in younger and older adults. *Journals of Gerontology: Psychological Sciences*, 48, 179–188.

Stone, M. (1960). Models for choice reaction time. *Psychometrika*, 25, 251–260.

Strayer, D. L., & Kramer, A. F. (1994). Aging and skill acquisition: Learning-performance distinctions. *Psychology and Aging*, 9, 589.

Strayer, D. L., Wickens, C. D., & Braune, R. (1987). Adult age differences in the speed and capacity of information processing: II. An electrophysiological approach. *Psychology and Aging*, 2, 99–110.

Strouse, A., Ashmead, D. H., Ohde, R. N., & Grantham, D. W. (1998). Temporal processing in the aging auditory system. *Journal of the Acoustical Society of America*, 104, 2385–2399.

Stuss, D. T., Stethem, L. L., & Poirier, C. A. (1987). Comparison of three tests of attention and rapid information processing across six age groups. *The Clinical Neuropsychologist*, 1, 139–152.

Sullivan, E. V., Rohlfing, T., & Pfefferbaum, A. (2010). Quantitative fiber tracking of lateral and interhemispheric white matter systems in normal aging: Relations to timed performance. *Neurobiology of Aging*, 31, 464.

Sullivan, M. P. (1999). The functional interaction of visual-perceptual and response mechanisms during selective attention in young adults, young-old adults, and old-old adults. *Attention, Perception, & Psychophysics*, 61, 810–825.

Sullivan, M. P., & Faust, M. E. (1993). Evidence of identity inhibition during selective attention in old adults. *Psychology and Aging*, 8, 589–598.

Sullivan, M. P., Faust, M. E., & Balota, D. A. (1994, April). *On the nature of identity negative priming in old adults and patients with probable Alzheimer's disease.* Paper presented at the Cognitive Aging Conference, Atlanta, GA.

Sullivan, M. P., Faust, M. E., & Balota, D. A. (1995). Identity negative priming in older adults and individuals with dementia of Alzheimer type. *Neuropsychology*, 9, 537–555.

Sundet, J. M., Barlaug, D. G., & Torjussen, T. M. (2004). The end of the Flynn effect?: A study of secular trends in mean intelligence test scores of Norwegian conscripts during half a century. *Intelligence*, 32, 349–362.

Süß, H. M., Oberauer, K., Wittmann, W. W., Wilhelm, O., & Schulze, R. (2002). Working-memory capacity explains reasoning ability—and a little bit more. *Intelligence*, 30, 261–288.

Sweeney, J. A., Rosano, C., Berman, R. A., & Luna, B. (2001). Inhibitory control of attention declines more than working memory during normal aging. *Neurobiology of Aging*, 22, 39–48.

Swift, C. G., & Tiplady, B. (1988). The effects of age on the response to caffeine. *Psychopharmacology*, 94, 29–31.

Tachibana, H., Aragane, K., & Sugita, M. (1996). Age-related changes in event-related potentials in visual discrimination tasks. *Electroencephalography and Clinical Neurophysiology: Evoked Potentials Section*, 100, 299–309.

Tainturier, M. J., Tremblay, M., & Lecours, A. (1989). Aging and the word frequency effect: A lexical decision investigation. *Neuropsychologia*, 27, 1197–1202.

#Tamkin, A. S., & Jacobsen, R. (1984). Age-related norms for the Hooper Visual Organization Test. *Journal of Clinical Psychology*, 40, 1459–1463.

Tanaka, H., & Seals, D. R. (2003). Invited Review: Dynamic exercise performance in Masters athletes: Insight into the effects of primary human aging on physiological functional capacity. *Journal of Applied Physiology*, 95, 2152–2162.

Tays, W. J., Dywan, J., Mathewson, K. J., & Segalowitz, S. J. (2008). Age differences in target detection and interference resolution in working memory: An event-related potential study. *Journal of Cognitive Neuroscience*, 20, 2250–2262.

*Taylor, J. K., & Burke, D. M. (2002). Asymmetric aging effects on semantic and phonological processes: Naming in the picture-word interference task. *Psychology and Aging*, 17, 662–676.

Taylor, J. L., Miller, T. P., & Tinklenberg, J. R. (1992). Correlates of memory decline: A 4-year longitudinal study of older adults with memory complaints. *Psychology and Aging*, 7, 185–193.

Taylor, P., Morin, R., Parker, K., Cohn, D., & Wang, W. (2009*), Growing old in America: Expectations vs. reality*. Washington, DC: Pew Research Center.

Teasdale, T. W., & Owen, D. R. (2005). A long-term rise and recent decline in intelligence test performance: The Flynn Effect in reverse. *Personality and Individual Differences*, 39, 837–843.

Tecce, J. J., Cattanach, L., Yrchik, D. A., Meinbresse, D., & Dessonville, C. L. (1982). CNV rebound and aging. *Electroencephalography and Clinical Neurophysiology*, 54, 175–186.

Teixeira, L. A. (2008). Categories of manual asymmetry and their variation with advancing age. *Cortex*, 44, 707–716.

*Thapar, A., Ratcliff, R., & McKoon, G. (2003). A diffusion model analysis of the effects of aging on letter discrimination. *Psychology and Aging*, 18, 415–429.

Thorndike, E. L., Bregman, E. O., Tilton, J. W., and Woodyard, E. (1928). *Adult Learning*. New York, NY: Macmillan.

Thornton, W. J. L., & Raz, N. (2006). Aging and the role of working memory resources in visuospatial attention. *Aging, Neuropsychology, and Cognition*, 13, 36–61.

Tipper, S. P. (1985). The negative priming effect: Inhibitory priming by ignored objects. *The Quarterly Journal of Experimental Psychology*, 37, 571–590.

Tipper, S. P. (1991). Less attentional selectivity as a result of declaring inhibition in older adults. *Bulletin of the Psychonomic Society*, 29, 45–47.

Tisserand, D. J., Visser, P. J., van Boxtel, M. P. J., & Jolles, J. (2000). The relation between global and limbic brain volumes on MRI and cognitive performance in healthy individuals across the age range. *Neurobiology of Aging*, 21, 569–576.

Titz, C., Behrendt, J., Menge, U., & Hasselhorn, M. (2008). A reassessment of negative priming within the inhibition framework of cognitive aging: There is more in it than previously believed. *Experimental Aging Research*, 34, 340–366.

Tombaugh, T. N. (2004). Trail Making Test A and B: Normative data stratified by age and education. *Archives of Clinical Neuropsychology*, 19, 203–214.

Tornay, F. J., & Milán, E. G. (2001). A more complete task-set reconfiguration in random than in predictable task switch. *The Quarterly Journal of Experimental Psychology*, 54A, 785–803.

Touron, D. R., & Hertzog, C. (2004). Distinguishing age differences in knowledge, strategy use, and confidence during strategic skill acquisition. *Psychology and Aging*, 19, 452.

*Touron, D. R., Hoyer, W. J., & Cerella, J. (2001). Cognitive skill acquisition and transfer in younger and older adults. *Psychology and Aging*, 16, 555–563.

Townsend, J. T., & Ashby, F. G. (1983). *The stochastic modeling of elementary psychological processes*. Cambridge, UK: Cambridge University Press.

Townsend, J. T., & Wenger, M. J. (2004). The serial-parallel dilemma: A case study in a linkage of theory and method. *Psychonomic Bulletin & Review*, 11, 391–418.

Treitz, F. H., Heyder, K., & Daum, I. (2007). Differential course of executive control changes during normal aging. *Aging, Neuropsychology, and Cognition*, 14, 370–393.

Trick, L. M., & Enns, J. T. (1998). Lifespan changes in attention: The visual search task. *Cognitive Development*, 13, 369–386.

Trick, L. M., Enns, J. T., & Brodeur, D. A. (1996). Life span changes in visual enumeration: The number discrimination task. *Developmental Psychology*, 32, 925.

Trick, L. M., & Pylyshyn, Z. W. (1993). What enumeration studies can show us about spatial attention: Evidence for limited capacity preattentive processing. *Journal of Experimental Psychology: Human Perception and Performance*, 19, 331.

Trick, L. M., & Pylyshyn, Z. W. (1994). Why are small and large numbers enumerated differently? A limited-capacity preattentive stage in vision. *Psychological Review*, 101, 80.

Treisman, A. M., & Gelade, G. (1980). A feature-integration theory of attention. *Cognitive Psychology*, 12, 97–136.

Troche, S. J., Gibbons, H., & Rammsayer, T. H. (2008). Identity and location priming effects and their temporal stability in young and older adults. *Aging, Neuropsychology, and Cognition*, 15, 281–301.

*Trott, C. T., Friedman, D., Ritter, W., Fabiani, M., & Snodgrass, J. G. (1999). Episodic priming and memory for temporal source: Event-related potentials reveal age-related differences in prefrontal functioning. *Psychology and Aging*, 14, 390–413.

*Tsang, P. S. (1998). Age, attention, expertise, and time-sharing performance. *Psychology and Aging*, 13, 323–347.

Tsang, P. S., & Shaner, T. L. (1998). Age, attention, expertise, and time-sharing performance. *Psychology and Aging*, 13, 323–347.

Tsuchida, N. (2005). Inhibition of return using location discrimination in two age groups. *Perceptual and Motor Skills*, 100, 554–558.

Tucker-Drob, E. M. (2011a). Global and domain-specific changes in cognition throughout adulthood. *Developmental Psychology*, 47(2), 331–343.

Tucker-Drob, E. M. (2011b). Neurocognitive functions and everyday functions change together in old age. *Neuropsychology*, 25, 368–377.

Tucker-Drob, E. M., Johnson, K. E., & Jones, R. N. (2009). The cognitive reserve hypothesis: A longitudinal examination of age-associated declines in reasoning and processing speed. *Developmental Psychology*, 45, 431–446.

*Tun, P. A., O'Kane, G., & Wingfield, A. (2002). Distraction by competing speech in young and older adult listeners. *Psychology and Aging*, 17, 453–467.

Tun, P. A., & Wingfield, A. (1994). Speech recall under heavy load conditions: Age, predictability, and limits on dual-task interference. *Aging and Cognition*, 1, 29–44.

*Tun, P. A., Wingfield, A., Rosen, M. J., & Blanchard, L. (1998). Response latencies for false memories: Gist-based processes in normal aging. *Psychology and Aging*, 13, 230–241.

Tun, P. A., Wingfield, A., & Stine, E. A. L. (1991). Speech-processing capacity in young and older adults: A dual-task study. *Psychology and Aging*, 6, 3–9.

Tun, P. A., Wingfield, A., Stine, E. A. L., & Mecsas, C. (1992). Rapid speech processing and divided attention: Processing rate versus processing resources as an explanation of age effects. *Psychology and Aging*, 7, 546–550.

Turner, M. L., & Engle, R. W. (1989). Is working memory capacity task dependent? *Journal of Memory and Language*, 28, 127–154.

Ulrich, R., Mattes, S., & Miller, J. (1999). Donders's assumption of pure insertion: An evaluation on the basis of response dynamics. *Acta Psychologica*, 102, 43–76.

Uludag, K., Dubowitz, D. J., Yoder, E. J., Restom, K., Liu, T. T., & Buxton, R. B. (2004). Coupling of cerebral blood flow and oxygen consumption during physiological activation and deactivation measured with fMRI. *NeuroImage*, 23, 148–155.

Uttl, B., & Graf, P. (1997). Color-word Stroop test performance across the adult life span. *Journal of Clinical and Experimental Neuropsychology*, 19, 405–420.

Uttl, B., Graf, P., & Cosentino, S. (2000). Exacting assessments: Do older adults fatigue more quickly? *Journal of Clinical and Experimental Neuropsychology*, 22, 496–507.

Van Asselen, M., & Ridderinkhof, K. R. (2000). Shift costs of predictable and unexpected set shifting in young and older adults. *Psychologica Belgica*, 40, 259–273.

Vance, D., Dawson, J., Wadley, V., Edwards, J., Roenker, D., Rizzo, M., & Ball, K. (2007). The accelerate study: The longitudinal effect of speed of processing training on cognitive performance of older adults. *Rehabilitation Psychology*, 52, 89–96.

Van der Elst, W., Van Boxtel, M. P., Van Breukelen, G. J., & Jolles, J. (2006). The Stroop Color-Word Test influence of age, sex, and education; and normative data for a large sample across the adult age range. *Assessment*, 13, 62–79.

Van Disseldorp, J., Faddy, M. J., Themmen, A. P. N., De Jong, F. H., Peeters, P. H. M., Van der Schouw, Y. T., & Broekmans, F. J. M. (2008). Relationship of serum antimüllerian hormone concentration to age at menopause. *Journal of Clinical Endocrinology & Metabolism*, 93, 2129–2134.

Van Gerven, P. W., Paas, F., Van Merriënboer, J. J., & Schmidt, H. G. (2003). Memory load and the cognitive pupillary response in aging. *Psychophysiology*, 41, 167–174.

#Van Gerven, P. W. M., Van Boxtel, M. P. J., Meijer W. A., Willems D., et al. (2007). On the relative role of inhibition in age-related working memory decline. *Aging Neuropsychology and Cognition* 14, 95–107.

van Ravenzwaaij, D., Brown, S., & Wagenmakers, E. J. (2011). An integrated perspective on the relation between response speed and intelligence. *Cognition*, 119, 381–393.

Vaughan, L., Basak, C., Hartman, M., & Verhaeghen, P. (2008). Aging and working memory inside and outside the focus of attention: Dissociations of availability and accessibility. *Aging, Neuropsychology, and Cognition*, 15, 703–724.

#Vega, A., & Parsons, O. A. (1967). Cross-validation of the Halstead-Reitan tests for brain damage. *Journal of Consulting Psychology*, 31, 619–625.

Verhaeghen, P. (2000). The parallels in beauty's brow: Time-accuracy functions and their implications for cognitive aging theories. In T. J. Perfect and E. A. Maylor (Eds.), *Models of cognitive aging* (pp. 50–86). Oxford, UK: Oxford University Press.

Verhaeghen, P. (2003). Aging and vocabulary score: A meta-analysis. *Psychology and Aging*, 18, 332–339.

Verhaeghen, P. (2011). Aging and executive control: Reports of a demise greatly exaggerated. *Current Directions in Psychological Science*, 20, 174–180.

Verhaeghen, P., & Basak, C. (2005). Ageing and switching of the focus of attention in working memory: Results from a modified N-Back task. *The Quarterly Journal of Experimental Psychology*, 58A, 134–154.

Verhaeghen, P., Borchelt, M., & Smith, J. (2003). The relation between cardiovascular and metabolic disease and cognition in very old age: Cross-sectional and longitudinal findings from the Berlin Aging Study. *Health Psychology*, 22, 559–569.

Verhaeghen, P., & Cerella, J. (2002). Aging, executive control, and attention: A review of meta-analyses. *Neuroscience and Biobehavioral Reviews*, 26, 849–857.

Verhaeghen, P., & Cerella, J. (2008). Everything we know about aging and response times: A meta-analytic integration. In S. M. Hofer & D. F. Alwin (Eds.), *The handbook of cognitive aging: Interdisciplinary perspectives* (pp. 134–150). Thousand Oaks, CA: Sage Publications.

Verhaeghen, P., Cerella, J, & Basak, C. (2006). Aging, task complexity, and efficiency modes: The influence of working memory involvement on age differences in response times for verbal and visuospatial tasks. *Aging, Neuropsychology, and Cognition*, 13, 254–280.

*Verhaeghen, P., Cerella, J., Semenec, S. C., Leo, M. A., Bopp, K. L., & Steitz, D. W. (2002). Cognitive efficiency modes in old age: Performance on sequential and coordinative verbal and visuospatial tasks. *Psychology and Aging*, 17, 558–570.

Verhaeghen, P., & De Meersman, L. (1998a). Aging and negative priming: A meta-analysis. *Psychology and Aging*, 13, 435–444.

Verhaeghen, P., & De Meersman, L. (1998b). Aging and the Stroop effect: A meta-analysis. *Psychology and Aging*, 13, 120–126.

Verhaeghen, P., Kliegl, R., & Mayr, U. (1997). Sequential and coordinative complexity in time-accuracy functions for mental arithmetic. *Psychology & Aging*, 12, 555–564.

Verhaeghen, P., & Salthouse, T. A. (1997). Meta-analyses of age-cognition relations in adulthood: Estimates of linear and non-linear age effects and structural models. *Psychological Bulletin*, 122, 231–249.

Verhaeghen, P., Steitz, D. W., Sliwinski, M. J., & Cerella, J. (2003). Aging and dual-task performance: A meta-analysis. *Psychology and Aging*, 18, 443–460.

Verleger, R. (1997). On the utility of P3 latency as an index of mental chronometry. *Psychophysiology*, 34, 131–156.

Verleger, R., Jaśkowski, P., & Wascher, E. (2005). Evidence for an integrative role of P3b in linking reaction to perception. *Journal of Psychophysiology*, 19, 165–181.

Verleger, R, Neukäter, W., Kömpf, D., & Vieregge, P. (1991). On the reasons for the delay of P3 latency in healthy elderly subjects. *Electroencephalography and Clinical Neurophysiology*, 79, 488–502.

Vetter, P., Butterworth, B., & Bahrami, B. (2011). A candidate for the attentional bottleneck: Set-size specific modulation of the right TPJ during attentive enumeration. *Journal of Cognitive Neuroscience*, 23, 728–736.

Vigil-Colet, A., & Codorniu-Raga, M. J. (2002). How inspection time and paper and pencil measures of processing speed are related to intelligence. *Personality and Individual Differences*, 33, 1149–1161.

Von Bertalanffy, L. (1938). A quantitative theory of organic growth (Inquiries on growth laws II). *Human Biology*, 10, 181–213.

Von Bertalanffy, L., & Pirozynski, W. J. (1952). Ontogenetic and evolutionary allometry. *Evolution*, 6, 387–392.

Vul, E., Harris, C., Winkielman, P., & Pashler, H. (2009). Puzzlingly high correlations in fMRI studies of emotion, personality, and social cognition. *Perspectives on Psychological Science*, 4, 274–290.

Wagenmakers, E.-J., van der Maas, H. L. J., & Grasman, R. P. P. P. (2007). An EZ-diffusion model for response time and accuracy. *Psychonomic Bulletin & Review*, 14, 3–22.

Walhovd, K. B., & Fjell, A. M. (2007). White matter volume predicts reaction time instability. *Neuropsychologia*, 45, 2277–2284.

Walhovd, K. B., Westlye, L. T., Amlien, I., Espeseth, T., Reinvang, I., Raz, N., . . . Fjell, A. M. (2011). Consistent neuroanatomical age-related volume differences across multiple samples. *Neurobiology of Aging*, 32, 916–932.

Walker, N., Philbin, D. A., & Fisk, A. D. (1997). Age-related differences in movement control: Adjusting submovement structure to optimize performance. *Journal of Gerontology: Psychological Sciences*, 52, 40.

Walsh, D. A., & Thompson, L. W. (1978). Age differences in visual sensory memory. *Journal of Gerontology*, 33, 383–387.

#Wasserstein, J., Zappulla, R., Rosen, J., & Gerstman, L. (1987). In search of closure: Subjective contour illusions, gestalt completion tests, and implications. *Brain and Cognition*, 6, 1–14.

Wasylyshyn, C., Verhaeghen, P., & Sliwinski, M. (2011). Aging and task switching: A meta-analysis. *Psychology and Aging*, 26, 15–20.

*Waters, G. S., & Caplan, D. (2001). Age, working memory, and on-line syntactic processing in sentence comprehension. *Psychology and Aging*, 16, 128–144.

Watson, D. G., Maylor, E. A., Allen, G. E., & Bruce, L. A. (2007). Early visual tagging: Effects of target-distractor similarity and old age on search, subitization, and counting. *Journal of Experimental Psychology: Human Perception and Performance*, 33, 549.

Watson, D. G., Maylor, E. A., & Bruce, L. A. (2005a). Effects of age on searching for and enumerating targets that cannot be detected efficiently. *The Quarterly Journal of Experimental Psychology*, 58A, 1119–1142.

Watson, D. G., Maylor, E. A., & Bruce, L. A. (2005b). Search, enumeration, and aging: Eye movement requirements cause age-equivalent performance in enumeration but not in search tasks. *Psychology and Aging*, 20, 226–240.

Watson, D. G., Maylor, E. A., & Bruce, L. A. (2005c). The efficiency of feature-based subitization and counting. *Journal of Experimental Psychology: Human Perception and Performance*, 31, 1449–1462.

*Watson, D. G., Maylor, E. A., & Manson, N. J. (2002). Aging and enumeration: A selective deficit for the subitization of targets among distractors. *Psychology and Aging*, 17, 496–504.

Weekers, R., & Roussel, F. (1946). Introduction a l'etude de la frequence de fusion en Clinique [Introduction to the study of flicker fusion frequency in a clinical context.]. *Ophthalmologica*, 112, 305–319.

*Wegesin, D. J., Ream, J. M., & Stern, Y. (2004). Explicit contamination contributes to aging effects in episodic priming: Behavioral and ERP evidence. *Journals of Gerontology: Psychological Sciences*, 59, 317–324.

*Weir, C., Bruun, C., & Barber, T. (1997). Are backward words special for older adults? *Psychology and Aging*, 12, 145–149.

Welford, A. T. (1958). *Ageing and human skill*. Westport, CN: Greenwood Press.

Welford, A. T. (1959). Psychomotor performance. In J. E. Birren (Ed.), *Handbook of aging and the individual* (pp. 562–613). Chicago, IL: University of Chicago Press.

Welford, A. T. (1961). Age changes in the times taken by choice, discrimination and the control of movement. *Gerontologia*, 5, 129–145.

Welford, A. T. (1977). Motor performance. In J. E. Birren and K. W. Schaie (Eds.), *Handbook of the psychology of aging* (pp. 450–496). New York, NY: Van Nostrand Reinhold.

West, R. L. (1996). An application of prefrontal cortex function theory to cognitive aging. *Psychological Bulletin*, 120, 272–292.

*West, R. (1999). Age differences in lapses of intention in the Stroop task. *Journals of Gerontology: Psychological Sciences*, 54, 34–43.

West, R., & Alain, C. (1999). Event-related neural activity associated with the Stroop task. *Cognitive Brain Research*, 8, 157–164.

West, R., & Alain, C. (2000). Effects of task context and fluctuations of attention on neural activity supporting performance of the Stroop task. *Brain research*, 873, 102–111.

West, R. L., Ball, K. K., Edwards, J. D., & Cissell, G. M. (1994, April). *Individual differences in negative priming: Evidence for preserved inhibitory processes in some older individuals*. Paper presented at the Cognitive Aging Conference, Atlanta, GA.

*West, R., & Baylis, G. C. (1998). Effects of increased response dominance and contextual disintegration on the stroop interference effect in older adults. *Psychology and Aging*, 13, 206–217.

*West, R., & Craik, F. I. M. (2001). Influences on the efficiency of prospective memory in younger and older adults. *Psychology and Aging*, 16, 682–696.

*West, R., Herndon, R. W., & Covell, E. (2003). Neural correlates of age-related declines in the formation and realization of delayed intentions. *Psychology and Aging*, 18, 461–473.

*West, R., Murphy, K. J., Armilio, M. L., Craik, F. I. M., & Stuss, D. T. (2002). Effects of time of day on age differences in working memory. *Journals of Gerontology: Psychological Sciences*, 57, 3–10.

West, R., & Travers, S. (2008). Differential effects of aging on processes underlying task switching. *Brain and Cognition*, 68, 67–80.

Wicherts, J. M., Dolan, C. V., Hessen, D. J., Oosterveld, P., Baal, G. C. M. van, Boomsma, D. I., & Span, M. M. (2004). Are intelligence tests measurement invariant over time? Investigating the nature of the Flynn effect. *Intelligence*, 32, 509–537.

Wickett, J. C., & Vernon, P. A. (2000). Replicating the movement time-extraversion link with a little help from IQ. *Personality and Individual Differences*, 28, 205–215.

Wild-Wall, N., Falkenstein, M., & Hohnsbein, J. (2008). Flanker interference in young and older participants as reflected in event-related potentials. *Brain Research*, 1211, 72–84.

Wilk, M.B., & Gnanadesikan, R. (1968). Probability plotting methods for the analysis of data, *Biometrika*, 55, 1–17.

Williams, B. R., Hultsch, D. F., Strauss, E. H., Hunter, M. A., & Tannock, R. (2005). Inconsistency in reaction time across the life span. *Neuropsychology*, 19, 88–96.

#Wilson, T. R. (1963). Flicker fusion frequency, age and intelligence. *Gerontologia*, 7, 200–208.

Wilson, R. S., Beckett, L. A., Barnes, L. L., Schneider, J. A., Bach, J., Evans, D. A., et al. (2002). Individual differences in rates of change in cognitive abilities of older persons. *Psychology and Aging*, 17, 179–193.

*Wingfield, A., Peelle, J. E., & Grossman, M. (2003). Speech rate and syntactic complexity as multiplicative factors in speech comprehension by young and older adults. *Aging, Neuropsychology, and Cognition*, 10, 310–322.

Witt, S. J., & Cunningham, W. R. (1979). Cognitive speed and subsequent intellectual development: A longitudinal investigation. *Journal of Gerontology*, 34, 540–546.

Witt, K., Daniels, C., Schmitt-Eliassen, J., Kernbichler, J., Rehm, S., Volkmann, J., & Deuschl, G. (2006). The impact of normal aging and Parkinson's disease on response preparation in task-switching behavior. *Brain Research*, 1114, 173–182.

Witthöft, M., Sander, N., Süß, H. M., & Wittmann, W. W. (2009). Adult age differences in inhibitory processes and their predictive validity for fluid intelligence. *Aging, Neuropsychology, and Cognition*, 16, 133–163.

Wolf, E., & Shraffa, A. M. (1964). Relationship between critical flicker frequency and age inflicker perimetry. *Archives of Ophthalmology*, 72, 832–843.

Worden, A., Walker, N., Bharat, K., & Hudson, S. (1997, March). Making computers easier for older adults to use: area cursors and sticky icons. In *Proceedings of the SIGCHI conference on human factors in computing systems* (pp. 266–271). ACM.

Wright, R. E. (1981). Aging, divided attention, and processing capacity. *Journal of Gerontology*, 36, 605–614.

*Wurm, L. H., Labouvie-Vief, G., Aycock, J., Rebucal, K. A., & Koch, H. E. (2004). Performance in auditory and visual emotional Stroop tasks: A comparison of older and younger adults. *Psychology and Aging*, 19, 523–535.

Yang, Q., Kapoula, Z., Debay, E., Coubard, O., Orssaud, C., & Samson, M. (2006). Prolongation of latency of horizontal saccades in elderly is distance and task specific. *Vision Research*, 46, 751–759.

Yeudall, L. T., Reddon, J. R., Gill, D. M., & Stefanyk, W. O. (1987). Normative data for the Halstead-Reitan neuropsychological tests stratified by age and sex. *Journal of Clinical Psychology*, 43, 346–367.

Ystad, M. A., Lundervold, A. J., Wehling, E., Espeseth, T., Rootwelt, H., Westlye, L. T., … Lundervold, A. (2009). Hippocampal volumes are important predictors of memory function in elderly women. *BMC Medical Imaging*, 9, 17.

Yule, G. U. (1903). Notes on the theory of association of attributes in statistics. *Biometrika*, 2, 121–134.

Zacks, R. T., Radvansky, G., & Hasher, L. (1996). Studies of directed forgetting in older adults. *Journal of Experimental Psychology: Learning, Memory, and Cognition*, 22, 143–156.

Zacks, J. L., & Zacks, R. T. (1993). Visual search times assessed without reaction times: A new method and an application to aging. *Journal of Experimental Psychology: Human Perception and Performance*, 19, 798–813.

Zeef, E. J., & Kok, A. (1993). Age-related differences in the timing of stimulus and response processes during visual selective attention: Performance and psychophysiological analyses. *Psychophysiology*, 30, 138–151.

Zeef, E. J., Sonke, C. J., Kok, A., Buiten, M. M., & Kenemans, J. (1996). Perceptual factors affecting age-related differences in focused attention: Performance and psychophysiological analyses. *Psychophysiology*, 33, 555–565.

Zelinski, E. M., & Lewis, K. L. (2003). Adult age differences in multiple cognitive functions: Differentiation, dedifferentiation, or process-specific change? *Psychology and Aging*, 18, 727–745.

Zhang, Y., Han, B., Verhaeghen, P., & Nilsson, L. G. (2007). Executive functioning in older adults with mild cognitive impairment: MCI has effects on planning, but not on inhibition. *Aging, Neuropsychology, and Cognition*, 14, 557–570.

Zimprich, D. (2002). Cross-sectionally and longitudinally balanced effects of processing speed on intellectual abilities. *Experimental Aging Research*, 28, 231–251.

Zimprich, D., & Martin, M. (2002). Can longitudinal changes in processing speed explain longitudinal age changes in fluid intelligence? *Psychology and Aging*, 17, 690–695.

INDEX